"This book shows the robustness
of the emerging design
paradigm and demonstrates that
it is a workable research program
across a broad range of disciplines.
A great introduction to
this exciting new movement."
**CHUCK COLSON**
*chairman, Prison Fellowship Ministries*

"This collection not only brings one
up to date on a vital issue,
but it is so stimulating that it should
lead to more groundbreaking investigations."
**DIOGENES ALLEN**
*Stuart Professor of Philosophy, Princeton Theological Seminary*

"*Mere Creation* goes far beyond the limitations
of classical natural theology, . . .
and it effectively cuts off at the knees
the misguided notion of creative evolution. . . .
This book, which requires rigorous thinking on every page,
is essential reading for the contemporary
Christian discussion with science.
Skip this volume at your own risk."
**PATRICK HENRY REARDON**
*senior editor,* Touchstone

"This book resonates with the excitement
of reopening urgent questions
that have long been suppressed by the dead hand
of philosophical dogmas
disguised as scientific truth.
It should be welcomed as an invitation
to a more honest exploration
of the world of which we are part."
**RICHARD JOHN NEUHAUS**
*editor in chief,* First Things

"This extremely important and insightful book
should be studied by every thoughtful person
who is interested in an honest inquiry
into the origin and existence of life."
**DEAN L. OVERMAN**
*author of* A Case Against Accident and Self-Organization

# MERE CREATION

## Science, Faith & Intelligent Design

edited by
## William A. Dembski

foreword by
## Henry F. Schaefer III

**InterVarsity Press**
Downers Grove, Illinois

InterVarsity Press
P.O. Box 1400, Downers Grove, IL 60515
World Wide Web: www.ivpress.com
E-mail: mail@ivpress.com

InterVarsity Press® is the book-publishing division of InterVarsity Christian Fellowship/USA®, a student movement active on campus at hundreds of universities, colleges and schools of nursing in the United States of America, and a member movement of the International Fellowship of Evangelical Students. For information about local and regional activities, write Public Relations Dept., InterVarsity Christian Fellowship/USA, 6400 Schroeder Rd., P.O. Box 7895, Madison, WI 53707-7895.

All Scripture quotations, unless otherwise indicated, are taken from the Holy Bible, New International Version®. NIV®. Copyright ©1973, 1978, 1984 by International Bible Society. Used by permission of Zondervan Publishing House. All rights reserved.

Figure 5.4 taken from A. G. Cairns-Smith, Genetic takeover and the mineral origins of life, copyright 1982 by A. G. Cairns-Smith. Reprinted with the permission of Cambridge University Press.

Figure 6.1 taken from Peter A. Lawrence, The making of a fly, copyright 1992 by Peter A. Lawrence. Reprinted with the permission of Blackwell Science Ltd.

Figure 6.2 taken from Richard Elinson, "Changes in developmental patterns: Embryos of amphibians with large eggs," in R. A. Raff and E. C. Raff, Development as an evolutionary process, copyright 1987 by R. A. Raff and E. C. Raff. Reprinted with the permission of John Wiley & Sons, Inc.

Figure 6.3 taken from Scott Gilbert, Developmental biology, 3rd ed., copyright 1991 by Scott Gilbert. Reprinted with the permission of Sinauer Associates. C. elegans cell lineage figure originally published in J. E. Sulston, J. Schierenberg, J. White and N. Thompson, "The embryonic cell lineage of the nematode Caenorhabditis elegans," Developmental biology 100 (1983): 64-119. Copyright 1983 by J. E. Sulston, J. Schierenberg, J. White and N. Thompson. Reprinted with permission of Academic Press, Inc.

Cover photograph: Julian Baum / Science Photo Library

ISBN 0-8308-1515-5

Printed in the United States of America ∞

**Library of Congress Cataloging-in-Publication Data**

Mere creation: science, faith & intelligent design / William A.
  Dembski, editor.
      p.    cm.
    Includes bibliographical references.
    ISBN 0-8308-1515-5 (pbk.: alk. paper)
    1. Science—Philosophy.  2. Religion and science.  3. Naturalism.
  4. Experimental design.  I. Dembski, William A., 1960-.
  Q175.M5413  1998
  501—dc21                                                                        98-20999
                                                                                      CIP

20   19   18   17   16   15   14   13   12   11   10   9   8   7   6   5   4

15   14   13   12   11   10   09   08   07   06   05   04   03   02   01   00   99

DEDICATED TO
M. P. SCHÜTZENBERGER
1920-1996

Marcel-Paul Schützenberger was a remarkable figure in the intellectual life of the late twentieth century. Within the community of mathematicians, he is well known for his fundamental and prophetic contributions to combinatorics, automata and coding theory, mathematical linguistics, the theory of noncommutative semigroups, and many areas of algebra. His most recent mathematical work is relevant to the theory of quantum groups. A man of endless curiosity, he was the first scientist of his stature publicly to question Darwin's theory of evolution, raising questions at the Wistar Symposium of 1967 about life and chance that biologists did not comprehend and that mathematicians could not answer. His criticisms were remarkable both for their subtlety and for the courage required to make them. In an interview published shortly before his death, he expanded upon his views, arguing with characteristic force and wit that while the mechanism of random variation and natural selection is credited with almost everything, it explains almost nothing, the theory's claims neatly canceled by its failures. Those who knew Marcel Schützenberger remember him as a man of champagne wit and penetrating intelligence; they remember as well a man of uncommon forbearance and personal dignity. Schützenberger's mathematical work will preserve his memory. His criticism of Darwin's theory of evolution will do more. It will preserve his spirit.

118709

# Foreword

## Henry F. Schaefer III

An unprecedented intellectual event occurred in Los Angeles on November 14-17, 1996. Under the sponsorship of Christian Leadership Ministries, Biola University hosted a major research conference bringing together scientists and scholars who reject naturalism as an adequate framework for doing science and who seek a common vision of creation united under the rubric of intelligent design. The two hundred participants, primarily academics, formed a nonhomogeneous group. Most had never met each other. Yet virtually all the participants questioned the reigning paradigm of biology—namely, that natural selection and mutation can account for the origin and diversity of all living things. At the same time virtually none of the conference participants were creationists of the sort one frequently reads about in the popular press. In particular a very large majority of the participants had no stake in treating Genesis as a scientific text.

Also remarkable for a group skeptical of Darwin's theory was its religious orientation. Many of the participants could be described as evangelical Christians. For example, I am a Presbyterian with strong convictions about the truthfulness of the sixty-six books of the Old and New Testaments. Nonetheless few if any of those at the conference could be described as fundamentalists in the sense of George Marsden's now classic *Fundamentalism and American Culture*. Moreover, a significant number of the participants were not Protestant at all, including Michael Behe (Roman Catholic), John Mark Reynolds (Eastern Orthodox) and David Berlinski (Jewish), whose work is included in this volume. In fact Phillip Johnson, who gave the concluding address at the conference, stated he would welcome to this group earnest atheists who are convinced there must be a better scientific explanation of life than the dominant mutation/selection scenario.

Prior to the conference, each participant received a set of conference goals. These included:

*To build a community of thought.* Many scholars and scientists who work in disciplines dominated by naturalism personally reject that philosophy and its methodological consequences. They want positive alternatives to naturalism yet do not see (or see only faintly) a broader intellectual community of their own. The conference should bring these scholars together to discuss their points of commonality and thereby create a network of like-minded colleagues intent on pursuing scientifically promising theistic alternatives in their own fields. Scientists who know they are not alone in dissenting from naturalism will be better equipped to encourage others to think differently.

*To share ideas and knowledge.* Science and knowledge acquisition generally have grown increasingly specialized. In many respects this division of labor is natural and healthy. Yet in a culture dominated by naturalism, it can also be pernicious. "Everyone knows," for instance, that neo-Darwinism is well established because the neo-Darwinians themselves have so assured the rest of the world. Theistic scholars recognize that the intellectual world itself is in chaos. Secularists are having difficulty justifying the most basic academic standards and programs. It is past time for theists to propose a way out for their secular colleagues. This conference should enable scientists in fields spanning the life sciences, earth sciences, astrophysics, history and philosophy of science, mathematics, and similar disciplines to communicate what they know about the shortcomings of governing naturalistic theories (e.g., neo-Darwinism). Far more importantly, however, conferees would learn in some detail of the work and thinking of others who do not presuppose naturalism in their intellectual work; what common problems are faced; what research should be undertaken; and how the group might interact with the scientific and intellectual world at large.

*To unite on common ground.* The Christian world is badly riven over the "creation-evolution" issue. Yet a surprising amount of common ground unites many (if not all) of the feuding parties. The conferees should seek a way of approaching the origins issue that will unify Christians. The conferees should provide a means to discover shared principles and ideas by letting disputants spend time together amicably in a private setting where reputations are not on the line. The conference would also seek to formulate a general position statement on origins ("Mere Creation") that could be widely endorsed by Christians. (To preserve freedom of inquiry, conference participants decided against formulating such a position statement. William Dembski's introductory chapter in this volume is the closest thing to such a statement.)

*To communicate to others.* Wonderful ideas left under a bushel do no good. The conference should produce tangible results that will accelerate the growth of scientific research programs unencumbered by naturalism, encouraging and disseminating scholarship both at the highest level and at the popular level via such activities as

preparing a book for publication, with chapters drawn from the conference papers (this goal has been met with publication of the present volume);

planning a major origins conference at a large university to engage scientific naturalists (this goal remains in the offing);

outlining a research program to encourage the next generation of scholars to work on theories beyond the confines of naturalism;

exploring the need for establishing fellowship programs, and encouraging joint research (Seattle's Discovery Institute is the key player here—see www.discovery.org);

providing resources for the new journal *Origins & Design* as an ongoing forum and a first-rate interdisciplinary journal with contributions by conference participants (see www.arn.org/arn);

preparing information usable in the campus environment of a modern university, such as expanding a World Wide Web origins site (see www.leaderu.com, www.origins.org, www.iclnet.org) and exploring video and other means of communication (see www.daystarcom.org).

Christian Leadership Ministries, the faculty ministry of Campus Crusade for Christ, sponsored this conference. Rich McGee, Christian Leadership Ministries' Director of Research and International Expansion, served as the conference director. To organize the conference, a steering committee was convened at Christian Leadership Ministries' headquarters outside Dallas in February 1996. The steering committee consisted of Michael Behe (associate professor of biological sciences, Lehigh University), Walter Bradley (professor of mechanical engineering, Texas A&M University), William Dembski (visiting fellow, Center for Philosophy of Religion, University of Notre Dame), Phillip Johnson (professor of law, University of California Law School, Berkeley), Sherwood Lingenfelter (provost, Biola University), Richard McGee, Stephen Meyer (associate professor of philosophy, Whitworth College), J. P. Moreland (professor of philosophy, Talbot School of Theology, Biola University), Paul Nelson (editor of *Origins & Design*), Pattle Pun (professor of biology, Wheaton College), John Mark Reynolds (assistant professor of philosophy, Biola University), Jeffrey Schloss (professor of biology and department chairman, Westmont College) and me. Paul Nelson chaired the steering committee. William Dembski was appointed to serve as academic editor. Together Rich McGee, Paul Nelson and William Dembski worked harder than anyone else on this conference. The resounding success of the conference can in large measure be attributed to them.

Many more people played a crucial role in this conference than can be mentioned here individually. The staff, administration and faculty of Biola University accommodated the participants wonderfully (special thanks are due to the provost, Sherwood Lingenfelter). The staff of Christian Leadership Ministries was marvelously efficient in coordinating the many behind-the-scenes details that can make or break a conference (Peter Culver and Keith Seabourn stand out). Thanks are due to Mark Whalon (Dept. of Biology, Michigan State University) and Alvin Plantinga (Dept. of Philosophy, University of Notre Dame) for moderating the biology and philosophy sessions, respectively. Thanks are due to Luder Whitlock, president of Reformed Theological Seminary, for giving the sermon on the Sunday morning of the conference. Thanks are also due to Bruce Chapman, president of the Discovery Institute, for contributing to this volume a postscript in which he lays out the broader cultural implications of intelligent design. Finally I want to commend all the organizations and ministries represented at the conference which have consistently stood against naturalism and have found their resolve strengthened through this conference. I want to draw special attention to Access Research Network, the Foundation for Thought and Ethics, Mars Hill Audio, World Magazine, the Pascal Centre (Canada) and the Discovery Institute's Center for the Renewal of Science and Culture.

# Introduction: Mere Creation

## William A. Dembski

Sticking the word *mere* in front of a concept can be a way of trivializing it. Thus to engage in "mere rhetoric" is to persuade for the sake of persuading, without considering the truth or merits of what is said. Sticking "mere" in front of a concept can, however, also be a way of getting at its essentials. Thus for C. S. Lewis, "mere Christianity" signified the essentials of Christianity— what minimally one must hold to be a Christian. The "mere" in "mere creation" needs to be interpreted in this second sense, where at issue is what minimally must be included under a doctrine of creation.

Why should Christians bother with "mere creation" when they already have a full-fledged doctrine of creation? Sadly, no such doctrine is in place. Instead we find a multiplicity of views on creation, many of which conflict and none of which commands anywhere near universal assent. As a result the Christian world is badly riven about creation. True, Christians are united about God being the ultimate source of the world, and thus they are united in opposing naturalism, the view that nature is self-sufficient. But this is where the agreement ends.

With so little agreement about creation, what is the point of trying to uncover its essentials? Short of the bland "God is responsible for the whole show," any proposed "essential feature" of creation is sure to come under fire. One advocate of creation thinks it is essential that God intervene in the causal structure of the world. Another thinks it is essential that God not upset the causal structure of the world. One advocate of creation thinks it is essential to read Genesis literally and accept a young earth. Another thinks it does not matter how old the earth is. It appears mere creation can achieve unity but only at the cost of sterility—by affirming platitudes and avoiding controversy.

There is, however, an alternate approach to unifying the Christian world about creation. Rather than look for common ground on which all Christians can agree, propose a theory of creation that puts Christians in the strongest possible position to defeat the common enemy of creation, to wit, naturalism. Throughout history common enemies have been invaluable for suspending in-house squabbles and uniting people who should otherwise be friends. Although approaching creation through its common enemy may seem opportunistic, it is quite illuminating. We learn a great deal about something by learning what it is not. Creation is not naturalism. By developing a theory of creation in opposition to naturalism, we learn a great deal about creation. Mere creation, then, is a theory of creation aimed specifically at defeating naturalism and its consequences.

Within Western culture, naturalism has become the default position for all serious inquiry. From biblical studies to law to education to science to the arts, inquiry is allowed to proceed only under the supposition that nature is self-contained. To be sure, this is not to require that we explicitly deny God's existence. God could, after all, have created the world to be self-contained. Nonetheless, for the sake of inquiry we are required to pretend that God does not exist and proceed accordingly. Naturalism affirms not so much that God does not exist as that God need not exist. It is not that God is dead so much as that God is absent. And because God is absent, intellectual honesty demands that we get about our work without invoking him (except, of course, when we need to pacify our religious impulses). This is the received wisdom, and it is pure poison.

How then to defeat naturalism? Naturalism is an ideology. Its key tenet is the self-sufficiency of nature. Within Western culture its most virulent form is known as scientific naturalism. Scientific naturalism locates the self-sufficiency of nature in the undirected natural laws of science. Accordingly scientific naturalism would have us to understand the universe entirely in terms of such laws. Thus in particular, since human beings are a part of the universe, who we are and what we do must ultimately be understood in naturalistic terms. This is not to deny our humanity. But it is to reinterpret our humanity as the consequence of brute material processes that were not consciously aiming at us. Nor is this to deny God. But it is to affirm that if God exists, he was marvelously adept at covering his tracks and giving no evidence that he ever interacted with the world. It remains logically permissible for the scientific naturalist to affirm God's existence but only by making God a superfluous rider on top a self-contained account of the world.

What evidence is there of God interacting with the world? How we answer this question is crucial to how effective we are going to be in overcoming naturalism, scientific or otherwise. As Christians we know naturalism is false. Nature is not self-sufficient. God created nature as well as any laws by which nature operates. Not only has God created the world, but also God upholds the world moment by moment. Daniel's words to Belshazzar hold equally for the dyed-in-the-wool naturalist: "Thou hast praised the gods of silver, and gold, of brass, iron, wood, and stone, which see not, nor hear, nor know: and the God in whose hand thy breath is, and whose are all thy ways, hast thou not glorified" (Dan 5:23 KJV). The world is in God's hand and never leaves his hand. Christians are not deists. God is not an absentee landlord.

That said, the question remains what evidence has God given of interacting with the world. This is where things get sticky. Because God is intimately involved with the world moment by moment, there is no question that God interacts with the world. This is a tenet of our faith that brooks no controversy. Controversy arises, however, once we ask whether God's interaction with the world is empirically detectable. It is one thing as a matter of faith to hold that God exists, interacts with and sovereignly rules the world. Alternatively one may argue on philosophical grounds that the world and its laws are not self-explanatory and therefore point to a transcendent source. But it is another thing entirely to assert that empirical evidence supports God's interaction with the world, rendering God's interaction empirically detectable. Theology and philosophy are legitimate ways for understanding God's interaction with the world. Nonetheless neither theology nor philosophy can answer the evidential question whether God's interaction with the world is empirically detectable.

To answer this question we must to look to science. The science we look to, however, needs to be unencumbered by naturalistic philosophy. If we prescribe in advance that science must be limited to undirected natural causes, then science will necessarily be incapable of investigating God's interaction with the world. But if we permit science to investigate intelligent causes (as many special sciences already do, e.g., forensic science and artificial intelligence), then God's interaction with the world, insofar as it manifests the characteristic features of intelligent causation, becomes a legitimate domain for scientific investigation.

There is an important contrast to keep in mind here. Science, we are told, studies natural causes whereas to introduce God is to invoke supernatural causes. This is the wrong contrast. The proper contrast is between undirected natural causes on the one hand and intelligent causes on the other. Intelligent causes can do things that undirected natural causes cannot. Undirected natural causes can throw scrabble pieces on a board but cannot arrange the pieces to form meaningful words or sentences. To obtain a meaningful arrangement requires an intelligent cause. Whether an intelligent cause operates within or outside nature (i.e., is respectively natural or supernatural) is a separate question from whether an intelligent cause has operated. For instance, we can reliably infer that a Shakespearean sonnet has an intelligent cause independently of whether Shakespeare actually lived, whether a space alien moved Shakespeare's quill, or whether an angel made the sonnet materialize magically.

## Intelligent Design

This distinction between undirected natural causes and intelligent causes has underlain the design arguments of past centuries. Throughout the centuries theologians have argued that nature exhibits features which nature itself cannot explain but which instead require an intelligence beyond nature. From church fathers like Minucius Felix and Gregory of Nazianzus (third and fourth centuries) to medieval scholars like Moses Maimonides and Thomas Aquinas (twelfth and thirteenth centuries) to Reformed thinkers like Thomas Reid and Charles Hodge (eighteenth and nineteenth centuries), we find theologians making design arguments, arguing from the data of nature to an intelligence that transcends nature.

Design arguments are old hat. Indeed design arguments continue to be a staple of philosophy and religion courses. The most famous of the design arguments is William Paley's watchmaker argument (see Paley's *Natural Theology*, published in 1802). According to Paley, if we find a watch in a field, the watch's adaptation of means to ends (i.e., the adaptation of its parts to telling time) ensure that it is the product of an intelligence and not the result of undirected natural processes. So too the marvelous adaptations of means to ends in organisms, whether at the level of whole organisms or at the level of various subsystems (Paley focused especially on the mammalian eye), ensure that organisms are the product of an intelligence.

Though they are intuitively appealing, design arguments had until recently fallen into disuse. This is now changing. Design is experiencing an explosive resurgence. Scientists are beginning to realize that design can be rigorously formulated as a scientific theory. What has kept design outside the scientific mainstream these last 130 years is the absence of precise methods for distinguishing intelligently caused objects from unintelligently caused ones. For design to be a fruitful scientific theory, scientists have to be sure they can reliably determine whether something is designed. Johannes Kepler, for instance, thought the craters on the moon were intelligently designed by moon dwellers. We now know that the craters were formed naturally. This fear of falsely attributing something to design only to have it overturned later has prevented design from entering science proper. With precise methods for discriminating intelligently from unintelligently caused objects, scientists are now able to avoid Kepler's mistake.

What has emerged is a new program for scientific research known as intelligent design. Within biology intelligent design is a theory of biological origins and development. Its fundamental claim is that intelligent causes are necessary to explain the complex, information-rich structures of biology and that these causes are empirically detectable. To say intelligent causes are empirically detectable is to say there exist well-defined methods that, on the basis of observational features of the world, are capable of reliably distinguishing intelligent causes from undirected natural causes. Many special sciences have already developed such methods for drawing this distinction— notably forensic science, artificial intelligence (cf. the Turing test), cryptography, archeology and the Search for Extraterrestrial Intelligence (cf. the movie *Contact*).

Whenever these methods detect intelligent causation, the underlying entity they uncover is information. Intelligent design properly formulated is a theory of information. Within such a theory, information becomes a reliable indicator of intelligent causation as well as a proper object for scientific investigation. Intelligent design thereby becomes a theory for detecting and measuring information, explaining its origin and tracing its flow. Intelligent design is therefore not the study of intelligent causes per se but of informational pathways induced by intelligent causes. As a result intelligent design presupposes neither a creator nor miracles. Intelligent design is theologically minimalist. It detects intelligence without speculating about the nature of the intelligence. Biochemist Michael Behe's "irreducible complexity," mathematician Marcel Schützenberger's "functional complexity" and my own "complex specified information" are alternate routes to the same reality.

The empirical detectability of intelligent causes renders intelligent design a fully scientific theory and distinguishes it from the design arguments of philosophers, or what has traditionally been called natural theology. Natural theology reasons from the data of nature directly to the existence and attributes of God—typically the trinitarian God of Christianity with all the usual perfections. Perhaps the weakest part of Paley's *Natural Theology* was his closing chapter in which he sings the praises of nature's delicate balance and how only a beneficent deity could have arranged so happy a creation. Darwin turned this argument on its head, focusing instead on the brutality of nature and seeing anything but the hand of a beneficent deity.

Intelligent design is at once more modest and more powerful than natural theology. From observable features of the natural world, intelligent design infers to an intelligence responsible for those features. The world contains events, objects and structures that exhaust the explanatory resources of undirected natural causes and that can be adequately explained only by recourse to intelligent causes. This is not an argument from ignorance. Precisely because of what we know about undirected natural causes and their limitations, science is now in a position to demonstrate design rigorously (see the chapters by Dembski, Meyer and Nelson in this volume). Thus what has been a long-standing but fuzzy philosophical intuition can now be cashed out as a robust program of scientific research. At the same time intelligent design resists speculating about the nature, moral character or purposes of this intelligence (here is a task for the theologian—to connect the intelligence inferred by the design theorist with the God of Scripture). This is one of the great strengths of intelligent design, that it distinguishes design from purpose. We can know that something is designed without knowing the ultimate or even proximate purpose for which it was designed. As Del Ratzsch notes in this volume, "The Smithsonian has an entire collection of obviously designed human artifacts, concerning the purposes of which no one has a clue."

What will science look like once intelligent causes are readmitted to full scientific status? The worry is that intelligent design will stultify scientific inquiry. For after determining that something is designed, what remains for the scientist to do? Even if there are reliable methods for deciding when something is designed and even if those methods tell us that some natural object is designed, so what? Suppose Paley was right about the mammalian eye exhibiting sure marks of intelligent causation. How would this recognition help us understand the eye any better as scientists? It would help quite a bit. For one thing, it would put a stop to all those unsubstantiated just-so stories that evolutionists spin out in trying to account for the eye through a gradual succession of undirected natural causes. By telling us the mammalian eye requires an intelligent cause, intelligent design precludes certain types of scientific explanation. This is a contribution to science, albeit a negative one.

Even so, intelligent design is hardly finished once it answers whether an object was designed. Another question immediately presents itself, namely, how was the object produced? Consider a Stradivarius violin. Not only do we know that it is designed, but also we know the designer—Stradivarius. Nevertheless to this day we are unable to answer the "how" question: we no longer know how to manufacture a violin as good as a Stradivarius, much less how Stradivarius himself went about making his violins. Lost arts are lost precisely because we are no longer able to answer the "how" question, not because we have lost the ability to detect design. Now the problem of lost arts is the problem of reverse engineering. Unlike the ordinary engineer who constructs an object from scratch, the reverse engineer is first given an object (in this case a violin) and then must show how it could have been constructed.

Intelligent design's positive contribution to science is to reverse engineer objects shown to be designed. The design theorist is a reverse engineer.

Unconstrained by naturalism, the design theorist finds plenty of natural objects attributable to design (this is especially true with biological objects). Having determined that certain natural objects are designed, the design theorist next investigates how they were produced. Yet because evidence of how they were produced is typically lacking (at least for natural objects), the design theorist is left instead with investigating how these objects could have been produced. This is reverse engineering.

In this vein, consider again the Stradivarius example. In attempting to reconstruct Stradivarius's art of violin making, the contemporary violin maker does well to learn as much as possible about Stradivarius's actual methods for producing violins. Nonetheless, because the extant account of Stradivarius's methods is incomplete, the contemporary violin maker can do no better than try to reinvent Stradivarius's methods. Without a complete record of Stradivarius's actual methods, one can never be sure of reconstructing his methods exactly. Still one can legitimately claim to have reinvented Stradivarius's methods if one is able to produce a violin as good as his.

To sum up, intelligent design consists in empirically detecting design and then reverse engineering those objects detected to be designed. The worry that intelligent design stifles scientific inquiry is therefore ill-founded. One can argue that many scientists are design theorists already, albeit in naturalistic clothing. In biology, for instance, very few researchers confine themselves to Miller-Urey type experiments, attempting to generate biological complexity solely through undirected natural processes. Most researchers studying biological complexity bring all their expertise and technological prowess to bear, especially when trying to reconstruct complex biological systems. As Paul Nelson aptly remarks, scientists ought to line their labs with mirrors to remind themselves that at every point they are in the labs designing and conducting their experiments. Intelligent design is one intelligence determining what another intelligence has done. There is nothing mysterious about this. The only reason it seems mysterious is because naturalism so pollutes our intellectual life.

### Theistic Evolution
Where does intelligent design fit within the creation-evolution debate? Intelligent design is logically compatible with everything from utterly discontinuous creation (e.g., God intervening at every conceivable point to create new species) to the most far-ranging evolution (e.g., God seamlessly melding all organisms together into one great tree of life). For intelligent design the first question is not how organisms came to be (though, as we have seen, this is a vital question for intelligent design) but whether organisms demonstrate clear, empirically detectable marks of being intelligently caused. In principle

an evolutionary process can exhibit such marks of intelligence as much as any act of special creation.

That said, intelligent design is incompatible with what typically is meant by theistic evolution. Theistic evolution takes the Darwinian picture of the biological world and baptizes it, identifying this picture with the way God created life. When boiled down to its scientific content, however, theistic evolution is no different from atheistic evolution, treating only undirected natural processes in the origin and development of life. Theistic evolution places theism and evolution in an odd tension. If God purposely created life through Darwinian means, then God's purpose was to make it seem as though life was created without purpose. Within theistic evolution, God is a master of stealth who constantly eludes our best efforts to detect him empirically. The theistic evolutionist believes that the universe is designed. Yet insofar as there is design in the universe, it is design we recognize strictly through the eyes of faith. Accordingly, the natural world in itself provides no evidence that life is designed. For all we can tell through our natural intellect, our appearance on planet Earth is an accident.

It may be that God has so arranged the physical world that our natural intellect can discover no reliable evidence of him. Yet if this is so, how could we know it? Scripture and church tradition are hardly univocal here. Throughout church history we find Christian thinkers who regard our natural intellect as hopelessly inadequate for finding even a scrap of reliable knowledge about God from nature and others who regard our natural intellect as able to extract certain limited, though still reliable, knowledge about God from nature. Thus in the early church we find Tertullian inveighing against our natural intellect, Basil the Great and Gregory of Nazianzus defending it. In the Middle Ages, we find Ockham's occasionalism undermining the powers of our natural intellect, Thomas Aquinas raising it to new heights. In the modern era we find Blaise Pascal, Søren Kierkegaard and Karl Barth making the *Deus absconditus* a fundamental plank of their theology, Isaac Newton, Thomas Reid and Charles Hodge asserting how wonderfully God is revealed in nature. The current theological fashion prefers an evolutionary God inaccessible to scientific scrutiny over a designer God whose actions in nature are clearly detectable.

How then do we determine whether God has so arranged the physical world that our natural intellect can discover reliable evidence of him? The answer is obvious: Put our natural intellect to the task and see whether indeed it produces conclusive evidence of design in nature. Doing so poses no threat to the Christian faith. It challenges neither the cross, the tomb, the resurrection on the third day, the ascension into heaven, the sitting at the right hand of the Father nor the second coming of Christ. Nature is silent about the revelation of Christ in Scripture. However, nothing prevents nature from independently testifying to the God revealed in Scripture (cf. Thomas Aquinas's *Summa Contra Gentiles* 3.38). Intelligent design does just this—it puts our natural intellect to work and thereby confirms that a designer of remarkable talents is responsible for the natural world. How this designer connects with the God of Scripture is then for theology to determine.

Intelligent design and theistic evolution therefore differ fundamentally about whether the design of the universe is accessible to our natural intellect. Design theorists say yes; theistic evolutionists say no. Why the disagreement? To be sure there is a scientific disagreement: Design theorists think the scientific evidence favors design whereas theistic evolutionists think it favors Darwin or one of his naturalistic successors. Nonetheless, in discounting intelligent design, theistic evolutionists tend also to appeal to philosophical and theological considerations. Pessimism about the powers of the natural intellect to transcend nature is a dominant theme in certain theological traditions (see the theology of Karl Barth). Often aesthetic criteria for how God should create or interact with the world take precedence—a worthy deity would not have done it that way! My own view is that it is much more shaky to speculate about what God would have done or what nature might in principle reveal than to go to nature and see what nature does reveal.

If theistic evolution finds no solace from intelligent design, neither does it find solace from the Darwinian establishment. For the Darwinian establishment the theism in theistic evolution is superfluous. For the hard-core naturalist, theistic evolution at best includes God as an unnecessary rider in an otherwise purely naturalistic account of life. Thus by Ockham's razor, since God is an unnecessary rider in our understanding of the natural world, theistic evolution ought to dispense with all talk of God outright and get rid of the useless adjective *theistic*. This is the received view within the Darwinian establishment.

It is for failing to take Ockham's razor seriously that the Darwinian establishment despises theistic evolution. Not to put too fine a point on it, the Darwinian establishment views theistic evolution as a weak-kneed sycophant that desperately wants the respectability that comes with being a full-blooded Darwinist but refuses to follow the logic of Darwinism through to the end. It takes courage to give up the comforting belief that life on earth has a purpose. It takes courage to live without the consolation of an afterlife. Theistic evolutionists lack the stomach to face the ultimate meaninglessness of life, and this failure of courage makes them contemptible in the eyes of full-blooded Darwinists (Richard Dawkins is a case in point).

Unlike full-blooded Darwinists, however, the design theorists' objection to theistic evolution rests not with what the term *theistic* is doing in the phrase "theistic evolution" but rather with what the term *evolution* is doing there. The design theorists' objection to theistic evolution is not that theistic evolution retains God as an unnecessary rider in an otherwise perfectly acceptable scientific theory of life's origins. Rather the design theorists' objection is that the scientific theory that is supposed to undergird theistic evolution, typically called the neo-Darwinian synthesis, is itself problematic.

The design theorists' critique of Darwinism begins with Darwinism's failure as an empirically adequate scientific theory and not with its supposed incompatibility with some system of religious belief. This point is vital to keep in mind in assessing intelligent design's contribution to the creation-evolution controversy. Critiques of Darwinism by creationists have tended to conflate science and theology. Design theorists want none of this. Their critique of Darwinism is not based on any supposed incompatibility between Christian revelation and Darwinism. Rather they begin their critique by arguing that Darwinism is on its own terms a failed scientific research program—that it does not constitute a well-supported scientific theory, that its explanatory power is severely limited, and that it fails abysmally when it tries to account for the grand sweep of natural history.

Darwinists will no doubt object to this characterization of their theory. For them Darwinism continues to be a fruitful theory and one whose imminent demise I am greatly exaggerating. There is no question that Darwin's mutation-selection mechanism constitutes a fruitful idea for biology, and one whose fruits have yet to be fully plundered. But Darwinism is more than just this mechanism. Darwinism is the totalizing claim that this mechanism accounts for all the diversity of life. The evidence does not support this claim. What evidence there is supports limited variation within fixed boundaries, or what typically is called microevolution. Macroevolution—the unlimited plasticity of organisms to diversify across all boundaries—even if it is true, cannot legitimately be attributed to the mutation-selection mechanism. To do so is to extrapolate the theory beyond its evidential base. This is always a temptation in science—to think that one's theory encompasses a far bigger domain than it does. In the heady early days of Newtonian mechanics, physicists thought Newton's laws provided a total account of the constitution and dynamics of the universe. Maxwell, Einstein and Heisenberg each showed that the proper domain of Newtonian mechanics was far more constricted. So too, the proper domain of the mutation-selection mechanism is far more constricted than most Darwinists would like to admit.

The following problems have proven utterly intractable not only for the mutation-selection mechanism but also for any other undirected natural process proposed to date: the origin of life, the origin of the genetic code, the origin of multicellular life, the origin of sexuality, the absence of transitional forms in the fossil record, the biological big bang that occurred in the Cambrian era, the development of complex organ systems and the development of irreducibly complex molecular machines. These are just a few of the more serious difficulties that confront every theory of evolution that posits only undirected natural processes. It is thus sheer arrogance for Darwinists like Richard Dawkins and Daniel Dennett to charge design theorists with being stupid or wicked or insane for denying the all-sufficiency of undirected natural processes in biology or to compare challenging Darwinism with arguing for a flat earth.

The strength of the design theorists' critique against Darwinism, however, rests not with their ability to find holes in the theory. To be sure, the holes are there and they create serious difficulties for the theory. The point, however, at which the design theorists' critique becomes interesting and novel is when they begin raising the following sorts of questions: Why does Darwinism, despite being so inadequately supported as a scientific theory, continue to garner the full support of the academic establishment? What continues to keep Darwinism afloat despite its many glaring faults? Why are alternatives that introduce design ruled out of court by fiat? Why must science explain solely by recourse to undirected natural processes? Who determines the rules of science? Is there a code of scientific correctness that instead of helping lead us into truth, actively prevents us from asking certain questions and thereby coming to the truth?

We are dealing here with something more than a straightforward determination of scientific facts or confirmation of scientific theories. Rather we are dealing with competing worldviews and incompatible metaphysical systems. In the creation-evolution controversy we are dealing with a naturalistic metaphysic that shapes and controls what theories of biological origins are permitted on the playing field in advance of any discussion or weighing of evidence. This metaphysic is so pervasive and powerful that it not only rules alternative views out of court but also cannot even permit itself to be criticized. The fallibilism and tentativeness that are supposed to be part of science find no place in the naturalistic metaphysic that undergirds Darwinism. It is this metaphysic then that constitutes the main target of the design theorists' critique of Darwinism and to which we turn next.

## The Importance of Definitions

The design theorists' critique of the naturalistic metaphysic that undergirds Darwinism can be reduced to an analysis of three words. They are *creation, evolution* and *science*. Let us start with the words *creation* and *evolution*. Suppose you are on a witness stand and are required to respond yes or no to two questions. The questions are these: Do you believe in creation? Do you believe in evolution? Could you respond to these questions with a simple yes or no and still feel satisfied that you had expressed yourself adequately? Probably not. The problem is that the words *creation* and *evolution* both have multiple senses.

For instance, creation can be construed in the narrow sense of a literal six-day creation as presented in Genesis 1 and Genesis 2. Creation can also be construed in the broad sense of asserting that God has created the world, where the question of how God created the world is set to one side. Similarly evolution can be construed as a fully naturalistic, purposeless process that by means of natural selection and mutation has produced all living things. Or evolution can mean nothing more than that organisms have changed over time (leaving the extent of change unspecified). Depending on how one construes the words *creation* and *evolution,* one's answer to the questions Do you believe in creation? and Do you believe in evolution? are likely to show quite a bit of variability.

It is the design theorists' contention that the Darwinian establishment, in order to maintain its political, cultural and intellectual authority, consistently engages in a fallacy of equivocation when it uses the terms *creation* and *evolution.* The fallacy of equivocation is the fallacy of speaking out of both sides of your mouth. It is the deliberate confusing of two senses of a term, using the sense that is convenient to promote one's agenda. For instance, when Michael Ruse in one of his defenses of Darwinism writes, "Evolution is Fact, Fact, Fact!" how is he using the term *evolution?* Is it a fact that organisms have changed over time? There is plenty of evidence to confirm that organisms have experienced limited change over time. Is it a fact that the full panoply of life has evolved through purposeless naturalistic processes? This might be a fact, but whether it is a fact is open to debate.

Suppose you do not accept the Darwinian picture of natural history, that is, you do not believe that the vast panoply of life evolved through undirected naturalistic processes. Presumably, then, you are a creationist. But does this make you a young earth creationist? Ever since Darwin's *Origin of Species* Darwinists have cast the debate in these terms: either you are with us, or you are a creationist, by which they mean a young earth creationist. But of course it does not follow, logically or otherwise, that by rejecting fully naturalistic evolution you automatically embrace a literal reading of Genesis 1 and Genesis 2. Rejecting fully naturalistic evolution does not entail accepting young earth creationism. The only thing one can say for certain is that to reject fully naturalistic evolution is to accept some form of creation broadly construed, that is, the belief that God or some intelligent designer is responsible for life. Young earth creationism certainly falls under this broad construal of creation but is hardly coextensive with it.

Let us now assume we have our terms straight. No more terminological confusions. No more fallacies of equivocation. No more straw men. From here on we are going to concentrate on the substance of the creation-evolution debate. Henceforth this debate will be over whether life exhibits nothing more than the outcome of undirected natural processes or whether life exhibits the activity of an intelligent cause—usually called a designer—who in creating life has impressed on it clear marks of intelligence. For simplicity let us refer to the first view as naturalistic evolution. As for the second view, we already know it as intelligent design. The key question to be resolved in the creation-evolution controversy is deciding which of these views is correct. How then to resolve this question?

The first thing to notice is that naturalistic evolution and intelligent design both make definite assertions of fact. To see this, let us get personal. Here you are. You had parents. They in turn had parents. They too had parents. And so on. If we run the video camera back in time, generation upon generation, what do we see? Do we see a continuous chain of natural causes that go from apes to small furry mammals to reptiles to slugs to slime molds to blue green algae and finally all the way back to a prebiotic soup, with no event in the chain ever signaling the activity of an intelligent cause? Or, as we trace back the genealogy, do we find events that clearly signal the activity of an intelligent cause? There exist reliable criteria for inferring the activity of intelligent causes. Does natural history display clear marks of intelligence and thereby warrant a design inference, or doesn't it? To answer this question one way is to embrace intelligent design; to answer it the other way is to embrace naturalistic evolution.

Darwinists are quite clear about rejecting intelligent design and affirming naturalistic evolution. For instance, in *The Meaning of Evolution* George Gaylord Simpson, one of the founders of the neo-Darwinian synthesis, asserts,

> Although many details remain to be worked out, it is already evident that all the objective phenomena of the history of life can be explained by purely naturalistic or, in a proper sense of the sometimes abused word, materialistic factors. They [that is, the objective phenomena of the history of life] are readily explicable on the basis of differential reproduction in populations [that is natural selection], and the mainly random interplay of the known processes of heredity [that is random mutation, the other major element in the Darwinian picture]. Therefore, man is the result of a purposeless and natural process that did not have him in mind.

Where does Simpson derive his confidence that naturalistic evolution is correct and intelligent design is incorrect? How can Simpson so easily elide the weaknesses in his theory and then with perfect equanimity assert "it is already evident that all the objective phenomena of the history of life can be explained by purely naturalistic factors"? And how does Simpson know that when the "many details that remain to be worked out" do get worked out, that they will not overthrow naturalistic evolution and instead confirm intelligent design? Science is after all a fallible enterprise. Where then does Simpson get his certainty?

To answer this question we need to examine how the Darwinian establishment employs the third word in our trio, namely, *science.* Although design theorists take the question Which is correct, naturalistic evolution or intelligent design? as a legitimate question, it is not treated as a legitimate question by the Darwinian establishment. According to the Darwinian establishment naturalistic evolution addresses a scientific question whereas intelligent design addresses a religious question. Thus, for the Darwinian establishment, intelligent design is a nonstarter. Naturalistic evolution and intelligent design taken together may be mutually exclusive and exhaustive, but naturalistic evolution is the only viable scientific option. Intelligent design must therefore be ruled out of court.

Why is this? The answer is simple. Science, according to the Darwinian establishment, by definition excludes everything except the material and the natural. It follows that all talk of purpose, design and intelligence is barred entry from the start. By defining science as a form of inquiry restricted solely to what can be explained in terms of undirected natural processes, the Darwinian establishment has ruled intelligent design outside of science. But suppose that a design theorist comes along and like most Americans thinks intelligent design is correct and naturalistic evolution is incorrect. (According to a Gallup poll close to 50 percent of Americans are creationists of a stricter sort, thinking that God specially created human beings; another 40 percent believe in some form of God-guided evolution; and only 9 percent are full-blooded Darwinists. This 9 percent, however, controls the academy.) The design theorist's first inclination might be to say, "No big deal. Intelligent design is at least as good an answer to biological origins as is naturalistic evolution. Science just happens to be limited in the questions it can pose and the answers it can give." Any such concession is deadly and turns science into the lap dog of naturalistic philosophy.

The problem is this. As Phillip Johnson rightly observes, science is the only universally valid form of knowledge within our culture. This is not to say that scientific knowledge is true or infallible. But within our culture, whatever is purportedly the best scientific account of a given phenomenon demands our immediate and unconditional assent. This is regarded as a matter of intellectual honesty. Thus to consciously resist what is currently the best scientific theory in a given area is, in the words of Richard Dawkins, to be either stupid, wicked or insane. Thankfully, Richard Dawkins is more explicit than most of his colleagues in making this point and therefore does us the service of not papering over the contempt with which the Darwinian establishment regards those who question its naturalistic bias.

It bears repeating: the only universally valid form of knowledge within our culture is science. Within late-twentieth-century Western society neither religion, nor philosophy, nor literature, nor music nor art makes any such cognitive claim. Religion in particular is seen as making no universal claims that are obligatory across the board. The contrast with science is stark. Science has given us technology—computers that work as much here as they do in the Third World. Science has cured our diseases. Whether we are black, red, yellow or white, the same antibiotics cure the same infections. It is therefore clear why relegating intelligent design to any realm other than science (e.g., religion) ensures that naturalistic evolution will remain the only intellectually respectable option for the explanation of life.

But there is a problem. Intelligent design and naturalistic evolution both inquire into definite matters of fact. If every cell were to have emblazoned on it the phrase "made by Yahweh," there would be no question about intelligent design being correct and naturalistic evolution being incorrect. Granted, cells do not have "made by Yahweh" emblazoned on them. But that is not the point. The point is that we would not know this unless we looked at cells under the microscope. For precisely this reason both intelligent design and naturalistic evolution must remain live scientific options, unfettered by artificial a priori requirements about what can count as legitimate explanations in biology.

Naturalistic evolution and intelligent design are real possibilities. What is more, as mutually exclusive and exhaustive possibilities, one of these positions has to be correct. The Darwinian establishment so defines science that naturalistic evolution alone can constitute a legitimate scientific answer to the question How did life originate and develop? Nonetheless, when Stephen J. Gould, Michael Ruse, Richard Dawkins, George Gaylord Simpson and their disciples assert that naturalistic evolution is true, they purport that naturalistic evolution is the conclusion of a scientific argument based on empirical evidence. But it is nothing of the sort. The empirical evidence is in fact weak, and the conclusion follows necessarily as a strict logical deduction once science is as a matter of definition restricted to undirected natural processes. Naturalistic evolution is therefore built directly into a naturalistic construal of science.

Logicians have names for this—circular reasoning and begging the question being the best known. The view that science must be restricted solely to undirected natural processes also has a name. It is called methodological naturalism. So long as methodological naturalism sets the ground rules for how the game of science is to be played, intelligent design has no chance of success. Phillip Johnson makes this point eloquently. So does Alvin Plantinga. In his work on methodological naturalism Plantinga remarks that if one accepts methodological naturalism, then naturalistic evolution is the only game in town.

Since naturalistic evolution is so poorly supported empirically and since intelligent design is having such a hard time passing for science, what is wrong with a simple profession of ignorance? In response to the question How did life originate and develop? what is wrong with saying we don't know? (Such a profession of ignorance was the reason Michael Denton's *Evolution: A Theory in Crisis* was panned by the Darwinian establishment.) As philosophers of science Thomas Kuhn and Larry Laudan have pointed out, for scientific paradigms to shift, there has to be a new paradigm in place ready to be shifted into. You cannot shift into a vacuum. Napoleon III put it this way: "One never really destroys a thing till one has replaced it." If you are going to reject a reigning paradigm, you have to have a new, improved paradigm with which to replace it. Naturalistic evolution is the reigning paradigm. But what alternative is there to naturalistic evolution? Logically the only alternative is intelligent design. But intelligent design, we are told, is not part of science.

There is a simple way out of this impasse, and that is to reject methodological naturalism. We need to realize that methodological naturalism is the functional equivalent of a full-blown metaphysical naturalism. Metaphysical naturalism asserts that nature is self-sufficient. Methodological naturalism asks us for the sake of science to pretend that nature is self-sufficient. But once science is taken as the only universally valid form of knowledge within a culture, it follows that methodological and metaphysical naturalism become functionally equivalent. What needs to be done, therefore, is to break the grip of naturalism in both guises, methodological and metaphysical. And this happens once we realize that it was not empirical evidence but the power of a metaphysical worldview that was all along urging us to adopt methodological naturalism in the first place.

### Conclusion

At the start of this chapter I described mere creation as a theory of creation aimed specifically at defeating naturalism and its consequences. We are finally in a position to give a precise definition of mere creation. Mere creation is a four-pronged approach to defeating naturalism. The prongs are as follows:

1. A scientific and philosophical critique of naturalism, where the scientific critique identifies the empirical inadequacies of naturalistic evolutionary theories and the philosophical critique demonstrates how naturalism subverts every area of inquiry that it touches;

2. A positive scientific research program, known as intelligent design, for investigating the effects of intelligent causes;

3. A cultural movement for systematically rethinking every field of inquiry that has been infected by naturalism, reconceptualizing it in terms of design; and

4. A sustained theological investigation that connects the intelligence inferred by intelligent design with the God of Scripture and therewith formulates a coherent theology of nature.

Where does mere creation stand currently? Through the work of Phillip Johnson and his colleagues, the scientific and philosophical critiques of naturalism are now well in hand. To be sure, naturalists continue to resist these critiques. Nevertheless the tide has turned. The naturalistic dream of turning science into applied materialist philosophy is no longer tenable. With the publication of Michael Behe's *Darwin's Black Box,* intelligent design has taken its first baby steps. Intelligent design is a fledgling science. Even so, intelligent design is a fledgling of enormous promise. Many books and articles are in the pipeline. I predict that in the next five years intelligent design will be sufficiently developed to deserve funding from the National Science Foundation. Whether it receives such funding will depend on how much progress is made on mere creation's third prong. Virtually every discipline and endeavor is presently under a naturalistic pall. To lift this pall will require a new generation of scholars and professionals who explicitly reject naturalism and consciously seek to understand the design God has placed in the world (see Bruce Chapman's postscript in this volume). Theologians will have the task of taking up all these developments, formulating a coherent theology of nature that makes sense not only of God creating, sustaining and acting in the world but also of God incarnating himself in Jesus Christ. The third and fourth prongs are for now the least developed.

The possibilities for transforming the intellectual life of our culture are immense. Daniel Dennett speaks of Darwinism as a "universal acid" that has fundamentally transformed every aspect of Western culture. Dennett is right. Darwin gave us a creation story, one in which God was absent and undirected natural processes did all the work. That creation story has held sway for more than a hundred years. It is now on the way out. When it goes, so will all the edifices that have been built on its foundation. But what will be built in its place? And who will do the building? Mere creation is a golden opportunity for a new generation of Christian scholars. In *The End of Christendom* Malcolm Muggeridge wrote, "I myself am convinced that the theory of evolution, especially to the extent to which it has been applied, will be one of the greatest jokes in the history books of the future. Posterity will marvel that so very flimsy and dubious an hypothesis could be accepted with the incredible credulity it has." The movement whose inception is represented in this volume promises to turn Muggeridge's posterity into today's generation.

# Part 1

## Unseating Naturalism

# 1

# Nature

*Designed or Designoid*

## WALTER L. BRADLEY

ICHARD DAWKINS BEGINS *CLIMBING MOUNT IMPROBABLE* BY CON-
trasting two rock formations (Dawkins 1996). The first is a weathered hillside in Hawaii that, when it is viewed from a certain
direction at a certain time of day at a certain time of the year,
casts a shadow that has a resemblance to John F. Kennedy. The second is the
magnificent Mount Rushmore in South Dakota, where the images of Presidents Washington, Jefferson, Theodore Roosevelt and Lincoln are clearly
seen from any angle at any time of the day, any season of the year. Obviously
the weathered hillside in Hawaii is the result of pure accident while the faces
on Mount Rushmore were carefully designed. Dawkins goes on to claim that
living systems in nature look as though they, like Mount Rushmore, were
designed but can be explained naturalistically. Dawkins calls such objects in
nature "designoids." The character of the cosmos, particularly the coincidence that the universal constants are indeed what they need to be to provide
a suitable home for life, must also be a designoid in Dawkins's thinking. In
fact Dawkins's materialistic philosophy would lead him to assign the label
*designoid* to all facets of nature that give the appearance of design, assuming
as he does the nonexistence of a creator or a designer (see Dawkins 1986).
The purpose of this chapter is to show that not every facet of nature that
appears designed is merely a designoid, but rather that nature includes facets
that may rightly be regarded as designed.

## Possible Designoids

We therefore consider three possible designoids.

1. The physical universe is surprising in the simple mathematical form it assumes. All the basic laws of physics and fundamental relationships can be described on one side of one sheet of paper because they are so few in number and so simple in form (see table 1.1).

2. The universal constants that are needed in these mathematical descriptions of the laws of nature (table 1.1) and the fundamental properties of matter in nature (such as unit charge, mass of electron, mass of proton, etc.) must be carefully prescribed if a universe suitable not just for life as we know it but suitable for life of any imaginable type is to be possible. The values of some of these constants are provided in table 1.2.

3. The existence of living systems requires the specification of some very complex boundary conditions, such as the sequencing required to get functional biopolymers. As Michael Polanyi noted some years ago, both machines and living systems transcend simple explanations based on the laws of chemistry and physics, requiring as they do highly improbable initial conditions or time independent boundary constraints (Polanyi 1967).

Polanyi illustrated his argument with a discussion of an automobile. The operation of every part of the automobile can be fully explained in terms of principles of chemistry and physics. When the piston is lowered, air and vaporized gasoline are drawn into the cylinder. This mixture is subsequently compressed as the piston rises to the top of its stroke. A spark ignites the mixture, allowing the reaction of the oxygen in the air with the gasoline, releasing a large amount of energy. This released energy causes tremendous pressure on the piston, which is then displaced downward. This downward motion is transmitted to the drive shaft as torque, which is then transmitted to the wheels of the car, completing the transformation of chemical energy in the gasoline into kinetic energy of the moving automobile. Every step can be nicely explained by the laws of chemistry and physics. Yet these laws cannot account for the existence (i.e., origin) of the automobile, but only for its operation. The highly unusual (boundary) conditions under which the chemical energy in the gasoline is converted into kinetic energy in the automobile are the result of careful design of the system and its component parts by a mechanical engineer who subsequently passed the drawings to a skilled machinist who fabricated the pieces and then gave them to a mechanic who assembled the pieces in just the right fashion. Human intelligence is a crucial factor in the existence of a functional automobile. Polanyi argues that living systems are far more complicated than the machines of people and thus provide an even greater challenge to the observer to explain their existence in terms of natural laws alone.

☐ Mechanics (Hamilton's Equations)

$$\dot{p} = -\frac{\partial H}{\partial q} \qquad \dot{q} = \frac{\partial H}{\partial p}$$

☐ Electrodynamics (Maxwell's Equations)

$$F^{\mu\nu} = \partial^{\mu} A^{\nu} - \partial^{\nu} A^{\mu}$$

$$\partial_{\mu} F^{n\nu} = j^{\nu}$$

☐ Statistical Mechanics (Boltzmann's Equations)

$$S = -h \int + \log f \, d\bar{v}$$

$$\frac{dS}{dt} \geq 0$$

☐ Quantum Mechanics (Schrödinger's Equations)

$$I h \, | \, \dot{\psi} \rangle = H \, | \, \psi \rangle$$

$$\Delta \times \Delta P \geq \frac{h}{2}$$

☐ General Relativity (Einstein's Equation)

$$G_{\mu\nu} = -8\pi G T_{\mu\nu}$$

Table 1.1   Fundamental Laws of Nature

## Universal Constants

| Boltzmann's constant | $k = 1.38 \times 10^{-23}$ J/°K |
| Planck's constant | $h = 6.63 \times 10^{-34}$ J/s |
| Speed of light | $c = 3.00 \times 10^{8}$ m/s |
| Gravitational constant | $G = 6.67 \times 10^{-11} \dfrac{N-m^2}{kg^2}$ |

## Properties of Matter

| Neutron rest mass | $M_n = 1.674 \times 10^{-27}$ kg |
| Electron rest mass | $M_e = 9.11 \times 10^{-31}$ kg |
| Proton rest mass | $M_p = 1.672 \times 10^{-27}$ kg |
| Electron or proton unit charge | $e = 1.6 \times 10^{-19}$ coul |
| Mass-energy relation | $c^2 = \dfrac{E}{m}$ J/kg |

## Fine Structure Constant

$$a_e = \frac{e^2}{\hbar c} = \frac{1}{137}$$

Table 1.2   Universal Constants

**Critical Issues in Designed or Designoid Systems**

At the human level the engineer can deal only with prescribing boundary conditions, having no control over the laws of nature, the universal constants or the fundamental properties of matter. It is important to emphasize that in the prescribing of boundary conditions, the challenge is not to establish order but rather complexity. Much of the discussion in the scientific literature does not make this distinction and thus wrongly argues that self-ordering can somehow solve the boundary condition problem. The regular arrangement of atoms in a crystal bear scant resemblance to the informational requirements of a biopolymer. Thaxton, Bradley and Olsen (1984) emphasized that the informational requirements needed to construct a crystal are quite small. Specify the requirements for the unit cell (the smallest subdivision of the crystal that retains all of the essential symmetry features) and then just repeat infinitum. However, to make a functional protein for a DNA molecule, one must specify the sequencing for a very large number of amino acid units in protein or bases in DNA. Function in biopolymers is inextricably connected to the specific aperiodic sequence of building blocks, and it is this specification of sequence to which I refer as biological information. This distinction is developed in detail by Steven C. Meyer in chapter five of this volume.

In an analogous way the same type of problem attends cosmology. A universe that is suitable to support life seems to require a very narrow prescription of the various universal constants. Whether biological and cosmological information can be accounted for in some naturalistic way, as claimed by Dawkins (1986, 1996), or is the result of activity by an intelligent designer who works on a cosmic scale, much like the mechanical engineer who designs a car, is the crucial issue to be addressed in this chapter and by the other chapters in this volume.

**Proposed Designoid Solutions to the Appearance of Cosmological and Biological Design**

The most prominent and promising proposed solution to the apparent design in cosmology are string theory and the unified field theory (Weinberg 1992). It is claimed that these theories may eventually explain why many of the universal constants have exactly the values that they must (cosmological information for our design or designoid universe) to provide a universe that is suitable not just for life as we know it but for life of any imaginable type.

During the last fifty years, however, at least seven natural explanations for biological design have been proposed to account for biological information: time plus chance; natural ordering due to equilibrium thermodynamics; irreversible (nonequilibrium) thermodynamics; intrinsic chemical bonding preferences; self-organizing systems; complexity from simple algorithms; and mutation or natural selection.

The three most prominent currently are Dawkins's incrementalist approach via mutation or natural selection (Dawkins 1986, 1996), Prigogine's irreversible thermodynamics of nonlinear systems (Prigogine 1980) and Kauffman's self-ordering systems (Kauffman 1993, 1995). Each claims to provide immediately or have the potential to provide eventually a naturalistic explanation that is adequate to account for biological information, making all biological appearances of design in actuality designoids. In what follows, each of these proposals will be critiqued to see to what degree they can immediately or may ultimately provide a sufficient cause to account for the informational results we see in the cosmos and in living systems, rendering the universe a designoid rather than a true design by an intelligent creator or designer.

**Design or Designoid: The Mathematical Form That Nature Takes**
It has been widely recognized for some time that nature assumes a form that is elegantly described by a relatively small number of simple, mathematical relationships, as previously noted in table 1.1. None of the various proposals presented later in this chapter to explain the complexity of the universe address this issue. Albert Einstein in a letter to a friend expressed his amazement that the universe takes such a form (Einstein 1956), saying:

> You find it strange that I consider the comprehensibility of the world to the degree that we may speak of such comprehensibility as a miracle or an eternal mystery. Well, a priori one should expect a chaotic world which cannot be in any way grasped through thought. . . . The kind of order created, for example, by Newton's theory of gravity is of quite a different kind. Even if the axioms of the theory are posited by a human being, the success of such an enterprise presupposes an order in the objective world of a high degree which one has no a priori right to expect. That is the "miracle" which grows increasingly persuasive with the increasing development of knowledge.

Alexander Polykov (1986), one of the top physicists in Russia, commenting on the mathematical character of the universe, said: "We know that nature is described by the best of all possible mathematics because God created it." Paul Davies, an astrophysicist from England, says, "The equations of physics have in them incredible simplicity, elegance and beauty. That in itself is sufficient to prove to me that there must be a God who is responsible for these laws and responsible for the universe" (Davies 1984). Successful development of a unified field theory in the future would only add to this remarkable situation, further reducing the number of equations required to describe nature, indicating even further unity and integration in the natural phenomena than have been observed to date.

## Design or Designoid: Setting the Values of the Universal Constants—Prescribing the Cosmological Information

The remarkable coincidences that the universal constants (see table 1.2) are just what they need to be to provide a universe suitable for life of any imaginable type have been well documented in a series of books published in the past ten years (e.g., Davies 1988; Tipler and Barrow 1986; Breuer 1991; Gribbins and Rees 1993). It is useful to highlight a few of these coincidences to illustrate the physical nature of cosmic informational requirements to provide a suitable home for life of any imaginable type. While life does not necessarily have to assume the form that it has on earth (or in our universe), it is possible to identify minimal requirements that would apply for life of any imaginable type. These would include such requirements as a reasonable amount of elemental diversity to provide for the molecular complexity to process energy, store information and replicate (which are minimal functions for living systems) and a reasonably stable source of energy such as is provided by our sun.

Brandon Carter in 1970 showed that a 2 percent reduction in the strong force and its associated constant would preclude the formation of nuclei with larger numbers of protons, making the formation of elements heavier than hydrogen impossible. On the other hand, if the strong force and associated constant were just 2 percent greater than it is, then all hydrogen would be converted to helium and heavier elements from the beginning, leaving the universe no water and no long-term fuel for the stars. The absolute value of the strong force constant, and more importantly, its value relative to the electromagnetic force constant is not "prescribed" by any physical theories, but it is certainly a critical requirement for a universe suitable for life (Breuer 1991, 183). Carter has also shown that the existence of a sun such as our own that provides the long-term source of energy required for the existence of life depends on the very precise specification of the gravity force constant, the electromagnetic force constant, the mass of the proton and the mass of the electron. It is remarkable that the values of these four apparently independent physical constants are exactly what they must be to provide for a long-term source of energy such as our sun provides.

The existence of elements heavier than beryllium is again the result of the remarkable coincidence first predicted by Hoyle (Hoyle et al. 1953) and later confirmed experimentally of a quantum energy level in carbon at exactly the value needed to provide for a very efficient conversion in a fusion reaction from beryllium (reacting with helium) to carbon and a partially efficient conversion of carbon (reacting with helium) to oxygen, leaving an ample supply of both. The existence of this precise energy level in carbon in turn is the consequence of the very precise values of the strong force and the electromagnetic force constants.

More than one hundred similar cosmological coincidences have been identified. Initially there was a tendency to attribute these coincidences to fortuitous accidents, as evidenced by an early quotation from Hoyle (1951, 103-4):

> I have often seen it stated that our situation on earth is providential. The argument goes like this. It is providential that the earth is of the right size and at the right distance from the sun. It is providential that the sun radiates the right kind of heat and light. It is providential that the right chemical substances occur on earth. A long list of this sort of statements could be compiled, and to some people it looks as if there is indeed something very strange and odd about our particular home in the universe. But I think that this outlook arises from a misunderstanding of the situation. Because if everything was not just right we should not be here. We should be somewhere else (or more likely, no where).

However, many scientists are no longer willing to attribute these coincidences to chance, as is evidenced by a much more recent quotation from Hoyle: "Such properties seem to run through the fabric of the natural world like a thread of happy coincidences. But there are so many odd coincidences essential to life that some explanation seems required to account for them" (Hoyle 1983, 220). Arno Penzias, Nobel laureate in physics and the director of Bell Laboratories until its recent fragmentation, makes this observation about the enigmatic character of the universe: "Astronomy leads us to a unique event, a universe which was created out of nothing, and delicately balanced to provide exactly the conditions required to support life. In the absence of an absurdly-improbable accident, the observations of modern science seem to suggest an underlying, one might say, supernatural plan" (Brock 1992).

In summary it is clear that providing a universe that is suitable for life requires a remarkable assignment of the values for the various universal constants. The source of this cosmological information requires some explanation. How may these remarkable coincidences be explained in terms of natural laws? At present none of the explanations to be discussed with regard to biological information and design have any bearing on cosmological information and design. It has been suggested that a unified field theory might show that certain of the constants are causally connected to each other so that they are not independently assigned. However, in such a theory the residual constants would almost certainly need to be prescribed even more narrowly. Why these constants happen to be exactly what they need to be when they could in principle assume any value does not seem to be reducible to a naturalistic cause or explanation.

## Design or Designoid: The Origin of Biological Information

We now consider the seven possible natural explanations for how biological information might be created.

*Random chance.* It was fashionable in the middle part of the twentieth century to attribute biological information and complexity to chance plus time (Monod 1972). However, as our understanding of the enormous biochemical complexity associated with the origin of life and the development of more complex life forms has matured, appeals to chance have gradually lost credibility. Appeals to chance have been further hurt by the recognition that the universe is not infinitely old. In fact the widespread acceptance of the big bang cosmology after the discovery of background radiation in 1965 caused chance to lose favor very quickly as a suitable explanation for the origin of life (Kenyon and Steinman 1969). It would be fair to say that chance is nothing more than the God of the gaps of the atheist, expressing as an article of faith what reason cannot demonstrate.

*Spontaneous ordering near equilibrium—phase changes.* It is common for proponents of naturalistic sources of biological information resulting in designoids to use analogies to simple phase changes in nature in which disordered systems become spontaneously ordered, as when randomly arranged water molecules become highly ordered molecules in an ice crystal or a snowflake. However, this solution can be easily understood to be the simple result of providing a chemical energy driving force that is sufficiently strong to overcome the natural tendency to disorder when the temperature is reduced to a sufficiently low value (below the melting point). The melting point in fact is thermodynamically determined by the ratio of the change in enthalpy (mainly chemical bonding energy) during the phase change divided by the associated change in the entropy of the system. Details of this argument have been presented elsewhere (Thaxton, Bradley, and Olsen 1984; Meyer, chap. 5 in this volume).

An analogy may be helpful. If I have a pool table with a dip in the center of the table and I gently agitate the table, I would expect in due course to find all of the balls in the dip in the center of the table, since this represents the position of lowest potential energy. However, this explanation is irrelevant to the formation of biopolymers and biological information for two reasons. First, the change in the enthalpy in the polymerization of biopolymers is positive (needs energy to be supplied, endothermic) rather than negative (gives off energy, exothermic), which would correspond to a hump in the center of the pool table. This makes the polymerization process much more difficult. Second and more importantly, the order in crystals has very little information and thus does a poor job of mimicking the specified aperiodicity in the sequencing of functional biopolymers, which is very information-intensive.

It is worth noting that all living systems live energetically well above equilibrium and require a continuous flow of energy to stay there (much as a hot water heater maintains hot water above the equilibrium temperature of the room). Equilibrium is associated with death in the biosphere, making any explanation of the origin of life that is based on equilibrium thermodynamics clearly incorrect. In summary phase changes such as water freezing into ice cubes or snowflakes is irrelevant to the processes necessary to generate biological information.

*Prigogine's spontaneous self-organization in irreversible thermodynamic systems far from equilibrium.* Prigogine's work is based on much more significant analysis and supporting experiments than is Dawkins's while making much more modest claims of progress. The self-organization Prigogine (Prigogine 1980; Prigogine, Nicolis, and Babloyantz 1972) can predict and demonstrate experimentally requires the following conditions: the system must be open and subject to a constant input and output of matter and energy, implying systems constrained to be far from equilibrium; various catalytic, cross-catalytic or feedback processes must be present in the system, insuring that the description of the system kinetics will include nonlinear differential equations; and certain well-defined values of imposed constraints must be imposed so that fluctuations are not damped but can grow.

The nature of the self-organization that is predicted and empirically demonstrated by Prigogine and others in this field of irreversible thermodynamics is spontaneous spatial ordering and/or time-dependent cycling in a system. While such behaviors constitute an increase in the complexity of the behavior of the system compared with that observed at equilibrium, it is more the type of order that we see in crystals, with little resemblance to the type of complexity that is seen in biopolymers.

Autocatalytic activity in RNA could provide the possibility of similar behavior in a biological system, if the system has the necessary constraints and system parameters specified. However, the nature of the outcome would be more polymerization of RNA-like chain segments but with no assistance in sequencing. Again, this whole approach does not seem capable of generating the aperiodic, specified complexity that is usually associated with biological information essential to life.

In an article dealing with self-organization in irreversible thermodynamic systems, Prigogine, Nicolis and Babloyantz (1972) indicated that they were "tempted to hope" that such phenomena might one day explain how one gets from molecules to man. Fourteen years later, in the most recent book highlighting their work in this area, Babloyantz (1986, 220) comments wistfully,

> The bold and audacious hypothesis which assumes that life has been created as a result of the self-organization of matter is new. At the present time it seems the only valid hypothesis which reconciles matter and life. Ultimately, such an idea must be confirmed in laboratory experiments. We are at the very beginning of such an endeavor, and the road from molecules to life is still very long and full of pitfalls. However, we are entitled to HOPE that sometime in the future it can be proved unambiguously that self-organized properties of reacting and flowing systems constitute the missing link in the evolution of molecules to man.

Prigogine's group has made remarkable progress in showing how highly constrained systems meeting certain parametric requirements can self-organize. However, this self-organization does not yet seem to provide any useful path to biological information.

*Physical or chemical forces in nature.* Steinman and Cole (1967) published a paper in the National Academy of Science's Proceedings that purported to demonstrate that sequencing of amino acids in proteins is not random (or by chance, which proved to be too improbable) but rather depends on the variations in the affinity of various amino acids for one another. Support for this hypothesis was presented which was based on the number of dipeptide bonds formed in a solution in which amino acids were allowed to react to form dipeptides. The observed dipeptide bond frequencies were then compared with the sequencing of amino acids for ten actual proteins and were found to correlate nicely. Thus for a time it was thought that this chemical affinity might be able to account for the amino acid sequencing in proteins.

Subsequent work by Kok, Taylor, and Bradley (1988), however, has clearly demonstrated that the original amino acid dipeptide bond frequencies for the ten actual proteins reported by Steinman and Cole were incorrect. Furthermore, when dipeptide bonds frequencies from 250 different proteins taken from the *Atlas of Protein Sequence and Structure* (Dayhoff 1965) were considered, the frequency was found to correlate much better with random statistical probabilities than with the experimentally measured dipeptide bond frequencies of Steinman and Cole.

There is a more fundamental reason for doubting that chemical affinities can account for biological information. If the steric interference between various proteins was strong enough to determine sequencing, then one would expect to get only one or possibly a few sequences. The great variety of sequences noted in different proteins argues strongly for an explanation other than intrinsic physical or chemical forces in nature. Furthermore, sequencing of bases in DNA could not have been explained in this way in any case since the backbone chain bonds are all identical, with the bases as side chains off the backbone.

*Kauffman and Santa Fe Institute's approach to complexity and self-organization.* As it has become more widely recognized that the complexity of even the simplest imaginable living thing defies piecewise assembly in a prebiotic soup or elsewhere, scientists have looked for promising alternative paradigms to the traditional "soup theory" to explain both the origin and development of the complexity that is ubiquitous in nature. Stuart Kauffman (1993, 1995) of the Santa Fe Institute is the leading proponent of the most popular new paradigm. Accordingly complexity results naturally from the self-organizing character of nature. In two recent books Kauffman (1993, technical; 1995, shorter and less technical presentation of the same ideas) argues that the origin of "life" is essentially inevitable, not vastly improbable as Jacques Monod (1972), Francis Crick (1981), Robert Shapiro (1986) and the present author have previously argued (Thaxton, Bradley, and Olsen 1984).

Kauffman defines "life" as a closed network of catalyzed chemical reactions that reproduce each molecule in the network—a self-maintaining and self-reproducing metabolism that does not require self-replicating molecules. Kauffman's ideas are based on computer simulations alone without any experimental support. He argues with his computer simulations that when a system of simple chemicals reaches a critical level of diversity and connectedness, it undergoes a dramatic transition, or phase change. Kauffman further postulates that molecules in such a system undergo a dramatic transition, combining to create larger molecules of increasing complexity and catalytic capability—Kauffman's definition of life.

Such computer models ignore important aspects of physical reality that, if they were included in the models, would make the models not only more complicated but also incapable of the self-organizing behavior that is desired by the modelers. For example, Kauffman's origin of life model requires a critical diversity of molecules so that there is a high probability that the production of each molecule is catalyzed by another molecule. For example, he posits $1/1,000,000$ as the probability a given molecule catalyzes the production of another molecule (which is too optimistic a probability based on catalyst chemistry). If one has a system of 1,000,000 molecules, then in theory it becomes highly probable that most molecules are catalyzed in their production, at which point this catalytic closure causes the system to "catch fire," effectively to come to life (Kauffman 1995, 64).

Einstein said that we want our models to be as simple as possible but not too simple (i.e., ignoring important aspects of physical reality). Kauffman's model for the origin of life ignores critical thermodynamic and kinetic issues that, if they were included in his model, would "kill" his "living system." For example, there are kinetic transport issues in taking Kauffman's system with 1,000,000 different types of molecules, each of which can be catalyzed in its production by approximately 1 type of molecule, and organizing it in such a way that the catalyst that produces a given molecule will be in the right proximity to the necessary reactants to be able to be effective. Kauffman's simple computer model ignores this enormous organizational problem that must precede the "spontaneous self-organization" of the system. Here he is assuming away (not solving) a system-level configurational entropy problem that is completely analogous to the molecular-level configurational entropy problem discussed in Thaxton, Bradley, and Olsen (1984).

Kauffman does acknowledge that polymerization of biopolymers goes uphill energetically, an important physical reality that is also ignored in his simple model. His three proposed solutions to this problem all complicate his simple model in ways that are untenable. For example, he suggests that coupling the energetically unfavorable polymerization reactions with other energetically favorable chemical reactions could solve the thermodynamic problem, but he fails to recognize that this dramatically increases the logistical problems in kinetic transport mentioned previously, solving the chemical energy (enthalpy) problem while enlarging the configurational entropy problem. Dehydration and condensation onto substrates, his other two possible solutions to the thermodynamic problems, also further complicate the logistics of allowing all of these 1,000,000 molecules to be organized into a system in which all catalysts are rightly positioned relative to reactants to provide their catalytic function, again significantly increasing the configurational entropy problem.

It would be useful to quantify the magnitude of increase in the configurational entropy barrier that is implicit in each of Kauffman's solutions to the physical shortcomings he acknowledges in his model, as well as the shortcomings he apparently does not recognize or at least acknowledge as Thaxton, Bradley, and Olsen (1984) have previously done for biopolymers. Unfortunately he does not provide sufficient details in his model to allow such a calculation to be made, and any calculation would be very model-specific. However, given the number of items to be arranged and the specificity needed to give function, it would most likely be much greater than that associated with a biopolymer.

Kauffman's (1995, chap. 3) origin-of-life discussion is entitled "A Chemical Creation Myth," which it truly is. Chapter four is entitled "Order for Free." But Kauffman's "self-ordering" only appears to be free because he ignores the thermodynamic and kinetic realities which incur the "real costs of this ordering."

John Horgan (1995) quotes W. Brian Arthur of the Santa Fe Institute as saying, "If Darwin had a computer on his desk, who knows what he could have discovered." Horgan then wryly comments, "What indeed: Charles Darwin might have discovered a great deal about computers and very little about nature." Horgan describes the entire field of complexity as being based on a seductive syllogism: There are simple sets of mathematical rules that when followed by a computer give rise to extremely complicated patterns. The world contains many extremely complicated patterns. Conclusion: Simple rules underlie many extremely complicated phenomena in the world. Horgan quotes John Maynard-Smith, one of the pioneers of mathematical biology, as referring to such simulation science as "fact-free science," where mentioning observational facts is considered to be in bad taste. Horgan concludes that given our lack of knowledge of how life might arise here or elsewhere, whether life began as Kauffman and his colleagues at the Santa Fe Institute say is entirely a matter of speculation, and all the computer simulations in the world cannot make it less so.

*Simple algorithms as a source of information.* In those portions of Kauffman's (1993, 1995) books that deal with evolution rather than the origin of life, he employs computer simulations of Boolean networks to show that simple algorithms can produce complex patterns. In a vague analogy to biology, he infers that nature can likewise produce biological complexity. However, one must not forget that the simple algorithms on which Kauffman bases the analogy operate on a very complex computer to produce the observed cyberspace complexity. The problem in nature is that one must find not only appropriately simple algorithms but also the computer in which the simple algorithm can operate to generate complexity. You do not get something (i.e., complexity) for nothing (i.e., a simple algorithm).

Dawkins (1986) also resorts to computer algorithms to support his argument that biological information can be generated easily via natural selection with a computer simulation entitled *The Blind Watchmaker.* What he demonstrates is that a very sophisticated computer system with a relatively simply algorithm can produce a variety of patterns on the computer screen, some surprisingly complex. This analogy fails to explain the origin of complexity in nature for two reasons. First, he begins with a very sophisticated computer bootlegging in a high degree of complexity to his starting point. Second, he has failed in the ten years since he first published *The Blind Watchmaker* book and computer simulation to point out any processes in nature that would be examples of his computer algorithms. If this is indeed how complexity is generated in nature, why are examples so hard to find?

In 1986 Dawkins offered one thousand dollars to the first person who could create an algorithm that could produce a certain biomorph. Both the first- and second-place finishers in this contest indicated that an algorithm alone could not produce the required biomorph (Pittman 1989). Without building "design" into the system to give some direction and constraint, the biomorph could not be produced, which is probably analogous to the real situation in nature.

*Dawkins's incremental approach to information generation.* Dawkins in his most recent books (1986, 1996) argues strongly that random mutations in combination with highly directed natural selection can account for all biological information. He presses his argument not with empirical data but with cleverly devised analogies from nature and from computer-generated biomorphs. What is the substance of these arguments?

In *Climbing Mount Improbable,* Dawkins cheerfully admits that living systems cannot possibly be created in one improbable step any more than Mount Improbable can be scaled on its nearly vertical face in one gigantic and improbable step. However, he argues that by coming up the back side in many small steps, it can be scaled. He acknowledges the difficulty in larger steps that require macromutations, expressing some differences with Gould about just how large of a mutation is likely to occur. For this analogy to be meaningful, however, Dawkins's tacit assumption is that there is a way to the top of the mountain that can be climbed like a well-honed footpath, a path carefully put into place by the park rangers so climbers can avoid any larger steps.

Mutations produce the change in information while natural selection is the source of improvement in the quality of the information. However, this process cannot take the larger steps that are associated with the origin of light-sensitive cells in an organism, for example. Thus Dawkins's journey to the top of Mount Improbable is possible only if the path can realistically be made in a large number of small steps. Michael Behe (1996) clearly demonstrates this is not the case, rendering Dawkins's argument untenable.

Dawkins's bold claims to tell us how Mount Improbable may be scaled offer no fundamental principles of promise regarding how biological information of the scale needed to explain macroevolution might be generated and absolutely no empirical support for his thesis that there is a footpath to the top of Mount Improbable with sufficiently small steps. In a recent letter to the editor of *The Independent* Brian Josephson, professor of physics at Cambridge University, summarizes Dawkins's approach:

> In such books as the *Blind Watchmaker,* a crucial part of the argument concerns whether there exists a continuous path, leading from the origins of life to man, each step of which is both favored by natural selection, and small enough to have happened by chance. It appears to be presented as a matter of logical necessity that such a path exists, but actually there is

no such logical necessity; rather, commonly made assumptions in evolution require the existence of such a path. (Josephson 1997)

**Conclusion**

Not only has science failed to provide naturalistic explanations for the mathematical form of nature, the coincidence of cosmological constants, and the emergence of living things, but also these facets of nature all demonstrate the essential element of design, namely, information. Various naturalistic explanations for this biological and cosmological information have been reviewed and found wanting.

Chance and intrinsic chemical properties of matter have both been considered and abandoned as unreasonable explanations for the complexity we see in the character of the universe and in biological systems. The ordering that results from a local decrease in enthalpy (as in a phase change) cannot account for cosmological or biological information but only for the kind of ordering that is seen in crystals.

Constraint of systems far from equilibrium can produce self-organization that takes the form of spatial ordering and/or cycling over time. However, neither biological information (e.g., aperiodic specificity in sequencing of biopolymers) nor cosmological information is created in such processes. The limited ordering and information produced in such systems is consistent with the information level of the constraints imposed on the system.

Self-organization in complex systems that consists of large numbers of chemicals coupled together have been demonstrated primarily in computer simulations. Again the complexity or information that can be produced in an actual system depends on logistically arranging the many chemical reactions that take place in a very complicated way so that the required coupling can occur. While this is not a problem in the computer, it would be a nightmare in a real system of 1,000,000 chemical reactions. In reality the information associated with the self-organization in such systems is almost certainly less than the informational requirements to make the necessary spatial arrangements. Again we see that there do not seem to be any free lunches in nature when one is trying to explain the origin of information.

Natural selection acting on mutationally induced random change in the genetic code can produce biological information where the steps are small, what we normally associate with microevolution. The origin of new systems such as sight, which begins with irreducible complexity of a light-sensitive cell, cannot be accounted for by mutation or natural selection alone. Only the gently rolling high pastures on the back side of Mount Improbable can be crossed by this process, and you cannot reach the top of Mount Improbable by passing only through gently rolling high pastures. No cosmological information (i.e., finely tuned cosmological constants) results from mutation or natural selection.

The similarity between such information in nature and the production of information by human intelligence argues persuasively for an intelligent creator or designer. Consistent with this hypothesis is the utter failure of all natural processes that have been identified to date to account for biological and cosmological information. Our best scientific evidence supports a universe that is designed and not merely a designoid.

## References

Babloyantz, A. 1986. *Molecules, dynamics and life.* New York: Wiley & Sons.

Behe, M. 1996. *Darwin's black box.* New York: Simon and Schuster.

Breuer, R. 1991. *The anthropic principle: Man as the focal point of nature.* Boston: Birkhauser.

Brock, D. L. 1992. *Our universe: Accident or design?* Wits, South Africa: Star Watch.

Crick, F. 1981. *Life itself.* New York: Simon and Schuster.

Davies, P. 1984. *Superforce.* New York: Simon and Schuster.

———. 1988. *The cosmic blueprint.* New York: Simon and Schuster.

Dawkins, R. 1986. *The blind watchmaker.* New York: Norton.

———. 1996. *Climbing Mount Improbable.* New York: Norton.

Dayhoff, M. O. 1965. *Atlas of protein sequence and structure.* Silver Springs, Md.: National Biomedical Research Foundation.

Einstein, A. 1956. *Lettres a Maurice Solovine.* Paris: Gauthier-Villars.

Gribbins, J., and M. Rees. 1989. *Cosmological coincidences: Dark matter, mankind and anthropic cosmology.* New York: Bantam.

Horgan, J. 1995. From complexity to perplexity. *Scientific American* 272, no. 6 (June):104-9.

Hoyle, F. 1951. *The nature of the universe.* New York: Harper.

———. 1983. *The intelligent universe.* London: Michael Joseph.

Hoyle, F., D. N. F. Dunbar, W. A. Wensel, and W. Whaling. 1953. *Physics Rev.* 192:649.

Josephson, B. 1997. Letter to the editor. *The Independent,* January 12.

Kauffman, S. 1993. *Origins of order: Self-organization and selection in evolution.* New York: Oxford University Press.

———. 1995. *At home in the universe: The search for laws of self-organization and complexity.* New York: Oxford University Press.

Kenyon, D. H., and G. Steinman. 1969. *Biochemical predestination.* New York: McGraw-Hill.

Kok, R. A., J. A. Taylor, and W. L. Bradley. 1988. A statistical examination of self-ordering of amino acids in proteins. *Origin of Life and Evolution Biosphere* 18:135-42.

Monod, J. 1972. *Chance and necessity.* New York: Vintage.

Pittman, T. 1989. Another look at the blind watchmaker. *Origins Research* (spring/summer):10-11.

Polanyi, M. 1967. Life transcending chemistry and physics. *Chemical and Engineering News,* November, 45:54-64.

Polykov, A. 1986. Scientists at the frontiers. *Fortune,* October 13, 47-57.

Prigogine, I. 1980. *From being to becoming.* New York: Freeman.

Prigogine, I., G. Nicolis, and A. Babloyantz. 1972. *Physics Today,* November, 23-31.

Shapiro, R. 1986. *Origins: A skeptic's guide to the creation of life in the universe.* New York: Simon and Schuster.

Steinman, G., and M. Cole. 1967. *Proceedings of National Academy of Science USA* 58:735.

Thaxton, C. B., W. L. Bradley, and R. L. Olsen. 1984. *Mystery of life's origin: Reassessing current theories.* Dallas: Lewis and Stanley.

Tipler, F. J., and J. D. Barrow. 1986. *The anthropic cosmological principle.* New York: Oxford University Press.

Weinberg, S. 1992. *Dreams of a final theory.* New York: Pantheon.

# 2

# Unseating Naturalism

## *Recent Insights from Developmental Biology*

## JONATHAN WELLS

W HEN CHARLES DARWIN WROTE IN 1859 THAT ALL LIVING THINGS are the undesigned byproducts of random variations and natural selection, he argued more from analogy than from evidence. By excluding design from the history of life, Darwin's theory provided for many people a scientific justification for rejecting theism and embracing naturalism. Yet Darwinian evolution did not come of age as a scientific theory until its synthesis with population genetics in the 1930s, and it did not achieve its present dominance until James Watson and Francis Crick provided a molecular basis for genetics with their discovery of the structure of DNA in the 1950s (Bowler 1989).

Neo-Darwinism is elegantly simple. The theory can be summarized in four propositions: every organism develops according to a program encoded in its genes (which is to say, its DNA); DNA is the hereditary material that transmits traits from organisms to their descendants; new traits occasionally arise because of DNA mutations; and natural selection produces both microevolution (within a species or genus) and macroevolution (above the species or genus level) by favoring advantageous traits and thereby increasing the frequency of their genes in the population.

Since neo-Darwinism ties together all aspects of the origin and history of life, Theodosius Dobzhansky claimed that "nothing in biology makes sense" except in the light of it (Dobzhansky 1973). The centrality of DNA in the modern formulation of the theory prompted Crick to call this molecule "the secret of life" (Judson 1979, 175). And the evidence from molecular biology led Jacques Monod to declare that Darwinian evolution "is at last securely founded," thus proving that human beings are "not the center of creation" but "a mere accident" (Judson 1979, 217; Wells 1992).

The modern synthesis of Darwin's theory with population and molecular genetics, however, left out embryology. Embryology was "second to none in importance" for Darwin, and along with homology provided him with such convincing evidence for descent with modification that he would have adopted his theory "even if it were unsupported by other facts or arguments" (Darwin 1936, 346, 352). Yet embryology was virtually ignored by the modern synthesis (Bowler 1989; Gilbert 1994; Sapp 1987).

By 1980 this situation was beginning to change. Using the favorite organism of population geneticists, the fruit fly *Drosophila melanogaster*, developmental biologists started to decipher the action of genes in embryonic development, and by 1995 they had determined the DNA sequences of dozens of genes involved in setting up the body pattern of insects. They also found remarkably similar DNA sequences in many other types of organisms, including mammals.

The same comparative approach that revealed the almost universal occurrence of similar DNA sequences also discovered some surprising facts about embryogenesis. Darwin had noted that vertebrate embryos resemble each other at a certain stage in their development and considered this resemblance to be evidence of common ancestry. In fact, however, in the early stages of their development vertebrate embryos are radically different from each other. In the 1980s comparative embryologists began to find many cases in which organisms with very similar morphologies follow radically dissimilar pathways in early development. Rather than regarding this as a threat to Darwin's theory, evolutionary biologists are now interpreting it as evidence that early development can be easily modified to produce macroevolutionary change.

Thus developmental genetics seems to have provided empirical confirmation of the neo-Darwinian proposition that organisms develop according to a program encoded in their DNA that evolved from a common ancestor through mutation and natural selection. And comparative embryology seems to have provided evidence that major changes in early development are relatively easy to achieve. According to a recent review of advances in evolutionary and developmental biology, "the evidence for evolution is better than ever" (Gilbert, Opitz, and Raff 1996, 368).

Or is it? In the opinion of some biologists, myself included, recent discoveries in developmental genetics and comparative embryology pose serious problems for neo-Darwinism. Those discoveries have been welcomed into the City of Darwin, but I predict that, like a Trojan horse, they will bring that city down. To illustrate my point I will survey recent data about homeotic genes, which neo-Darwinists consider to be their best evidence that evolution modifies development by altering genetic programs, and show that those data raise more questions than they answer. I will also review recent advances in comparative embryology, which Darwin thought provided such convincing support for his theory, and show that those advances point to the need for a radically new approach to the study of living organisms. The best foundation for this new approach, I will argue, is not naturalism but design.

**Homeotic Genes**

More than a century ago biologists observed that parts of some animals occasionally develop like body parts normally found elsewhere in the organism. For example, the antenna of an insect sometimes develops as a leg, or a leg as an antenna. Such transformations were dubbed "homeotic" by William Bateson to indicate that the affected part has become "like" some other part of the organism (Bateson 1894). With the rise of modern genetics, such transformations were traced to mutations in homeotic genes that specify the identities of certain groups of cells during embryonic development.

One of the most famous homeotic mutations is *Antennapedia (Antp)*, so called because fruit flies that possess it grow legs on their heads where there would normally be antennae. (Another sort of mutation in the same gene can cause an antenna to grow from the thorax where there would normally be a leg.) The DNA sequence of *Antp* was determined in 1983, and it turned out to include a 180-base pair segment that was about 75 percent identical to segments in several other homeotic genes that were sequenced at about the same time. This segment was dubbed a homeobox, and it encodes a protein subunit called a homeodomain, which binds to DNA. Apparently homeotic genes affect development by regulating the expression of DNA.

For many biologists the neo-Darwinian proposition that development is controlled by a program encoded in the DNA was confirmed by the molecular characterization of homeotic genes. Developmental biologist Walter Gehring, codiscoverer of the homeobox, confidently reported in 1987 that "organisms develop according to a precise developmental program that specifies their body plan in great detail and also determines the sequence and timing of the developmental events. This developmental information is stored in the nucleotide sequences of the DNA" (Gehring 1987, 1245).

The eight principal homeotic genes in fruit flies (one of which is *Antp*) are differentially expressed along the anterior-posterior axis of the embryo. In other words, the product of one is found in the anterior part of the head, the product of a second is found just behind that, the product of a third behind the second, and so on (see figure 2.1). Apparently this differential expression pattern specifies the identities of cells along the body axis, and when the pattern is disrupted by homeotic mutations, cells assume incorrect identities (such as legs rather than antennae). By 1990 it was determined that these eight homeotic genes in the fruit fly are located on a single chromosome, where (remarkably!) they are arranged in the same order as their expression pattern in the embryo. Together, the eight genes in *Drosophila* have been dubbed the homeotic gene complex (HOM-C; Duboule 1994; Gilbert 1994).

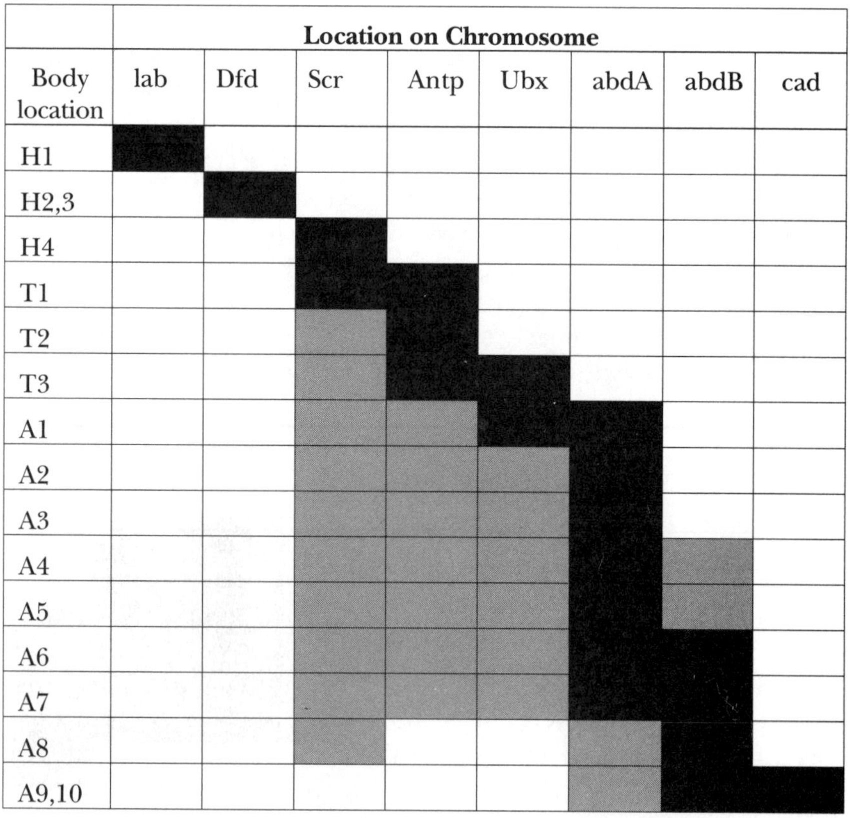

| Body location | Location on Chromosome | | | | | | | |
|---|---|---|---|---|---|---|---|---|
| | lab | Dfd | Scr | Antp | Ubx | abdA | abdB | cad |
| H1 | | | | | | | | |
| H2,3 | | | | | | | | |
| H4 | | | | | | | | |
| T1 | | | | | | | | |
| T2 | | | | | | | | |
| T3 | | | | | | | | |
| A1 | | | | | | | | |
| A2 | | | | | | | | |
| A3 | | | | | | | | |
| A4 | | | | | | | | |
| A5 | | | | | | | | |
| A6 | | | | | | | | |
| A7 | | | | | | | | |
| A8 | | | | | | | | |
| A9,10 | | | | | | | | |

**Figure 2.1  Embryonic Expression of the HOM-C Genes of the Fruit Fly**
**Adapted from Gilbert 1994**

In the past few years similar genes have been found in many other kinds of animals. Surprisingly, the similarities often include not only the DNA sequences of individual genes but also their order on the chromosome and their expression patterns in the embryo. Vertebrates, for example, have a cluster of genes (called the *Hox* complex) similar to the HOM-C of *Drosophila,* arranged in the same order on the chromosome and expressed in the same order along the anterior-posterior axis of the embryo (see figure 2.2). Although the correspondence is not exact, the similarities are striking; by interfering with the expression of *Hox-6* (the vertebrate counterpart of *Antp),* the anterior spinal cord in frogs can be morphologically transformed into hindbrain structures (Wright et al. 1989), and *Hox-6* from a mouse can mimic some of the functions of *Antp* when it is artificially transferred to a fly embryo (Gilbert 1994).

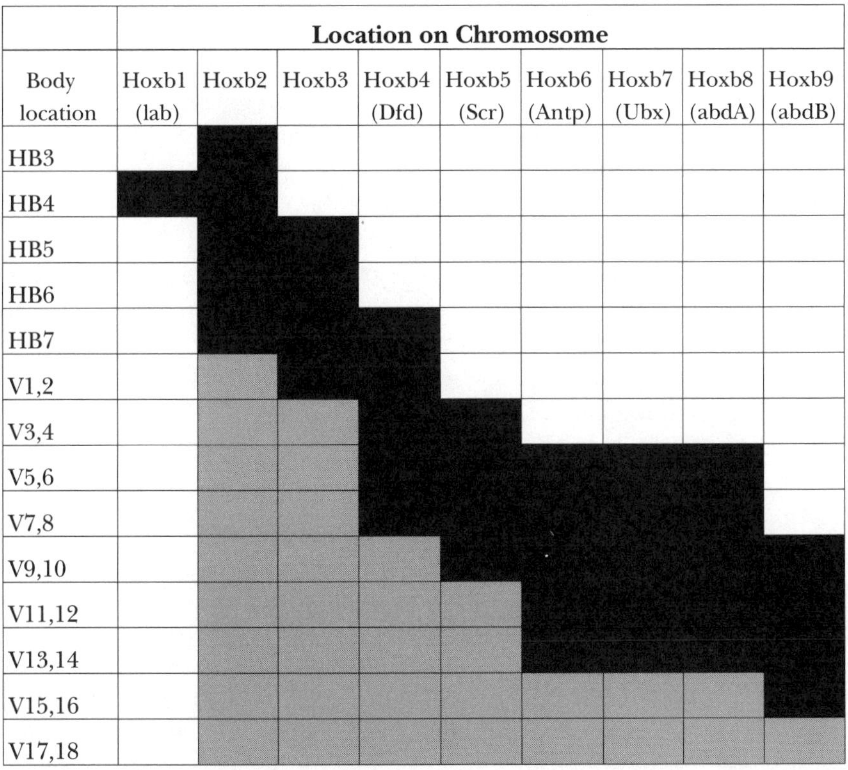

| Body location | Location on Chromosome | | | | | | | | |
|---|---|---|---|---|---|---|---|---|---|
| | Hoxb1 (lab) | Hoxb2 | Hoxb3 | Hoxb4 (Dfd) | Hoxb5 (Scr) | Hoxb6 (Antp) | Hoxb7 (Ubx) | Hoxb8 (abdA) | Hoxb9 (abdB) |
| HB3 | | ■ | | | | | | | |
| HB4 | ■ | ■ | | | | | | | |
| HB5 | | ■ | ■ | | | | | | |
| HB6 | | ■ | ■ | | | | | | |
| HB7 | | ■ | ■ | ■ | | | | | |
| V1,2 | | ▓ | ■ | ■ | ■ | ■ | | | |
| V3,4 | | ▓ | ▓ | ■ | ■ | ■ | | | |
| V5,6 | | ▓ | ▓ | ■ | ■ | ■ | ■ | ■ | |
| V7,8 | | ▓ | ▓ | ▓ | ■ | ■ | ■ | ■ | ■ |
| V9,10 | | ▓ | ▓ | ▓ | ▓ | ■ | ■ | ■ | ■ |
| V11,12 | | ▓ | ▓ | ▓ | ▓ | ▓ | ■ | ■ | ■ |
| V13,14 | | ▓ | ▓ | ▓ | ▓ | ▓ | ▓ | ■ | ■ |
| V15,16 | | ▓ | ▓ | ▓ | ▓ | ▓ | ▓ | ▓ | ■ |
| V17,18 | | ▓ | ▓ | ▓ | ▓ | ▓ | ▓ | ▓ | ▓ |

Figure 2.2 **Embryonic Expression of the Hox Genes of the Mouse**
**Adapted from Gilbert 1994**

There are other homeotic genes that are not in the HOM/*Hox* complexes. One such gene is *Pax-6*, which primarily affects eye development. *Pax-6* made the news in 1995 when Walter Gehring and his colleagues used it to induce eyes in unusual parts of the fly, such as the antennae and legs. Since it had previously been shown that *Pax-6* is similar in flies and mammals (including humans) and that sequences similar to the DNA-binding domain of *Pax-6* are present even in worms and squids (Quiring et al. 1994), Gehring and his colleagues concluded that they had found "the master control gene for eye morphogenesis" that is "universal" among multicellular animals (Halder, Callaerts, and Gehring 1995, 1792).

Darwinian biologists are excited about these recent advances. Not only have developmental geneticists succeeded in characterizing genes that have dramatic effects in embryogenesis, but also they have shown that these genes are probably present in all multicellular animals. According to biologist Sean Carroll, "One of the most important biological discoveries of the past decade is that arthropods and chordates, and indeed most or all other animals, share a special family of genes, the homeotic (or *Hox*) genes, which are important for determining body pattern" (Carroll 1995, 479). It seems as though the neo-Darwinian proposition that "novel morphological forms in animal evolution result from changes in genetically encoded programs of developmental regulation" (Davidson, Peterson, and Cameron 1995, 1319) has been empirically confirmed.

Or has it? Although most Darwinian biologists have not yet realized it, the very universality of homeotic genes invalidates the grand claims that are made for them. Here is why: If biological structures are determined by their genes, then different structures must be determined by different genes. If the same gene can "determine" structures as radically different as a fruit fly's leg and a mouse's brain or an insect's eyes and the eyes of humans and squids, then that gene is not determining much of anything.

Consider the analogy of an ignition switch in a vehicle. One might find similar ignition switches in vehicles such as automobiles, boats and airplanes, which are otherwise very different from each other. Perhaps in some sense an ignition switch can be called a master control; but except for telling us that a vehicle can be started by turning on an electrical current, it tells us nothing about that vehicle's structure and function.

Or perhaps a better analogy would be computer dip switches. A dip switch is a bank of binary toggle switches that can be set in various combinations to specify alternate states of a computer component, such as its electronic address. Many components might contain identical banks of switches, just as the cells in an organism contain identical homeotic genes; those components can be distinguished by the different settings of their dip switches, just as cells in the organism can be distinguished by differences in the expression of their homeotic genes. Again, a dip switch might be called a master control; but except for specifying alternate states of a computer component, dip switches explain nothing about that component's circuitry or operation.

Similarly, except for telling us how an embryo directs its cells into one of several built-in developmental pathways, homeotic genes tell us nothing about how biological structures are formed. As homeotic genes turn out to be more and more universal, the control they exercise in development turns out to be less and less specific.

Since HOM/*Hox* genes affect such radically different structures, some biologists (pointing out that both the fly's body and the mouse's brain are segmented) have suggested that their function is to specify segment identity. But *Antp*-like homeoboxes and HOM-C-like clusters have been found in animals with no segmentation at all (Holland and Hogan 1986; Kenyon and Wang 1991; Schierwater et al. 1991); and most evolutionary biologists are convinced that the segmentation of the fly's body arose independently of the segmentation in the mouse's brain (Barnes et al. 1988; Clark 1964; Hyman 1951; Jefferies 1986; Willmer 1990).

Likewise, since *Pax-6* affects such radically different structures as compound (multifaceted) insect and camera-like vertebrate eyes, some biologists have suggested that its original function was to specify an ancestral light-sensitive spot. But fruit flies possess simple eyes as well as compound eyes, and their simple eyes (the closest thing they have to light-sensitive spots) are unaffected by *Pax-6* (Halder, Callaerts, and Gehring 1995); and although some biologists are convinced that similarities among visual pigments in a variety of animals suggest a common ancestor (Martin et al. 1986), evolutionary biologists L. von Salvini-Plawen and Ernst Mayr concluded from a survey of the morphological and phylogenetic evidence that "the earliest invertebrates, or at least those that gave rise to the more advanced phyletic lines, had no photoreceptors" and that "photoreceptors have originated independently in at least 40, but possibly up to 65 or more different phyletic lines" (Salvini-Plawen and Mayr 1977, 10:253-54).

In other words, the universality of homeotic genes is supposed to be due to their presence in a common ancestor, but the preponderance of the evidence suggests that the common ancestor lacked the features that those homeotic genes now supposedly control. From a Darwinian perspective this is a serious problem. According to neo-Darwinism, complex gene sequences gradually evolve by conferring selective advantages on the organisms that possess them. But gene sequences confer selective advantages only if they program the development of useful adaptations. If a primitive animal possessed homeotic genes but lacked all of the adaptations now associated with them, then those genes must have originated prior to those adaptations. How then did homeotic genes evolve?

Neo-Darwinists can maintain that such genes evolved by encoding primitive adaptations that remain to be discovered, but this is ad hoc speculation. The bottom line is that each new piece of evidence demonstrating the universality of homeotic genes (and thus their independence from any particular adaptation) makes their presence in a putative common ancestor more difficult for neo-Darwinists to explain. Ironically the very discoveries that Darwinian biologists now find so exciting are adding to the list of difficulties for their theory.

If, instead, homeotic genes are the product of intelligent design, this particular difficulty disappears. Once design is admitted, there is no obstacle to saying that a complex gene sequence can originate quickly, based on future rather than past usefulness, and that its designer can incorporate it into a wide variety of organisms that otherwise share few structural similarities. Just as an engineer would not be surprised to find similar ignition switches in different kinds of vehicles produced by the same manufacturer, so biologists who admit design need not be surprised to find similar homeotic genes in most or all types of animals.

Thus a design approach is better able than neo-Darwinism to accommodate recent discoveries in developmental genetics. The superiority of a design perspective is also apparent in the light of recent discoveries in comparative embryology.

**Comparative Embryology**
Darwin considered some of the best evidence for his theory to be the striking resemblance of vertebrate embryos at an early stage of their development. He wrote in *The Origin of Species* that "the embryos of mammals, birds, fishes, and reptiles" are "closely similar, but become, when fully developed, widely dissimilar." He argued that the best explanation for their embryonic similarity was that such animals "are the modified descendants of some ancient progenitor." According to Darwin, "the embryonic or larval stages show us, more or less completely, the condition of the progenitor of the whole group in its adult state" (Darwin 1936, 338, 345).

Darwin believed that evolutionary changes tend to occur in the later stages of development and are gradually pushed back into embryogenesis, with the result that embryonic development bears the imprint of past evolution (in Ernst Haeckel's words, "ontogeny recapitulates phylogeny"). The doctrine of recapitulation fits so nicely with Darwin's theory that it has endured to the present and can be found in many modern biology textbooks. But it was clear to embryologists even during Darwin's lifetime that it did not fit the facts. Nineteenth-century embryologist Karl Ernst von Baer pointed out that although vertebrate embryos resemble each other at one point in their development, they never resemble the adult of any species, present or past. The most that can be said is that embryos in the same major group (such as the vertebrates, which include fishes, reptiles, birds and mammals) tend to resemble each other at a certain stage before they develop the distinguishing characteristics of their class, genus and species (Gould 1977; Hall 1992; Raff 1996).

Darwin and his followers ignored these difficulties, however, and the modern synthesis excluded embryology entirely. Only in the past twenty years, with the rise of developmental genetics, has comparative embryology attracted significant interest from evolutionary biologists. One result of this renewed interest has been the recognition that patterns of early development do not fit the Procrustean bed of recapitulationism.

Although it is true that vertebrate embryos are somewhat similar at one stage of their development, at earlier stages they are radically dissimilar. After fertilization, animal embryos first undergo a process called cleavage, in which the fertilized egg divides into hundreds or thousands of separate cells. During cleavage, embryos acquire their major body axes (e.g., anterior-posterior, or head to tail, and dorsal-ventral, or back to front). Each major group of animals follows a distinctive cleavage pattern; among vertebrates, for example, mammals, birds, fishes and reptiles cleave very differently.

Animal embryos then enter the gastrulation stage, during which their cells move relative to each other, rearranging themselves to generate basic tissue types and establish the general layout of the animal's body. The consequences of this process are so significant that embryologist Lewis Wolpert has written that "it is not birth, marriage, or death, but gastrulation which is truly the important event in your life" (Wolpert 1991, 12). Like cleavage patterns, gastrulation patterns vary markedly among the major groups of animals, including the different classes of vertebrates (Elinson 1987).

Only after gastrulation do the embryos of mammals, birds, fishes and reptiles begin to resemble each other. In the pharyngula stage, every vertebrate embryo looks vaguely like a tiny fish, with a prominent head and a long tail. The neck region of a vertebrate pharyngula also has a series of pharyngeal pouches, or tiny ridges, which recapitulationists misleadingly refer to as gill slits. Although in fish embryos these go on to form gills, in other vertebrates they develop into various other head structures such as the inner ear and parathyroid gland (Lehman 1987). The embryos of mammals, birds and reptiles never possess gills.

Therefore Darwin's belief in recapitulation is belied by the evidence.

Embryologists have occasionally pointed this out (de Beer 1958; Garstang 1922), but their admonitions have fallen mostly on deaf ears. As recently as 1976, biologist William Ballard (who, according to Richard Elinson, coined the term *pharyngula* [Elinson 1987]), lamented the fact that so much energy continues to be "diverted into the essentially fruitless 19th century activity of bending the facts of nature to support second-rate generalities." Ballard concluded that it is "only by semantic tricks and subjective selection of evidence" that one can argue that the cleavage and gastrulation stages of the various classes of vertebrates "are more alike than their adults" (Ballard 1976, 38).

Since 1980, with the rapprochement between developmental and evolutionary biology, there has been a growing recognition that the early stages of embryogenesis contradict Darwin's view. Rather than seeing the embryological evidence as a threat to evolutionary theory, however, Darwinian biologists now welcome it as a new source of support. Their reasoning goes something like this: major evolutionary changes require major changes in development; if similar morphologies (such as a pharyngula) can be reached by very different developmental pathways, as in the vertebrates, then early development must be more changeable than we thought; since early development is so changeable, then large-scale evolution must be relatively easy to achieve. As developmental and evolutionary biologist Rudolf Raff puts it, the "evolutionary freedom of early ontogenetic stages is significant in providing novel developmental patterns and life histories. These stages also contain an unexplored potential for the discovery of mechanisms of evolution of . . . animal body plans" (Raff 1996, 211). To explore this potential, Raff and others are now collecting and studying a wide variety of organisms in which similar morphologies are produced by very different developmental pathways.

For example, most sea urchins develop indirectly, passing through a feeding larva stage before they metamorphose into adults; but about 20 percent of the species that have been studied so far bypass the feeding larva stage and develop directly into adults. Raff and his colleagues have analyzed in detail the developmental differences between two Australian sea urchins of the genus *Heliocidaris*. Adults of the two species are morphologically similar and occupy the same habitat, yet one develops by means of a typical feeding larva while the other develops directly into an adult (Wray and Raff 1989). Direct development is not simply a matter of accelerating the formation of adult features but involves significant alterations in such fundamental processes as cleavage, gastrulation, embryonic axis specification and cell fate determination. Raff and his coworkers note that "the dramatic differences in embryonic development displayed by the two *Heliocidaris* species are usually thought to be restricted to higher taxonomic levels" (Raff 1987; Henry and Raff 1990, 68).

Similar cases of direct development are common in such diverse groups as mollusks, brachiopods, bryozoans, ascidians and frogs (Raff 1987). Although most people think of frogs as developing indirectly, through a tadpole stage, many species develop directly. One well-studied example is the South American marsupial frog, *Gastrotheca riobambae*. Marsupial frogs brood their fertilized eggs in a pouch on the female's back; in some species the embryos emerge from the pouch as tadpole larvae, while in others (such as *Gastrotheca riobambae*) they emerge as fully formed froglets. Surprisingly, early development in *Gastrotheca riobambae* is radically different from that of indirect developers. Although cleavage is similar, gastrulation leads to the formation of an embryonic disc from which most of the frog's body is derived (Del Pino and Elinson 1983). According to Elinson, this "is more reminiscent of reptile or bird development than of amphibian development" (Elinson 1987, 10).

So the embryos of many types of animals can reach similar morphologies by very different routes. Vertebrate embryos that resemble each other at the pharyngula stage differ radically from each other during the cleavage and gastrulation stages that precede it; sea urchins that are morphologically similar in adulthood may follow dramatically different developmental pathways to get there; and early embryogenesis in some frogs resembles that of reptiles and birds more than that of amphibians. Many biologists celebrate this variability in early development as providing an opportunity for macroevolutionary change. Others, myself included, see it as deepening the mystery of how embryos attain their final form.

From a naturalistic perspective, development supposedly proceeds mechanistically, like a ball rolling down a hill. Changes in developmental pathways are likely to produce alterations in the final outcome, and the earlier the changes, the more drastic the alterations. It would not be surprising, perhaps, if balls released in a specific direction consistently found their way to the same spot at the bottom of the hill; but it would be very surprising if balls that were diverted from their original trajectory, especially near the starting point, still found their way to the same spot. It would be even more surprising if similar coincidences were noted for many different kinds of balls at many different starting points.

From a design perspective, however, it is possible to regard development as an end-directed process. If organisms are designed, which is to say produced according to a preconceived plan, then in some sense their final form precedes their embryonic development. Rather than rolling freely down the hill, the developmental ball is attracted to its final resting place, which it could conceivably reach by a variety of routes unless it is prevented from doing so by obstacles along the way. Such thinking is anathema to neo-Darwinism, but before Darwin it was commonplace for embryologists to regard development as an end-directed process. Saying that final form guides embryogenesis does not settle the matter. As naturalistic critics point out, unless organic forms can be characterized in such a way as to guide fruitful research, they are scientifically useless.

Besides, Darwinian biologists respond, final forms are unnecessary, because development is guided by a genetic program encoded in the organism's DNA. When they are pressed for details, advocates of genetic programs often list homeotic genes as their premier examples; but as I have argued, the functions of those particular DNA sequences are disappointingly nonspecific. The insufficiency of a few examples does not necessarily invalidate the whole notion of a genetic program. It turns out, however, that there are other objections to it as well.

**Genetic Programs or Organic Forms?**
Although molecular biology has demonstrated conclusively that DNA carries the genetic code for the amino acid sequence of proteins, this is not sufficient to specify a whole organism. Combining DNA with all the ingredients necessary for protein synthesis does not make a cell.

Why not? Consider the analogy of building a house. One needs to specify and provide the building materials: boards of particular sizes and shapes, nails, insulation, shingles, windows, doors, electrical wires, pipes and so on. One also needs to specify the order in which components should be assembled, because the foundation must be completed before the walls and roof are erected and the plumbing and wiring are installed. Most important, one needs to specify the intended floor plan, because the individual materials could be combined in a number of different ways. Molecular biology has shown that an organism's DNA specifies the building materials. It turns out, however, that the assembly instructions are largely in other components of the cell, and that the floor plan has not yet been discovered.

Conceptually it is difficult to imagine how DNA could encode a floor plan, at least in eukaryotes. The DNA in the nucleus directs the production of messenger RNAs and proteins, which are then transported throughout the cell. In order to perform their functions these molecules must become localized in specific regions of the cell, and this depends on prior localization of receptors anchored to the membrane or on directed transport by the cytoskeleton (Alberts et al. 1989). The spatial patterning of membrane receptors and the organization of the cytoskeleton must precede the localization of molecules produced in the nucleus. The building blocks that make up the membrane and the cytoskeleton are themselves specified by DNA; but the three-dimensional structure of large aggregates of these building blocks is not determined by the structure of individual subunits any more than the floor plan of a house is determined by the shape of its bricks.

Consider, for example, the cytoskeleton, which consists of microtubules, intermediate filaments and microfilaments. All of these are assembled from protein subunits that the cell produces from templates in its DNA. But the assembly of these subunits into three-dimensional structures is a dynamic process which depends on intracellular nucleating sites and environmental cues, and which responds to the changing needs of the cell. Every time a cell changes its shape or divides to produce another cell, it must substantially rearrange its cytoskeleton, even though the subunits themselves are not altered. And even though all the cells in a multicellular organism use the same subunits, they assemble their cytoskeletons in different ways to produce morphologically different tissues.

Thus the generation of shape, or morphogenesis, is not reducible to subunit structure. Developmental biologist Brian Goodwin writes that "genes are responsible for determining which molecules an organism can produce," but this "fails to address the basic problem posed by morphogenesis, namely, how distinctive spatial order arises in embryos." He concludes that "the molecular composition of organisms does not, in general, determine their form" (Goodwin 1985, 32).

Shape is not the only variable unspecified by the DNA. In multicellular organisms, cell types differ in physiology as well as morphology. For example, liver cells, muscle cells and nerve cells are not only shaped differently but also manufacture different proteins and perform very different biochemical functions. Yet they all contain the same DNA, which they inherited from the fertilized egg. Whatever is producing the differences in these cells, it must be something other than their DNA. Developmental biologist H. F. Nijhout writes that "the only strictly correct view of the function of genes is that they supply cells, and ultimately organisms, with chemical materials." Furthermore the function of homeotic and other regulatory genes "is ultimately no different from that of structural genes, in that they simply provide efficient ways of ensuring that the required materials are supplied at the right time and place" (Nijhout 1990, 444).

In many organisms the region of the egg from which a cell develops determines what type of cell it will become. In such organisms there is evidence that cell differentiation is due to factors that are regionally localized in the fertilized egg. But such regional localization precedes gene activity in the cells whose developmental pathways it determines. In many organisms (such as sea urchins and frogs) early development is independent of the

DNA in the fertilized egg and can proceed even if all of it is removed or inactivated (Gilbert 1994). In other words, even in those organisms in which cellular differences can be traced directly to regional differences in the fertilized egg, the floor plan is independent of the DNA.

If the organism's floor plan is not in its DNA, where is it? Other features of an embryo that can carry developmental information include the cytoskeleton, the membrane and the cytoplasm. When a sperm fertilizes an egg, in many cases it transmits not only DNA but also a nucleating center, or centrosome, for the embryonic cytoskeleton. A parthenogenic frog can be produced by pricking an egg with a needle dipped in sperm homogenate; it turns out, however, that the needle does not need to introduce any DNA but only a functional centrosome (Klotz et al. 1990). Experiments with vertebrate tissues show that dividing cells transmit cytoskeletal patterns to their descendants that determine the spatial orientation of cells in those tissues (Locke 1990).

Membranes also carry morphogenetic information that can be inherited independently of DNA. Biological membranes are not merely featureless bags but include proteins and other molecules that are spatially distributed in highly structured patterns; and when a cell divides, its progeny inherit not only its DNA but also a membrane pattern. Experiments with protozoa (single-celled organisms possessing nuclei) show that surgical modifications of the membrane pattern can be passed on for many generations even though the organism's DNA has not been altered (Nanney 1983; Nelsen, Frankel, and Jenkins 1989).

So there are clearly other factors involved in heredity and development besides DNA. By itself this observation would not require the formulation of a radically new theory of evolution. Although it is incompatible with reductionistic, DNA-based neo-Darwinism, it is not necessarily incompatible with the more general notion of descent with modification. Biologist Sydney Brenner, who originally coined the term "genetic program," then later repudiated it for being too simplistic, did not abandon his commitment to Darwinian evolution, much less its underlying naturalism (Brenner 1973; Lewin 1984).

If the program for embryonic development is not in the genes, however, but at least partly in the cytoskeleton, the membrane and the cytoplasm, it becomes more difficult to explain how different developmental pathways could lead to similar results. Cleavage patterns are heavily dependent on the cytoskeleton, and the orientation of centrosomes in embryonic cells determines whether cleavage will be characteristic of mollusks, frogs or mammals. Gastrulation requires cell movements and cell shape changes that are heavily dependent on cytoskeleton reorganization. Cytoskeletal differences could account for differences in cleavage and gastrulation, but it seems very unlikely that they could then also account for later similarities. Yet sea urchins that exhibit different cleavage patterns develop into morphologically similar adults, and a gastrulation pattern normally seen in fishes can produce a frog.

Similar reasoning applies to the membrane and cytoplasm. In some types of organisms, differences in cell fate are largely determined by regionalization in the egg. Such differences are usually evident in early cleavage, and this is to be expected, since patterns in the membrane or cytoplasm that underlie regionalization are directly transferred in the process of cell division. It seems unlikely that such patterns could determine the final outcome of embryogenesis without noticeably affecting the intervening stages. Yet similar sea urchins can exhibit remarkable differences in cell fate determination during early development.

Consider once again the analogy of building a house. Some houses are built from a pile of lumber delivered to the job site; pieces are cut and nailed together one by one as the house gradually takes shape. Nowadays, however, more and more houses are built by assembling entire sections at centralized factories, then trucking them to the job site and erecting them in the course of an afternoon. The finished houses may be quite similar, and the list of materials that went into them might be identical, but the construction processes are quite different.

If an organism were a house, its DNA would specify the building materials, and the inherited arrangement of its cytoskeleton, membrane and cytoplasm would help to specify the order in which those materials are assembled. But the floor plan is determined neither by the building materials nor by the order in which they are assembled. Where then is the floor plan of the organism?

Physicists are better equipped than biologists to deal with a question like this, because physicists are more accustomed to thinking in terms of forms. Atoms and molecules are collections of electrons, protons and neutrons, but such particles cannot be combined in arbitrary ways. Instead they can only assume certain discrete configurations, as described by the equations of quantum mechanics. Although a particular configuration is mathematically specified, it may be reached by more than one pathway. Apparently organisms too can assume only certain discrete configurations, though these may be attainable by alternate pathways. In other words, there may be embryological equivalents of quantum-mechanical equations. Some as-yet-undiscovered law of development may do for embryos what quantum mechanics does for atoms and molecules.

A vague hint of what is to come might be found in complexity theory, in which physicists use the term *attractor* to describe stable points, curves or surfaces toward which complex movements tend to gravitate. For example, a pendulum slowing down because of friction gravitates (in this case, literally) toward an attractor (the point at which it is closest to the center of the earth). Even complex movements of fluids sometimes appear to form stable curves or surfaces, which complexity theorists have dubbed "strange attractors" because (unlike the pendulum's resting place) they are not specified by any known natural law. Yet the phenomena are reproducible (Gleick 1987).

Some biologists are now attempting to apply complexity theory to embryonic development (Goodwin 1994). Whether the solution will emerge from complexity theory or a more radical approach, however, it is not likely to emerge in the context of neo-Darwinism. Biologists who regard molecules as the only real entities and relentlessly attempt to reduce embryonic development to molecules in motion cannot take seriously the possibility that there are organic forms that are analogous to the allowed configurations of quantum mechanics or the attractors of complexity theory.

The sort of thinking that could account for recent discoveries in comparative embryology and open the way to future progress in biology is alien to neo-Darwinism. Instead creative thinking is much more likely to flourish in an intellectual environment in which organisms are regarded as designed. If an organism is designed, then the idea for it preceded its existence, and formal and final causes are real. To be sure, one can regard organisms as designed and still try to treat them as molecules in motion; but one is also liberated, even encouraged, to regard them as much more.

### Conclusion: Toward a New Paradigm

According to Thomas Kuhn, science normally functions within a "paradigm," a general theory that has successfully answered some important questions and that lays out a research program for further investigation (Kuhn 1970). Typically the general theory integrates specific inferences from various scientific disciplines and includes philosophical assumptions as well. Thus the Ptolemaic paradigm that dominated Western science until the sixteenth century integrated not only medieval astronomy but also Aristotelian physics and a geocentric cosmology.

Kuhn aroused the ire of many scientists when he argued that paradigms have philosophical and psychological components and are not readily discarded in the face of anomalous evidence. All of us, especially scientists, like to think of ourselves as reasonable people, willing to change our minds when we are confronted with contrary data. Kuhn, however, presented historical evidence that scientists generally resist or ignore anomalies and act to preserve the paradigm within which they conduct their research. For example, by the sixteenth century there were many observations inconsistent with a simple model of planets and stars revolving around the earth; yet rather than discard the Ptolemaic paradigm, astronomers continually adjusted it by adding epicycles, ad hoc corrections to the original theory.

Neo-Darwinism integrates data and inferences from a variety of scientific disciplines; it incorporates philosophical assumptions (such as naturalism); and its research program currently guides the work of most biologists. If Kuhn was correct, we may expect to see Darwinian biologists, like Ptolemaic astronomers, dealing with anomalous evidence by adding epicycles to their theory.

Anomalous evidence from developmental biology has been accumulating at an accelerating rate since 1980. The anomalies are not isolated results reported in obscure publications; instead they have been reproduced in many reputable laboratories and reported in the best peer-reviewed journals. In their zeal to confirm neo-Darwinism, some of the most talented biologists in the world have devoted years of work to analyzing the developmental effects of homeotic genes or searching for them in every conceivable type of organism. Each new discovery is featured prominently in the scientific press and celebrated as another nail in the coffin of those who oppose Darwinism. Ironically, however, these new discoveries about homeotic genes are subverting the paradigm that inspired them, because as those genes turn out to be more and more universal, the control they exercise in development turns out to be less and less specific and their origin more and more difficult to explain from a Darwinian perspective. Neo-Darwinists are left with ad hoc speculations about how homeotic gene sequences might have evolved before the adaptations which they now control; but these are merely the epicycles of a dying paradigm.

Recent discoveries that radically different developmental pathways can produce strikingly similar morphologies have not received the same enthusiastic press coverage as homeotic genes; but they too are highly reproducible and have been reported in the best peer-reviewed journals. These anomalies directly contradict what Darwin considered to be some of the best evidence for his theory. Yet modern Darwinians brush aside the contradiction and marvel at the ease with which early development can be modified. They speculate that they have found the mechanism of macroevolution, but their commitment to the Darwinian paradigm blinds them to the obvious question: How can such radical modifications produce similar outcomes?

Recent advances in developmental biology thus point to an impending paradigm shift. Advances in other fields do too, but the insights from developmental biology point so convincingly to a scientific revolution that (to steal a phrase from Darwin himself) "I should without hesitation adopt this view, even if it were unsupported by other facts or arguments" (Darwin 1936, 352). According to Kuhn, however, the shift cannot take place until a competing paradigm wins out over the old one.

The new paradigm, it seems to me, will be based on design. A design paradigm can account far better than naturalistic Darwinism for the origin of complex genes and their presence in a wide variety of organisms. A design paradigm can nurture the sort of formal and teleological thinking that will enable biologists to discover the laws of development that have so far eluded them. In order for a design paradigm to out-compete Darwinism, however, it will have to be developed to the point where it is philosophically rigorous and scientifically fruitful. I am confident that this can be done and that this conference will be a giant step in that direction.

## References

Alberts, B., D. Bray, J. Lewis, M. Raff, K. Roberts, and J. D. Watson. 1989. *Molecular biology of the cell.* 2nd ed. New York: Garland.

Ballard, W. W. 1976. Problems of gastrulation: Real and verbal. *BioScience* 26:36-39.

Barnes, R. S. K., P. Calow, P. J. W. Olive, and D. W. Golding. 1988. *The invertebrates: A new synthesis.* Oxford: Blackwell Scientific.

Bateson, W. 1894. *Materials for the study of variation treated with especial regard to discontinuity in the origin of species.* London: Macmillan.

Bowler, P. J. 1989. *Evolution: The history of an idea.* Rev. ed. Berkeley, Calif.: University of California Press.

Brenner, S. 1973. The genetics of behavior. *British Medical Bulletin* 29:269-71.

Carroll, S. B. 1995. Homeotic genes and the evolution of arthropods and chordates. *Nature* 376:479-85.

Clark, R. B. 1964. *Dynamics in Metazoan evolution: The origin of the coelom and segments.* Oxford: Clarendon Press.

Darwin, C. [1859] 1936. *On the origin of species.* 1859. Reprint, New York: Modern Library.

Davidson, E. H., K. J. Peterson, and R. A. Cameron. 1995. Origin of bilaterian body plans: Evolution of developmental regulatory mechanisms. *Science* 270:1319-25.

de Beer, G. 1958. *Embryos and ancestors.* 3rd ed. Oxford: Clarendon Press.

Del Pino, E. M., and R. P. Elinson. 1983. A novel developmental pattern for frogs: Gastrulation produces an embryonic disc. *Nature* 306:589-91.

Dobzhansky, T. 1973. Nothing in biology makes sense except in the light of evolution. *The American Biology Teacher* 35:125-29.

Duboule, D., ed. 1994. *Guidebook to the homeobox genes.* Oxford: Oxford University Press.

Elinson, R. P. 1987. Change in developmental patterns: Embryos of amphibians with large eggs. In *Development as an evolutionary process.* Ed. R. A. Raff and E. C. Raff. Vol. 8 of *MBL Lectures in Biology.* 12 vols. New York: Alan Liss. 8:1-21.

Garstang, W. 1922. The theory of recapitulation: A critical restatement of the biogenetic law. *Journal of the Linnean Society (Zoology)* 35:81-101.

Gehring, W. J. 1987. Homeo boxes in the study of development. *Science* 236:1245-52.

Gilbert, S. F. 1994. *Developmental biology.* 4th ed. Sunderland, Mass.: Sinauer.

Gilbert, S. F., J. M. Opitz, and R. A. Raff. 1996. Resynthesizing evolutionary and developmental biology. *Developmental Biology* 173:357-72.

Gleick, J. 1987. *Chaos: Making a new science.* New York: Penguin.

Goodwin, B. C. 1985. What are the causes of morphogenesis? *Bioessays* 3:32-36.

———. 1994. *How the leopard changed its spots.* New York: Charles Scribner's Sons.

Gould, S. J. 1977. *Ontogeny and phylogeny.* Cambridge, Mass.: Belknap Press.

Halder, G., P. Callaerts, and W. J. Gehring. 1995. Induction of ectopic eyes by targeted expression of the *eyeless* gene in *Drosophila. Science* 267:1788-92.

Hall, B. K. 1992. *Evolutionary developmental biology.* London: Chapman and Hall.

Henry, J. J., and R. A. Raff. 1990. Evolutionary change in the process of dorsoventral axis determination in the direct developing sea urchin, *Heliocidaris erythrogramma. Developmental Biology* 141:55-69.

Holland, P. W. H., and B. L. M. Hogan. 1986. Phylogenetic distribution of *Antennapedia*-like homeo boxes. *Nature* 321:251-53.

Hyman, L. H. 1951. *The invertebrates,* 2, *Platyhelminthes and Rhynchocoela.* New York: McGraw-Hill.

Jefferies, R. P. S. 1986. *The ancestry of the vertebrates.* London: British Museum (Natural History).

Judson, H. F. 1979. *The eighth day of creation.* New York: Simon and Schuster.

Kenyon, C., and B. Wang. 1991. A cluster of *Antennapedia*-class homeobox genes in a nonsegmented animal. *Science* 253:516-17.

Klotz, C., M.-C. Dabauvalle, M. Paintrand, T. Weber, M. Bornens, and E. Karsenti. 1990. Parthenogenesis in *Xenopus* eggs requires centrosomal integrity. *Journal of Cell Biology* 110:405-15.

Kuhn, T. S. 1970. *The structure of scientific revolutions.* 2nd ed. Chicago: University of Chicago Press.

Lehman, H. E. 1987. *Chordate development.* 3rd ed. Winston-Salem, N.C.: Hunter Textbooks.

Lewin, R. 1984. Why is development so illogical? *Science* 224:1327-29.

Locke, M. 1990. Is there somatic inheritance of intracellular patterns? *Journal of Cell Science* 96:563-67.

Martin, R. L., C. Wood, W. Baehr, and M. L. Applebury. 1986. Visual pigment homologies revealed by DNA hybridization. *Science* 232: 1266-69.

Nanney, D. L. 1983. The ciliates and the cytoplasm. *Journal of Heredity* 74:163-70.

Nelsen, E. M., J. Frankel, and L. M. Jenkins. 1989. Nongenic inheritance of cellular handedness. *Development* 105:447-56.

Nijhout, H. F. 1990. Metaphors and the role of genes in development. *Bioessays* 12:441-46.

Quiring, R., U. Walldorf, U. Kloter, and W. J. Gehring. 1994. Homology of the *eyeless* gene of *Drosophila* to the *small eye* gene in mice and *Aniridia* in humans. *Science* 265:785-89.

Raff, R. A. 1987. Constraint, flexibility and phylogenetic history in the evolution of direct development in sea urchins. *Developmental Biology* 119:6-19.

———. 1996. *The shape of life: Genes, development and the evolution of animal form.* Chicago: University of Chicago Press.

Salvini-Plawen, L. von, and E. Mayr. 1977. On the evolution of photoreceptors and eyes. *Evolutionary Biology* 10:207-63.

Sapp, J. 1987. *Beyond the gene: Cytoplasmic inheritance and the struggle for authority in genetics.* Oxford: Oxford University Press.

Schierwater, B., M. Murtha, M. Dick, F. H. Ruddle, and L. W. Buss. 1991. Homeoboxes in cnidarians. *Journal of Experimental Zoology* 260:413-16.

Wells, J. 1992. The history and limits of genetic engineering. *International Journal on the Unity of the Sciences* 5:137-50.

Willmer, P. 1990. *Invertebrate relationships: Patterns in animal evolution.* Cambridge: Cambridge University Press.

Wolpert, L. 1991. *The triumph of the embryo.* Oxford: Oxford University Press.

Wray, G. A., and R. A. Raff. 1989. Evolutionary modification of cell lineage in the direct-developing sea urchin *Heliocidaris erythrogramma*. *Developmental Biology* 132:458-70.

Wright, C. V. E., K. W. Y. Cho, J. Hardwicke, R. H. Collins, and E. M. De Robertis. 1989. Interference with function of a homeobox gene in *Xenopus* embryos produces malformations of the anterior spinal cord. *Cell* 59:81-93.

# Part 2

## Design Theory

# 3

# "You Guys Lost"

## Is Design a Closed Issue?

## NANCY R. PEARCEY

T HE SETTING WAS ONE OF THOSE NOTORIOUSLY COLORFUL DEBATES over evolution that scientists hate but the public loves. The combatants in this case were anthropologist Vincent Sarich and creationist Duane Gish. Eventually Sarich turned to Gish in exasperation and denounced the debate as an exercise in redundancy. After all, he said, the same debate was conducted a hundred years ago, and "you guys lost" (Dembski n.d., 2). In other words, Sarich was saying, creation was discredited in the nineteenth century by Darwin, so why are you resurrecting a dead issue?

It is commonly assumed that the battle over Darwinism was waged in the nineteenth century and that Darwin won the day because his theory was supported by the scientific evidence. To cite just two examples, zoologist Ernst Mayr asserts that "Darwin solved the problem of teleology, a problem that had occupied the best minds for the 2000 years since Aristotle" (Mayr 1964, xviii). Douglas Futuyma writes that "by coupling undirected, purposeless variation to the blind, uncaring process of natural selection, Darwin made theological or spiritual explanations of the life processes superfluous" (Futuyma 1986, 3). In the modern world Darwin's theory tends to be accepted by each new generation for the simple reason that it is part of the outlook in which we are reared and educated.

Yet I suggest that there are good reasons for returning to the site of battle and asking whether it was won fair and square. I propose to show that the battle was not won by Darwin in the sense normally intended: I will argue that Darwin was a turning point in biology not so much because the empirical evidence was persuasive but primarily because his theory proved useful in advancing a particular philosophy—a philosophy of science first of all and in many cases a general metaphysical position as well.

In modern culture science is accorded intellectual authority to define the way the world really is. The persuasive power of Darwinian theory stems from the aura of scientific factuality that surrounds it. If it can be shown that historically the primary motivation for advancing Darwin's cause was not so much scientific as philosophical, then the theory loses much of its persuasive force. For scientists have authority to tell us how the natural world functions, but they have no comparable authority to tell us what philosophy we ought to hold. If the motivation for accepting Darwinism was primarily philosophical, then we in the twentieth century are justified in calling for a resurrection of the old debate.

In this chapter I will first examine the writings of Darwin's core supporters in the nineteenth century. Contrary to a common misconception, Darwin did not win over many contemporaries to his theory. Even those who identified themselves as supporters often did not accept his theory of natural selection. It was not until the 1930s and 1940s, with the development of the modern synthesis (i.e., the combination of Darwin's theory with genetics), that natural selection was finally accepted as the central mechanism of evolution. Those who insist that Darwin closed the issue are anachronistically reading back into history the views held by most modern biologists.

Why then did Darwin become the focal point of debate in the nineteenth century, even for many who did not accept his theory? The answer has to do with a shift in the philosophy of science from an older epistemology that allowed for mind as a real cause in nature to a new epistemology that admitted nothing but natural causes. Darwin's theory seemed to show that a completely naturalistic account of living things was possible; as a result it attracted many supporters whose main interest was in promoting naturalism, even if they shrugged off the theory's scientific details. By probing the writings of the early Darwinists, I propose to show that their motivation was in fact primarily philosophical.

Second, I will look briefly at those who adopted a peacekeeping strategy, seeking to reconcile design and Darwin. What effects did their efforts have historically?

Third, I will analyze one of the most important strategies Darwin and his supporters used in order to discredit design. As the battle became more heated, they sought to make design implausible by casting it as perpetual miracle. In so doing they set up a straw man that continues to be useful to modern-day Darwinists.

Finally, I will suggest that the success of Darwin and his cohorts in the nineteenth century had much to do with their political expertise. They understood clearly that the battle is not only about ideas but also about institutions and power.

## The Non-Darwinian Darwinians

The argument that Darwin won the day in the nineteenth century, so why don't we all go home, ignores a key fact: namely, that Darwin did not win over most of his contemporaries. His theory was accepted by only a handful of scientists for a good three-quarters of a century, and then only after Mendelian genetics had provided a clearer understanding of heredity. The majority of Darwin's contemporaries came to agree that some form of evolution or development had occurred, but they championed other mechanisms and causes to explain the process. Generally they insisted either that God was directing the process or that it was propelled forward by some internal directing force.

Historian Peter Bowler goes so far as to suggest that the Darwinian revolution would be more accurately labeled the non-Darwinian revolution. Bowler argues that Darwin should be seen as "a catalyst that helped bring about the transition to an evolutionary viewpoint" but not to Darwinian evolution. Most commonly evolution was seen as an orderly, lawful, goal-directed and purposeful process analogous to the development of an embryo to an adult—"the preordained unfolding of a rationally ordered plan," often a divine plan. As Bowler puts it, "once convinced that evolution did occur, they [Darwin's followers] turned their backs on Darwin's message and got on with the job of formulating their own theories of how the process worked" (Bowler 1988, 4-5, 10-11, 30-31, 50, 66-67; Moore 1979; Richards 1992).

Ironically even those who championed Darwin's cause and who regarded themselves as Darwinians did not generally adopt his theory. That is, they did not accept his proposed mechanism for evolution, which gave pride of place to natural selection. Many were Lamarckians or speculated on other mechanisms for evolution. These historical facts provoke a question: If even Darwin's supporters were not attracted to his proposed scientific mechanism, what was his appeal?

The answer is that Darwin demonstrated how one might frame a completely naturalistic account of living things, an accomplishment that was attractive to those whose metaphysical stance was naturalistic and to others who felt that science at least should be completely naturalistic. Though his supporters did not think Darwin had succeeded in identifying the mecha-nism of evolution, still he had shown how one must reason in order to succeed eventually. He had focused on presently observable processes (proc-esses of "ordinary generation," as he put it) and extrapolated those processes into the past. It was not the specifics of Darwin's theory but his naturalistic methodology that attracted support.

For some time pressure had been building to frame a naturalistic ap-proach to biology. Since the triumph of Newtonian physics, many scientists had announced their intention of extending the domain of natural law to all other fields. But the complexities of living things had defied all attempts to fit them into the naturalistic mold. As Huxley asked plaintively in 1860, "Shall Biology alone remain out of harmony with her sister sciences?" (Huxley 1879). For those caught in this dilemma, Darwin came to the rescue. His goal was to show how biology might be transformed to fit the naturalistic ideal dominant in other fields of science. And not only biology but also the human sciences, since his theory included human origins in explaining all life by completely naturalistic causes.

Neal Gillespie sums up the point neatly:

It is sometimes said that Darwin converted the scientific world to evolution by showing them the process by which it had occurred. Yet the uneasy reservations about natural selection among Darwin's contemporaries and the widespread rejection of it from the 1890s to the 1930s suggest that this is too simple a view of the matter. It was more Darwin's insistence on *totally natural explanations* than on natural selection that won their adherence. (Gillespie 1979, 147, emphasis added)

Robert Young makes a similar point. The principal effect of the nine-teenth-century debate, he writes, was not providing an acceptable mecha-nism for evolutionary change. Rather it was "eliciting faith in the philosophical principle of the uniformity of nature"—bringing "the earth, life, and man under the domain of natural laws" (Young 1985, 82, 122, 120). From the 1860s to the 1930s, acceptance of Darwin's theory of natural selection declined while adherence to naturalism as a founda-tional assumption in biology increased. As Young puts it, there was ongoing debate about the mechanism of evolution, but "the uniformity of nature was progressively assumed to apply to the history of life, including the life and mind of man." Both the primary motivation for supporting Darwin and the principal effect of his work was not so much scientific as philosophical.

**Charles Darwin**

This interpretation is borne out by examining the writings of key nineteenth-century Darwinians, beginning with Darwin himself. The typical account, certainly in popular works, portrays Darwin as a man forced to the theory of natural selection by the weight of the facts. But professional historians tell a different story. Long before formulating his theory, Darwin nurtured a sympathy for philosophical naturalism. He was therefore predisposed toward a naturalistic theory of evolution even when the evidence itself was weak or inconclusive.

In a personal letter Darwin describes his gradual loss of religious belief and slide into naturalism. By the late 1830s he writes that he had come to consider the idea of divine revelation in the Old Testament "utterly incredible." He had also rejected the biblical concept of miracles. In his words, "The more we know of the fixed laws of nature the more incredible do miracles become." This commitment to "the fixed laws of nature" preceded Darwin's major scientific work and made it virtually inevitable that he would interpret the evidence through a naturalistic lens.

Gillespie notes the same progression. Once Darwin had decided in the late 1830s that "creationist explanations in science were useless," Gillespie writes, then "transmutation was left as virtually the only conceivable means of species succession." When Darwin began to consider the origin of species, "he did so as an evolutionist because he had first become a positivist, and only later did he find the theory to validate his conviction" (Gillespie 1979, 46).

Even when he found the theory, Darwin was aware that it could not be confirmed directly. Modern Darwinians often imply that the theory is so clearly supported by the facts that anyone who fails to concur must be intellectually dishonest or deranged. But Darwin was not so dogmatic. He described his theory as an inference grounded chiefly on analogy. And he praised the author of one review for seeing "that the change of species cannot be directly proved and that the doctrine must sink or swim according as it groups and explains phenomena" (Darwin 1899, 2:155). In an 1863 letter, he amplified by pointing out that evolution by natural selection was "grounded entirely on general considerations" such as the difference between contemporary organisms and fossil organisms. "When we descend to details," he wrote, "we can prove that no one species has changed [i.e., we cannot prove that a single species has changed]; nor can we prove that the supposed changes are beneficial, which is the groundwork of the theory. Nor can we explain why some species have changed and others have not" (Darwin 1899, 2:210). In other words, Darwin was aware that the scientific evidence was short of compelling.

The key to Darwin's own thinking is his philosophical commitment. Consider his stance on the origin of life. In the last sentence of the *Origin of*

*Species* Darwin resorted to Pentateuchal language, speaking of life, "with its several powers, having been originally breathed into a few forms or into one." (In a later edition he added "by the Creator.") But over time Darwin drifted toward a more consistently naturalistic position, provisionally accepting the spontaneous generation of life from inorganic material despite a striking absence of evidence for the theory at the time. In an 1882 letter, he wrote: "Though no evidence worth anything has as yet, in my opinion, been advanced in favour of a living being, being developed from inorganic matter, yet I cannot avoid believing the possibility of this will be proved some day in accordance with the law of continuity." Here is the naturalist's faith: Darwin is confident that a naturalistic theory will be found, not because the facts point in that direction but because he believes in the "continuity" of natural causes (Darwin 1903, 2:171).

This belief achieved almost religious status for Darwin. Years later William Darwin was to describe his father's attitude toward nature in near-devotional terms: "As regards his respect for the laws of Nature," William wrote of his father, "it might be called reverence if not a religious feeling. No man could feel more intensely the vastness and the inviolability of the laws of nature" (Durant 1985, 18). Darwin's intellectual journey seems to illustrate the adage that if one rejects a Creator, inevitably one puts something else in its place. In Darwin's case, he assigned godlike powers to the laws of nature.

To the end of his life Darwin struggled with a residual belief in theism, so there is some question whether he held strictly to metaphysical naturalism. But there is no question that at least he held to methodological naturalism in science. He did not argue that design was a weak theory or even a false theory; he argued that it was not a scientific theory at all. In 1856 he wrote to Asa Gray: "to my mind to say that species were created so and so is no scientific explanation, only a reverent way of saying it is so and so" (Darwin 1899, 1:437). As philosopher of biology David Hull writes, Darwin dismissed special creation "not because it was an incorrect scientific explanation but because it was not a proper scientific explanation at all" (Hull 1973, 26).

When Darwin's own ideas were attacked, he defended them by arguing that at least his proposed theory was naturalistic—which begged the question. As Young writes, "Whenever [Darwin] was really in trouble . . . he appealed to the very principle which was at issue, the uniformity of nature." Young then quotes John Tyndall in his Belfast Address in 1874: "'The strength of the doctrine of Evolution consists, not in an experimental demonstration (for the subject is hardly accessible to this mode of proof), but in its general harmony with scientific thought'" (Young 1985, 98). The underlying assumption is that genuinely scientific thought must be naturalistic. And once that assumption is granted, some form of naturalistic evolution will win the day by default.

## Herbert Spencer

In his autobiography Herbert Spencer recounts in excruciating detail the process by which he developed a naturalistic outlook, beginning when he was a boy. Over time, he writes, "a breach in the course of [physical] causation had come to be, if not an impossible thought, yet a thought never entertained" (Spencer 1904, 1:172). As in Darwin's case, members of Spencer's family described his adherence to naturalism in near-religious terms. His father drew a parallel between the son's naturalism and the father's own religion: "From what I see of my son's mind, it appears to me that the laws of nature are to him what revealed religion is to us, and that any wilful infraction of those laws is to him as much a sin as to us is disbelief in what is revealed" (Spencer 1904, 1:655).

This semireligious attachment to naturalism explains why Spencer eventually became a tireless promoter of Darwinism. It was not because he was persuaded by Darwin's scientific theory; he rejected Darwinism and embraced Lamarckianism. Yet Spencer saw clearly that once he had embraced philosophical naturalism, he had no alternative but to accept some form of naturalistic evolution. As he puts it, having discarded orthodox Christianity, he developed an "intellectual leaning towards belief in natural causation everywhere operating." And in that naturalistic leaning, "doubtless . . . a belief in evolution at large was then latent." Why latent? Because "anyone who, abandoning the supernaturalism of theology, accepts in full the naturalism of science, tacitly asserts that all things as they now exist have been evolved." Spencer accepted naturalism first and then accepted evolution as a logical consequence. He goes on: "The doctrine of the universality of natural causation, has for its inevitable corollary the doctrine that the Universe and all things in it have reached their present forms through successive stages physically necessitated" (Spencer 1904, 2:7). Just so: Once one accepts the philosophy of naturalism, some form of naturalistic evolution is an "inevitable corollary." Finding a plausible scientific theory is secondary.

In Spencer's writings we get a glimpse of the intellectual pressure that impelled him toward a naturalistic view of evolution. "I cheerfully acknowledge," he writes in *The Principles of Psychology*, that the hypothesis of evolution is beset by "serious difficulties" scientifically. Yet, "save for those who still adhere to the Hebrew myth, or to the doctrine of special creations derived from it, there is no alternative but this hypothesis or no hypothesis." And no one can long remain in "the neutral state of having no hypothesis" (Spencer 1896, 1:466n).

Similarly, in an 1899 letter, he writes that already decades earlier, "in 1852 the belief in organic evolution had taken deep root"—not for scientific reasons but because of "the necessity of accepting the hypothesis of Evolution when the hypothesis of Special Creation has been rejected." He concludes with these telling words: "The Special Creation belief had dropped out of my mind many years before, and I could not remain in a suspended state: acceptance of the only conceivable alternative was peremptory" (Duncan 1908, 2:319). Here is a candid admission that Spencer was driven by a sense of philosophical necessity—naturalistic evolution was "the only conceivable alternative" to creation—more than by a dispassionate assessment of the scientific evidence.

## Thomas H. Huxley

Thomas Huxley christened himself Darwin's bulldog and offered his natural "combativeness," as he put it, in service to the cause. So it may come as a surprise to learn that Huxley was never convinced that Darwin's theory of natural selection amounted to much scientifically; Huxley argued that the effectiveness of the mechanism would not be proved until a new species had been produced by artificial selection. By the 1870s he was even speculating on the existence of a "law of variation" that would somehow direct evolution, an idea he favored over Darwin's concept of random variations.

What then gave Huxley his bulldog determination to fight for Darwin? The answer is once again largely philosophical. Before his encounter with Darwin, Huxley writes, "I had long done with the Pentateuchal cosmogony." He had also surveyed early forms of evolutionary theory, finding them all unsatisfactory. And yet, he writes, he continued to nurse a "pious conviction that Evolution, after all, would turn out true" (Huxley 1903, 1:241, 243).

When Darwin published the *Origin of Species,* Huxley welcomed it as a vindication of that "pious conviction." As his son Leonard Huxley writes, "Under the suggestive power of the *Origin of Species,*" his father experienced "the philosophic unity he had so long been seeking" (Huxley 1903, 2:1). Huxley himself recalls that the *Origin* "did the immense service of freeing us for ever from the dilemma—Refuse to accept the creation hypothesis, and what have you to propose that can be accepted by any cautious reasoner?" (Huxley 1903, 1:246). Apparently Huxley, like Spencer, was so eager to be freed from that dilemma that he was willing to champion any naturalistic theory, even one he himself found scientifically implausible, so long as it provided an alternative to creation.

Consider Huxley's response to spontaneous generation. His son notes that "there was no evidence that anything of the sort had occurred recently." (Louis Pasteur had discredited all currently held theories of spontaneous generation.) Nevertheless his father persisted in believing that "at some remote period, life had arisen out of inanimate matter"—not because of any scientific evidence but as "an act of philosophic faith" (Huxley 1903, 2:16).

Huxley was especially sensitive to pressures to bring biology under the naturalistic framework that had become dominant in other fields of science. Geology had recently been placed on a new philosophical footing by Charles Lyell, and Huxley writes that Lyell's *Principles of Geology* persuaded him that new life forms must be generated by "ordinary agencies" at work today (by which he meant natural agencies). In his words, "consistent uniformitarianism postulates Evolution as much in the organic as in the inorganic world" (Huxley 1903, 1:243). In 1859 he wrote to Lyell: "I by no means suppose that the transmutation hypothesis is proven or anything like it. But . . . I would very strongly urge upon you that it is the logical development of Uniformitarianism, and that its adoption would harmonize the spirit of Paleontology with that of Physical Geology" (Huxley 1903, 1:252). That spirit was a consistent and relentless naturalism. As Huxley wrote elsewhere, the "whole theory crumbles to pieces" if one denies "the uniformity and regularity of natural causation for illimitable past ages" (Darwin 1899, 1:553).

Huxley was what Bowler terms a "pseudo-Darwinian": someone who rallied to Darwin for philosophical reasons even while remaining unconvinced of his scientific theory. In Bowler's words, Huxley was "guaranteed" to support Darwinism because of his "empiricist philosophy" (Bowler 1988, 70, 72). Or, as Gillespie puts it, he "leaned toward transmutation from intellectual necessity" (Gillespie 1979, 33). Huxley expresses his philosophical credo eloquently in *Man's Place in Nature* (1864): "Even leaving Mr. Darwin's views aside, the whole analogy of natural operations furnish so complete and crushing an argument against the intervention of any but what are called secondary causes, in the production of all the phenomena of the universe; that . . . I can see no reason for doubting that all are coordinate in terms of nature's great progression, from formless to formed, from the inorganic to the organic, from blind force to conscious intellect and will" (Huxley 1896, 151). As he put it more simply in a speech, if the world is governed by uniformly operating laws, then the successive populations of beings "*must* have proceeded from one another in the way of progressive modification" (Huxley 1859, 35, emphasis in original). If one accepts philosophical naturalism, then something very much like Darwinism must be true a priori. This explains why Huxley was willing to do battle for Darwin, without being overly concerned about the scientific details.

## Deduction from a Philosophy

"You guys lost" may be a fair assessment of the intellectual battle in the nineteenth century. But the question is how the battle was lost. It is often said that what made Darwin unique is that he provided a genuinely scientific mechanism for evolution—that others had proposed vague or idealist causes but in natural selection Darwin provided the first genuinely empirical mechanism. Yet, since most of Darwin's supporters did not accept his theory, that cannot be the reason for his success. I have argued that the battle was rigged—that Darwinism won less because it fit the empirical data than because it provided a scientific rationale for those already committed to a purely naturalistic account of life.

Both Darwin's supporters and opponents understood that philosophical naturalism was the central issue. Among opponents, Princeton theologian Charles Hodge wrote an essay titled *What Is Darwinism?* He answered bluntly that Darwinism is tantamount to atheism: "Natural selection is selection made by natural laws, working without intention and design." And "the denial of design in nature is virtually the denial of God" (Hodge 1994, 85, 155). Among supporters, Karl Vogt noted happily that Darwin's theory "turns the Creator—and his occasional intervention in the revolutions of the earth and in the production of species—without any hesitation out of doors, inasmuch as it does not leave the smallest room for the agency of such a Being" (cited in Hodge 1994, 110). Emil du Bois-Reymond wrote: "The possibility, ever so distant, of banishing from nature its seeming purpose, and putting blind necessity everywhere in the place of final causes, appears, therefore, as one of the greatest advances in the world of thought." To have "eased" this problem, du Bois-Reymond concludes, will be "Charles Darwin's greatest title to glory" (du Bois-Reymond, cited in Merz 1904, 1:435n). And finally, August Weismann: "We must assume natural selection to be the principle of the explanation of the metamorphoses because all other apparent principles of explanation fail us, and it is inconceivable that there should be another capable of explaining the adaptation of organisms without assuming the help of a principle of design" (cited in Lunn 1931, 101). Apparently only Darwinism would keep biology safe from design.

### Darwin and Design

Is it necessary, however, to drive such a sharp wedge between design and natural causes? Many if not most of the scientists in the Darwinian and post-Darwinian era sought some kind of middle ground. They gave God a directing role in evolution and asserted his constant supervision over the process. They located design not in the "contrivances" of living things (to use Paley's word) but in the laws that created those contrivances.

Gillespie calls this position nomothetic creation (creation by law) or providential evolution, depending on how much leeway is allowed to divine initiative. This category would include men such as Asa Gray, Charles Kingsley, the Duke of Argyll, St. George Jackson Mivart, Baden Powell,

Robert Chambers and Richard Owen. Despite important differences among these men, they agreed that natural laws are expressions of divine purpose and that God or mind directs or preordains the course of evolution. John Herschel states the position clearly: "An intelligence, guided by a purpose, must be continually in action to bias the directions of the steps of change—to regulate their amount—to limit their divergence—and to continue them in a definite course. We do not believe that Mr. Darwin means to deny the necessity of such intelligent direction" (Herschel 1867, 12n).

But Mr. Darwin did mean to deny the necessity of such intelligent direction. The design argument pointed to characteristics of living things that seemed analogous to the products of an intelligent mind, with its capacity for forethought, purpose and design. The challenge Darwin took on was to identify completely natural processes capable of mimicking the products of a mind. Gillespie describes Darwin's goal:

> It has been generally agreed (then [in Darwin's day] and since) that Darwin's doctrine of natural selection effectively demolished William Paley's classical design argument for the existence of God. By showing how blind and gradual adaptation could counterfeit the apparently purposeful design that Paley . . . and others had seen in the contrivances of nature, Darwin deprived their argument of the analogical inference that the evident purpose to be seen in the contrivances by which means and ends were related in nature was necessarily a function of mind.

Put simply, Darwin proposed to show that purposeless nature could "counterfeit purpose" (Gillespie 1979, 83-85).

Hence Darwin emphatically rejected any attempt to sneak purpose in by the back door, so to speak. Consider his response to Asa Gray, who wedded Darwinian theory to fairly conservative Christian theology. Gray denied that variation, the raw material of natural selection, was random; instead he opted for a teleological view of evolution. In fact Gray fancied that he comprehended the implications of Darwin's theory better than Darwin himself. In a letter written in 1863, he confessed to a bit of cunning: "Under my hearty congratulations of Darwin for his striking contributions to teleology, there is a vein of petite malice, from my knowing well that he rejects the idea of design, while all the while he is bringing out the neatest illustrations of it" (Gray 1973, 2:498).

But Darwin's response to Gray's notion of divine direction was unequivocal. In a letter to Lyell he wrote, "If I were convinced that I required such additions to the theory of natural selection, I would reject it as rubbish." Two years later he wrote again to Lyell: "The view that each variation has been providentially arranged seems to me to make Natural Selection entirely superfluous, and indeed takes the whole case of the appearance of new species out of the range of science." To say variations are divinely ordained adds nothing scientifically, Darwin went on: it "seems to me mere verbiage." He summed up his view by charging that "Gray's notion [of guided variations] seems to me to smash the whole affair" (Darwin 1899, 2:6-7, 28; 1903, 1:191-92).

Notice that Darwin's objections to providential evolution are twofold. First, it makes natural selection "superfluous," "rubbish," "mere verbiage." Natural selection was intended to replace design; the presence of both is redundant. As Darwin wrote in his autobiography, "The old argument from design in nature, as given by Paley, which formerly seemed to me so conclusive, fails, now that the law of natural selection has been discovered. . . . There seems to be now more design in the variability of organic beings and in the action of natural selection, than in the course which the wind blows. Everything in nature is the result of fixed laws" (Barlow 1958, 87). The effort to superimpose divine direction onto a completely naturalistic process Young labels "theistic naturalism," an oxymoron that has resurfaced in recent debates.

Second, Darwin objected that adding divine purpose to evolution takes the discussion "out of the range of science." The implication is that science cannot countenance intelligent causation in any form. In Darwin's mind, divinely ordained evolution was no different in principle from direct creation. Both were inadmissible in science. As Hull notes, "Darwin insisted on telling a totally consistent naturalistic story or none at all" (Hull 1973, 54).

Those who reformulated Darwin to accommodate design were hoping to prevent the takeover of the idea of evolution by philosophical naturalism. They sought to extract the scientific theory from the philosophy in which it was embedded. But the two proved inseparable, and ironically the effect of their effort was precisely the opposite of what they had hoped: It sped the acceptance of philosophical naturalism. As Hull writes, "The architects of the demise of teleology were not atheistic materialists but pious men . . . who thought they were doing religion a good service" in restricting God to working through natural laws. "What these men did not realize was that by pushing God further and further into the background as the unknowable author of natural law, . . . they had prepared the way for his total expulsion" (Hull 1973, 63, 65).

Gillespie tells the same story. The restructuring of the design argument to adapt to evolution, he writes, was an important "step in the secularization of science and its eventual intellectual separation from theology." The idea of designed or directed evolution "eased a generation of often reluctant scientists into a 'naturalistic' and ultimately positivistic world view." In this naturalistic worldview God had no significant function, and divine action was not required for a true understanding of the world. As a result religious belief became "private, subjective, and artificial"; God "was, at best, a gratuitous philosophical concept derived from a personal need" (Gillespie 1979, 119-20, 16).

Once God had been reduced to a "gratuitous philosophical concept" based on personal need, Darwin and his cohorts could afford to be tolerant toward religious believers. In the mid-1870s, Young writes, there were signs of the "benevolent tolerance of the victors" (Young 1985, 110-12). Religious believers could be treated gently so long as they agreed that God did absolutely nothing in the natural world studied by science. As Gillespie explains, the strategy of relocating design from contrivances to laws "gave the game to the positivist." It removed from the idea of design "any identifiable sign of divine action"—stripped it of any empirical content (Gillespie 1979, 149). And to those who clung to such a tame and vacuous concept of design, even the most aggressive Darwinist could afford to be indulgent.

### "Every Trifling Detail"
Another important facet of the nineteenth-century debate is the strategy employed to discredit design and to redefine science in strictly naturalistic terms. As the debate intensified Darwin and his allies increasingly identified creation with perpetual miracle. Historically Paley and other proponents of design had insisted on the reality of both primary and secondary causality at work in the world. But the Darwinians ignored that history. Instead they presented design as the denial of all secondary causes. They portrayed a designed world as a world at the mercy of divine caprice and arbitrary whim.

For example, in the *Origin of Species* Darwin describes his opponents as holding that each variety of finch on the Galápagos Islands sprang full-blown from the Creator's hand. Moreover, he also describes his opponents as holding that the islands' unusual flora and fauna were "created in the Galapagos Archipelago, and nowhere else" (Darwin 1964, 398; see also 352, 365). Design was presented as the belief that God had created each minor variety in its present location—giraffes in Africa, tigers in Asia and buffalo in America. Darwin referred to this as the theory of "multiple centres of creation," and in the *Origin* he demolished it.

Interestingly Darwin concedes that at the time the idea of creation in situ rested on empirical, not theological, grounds (Darwin 1964, 365-66). For example, it appeared to be the only explanation for the existence of the same species on both sides of the Atlantic Ocean. Surely no organism was capable of migrating across thousands of miles of salt water. Be that as it may, Darwin focused his argument on places such as the Galápagos Archipelago, where evidence for migration was strong. Was it really plausible that each variety of finch and tortoise had been specially created for each of the tiny islands, some of which were, in Darwin's words, hardly more than "points of rock"? For myself, he stated, "I disbelieve in . . . innumerable acts of creation" (Darwin 1903, 1:173).

Much of the *Origin of Species* is taken up with arguments for variability and migration. The idea of separate creations would be more plausible, Darwin noted in his journal, if each island had a completely unique set of plants and animals. But since many of the organisms were variations on a common theme, it was difficult to resist the conclusion that they descended from a single set of ancestral species that originally migrated to the islands. This and other patterns of geographical distribution, Darwin insisted, were "utterly inexplicable on the ordinary view of the independent creation of each species." He warned that anyone who rejected the idea of migration "rejects the *vera causa* of ordinary generation with subsequent migration, and calls in the agency of a miracle" (Darwin 1964, 355, 406, 352).

What do we say to all this? The views Darwin attributes to proponents of design are so foreign that we have to read our history books to learn about them. No design theorist today denies the reality of variation or migration. The consensus among even the strictest biblical creationists is that the Galápagos finches were not separately created but represent variations within a single species. For example, James Coppedge dismisses them as "only minor adaptation within types, as would be expected in any design of creation" (Coppedge 1973, 87). Wayne Frair and Percival Davis note that the finches "may serve as an example of diversification" but "not evolution in the usual sense, because the changes were relatively minor" (Frair and Davis 1983, 72). Walter Lammerts, who made detailed measurements of a large collection of Darwin's finches, notes that they exhibit complete intergradation of bill and body size. He concludes that the birds constitute a single species, "broken up into various island forms as a result of chance arrangement of their original variability potential" (Lammerts 1970, 361).

Clearly design does not require the rejection of either variability or migration. In fact historians have been hard put to explain why Darwin was so preoccupied with a position that in his own day naturalists had all but abandoned. Some historians attribute it to Darwin's ignorance of the current state of the debate; others think he was setting up a straw man. I suggest he was framing a false choice between perpetual miracle and completely closed naturalistic world. His argument ran like this: Either invoke direct divine action to explain every phenomenon in biology ("call in the agency of a miracle") or else admit that every phenomenon can be explained by natural processes of "ordinary generation."

Darwin urged this false choice again and again. In *The Descent of Man* he acknowledged that "our minds refuse to accept" an explanation of the universe based on the idea of "blind chance." Yet the alternative, he went on, is to believe that "every slight variation of structure,—the union of each pair in marriage,—the dissemination of each seed,—and other such events, have all been ordained for some special purpose" (Darwin 1896, 613). Darwin wrote to Sir John Herschel: "One cannot look at this Universe with all living productions & man without believing that all has been intelligently designed; yet when I look to each individual organism, I can see no evidence of this. For, I am not prepared to admit that God designed the feathers in the tail of the rock-pigeon to vary in a highly peculiar manner in order that man might select such variations & make a Fan-tail" (de Beer 1959, 35).

In pressing the point Darwin could not resist ridicule. In a book on the fertilization of orchids, he described proponents of design as those who view "every trifling detail of structure as the result of the direct interposition of the Creator" (Darwin 1862, 2). In a letter to Asa Gray he wrote: "I cannot think that the world, as we see it, is the result of chance; and yet I cannot look at each separate thing as the result of Design." He confessed that he could not believe pigeon tail feathers were led to vary "in order to gratify the caprice of a few men" (Darwin 1899, 2:146). He asked Lyell: Could he really think that the deity had intervened to cause variations in domestic pigeons "solely to please man's silly fancies"? (Darwin 1899, 2:97).

The argument became downright silly when Darwin challenged his friends to say whether God had designed his nose. He wrote to Lyell asking whether he believed that the shape of his nose "was ordained and 'guided by an intelligent cause'" (Darwin 1903, 1:193-94). In a similar vein he asked Gray: "Do you believe that when a swallow snaps up a gnat that God designed that that particular swallow should snap up that particular gnat at that particular instant?" (Darwin 1899, 1:284).

In these facetious comments Darwin was ignoring centuries of debate among Christians over the balance between God's direct activity and the action of created causes. As Anglican theologian E. L. Mascall writes, "The main tradition of classical Christian philosophy, while it insisted upon the universal *primary causality* of God in all the events of the world's history, maintained with equal emphasis the reality and the authenticity of *secondary causes*" (Mascall 1965, 198). Scottish theologian Thomas Torrance sums up this balanced view by speaking of the "contingent order" of creation. Contingency refers to the fact that the creation is not autonomous. It is not self-originating or self-sustaining; it was created by God and depends continually upon his power. Order refers to the fact that God does not work in the world by perpetual miracle. He has set up a network of secondary causes that act in regular and consistent patterns (Torrance 1981; see also the phrase "relative autonomy" in Kaiser 1991, 15, 131). As Christopher Kaiser points out, attempts to conceptualize this balance have carried on since the time of the church fathers—notably Basil of Caesarea in the fourth century (Kaiser 1991, 4-7). Darwin ignored this rich history and slashed the Gordian knot by insisting that one must choose either God or nature. Give any quarter to divine activity, he implied, and the entire world becomes an arena of perpetual and arbitrary miracle. Allow that minor variation and diversification can be accounted for by natural processes, and one must place all the world and all life solely under the domain of natural law.

This false dichotomy continues to be useful to Darwinists. Admit that natural processes account for the diversification of finch beaks or peppered moths or fruit flies, we are told, and one is logically committed to admitting that the same processes are adequate to create birds and fruit flies in the first place. Only recently has this strategy begun to wear thin, with biologists recognizing that minor variation is not the means of producing major innovations. Simply put, microevolution is not the mechanism for macroevolution. Yet examples of microevolution continue to be exhibited as the prime factual evidence supporting naturalistic theories of evolution.

### The Politics of Science

In considering how Darwin won the day, we must not ignore politics. The changes sought by nineteenth-century Darwinists were not only intellectual but also institutional. The older epistemology of science accommodated both religion and science; it allowed theology to place limits on the ideas acceptable in science. Once again this was a balance rooted as far back as the church fathers. The second-century apologists accepted as much as they could of the science of their day (which was a product of Greek philosophy), but they insisted on certain limits. For example, they rejected the idea that the universe is eternal and instead insisted on an absolute beginning, on God's creation of the world ex nihilo (Norris 1965).

But the new naturalistic epistemology promoted by the Darwinists was aggressively autonomous. It demanded that science be completely independent of theology. Gillespie writes: "The very existence of a rival science or of an alternative mode of knowledge was intolerable to the positivist." Darwin was "intolerant of all other claims to scientific knowledge. Anyone not of his tribe was a charlatan, an imposter." As a result these disagreements did not remain merely academic; they precipitated a struggle for power over social institutions. As Gillespie explains,

> It was not enough to drive out the old ideas. Their advocates had to be
> driven out of the scientific community as well. . . . In order for the world
> to be made safe for positive science, its practitioners had to occupy the
> seats of power as well as win the war of ideas. Both were necessary to the

establishment of a new scientific orthodoxy. (Gillespie 1979, 152-53) Many scientists are understandably uncomfortable with the idea that skill in politics and public relations help a theory gain acceptance. They like to believe that the dominant factor in the success of a theory is the objective evidence in its favor. Yet sociologists of knowledge are right in stressing that science is to some extent a social process and that an advantage is gained by those who are skillful at controlling the social process, at attracting supporters while isolating opponents.

In hindsight the strategies pursued by the nineteenth-century Darwinists are clear. Before publishing the *Origin of Species,* Darwin carefully cultivated a nucleus of biologists who were prepared to support his work. These early converts then followed basic political strategies: They presented a unified front in public; they conceded minor points in order to make major points; they were willing to accept as allies people who disagreed over the details; they minimized open controversy that might alienate doubters and fence sitters while cultivating younger scientists who were open to the new ideas. In this way the Darwinians gradually gained a majority. Their supporters were able to influence the educational system as teachers. They took control of the editorial process at scientific periodicals so that editors and referees became willing to accept papers from a Darwinian viewpoint. The journal *Nature* was founded at least in part as a vehicle for spreading the Darwinian message. Darwin won the day in part because his supporters were adept at employing public-relations tactics, and they outmaneuvered their rivals (Bowler 1988, 68-71).

It would appear that latter-day design theorists have caught on. The movement has capable leadership—such as that provided by Phillip Johnson—has launched a professional journal *(Origins and Design),* has started a fellowship program at the Discovery Institute, has founded an honors program at Biola and is holding professional conferences (the Mere Creation Conference in 1996). I suggest that we are well on our way to building our own institutions, and there is surely reason to hope that we may one day turn the tide.

In closing I would like to pose a sampling of questions that emerge from a survey of the history of the evolution debate. Since the nineteenth century these have been among the most frequently raised objections to design, yet they have not been adequately answered by design theorists.

*An understanding of history.* The nineteenth century marked the birth of historical consciousness in every field, from philosophy to the sciences. But the notion of design was essentially static, and as a result it was swept away by theories that offered some account of the history of life. How do updated versions of design get beyond a static view of life and account for history?

*Mind as cause.* What exactly is meant in speaking of a mind or intelligence acting in nature? What is primary causality? How is such a notion scientific? Does such a notion introduce sheer "mystery" and "caprice," as Gillespie puts it? One of Darwin's margin notes from 1838 reads as follows: "The explanation of types of structure in classes—as resulting from the *will* of the deity, to create animals on certain plans—is no explanation—it has not the character of a physical law / & is therefore utterly useless—it foretells nothing / because we know nothing of the will of the Deity" (cited in Brooke 1985, 46). Darwin is right: We cannot know the will of God. How then can it be scientific to speak of divine intention and divine action in the world?

*Does design imply an end to scientific inquiry?* Sir Joseph Dalton Hooker said he embraced Darwinism—what he called the "newest doctrines"—"not because they are the truest but because they do give you room to reason and reflect." By contrast the old doctrines of design "are so many stops to further inquiry; if they are admitted as truths, why there is an end of the whole matter, and it is no use hoping ever to get to any rational explanation of origin or dispersion of species—so I hate them" (Huxley 1981, 1:481-82). Hooker's view is shared by many people today: that is, to attribute something to design is not to explain it at all. It is to throw in the towel, to halt inquiry, to give up hope of any rational explanation. How do modern design theorists answer this objection?

*Does the concept of design have any empirical content?* In the *Origin of Species* Darwin twits the design theorists of his day for allowing that some structures result from secondary causes while insisting that others are designed but offering no principle for distinguishing between the two. Why not attribute all of them to secondary causes? he asks. In his words: "Several eminent naturalists have of late published their belief that a multitude of reputed species in each genus are not real species; but that other species are real, that is, have been independently created. This seems to me a strange conclusion to arrive at. They admit that a multitude of forms, which till lately they themselves thought were special creations . . . have been produced by variation, but they refuse to extend the same view to other and very slightly different forms. Nevertheless they do not pretend that they can define, or even conjecture, which are the created forms of life, and which are those produced by secondary laws. They admit variation as a *vera causa* in one case, they arbitrarily reject it in another, without assigning any distinction in the two cases" (Darwin 1964, 482). If design theorists insist on the reality of both primary and secondary causality, what principle do we offer for distinguishing between their effects?

*The problem of evil.* Darwin wrote there was just "too much misery in the world" for him to believe in design: "I cannot persuade myself that a beneficent and omnipotent God would have designedly created the Ichneumonidae with the express intention of their feeding within the living bodies of Caterpillars, or that a cat should play with mice" (Darwin 1899, 105). Other examples were "the young cuckoo ejecting its foster-brother" and "ants making slaves" (Darwin 1964, 242-44). How do contemporary design theorists explain the presence of evil in a designed world?

*What philosophy of science does design theory entail?* Hull writes that older theories of design rested on two pillars: a Baconian understanding of induction, with its claim of guaranteeing absolute certainty, and an essentialist metaphysic. James Moore echoes the same theme, describing Christian anti-Darwinists as those who sought "ultimate certainty through inductive inferences," with the corollary belief that the world "contains a finite number of fixed natural 'kinds'" (Moore 1979, 205-6, 346). Does the notion of design require us to embrace these philosophical positions?

## References

Barlow, N., ed. 1958. *The autobiography of Charles Darwin 1809-1882 with original omissions restored.* New York: Norton.

Bowler, P. 1988. *The non-Darwinian revolution: Reinterpreting a historical myth.* Baltimore: Johns Hopkins University Press.

Brooke, J. H. 1985. The relations between Darwin's science and his religion. In *Darwinism and divinity: Essays on evolution and religious belief,* ed. J. Durant. New York: Basil Blackwell, p. 46.

Coppedge, J. F. 1973. *Evolution: Possible or impossible?* Grand Rapids, Mich.: Zondervan.

Darwin, C. 1862. *On the various contrivances by which British and foreign orchids are fertilized by insects and on the good effects of intercrossing.* London: John Murray.

———. 1896. *The descent of man and selection in relation to sex.* 2nd ed. New York: D. Appleton.

———. 1964. *On the origin of species.* 1859. Reprint, Cambridge, Mass.: Harvard University Press.

Darwin, F., ed. 1899. *Life and letters of Charles Darwin.* 2 vols. New York: D. Appleton and Co.

———. 1903. *More letters of Charles Darwin.* New York: D. Appleton and Co.

de Beer, G., ed. 1959. *Notes and records of the Royal Society of London* 14, no. 1.

Dembski, W. n.d. Not even false? Reassessing the demise of British natural theology. Princeton, N.J.: Center for Interdisciplinary Studies.

du Bois-Reymond, E. 1904. Darwin versus Galiani. Cited in J. T. Merz, *A history of European thought in the nineteenth century.* 4 vols. New York: Dover Publications.

Duncan, D.. ed. 1908. *Life and letters of Herbert Spencer.* 2 vols. New York: D. Appleton and Co.

Durant, J. 1985. Darwinism and divinity: A century of debate. In *Darwinism and divinity: Essays on evolution and religious belief,* ed. J. Durant. New York: Basil Blackwell, pp. 9-39..

Frair, W., and P. Davis. 1983. *A case for creation.* Chicago: Moody Press.

Futuyma, D. 1986. *Evolutionary biology.* 2nd ed. Sunderland, Mass.: Sinauer.

Gillespie, N. C. 1979. *Charles Darwin and the problem of creation*. Chicago: University of Chicago Press.

Gray, J. L., ed. 1973. *Letters of Asa Gray*. 2 vols. New York: Burt Franklin.

Herschel, J. 1867. *Physical geography of the globe*. Edinburgh: Adam and Charles Black.

Hodge, C. 1994. *What is Darwinism? And other writings on science and religion*, ed. M. A. Noll and D. N. Livingstone. 1874. Reprint, Grand Rapids, Mich.: Baker.

Hull, D. L. 1973. *Darwin and his critics: The reception of Darwin's theory of evolution by the scientific community*. Cambridge, Mass.: Harvard University Press.

Huxley, L., ed. 1903. *Life and letters of Thomas Henry Huxley*. 3 vols. New York: Macmillan.

———. 1981. *Life and letters of Sir Joseph Dalton Hooker*. London: John Murray.

Huxley, T. H. 1859. Science and religion. *The Builder* 17.

———. 1879. *Lay sermons, addresses and reviews*. New York: D. Appleton and Co.

———. 1896. *Man's place in nature*. New York: D. Appleton and Co.

Kaiser, C. 1991. *Creation and the history of science*. Grand Rapids, Mich.: Eerdmans.

Lammerts, W. 1970. The Galapagos Island finches. In *Why not creation?* ed. W. Lammerts. Grand Rapids, Mich.: Baker, pp. 354-66.

Lunn, A. 1931. *The flight from reason*. New York: Dial Press.

Mascall, E. L. 1965. *Christian theology and natural science*. Hamden, Conn.: Archon Books.

Mayr, E. 1964. Introduction to *On the origin of species*, by C. Darwin. 1859. Reprint, Cambridge, Mass.: Harvard University Press.

Moore, J. R. 1979. *The post-Darwinian controversies: A study of the Protestant struggle to come to terms with Darwin in Great Britain and America 1870-1900*. Cambridge: Cambridge University Press.

Norris, R. A. 1965. *God and world in early Christian theology*. London: Adam and Charles Black.

Richards, R. J. 1992. *The meaning of evolution: The morphological construction and ideological reconstruction of Darwin's theory*. Chicago: University of Chicago Press.

Spencer, H. 1896. *The principles of psychology*, 2 vols. New York: D. Appleton and Co.

———. 1904. *An autobiography*, 2 vols. New York: D. Appleton and Co.

Torrance, T. F. 1981. Divine and contingent order. In *The sciences and theology in the twentieth century*, ed. A. R. Peacocke. Notre Dame, Ind.: University of Notre Dame Press, pp. 81-97.

Young, R. M. 1985. *Darwin's metaphor: Nature's place in Victorian culture*. Cambridge: Cambridge University Press.

# 4

# Redesigning Science

## WILLIAM A. DEMBSKI

S TEPHEN JAY GOULD RECENTLY HAD A NIGHTMARE. THE NIGHTMARE
began with Phillip Johnson just having been elected to the
National Academy of Sciences. As the nightmare progressed Gould
found he was no longer teaching at Harvard but instead was now
head of a cheesy evolution think tank in San Francisco known as the NCSE
(National Center for Scientific Evolution). Across America the tide had
turned against evolutionists. A movement known as intelligent design had
caught the popular imagination and in a remarkably short time displaced
Gould and his fellow evolutionists. With the National Science Foundation
now firmly in the hands of Phillip Johnson's cronies, Gould's research
monies dried up, and to make ends meet Gould was forced to give tours of
the Burgess Shale and the Galápagos Islands. Gould's nightmare ended with
Gould braving the intense heat of the Galápagos Islands, seated atop a
volcanic heap, sipping some pink lemonade and longing for the halcyon
days when science was still free from that blight known as intelligent design.

We are a long way from seeing Gould's nightmare realized. Nor is it a
nightmare we should want to see realized, at least not in all its details. The
nightmare, however, raises a serious question: What is science going to look
like once intelligent design succeeds? To answer this question we need first
to be clear what intelligent design is. Intelligent design is neither repackaged

creationism nor religion masquerading as science. Intelligent design is a theory for making sense of intelligent causes. As such, intelligent design formalizes and makes precise something we do all the time. All of us are all the time engaged in a form of rational activity that, without being tendentious, can be described as inferring design. Inferring design is a common and well-accepted human activity. People find it important to identify events caused through the purposeful, premeditated action of an intelligent agent and to distinguish such events from events due to either law or chance. Intelligent design unpacks the logic of this everyday activity and applies it within the special sciences. There is no magic, no vitalism, no appeal to occult forces. Inferring design is common, rational and objectifiable. The purpose of this chapter is to sketch the foundation for a theory of intelligent design.

The key step is to delineate a method for detecting design. Such a method exists. We use it implicitly all the time. The main task of this chapter is make this method explicit and then to justify it. The method takes the form of a three-stage explanatory filter. Given something we think might be designed, we submit it to the filter. If it successfully passes all three stages of the filter, then we are warranted asserting it is designed. Roughly speaking the filter asks three questions, and in the following order: Does a law explain it? Does chance explain it? Does design explain it?

To see how the filter works in practice, consider the case of Nicholas Caputo (*New York Times,* July 23, 1985, B1). In 1985 Nicholas Caputo was brought before the New Jersey Supreme Court. The Republican Party had filed suit against him, claiming Caputo had consistently rigged the ballot lines in Essex County, New Jersey, where he was county clerk. It is a known fact that first position on a ballot increases one's chances of winning an election (other things being equal, voters are more likely to vote for the first person on a ballot line than for the others). Since in 40 out of 41 cases Caputo positioned the Democrats first on the ballot line, the Republicans argued that in selecting the order of ballots, Caputo had intentionally favored his own Democratic Party. In short, the Republicans claimed Caputo had cheated.

The question before the New Jersey Supreme Court was, Did Caputo actually rig the order, or was it without malice and forethought on his part that the Democrats happened 40 out of 41 times to appear first on the ballot? Since Caputo denied wrongdoing, and since he conducted the drawing of ballots so that witnesses were unable to observe how he actually drew the ballots, determining whether Caputo rigged the order of ballots becomes a matter of evaluating the circumstantial evidence connected with this case. How then is this evidence to be evaluated?

In determining how to explain the remarkable coincidence of Nicholas Caputo's selecting the Democrats 40 out of 41 times to head the ballot line, the court had three options to consider.

*Law.* Unbeknownst to Caputo, he was not employing a reliable random process to determine ballot order. Caputo was in the position of someone who thinks she is flipping a fair coin when in fact she is flipping a double-headed coin. Just as flipping a double-headed coin is going to yield a long string of heads, so Caputo, using his faulty method for ballot selection, generated a long string of Democrats coming out on top.

*Chance.* In selecting the order of political parties on the state ballot, Caputo employed a reliable random process that did not favor one political party over another. The fact that the Democrats came out on top 40 out of 41 times was simply a fluke. It occurred by chance.

*Design.* Caputo, knowing full well what he was doing and intending to aid his own political party, purposely rigged the ballot line selection process so that the Democrats would consistently come out on top. In short, Caputo cheated.

The first option—that Caputo chose poorly his procedure for selecting ballot lines, so that instead of genuinely randomizing the ballot order, it just kept putting the Democrats on top—was dismissed by the court because Caputo himself had claimed to use a randomization procedure in selecting ballot lines. And since there was no reason for the court to think that Caputo's randomization procedure was at fault, the key question therefore became whether Caputo put this procedure into practice when he made the ballot line selections or whether he purposely circumvented this procedure in order for the Democrats consistently to come out on top. And since Caputo's actual drawing of ballot lines was obscured to witnesses, it was this question that the court had to answer.

With the law explanation eliminated, the court next decided to dispense with the chance explanation. Having noted that the chances of picking the same political party 40 out of 41 times were less than 1 in 50 billion, the court concluded, "Confronted with these odds, few persons of reason will accept the explanation of blind chance." This certainly seems right. Nevertheless a bit more needs to be said. The problem is that exceeding improbability is by itself not enough to preclude something from happening by chance. Whenever I am dealt a bridge hand, I participate in an exceedingly improbable event. Whenever I play darts, the precise position where the darts land represents an exceedingly improbable configuration. Just about anything that happens is exceedingly improbable once we factor in all the other ways what happened might have happened. The problem then does not reside simply in the event's being improbable.

All the same, without a causal story detailing what happened, improbability remains a crucial ingredient for eliminating chance. For suppose that Caputo actually was cheating from the beginning of his career as Essex

County Clerk. Suppose further that the one case where Caputo placed the Democrats second on the ballot line did not occur until after his third time around selecting ballot lines. Thus for the first three ballot line selections of Caputo's career the Democrats all came out on top, and they came out on top precisely because Caputo rigged it that way. Nevertheless, on the basis of three ballot selections and without direct evidence of Caputo's cheating, an outside observer would be in no position to decide whether Caputo was cheating or selecting the ballots honestly.

The problem is that with only three ballot line selections, the probabilities are too large to reliably eliminate chance as an explanation. The probability of randomly selecting the Democrats to come out on top given that their only competition is the Republicans is in this case 1 in 8. Because three Democrats in a row could easily happen by chance, we would be acting in bad faith if we did not give Caputo the benefit of the doubt in the face of such large probabilities. Small probabilities are therefore a necessary condition for eliminating chance, even though they are not a sufficient condition.

The question therefore remains, What besides small probabilities do we need to have convincing evidence that Caputo was cheating? If we are going to eliminate chance as an explanation, the probabilities have to be small, for otherwise we could just as well attribute the event to chance. Yet having determined that the event would have an exceedingly small probability in case it were due to chance, what more do we need to eliminate chance as an explanation? Invariably what is needed to eliminate chance is that the event in question conform to a pattern. Not just any pattern will do, however. Some patterns can legitimately be employed to eliminate chance whereas others cannot. The basic intuition underlying the distinction between patterns that alternately succeed or fail to eliminate chance is, however, motivated easily enough.

Consider the case of an archer. Suppose an archer stands 50 meters from a large wall with bow and arrow in hand. The wall, let us say, is sufficiently large that the archer cannot help but hit it. Now suppose every time the archer shoots an arrow at the wall, she paints a target around the arrow, so that the arrow is squarely in the bull's-eye. What can be concluded from this scenario? Absolutely nothing about the archer's ability as an archer. The fact that the archer is in each instance squarely hitting the bull's-eye is utterly bogus. She is matching a pattern; but it is a pattern that she fixes only after she has shot the arrow. The pattern is thus purely ad hoc. But suppose instead that the archer paints a fixed target on the wall and then shoots at it. Suppose she shoots one hundred arrows and that each time she hits a perfect bull's-eye. What can be concluded from this second scenario? In the words of the New Jersey Supreme Court, "confronted with these odds, few persons of reason will accept the explanation of blind chance." Confronted with this second scenario we are obligated to infer that here is a world-class archer.

This method of eliminating chance is of course extremely common in statistics, where it is known as setting a rejection region prior to an experiment. In statistics, if the outcome of an experiment (= event) falls within the rejection region (= pattern), the chance hypothesis supposedly responsible for the outcome is rejected (i.e., chance is eliminated). A little reflection, however, makes clear that a pattern need not be given prior to an event to warrant eliminating chance. Consider, for instance, Alice and Bob on the occasion of their fiftieth wedding anniversary. Their six children show up bearing gifts. Each gift is part of a matching set of china. There is no duplication of gifts, and together the gifts form a complete set of china. Suppose Alice and Bob were satisfied with their old set of china and had no inkling prior to opening their gifts that they might expect a new set of china. Alice and Bob are therefore without a relevant pattern whither to refer their gifts prior to actually receiving them from their children. Nevertheless Alice and Bob will not attribute the gifts to random acts of kindness (i.e., to chance). Rather Alice and Bob will attribute the new set of china to the collusion of their children (i.e., to design). Granted, Alice and Bob have been given no pattern prior to receiving the gifts. Yet on receiving the gifts, Alice and Bob discern a pattern that, though it is discerned after the fact, cannot be reasonably explained apart from the collusion of their children.

In the presence of small probabilities, patterns given prior to events always eliminate chance. In the presence of small probabilities, patterns identified after events may or may not eliminate chance. Thus Alice and Bob were able to eliminate chance after the fact. But suppose I flip a coin a thousand times and subsequently record the sequence of coin tosses on paper. The sequence I flipped (= event) conforms to the sequence recorded on paper (= pattern). Moreover, the sequence I flipped is vastly improbable (the probability is approximately $10^{-300}$). Nevertheless it is clear that the pattern to which these coin flips conform was artificially concocted and as it stands cannot legitimately warrant eliminating chance. The pattern was simply read off the event.

Patterns may therefore be divided into two types, those that in the presence of small probabilities warrant the elimination of chance and those that despite the presence of small probabilities do not warrant the elimination of chance. The first type of pattern will be called a *specification,* the second a *fabrication.* Specifications are therefore the non-ad hoc patterns that can legitimately be used to eliminate chance and warrant a design inference. In contrast fabrications are the ad hoc patterns that cannot legitimately be used to eliminate chance. Thus when the archer paints a fixed target on the wall and thereafter shoots at it, she specifies the event of hitting a bull's-eye. When she repeatedly hits the bull's-eye, we are therefore warranted in attributing her success not to luck but rather to her skill as an archer. When the archer paints a target around her arrow after each shot, squarely positioning each arrow in the bull's-eye, she fabricates the event of hitting the bull's-eye. Thus even though she repeatedly hits the bull's-eye, we are not warranted attributing her "success" in hitting the bull's-eye to anything other than luck. In the latter scenario her skill as an archer therefore remains an open question.

How do these considerations apply to the case of Nicholas Caputo? By selecting the Democrats to head the ballot 40 out of 41 times, Caputo has participated in an event of probability less than 1 in 50 billion. Yet as we have noted, exceedingly improbable things happen all the time. Hence by itself Caputo's participation in an event of probability less than 1 in 50 billion is no cause for alarm. The crucial question therefore is whether this event is also specified. Does this event follow a non-ad hoc pattern so that we can legitimately eliminate chance? But of course the event is specified: that Caputo is a Democrat, that it is in Caputo's interest to see the Democrats appear first on the ballot, that Caputo controls the ballot lines, and that Caputo would by chance be expected to assign Republicans top ballot line as often as Democrats all conspire to specify Caputo's ballot line selections and render his selections incompatible with chance (for the details of how Caputo's ballot line selections are specified see Dembski 1998, chap. 5).

**The Explanatory Filter**
In general, whenever we are called to explain an event, we must choose from three distinct modes of explanation. These modes of explanation may conveniently be dubbed law, chance and design. We have already seen these modes of explanation illustrated in the case of Nicholas Caputo. Insofar as they cover our various explanatory options, these three modes of explanation are mutually exclusive and exhaustive. To attribute an event to a law is to say that the event will almost always happen given certain antecedent circumstances. To attribute an event to chance is to say that its occurrence is characterized by some (perhaps not fully specified) probability distribution according to which the event might equally well not have happened. To attribute an event to design is to say that it cannot plausibly be referred to either law or chance. In characterizing design as the set-theoretic complement of the disjunction law-or-chance, one therefore guarantees that these three modes of explanation will be mutually exclusive and exhaustive. It remains to show that this eliminative approach to design (i.e., as the negation of law and chance) corresponds to design in the ordinary sense (i.e., as the product of intelligence).

When we are called to explain an event, we therefore have a decision to make. Are we going to attribute it to law or chance or design? To answer this question, our species deploys a standard operating procedure that discriminates among these competing modes of explanation. Figure 4.1 summarizes this procedure and will be referred to as the explanatory filter. To use the explanatory filter we start with an event $E$. Our object is to explain $E$—whether to attribute $E$ to law or chance or design. We therefore hand $E$ over to the explanatory filter. The filter consists of two types of nodes, initial and terminal nodes represented by ovals and decision nodes represented by diamonds. Thus we start $E$ off at the node labeled start. From start $E$ moves to the first decision node. This node asks whether $E$ is highly probable (hence the label HP).

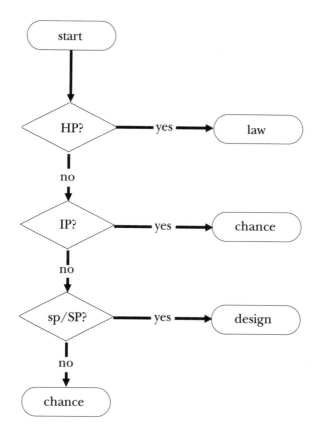

**Figure 4.1 The Explanatory Filter**

To say that $E$ is highly probable is to say that given certain antecedent circumstances, $E$ will for all practical purposes always happen. To characterize such events as highly probable (i.e., as HP events) serves as a convenient way of incorporating deterministic and nondeterministic natural laws within a single framework. For instance, the event of a bullet firing when a gun's trigger is pulled and the event of getting at least one head when a fair coin is tossed a hundred times are both HP events. Generally we regard the first event as nonprobabilistic, the second as probabilistic. My own preference is to think of all laws in nature as potentially probabilistic, with the nonprobabilistic case assimilated to the probabilistic case in which probabilities collapse to 0 and 1.

Thus if $E$ happens to be an HP event, we stop and attribute $E$ to law. Law is always the first line of defense. If we can explain by means of law, chance and design are automatically precluded. Similarly chance is always the second line of defense. If we cannot explain by means of law but can explain by means of chance, then design is automatically precluded. There is thus an order of priority to explanation. Within this order law has top priority, chance second and design last.

It needs to be stressed, however, that this order of priority among competing modes of explanations has nothing to do with one explanation being somehow preferable or better than another. We are not offering a better explanation of Nicholas Caputo's "golden arm" (as his talent for selecting ballot lines was affectionately called) by attributing it to law or chance as opposed to design. Presumably one or the other of these explanations is correct, so that the preferable one is going to be the one that is correct. Nevertheless, as a matter of explanatory priority, we look to law or chance before we invoke design.

Explanatory priority is a case of Ockham's razor. Accordingly, when any one of the three modes of explanation fails adequately to explain an event, we move to the mode of explanation at the next level of complication. Note that explanations that appeal to law are simplest, for they admit no contingency, claiming things always happen that way. Explanations that appeal to chance add a level of complication, for they admit contingency but one characterized by probability. Most complicated are those explanations that appeal to design, for they admit contingency but not one characterized by probability.

Returning now to the event $E$ as it proceeds through the explanatory filter, suppose $E$ is not an HP event and has therefore passed to the next decision node, the node labeled IP. What needs to be determined now is whether $E$ is an event of intermediate probability. Events of intermediate probability, or what I am calling IP events, are the events we can regularly expect to occur by chance in the ordinary circumstances of life. Rolling snake eyes with a pair of fair dice constitutes an IP event. Even someone winning a lottery where the probability of winning is as little as one in ten million will constitute an IP event once we factor in all the other people playing the lottery. IP events are sufficiently probable to give us no reason to suspect they were the result of something other than chance. Thus if an event $E$ reaches the second decision node and is judged to be an IP event, we stop and attribute $E$ to chance.

But suppose that $E$ is neither an HP nor an IP event. By a process of elimination $E$ will therefore make it all the way to the third and final decision node. In this case $E$ is an event of small probability, or what I am calling an SP event. Our naive intuition is that SP events are so unlikely as not to occur by chance. To take an extreme example, consider the possibility of a thermodynamic accident whereby a loaded gun (say a perfect replica of a .357 Magnum, complete with bullets) materializes in your hand, gets aimed at your favorite enemy, fires and kills him. Strictly speaking the laws of physics do not preclude such an event from happening by chance. Nevertheless, a court will surely convict you of willful homicide. Why does a court refuse to exonerate you by attributing such an event to chance? How would a jury respond to a defense that argues the gun simply materialized?

Our first intuition then is that SP events do not happen by chance and can be safely ignored. But to see that this cannot quite be right, consider the following naive formulation of this intuition as found in the work of the French probabilist Emile Borel (1962, 28):

> We may be led to set at $10^{-50}$ the value of negligible probabilities on the cosmic scale. When the probability of an event is below this limit, the opposite event may be expected to occur with certainty, whatever the number of occasions presenting themselves in the entire universe. The number of observable stars is of the order of magnitude of a billion, or $10^9$, and the number of observations which the inhabitants of the earth could make of these stars, even if all were observing, is certainly less than $10^{20}$. [An event] with a probability of $10^{-50}$ will therefore never occur, or at least never be observed.

There is a problem here. Suppose I flip a fair coin 1,000 times (by "fair" I mean the coin has distinguishable sides and is evenly balanced). As I flip the coin, I note the outcome of each toss. There are $2^{1000}$, or approximately $10^{300}$, equiprobable ways I might have flipped the coin. I have therefore participated in an event with probability 1 in $10^{300}$. Because this probability is well below Borel's 1 in $10^{50}$, the preceding passage appears to say that the event I just experienced did not happen. Yet given that I flip a coin 1,000 times, some exceedingly unlikely event has to happen, to wit, an SP event.

Our intuition is that SP events are so improbable that they cannot happen by chance. Yet we cannot deny that exceedingly improbable events (i.e., SP events) happen by chance all the time. To resolve the paradox we need to introduce an extraprobabilistic notion, a notion I referred to as specification. If a probabilistic set-up, like tossing a coin 1,000 times, entails that an SP event will occur, then necessarily some extremely improbable event will occur. If, however, independently of the event we are able to specify it, then we are justified in eliminating chance as the proper mode of explanation. It is the specified SP events (abbreviated sp/SP) that cannot properly be attributed to chance. In *The Blind Watchmaker* Richard Dawkins (1987, 8) provides some helpful illustrations of sp/SP events:

> Hitting upon the lucky number that opens the bank's safe is the equivalent, in our analogy, of hurling scrap metal around at random and happening to assemble a Boeing 747. Of all the millions of unique and, with hindsight equally improbable, positions of the combination lock, only one opens the lock. Similarly, of all the millions of unique and, with hindsight equally improbable, arrangements of a heap of junk, only one (or very few) will fly. The uniqueness of the arrangement that flies, or that opens the safe, [has] nothing to do with hindsight. It is *specified in advance.*

Specifications are common in statistics, where they are known as rejection regions. The basic problem of statistics is the testing of probabilistic hypotheses. Statisticians are continually confronted with situations in which some probability distribution is said to be operating and then are given the task of finding out whether that probability distribution is indeed operating. To do this statisticians set up a rejection region and then take a sample. If the observed sample falls within the rejection region, the presumption is that the probability distribution in question was not operating to produce the sample. If the observed sample falls outside the rejection region, the probability distribution in question is taken at least provisionally to be adequate in accounting for the sample (for an account of statistical reasoning see Hacking 1965 as well as Howson and Urbach 1993; Mood et al. [1974, 401-81] is specifically devoted to hypothesis testing).

There is, however, an important difference between the logic of the explanatory filter and the logic of statistical hypothesis testing: by ending up at the terminal node of the filter labeled "design," one sweeps the field clear of all relevant chance explanations. This contrasts with statistical hypothesis testing, where eliminating one chance hypothesis opens the door to others. The sp/SP events of the explanatory filter exclude chance decisively, whereas the events that fall within the rejection regions of statistics indicate that some probability distribution other than the one originally suspected may be operating.

For an event $E$ to pass to the third decision node of the explanatory filter, it is therefore not enough to know that $E$ has small probability with respect to some arbitrarily chosen probability distribution. Rather we must know that whatever probability distribution may have been responsible for the event $E$, it was not one for which $E$ was either an HP or an IP event. Thus unlike the statistician, who is typically operating from a position of ignorance in trying to figure out what probability distribution is producing the samples he or she observes, before we even begin to send the event $E$ through the explanatory filter, we need to know what probability distribution(s), if any, were operating to produce the event. To put it another way, the design theorist is in the business of categorically eliminating chance in accounting for $E$ whereas the statistician is in the business of ruling out individual probability distributions that might account for $E$.

If this distinction between statistical inferences and design inferences seems obscure, an example suggested by Dawkins may clarify matters. Suppose we must explain why a certain bank's safe that was closed earlier happens now to be open. Let us assume the safe has a combination lock that is marked with a hundred numbers ranging from 00 to 99 and for which five turns in alternating directions are required to open the lock. We assume that precisely one sequence of alternating turns is capable of opening the lock (e.g., 34-98-25-09-71). There are thus ten billion possible combinations of which precisely one succeeds in opening the lock (or as Dawkins put it, "of all the millions of unique and, with hindsight equally improbable, positions of the combination lock, only one opens the lock").

Suppose we now take the opening of the bank's safe, an event we will denote by $E$, and feed it into the explanatory filter. How does E fare at the first decision node? Since no law accounts for the opening of safes with combination locks, $E$ is not an HP event (the opening of the combination lock is compatible with natural laws but is hardly explained by natural laws). $E$ therefore moves past the first decision node. How does $E$ fare at the second decision node? With ten billion possibilities, only one of which opens the safe, random twirling of the combination lock's dial is exceedingly unlikely to open the lock. $E$ is therefore not an IP event but an SP event. $E$ therefore moves past the second decision node and lands at the third decision node labeled sp/SP. Now the crucial thing to observe is that the status of $E$ as an SP event is secure. Unlike the statistician who frequently has little knowledge about the precise probability distribution governing an event, we have a great deal of prior knowledge about locks in general and combination locks in particular before the specific combination lock we are considering crosses our path. A probability of one in ten billion properly characterizes the opening of this lock by chance.

As an SP event, $E$ has moved to the third and final decision node. With $E$ at the third decision node, the crucial question now becomes whether $E$ was specified. Is $E$ an sp/SP event or merely an SP event? If it is the latter, then the opening of the bank's safe can legitimately be attributed to chance. But $E$ is indeed specified, for the construction of the lock's tumblers specifies which one of the ten billion combinations will open the lock. $E$ is therefore an sp/SP event and passes to the terminal node labeled "design." In this way design becomes the proper mode of explanation for the opening of the safe.

To sum up, the explanatory filter faithfully represents the ordinary practice of humans in sorting through events whose mode of explanation is alternately law or chance or design. In particular, passage through the flowchart to the terminal node labeled design encapsulates:

> how copyright and patent offices identify theft of intellectual property,
>
> how insurance companies prevent themselves from being cheated,
>
> how detectives employ circumstantial evidence to incriminate a guilty person,
>
> how forensic scientists are able reliably to place individuals at the scene of a crime,
>
> how skeptics debunk the claims of parapsychologists,
>
> how scientists identify cases of data falsification,
>
> how the Search for Extraterrestrial Intelligence (SETI) program seeks to identify the presence of extraterrestrial life, and
>
> how statisticians and computer scientists distinguish random from nonrandom strings of digits.

Entire human industries would be dead in the water without the explanatory filter. Much is riding on the explanatory filter. Using the filter, our courts have sent people to the electric chair. A rigorous elucidation of the filter, and especially the decision node labeled sp/SP, is therefore of more than academic interest. For a thorough treatment of this problem see Dembski (1998).

### Why the Filter Works

Up to now I have described how the explanatory filter works and have given a few examples where it successfully detects design. What I want to do in the remainder of this chapter is show why the filter works. The filter is a criterion for distinguishing intelligent from unintelligent causes. Here I am using the word *criterion* in its strict etymological sense as a method for deciding or judging a question. The explanatory filter decides when something is intelligently caused and when it is not. Does it decide such questions reliably? This is the key question.

As with any criterion, we need to make sure that whatever judgments the filter renders agree with reality. A criterion for judging the quality of wines is worthless if it judges the rot-gut consumed by winos superior to a fine French Bordeaux. The reality is that a 1973 Chateau Mouton Rothschild is superior to a jug of muscatel, and any criteria for discriminating among wines better indicate as much.

Or consider medical tests. Any medical test is a criterion. A perfectly reliable medical test would detect the presence of a disease whenever it is indeed present and fail to detect the disease whenever it is absent. Unfortunately no medical test is perfectly reliable, and so the best we can do is keep the proportion of false positives and false negatives as low as possible.

All criteria, not just medical tests, face the problem of false positives and false negatives. A criterion attempts to classify individuals with respect to a target group (in the case of medical tests, those who have a certain disease). When the criterion classifies an individual as a member of the target group who should not be there, it commits a false positive. Alternatively, when the criterion fails to classify an individual as a member of the target group who should be there, it commits a false negative.

Take medical tests again. A medical test checks whether an individual has a certain disease. The target group comprises all those individuals who have the disease. When the medical test classifies an individual who does not have the disease with those who do, it commits a false positive. When the medical test classifies an individual who does have the disease with those who do not, it commits a false negative.

Let us now apply these observations to the explanatory filter. The explanatory filter is a criterion for detecting design. Is it a reliable criterion? The target group for the explanatory filter comprises all things intelligently caused. How accurate is the explanatory filter at correctly assigning things to this target group and correctly omitting things from it? The things we are trying to explain have causal stories. In some of those causal stories intelligent causation is indispensable, whereas in others it is dispensable. An inkblot can be explained without appealing to intelligent causation; ink arranged to form meaningful text cannot. When the explanatory filter assigns something to the target group, can we be confident that it actually is intelligently caused? If not, we have a problem with false positives. When the explanatory filter fails to assign something to the target group, can we be confident that no intelligent cause underlies it? If not, we have a problem with false negatives.

Consider first the problem of false negatives. When the explanatory filter fails to detect design in a thing, can we be sure no intelligent cause underlies it? The answer to this question is no. For determining that something is not designed, the explanatory filter is not a reliable criterion. False negatives are a problem for the explanatory filter. This problem of false negatives, however, is endemic to detecting intelligent causes.

One difficulty is that intelligent causes can mimic law and chance, thereby rendering their actions indistinguishable from those of unintelligent causes. A bottle of ink may fall off a cupboard and spill onto a sheet of paper. Alternatively, a human agent may deliberately take a bottle of ink and pour it over a sheet of paper. The resulting inkblot may look identical in both instances but in the one case results by chance, in the other by design.

Another difficulty is that detecting intelligent causes requires background knowledge on our part. It takes an intelligent cause to know an intelligent cause. But if we do not know enough, we will miss it. Consider a spy listening in on a communication channel whose messages are encrypted. Unless the spy knows how to break the cryptosystem used by the parties on whom he is eavesdropping, any messages passing the communication channel will be to him unintelligible and might in fact be meaningless.

The problem of false negatives therefore arises either when an intelligent agent has acted (whether consciously or unconsciously) to conceal one's actions or when an intelligent agent in trying to detect design has insufficient background knowledge to determine whether design is present. Detectives face this problem all the time. A detective confronted with a murder needs first to determine whether a murder has indeed been committed. If the murderer was clever and made it appear that the victim died by accident, then the detective will mistake the murder for an accident. So too, if the detective is stupid and misses certain obvious clues, the detective will mistake the murder for an accident. In mistaking a murder for an accident, the detective commits a false negative. Contrast this, however, with a detective facing a murderer intent on revenge and who wants to leave no doubt that the victim was intended to die. In this case the problem of false negatives is unlikely to arise (though we can imagine an incredibly stupid detective, like Chief Inspector Clouseau, mistaking a rather obvious murder for an accident).

Intelligent causes can do things that unintelligent causes cannot and can make their actions evident. When for whatever reason an intelligent cause fails to make its actions evident, we may miss it. But when an intelligent cause succeeds in making its actions evident, we take notice. This is why false negatives do not invalidate the explanatory filter. The explanatory filter is fully capable of detecting intelligent causes intent on making their presence evident. Masters of stealth intent on concealing their actions may successfully evade the explanatory filter. But masters of self-promotion intent on making sure their intellectual property gets properly attributed find in the explanatory filter a ready friend.

And this brings us to the problem of false positives. Even though the explanatory filter is not a reliable criterion for eliminating design, it is, I shall argue, a reliable criterion for detecting design. The explanatory filter is a net. Things that are designed will occasionally slip past the net. We would prefer that the net catch more than it does, omitting nothing due to design. But given the ability of design to mimic unintelligent causes and the possibility of our own ignorance passing over things that are designed, this problem cannot be fixed. Nevertheless we want to be very sure that whatever the net does catch includes only what we intend it to catch, to wit, things that are designed. Only things that are designed had better end up in the net. If this is the case, we can have confidence that whatever the filter attributes to design is indeed designed. If things end up in the net that are not designed, the filter will be worthless.

I want to argue that the explanatory filter is a reliable criterion for detecting design. Alternatively I want to argue that the explanatory filter successfully avoids false positives. Thus whenever the explanatory filter attributes design, it does so correctly. Let us now see why this is the case. I offer two arguments. The first is a straightforward inductive argument: in every instance where the explanatory filter attributes design and where the underlying causal story is known, it turns out design is present; therefore design actually is present whenever the explanatory filter attributes design. The conclusion of this argument is a straightforward inductive generalization. It has the same logical status as concluding that all ravens are black given that all ravens observed to date have been found to be black.

The naturalist is likely to object at this point, claiming that the only things we can know to be designed are artifacts manufactured by intelligent beings who are in turn the product of blind evolutionary processes. Hence to use the explanatory filter to extrapolate design beyond such artifacts is illegitimate. To echo Dawkins, this is a transparently feeble argument. It is circular reasoning to invoke naturalism to underwrite an evolutionary account of intelligence and then in turn to employ this account of intelligence to insulate naturalism from critique. Naturalism is a metaphysical position, not a scientific theory based on evidence. Any account of intelligence it entails is therefore suspect and needs to be subjected to independent checks. The explanatory filter provides one such check.

If we dismiss, as we ought, the naturalist's evolutionary account of intelligence, a more serious objection remains. I am arguing inductively that the explanatory filter is a reliable criterion for detecting design. The conclusion of this argument is that whenever the filter attributes design, design is present. The premise of this argument is that whenever the filter attributes design and the underlying causal story can be verified, design is present.

Even though the conclusion follows as an inductive generalization from the premise, the premise itself seems false. There are a lot of coincidences that seem best explained without invoking design. Consider, for instance, the Shoemaker-Levy comet. The Shoemaker-Levy comet crashed into Jupiter exactly twenty-five years to the day after the Apollo 11 moon landing. What are we to make of this coincidence? Do we really want to explain it in terms of design? What if we submitted this coincidence to the explanatory filter and out popped design? Our intuitions strongly suggest that the comet's trajectory and NASA's space program were operating independently and that at best this coincidence should be referred to chance, not design.

This objection is readily met. The fact is that the explanatory filter does not yield design all that easily, especially if the probabilities are kept small. It is not the case that unusual and striking coincidences automatically yield design from the explanatory filter. Martin Gardner (1972) is no doubt correct when he notes, "The number of events in which you participate for a month, or even a week, is so huge that the probability of noticing a startling correlation is quite high, especially if you keep a sharp outlook." The implication he means to draw, however, is incorrect, namely, that therefore startling correlations or coincidences may uniformly be relegated to chance. The fact that the Shoemaker-Levy comet crashed into Jupiter exactly twenty-five years to the day after the Apollo 11 moon landing is a coincidence best referred to chance. But the fact that Mary Baker Eddy's writings on Christian Science bear a remarkable resemblance to Phineas Parkhurst Quimby's writings on mental healing is a coincidence that cannot be explained by chance and is properly explained by positing Quimby as a source for Eddy (see Martin 1985, 127-30).

The explanatory filter is robust and easily resists counterexamples of the Shoemaker-Levy variety. Assuming, for instance, that the Apollo 11 moon landing serves as a specification for the crash of Shoemaker-Levy into Jupiter (a generous concession at that), and that the comet could have crashed at any time within a period of a year, and that the comet crashed to the very second precisely twenty-five years after the moon landing, a straightforward probability calculation indicates that the probability of this coincidence is no smaller than $10^{-8}$. This is not all that small a probability, especially when considered in relation to all the events astronomers are observing in the solar system. Certainly this probability is nowhere near the universal probability bound of $10^{-50}$ proposed by Borel. I have yet to see a convincing application of the explanatory filter in which coincidences better explained by chance get attributed to design. I challenge anyone to exhibit a specified event of probability less than Borel's universal probability bound for which intelligent causation can be convincingly ruled out.

## The Nature of Intelligent Causation

My second argument showing that the explanatory filter is a reliable criterion for detecting design considers the nature of intelligent causation and specifically what it is about intelligent causes that makes them detectable. Even though induction confirms that the explanatory filter is a reliable criterion for detecting design, induction does not explain why the filter works. What about the inner workings of the filter makes it a suitable instrument for detecting design? The logic of the explanatory filter is largely eliminative—eliminating law and chance. What is it about eliminating law and chance that purchases design? If the filter is going to be employed with confidence to detect design, it cannot be an inscrutable algorithm, mechanically delivering the right answers but offering no clue why it works. That design and nothing else should remain once the filter eliminates law and chance is not immediately apparent. And yet I shall argue that this is precisely the case.

To see why the filter is exactly the right instrument for detecting design, we need to probe the nature of intelligent causation. The principal characteristic of intelligent causation is choice. Whenever an intelligent cause acts, it chooses from a range of competing possibilities. This is true not just of humans but of animals as well as of extraterrestrial intelligences. A rat navigating a maze must choose whether to go right or left at various points in the maze. When SETI researchers attempt to discover intelligence in the extraterrestrial radio transmissions they are monitoring, they assume an extraterrestrial intelligence could have chosen any number of possible radio transmissions and then attempt to match the transmissions they observe with certain patterns as opposed to others (see Drake and Sobel 1992). Whenever a human being utters meaningful speech, a choice is made from a range of possible sound combinations that might have been uttered. Intelligent causation always entails discrimination, choosing certain things, ruling out others.

Given this characterization of intelligent causes, the next question is how to recognize their operation. Intelligent causes act by making a choice. How do we know when an intelligent cause has so acted? A bottle of ink spills accidentally onto a sheet of paper; someone takes a fountain pen and writes a message on a sheet of paper. In both instances ink is applied to paper. In both instances one among an almost infinite set of possibilities is realized. In both instances a choice is made; one possibility is selected and the rest are ruled out. Yet in one instance we infer design; in the other we do not. What is the relevant difference? Not only do we need to observe that a choice has been made, but also we ourselves need to be able to specify that choice. It is not enough that one possibility has been chosen and others have been ruled out. We ourselves need to be able to make the same choice. Wittgen-stein (1980, 1e) illustrated this point as follows: "We tend to take the speech of a Chinese for inarticulate gurgling. Someone who understands Chinese will recognize *language* in what he hears. Similarly I often cannot discern the *humanity* in man."

In hearing a Chinese utterance, someone who understands Chinese not only recognizes that a choice was made from the range of all possible utterances but also is able to specify the utterance that was made as coherent Chinese speech. Contrast this with someone who does not understand Chinese. In hearing a Chinese utterance, someone who does not understand Chinese also recognizes that a choice was made from the range of all possible utterances. But this time, because the person lacks the ability to understand Chinese, he or she is unable to specify the utterance as coherent speech. To someone who does not understand Chinese, the utterance is gibberish. To be sure, uttering gibberish always constitutes a choice from the range of all possible utterances. Nonetheless, gibberish corresponds to nothing we can understand in any language and so cannot be specified. As a result gibberish is never taken for intelligent communication but always for what Wittgen-stein calls "inarticulate gurgling."

This choosing of one among several competing possibilities, ruling out the rest and specifying the one that was chosen encapsulates how we recognize intelligent causes, or equivalently, how we detect design. Psycholo-gists who study animal learning and behavior have known this all along. For these psychologists, known as learning theorists, learning is discrimination (see Mazur 1990; Schwartz 1984). To learn a task an animal must acquire the ability to choose behaviors suitable for the task as well as the ability to rule out behaviors unsuitable for the task. Moreover, for a psychologist to recog-nize that an animal has learned a task, it is necessary not only to observe the animal making the appropriate discrimination but also to specify this dis-crimination.

Thus to recognize whether a rat has successfully learned how to traverse a maze, a psychologist must first specify which sequence of right and left turns conducts the rat out of the maze. No doubt a rat randomly wandering a maze also discriminates a sequence of right and left turns. But by randomly wandering the maze, the rat gives no indication that it can discriminate the appropriate sequence of right and left turns for exiting the maze. Conse-quently the psychologist studying the rat will have no reason to think the rat has learned how to traverse the maze. Only if the rat executes the sequence of right and left turns specified by the psychologist will the psychologist recognize that the rat has learned how to traverse the maze. It is precisely the learned behaviors we regard as intelligent in animals. Hence it is no surprise that the same scheme for recognizing animal learning recurs for recognizing intelligent causes generally, to wit: choosing one among several competing possibilities, ruling out the others and specifying the one chosen.

This general scheme for recognizing intelligent causes is but a thinly disguised form of the explanatory filter: In order for the filter to eliminate law, one must establish that a multiplicity of possibilities is compatible with the given antecedent circumstance (recall that law admits only one possible consequence for the given antecedent circumstance; hence to eliminate law is to establish a multiplicity of possible consequences). Next, in order for the filter to eliminate chance, one must establish that the possibility chosen after the others were ruled out was also specified. So far the match between this general scheme for recognizing intelligent causation and how the explanatory filter detects design is exact. Only one loose end remains: the role of small probabilities. Although small probabilities figure prominently in the explanatory filter, their role in this general scheme for recognizing intelligent causation is not immediately obvious. In this scheme a choice is made among several competing possibilities, the rest are ruled out, and the possibility chosen is specified. Where in this scheme are the small probabilities?

The answer is that they are there implicitly. To see this, consider again a rat traversing a maze, but now take a very simple maze in which two right turns conduct the rat out of the maze. How will a psychologist studying the rat determine whether it has learned to exit the maze? Just putting the rat in the maze will not be enough. Because the maze is so simple, the rat could by chance happen to take two right turns and thereby exit the maze. The psychologist will therefore be uncertain whether the rat learned to exit this maze or whether the rat was lucky. But contrast this now with a complicated maze in which a rat must take just the right sequence of left and right turns to exit the maze. Suppose the rat must take one hundred appropriate right and left turns and that any mistake will prevent the rat from exiting the maze. A psychologist who sees the rat take no erroneous turns and in short order exit the maze will be convinced that the rat has indeed learned how to exit the maze and that this was not dumb luck. With the simple maze there is a substantial probability that the rat will exit the maze by chance; with the complicated maze this is exceedingly improbable.

My second argument for showing that the explanatory filter is a reliable criterion for detecting design may now be summarized as follows: The explanatory filter is a reliable criterion for detecting design because it coincides with how we recognize intelligent causation generally. In general, to recognize intelligent causation we must observe a choice among competing possibilities, note which possibilities were not chosen and then be able to specify the possibility that was chosen. What is more, the competing possibilities that were ruled out must be live possibilities and sufficiently numerous so that specifying the possibility that was chosen cannot be attributed to chance. In terms of probability this means that the possibility that was specified has small probability. All the elements in this general scheme for recognizing intelligent causation (i.e., choosing, ruling out and specifying) find their counterpart in the explanatory filter. It follows that the filter formalizes what we have been doing when we recognize intelligent causes. The explanatory filter pinpoints what we need to be looking for when we detect design.

As a postscript, I call the reader's attention to the etymology of the word *intelligent*. The word *intelligent* derives from two Latin words, the preposition *inter*, meaning "between," and the verb *lego*, meaning "to choose or select." Thus according to its etymology, intelligence consists in choosing between. It follows that the etymology of the word *intelligent* parallels the formal analysis of intelligent causation inherent in the explanatory filter. Intelligent design is therefore a thoroughly apt phrase, signifying that design is inferred precisely because an intelligent cause has done what only an intelligent cause can do, to wit, make a choice.

## Acknowledgment

I wish to thank Stephen C. Meyer and Paul A. Nelson for helpful discussions. Their comments and insights have greatly improved this chapter.

## References

Borel, E. 1962. *Probabilities and life*. Translated by M. Baudin. New York: Dover Publications.

Dawkins, R. 1987. *The blind watchmaker*. New York: Norton.

Dembski, W. A. 1998. *The design inference: Eliminating chance through small probabilities*. Cambridge: Cambridge University Press.

Drake, F., and D. Sobel. 1992. *Is anyone out there? The scientific search for extraterrestrial intelligence*. New York: Delacorte Press.

Gardner, M. 1972. Arthur Koestler: Neoplatonism rides again (review of *The roots of coincidence*). *World* 1 (August):87–89.

Hacking, I. 1965. *Logic of statistical inference*. Cambridge: Cambridge University Press.

Howson, C., and P. Urbach. 1993. *Scientific reasoning: The Bayesian approach*. 2nd ed. La Salle, Ill.: Open Court.

Martin, W. 1985. *The kingdom of the cults*. Rev. ed. Minneapolis: Bethany House.

Mazur, J. E. 1990. *Learning and behavior*. 2nd ed. Englewood Cliffs, N.J.: Prentice-Hall.

Mood, A. M., F. A. Graybill, and D. C. Boes. 1974. *Introduction to the theory of statistics*. 3rd ed. New York: McGraw-Hill.

Schwartz, B. 1984. *Psychology of learning and behavior*. 2nd ed. New York: Norton.

Wittgenstein, L. 1980. *Culture and value*. Edited by G. H. von Wright. Translated by P. Winch. Chicago: University of Chicago Press.

# 5

# The Explanatory Power of Design

## *DNA and the Origin of Information*

### STEPHEN C. MEYER

SINCE THE LATE NINETEENTH CENTURY MOST BIOLOGISTS HAVE rejected the idea that biological organisms display evidence of intelligent design. While many acknowledge the appearance of design in biological systems, they insist that Darwinism, or neo-Darwinism, can give a full account for how this appearance arose naturalistically—i.e., without invoking a directing intelligence or agency. Following Darwin, modern neo-Darwinists generally accept that natural selection acting on random variation (or mutations) suffices to explain the appearance of design in living organisms. As evolutionary biologist Francisco Ayala has explained,

> The functional design of organisms and their features would . . . seem to argue for the existence of a designer. It was Darwin's greatest accomplishment [however] to show that the directive organization of living beings can be explained as the result of a natural process, natural selection, without any need to resort to a Creator or other external agent. (Ayala 1994, 4-5)

Yet whatever the explanatory efficacy of the Darwinian program, the appearance of design in at least one important domain of biology cannot be so easily dismissed. Since the late 1950s advances in molecular biology and biochemistry have revolutionized our understanding of the miniature world within the cell. Modern molecular biology has revealed that living cells—the fundamental units of life—possess the ability to store, edit and transmit information and to use information to regulate their most fundamental metabolic processes. Far from characterizing cells as simple "homogeneous globules of plasm," as did Ernst Haeckel (Haeckel 1905, 111) and other nineteenth-century biologists, modern biologists now describe cells as, among other things, "distributive real-time computers" and complex information processing systems.

Darwin, of course, neither knew about these intricacies nor sought to explain their origin. Instead, his theory of biological evolution sought to explain how life could have grown gradually more complex *starting* from "one or a few simple forms." Strictly speaking, therefore, those who insist that the Darwinian mechanism can explain the appearance of design in biology naturalistically overstate their case. The complexities within the microcosm of the cell beg for some kind of explanation, yet they lie beyond the purview of strictly biological evolutionary theory which assumes, rather than explains, the existence of the first life and the information it would have required.

This essay will argue that the complexity and specifity of even the simplest living cells suggest more than just apparent design. Indeed, it will argue that actual or "intelligent" design now constitutes the best explanation for the origin of the information required to make a living cell in the first place. In so doing, this essay will also critique naturalistic theories of chemical, rather than biological, evolution. Whereas biological evolutionary theories such as Darwinism or neo-Darwinism seek to explain the origin of new biological forms from preexisting forms, theories of chemical evolution seek to explain the ultimate origin of life starting from inanimate matter.

The discussion that follows will evaluate and compare the explanatory power of competing classes of explanation with respect to the origin of biological information. It will show the causal inadequacy of explanations based upon both chance and necessity (and the two working in combination). As it happens, the recent history of origin-of-life research can be understood nicely by reference to Jacques Monod's famous categories "chance" and "necessity," which were addressed by William Dembski in his discussion of the explanatory filter in the previous chapter. From the 1920s to the mid-1960s, chemical evolutionary theories emphasized the creative role of random variations (i.e., chance)—often working in tandem with so-called prebiotic natural selection. Since the late 1960s, theorists have instead generally invoked deterministic "self-oganizational properties," i.e., necessity or law, the other naturalistic node on Dembski's explanatory filter (see previous chapter). This essay will trace the recent history of origin-of-life research to show the inadequacy of scenarios invoking either chance or necessity (or the combination) as causal mechanisms for the origin of information. It will then argue that a third type of explanation—intelligent design—provides a better explanation for the origin of the information, including the information content present in large bio-macromolecules such as DNA, RNA and proteins.

## The Problem of Life's Origin

After Darwin published the *Origin of Species* in 1859, many scientists began to think about a problem that Darwin had not addressed,[1] namely, how life had arisen in the first place. While Darwin's theory purported to explain how life could have grown gradually more complex starting from "one or a few simple forms," it did not explain nor did it attempt to explain where life had originated.

Yet scientists in the 1870s and 1880s assumed that devising an explanation for the origin of life would be fairly easy. For one thing, they assumed that life was essentially a rather simple substance called protoplasm that could be easily constructed by combining and recombining simple chemicals such as carbon dioxide, oxygen and nitrogen. Thus Haeckel and others would refer to the cell as a simple "homogeneous globule of plasm" (Haeckel 1905, 111; Huxley 1869, 129-45). To Haeckel a living cell seemed no more complex than a blob of gelatin. His theory of how life first came into existence reflected this simplistic view. His method likened cell "autogony," as he called it, to the process of inorganic crystallization (Haeckel 1866, 179-80; 1892, 411-13; Kamminga 1980, 60, 61). Haeckel's English counterpart, T. H. Huxley, proposed a simple two-step method of chemical recombination to explain the origin of the first cell (Huxley 1869, 138-39). Just as salt could be produced spontaneously by adding sodium to chloride, so, thought Haeckel and Huxley, could a living cell be produced by adding several chemical constituents together and then allowing spontaneous chemical reactions to produce the simple protoplasmic substance that they assumed to be the essence of life.

## Orthodox Chemical Evolutionary Theory: The Oparin Scenario

During the 1920s and 1930s a more sophisticated version of this so-called chemical evolutionary theory was proposed by a Russian biochemist named Alexander I. Oparin. Oparin had a much more accurate understanding of the complexity of cellular metabolism, but neither he nor any one else in the 1930s fully appreciated the complexity of the molecules such as protein and DNA that make life possible. Oparin, like his nineteenth-century predecessors, suggested that life could have first evolved as the result of a series of chemical reactions. Unlike his predecessors, however, he envisioned that this process of chemical evolution would involve many more chemical transformations and reactions and many hundreds of millions or even billions of years.

Oparin's theory envisioned a series of chemical reactions (see figure 5.1) that he thought would enable a complex cell to assemble itself gradually and naturalistically from simple chemical precursors. Oparin believed that simple gases such as ammonia ($NH_3$), methane ($CH_4$), water ($H_2O$), carbon dioxide ($CO_2$) and hydrogen ($H_2$) would have rained down to the early oceans and combined with metallic compounds extruded from the core of the earth (Oparin 1938, 64-103). With the aid of ultraviolet radiation from the sun, the ensuing reactions would have produced energy-rich hydrocarbon compounds (Oparin 1938, 98, 107, 108). These in turn would have combined and recombined with various other compounds to make amino acids, sugars, phosphates and other building blocks of the complex molecules (such as proteins) necessary to living cells (Oparin 1938, 133-35). These constituents would eventually arrange themselves into simple cell-like enclosures that Oparin called coacervates (Oparin 1938, 148-59). Oparin then proposed a kind of Darwinian competition for survival among his coacervates. Those that developed increasingly complex molecules and metabolic processes would have survived and grown more complicated. Those that did not would have dissolved (Oparin 1938, 195-96).

Thus cells would have become gradually more and more complex as they competed for survival over billions of years. Like Darwin, Oparin employed time, chance and natural selection to account for the origin of complexity from initial simplicity. Moreover, nowhere in his scenario did mind or intelligent design or a Creator play any explanatory role. For Oparin, a committed Marxist (Graham 1973, 262-63; Araujo 1981, 19), such notions were explicitly precluded from scientific consideration. Matter interacting chemically with other matter, if given enough time and the right conditions, could produce life. Complex cells could be built from simple chemical precursors without any guiding personal or intelligent agency.

## The Miller-Urey Experiment

The first experimental support for Oparin's hypothesis came in December 1952. While doing graduate work under Harold Urey at the University of Chicago, Stanley Miller conducted the first experimental test of the Oparin chemical evolutionary model. Miller circulated a gaseous mixture of methane ($CH_4$), ammonia ($NH_3$), water vapor ($H_2O$) and hydrogen ($H_2$) through a glass vessel containing an electrical discharge chamber (Miller 1953, 528-29). Miller sent a high-voltage charge of electricity into the chamber via tungsten filaments in an attempt to simulate the effects of ultraviolet light on prebiotic atmospheric gases. After two days Miller found a small (2 percent) yield of amino acids in the U-shaped water trap he used to collect reaction products at the bottom of the vessel. While Miller's initial experiment yielded only three of the twenty amino acids that occur naturally in proteins, subsequent experiments performed under similar conditions have produced all but one of the others. Other simulation experiments have pro-

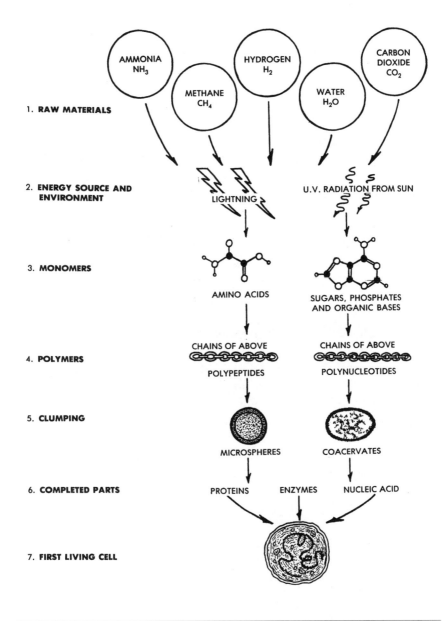

**1. RAW MATERIALS**

**2. ENERGY SOURCE AND ENVIRONMENT**

**3. MONOMERS**

**4. POLYMERS**

**5. CLUMPING**

**6. COMPLETED PARTS**

**7. FIRST LIVING CELL**

**Figure 5.1** Chemical evolutionary theorists envision life developing from simple chemicals in a series of steps such as these. Courtesy of John Wiester.

duced fatty acids and the nucleotide bases found in DNA and RNA but not the sugar molecules deoxyribose and ribose necessary to build DNA and RNA molecules (Thaxton and Bradley 1994, 182; Shapiro 1988, 71-95; Ferris 1987, 30; Thaxton, Bradley, and Olsen 1984, 24-38; Harada and Fox 1964, 335; Lemmon 1970, 95-96).

Miller's success in producing biologically relevant building blocks under ostensibly prebiotic conditions was heralded as a great breakthrough. His experiment seemed to provide experimental support for Oparin's chemical evolutionary theory by showing that an important step in Oparin's scenario— the production of biological building blocks from simpler atmospheric gases— was possible on the early earth. Miller's work inspired many similar simulation experiments and an unprecedented optimism about the possibility of developing an adequate naturalistic explanation for the origin of life.

Thanks largely to Miller's experimental work, chemical evolution is now routinely presented in both high school and college biology textbooks (e.g., Alberts et al. 1983, 4; Lehninger 1975, 23) as the accepted scientific explanation for the origin of life. Yet chemical evolutionary theory is now known to be riddled with difficulties, and Miller's work is understood by the origin-of-life research community itself to have little if any relevance to explaining how amino acids, let alone proteins or living cells, could have arisen on the early earth.

## Problems with the Oparin/Miller Hypothesis
Despite its status as textbook orthodoxy, the Oparin chemical evolutionary theory has in recent years encountered severe, even fatal, criticisms on many fronts. First, geochemists have failed to find evidence of the nitrogen-rich prebiotic soup required by Oparin's model.[2] Second, the remains of single-celled organisms in the very oldest rocks testify that, however life emerged, it did so relatively quickly; that is, fossil evidence suggests that chemical evolution had little time to work before life emerged on the early earth.[3] Third, new geological and geochemical evidence suggests that prebiotic atmospheric conditions were hostile, not friendly, to the production of amino acids and other essential building blocks of life. Fourth, the revolution in the field of molecular biology has revealed so great a complexity and specificity of design in even the simplest cells and cellular components as to defy materialistic explanation. Even scientists known for a staunch commitment to materialistic philosophy now concede that materialistic science in no way suffices to explain the origin of life (Dose 1988, 348-56; Shapiro 1986). As origin-of-life biochemist Klaus Dose has said, "More than 30 years of experimentation on the origin of life in the fields of chemical and molecular evolution have led to a better perception of the immensity of the problem of the origin of life on Earth rather than to its

solution. At present all discussions on principle theories and experiments in the field either end in stalemate or in a confession of ignorance" (Dose 1988, 348-56; cf. Crick 1981, 88).

To understand the crisis in chemical evolutionary theory, it will be necessary to explain in more detail the latter two difficulties, namely, the problem of hostile prebiotic conditions and the problem posed by the complexity of the cell and its components.

When Miller conducted his experiment simulating the production of amino acids on the early earth, he presupposed that the earth's atmosphere was composed of a mixture of what chemists call reducing gases such as methane ($CH_4$), ammonia ($NH_3$) and hydrogen ($H_2$). He also assumed that the earth's atmosphere contained virtually no free oxygen. Miller derived his assumptions about these conditions from Oparin's 1936 book (Miller 1953, 528-29). In the years following Miller's experiment, however, new geochemical evidence made it clear that the assumptions that Oparin and Miller had made about the early atmosphere could not be justified. Instead evidence strongly suggested that neutral gases such as carbon dioxide, nitrogen and water vapor (Walker 1977, 210, 246; 1978, 22; Kerr 1980, 42-43; Thaxton, Bradley, annd Olsen 1984, 73-94)—not methane, ammonia and hydrogen—predominated in the early atmosphcre. Morcovcr, a number of geochemical studies showed that significant amounts of free oxygen were also present even before the advent of plant life, probably as the result of volcanic outgassing and the photodissociation of water vapor (Berkner and Marshall 1965, 225; Brinkman 1969, 53-55; Dimroth and Kimberly 1976, 1161; Carver 1981, 136; Holland, Lazar, and McCaffrey 1986, 27-33; Kastings, Liu, and Donahue 1979, 3097-3102; Kerr 1980, 42-43; Thaxton, Bradley, and Olsen 1984, 73-94).

This new information about the probable composition of the early atmosphere has forced a serious reevaluation of the significance and relevance of Miller-type simulation experiments. As had been well know even before Miller's experiment, amino acids will form readily in an appropriate mixture of reducing gases. In a chemically neutral atmosphere, however, reactions among atmospheric gases will not take place readily, and those reactions that do take place will produce extremely low yields of biological building blocks.[4] Further, even a small amount of atmospheric oxygen will quench the production of biologically significant building blocks and cause any biomolecules otherwise present to degrade rapidly.

### The Molecular Biological Revolution and the Origin of Information

Yet a more fundamental problem remains for all chemical evolutionary scenarios. Even if it could be demonstrated that the building blocks of essential molecules could arise in realistic prebiotic conditions, the problem of assembling those building blocks into functioning proteins or DNA chains would remain. This problem of explaining the specific sequencing and thus the information within biopolymers lies at the heart of the current crisis in materialistic evolutionary thinking.

In the early 1950s, the molecular biologist Fred Sanger determined the structure of the protein molecule insulin. Sanger's work made clear for the first time that each protein found in the cell comprises a long and definitely arranged sequence of amino acids. The amino acids in protein molecules are linked together to form a chain, rather like individual railroad cars composing a long train. Moreover, the function of all such proteins, whether as enzymes, signal transducers or structural components in the cell, depends upon the specific sequencing of the individual amino acids (Alberts et al. 1983, 91-141), just as the meaning of an English text depends upon the sequential arrangement of the letters. The various chemical interactions between amino acids in any given chain will determine the three-dimensional shape or topography that the amino acid chain adopts. This shape in turn determines what function, if any, the amino acid chain can perform within the cell.

For a functioning protein, its three-dimensional shape gives it a hand-in-glove fit with other molecules in the cell, enabling it to catalyze specific chemical reactions or to build specific structures within the cell. The proteins histone 3 and 4, for example, fold into very well-defined three-dimensional shapes with a precise distribution of positive charges around their exteriors. This shape and charge distribution enable them to form part of the spool-like nucleosomes that allow DNA to coil efficiently around itself and to store information (Lodish et al. 1995, 347-48). The information storage density of DNA, thanks in part to nucleosome spooling, is several trillion times that of our most advanced computer chips (Gitt 1989, 4).

To get a feel for the specificity of the three-dimensional charge distribution on these histone proteins, imagine a large wooden spool with grooves on the surface. Next picture a helical cord made of two strands. Then visualize wrapping the cord around the spool so that it lies exactly into perfectly hollowed-out grooves. Finally, imagine the grooves to be hollowed so that they exactly fit the shape of the coiled cord, with thicker parts nestling into deeper grooves, thinner parts into more shallow ones. In other words, the irregularities in the shape of the cord exactly match irregularities in the hollow grooves. In the case of histone and DNA there are not actually grooves, but there is an uncanny distribution of positively charged regions on the surface of the histone proteins that exactly matches the negatively charged regions of the double-stranded DNA that coils around it (Lodish et al. 1995, 347-48). Proteins that function as enzymes or that assist in the processing of information stored on DNA strands often have an even greater specificity of fit with the molecules to which they must bind. Almost all proteins function as a result of an extreme hand-in-glove three-dimensional specificity that derives from the precise sequencing of the amino acid building blocks.

The discovery of the complexity and specificity of protein molecules has raised serious difficulties for chemical evolutionary theory, even if an abundant supply of amino acids is granted for the sake of argument. Amino acids alone do not make proteins, any more than letters alone make words, sentences or poetry. In both cases the sequencing of the constituent parts determines the function or lack of function of the whole. In the case of human languages the sequencing of letters and words is obviously performed by intelligent human agents. In the cell the sequencing of amino acids is directed by the information—the set of biochemical instructions—encoded on the DNA molecule.

## Information Transfer: From DNA to Protein

During the 1950s and 1960s, at roughly the same time molecular biologists began to determine the structure and function of many proteins, scientists were able to explicate the structure and function of DNA, the molecule of heredity. After James Watson and Francis Crick elucidated the structure of DNA (Watson and Crick 1953, 737), molecular biologists soon discovered how DNA directs the process of protein synthesis within the cell. They discovered that the specificity of amino acids in proteins derives from a prior specificity within the DNA molecule—from information on the DNA molecule stored as millions of specifically arranged chemicals called nucleotides or bases along the spine of DNA's helical strands (see figure 5.2). Chemists represent the four nucleotides with the letters A, T, G and C (for adenine, thymine, guanine and cytosine).

As in the case of protein, the sequence specificity of the DNA molecule strongly resembles the sequence specificity of human codes or languages. Just as the letters in the alphabet of a written language may convey a particular message depending on their sequence, so too do the sequences of nucleotides or bases in the DNA molecule convey precise biochemical messages that direct protein synthesis within the cell. Whereas the function of the protein molecule derives from the specific arrangement of twenty different amino acids (a twenty-letter alphabet), the function of DNA depends upon the arrangement of just four bases. Thus it takes a group of three nucleotides (or triplets, as they are called) on the DNA molecule to specify the construction of one amino acid. This process proceeds as long chains of nucleotide triplets (the genetic message) are first copied during a process known as DNA transcription and then transported (by the molecular messenger m-RNA) to a complex organelle called a ribosome (Borek 1969, 184). At the ribosome site the genetic message is translated with the aid of an ingenious adaptor molecule called transfer-RNA to produce a growing amino acid chain (Alberts et al. 1983, 108-9; see figure 5.3). Thus the sequence specificity in DNA begets sequence specificity in proteins. Or put differently, the sequence specificity of proteins depends upon a prior specificity—upon information—encoded in DNA.

**Naturalistic Approaches to the Problem of the Origin of Information**
The explication of this system by molecular biologists in the 1950s and 1960s has raised the question of the ultimate origin of the specificity—the information—in both DNA and the proteins it generates. Many scientists now refer to the information problem as the Holy Grail of origin-of-life biology (Thaxton and Bradley 1994, 190). As Bernd-Olaf Küppers recently stated, "the problem of the origin of life is clearly basically equivalent to the problem of the origin of biological information" (Küppers 1990, 170-72). As mentioned previously, the information contained or expressed in natural lan-

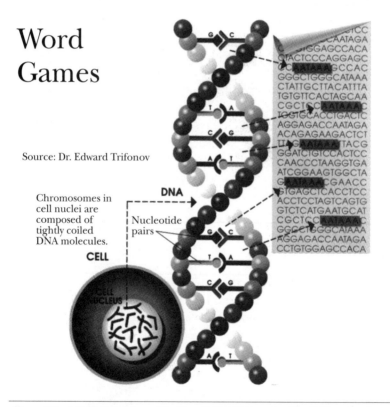

Figure 5.2   **A DNA Molecule and the Genetic Text It Contains.** The DNA molecule stores information in the form of many specifically arranged chemicals called *nucleotides* (represented by A, T, G and C). The genetic text (pictured as a scroll on the far right) is read along the spine or long axis of the molecule. Courtesy of Doug Stevens and *Insight* magazine.

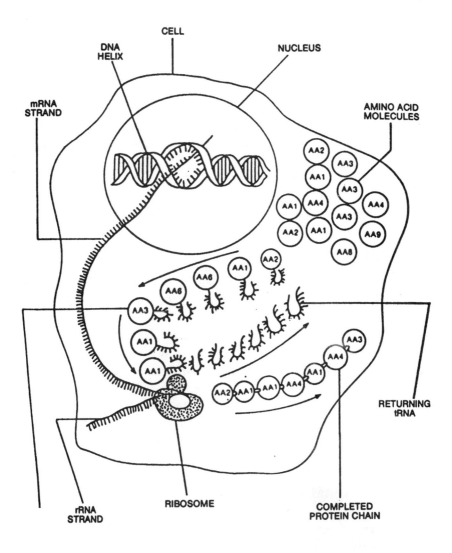

**Figure 5.3   The Intricate Machinery of Protein Synthesis.** The genetic messages encoded on the DNA molecule are copied and then transported by messenger RNA to the ribosome complex. There the genetic message is read and translated with the aid of other large biomolecules (transfer RNA and specific enzymes) to produce a growing amino acid chain. Courtesy of I. L. Cohen of New Research Publications from *Darwin Was Wrong: A Study in Probabilities.*

guages and computer codes is the product of intelligent minds. Minds routinely create informative arrangements of matter. Yet since the mid-nineteenth century scientists have sought to explain all phenomena by reference to exclusively material causes (Gillespie 1979; Meyer 1994a, 29-40; Meyer 1993, A14; Johnson 1991; Ruse 1982, 72-78). Since the 1950s three broad types of naturalistic explanation have been proposed by scientists to explain the origin of information.

**Biological Information: Beyond the Reach of Chance**
After the revolutionary developments within molecular biology in the 1950s and early 1960s made clear that Oparin had underestimated the complexity of life, he revised his initial theory. He sought to account for the sequence specificity of the large protein, DNA and RNA molecules (known collectively as biomacromolecules or biopolymers). In each case the broad outlines of his theory remained the same, but Oparin invoked the notion of natural selection acting on random variations within the sequences of the biopolymers to account for the emergence of the specificity within these molecules (Kamminga 1980, 326; Oparin 1968, 146-47). Others invoked the idea of a chance formation for these large information-bearing molecules by speaking of them as "frozen accidents" (Crick 1968, 367-79; Kamminga 1980, 303-4).

While many outside origin-of-life biology may still invoke chance as a causal explanation for the origin of biological information, few serious researchers still do (de Duve 1995, 112). Since molecular biologists began to appreciate the sequence specificity of proteins and nucleic acids in the 1950s and 1960s, many calculations have been made to determine the probability of formulating functional proteins and nucleic acids at random. Various methods of calculating probabilities have been offered (Morowitz 1968, 5-12; Cairns-Smith 1971, 92-96; Hoyle and Wickramasinghe 1981, 24-27; Shapiro 1986, 117-31; Yockey 1981, 13-31; Yockey 1992, 246-58; Bowie and Sauer 1989, 2152-56; Bowie et al. 1990, 1306-10; Reidhaar-Olson and Sauer 1990, 306-16). For the sake of argument these calculations have generally assumed extremely favorable prebiotic conditions (whether realistic or not) and theoretically maximal reaction rates among the constituent monomers (i.e., the constituent parts of the proteins, DNA and RNA). Such calculations have invariably shown that the probability of obtaining functionally sequenced biomacromolecules at random is, in Prigogine's words, "vanishingly small . . . even on the scale of . . . billions of years" (Prigogine, Nicolis, and Babloyantz 1972, 23).[5] As Cairns-Smith (1971, 95) wrote:

> Blind chance . . . is very limited. Low-levels of cooperation he [i.e., blind
> chance] can produce exceedingly easily (the equivalent of letters and

small words), but he becomes very quickly incompetent as the amount of organization increases. Very soon indeed long waiting periods and massive material resources become irrelevant.

Consider the probabilistic hurdles that must be overcome to construct even one short protein molecule of about 100 amino acids in length. (A typical protein consists of about 300 amino acids, and some are very much longer; Alberts et al. 1983, 118). First, all amino acids must form a chemical bond known as a peptide bond so as to join with other amino acids in the protein chain. Yet in nature many other types of chemical bonds are possible between amino acids; peptide and nonpeptide bonds occur with roughly equal probability. Thus at any given site along a growing amino acid chain the probability of having a peptide bond is roughly 1/2. The probability of attaining four peptide bonds is: $(1/2 \times 1/2 \times 1/2 \times 1/2) = 1/16$ or $(1/2)^4$. The probability of building a chain of one hundred amino acids in which all linkages involve peptide linkages is $(1/2)^{100}$ or roughly 1 chance in $10^{30}$.

Second, in nature every amino acid has a distinct mirror image of itself, one left-handed version or L-form, and one right-handed version, or D-form. These mirror-image forms are called optical isomers. Functioning proteins tolerate only left-handed amino acids, yet the right-handed and left-handed isomers occurs in nature with roughly equal frequency. Taking this into consideration compounds the improbability of attaining a biologically functioning protein. The probability of attaining at random only L-amino acids in a hypothetical peptide chain 100 amino acids long is again $(1/2)^{100}$ or roughly 1 chance in $10^{30}$. The probability of building a 100 amino acid length chain at random in which all bonds are peptide bonds and all amino acids are L-form would be $(1/4)^{100}$ or roughly 1 chance in $10^{60}$ (zero for all practical purposes given the time available on the early earth).

Functioning proteins have a third independent requirement, the most important of all: their amino acids must link up in a specific sequential arrangement, just like the letters in a meaningful sentence. In some cases changing even one amino acid at a given site can result in a loss of protein function. Moreover, because there are 20 biologically occurring amino acids, the probability of getting a specific amino acid at a given site is small (i.e., 1/20; the probability is even lower because there are many nonproteineous amino acids in nature). On the assumption that all sites in a protein chain require one particular amino acid, the probability of attaining a particular protein 100 amino acids long would be $(1/20)^{100}$ or roughly 1 chance in $10^{130}$.

We know now, however, that some sites along the chain do tolerate several of the twenty proteineous amino acids, while others do not. The biochemist Robert Sauer of MIT has used a technique known as "cassette mutagenesis" to determine just how much variance among amino acids can be tolerated at any given site in several proteins. His results have shown that, even taking the possibility of variance into account, the probability of achieving a functional sequence of amino acids[6] in several functioning proteins at random is still "vanishingly small," roughly 1 chance in $10^{65}$—an astronomically large number (there are $10^{65}$ atoms in our galaxy; Reidhaar-Olson and Sauer 1990, 306-16). In light of these results, biochemist Michael Behe has compared the odds of attaining proper sequencing in a 100 amino acid length protein to the odds of a blindfolded man finding a single marked grain of sand hidden in the Sahara Desert not once but three times (Behe 1994, 68-69). Moreover, if one also factors in the probability of attaining proper bonding and optical isomers, the probability of constructing a rather short functional protein at random becomes so small as to be effectively zero (1 chance in $10^{125}$) even given our multibillion-year-old universe (Borel 1962, 28; Dembski 1998). All these calculations thus reinforce the opinion that has prevailed since the mid-1960s within origin-of-life biology: Chance is not an adequate explanation for the origin of biological specificity. What P. T. Mora said (1963, 215) still holds:

> Statistical considerations, probability, complexity, etc., followed to their logical implications suggest that the origin and continuance of life is not controlled by such principles. An admission of this is the use of a period of practically infinite time to obtain the derived result. Using such logic, however, we can prove anything.

**Prebiotic Natural Selection: A Contradiction in Terms**

At nearly the same time that many researchers became disenchanted with chance explanations, theories of prebiotic natural selection also fell out of favor. Such theories allegedly overcome the difficulties attendant pure chance theories by providing a mechanism by which complexity-increasing events in the cell would be preserved and selected. Yet these theories share many of the difficulties that afflict purely chance-based theories.

Oparin's revised theory, for example, claimed that a kind of natural selection acted upon random polymers as they formed and changed within his coacervate protocells (Oparin 1968, 146-47). As more complex molecules accumulated, they presumably survived and reproduced more prolifically. Nevertheless Oparin's discussion of differential reproduction seemed to presuppose a preexisting mechanism of self-replication. Self-replication in all extant cells depends upon functional and therefore to a high degree sequence-specific proteins and nucleic acids. Yet the origin of these molecules is precisely what Oparin needed to explain. Thus many rejected the postulation of prebiotic natural selection as question begging (Mora 1965,

311-12; Bertalanffy 1967, 82). Functioning nucleic acids and proteins (or molecules approaching their complexity) are necessary to self-replication, which in turn is necessary to natural selection. Yet Oparin invoked natural selection to explain the origin of proteins and nucleic acids. As the evolutionary biologist Theodosius Dobzhansky would proclaim, "prebiological natural selection is a contradiction in terms" (Dobzhansky 1965, 310). Or as H. H. Pattee (1970, 123) put it:

> there is no evidence that hereditary evolution occurs except in cells which already have the complete complement of hierarchical constraints, the DNA, the replicating and translating enzymes, and all the control systems and structures necessary to reproduce themselves.

In any case, functional sequences of amino acids (i.e., proteins) cannot be counted on to arise via random events, even if some means of selecting them exists after they have been produced. Natural selection can only select what chance has first produced, and chance, at least in a prebiotic setting, seems an implausible agent for producing the information present in even a single functioning protein or DNA molecule. Oparin attempted to circumvent this problem by claiming that the first polymers need not have been terribly specific. But lack of polymer specificity produces "error catastrophes" that efface the accuracy of self-replication and eventually render natural selection impossible. Further, the mathematician von Neumann (1966) showed that any system capable of self-replication would need to contain subsystems that were functionally equivalent to the information storage, replicating and processing systems found in extant cells. His calculations and similar ones by Wigner (1961, 231-35), Landsberg (1964, 928-30) and Morowitz (1966, 446-59; 1968, 10-11) showed that random fluctuations of molecules in all probability would not produce the minimal complexity needed for even a primitive replication system. The improbability of developing a replication system vastly exceeds the improbability of developing the protein or DNA components of such a system. Thus appeals to prebiotic natural selection increasingly appear indistinguishable from appeals to chance.

Nevertheless, Richard Dawkins (Dawkins 1986, 47-49) and Bernd-Olaf Küppers (Küppers 1987, 355-69) recently have attempted to resuscitate prebiotic natural selection as an explanation for the origin of biological information. Both accept the futility of naked appeals to chance and invoke what Küppers calls a "Darwinian optimization principle." Both use a computer to demonstrate the efficacy of prebiotic natural selection. Each selects a target sequence to represent a desired functional polymer. After creating a crop of randomly constructed sequences and generating variations among them at random, they then program the computer to select those sequences that match the target sequence most closely. The computer then amplifies the production of those sequences and eliminates the others (thus simulating differential reproduction) and repeats the process. As Küppers puts it,

> Every mutant sequence that agrees one bit better with the meaningful or reference sequence . . . will be allowed to reproduce more rapidly. (Küppers 1987, 366)

In Küppers's case, after a mere thirty-five generations his computer succeeded in spelling his target sequence, "NATURAL SELECTION."

Despite superficially impressive results, these "simulations" conceal an obvious flaw: molecules *in situ* do not have a target sequence in mind, nor will they confer any selective advantage on a cell and thus differentially reproduce until they combine in a functionally advantageous arrangement. Thus, nothing in nature corresponds to the role that the computer plays in selecting functionally nonadvantageous sequences that happen to agree "one bit better" than others with a target sequence. The sequence "NORMAL ELECTION" may agree more with "NATURAL SELECTION" than does the sequence "MISTRESS DEFECTION," but neither of the two yields any advantage in communication over the other if, that is, we are trying to communicate something about natural selection. If so, both are equally ineffectual. Similarly, a nonfunctional polypeptide would confer no selective advantage on a hypothetical protocell, even if its sequence happens to "agree one bit better" with an unrealized target protein than some other nonfunctional polypeptide.

Indeed, both Küppers's and Dawkins's published results of their simulations show the early generations of variant phrases awash in nonfunctional gibberish. In Dawkins's simulation, not a single functional English word appears until after the tenth iteration (unlike the more generous example above, which starts with actual albeit incorrect words). Yet to make distinctions on the basis of function among sequences that have no function whatsoever would seem quite impossible. Such determinations can only be made if considerations of proximity to possible future function are allowed, but this requires foresight that molecules do not have. A computer, programmed by a human being, *can* perform these functions. To imply that molecules can as well only illicitly personifies nature. Thus, if these computer simulations demonstrate anything, they subtly demonstrate the need for intelligent agents to elect some options and exclude others—that is, to create information.

### Self-Organizational Scenarios

Because of the difficulties with appeals to prebiotic natural selection, many origin-of-life theorists after the mid-1960s attempted to address the problem of the origin of biological information in a new way. Rather than invoking prebiotic natural selection or "frozen accidents" (Crick 1968, 367-79; Kamminga 1980,

303-4), many theorists suggested that the laws of nature and chemical attraction may themselves be responsible for the information in DNA and proteins. Some have suggested that simple chemicals might possess "self-ordering properties" capable of organizing the constituent parts of proteins, DNA and RNA into the specific arrangements they now possess (Morowitz 1968). Steinman and Cole, for example, suggested that differential bonding affinities or forces of chemical attraction between certain amino acids might account for the origin of the sequence specificity of proteins (Steinman and Cole 1967, 735-41; Steinman 1967, 533-39; for recent criticism see Kok, Taylor, and Bradley 1988, 135-42). Just as electrostatic forces draw sodium ion (Na+) and chloride ions (Cl-) together into highly ordered patterns within a crystal of salt (NaCl), so too might amino acids with special affinities for each other arrange themselves to form proteins. This idea was developed in *Biochemical Predestination* by Kenyon and Steinman (1969). They argued that the origin of life might have been "biochemically predestined" by the properties of attraction that exist between constituent chemical parts, particularly between amino acids in proteins (Kenyon and Steinman 1969, 199-211, 263-66).

In 1977 another self-organizational theory was proposed by Prigogine and Nicolis based on a thermodynamic characterization of living organisms. In *Self Organization in Nonequilibrium Systems,* they classified living organisms as open, nonequilibrium systems capable of "dissipating" large quantities of energy and matter into the environment (Prigogine and Nicolis 1977, 339-53, 429-47). They observed that open systems driven far from equilibrium often display self-ordering tendencies. For example, gravitational energy will produce highly ordered vortices in a draining bathtub; thermal energy flowing through a heat sink will generate distinctive convection currents or "spiral wave activity." Prigogine and Nicolis then argued that the organized structures observed in living systems might have similarly self-originated with the aid of an energy source. In essence they conceded the improbability of simple building blocks arranging themselves into highly ordered structures under normal equilibrium conditions. But they suggested that under nonequilibrium conditions, where an external source of energy is supplied, biochemical building blocks might arrange themselves into highly ordered patterns.

## Order Versus Information

For many current origin-of-life scientists, self-organizational models (see, e.g., Kauffman 1993; de Duve 1995) now seem to offer the most promising approach to explaining the origin of biological information. Nevertheless critics have called into question both the plausibility and the relevance of self-organizational models. Perhaps the most prominent early advocate of self-organization, Dean Kenyon, has now explicitly repudiated such theories as both incompatible with empirical findings and theoretically incoherent (Kok, Taylor, and Bradley 1988, 135-42).

First, empirical studies have shown that some differential affinities do exist between various amino acids (i.e., particular amino acids do form linkages more readily with some amino acids than others; Steinman and Cole 1967, 735-41; Steinman 1967, 533-39). Nevertheless these differences do not correlate to actual sequencing in large classes of known proteins (Kok, Taylor, and Bradley 1988, 135-42). In short, differing chemical affinities do not explain the multiplicity of amino acid sequences that exist in naturally occurring proteins or the sequential ordering of any single protein.

In the case of DNA this point can be made more dramatically. Figure 5.4 shows the structure of DNA depends upon several chemical bonds. There are bonds, for example, between the sugar and the phosphate molecules that form the two twisting backbones of the DNA molecule. There are bonds fixing individual nucleotide bases to the sugar-phosphate backbones on each side of the molecule. There are also hydrogen bonds stretching horizontally across the molecule between nucleotide bases making so-called complementary pairs. These bonds, which hold two complementary copies of the DNA message text together, make replication of the genetic instructions possible. Most importantly, however, notice that there are *no* chemical bonds between the nucleotide bases that run along the spine of the helix. Yet it is precisely along this axis of the molecule that the genetic instructions in DNA are encoded (Alberts et al. 1983, 105). In other words, the chemical constituents that are responsible for the message text in DNA do not interact chemically in any significant way.

Further, just as magnetic letters can be combined and recombined in any way to form various sequences on a metal surface, so too can each of the four bases A, T, G and C attach to any site on the DNA backbone with equal facility, making all sequences equally probable (or improbable). Indeed, there are no differential affinities between any of the four bases and the binding sites along the sugar-phosphate backbone. The same type of so-called "n-glycosidic" bond occurs between the base and the backbone regardless of which base attaches. All four bases are acceptable; none is preferred. As Küppers has noted,

> the properties of nucleic acids indicates that all the combinatorially possible nucleotide patterns of a DNA are, from a chemical point of view, equivalent. (Küppers 1987, 364)

Thus, "self-organizing" bonding affinities cannot explain the sequential ordering of the nucleotide bases in DNA because (1) there are *no* bonds between bases along the message-bearing axis of the molecule, and (2) there are no *differential* affinities between the backbone and the various bases that could account for variations in sequencing. Because the same holds for RNA molecules, researchers who speculate that life began in an "RNA world" have also failed to solve the sequencing problem[7]—that is, the problem of explaining how information present in all functioning RNA molecules could have arisen in the first place.

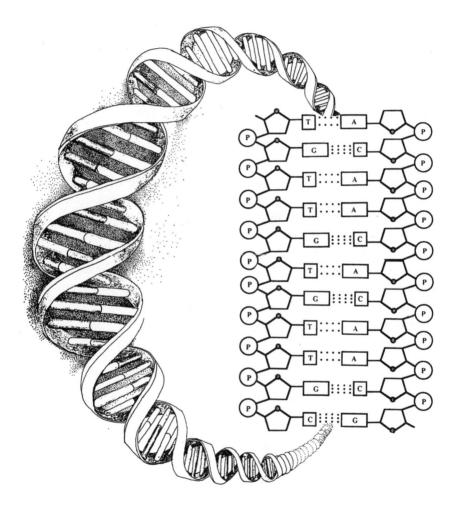

**Figure 5.4  The Bonding Relationships Between the Chemical Constituents of the DNA Molecule.** Sugars (designated by the pentagons) and phosphates (designated by the circled Ps) are linked chemically. Nucleotide bases (A's, T's, G's and C's) are bonded to the sugar-phosphate backbones. Nucleotide bases are linked by hydrogen bonds (designated by dotted double or triple lines) across the double helix. But no chemical bonds exist between the nucleotide bases along the message-bearing spine of the helix. Courtesy of Fred Hereen, Daystar Publications.

For those who want to explain the origin of life as the result of self-organizing properties intrinsic to the material constituents of living systems, these rather elementary facts of molecular biology have devastating implications. The most logical place to look for self-organizing properties to explain the origin of genetic information is in the constituent parts of the molecules carrying that information. But biochemistry and molecular biology make clear that forces of attraction between the constituents in DNA, RNA and proteins do not explain the sequence specificity of these large information-bearing biomolecules.

Significantly, information theorists insist that there is a good reason for this. If chemical affinities between the constituents in the DNA message text determined the arrangement of the text, such affinities would dramatically diminish the capacity of DNA to carry information. To illustrate, imagine receiving the following incomplete message over the wire: the "q-ick brown fox jumped over the lazy dog." Obviously someone who knew the conventions of English could determine which letter had been rubbed out in the transmission. Because $q$ and $u$ always go together by grammatical necessity, the presence of one indicates the probable presence of the other in the initial transmission of the message. The $u$ in all English communications is an example of what information theorists call "redundancy." Given the grammatical rule "$u$ must always follow $q$," the addition of the $u$ adds no new information when $q$ is already present. It is redundant or unnecessary to determining the sense of the message (though not to making it grammatically correct).

Now consider what would happen if the individual nucleotide letters (A, T, G, C) in a DNA molecule did interact by chemical necessity with each other. Every time adenine (A) occurred in a growing genetic sequence, it would attract thymine (T) to it. Every time cytosine (C) occurred, guanine (G) would follow.[8] As a result the DNA message text would be peppered with repeating sequences of A's followed by T's and C's followed by G's. Rather than having a genetic molecule capable of unlimited novelty with all the unpredictable and aperiodic sequences that characterize informative texts, we would have a highly repetitive text awash in redundant sequences, much as happens in crystals. In a crystal the forces of mutual chemical attraction do completely explain the sequential ordering of the constituent parts and consequently crystals cannot convey novel information. Sequencing in crystals is highly ordered or repetitive but not informative. Once one has seen Na followed by Cl in a crystal of salt, for example, one has seen the extent of the sequencing possible. In DNA, however, where any nucleotide can follow any other, innumerable novel sequences are possible, and a countless variety of amino acid sequences can be built.

The forces of chemical necessity, like grammatical necessity in the q-and-u example, produce redundancy or monotonous order but reduce the capacity to convey information and create novelty. As Polanyi has said:

> Suppose that the actual structure of a DNA molecule were due to the fact that the bindings of its bases were much stronger than the bindings would be for any other distribution of bases, then such a DNA molecule would have no information content. Its code-like character would be effaced by an overwhelming redundancy. . . . Whatever may be the origin of a DNA configuration, it can function as a code only if its order is not due to the forces of potential energy. It *must be* as physically indeterminate as the sequence of words is on a printed page. (Polanyi 1968, 1309, emphasis added)

So, if chemists had found that bonding affinities between the nucleotides in DNA produced nucleotide sequencing, they would have also found that they had been mistaken about DNA's information-bearing properties. To put the point quantitatively, to the extent that forces of attraction between constituents in a sequence determine the arrangement of the sequence, to that extent will the information-carrying capacity of the system be diminished.[9] As Dretske has explained:

> As $p(s_i)$ [the probability of a condition or state of affairs] approaches 1 the amount of information associated with the occurrence of $s_i$ goes to 0. In the limiting case when the probability of a condition or state of affairs is unity [$p(s_i) = 1$], no information is associated with, or generated by, the occurrence of $s_i$. This is merely another way to say that no information is generated by the occurrence of events for which there are no possible alternatives. (Dretske 1981, 12)

Bonding affinities, to the extent they exist, militate against the maximization of information (Yockey 1981, 18). They cannot therefore be used to explain the origin of information. Affinities create mantras, not messages.

The tendency to conflate the qualitative distinction between order and information has characterized self-organizational research efforts and calls into question the relevance of such work to the origin of life. As Yockey has argued, the accumulation of structural or chemical order does not explain the origin of biological complexity (i.e., genetic information).[10] He concedes that energy flowing through a system may produce highly ordered patterns. Strong winds form swirling tornadoes and the eyes of hurricanes; Prigogine's thermal baths do develop interesting "convection currents"; and chemical elements do coalesce to form crystals. Self-organizational theorists explain well what does not need explaining. What needs explaining is not the origin of order (in the sense of symmetry or repetition) but the origin of information—the highly improbable, aperiodic and yet specified sequences that make biological function possible.

To illustrate the distinction between order and information compare the sequence ABABABABABABAB to the sequence THE BIG RED HOUSE IS ON FIRE! The first sequence is repetitive and ordered but not complex or informative. The second sequence is not ordered in the sense of being repetitious, but it is complex and also informative. The second sequence is complex because its characters do not follow a rigidly repeating or predictable pattern; that is, it is aperiodic. It is also informative because, unlike a merely complex sequence such as RFSXDCNCTQJ, the particular arrangement of characters is highly exact or specified so as to perform a (communication) function. Systems that are characterized by both specificity and complexity (what information theorists call "specified complexity") have "information content." Since such systems have the qualitative feature of complexity (aperiodicity), they are qualitatively distinguishable from systems characterized by simple periodic order. Thus attempts to explain the origin of order have no relevance to discussions of the origin of specified complexity or information content. Significantly, the nucleotide sequences in the coding regions of DNA have by all accounts a high information content—that is, they are both highly specified and complex, just like meaningful English sentences (Thaxton and Bradley 1994, 173-210; Thaxton, Bradley and Olsen 1984, 127-66; Yockey 1992, 242-93).

Conflating order and information (or specified complexity) has led many to attribute properties to brute matter that it does not possess. While energy in a system can create patterns of symmetric order such as whirling vortices, there is no evidence that energy alone can encode functionally specified sequences, whether biochemical or otherwise. As Yockey (1977, 380) warns:

> Attempts to relate the idea of order . . . with biological organization or specificity must be regarded as a play on words which cannot stand careful scrutiny. Informational macromolecules can code genetic messages and therefore can carry information because the sequence of bases or residues is affected very little, if at all, by [self-organizing] physico-chemical factors.

### The Return of the Intelligent Design Hypothesis

The preceding discussion suggests that the properties of the material constituents of DNA, like those of any information-bearing medium, are not responsible for the information conveyed by the molecule. In all informational systems, the information content or message is neither deducible from the properties of the material medium nor attributable to them. The properties of matter do not explain the origin of the information.

To amplify this point, consider first that many different materials can express the same message. The headline of this morning's *New York Times* was written with ink on paper. Nevertheless, many other materials could have been used to convey the same message. The information in the headline could have been written with chalk on a board, with neon-filled tubes in a series of signs, or by a skywriter over New York harbor. Clearly the peculiar chemical properties of ink are not necessary to convey the message. Neither are the physical properties (i.e., the geometric shapes) of the letters necessary to transmit the information. The same message could have been expressed in Hebrew or Greek using entirely different alphabetic characters.

Conversely the same material medium and alphabetic characters can express many different messages; that is, the medium is not sufficient to determine the message. In November of an election year the *Times* will use ink and English characters to tell the reading public that either a Democrat, a Republican or a third-party candidate has won the presidential election. Yet the properties of the ink and the twenty-six letters available to the typesetter will not determine which headline will be published by the *Times*. Instead the ink and English characters will permit the transmission of whatever headline the election requires, as well as a vast ensemble of other possible arrangements of text, some meaningful and many more not. Neither the chemistry of the ink nor the shapes of the letters determines the meaning of the text. In short, the message transcends the properties of the medium.

The information in DNA also transcends the properties of its material medium. Because chemical bonds do not determine the arrangement of nucleotide bases, the nucleotides can assume a vast array of possible sequences and thereby express many different messages. (Conversely various materials can express the same messages, as happens in variant versions of the genetic code or when laboratory chemists use English instructions to direct the synthesis of naturally occurring proteins.) Thus, again, the properties of the constituents do not determine the function—the information transmitted—by the whole. As Polanyi (1968, 1309) has said, "As the arrangement of a printed page is extraneous to the chemistry of the printed page, so is the base sequence in a DNA molecule extraneous to the chemical forces at work in the DNA molecule."

If the properties of matter (i.e., the medium) do not suffice to explain the origin of information, what does? Blind chance is a possibility but not, as we have seen in the case of DNA and proteins, where the amount of information or the improbability of arrangement gets too immense. The random selection and sequencing of Scrabble pieces out of a grab bag might occasionally produce a few meaningful words such as cat or ran. Nevertheless undirected selection will inevitably fail as the numbers of letters required to make a text increases. Fairly soon chance becomes clearly inadequate, as origin-of-life biologists have almost universally acknowledged.

Some have suggested that the discovery of new scientific laws might explain the origin of biological information. But this suggestion betrays confusion on two counts. First, scientific laws do not generally explain or cause natural phenomena; they describe them. For example, Newton's law of gravitation described but did not explain the attraction between planetary bodies. Second, scientific laws describe (almost by definition) highly regular phenomena—that is, order. Thus to say that any scientific law can describe or generate an informational sequence is essentially a contradiction in terms. The patterns that laws describe are necessarily highly ordered, not complex. Thus, like crystals, all law-like patterns have an extremely limited capacity to convey information. One might perhaps find a complex set of material conditions capable of generating high information content on a regular basis, but everything we know suggests that the complexity and information content of such conditions would have to equal or exceed that of any system produced, thus again begging the question about the ultimate origin of information.

For example, the chemist J. C. Walton has argued (echoing earlier articles by Mora) that even the self-organization produced in Prigogine-style convection currents does not exceed the organization or information represented by the experimental apparatus used to create the currents (Walton 1977, 16-35; Mora 1965, 41). Similarly, Maynard-Smith (1979, 445-46) and Dyson (1985, 9-11, 35-39, 65-66, 78) have shown that Manfred Eigen's (Eigen and Schuster 1977, 541-65; 1978a, 7-41; 1978b, 341-69) so-called hypercycle model for generating information naturalistically is subject to the same law of information loss. They show, first, that Eigen's hypercycles presuppose a large initial contribution of information in the form of a long RNA molecule and some forty specific proteins. More significantly, they show that because hypercycles lack an error-free mechanism of self-replication, they become susceptible to various error-catastrophes that ultimately diminish, not increase, the information content of the system over time.

Instead our experience with information-intensive[11] systems, especially codes and languages, indicates that such systems always come from an intelligent source—that is, from mental or personal agents. This generalization holds not only for the information present in languages and codes but also for the nongrammatical information (also describable as specified complexity) inherent in machines or expressed in works of art. Like the text of a newspaper, the parts of a supercomputer and the faces on Mount Rushmore require many instructions to specify their shape or arrangement[12] and consequently have a high information content. Each of these systems is also, not coincidentally, the result of intelligent design, not chance or material forces.

Our generalization about the cause of information has ironically received confirmation from origin-of-life research itself. During the last forty years, every naturalistic model proposed has failed to explain the origin of information.[13] Thus mind or intelligence or what philosophers call "agent causation" now stands as the only cause known to be capable of creating an information-rich system, including the coding regions of DNA, functional proteins and the cell as a whole.

Because mind or intelligent design is a necessary cause of an informative system, one can detect (or, logically, retrodict) the past action of an intelligent cause from the presence of an information-intensive effect, even if the cause itself cannot be directly observed (Meyer 1990, 79-99). Since information requires an intelligent source, the flowers spelling "Welcome to Victoria" in the gardens of Victoria harbor lead visitors to infer the activity of intelligent agents even if they did not see the flowers planted and arranged. Similarly the specifically arranged nucleotide sequences—the encoded information—in DNA imply the past action of an intelligent mind, even if such mental agency cannot be directly observed.

Moreover, the logical calculus underlying such inferences follows a valid and well-established method used in all historical and forensic sciences. In historical sciences knowledge of the present causal powers of various entities and processes enables scientists to make inferences about possible causes in the past. When a thorough study of various possible causes turns up just a single adequate cause for a given effect, historical or forensic scientists can make fairly definitive inferences about the past (Meyer 1990, 79-99; Sober 1988, 4-5; Scriven 1966, 249-50). Several years ago, for example, one of the forensic pathologists from the original Warren Commission that investigated the assassination of President John F. Kennedy spoke out to quash rumors about a second gunman firing from in front of the motorcade. Apparently the bullet hole in the back of President Kennedy's skull evidenced a distinctive beveling pattern that clearly indicated its direction of entry. In this case it revealed definitely that the bullet had entered from the rear. The pathologist called the beveling pattern a "distinctive diagnostic" to indicate a necessary causal relationship between the direction of entry and the presence of the beveling.

Inferences based on knowledge of necessary causes (distinctive diagnostics) are quite common in historical and forensic sciences and often lead to the detection of intelligent as well as natural causes. Since Criminal X's fingers are the only known cause of Criminal X's fingerprints, X's prints on the murder weapon incriminate him with a high degree of certainty. In the same way, since intelligent design is the only known cause of information-rich systems, the presence of information, including the information-rich nucleotide sequences in DNA, implies an intelligent source.

Scientists in many fields recognize the connection between intelligence and information and make inferences accordingly. Archaeologists assume a mind produced the inscriptions on the Rosetta stone. Evolutionary anthropologists try to demonstrate the intelligence of early hominids by arguing that certain chipped flints are too improbably specified to have been produced by natural causes. NASA's Search for Extraterrestrial Intelligence (SETI) 14 presupposed that information imbedded in electromagnetic signals from space would indicate an intelligent source (McDonough 1987). As yet, however, radio astronomers have not found information-bearing signals coming from space. But closer to home, molecular biologists have identified encoded information in the cell. Consequently the presence of information in DNA justifies making what probability theorist William A. Dembski (1998) calls *the design inference* (see also Behe 1996; Kenyon and Mills 1996, 9-16; Ayoub 1996, 19-22; Moreland 1994; Bradley 1988, 72-83; Augros and Stanciu 1987; Denton 1986, 326-43; Thaxton, Bradley and Olsen 1984; Ambrose 1982; Walton 1977, 16-35).

### An Argument from Ignorance?

Against all that has been said, many have maintained that this argument from information content to design constitutes nothing more than an argument from ignorance. Since we don't yet know how biological information could have arisen we invoke the mysterious notion of intelligent design. Thus, say objectors, intelligent design functions not as a legitimate inference or explanation but as a kind of place holder for ignorance.

And yet, as Dembski has demonstrated (Dembski 1998, 9-35, 62-66) we often infer the causal activity of intelligent agents as the best explanation for events and phenomena. Moreover, we do so rationally, according to objectifiable, if often tacit, information and complexity theoretic criteria. His examples of design inferences—from archeology and cryptography to fraud detection and criminal forensics—show that we make design inferences all the time, often for a very good reason (Dembski 1998, 9-35). Intelligent agents have unique causal powers that nature does not. When we observe effects that we know only agents can produce, we rightly infer the antecedent presence of a prior intelligence even if we did not observe the action of the particular agent responsible. In other words, Dembski has shown that designed events leave a complexity and information-theoretic signature that allows us to detect intelligent design reliably. Specifically, when systems or artifacts have a high information content or (in his terminology) are both highly improbable and specified, intelligent design necessarily played a causal role in the origin of the system in question.

While admittedly the design inference constitutes a provisional, empirically-based conclusion and not a proof (science can provide nothing more), it most emphatically does not constitute an argument from ignorance. Instead, the design inference from biological information constitutes an "inference to the best explanation." Recent work on the method of "inference to the best explanation" (Lipton 1991; Meyer 1994b, 88-94) suggests that determining which among a set of competing possible explanations constitutes the best depends upon assessments of the causal powers of competing explanatory entities. Causes that have the capability to produce the evidence in question constitute better explanations of that evidence than those that do not. This essay has evaluated and compared the causal efficacy of three broad categories of explanation—chance, necessity (and chance and necessity combined) and design—with respect to their ability to produce high information content. As we have seen, neither chance- nor necessity-based scenarios (nor those that combine the two) possess the ability to produce biological information in a prebiotic context. This result comports with our ordinary, uniform human experience. Brute matter—whether acting randomly or by necessity—does not have the capability to produce information-intensive systems or sequencing.

Yet it is not correct to say that we do not know how information arises. We know from experience that intelligent agents create information all the time. Indeed, experience teaches that whenever high information content is present in an artifact or entity whose causal story is known, invariably creative intelligence—design—has played a causal role in the origin of that entity. Moreover, citing the activity of an intelligent agent really does explain the origin of certain features such as, for example, the faces on Mount Rushmore or the inscriptions on the Rosetta Stone. (Imagine the absurdity of an archeologist who refused to infer an intelligent cause for the incriptions on the Rosetta Stone because such an inference would constitute a scribe-of-the gaps fallacy.) Inferences to design need not depend upon our ignorance, but instead are often justified by our knowledge of the demonstrated causal powers of nature and agency, respectively. Recent developments in the information sciences formalize this knowledge, helping us to make inferences about the causal histories of various artifacts, entities or events based upon the information-theoretic signatures they exhibit (Dembski 1998, 62-66). Thus knowledge (albeit provisional) of established cause-effect relationships, not ignorance, justifies the design inference as the best explanation for the origin of biological information in a prebiotic context.

**Conclusion**

During the last forty years, molecular biology has revealed a complexity and intricacy of design that exceeds anything that was imaginable during the late nineteenth century. We now know that organisms display any number of distinctive features of intelligently engineered "high-tech" systems: information storage and transfer capability; functioning codes (Wolfe 1993,

671-79); sorting and delivery systems (Wolfe 1993, 835-44); regulatory and feedback loops; signal transduction circuitry (Wolfe 1993, 237-53); and everywhere complex, mutually interdependent networks of parts (Behe 1996). Indeed, the complexity of the biomacromolecules discussed in this essay does not begin to exhaust the full complexity of living systems.

Norbert Wiener once said, "Information is information, neither energy nor matter. No materialism that fails to take account of this can survive the present day" (quoted in Gitt 1989, 5). The informational properties of living systems suggest that "no materialism" can suffice to explain the origin of life. Indeed, as molecular biology and the information sciences have revolutionized our understanding of the complexity of life, they have also made it progressively more difficult to conceive how life might have arisen naturalistically. The complexity and specificity of DNA, RNA and proteins simply exceed the creative capacities of the explanatory entities that scientific materialists employ. The origin-of-life research community has generated a multiplicity of explanations involving either random and/or deterministic interactions of matter and energy. It has refused on principle to consider explanations that involve intelligent design.

Yet this methodological commitment to naturalistic explanation at all costs has created an unnecessary impasse. Experience teaches that information-rich systems (or to use Dembski's terminology, "small probability specifications") invariably result from intelligent causes, not naturalistic ones. Yet origin-of-life biology has artificially limited its explanatory search to the naturalistic nodes of causation on Dembski's explanatory filter: chance and necessity. Finding the *best* explanation, however, requires invoking causes that have the power to produce the effect in question. When it comes to information, we know of only one such cause. For this reason, the biology of the information age now requires a new science of design.

## Notes

[1] See Darwin 1871.

[2] As the result of geological and geochemical studies of the earliest Precambrian rocks scientists now question whether an oceanic medium full of biological precursors (i.e., the so-called prebiotic soup required by Oparin's scenario) ever existed. In 1973 Brooks and Shaw argued that if an amino and nucleic acid-rich ocean had existed, it would have left large deposits of nitrogen-rich minerals (nitrogenous cokes) in metamorphosed Precambrian sedimentary rocks. No evidence of such deposits exists, however. In the words of Brooks, "the nitrogen content of early PreCambrian organic matter is relatively low (less than .015%). From this we can be reasonably certain that: there never was any substantial amount of 'primitive soup' on Earth when PreCambrian sediments were formed; if such a soup ever existed it was only for a brief period of time" (Brooks 1985, 118).

[3]Though in 1936 Oparin did not specify when he believed life first emerged, the gradual process of evolutionary development he described clearly implied that the earth had long existed in a lifeless state (perhaps several hundreds or even thousands of million years) in order to allow for the gradual development of molecular and metabolic complexity via natural selection. After the 1960s, however, a series of new fossil finds forced scientists to revise progressively downward their estimates of the time available for chemical evolution on earth (Schopf and Barghoorn 1967, 508-11; Brooks and Shaw 1973, 267-305, 361; Dickerson 1978, 70; Knoll and Barghoorn 1977, 396-98; Lowe 1980, 441-43; Walter, Buick, and Dunlop 1980, 443-45; Brooks 1985, 104-16). Fossilized mats of stromatolites and the remains of various one-celled microorganisms were found in some of the world's oldest Precambrian rocks in Australia, South Africa and Greenland. These finds suggested that one-celled life first existed at least as early as 3.5 billion and perhaps as early as 3.85 billion years ago (Pflug and Jaeschke-Boyer 1979, 483-86; Bridgewater et al. 1981, 51-53) or within as few as 150 million years of the earth's cooling according to geological and astronomical estimates (Maher and Stevenson 1988, 612-14; Brooks and Shaw 1973, 73; Thaxton, Bradley, and Olsen 1984, 69-72). This drastic diminution of the time considered available for the occurrence of chemical evolution challenged the plausibility of Oparin's assumption of a long-lifeless terrestrial environment. It also calls into question all chemical evolutionary theories that rely heavily on time and chance to explain the origin of biological complexity.

[4]Thaxton and Bradley have shown that polymerizing amino acids under reducing conditions releases 200 kcal of energy per mole, whereas polymerizing amino acids in neutral conditions requires an input of 50 kcal of energy per mole (Thaxton and Bradley 1994, 184).

[5]Prigogine's full statement is, "The probability that at ordinary temperatures a macroscopic number of molecules is assembled to give rise to the highly ordered structures and to the coordinated functions characterizing living organisms is vanishingly small. The idea of spontaneous genesis of life in its present form is therefore highly improbable, even on the scale of the billions of years during which prebiotic evolution occurred."

[6]Sauer counted sequences that folded into stable three-dimensional configurations as functional, though many sequences that fold are not functional. Thus his results underestimate the probabilistic difficulty.

[7]A recent article heralding a breakthrough for RNA-world scenarios makes this clear. After telling how RNA researcher Jack Szostak had succeeded in engineering RNA molecules with a broader range of catalytic properties than previously known, science writer John Horgan makes a candid admission: "Szostak's work leaves a major question unanswered: How did RNA, self-catalyzing or not, arise in the first place?" (Horgan 1996, 27; see also Shapiro 1988, 71-95; Zaug and Cech 1986, 470-75; Cech 1989, 507-8).

[8]This in fact happens where adenine and thymine do interact chemically in the complementary base pairing across the message-bearing axis of the DNA molecule.

[9]The information-carrying capacity of any symbol in a sequence is inversely proportional to the probability of its occurrence. The informational capacity of a sequence as a whole is inversely proportional to the product of the individual probabilities for each member in the sequence. Since chemical affinities between constituents (symbols) increase the probability of the occurrence of one given another (i.e.,

necessity increases probability), such affinities decrease the information-carrying capacity of a system in proportion to the strength and relative frequency of such affinities within the system.

[10]Orgel has drawn a similar distinction between order and/or the randomness that characterizes inanimate chemistry and what he calls the "specified complexity" of informational biomolecules (Orgel 1973, 189-90; see also Thaxton, Bradley, and Olsen 1984, 130-40).

[11]This qualification means to acknowledge that chance can produce low levels of information.

[12]Defining information as the number of instructions required to specify a structure allows scientists to distinguish sequences that are merely mathematically improbable from functional sequences or meaningful text. Classical information theory as developed in the 1940s by Claude Shannon could not distinguish merely improbable sequences from those that conveyed a message (e.g., we hold these truths to be self-evident versus ntnyhiznlhteqkhgdsjh). Shannon's theory could measure the information-carrying capacity of a given sequence of symbols but not the information content. This is significant because random (natural) processes might produce an improbable but unspecified system. Nevertheless recent reformulations of the design argument based on the presence of information in DNA have been based upon evaluations of information content, not carrying capacity. As such they do not commit the fallacy of equivocation (see Thaxton and Bradley 1994, 200-210; Thaxton, Bradley, and Olsen 1984, 127-66).

[13]For good summary and critique of different approaches see especially Dose 1988, 348-56; Yockey 1992, 259-93; Thaxton, Bradley, and Olsen 1984; Shapiro 1986. For a contradictory hypothesis see Kauffman 1993, 287-341.

[14]Less exotic and more successful design detection occurs routinely in both science and industry. Fraud detection, forensic science and cryptography all depend upon the application of probabilistic or information-theoretic criteria of intelligent design (see Wilford 1994, A10; Edwards 1986, 295-312; Hilts 1992, C9; Patterson 1987).

**Bibliography**

Alberts, B., D. Bray, J. Lewis, M. Ralf, K. Roberts, and J.D. Watson. 1983. *Molecular biology of the cell.* New York: Garland.

Ambrose, E. J. 1982. *The nature and origin of the biological world.* New York: Halstead Press.

Araujo, L. 1981. Interview with A. I. Oparin in *Uno Mas Uno* [Mexico City newspaper], May 7.

Augros, R., and G. Stanciu. 1987. *The new biology.* Boston: Shambala.

Ayala, F. 1994. *Creative evolution,* ed. John H. Campbell and J. W. Schoff. New York: Jones and Bartlett.

Ayuob, G. 1996. On the design of the vertebrate retina. *Origins & Design* 17 (1):19-22.

Behe, M. 1993. Molecular machines: Experimental support for the design inference. Unpublished paper presented to ASA Intelligent Design Symposium, August 9.

———. 1994. Experimental support for regarding functional classes of proteins to be highly isolated from each other. In *Darwinism: Science or philosophy,* ed. J. Buell and G. Hearn, 60-71. Dallas: Foundation for Thought and Ethics.

———. 1996. *Darwin's black box: The biochemical challenge to evolution.* New York: Free Press.

Berkner, L. C., and L. L. Marshall. 1965. On the origin and rise of oxygen concentration in the earth's atmosphere. *Journal of Atmospheric Science* 22:225-61.

Bertalanffy, L. V. 1967. *Robots, men and minds.* New York: George Braziller.

Borek, E. 1969. *The code of life.* New York: Columbia University Press.

Borel, E. 1962. *Probabilities and life.* Translated by M. Bandin. New York: Dover.

Bowie, J., and R. Sauer. 1989. Identifying determinants of folding and activity for a protein of unknown structure. *Proceedings of the National Academy of Sciences USA* 86:2152-56.

Bowie, J., J. Reidhaar-Olson, W. Lim, and R. Sauer. 1990. Deciphering the message in protein sequences: Tolerance to amino acid substitution. *Science* 247:1306-10.

Bradley, W. L. 1988. Thermodynamics and the origin of life. *Perspectives on Science and Christian Faith* 40 (2):72-83.

Bridgewater, D., J. H. Allaart, J. W. Schopf, C. Klein, M. R. Walter, E. S. Barghoorn, P. Strother, A. H. Knoll, and B. E. Gorman. 1981. *Nature* 289:51-53.

Brinkman, R. T. 1969. Dissociation of water vapor and evolution of oxygen in the terrestrial atmosphere. *Journal of Geophysical Research* 74:5354-68.

Brooks, J. 1985. *Origins of life.* Sydney: Lion.

Brooks, J., and G. Shaw. 1973. *Origin and development of living systems.* New York: Academic Press.

Cairns-Smith, A. G. 1971. *The life puzzle.* Edinburgh: Oliver and Boyd.

Carver, J. H. 1981. Prebiotic atmospheric oxygen levels. *Nature* 292:136-38.

Cech, T. R. 1989. Ribozyme self-replication? *Nature* 339:507-8.

Conant, J. B. 1953. *Modern science and modern man.* Garden City, N.Y.: Doubleday, Anchor Books.

Crick, F. 1968. The origin of the genetic code. *Journal of Molecular Biology* 38:367-79.

———. 1981. *Life itself.* New York: Simon and Schuster.

Darwin, C. 1871. Letter to Hooker. Courtesy of Mr. Peter Gautrey. Cambridge University Library, Darwin Archives, Manuscripts Room.

———. 1984. *The origin of species by means of natural selection.* 1859. Reprint, Harmondsworth, England: Penguin.

Dawkins, R. 1986. *The blind watchmaker.* London: Longman.

Day, W. 1984. *Genesis on planet earth.* New Haven, Conn.: Yale University Press.

de Duve, C. 1995. *Vital dust: Life as a cosmic imperative.* New York: Basic Books.

———. 1996. The constraints of chance. *Scientific American* 274 (January):112.

Dembski, W. A. 1998. *The design inference: Eliminating chance through small probabilities.* Cambridge: Cambridge University Press.

Denton, M. 1986. *Evolution: A theory in crisis.* London: Adler and Adler.

Dickerson, R. E. 1978. Chemical evolution and the origin of life. *Scientific American* 239 (September): 70-85.

Dimroth, E., and M. M. Kimberly. 1976. Pre-Cambrian atmospheric oxygen: Evidence in sedimentary distribution of carbon, sulfur, uranium and iron. *Canadian Journal of Earth Sciences* 13:1161-85.

Dobzhansky, T. 1965. Discussion of G. Schramm's Paper. In *The origins of prebiological systems and of their molecular matrices,* ed. S. W. Fox, 309-15. New York: Academic Press.

Dose, K. 1988. The origin of life: More questions than answers. *Interdisciplinary Science Review* 13:348-56.

Dretske, F. 1981. *Knowledge and the flow of information.* Cambridge, Mass.: MIT Press.

Dyson, F. 1985. *Origins of life.* Cambridge: Cambridge University Press.

Edwards, A. W. F. 1986. Are Mendel's results really too close? *Biological Reviews* 61:295-312.

Eigen, M., W. Gardner, P. Schuster, and R. Winkler-Oswaititich. 1981. The origin of genetic information. *Scientific American* 244 (April): 88-118.

Eigen, M., and P. Schuster. 1977. The hypercycle; A principle of natural self-organization. Part A: Emergence of the hypercycle. *Naturwissenschaften* 64:541-65.

———. 1978a. The hypercycle: A principle of natural self-organization. Part B: The abstract hypercycle. *Naturwissenschaften* 65:7-41.

———. 1978b. The hypercycle: A principle of natural self-organization. Part C: The realistic hypercycle. *Naturwissenschaften* 65:341-69.

Ferris, J. P. 1987. Prebiotic synthesis: Problems and Challenges. *Cold Spring Harbor Symposia on Quantitative Biology* 52:30-32.

Gillespie, N. C. 1979. *Charles Darwin and the problem with creation.* Chicago: University of Chicago Press.

Gitt, W. 1989. Information: The third fundamental quantity. *Siemens Review* 56 (6):2-7.

Graham, L. 1973. *Science and philosophy in the Soviet Union.* London: Alfred A. Knopf.

Haeckel, E. 1866. *Generelle morphologie der organismen.* Vol. 1. Berlin: G. Reimer.

———. 1892. *The history of creation.* Translated by E. R. Lankester. London: Truber & Co.

———. 1905. *The wonders of life.* Translated by J. McCabe. London: Watts.

Harada, K., and S. Fox. 1964. Thermal synthesis of amino acids from a postulated primitive terrestrial atmosphere. *Nature* 201:335-37.

Hilts, P. J. 1992. Plagiarists take note: Machine is on guard. *New York Times,* January 7, C9 [Science Times].

Holland, H. D., B. Lazar, and M. McCaffrey. 1986. Evolution of the atmosphere and oceans. *Nature* 320:27-33.

Horgan, J. 1996. The world according to RNA. *Scientific American* (January):27.

Hoyle, F., and S. Wickramasinghe. 1981. *Evolution from space.* London: J. M. Dent.

Huxley, T. H. 1869. On the physical basis of life. *The Fortnightly Review* 5:129-45.

Johnson, P. 1991. *Darwin on trial.* Washington, D.C: Regnery Gateway.

Judson, H. 1979. *The eighth day of creation.* New York: Simon and Schuster.

Kamminga, H. 1980. *Studies in the history of ideas on the origin of life.* Ph.D. thesis, University of London.

Kasting, J. F., S. C. Liu, and T. M. Donahue. 1979. Oxygen levels in the prebiological atmosphere. *Journal of Geophysical Research* 84:3097-3102.

Kauffman, S. 1993. *The origins of order.* Oxford: Oxford University Press.

Kenyon, D. 1985. Going beyond the naturalistic mindset in origin-of-life research. Paper presented to Christianity Challenges the University Conference. Dallas: February 9-10.

Kenyon, D., and G. Steinman. 1969. *Biochemical predestination.* New York: McGraw-Hill.

Kenyon, D., and P. W. Davis. 1993. *Of pandas and people: The central question of biological origins.* Dallas: Haughton.

Kenyon, D., and G. Mills. 1996. The RNA world: A critique. *Origins & Design* 17 (1):9-16.

Kerr, R. 1980. Origin of life: New ingredients suggested. *Science* 210:42-43.

Kitcher, P. 1982. *Abusing science.* Cambridge, Mass.: MIT Press.

Knoll, A. H., and E. S. Barghoorn. 1977. Archean microfossils showing cell division from the swaziland system of South Africa. *Science* 198:396-98.

Kok, R. A., J. A. Taylor, and W. L. Bradley. 1988. A statistical examination of self-ordering of amino acids in proteins. *Origins of Life and Evolution of the Biosphere* 18:135-42.

Küppers, B. 1987. On the prior probability of the existence of life. In *The probabilistic revolution*, ed. Kruger et. al., 355-69. Cambridge, Mass.: MIT Press.

———. 1990. *Information and the origin of life*. Cambridge, Mass.: MIT Press.

Landsberg, P. T. 1964. Does quantum mechanics exclude life? *Nature* 203:928-30.

Lehninger, A. L. 1975. *Biochemistry*. New York: Worth.

Lemmon, R. 1970. Chemical evolution. *Chemical Review* 70:95-96.

Lipton, P. 1991. *Inference to the best explanation*. New York: Routledge.

Lodish, H., D. Baltimore, A. Berk, S. L. Zipursky, P. Matsudaira, and J. Darnell. 1995. *Molecular cell biology*, 347-49. New York: Freeman.

Lowe, D. R. 1980. Stromatolites 3,400-myr old from the archean of Western Australia. *Nature* 284:441-43.

McDonough, T. R. 1987. *The search for extraterrestrial intelligence: Listening for life in the cosmos*. New York: Wiley.

Macnab, R. 1978. Bacterial mobility and chemotaxis: The molecular biology of a behavioral system. *CRC Critical Reviews in Biochemistry* 5:291-341.

Maher, K., and D. Stevenson. 1988. Impact frustration of the origin of life. *Nature* 331:612-14.

Maynard-Smith, J. 1979. Hypercycles and the origin of life. *Nature* 280:445-46.

Meyer, S. C. 1990. *Of clues and causes: A methodological interpretation of origin of life studies*. Ph.D. thesis, Cambridge University.

———. 1993. A Scopes trial for the '90s. *Wall Street Journal*, December 6, A14. See also The harmony of natural law, January 17, Letters to the editor, A9.

———. 1994a. Laws, causes and facts: A response to Professor Ruse. In *Darwinism: Science or philosophy*, ed. J. Buell and G. Hearn, 29-40. Foundation for Thought and Ethics: Dallas.

———. 1994b. The methodological equivalence of design and descent: Can there be a scientific theory of creation? In *The creation hypothesis*, ed. J. P. Moreland, 67-112, 300-312. Downers Grove, Ill.: InterVarsity Press.

———. 1996. Demarcation and design: The nature of historical reasoning. In *Facets of faith and science*, 4, *Interpreting God's action in the world*, ed. J. van der Meer, 91-130. Lanham, Md.: University Press of America.

Miller, S. L. 1953. A production of amino acids under possible primitive earth conditions. *Science* 117:528-29.

Mora, P. T. 1963. Urge and molecular biology. *Nature* 199:212-19.

———. 1965. The folly of probability. In *The origins of prebiological systems and of their molecular matrices*, ed. S. W. Fox, 39-64, 310-15. New York: Academic Press.

Moreland, J. P., ed. 1994. *The creation hypothesis*. Downers Grove, Ill.: InterVarsity Press.

Morowitz, H. J. 1966. The minimum size of the cell. In *Principles of biomolecular organization*, ed. G. E. W. Wolstenhome and M. O'Connor, 446-59. London: Churchill.

Nelson, P. 1968. *Energy flow in biology*. New York: Academic Press.

———. 1996. Anatomy of a still-born analogy. *Origins and Design* 17 (3):12.

Oparin, A. I. 1938. *The origin of life*. Translated by S. Morgulis. New York: Macmillan.

———. 1968. *Genesis and evolutionary development of life*. Translated by E. Maass. New York:

Academic Press.

Orgel, L. E. 1973. *The origins of life on earth.* New York: Wiley.

Pattee, H. H. 1970. The problem of biological hierarchy. In *Towards a theoretical biology,* ed. C. H. Waddington, 3:117-36. Edinburgh: Edinburgh University Press.

Patterson, W. 1987. *Mathematical cryptology for computer scientists and mathematicians.* Totowa, N.J.: Rowman and Littlefield.

Pflug, H. D., and H. Jaeschke-Boyer. 1979. Combined structural and chemical analysis of 3,800-myr-old microfossils. *Nature* 280:483-85.

Prigogine, I., and G. Nicolis. 1977. *Self organization in nonequilibrium systems.* New York: Wiley.

Prigogine, I., G. Nicolis, and A. Babloyantz. 1972. Thermodynamics of evolution. *Physics Today* 25 (November):23-31.

Polanyi, M. 1967. Life transcending physics and chemistry. *Chemical Engineering News,* August 21, 54-66.

————. 1968. Life's irreducible structure. *Science* 160:1308-12.

Reidhaar-Olson, J., and R. Sauer. 1990. Functionally acceptable substitutions in two alpha-helical regions of lambda repressor. *Proteins: Structure, Function and Genetics* 7:306-16.

Ruse, M. 1982. Creation science is not science. *Science, Technology and Human Values* 7 (40):72-78.

Schopf, J. W., and E. S. Barghoorn. 1967. Alga-like fossils from the early precambrian of South Africa. *Science* 156:508-11.

Scott, A. 1986. *The creation of life.* Oxford: Oxford University Press.

Scriven, M. 1959. Explanation and prediction in evolutionary theory. *Science* 130:477-82.

————. 1966. Causes, connections and conditions in history. In *Philosophical analysis and history,* ed. W. Dray, 238-64. New York: Harper & Row.

Shapiro, R. 1986. *Origins.* London: Heinemann.

————. 1988. Prebiotic ribose synthesis: A critical analysis. *Origins of Life and Evolution of the Biosphere* 18:71-85.

Sober, E. 1988. *Reconstructing the past.* Cambridge, Mass.: MIT Press.

Steinman, G. 1967. Sequence generation in prebiological peptide synthesis. *Arch. Biochem. Biophys.* 121:533-39.

Steinman, G., and M. N. Cole. 1967. *Proceedings of the National Academy of Sciences USA* 58:735-41.

Thaxton, C. B., and W. L. Bradley. 1994. Information and the origin of life. In *The creation hypothesis,* ed. J. P. Moreland, 173-210. Downers Grove, Ill.: InterVarsity Press.

Thaxton, C. B., W. L. Bradley, and R. L. Olsen. 1984. *The mystery of life's origin: Reassessing current theories.* Dallas: Lewis and Stanley.

von Neumann, J. 1966. Theory of self-reproducing automata. Edited and completed by A. Berks. Urbana, Ill.: University of Illinois Press.

Walker, J. C. G. 1977. *Evolution of the atmosphere.* New York: Macmillan.

Walter, M. R., R. Buick, and J. S. R. Dunlop. 1980. Stromatolites 3,400-3,500 myr old from the North Pole area, Western Australia. *Nature* 284:443-45.

Walton, J. C. 1977. Organization and the origin of life. *Origins* 4:16-35.

Watson, J., and F. Crick. 1953. A structure for deoxyribose nucleic acid. *Nature* 171:737-38.

Whitehead, A. N. 1926. *Science and the modern world.* New York: Macmillan.

Wieland, C. 1995. The marvelous "message molecule." *Creation* 17 (4):11-13.

Wigner, E. 1961. The probability of the existence of a self-reproducing unit. In *The logic of personal knowledge: Essays presented to Michael Polanyi,* 231-35. London: Kegan and Paul.

Wilford, J. N. 1994. An ancient "lost city" is uncovered in Mexico. *New York Times,* February 4, A10.

Wolfe, S. L. 1993. *Molecular and cellular biology.* Belmont, Calif.: Wadsworth.

Yockey, H. P. 1977. A calculation of the probability of spontaneous biogenesis by information theory. *Journal of Theoretical Biology* 67:377-98.

———. 1981. Self organization origin of life scenarios and information theory. *Journal of Theoretical Biology* 91:13-31.

———. 1992. *Information theory and molecular biology.* Cambridge: Cambridge University Press.

Zaug, A. J., and T. R. Cech. 1986. The intervening sequence RNA of *tetrahymena* is an enzyme. *Science* 231:470-75.

# 6

# Applying Design
# Within Biology

## PAUL A. NELSON

**N**O ONE, NOT EVEN DAVID HUME, IS GOING TO WONDER HOW WE should explain that famous pocket watch lying on the heath. Watches are intelligently caused, by design, and this inference is robust, to the degree that "no man can be so hardened in absurd systems as at all times to reject it" (Hume 1980, 77). No one, for that matter, is going to wonder about the cause of largely identical essays turned in for credit by two students as their supposedly independent work, nor about fruit trees growing in long parallel rows, nor even, perhaps, about one hundred or so model airplanes crashing in Marseilles for no apparent reason, just near the house of an avowed model airplane hater.[1]

But when we come to organisms and to the hypothesis of intelligent design, then we must, received opinion holds, be "apprehensive that we have here got quite beyond the reach of our faculties" (Hume 1980, 7). To infer design in biology, this apprehension worries, we must know that we have exhausted all possible natural causes at the first and second nodes of what William Dembski (1998) calls the explanatory filter. Yet we can never be certain that all possibilities have been tried. Thus design must ever be an explanation from ignorance, attempting to prove a negative and vulnerable at every instant to being overturned by fresh knowledge in science. This worry, I think, probably more than any other objection, keeps otherwise interested scientists and philosophers from embracing design as an explanation.

What is not often grasped is the logical identity of these two situations. That is, no one should wonder about the unknown natural cause of pocket watches, we say—but why not? After all, the space of yet-to-be-discovered natural causes that generate pocket watches remains unexplored by scientists. It remains unexplored by generally everyone.

But that is absurd, comes the rejoinder. We *know* that pocket watches are intelligently caused, as certainly as we know anything. We have no reason to look for another explanation.

Indeed. We discharge our responsibility to discover the natural cause of pocket watches, if we think about it at all (and who does?), not because we have exhausted the space of all natural possibilities. That would be impossible in any case. Rather we do not look for the natural cause of watches, or computer programs, or tennis shoes, because no one has given us any reason to look for such a cause. And no one has given us any reason, because, of course, there is none.

In this chapter I shall argue that received opinion about the special epistemological handicaps attached to design as a scientific explanation is desperately confused. I shall do so by considering some examples from biology. When skeptics of design worry that the hypothesis shuts off scientific inquiry about the origin of an object or pattern prematurely, they do not have any good or even fair-to-middling natural cause explanation waiting in the wings. If an adequate natural cause were available, design could not have been postulated. Rather skeptics of design adopt standards of apodictic certainty that they themselves would reject as wholly unreasonable if the same yoke were laid on their shoulders, and they ask design theorists to solve problems or explain phenomena that have already resisted the available natural cause explanations but moreover for which good reasons can be given not to expect a natural cause explanation. Skeptics of design ask design theorists to go fishing for causes where there is no reason to think the fish will be caught: certainly the skeptics have caught none. The skeptic of design, a philosophical or methodological naturalist, typically, asks us to pursue the naturalistic program of explanation without reason.[2]

In urging this approach to the design hypothesis, I want to encourage the reader to think about design as a positive explanation, robust and tractable, reached by ordinary methods of inference and facing no special difficulties beyond the problem of induction—a problem that obtains for all rational inquiry and thus counts against everyone in general and no one in particular.[3]

Design is ordinary science. The philosophical myth that design is negative knowledge was foisted on us by the massive failure of nerve about this mode of reasoning in the nineteenth century, from which we are only now slowly recovering, but above all by the presumption of naturalism (Gillespie 1979; Hull 1983), which caused that historical failure of nerve. Design theorists do have a genuine responsibility, set by their own method, to consider natural causes. They discharge that responsibility, however, when they survey thoroughly what is known about natural causes: that is, when they consider what is empirically the case, as ordinary reasoners must.

The design theorist has no responsibility to naturalism. That is the business—the special difficulty, if you will—of the philosophical and methodological naturalist.

## The Explanatory Filter and Biological Explanation

Near the end of the *Origin of Species,* Charles Darwin chides his creationist opponents in the following terms:

> Several eminent naturalists have of late published their belief that a multitude of reputed species in each genus are not real species; but that other species are real, that is, have been independently created. This seems to me a strange conclusion to arrive at. They admit that a multitude of forms, which till lately they themselves thought were special creations . . . have been produced by variation, but they refuse to extend the same view to other and very slightly different forms. Nevertheless, they do not pretend that they can define, or even conjecture, which are the created forms of life, and which are those produced by secondary causes. They admit variation as a *vera causa* in one case, they arbitrarily reject it in another, without assigning any distinction in the two cases. (Darwin 1964, 482)

If we may generalize "creation" to "design," this view asserts that the design hypothesis is empirically empty. The hypothesis is powerless to discriminate between naturally and intelligently caused phenomena. This indictment differs from the worry outlined by Hume and is altogether more serious.

The explanatory filter (Dembski 1998), however, reliably discriminates between naturally and intelligently caused phenomena. It does so because naturally caused phenomena are trapped by their corresponding causes or mechanisms, necessarily, as a matter of method, at the first and second analytical nodes of the filter. Thus any object or pattern for which we have a sufficient natural cause cannot be assigned to design. I will not recapitulate the logical structure of the explanatory filter (see Dembski, chap. 4 in this volume) but want instead to explicate how it might function in biological explanation.

Consider, as the phenomenon or pattern to be explained, the genotype frequencies of the *esterase-6* locus in a population of the fruit fly *Drosophila melanogaster*.[4] The frequencies have the following proportions:

| | | |
|---|---|---|
| $E6^F/E6^F$ | (FF) | .1281 |
| $E6^F/E6^S$ | (FS) | .4596 |
| $E6^S/E6^S$ | (SS) | .4123 |

These proportions correspond to the pattern expected under the Hardy-Weinberg law (Hartl 1981), which, given certain conditions, holds that the distribution of alleles in any randomly mating, sexually reproducing population will be the expansion of the binomial $(p + q)^2$, or $p^2 + 2pq + q^2 = 1$, thus accounting for all frequencies at a genetic locus.

Is the immediate origin of the genotype frequency of the *esterase-6* locus best explained by design? No. It is best explained by the principle with which it collides as soon as we feed it into the filtering mesh of our biological knowledge: namely, given certain conditions, allelic frequencies will naturally, or as a matter of course, distribute themselves according to the expansion of the binomial $(p + q)^2$. The Hardy-Weinberg law is thus one strand in the great network of our biological knowledge, itself only one aspect of the much larger network of our causal knowledge, which constitutes the first node of the explanatory filter. Causal laws and regularities such as the Hardy-Weinberg law will trap certain events and patterns—those which happen deterministically or nearly deterministically as a matter of course—as they enter the filter to be explained.

Now consider another phenomenon to be explained: the omnipresence of the gene *bicoid* in populations of *Drosophila melanogaster*. First, some background. After a fly embryo (or oocyte) is fertilized, *bicoid* messenger RNA, located at the anterior or head pole of the embryo, is translated into protein, which then diffuses toward the posterior or rear pole of the embryo. This diffusion sets up a gradient about halfway down the body (see figure 6.1).

The gene *bicoid* encodes a homeodomain, a 60 amino-acid DNA binding protein motif. As this protein diffuses through the embryo, it acts as a body plan morphogen, meaning its presence is needed very near the top of the chain of developmental decisions establishing the head and thorax structures of the fly. This functional necessity has been well-established experimentally: when *bicoid* is deleted or otherwise missing, fly embryos develop with posterior (telson or tail) structures at both ends (Nusslein-Volhard and Wieschaus 1980).

Thus *bicoid* is a gene whose protein product *Drosophila* cannot do without. If it is missing, the resulting embryos die. In the real-time chronicle geneticists and developmental biologists have uncovered about how fruit flies come

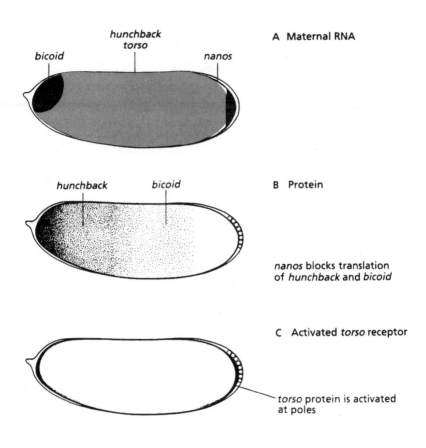

**Figure 6.1  Fruit Fly Embryo**

to be, "*bicoid* clearly sits at the top of the hierarchy, *as there seems to be no way to organize a coherent body plan without it*" (Lawrence and Struhl 1996, 957, emphasis added).

So how did *bicoid* itself come to be originally? Here the explanatory situation immediately becomes vastly and interestingly more complicated. As Jonathan Wells (1998) points out, neo-Darwinism explains the origin of novel gene sequences by the selective advantages those genes confer on their possessors. But *bicoid* displays its selective advantage, if you will, only when a *Drosophila* embryo successfully develops into an adult fly. That is, the normal or proper functional role of *bicoid* is entirely end-determined. Bicoid functions to enable *hunchback*, *giant* and additional pattern formation genes, lying causally downstream from *bicoid*, to function, which in turn enable other developmental events, and so on, right down to, if all goes well, a fruit fly.

What, on the neo-Darwinian picture of the history of life, was *bicoid*'s initial selective role when it first evolved? The gene has been cloned and sequenced; it contains a homeobox, which, as noted, encodes a DNA-binding protein. So we know that; we know that *bicoid* bears some homology to DNA-binding proteins in other, very different organisms (e.g., *goosecoid* in vertebrates; Manak and Scott 1994, 62); and of course we have a considerable body of experimental knowledge about the role of *bicoid* as a *Drosophila* morphogen. And that is about all we know.

### Diversity in Early Development, Functional Constraints and the Paradox of Conservation

Well, not exactly. According to neo-Darwinism, all metazoans (animals) share a common multicellular ancestor. That is, the first organism to evolve "an increase in geometrical complexity between egg and adult," to employ John Maynard Smith's (1983, 33) brief definition of development, gave rise to all other organisms having such an increase in complexity. It is also generally believed, from strong experimental and observational evidence, that the processes of development are inherently conservative. On this view disruptions of development are for the most part increasingly severe or deleterious the earlier they occur. The reason, as Leigh Van Valen argues, is that development "ramifies out; later developmental decisions depend on earlier ones which are much fewer and have consequences which interact" (Van Valen 1988, 173). Disrupt *bicoid* in flies, for instance, and lethality follows. Earlier developmental decisions or events are thus entrenched, relative to what lies causally downstream from them, and carry a heavier generative responsibility. As Leo Buss (1987, 33) puts it,

> It is axiomatic that a random alteration introduced early in ontogeny will likely be manifested in a cascade of subsequent morphogenetic events, whereas a modification introduced later in ontogeny can have relatively minor effects.

We may refer to the first theory, the common descent of the metazoans, by common descent (CD), and to the second, the functional conservation of development, by William Wimsatt's (1986) term "generative entrenchment" (GE).

On coupling common descent theoretically with generative entrenchment, we would expect to find that the earliest developmental events of different species, when sampled across the metazoan phyla, should be more alike than the later developmental events. As D. T. Anderson (1987, 149) frames this observational expectation,

> the highly integrated stepwise nature of animal development causes it to be in many respects an extremely conservative process. Basic developmen-

tal events established during the early evolution of a group are maintained repetitively over hundreds of millions of years, since any change in them would spell extinction. . . . For these basic developmental processes, once established, the rate of evolution has been minimal.

This may be represented schematically as

CD + GE → Conservation of early development

On turning to the observations, however, we find striking differences in early development (see figure 6.2 for some examples strictly within the

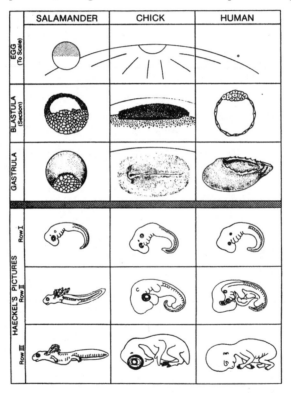

**Figure 6.2** In October 1994, during a conference at Indiana University, Jonathan Wells and I happened to sit at dinner with Richard Elinson, the author of this figure. Elinson, a developmental biologist at the University of Toronto, remarked that this (1987) diagram had been more widely reproduced and cited than anything else he had published. He feared he would go down in scientific history, he said, mainly as "the author of that amazing figure." It is not hard to see why. Since the late nineteenth century, biology textbooks, following the lead of Haeckel, have tended to feature only the lower half of this figure, showing apparent similarities in the development of vertebrates from what is known as the pharyngula stage (row I) onward. Yet the earlier stages (upper half of figure), which lay the groundwork for all that follows, differ markedly. Note, for example, the divergence in egg diameters and patterns of gastrulation.

vertebrates). Developmental biologist Eric Davidson (1990, 365) remarks on these differences, calling them "anything but trivial and superficial," and observes that

> those . . . who have attempted to deal with more than one embryonic form, have been struck by the amazing variety in the modes of embryonic development that exist in the various phylogenetic reaches of the Animal Kingdom.

In a later paper, describing the wide range of metazoan developmental architectures as "intellectually disturbing," Davidson notes that "there are several quite different processes by which gastrula-stage embryos are generated from eggs," some of which he indicates:

> *Caenorhabditis elegans* embryos have an invariant cell lineage while the cell lineage of a chicken or mouse or fish embryo is always different from that of another of the same species; portions of sea urchin or jellyfish embryos can regulate to generate whole new embryos, while equivalent portions of ascidian or annelid embryos cannot; *Drosophila* embryos specify elegant spatial patterns of gene expression before there are any cells to interact, while in *Xenopus* or sea urchin embryos the initial spatial diversification of gene expression depends causally and extensively on intercellular interactions. (Davidson 1991, 1)

And again (Davidson 1994, 604):

> The initial embryonic specification strategies employed by organisms of different phylogenetic groups actually differ from one another to a surprising extent, however. In some embryos, specification depends on intercellular interaction during cleavage, while in others this cannot be so since specification occurs while the nuclei are syncytial; some rely on invariant cell lineages, while others develop from populations of migratory cells of no fixed lineage; some generate autonomously specified founder cells, while others have none; and so forth.

Davidson's assessment of the empirical situation is shared by other observers. Arguing that early conservation is a "false view," Keith Thomson urges that "in fact, early stages in development in different lineages differ markedly, and that is where divergences in phenotype are set in place" (1992, 111). Developmental biologist Rudolf Raff and his colleagues note that "eggs, cleavage, gastrulation and germ layer formation are very different in amphibians, birds and mammals," adding that early development in these groups "actually appears to be less constrained" than later development (Raff, Wray, and Henry 1991, 189). Reviewing one evolutionary formulation of von Baer's theorem, which predicts early conservation—"during their ontogenies the members of twin taxa follow the same course up to the stage where they diverge into separate taxa"—embryologist Wolfgang Dohle (1988, 285) comments, somewhat acidly,

Everybody who is even slightly acquainted with ontogenetic facts know that there are hundreds of examples to which this theorem does not apply. In many polychaete and prosobranch genera one species develops through a planktonic larva, whereas another species has direct development. The telolecithal cephalopod eggs cleave in a bilateral manner without any similarity to the spiral cleavage of other related Mollusca. Triclad eggs have a blastomeric anarchy, whereas the adults very closely resemble the polyclads which show spiral cleavage. This list could easily be elongated.

Thus for many theorists the prediction of early developmental conservation among the metazoans, entailed by the conjunction of common descent and generative entrenchment, is false. This may be represented schematically as

CD + GE → ? ← Divergence of early development

Let us pause for a moment. Recall that we have good reason to think the processes of development in animals are functionally constrained. In any hierarchy of decisions, those decisions or events lying at the root of the causal tree will be functionally entrenched relative to those further out on the branches—and animals are built, generation by generation, in exactly this stepwise fashion. Recall also, as we have just noted, that early development is strikingly diverse in the animals. How then did these remarkable differences evolve from a common ancestor? This question is the daily bread of evolutionary developmental biologists. Richard Elinson (1987, 3), for instance, notes that early development "presents us with a conundrum: If early embryogenesis is conservative, how did such major changes in the earliest events of embryogenesis occur?"

Elinson's question is given a really wicked twist by the apparent nucleotide sequence conservation of key embryonic regulators. As Wells (1998) notes, the remarkable conservation of the HOM/hox complex between such disparate forms as *Drosophila* (flies) and *Mus* (mouse) (Manak and Scott 1994), and indeed the presence of homeobox genes in all the metazoan phyla (Ruddle et al. 1994) have been taken by neo-Darwinians as powerful evidence that all animals stemmed from a common multicellular ancestor that itself possessed the genes in question (Scott 1994).

Yet on nearly any construal of common descent these data should be deeply puzzling. We might describe the puzzle under heading of "the paradox of conservation," a puzzle perhaps first noticed by Miklos and John (1987, 273) as they commented on the homeodomain itself, the DNA-binding protein domain:

Since the homeobox domain has been so well conserved between organisms such as yeast (which is not segmented) and man, and indeed has good homology to DNA binding proteins in prokaryotes, its evolutionary significance in morphogenetic terms is difficult to evaluate. Since these organisms differ considerably in phenotype, there must be modes of escaping from this strict conservatism, if indeed it is the homeo-box domain which is so important.

Several years later, surveying a much greater range of examples, Scott (1994, 1121) raised the same puzzle, albeit now referring to the conservation of the *Hox* gene clusters:

> Animal architecture is guided by many conserved regulators, among them homeobox genes that have related functions in mammals, insects, and worms. The surprising conservation of the regulators stands in stark contrast to the diversity of animal form. . . . However, if *Hox* genes are conserved, what is not conserved? What makes animals different, the regulation of *Hox* genes or their effects on the genes they control?

Davidson lays his finger precisely on the problem:

> An extreme interpretation is that the common recurrence in diverse animals of particular elements of developmental circuitry signify that these are actually the only really important aspects of development, just because they *are* so general. Thus the basic nature of all forms of development is the same; know one, know them all; the rest is just details. Developmental biologists of the future might well invert this argument, however. *Obviously animals do develop differently.* They utilize differently assembled morphogenetic programs, and particular downstream batteries of structural genes, defined by natural selection. Sooner or later we need to understand the genetic mechanisms that program the development of phylogenetically distinct kinds of animal, and of their specific morphological structures. (Davidson 1994, 610, second emphasis added)

Met with this situation, many theorists have solved the puzzle by arguing that generative entrenchment is exception-ridden and should be held lightly. Taking common descent as given, this position places what is in effect a negation sign or at least a question mark in front of generative entrenchment. "So the dilemma is easily resolved," argues Thomson (1992, 112), favoring this solution. "Because early stages have changed, they must be capable of change." Van Valen, rephrasing the same point and remarking that it reminds him "a bit of Descartes," notes that "early development does often change; therefore it can" (1988, 329). As Thomson (1988, 121-22) argues,

> There is . . . a very widely held notion that evolutionary changes cannot be caused by changes in the deeper, more fundamental events of development. Such changes are often thought inevitably to be lethal. After all,

so the argument goes, very many variants that seem to be caused at relatively late stages are lethal; safely changing more fundamental stages must be even more risky. The whole notion of "macromutation" that would significantly alter the early course of development is, in this view, fanciful. . . . Despite these traditional skeptical views, it seems inescapable that changes in early development are possible and we have to find out how they occur, rather than attempt to dismiss them.

Note that this position rests entirely on the assumption of common descent. There is little if any experimental evidence that "changes in early development are possible." I know of only a single example of heritable changes in metazoan cleavage patterns;[5] and although early development in some organisms can often be mechanically perturbed, the system compensates, if it is capable of recovering from the insult, by returning to its preestablished trajectory toward the adult phenotype. Such perturbations, however, are not heritable.

Other authors favor another solution to the dilemma. Perhaps significant temporal asymmetries exist in evolutionary processes. Thus, although generative entrenchment generally does obtain now and is a reliable generalization about the functional constraints on development in extant organisms, it did not obtain at critical periods in the past. As Gregory Wray (1992, 131), an opponent of this view, glosses it,

> The Cambrian "explosion" of body plans is perhaps the single most striking feature of the metazoan fossil record. The rapidity with which phyla and classes appeared during the early Paleozoic, coupled with much lower rates of appearance for higher taxa since, poses an outstanding problem in macroevolution. One explanation for this pattern is that developmental programs have become too constrained by interaction since the early radiation of metazoans to allow the origin of new body plans.

During the Cambrian explosion, argue Foote and Gould (1992, 1816), "surviving designs stabilized through some form of genetic and developmental locking"—and thus the "unusual speed and flexibility in Cambrian evolution" was "followed by constraint upon fundamental anatomical change." This window of opportunity for profound evolutionary change, however, has long been closed. That the window has closed can be seen, Foote and Gould argue, from "the fact that morphological disparity has not increased dramatically since the Cambrian" (1992, 1816) but also (and more important for our analytical purposes) from the extreme difficulty of observing viable major developmental mutants today. The possibilities for fundamental evolutionary change appear to have narrowed considerably:

It seems very likely that the novelty producible from a chicken is considerably less "novel" than that producible from a poorly integrated, simple metazoan ontogeny of the later Precambrian. . . . The general result of the growth of developmental inertia has been to make the biosphere, as a whole, less amenable to change. . . . After the initial burst of body plan formation, successful profound ontogenetic changes soon became much less common as internal and external contingencies accumulated (i.e., as ontogenies "hardened" and ecosystems became more "niche-packed"). (McKinney and McNamara 1991, 339-40, 363)

While "significant changes in development are required by any model for the Cambrian radiation," Douglas Erwin (1994, 208) notes, "this [temporally asymmetric] model suggests that such changes were a primary forcing mechanism driving the extensive morphological innovation"—perhaps because the organization of the early metazoan genome was in some way distinctive:

> There seems to be no alternative but to seek some unusual feature of the primitive genome that would allow it to change in such a way that large coordinated viable morphological changes could take place over short periods of geological time. (Campbell and Marshall 1987, 97)[6]

## Biological Specification

We might now summarize the preceding section as follows. We began with the question, How did the gene *bicoid* originally come to be? No answer is forthcoming from neo-Darwinism or from the filtering mesh of our biological knowledge taken broadly. The object to be explained passes straight through the first node of the explanatory filter (and no contemporary biologist would seriously entertain a chance mechanism for its origin, so we pass straight through the second node as well). Rather we have stumbled into a landscape of paradoxes. Key embryonic regulators, apparently similar at the genetic level, are employed in building very different morphological endpoints throughout the Metazoa. Flies and mice are, well, flies and mice. As Manak and Scott (1994, 67) put it,

> The Hox clusters remain the most remarkable example of conservation of regulatory genes involved in development. . . . The major problem that we face is in trying to understand what it means for a gene to define a certain region of the body. What is in common between the thorax of a fly and a human?

Furthermore, all experimental evidence indicates that development, when perturbed, either shuts down, causing lethality, or returns via alternate and redundant pathways to its primary trajectory. Lastly, the overall developmental architectures of large groups of animals are remarkably divergent (see figure 6.3, comparing *C. elegans* and *Drosophila*).

This suggests three tentative conclusions:

1. The theory of the common descent of the animals is false.

2. The neo-Darwinian mechanism is causally insufficient for the phenomena it must explain.

3. The theory that genes provide the program of development is probably in need of some serious rethinking.

Now the second and third conclusions would raise few eyebrows in the biological community. Outside of textbooks and perhaps PBS television programs, the insufficiency of the mutation/selection mechanism is widely acknowledged, indeed by many neo-Darwinians themselves. Bruce Wallace (1984, 70), for instance, notes the functional problems entailed in modifying any body plan:

> The *Bauplan* [body plan] of an organism . . . can be thought of as the arrangement of genetic switches that control the course of the embryonic and subsequent development of the individual; such control must operate properly both in time generally and sequentially in the separately differentiated tissues. Selection, both natural and artificial, that leads to morphological change and other developmental modification does so by altering the settings and triggerings of these switches. . . . The extreme difficulty encountered when attempting to transform one organism into another but still functional one lies in the difficulty in resetting a number of the many controlling switches in a manner that still allows for the individual's orderly (somatic) development.[7]

And the third point, that DNA may not provide "the program of development," might surprise some biologists but does not shock (see, e.g., Goodwin 1994).

Nor is the first point, for that matter, entirely a forbidden inference. Perhaps the Metazoa are actually polyphyletic (meaning arising from multiple, independent lineages) and never shared a common multicellular ancestor. This view, as defended for instance by the English zoologist Pat Willmer, postulates that multicellularity may have evolved independently in separate lineages. Any phylogenetic diagram purporting to represent the origin of the animal phyla, Willmer (1990, 361) argues, "cannot be a vine, or a neatly dichotomous tree." Rather, properly interpreted, "the comparative evidence indicates that the history of the animals must branch like a field of grass low down. . . . The overall effect is therefore not that of a neat lawn of grass, but rather of an old-fashioned meadow, where a few hardy perennial designs flourish and branch amongst the grasses" (Willmer 1990, 361).

More prosaically:

> Many kinds of invertebrate do appear to have been "invented" several times over, with particular designs reappearing repeatedly. Given the lack

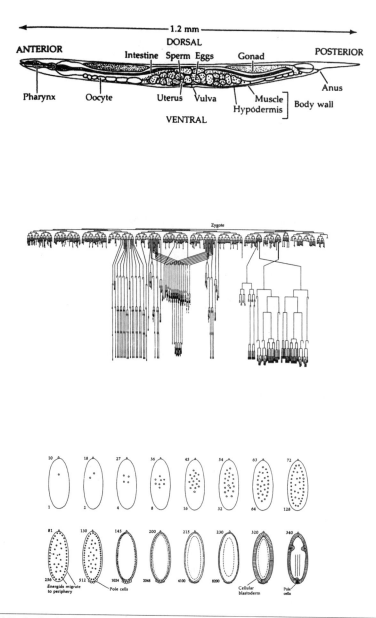

**Figure 6.3**  In the development of the nematode *C. elegans* (top diagram shows its adult phenotype), the zygote (middle diagram; zygote is the single-celled starting point) begins to divide immediately into daughter cells, which themselves divide further into a canonical and precise cell lineage. In *Drosophila* (bottom diagram), the nuclei in the egg first divide and then migrate to the periphery long before any cell division occurs. There are no cell membranes other than the egg membrane itself until about three hours into development. Figures from Gilbert 1991.

of any convincing homologies amongst lower groups, and the obvious advantages of a large size concomitant on multicellularity, one cannot avoid the inference that this also applies to the most fundamental design feature of all: metazoan status itself was achieved more than once, so that "animals" as a whole are polyphyletic. (Willmer 1990, 359)[8]

The forbidden inference is the one I find arising most naturally from the evidence, namely, design:

4. The gene (and protein) *bicoid* was intelligently designed and functions to enable orderly development in *Drosophila*.

In *bicoid*, we have found a biological specification. To put it simply, if you want *Drosophila melanogaster* at all, you had better have a functional copy of *bicoid* ready and waiting in the maternal genetic library. More formally, we might define biological specification as follows (I take this definition to be both necessary and sufficient for any specification):

Any element of an organism necessary for viability (meaning survival and reproduction) in any environment in which that organism may exist.

Biologists are, among their other explanatory tasks, already in the business of discovering these specifications. They do so typically by mapping the necessity relations that obtain among the elements of organisms, where viability exists as the analytical background which must be preserved. "The grave's a fine and private place," wrote Andrew Marvell (1620-1678), to his coy mistress, "but none, I think, do there embrace"—nor eat, mate, metabolize, and so on. Viability is thus a universal necessary condition, within biology, for functional analysis. It is also, for that matter, a necessary condition for any theory of origins. Evolutionary hypotheses that require inviable transitions can be disqualified as explanations on those grounds alone. Here we might call briefly on a recent paper by Arno Wouters (1995), on "viability explanation," to show how viability plays a role (analytically) essentially independent of other biological modes of explanation—in particular of neo-Darwinism.

Consider the human brain stem, specifically the medulla oblongata, which controls respiration and heart function. Viability explanation, as Wouters (1995, 441-42) construes it, is a "three step activity." One asks, for any trait *x*, such as the medulla oblongata,

1. Would a problem be created, for the survival and reproduction of this organism, if *x* were absent?

2. If so, what would that problem be?

3. How does the presence of trait *x* solve the problem?

Using such functional counterfactuals, one probes the causal relationships within an organism. In the case of the medulla oblongata, its absence would *[ceteris paribus[9]]* spell nonviability (death), as two essential functions, breathing and blood circulation, lie causally downstream from it. "Viability explanations, therefore," Wouters continues, "establish the necessity of the trait to be explained in the sense that if the organism *as it is* would lack that trait [it] would not be able to survive and reproduce" (1995, 444).[10]

This mode of analysis, widespread in the biological literature, has, Wouters notes (1995, 444), an explanatory force that is *sui generis:*

> Developmental, physiological and capacity explanations explain respectively how a certain trait came into being, how a certain type of event is brought about or how a task is performed in the individual. Adaptational explanations explain why a certain trait became prevalent in the lineage. All four are concerned with the mechanisms that bring about a certain state or capacity. Viability explanations, however, expose the way in which the traits of an organism and its environment depend on each other, but they do not show how the trait was brought about, neither in its ontogeny, nor in evolution. Although viability explanations do not explain how traits came into being, they are nevertheless genuinely explanatory, because they fit the trait to be explained into our picture of the organism's system of functional interdependencies.

The education of a medical student, for instance, will consist in large measure of learning which functional relations (molecular, cellular, physiological and anatomical) constitute necessary conditions for viability in humans. Those relations and the lower-level elements they presuppose will thereafter exist as deeply entrenched nodes, so to speak, in that physician's own conceptual universe. Viability is the *telos* from which the patient must not be allowed to slide.

More generally, consider the schema in figure 6.4, illustrative of Wouter's notion of viability explanation. The schema shows that the causal path from perturbation to lethality runs from the lower-level element—partly impaired or missing altogether—upwards through the functional hierarchy of the organism.

Consider, as another example, ß cell glucokinase in mice, as perturbed by Grupe et al.:

> The secretion of insulin is contributed by the rate of glucose metabolism in the pancreatic ß cells. As phosphorylation by glucokinase (GLK) appears to be the rate-limiting step for glucose catabolism in ß cells, this enzyme may be the glucose sensor. To test this possibility and to resolve the relative roles of liver and ß cell GLK in maintaining glucose levels, *we have generated mice completely deficient in GLK* and transgenic mice in which GLK is expressed only in ß cells. In mice with only one GLK allele, blood glucose levels are elevated and insulin secretion is reduced. *GLK-deficient mice die perinatally with severe hypergylcemia.* . . . These mice demonstrate *the critical need for β cell GLK* in maintaining normal glucose levels. (Grupe et al. 1995, 69, emphasis added)

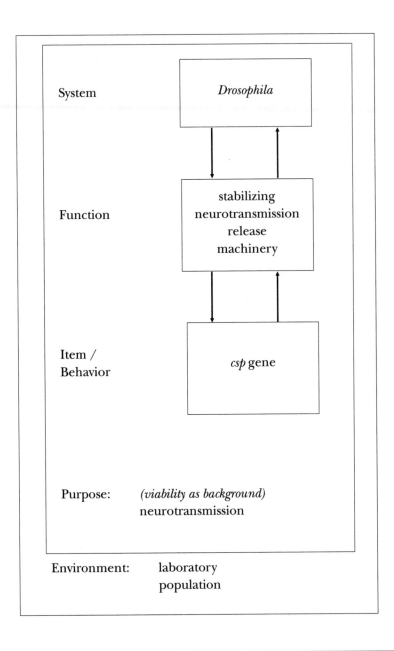

**Figure 6.4   Neurotransmitters in Flies**
"The *csp* gene of *Drosophila* encodes proteins homologous to the synaptic vesicle proteins in *Torpedo*. . . . Deletion of the *csp* gene in *Drosophila* causes a temperature-sensitive block of synaptic transmission, followed by paralysis and premature death" (Zinsmaier et al., 1994, 977).

In these cases and in a wide array of others in the biological literature, the primary mode of analysis takes the form *perturb this element, and then ask the organism about the consequences.* Where lethality occurs, one has uncovered (at least synchronically) an essentially entrenched, or fixed, functional element. One has uncovered, that is, a biological specification.

Conversely one may uncover a situation like the following:

The contribution of histone H1 to mitotic chromosome condensation was examined with the use of a cell-free extract from *Xenopus* eggs, which transforms condensed sperm nuclei into metaphase chromosomes. When H1 was removed from the extract, the resultant metaphase chromosomes were indistinguishable from those formed in complete extract. Nucleosomal spacing was the same for both. Thus, *H1 is not required for the structural reorganization that leads to condensed metaphase chromosomes* in this egg extract. (Ohsumi et al. 1993, 2033, emphasis added)

Here, for the purpose specified as chromosome formation, the element histone H1 is inessential.[11] (It may of course have other roles.) As noted, typically the perturbed elements in these experiments are lower-level entities—isolated genes and their protein products—functioning in higher-level systems (e.g., nerve signal transmission, cell growth, cell division). These higher-level systems are themselves constitutive of viability.

In summary, I think there can be little question that Wouters (1995, 453) is correct:

Viability explanations are really explanatory because they fit traits into individual level, [historically] non-causal, functional dependencies, but they do not explain how these traits came into being.[[12]] Viability explanation proceeds by means of calculation and experiment, the results of which are conveyed by means of a functional counterfactual. The truth of this counterfactual is independent of the history of the traits to which the counterfactual refers.

Two conclusions that Wouters does not draw but that follow directly from his analysis, concern development and evolution. First, the developing embryo is obviously alive, and it must continue to remain so to reach the adult phenotype. Thus development is fully assimilable to viability analysis, and in fact the experimental perturbation of development in systems such as *Drosophila* or the nematode *C. elegans* proceeds in great measure by searching for lethal mutations. Secondly, viability is both logically and empirically prior to any evolutionary considerations. No dead organism, or more precisely no population of dead organisms, ever evolved. Thus viability analysis provides an independent theoretical check on our speculations about the history of life—but only if we are willing to listen.

**Organisms Under Two Differing Modes of Analysis**

> The difficulty, as often happens, lies not with developing models of how evolution could operate, but with learning how evolution actually operates. (Erwin 1994, 290)

I claimed that received opinion about the shortcomings of design as a biological explanation was desperately confused, in the main because methodological naturalists encourage design theorists (indeed everyone) to search for natural mechanisms and causes of evolutionary change without providing any reason, in the face of disconfirming evidence, to believe that those causes or mechanisms exist. Our short odyssey with *bicoid* suggests, I think, that *bicoid* exists because it is a biological specification demonstrably necessary for fruit flies themselves to exist. The arrow of causality runs from element (gene) to system (fly) and back again. This is not woolly-minded vitalism. It is the plain testimony of the evidence. It was the system as a whole, that is, the fruit fly, that came to be originally. The only sufficient cause for such specified systems of small probability is design. If we want to tell another story about the origin of *bicoid*, we need to explain how a DNA-binding protein in an unknown organism came to be liberated from its original unknown function and began to act as a developmental regulator, somehow enlisting downstream elements—but how were they previously regulated? and what were they doing?—and sooner or later any pretense of explanation disappears under what Behe (1996, 177) calls "a choking complexity."

But I suspect many biologists will come away unsatisfied. Let me conclude then by suggesting a framework for conceiving the larger dimensions of the problem I have been sketching. When nearly all biologists look at organisms—since the Darwinian revolution, certainly—they see them historically. "In general, organisms can be understood," wrote E. S. Russell (1982, 233), glossing Darwin's conception of the organic realm, "only if we take into account the cardinal fact that they are historical beings." This historical outlook, almost entirely lacking in Paley and Cuvier and only partially adumbrated in the transcendental evolutionists, is exemplified by the succession for *Homo sapiens* that any biologist could recite, where each term marks off a larger and historically earlier clade:

*Homo sapiens*
Primate
Mammal
Amniote
Tetrapod
Chordate
Deuterostome
Metazoan

Eukaryote

. . . .

(origin of life)

Darwin would have recognized this as the "great law" of unity of type (1964, 206), which since the *Origin of Species* has been understood preeminently according to the theory of common descent: the common ancestry of all organisms, recent and extinct. The systematic hierarchy is thus, post-Darwin, understood by most biologists to indicate a hierarchy of actual history, namely, material descent.

But Darwin recognized a second "great law," this stemming from Cuvier, namely, conditions of existence.[13] What characters or features does this organism (*Homo sapiens,* say) require for its very existence, for its essential viability? Consider an example, typifying a mode of analysis that daily fills the biological literature:

> The presence of two X chromosomes in the female and only one in the male creates a problem of no small magnitude. Since the X and Y chromosomes are for the most part not homologous, females have twice the dose of X-chromosomes found in the male, simply because they have two X chromosomes to the male's one. (Jenkins 1979, 48)

What to do? Shut down one of the X chromosomes in females, achieving dosage compensation—and this requires a mechanism. One can dissect that mechanism genetically to determine its causal structure: in brief, to discover which elements or constituents are required for function (X inactivation), a function (dosage compensation) that is in its turn required by the genetics and physiology of the organism as a whole. Thus, decomposing the function of X inactivation in mammals into its causal elements, Penny et al. (1996, 131) report:

> The *Xist* gene has been proposed as a candidate for the X inactivation centre, the master regulatory switch locus that controls X chromosome inactivation. So far this hypothesis has been supported solely by indirect evidence. Here we describe gene targeting for *Xist,* and provide evidence for its absolute requirement in the process of X chromosome inactivation.

Mammals require dosage compensation (X inactivation), which requires the gene *Xist.* This is knowledge that must be reconciled with whatever history we postulate for the mammals.

Now most biologists, I conjecture, presuppose that these modes of biological analysis are entirely consonant. After all, they reason, the common descent of all organisms is true, and here we are: humans, archaebacteria, oak trees, snails and starfish, viably reproducing and competing and going about the business of organisms generally. Any conflict between these modes of analysis therefore can be only apparent.

But consider Raff's recent (1996, 6) historical reading of Cuvier's famous *embranchements,* the four essentially different architectures that, Cuvier argued, fundamentally divide the animals into discrete groups:

Cuvier's definitions of these embranchements [the radiates, mollusks, articulates and vertebrates] were based on characteristic modes of organization of the nervous system, and they have a rough correspondence to the phyla we currently recognize. Cuvier considered the nervous system to be the primary functional system, and thus its organization the critical feature of each body plan. Like the fundamentally different developmental pathways defined by von Baer, the embranchements of Cuvier argued against evolution. For Cuvier it was not just that the embranchements were different in morphology; integrated function also was crucial. Cuvier believed that the radically different organizations of the four embranchements could not change from one to another without a fatal loss of integrated function during the transition. This argument is still a forceful one.

Still forceful, I would argue, because the problem Cuvier grasped is very much alive today. The observation that early development is refractory to mutational change is a finding about *biological possibility and impossibility,* where viability defines the sphere of the possible. Cuvier saw his embranchements as functionally constrained in their range of possible variation, and to a remarkable extent, given the vast shift in underlying philosophies, neo-Darwinians share the same outlook.

But neo-Darwinians are also saddled with a defective metaphysics of scientific explanation, namely, methodological naturalism. Thus golden ages of evolution are postulated (e.g., the Cambrian explosion), in the complete absence of any mechanistic understanding, to accommodate the demands of a philosophy of nature that holds, in the face of abundant disconfirming evidence, that complex things come into existence by undirected mutation and selection from simpler things. Yet, however unlikely they may be, these golden ages of macroevolution are preferred by neo-Darwinians to taking at face value the demonstrable limits of organismal structure and function—for those limits imply the primary discontinuity of organisms one from another. Under the naturalistic philosophy of nature and hence of scientific explanation, however, there can be no primary, or designed, organismal discontinuity—living things coming into existence by intelligent causation—because that would be magic. What exists could only have been derived materially from other bundles of matter by natural causes. It must be so: design is magic.

Design is not magic. In 1857, the object *On the Origin of Species,* a text of some 490 pages in the first edition, did not exist. In 1859 it did. If the earth were swept clean of observers and of all historical records, it would still be the case that at a time $t_1$ a certain specified object of small probability did not exist and at time $t_2$ it did—because a mind acted and left its trace on the world in a distinctive pattern. For the origin of books, design is ordinary, explanatory science. We ought to rediscover that design is ordinary science for the origin of organisms, too.

I believe the path out of the neo-Darwinian thicket lies in the concepts of biological possibility and impossibility. The epigraph from Erwin (1994, 290) can be modified. The path to knowledge and understanding in biology lies not with speculating about how organisms *could* vary—that is, evolve from other, essentially different organisms—but with learning how organisms *actually do* vary. And that should be discovered by observation and experiment, because learning how organisms actually vary must inevitably govern our theories about how they could vary.

## Notes

[1] On January 14, 1994, the Associated Press reported from France that Rene Le Mancq, 62, "had been charged with using radio waves to crash more than 100 model airplanes." Le Mancq, an electronics teacher, lived in Marseilles next door to a model airplane club, with whom he often feuded about the noise of model planes flying over his property. In 1980 Le Mancq won a court decree limiting the number of model planes that could be flown at the same time. The decree, it seems, failed to satisfy him. "In 1992 and 1993," the AP report continues, "more than 100 planes flown by club members crashed for no apparent reason." Suspicion inevitably fell on Le Mancq.

[2] Many motivations may be pressed on one by the naturalist, especially the argument that any science that balks at the unknown will never move beyond where it currently sits. But we determine which unknowns are worth pursuing and which are not on the promise of actually finding something. And that is precisely what the naturalist has not delivered. More to the point, however, the naturalist prods us to keep searching for a natural cause when we may already be sitting on the true (intelligent design) cause. "At the end of my garden stand some birch trees," the probabilist A. W. F. Edwards (1992, 203) writes, "exhibiting no particular pattern when viewed from the house. One day my young daughter returned from the end of the garden with the comment 'When you look at the birches from *there*' (pointing down the garden) 'they stand in lines. *They must have been planted.*' She was surprised to find the trees exhibiting a pattern; an alternative explanation [to chance] sprang to mind, and a quick subconscious likelihood calculation (I presume) persuaded her to accept it." At the risk of sounding uncharitable, I see the naturalist as prodding this child to try harder with her scientific imagination. What is the natural cause of those rows of birch trees?

[3] To give the problem of induction the formulation it deserves: You had better watch out because you could always be wrong.

[4] An esterase is any enzyme that hydrolyses (breaks) an ester into an alcohol and an acid.

[5]In the snail *Limnaea peregra* (Gilbert 1991, 86), the direction of cleavage and hence of shell coiling may switch from right-handed to left-handed depending on the genotype of the mother. Jonathan Wells has argued to me (in conversation) that *Limnaea* is the proverbial exception that proves the rule. The nearly complete absence of any experimental literature demonstrating the heritable modification of cleavage patterns in animals is remarkable, in that this evidential lacuna is so little known.

[6]A philosophically noteworthy aspect of this view is its wariness of uniformitarian reasoning. "Of course, we are conditioned to think of evolutionary change in a uniformitarian way," argue Campbell and Marshall (1987, 73), "but we should acknowledge that this is a philosophical, and not a scientific, point of view." Or, as Douglas Erwin (1993, 271) frames the point, "Evolution is frequently, if implicitly, viewed as a uniformitarian process in which the mechanisms, rates and effects are time-homogeneous. In other words, there is no expectation that there were unusual mechanisms of change involved in the metazoan radiation, for example, or that natural selection produced a broader range of outcomes in the past than is true today. It may be time to revise this assumption, realizing that many of the constraints on the evolutionary process arose at specific points in the history of life and established frameworks for subsequent evolutionary change."

[7]Thus the problem of the de novo origin of body plans, for most people the essence of evolution, lies entirely outside the neo-Darwinian framework. It remains there because neo-Darwinism has been unable to integrate the realities of development with the mutation/selection mechanism. See for instance Arthur (1988, 19): "The modern synthesis lacks a coherent developmental component"; Raff and Kaufman (1991, 336): "Our own ability to synthesize . . . is severely limited by a currently poor understanding of the way in which genes direct the morphogenesis of even simple metazoan structures and of the nature of high-level genetic regulatory interactions"; John and Miklos (1988, 336): "It is when one attempts to examine the molecular basis of morphogenesis that the irrelevance of neo-Darwinian theory is put into real perspective. The theory can predict what is likely to survive once it has appeared, but it has absolutely nothing to say about the origin of change.... In our view, we need to put our major efforts into molecular embryology where the quintessence of morphological novelty must obviously lie"; and Müller and Wagner (1991, 252): "The majority of open questions . . . lie in the realm of the developmental context in which genetic changes can trigger a change of structure. It is unlikely that explanations for the origin of morphological novelties can be successful without the inclusion of the generative properties of developmental systems." As Arthur (1987, 180) sums the problem, "[O]ne can argue that there is no *direct* evidence for the Darwinian origin of a body plan—black *Biston betularia* [peppered moths] certainly do not constitute one! Thus in the end we have to admit that we do not really know how body plans originate."

[8]Erwin (1993, 263-64), more tentatively than Willmer, also considers the possibility of polyphyly: "The intriguing but inescapable conclusion from this analysis is that if 'protists' possess most of the requirements for development, several lineages *could* have independently achieved at least early grades of complex multicellular organization. Thus there may well have been other lineages with aspects of complex development earlier in the history of life and thus the apparent monophyly of the extant fungi, metaphyte and metazoan clades may be a historical artifact, rather

than reflecting the appearance of unique innovations in the three clades. There is no reason on developmental grounds to dismiss Seilacher's suggestion (1984, 1989) that the Ediacaran fauna were a metazoan-grade of organization independently derived from some 'simpler' eukaryote and unrelated to Metazoa, nor to reject Christen et al.'s (1991a, b) argument from analysis of 28S rRNA that living Metazoa are polyphyletic." See also Zuckerkandl (1994, 675): "Through gene evolution, parallel evolution can have occurred even at the lowest macroevolutionary level, the evolution of Bauplans, in early metazoan times. . . . Through the duplication of certain regulatory genes, metazoa may have evolved a number of times, in a manner of speaking, from scratch."

[9]Assuming that no functional equivalent is substituted interventionally, as occurs with major organ systems (e.g., the heart and lungs) during medical transplant operations.

[10]Wouters errs, I think, in arguing that viability explanations proceed exclusively by postulating hypothetical organisms. "This hypothetical organism is exactly like a real organism," he writes (1995, 442), "except that it lacks the trait to be explained (e.g., a large organism without a circulatory system or a male stickleback that does not ventilate the nest)." Such counterfactuals may presuppose hypothetical organisms in many cases, but viability analyses in the biological literature proceed by perturbing the elements of real organisms as well, to assess functional relationships.

[11]With the development of homologous recombination (genetic knockout) techniques in mice have come conceptual puzzles about apparently inessential genes and proteins. "Tenascin-C [an extracellular matrix protein] has various effects on the adhesion and migration of cells *in vitro* and is widely expressed both during development and in various physiological and pathological processes. It was, therefore, a considerable surprise when mice in which the tenascin-C gene had been ablated developed to term and were overtly normal and fertile" (Hynes 1994, 570). Hynes speculates that "the failure to observe an obvious phenotypic defect . . . reflects the inadequacy of the assays" but allows that unexpected levels of genetic redundancy may also explain the puzzle. "[N]umerous experimental systems," Pickett and Meeks-Wagner (1995, 1347) note, "have recently revealed unsuspected levels of complexity within genetic regulatory pathways. Perhaps most surprising is the result that loss-of-function mutations engineered within many regulatory genes have little or no effect on phenotype. Although the lack of phenotype suggests that these genes are not essential to the processes under consideration, new evidence indicates that these mutations are partly or completely compensated for by the activity of other genes."

[12]Christopher Boorse (1984, 373) has previously stressed the independence of viability modes of biological explanation from evolutionary considerations. "The modern theory of evolution," he argues, "is of recent vintage; talk of functions had been going on for a long time before it appeared. When Harvey, say, claimed that the function of the heart is to circulate the blood, he did not have natural selection in mind. Nor does this mean that pre-evolutionary physiologists must therefore have believed in a divine designer. The fact is that in talking of physiological functions, they did not mean to be making historical claims at all. They were simply describing the organization of a species as they found it. This approach to physiology is still the standard one. Even today physiological function statements are not usually supported by, or regarded as refutable by, evolutionary evidence."

[13]Russell argues that Darwin misrepresents Cuvier on the content of conditions of existence. "It is clear," Russell writes, "that Darwin took the phrase 'Conditions of Existence' to mean the environmental conditions, and the law of the Conditions of Existence to mean the law of adaptation to environment. But that is not what Cuvier meant by the phrase: he understood by it the principle of the co-ordination of the parts to form the whole, the essential condition for the existence of any organism whatsoever. . . . Of this thought there is in Darwin little trace" (Russell 1982, 239). There is little trace, but not, I think, because Darwin fails to understand Cuvier. Rather Darwin has explicitly recast conditions of existence in selective terms and in so doing changes the law's meaning profoundly. The necessary functional invariance Cuvier posited is fundamentally incongruent with Darwin's transformist view.

## References

Anderson, D. T. 1987. Developmental pathways and evolutionary rates. In *Rates of Evolution*, ed. K. S. W. Campbell and M. F. Day, 143-55. London: Allen and Unwin.

Arthur, W. 1987. *Theories of life*. London: Pelican.

———. 1988. *A theory of the evolution of development*. New York: Wiley.

Behe, M. 1996. *Darwin's black box: The biochemical challenge to evolution*. New York: Free Press.

Boorse, C. 1984. Wright on Functions. In *Conceptual issues in evolutionary biology*, ed. E. Sober, 369-85. Cambridge, Mass.: MIT Press.

Buss, L. 1987. *The evolution of individuality*. Princeton, N.J.: Princeton University Press.

Campbell, K. S. W., and C. R. Marshall. 1987. Rates of evolution among Paleozoic echinoderms. In *Rates of evolution*, ed. K. S. W. Campbell and M. F. Day, 61-100. London: Allen and Unwin.

Darwin, C. 1964. *On the Origin of Species*. 1859. Reprint, London: J. Murray; Cambridge, Mass.: Harvard University Press.

Davidson, E. 1990. How embryos work: A comparative view of diverse modes of cell fate specification. *Development* 108:365-89.

———. 1991. Spatial mechanisms of gene regulation in metazoan embryos. *Development* 113:1-26.

———. 1994. Molecular biology of embryonic development: How far have we come in the last ten years? *BioEssays* 16:603-15.

Dembski, W. A. 1998. *The design inference: Eliminating chance through small probabilities*. Cambridge: Cambridge University Press.

Dohle, W. 1988. Review of Løvtrup, Darwinism. *Journal of Evolutionary Biology* 1:283-85.

Edwards, A. W. F. 1992. *Likelihood*. Expanded ed. Baltimore: Johns Hopkins University Press.

Elinson, R. 1987. Changes in developmental patterns: Embryos of amphibians with large eggs. In *Development as an evolutionary process*, ed. R. A. Raff and E. C. Raff, 1-21. New York: Alan Liss.

Erwin, D. 1993. The origin of metazoan development: A palaeobiological perspective. *Biological Journal of the Linnean Society* 50:255-74.

———. 1994. Early introduction of major morphological innovations. *Acta Palaeontologica Polonica* 38 (1994):281-94.

Foote, M., and S. J. Gould. 1992. Cambrian and recent morphological disparity. *Science* 258:1816.

Gilbert, S. 1991. *Developmental biology.* 3rd ed. Sunderland, Mass.: Sinauer.

Gillespie, N. C. 1979. *Charles Darwin and the problem of Creation.* Chicago: University of Chicago Press.

Goodwin, B. 1994. *How the leopard changed its spots.* New York: Scribners.

Grupe, A., B. Hultgren, A. Ryan, Y. H. Ma, M. Bauer, and T. A. Stewart. 1995. Transgenic knockouts reveal a critical requirement for pancreatic ß cell glucokinase in maintaining glucose homeostasis. *Cell* 83:69-78.

Hartl, D. 1981. *A primer of population genetics.* Sunderland, Mass.: Sinauer.

Hull, D. 1983. Darwin and the nature of science. In *Evolution from molecules to men,* ed. D. S. Bendall, 63-80. Cambridge: Cambridge University Press.

Hume, D. 1980. *Dialogues concerning natural religion.* 1779. Indianapolis, Ind.: Hackett.

Hynes, R. O. 1994. Genetic analysis of cell-matrix interactions in development. *Current Biology* 4:569-74.

Jenkins, J. B. 1979. *Genetics.* 2nd ed. Boston: Houghton Mifflin.

John, B., and G. L. G. Miklos. 1988. *The eukaryote genome in development and evolution.* London: Allen and Unwin.

Lawrence, P. A., and G. Struhl. 1996. Morphogens, compartments and pattern: Lessons from Drosophila? *Cell* 85:951-61.

McKinney, M. L., and K. J. McNamara. 1991. *Heterochrony: The evolution of ontogeny.* New York: Plenum.

Manak, J. R., and M. P. Scott. 1994. A class act: Conservation of homeodomain protein functions. In *The evolution of developmental mechanisms,* ed. M. Akam, P. Holland, P. Ingham, and G. Wray, 61-77. Cambridge: The Company of Biologists Limited.

Maynard-Smith, J. 1983. Evolution and development. In *Development and evolution,* ed. B. C. Goodwin, N. Holder, and C. C. Wylie, 33-45. Cambridge: Cambridge University Press.

Miklos, G. L. G., and B. John. 1987. From genotype to phenotype. In *Rates of evolution,* ed. K. S. W. Campbell and M. F. Day, 263-82. London: Allen & Unwin.

Müller, G. B., and G. Wagner. 1991. Novelty in evolution: Restructuring the concept. *Annual Reviews in Ecology and Systematics* 22:229-56.

Nusslein-Volhard, C., and E. Wieschaus. 1980. Mutations affecting segment number and polarity in Drosophila. *Nature* 287:795-801.

Ohsumi, Keita, Chiaki Katagiri, Takeo Kishimoto. 1993. Chromosome Condensation in *Xenopus* Mitotic Extracts Without Histone 1. *Science* 262:2033-2035.

Penny, G. D., G. F. Kay, S. A. Sheardown, S. Rastan, and N. Brockdorff. 1996. Requirement for *Xist* in X chromosome inactivation. *Nature* 379:131-37.

Pickett, F. B., and D. R. Meeks-Wagner. 1995. Seeing double: Appreciating genetic redundancy. *The Plant Cell* 7:1347-56.

Raff, R. 1996. *The shape of life: Genes, development and the evolution of animal form.* Chicago: University of Chicago Press.

Raff, R., and T. Kaufman. 1991. *Embryos, genes and evolution.* 2nd ed. Bloomington, Ind.: Indiana University Press.

Raff, R., G. Wray, and J. J. Henry. 1991. Implications of radical evolutionary changes in early development for concepts of developmental constraint. In *New Perspectives in Evolution,* ed. L. Warren and H. Koprowski, 189-207. New York: Wiley-Liss.

Ruddle, F. H., J. L. Bartels, K. L. Bentley, C. Kappen, M. T. Murtha, and J. W.

Pendleton. 1994. Evolution of *Hox* genes. *Annual Review of Genetics* 28:423-42.

Russell, E. S. 1982. *Form and function*. London: John Murray, 1916. Reprint, Chicago: University of Chicago Press.

Scott, M. P. 1994. Intimations of a creature. *Cell* 79:1121-24.

Thomson, K. S. 1988. *Morphogenesis and evolution*. Oxford: Oxford University Press.

———. 1992. Macroevolution: The morphological problem. *American Zoologist* 32:106-12.

Van Valen, L. 1988. How do major evolutionary changes occur? *Evolutionary Theory* 8:173-76.

Wallace, B. 1984. Adaptation, neo-Darwinian tautology and population fitness: A reply. *Evolutionary Biology* (ed. M. H. Hecht, B. Wallace, and G. T. Prance) 17:59-71.

Wells, J. 1998. Unseating naturalism: Recent insights from developmental biology. *Mere Creation*, ed. W. A. Dembski, chap. 2. Downers Grove, Ill.: InterVarsity Press.

Willmer, P. 1990. *Invertebrate relationships*. Cambridge: Cambridge University Press.

Wimsatt, W. C. 1986. Developmental constraints, generative entrenchment and the innate-acquired distinction. In *Integrating scientific disciplines*, ed. W. Bechtel. Dordrecht: Martinus-Nijhoff. (Pagination from corrected and expanded version, unpublished, 1990.)

Wouters, A. 1995. Viability explanation. *Biology and Philosophy* 10:435-37.

Wray, G. 1992. Rates of evolution in developmental processes. *American Zoologist* 32:123-34.

Zinsmaier, K. E., K. K. Eberle, E. Buchner, N. Walter, and S. Benzer. 1994. Paralysis and early death in cysteine string protein mutants of *Drosophila*. *Science* 263:977-80.

Zuckerkandl, E. 1994. Molecular pathways to parallel evolution: I. gene nexuses and their morphological correlates. *Journal of Molecular Evolution* 39:661-78.

# Part 3

## Biological Design

# 7

# Intelligent Design Theory as a Tool for Analyzing Biochemical Systems

## MICHAEL J. BEHE

WE ARE PRIVILEGED TO LIVE IN A TIME OF UNPRECEDENTED PROgress in biology. Plants and animals have been studied since antiquity, yet for the great majority of that time naturalists were completely in the dark about the way living things actually work. Only with the discovery of the molecular basis of life has science been able to address questions about life's basic mechanisms. Science has learned over the past four decades that the many cellular tasks required to sustain life are carried out by machines—literally, molecular machines. In *Darwin's Black Box* I discussed several such machines. I showed that they are irreducibly complex—that is, they require a number of closely matched components before they can function—and thus are mammoth barriers to gradualistic, Darwinian evolution. I further argued that such irreducibly complex systems are best interpreted as the result of deliberate intelligent design.

In this chapter I want to proceed from that point to consider the likelihood of design for other biochemical systems. That is, given that some cellular systems were in fact designed, what can be said about other biochemical systems in which design is less obvious? The focus will be on how a theory of intelligent design can illuminate the structure of biochemical systems and how it can usefully direct future research.

But before going on to the new systems I will briefly review my argument from *Darwin's Black Box.* Let me begin by discussing the reasoning by which I reach a conclusion of design, as well as two examples of biochemical design: the bacterial flagellum and intracellular transport.

## Conceptual Tools

I want to start by discussing two concepts that I hope will not be controversial. They are the concept of irreducible complexity and that of minimal function. Both irreducible complexity and minimal function will be important in trying to distinguish what features of a biochemical system may have been designed and which may have arisen solely by natural mechanisms.

The concept of minimal function provides a way to recognize that a device in the real world has to work at a certain minimal level of efficiency to be of any practical use. As an example, suppose that the world's first outboard motor had been designed and was being marketed. The motor functioned smoothly—burning gasoline at a controlled rate, transmitting the force along an axle and turning the propeller. However, the propeller rotated at only one revolution per hour. This is an impressive technological feat; after all, burning gasoline in a can next to a propeller does not turn it at all. Nonetheless few people would purchase such a machine, because it fails to perform at a level suitable for its purpose.

Our second concept is irreducible complexity. An irreducibly complex system is one that requires several closely matched parts in order to function and where removal of one of the components effectively causes the system to cease functioning. A good example of such a system is a mechanical mousetrap. Mousetraps that you can buy in a grocery store consist of a number of distinguishable parts. There are a flat wooden platform to act as a base; a metal hammer, which pins the mouse against the base when the hammer is tripped, crushing the mouse; a spring with extended ends to press against the platform and the hammer when the trap is charged; a sensitive catch that releases when slight pressure is applied, and a metal bar that connects to the catch and holds the hammer back when the trap is charged. There are also assorted staples to hold the system together.

The mousetrap depends critically on the presence of all five of its components; if there were no spring, the mouse would not be pinned to the base; if there were no platform, the other pieces would fall apart; and so on. The function of the mousetrap requires all the pieces: you cannot catch a few mice with just a platform, add a spring and catch a few more mice, add a holding bar and catch a few more. All of the components have to be in place before any mice are caught. Thus the mousetrap is irreducibly complex. Furthermore, the components of the mousetrap are closely matched to each other: if the holding bar were too short, it would not reach the catch, and the system would be utterly useless. If the ends of the spring did not wrap around in the precise manner they do, the trap could not be loaded. If the catch were too big or too rounded, it would not be tripped when a mouse grabbed a piece of cheese (probably half of the time I set a trap the mouse steals the cheese without tripping it).

Let me interject a note of caution: some systems require several pieces but not ones that need to be closely matched. For example, suppose you were walking in the woods and came across an old log where the wind had blown a tree branch onto it, and the branch was perpendicular to the log. Here you have an irreducibly complex system—a lever and fulcrum. If there were a boulder nearby, you possibly could use the lever and fulcrum to move it. So some systems require several parts but not closely matched ones.

Closely matched, irreducibly complex systems are huge stumbling blocks for Darwinian evolution because they cannot be put together directly by improving a given function over many steps, as Darwinian gradualism would have it, where the function works by the same mechanism as the completed structure. The only possible recourse to a gradualist is to speculate that an irreducibly complex system might have come together through an indirect route—perhaps the mousetrap started out as a washing board, was changed into an orange crate, and somehow ended up as a mousetrap. One can never completely rule out such an indirect scenario, which is tantamount to trying to prove a negative. However, the more complex a system, the more difficult it becomes to envision such indirect scenarios, and the more examples of irreducible complexity we meet, the less and less persuasive such indirect scenarios become. It cannot be that everything in life started out as something else.

Closely matched, irreducibly complex systems not only are tall problems for Darwinism but also are the hallmarks of intelligent design. What is design? In my definition, design is simply the purposeful arrangement of parts. You cannot tell just by looking at something that it has not been designed—anything might have been designed. The coats on a rack in a restaurant may have been arranged just so by the owner before you came in. The trash and tin cans along the edge of a highway may have been placed by an artist trying to make an environmental statement. Apparently chance meetings between people might be the result of a grand design (conspiracy theorists thrive on postulating such designs). On the campus of my university there are sculptures which, if I saw them lying beside the road, I would guess were the result of chance blows to a piece of scrap metal, but they were designed.

The upshot of this conclusion—that anything could have been purposely arranged—is that we cannot know that something has not been designed.

The scientific problem then becomes, How do we confidently detect design? When is it reasonable to conclude, in the absence of firsthand knowledge or eyewitness accounts, that something has been designed?

For discrete physical systems—if there is not a gradual route to their production—design is evident when a number of separate, interacting components are ordered in such a way as to accomplish a function beyond the individual components. The greater the specificity of the interacting components required to produce the function, the greater is our confidence in the conclusion of design. A mousetrap is an obvious result of design. Any person, even someone who had not seen such a device before, would quickly conclude that a mousetrap was designed because of the way its parts interact to perform a function.

## Irreducible Complexity in Biochemistry

Let us now switch our focus from the everyday world to the biochemical world of the cell. To understand how life works you have to descend from the level of the whole organism to the level of the cell and subcellular systems. Biochemistry is the basis of life—it is the study of the molecules that make up living tissues and cells. Within the past four decades science has advanced to the point where it has been able to isolate many of the components of the cell and understand in some detail how they work. With the background discussion in place we must now ask whether any biochemical systems are irreducibly complex. It turns out that many are. I will describe just two such systems. For more examples consult *Darwin's Black Box* or any undergraduate biochemistry textbook.

The first system I will consider is the familiar bacterial flagellum. The flagellum is an organelle that allows many bacteria to swim. It was shown about twenty-five years ago that, remarkably, the flagellum is a propeller that is rotated by a motor. The mechanical requirements of such a system are quite complex. Instead of describing this fantastic apparatus in my own words, I will quote a recent review of the flagellum written by Lucy Shapiro (1995) of the Department of Developmental Biology at Stanford University.

A rotating propeller at the cell surface, driven by a transmembrane proton gradient, provides many bacteria with the ability to move and thus respond to environmental signals. To acquire this powerful capability, the bacterial cell is faced with the challenge of building a tiny rotary engine at the base of the propeller. Although the motor is anchored in the cytoplasmic membrane, a significant portion of the entire mechanism extends into the cytoplasm and, at the other end, out into the environment. At least 20 individual proteins are used as parts for this complex structure and another 30 are used for its construction, function, and maintenance (525).

   To carry out the feat of coordinating the ordered expression of about 50 genes, delivering the protein products of these genes to the construction site, and moving the correct parts to the upper floors while adhering to the design specifications with a high degree of accuracy, the cell requires impressive organizational skills. The construction scheme must deal with fundamental questions in structural and developmental biology: How does the cell measure the length of a component made up of polymerized subunits? When the appropriate length is reached, how does the cell turn off the assembly of one part of the structure and switch on the assembly of the next part? Are there checkpoint mechanisms that determine whether one flagellum component has been completed and that it is okay to start construction of the next component? How is this information conveyed to the expression of the flagellar genes? Because the assembly of the flagellum proceeds in large measure by the passage of structural proteins through a central channel to its distal tip, what is the export mechanism and how does it choose the proteins that are allowed entry into the pipeline?

As you can see from Shapiro's review, many discrete parts have to be in place to produce a functioning flagellum. Clearly the necessary pieces of the flagellum itself have to be in place. If there is no whip protein, the bacterium cannot swim. If there is no rotary motor, then the flagellum lies in rigor mortis. If there is no base, then the flagellum has nothing to hang on to when it tries to turn. Furthermore, the parts themselves are mulitfunctional. The rotary motor uses a flow of acid to power it, like a hydroelectric dam uses a flow of water to power its turbines. Several models have been proposed to explain how the motor works; none of them are simple.

   Thus the flagellum itself is irreducibly complex. However, a simple examination of the flagellum shows only a portion of the components required for a functioning organelle. As Shapiro's review made clear, the assembly of this bulky machine is a significant logistical task. We must remember that the cell is essentially a completely automated factory, so all assembly has to be done by highly sophisticated robots, not by magic.

   My second example of an irreducibly complex biochemical system is the one that targets proteins for delivery to subcellular compartments (Alberts et al. 1994, 551-650). The eukaryotic cell contains a number of membrane-enclosed areas that perform specialized tasks. These include lysosomes for digestion, Golgi vesicles for export, and others. Unfortunately the machinery for making proteins is outside these compartments, so how do the proteins that perform tasks in subcellular compartments find their way to their destination? It turns out that proteins that will wind up in subcellular compartments contain a special amino acid sequence near the beginning called a signal sequence. As the proteins are being synthesized, a complex molecular assemblage called the signal recognition particle, or SRP, binds to the signal sequence. This causes synthesis of the protein to halt temporarily. During the pause in protein synthesis the SRP binds the transmembrane SRP receptor, which causes protein synthesis to resume and which allows passage of the protein into the interior of the endoplasmic reticulum (ER). As the protein passes into the ER the signal sequence is cut off.

For many proteins the ER is just a waystation on their travels to their final destinations. Proteins that will end up in a lysosome are enzymatically tagged with a carbohydrate residue called mannose-6-phosphate while still in the ER. An area of the ER membrane then begins to concentrate several proteins; one protein, clathrin, forms a sort of geodesic dome called a coated vesicle, which buds off from the ER. In the dome there is also a receptor protein that binds to both the clathrin and to the mannose-6-phosphate group of the protein that is being transported. The coated vesicle then leaves the ER, travels through the cytoplasm and binds to the lysosome through another specific receptor protein. Finally, in a maneuver involving several more proteins, the vesicle fuses with the lysosome, and the protein is at its destination.

During its travels our protein interacted with dozens of macromolecules to achieve one purpose: its arrival in the lysosome. Virtually all components of the transport system are necessary for the system to operate, and therefore the system is irreducible. The consequences of even a single gap in the transport chain can be seen in the hereditary defect known as I-cell disease. It results from a deficiency of the enzyme that places the mannose-6-phosphate on proteins to be targeted to the lysosomes. I-cell disease is characterized by progressive retardation, skeletal deformities and early death.

**The Professional Literature**
What has science had to say so far about these stunningly complex biochemical systems? A good place to look for an answer is the *Journal of Molecular Evolution*. *JME* was begun specifically to deal with the topic of how evolution occurs on the molecular level. It has high scientific standards and is edited by prominent figures in the field. In the February 1996 issue of *JME* there were published fourteen articles; of these, all fourteen were concerned simply with the comparison of protein or DNA sequences. A sequence comparison is an amino acid-by-amino acid comparison of two different proteins or a nucleotide-by-nucleotide comparison of two different pieces of DNA, noting the positions at which they are identical or similar and the places where they are not. Although it is useful for determining possible lines of descent, which is an interesting question in its own right, comparing

sequences cannot show how a complex biochemical system achieved its function—the question that most concerns us. By way of analogy, the instruction manuals for two different models of computer put out by the same company might have many identical words, sentences and even paragraphs, suggesting a common ancestry (perhaps the same author wrote both manuals), but comparing the sequences of letters in the instruction manuals will never tell us if a computer can be produced step by step starting from a typewriter.

None of the papers discussed detailed models for intermediates in the development of complex biomolecular structures. In the past ten years *JME* has published more than a thousand papers. Of these, about one hundred discussed the chemical synthesis of molecules thought to be necessary for the origin of life, about fifty proposed mathematical models to improve sequence analysis, and about eight hundred were analyses of sequences. There were zero papers discussing detailed models for intermediates in the development of complex biomolecular structures. This is not a peculiarity of *JME*. No papers are to be found that discuss detailed models for intermediates in the development of complex biomolecular structures, whether in the *Proceedings of the National Academy of Science, Nature, Science,* the *Journal of Molecular Biology* or, to my knowledge, any science journal.

The idea of Darwinian molecular evolution is not based on science. There is no publication in the scientific literature—in journals or books—that describes how molecular evolution of any real, complex, biochemical system either did occur or even might have occurred. There are assertions that such evolution occurred, but absolutely none are supported by pertinent experiments or calculations. Since there is no authority on which to base claims of knowledge, it can truly be said that the assertion of Darwinian molecular evolution is merely bluster.

**Foundation**
These are the facts that I offer to reach a conclusion of intelligent design: the irreducible complexity of the bacterial flagellum and the intermolecular transport system, as well as the utter sterility of Darwinian theory in explaining their origins. Although many scientists entertain hopes about the future prospects of explaining these biochemical systems within a Darwinian framework, at the very least I have established that preferring a theory of intelligent design to explain those systems is not unreasonable. If in the future other researchers demonstrate experimentally that the flagellum or vesicular transport can arise by a nondirected process, then I shall admit intelligent design theory is wrong. But I am not overly worried about that prospect, and in the meantime I do not want to sit on my hands waiting for laboratories to

make good on their promissory notes.

I shall therefore use the conclusion of intelligent design as a jumping-off point. Specifically I want to explore the following question: Given that some biochemical systems were designed by an intelligent agent, and given the tools by which we came to that conclusion, how do we analyze other biochemical systems that may be more complicated and less discrete than the ones we have so far discussed? To give an idea of the general direction that I think intelligent design theory should head in biochemistry, I would like to describe the process by which DNA is replicated in modern cells and suggest some questions and approaches that a design theorist could explore. But first let me give some background information about the structure of DNA.

## Nucleic Acid Structure

Nucleic acids are polymers of a small number of building blocks, called nucleotides (Voet and Voet 1995, 849-69). A nucleotide itself has several parts. The first part is a carbohydrate, either ribose (in RNA) or deoxyribose (in DNA). To deoxyribose is attached one of four bases, either adenine (A), cytosine (C), guanine (G) or thymine (T). Attached to a different part of the carbohydrate ring (to the $5'$-OH group, which is pronounced the "five-prime hydroxyl" group) is a phosphate group. The sugar-phosphate portion of a nucleotide is analogous to the backbone portion of an amino acid, and the base is analogous to an amino acid side chain. It is only in its base that one nucleotide differs from another.

Two nucleotides can be joined chemically by reacting the phosphate of one nucleotide with the $3'$-OH group of the carbohydrate portion of the second nucleotide. This still leaves a free phosphate group on one end and a free $3'$-OH group on the other end, which can be further reacted with other nucleotides. Repetition of this process can generate very long polynucleotides. One single molecule of DNA can range from several thousand to about a billion nucleotides. The sequence of a polynucleotide is conventionally written starting from the $5'$ end to the $3'$ end.

Cellular DNA is found as an association of two separate strands (the famous double helix) that are strongly held together by an electrostatic force called hydrogen bonding. If A and T are correctly oriented they can form two hydrogen bonds with each other, and G can form three hydrogen bonds with C. In cells, wherever there is a G in one strand of DNA there is a C in the second strand and vice versa; and wherever there is an A in one strand there is a T in the second strand and vice versa. Thus the two strands are called complementary to each other. To be correctly oriented for hydrogen bonding the two strands must be pointed in different directions, with one running 5′ to 3′ from left to right and the other going 5′ to 3′ from right to left.

The amount of DNA in a cell varies roughly with the complexity of the organism. Bacteria have about several million nucleotides of DNA. The amount of eukaryotic DNA ranges from a low of several tens of millions of nucleotides in fungi to a high of several hundred billion in some flowering plants. Humans come in at around three billion nucleotides.

## Analysis of Replication

There comes a time in the life of every cell when it turns to thoughts of division. One major consideration in cell division is ensuring that the genetic information be copied and handed down uncorrupted; a great deal of effort is invested in that task (Voet and Voet 1995, 1020-45).

DNA replication is an enormously complex process with many different components that interact to ensure the faithful passing down of genetic information to the next generation. A large number of parts have to work together to that end. In the absence of one or more of a number of the components, DNA replication is either halted completely or significantly compromised, and the cell either dies or becomes quite sick.

However, DNA replication is not irreducibly complex in its entirety in the same way that the biochemical systems I spoke of previously (the flagellum and intracellular transport) are irreducibly complex. In those systems many components had to work together to produce a single function. In DNA replication, however, only one of the components actually performs the task of making a new DNA molecule—the polymerase enzyme. Furthermore, many of the additional components of the replication machinery form conceptually discrete subassemblies with conceptually discrete functions. The task of intelligent design theory in analyzing a system like DNA replication is to tease apart the components, determine the extent of their integration, and come to a tentative conclusion about what parts of the system are irreducibly complex, what level of performance for each part is needed for minimal function, whether discrete subassemblies have any useful function by themselves, or whether they are necessarily parts of larger systems. Additionally intelligent design theory wants to probe the plasticity of designed systems: can closely related systems have been produced by natural processes such as drift or natural selection, or is there reason to believe that they also were designed?

In the remainder of this chapter I am going to point out what strike me as interesting aspects of DNA replication for future investigation, as well as suggest a few questions and some possible lines of research.

## DNA Polymerase I

The simplest system that can replicate DNA in a test tube consists of a single enzyme called a DNA polymerase. The polymerase that Arthur Kornberg isolated in the 1950s (known as PolI) was able to take nearly any DNA that he threw into the test tube and, when supplied with activated nucleotides, replicate the DNA (Kornberg and Baker 1992, 101-5). However, there were problems with PolI: the DNA that it made contained some unusual features. When viewed by electron microscopy the product of DNA synthesis was frequently branched; it was not the linear molecule that Kornberg and others started with. After some work it was determined that the branching was due to the polymerase copying one strand and displacing the other. Occasionally during the displacement the protein would hop over to the displaced strand and begin to use that as a template instead of the strand it started with. Thus, although replication could proceed, the product of replication was not the same as the starting material—sequences of DNA got scrambled in the process.

The question that arises to a design theorist is whether the first cell might have contained only one simple polymerase. The considerations are that the polymerase would have been prone to just the errors that Kornberg came across when studying DNA polymerase I in isolation. Such a primitive polymerase would not be able to copy long DNA faithfully. It may, however, have copied shorter DNA reasonably well. For example, Kornberg showed that PolI could replicate the circular, single-stranded DNA bacteriophage _X174 and produce circular DNA that was capable of infecting bacterial cells. (I should add that not all DNA polymerases can do this. For example, PolIII, which does the bulk of the replicating job in bacterial cells, has never been seen to replicate any DNA to completion without the aid of other proteins. It always gets stuck. Apparently some common DNA structures cause the enzyme to stall irrecoverably.) This shows that a simple polymerase can produce biologically active DNA, but the DNA must be rather short. The bacteriophage _X174 can code for only ten genes. The simplest free-living organism we know of, the mycoplasma, contains hundreds of genes. To be certain that a simple polymerase is enough to replicate the genome of a self-sufficient cell, we must determine the probable length of the simplest cell's DNA—not an easy task, but perhaps doable with some effort.

A second consideration is that DNA polymerase I is not a simple enzyme. Rather, in Kornberg's phrase, it is "three enzymes in one." Besides the polymerizing activity, PolI can also degrade DNA in two different ways: it can degrade the DNA starting from a $3'$-end and working back toward the $5'$-end; and it can degrade starting at the $5'$-end and working back toward the $3'$-end. These different activities (polymerizing, $5'$-, and $3'$-nuclease) are done by three different, discrete regions of the molecule. It is kind of like having a key chain that has a key, a lighter and a pocket knife attached.

The $3'\_5'$ exonuclease activity plays a critical role in replication: it allows the enzyme to proofread the new DNA and cut out any mistakes it has made. Although the polymerase reads the sequence of the old DNA to produce new DNA, it turns out that simple base pairing allows about one mistake per thousand base pairs copied. Proofreading reduces errors to about one in a million base pairs. The question for design theorists is whether a proofreading exonuclease had to be present in the very first cell. That is, could the first cell, with its required complement of genes coded for by DNA, have successfully reproduced for a significant number of generations without a proofreading function? In order to answer this question again the minimum number of genes in the first cell and the minimum length of DNA have to be known. Then it can be calculated how fast the information would be degraded in the absence of proofreading. Bacterial mutants that are missing PolI can grow in minimal media but not rich media. In other words, they can grow slowly but not quickly. Evidently the strain put on the system by reproducing DNA rapidly exceeds the ability of the mutant to correct and repair new DNA. Variations on this experimental system may allow intelligent design theorists to probe these questions.

The third activity of DNA polymerase I, the $5'\_3'$ exonuclease activity is only indirectly involved in DNA replication. It is responsible for removing the short pieces of RNA that the cell uses to prime replication, allowing the polymerase function to fill in the gaps. This is clearly an advanced function and would not have been expected to be part of a simple polymerase (if a system much simpler than present cells is possible.) However, a question for intelligent design theorists is whether a simpler system, one with a simple polymerase, could switch over to a more complex system. That is, if a primitive cell was using just the polymerase activity (and maybe the proofreading activity) of PolI to replicate its DNA, is it even possible or likely that such a polymerase could be switched in midstream, so to speak, to an enzyme that degrades RNA and fills in gaps? A possible experimental approach to this question is to take mutants in which the $5'\_3'$ activity has been deleted (such mutants are viable) and determine if the activity can be reestablished. (There may be difficulties with this approach, but it is a place to start.)

### Clamp Protein and Loader

Let us now look at another feature of the modern DNA replication machinery (Marians 1992). Most enzymes work by randomly colliding with their substrate (the chemical that they are going to transform), catalyzing a reaction and dissociating from the product. If that were the case with DNA polymerase, then it would bind to DNA, add a nucleotide to the new chain that was being made and then fall off the chain. In order to put the next nucleotide onto the growing chain, the enzyme would again have to find its way back to the growing end, bind, bind a nucleotide and catalyze the addition. This same cycle would have to repeat itself a very large number of times to complete the new DNA chain. Modern polymerases do not do this, however. They catalyze the addition of a nucleotide but do not then fall off the DNA. Rather they stay bound to it until the next nucleotide comes in, and then they catalyze its addition to the chain, and they again stay bound. The ability of an enzyme to stay stuck to the DNA chain for multiple rounds of catalysis is called "processivity." The processivity of different modern DNA polymerases ranges from about 10 to about 100. That is, they stay stuck for an average of 10-100 nucleotide additions, and then they fall off and have to find their way back again. If this happened in the cell it would slow replication enormously. In the cell polymerases stay on the DNA until their job is completed, which might be only after millions of nucleotides have been joined. Their processivity in the cell is at least a hundred thousand times greater than it is in a test tube.

It turns out that in all cells there are things called clamp proteins. It was shown a few years ago that several copies of clamp protein join together to form a doughnut shape, where the hole in the middle is big enough to accommodate DNA. When the clamp is on DNA, it binds to the DNA polymerase and keeps it held bound until it reaches the end of its polymerizing job. However, clamp protein alone cannot bind to DNA. It has to be loaded onto the DNA by several other proteins that are part of the replication complex. The sequence goes this way: DNA polymerase III binds to DNA, the other proteins bind to DNA polymerase, and clamp protein binds to the other proteins. In a process that requires the expenditure of energy, the other proteins then place the clamp onto the DNA where it stabilizes the DNA, increasing its processivity to very high levels.

Such a system raises a number of questions for the design theorist. The first question is whether or not the clamp/clamp-loader system is irreducibly complex. This is not as straightforward a question as for the bacterial flagellum or intracellular transport. First of all, we have to define a function for the subsystem. Is the function to load a clamp, or to increase polymerase processivity, or to simply bind DNA? Depending on what we think is the function, we might decide that the system is or is not irreducibly complex. The next question is what are all the parts of the system. The roles of several of the proteins in the clamp-loader system are not known, and the mechanism of the process is still unclear. Questions about this will have to be informed by continuing investigation of the workings of the replication apparatus. Even when these questions are answered, however, many others will remain. For example, even if the system is somehow not irreducibly complex, could it nonetheless have developed incrementally? If the clamp first acquired the ability to bind to DNA, would it have been disallowed because it would be a roadblock to the polymerase? If the loading proteins first attached themselves to the polymerase, why would they have done so? Would they have interfered with its function of making DNA? If the clamp loader were first attached to the polymerase, and then a clamp protein acquired the ability to bind to the loader, and then the system first began loading the clamp, would the dramatic increase in processivity have been a help or a hindrance? If a cell were somehow used to making DNA slowly, would the ability to make it rapidly tax the control systems of the cell or the metabolic pathways that provide activated nucleotides?

**Topological Problems**

Let us turn to another aspect of replication (Lohman and Ferrari 1994; Lohman and Bjornson 1996; Wang 1996). DNA is a double helix. In order to read the information in DNA the cell has to pull apart the two strands so that the new strand it is synthesizing can physically interact with the template DNA. Pulling apart the strands creates a number of problems. First of all, the two strands like to be together—they stick to each other just as if they had tiny magnets up and down their length. In order to pull apart the DNA you have to tug on it; you have to put energy into the system. In modern cells a protein binds to a specific spot along the DNA, and the protein proceeds to open up the double strand. A second protein, called a helicase, now comes along. Helicase is like a snowplow; it is a molecular machine that plows down the middle of the double helix, pushing apart the two strands. This allows the polymerase and associated proteins to travel along behind it in ease and comfort.

There is a problem, though, with this setup. If you push apart two DNA strands they generally do not float around separately. If they are close to one another they will rapidly snap back and form a double strand again almost as soon as the helicase passes. Even if the strands are not near each other, a single strand will usually fold up and form hydrogen bonds with itself—in other words, a tangled mess. So it is not enough to push apart the two strands of DNA; there must also be a way to keep the strands apart once they have been separated.

In modern cells this job is done by single-strand binding protein, or SSB. As the helicase separates the strands of DNA, SSB coats them. The binding of SSB prevents the strands from rejoining until the new DNA strand has been made.

There is another difficulty in being a double helix. It can be illustrated with a simple example. Take two intertwined shoe laces and ask a friend to hold them together at each end. Now take a pencil, insert it between the strands near one end, and start pushing it down toward the other end. As you can see, shoestrings behind the pencil become melted, in the jargon of biochemistry. The shoestrings ahead of the pencil become more and more tangled. It becomes harder and harder to push the pencil forward.

Helicase and polymerase encounter the same problem with DNA. It does not matter whether you are talking about intertwined strings or intertwined DNA strands; the problem of tangling is the result of the topological interconnectedness of the two strands. If this problem persisted for very long in a modern cell, DNA replication would grind to a halt. However, the cell contains several enzymes, called topoisomerases, to take care of the difficulty. The way in which they do so can be illustrated with an enzyme called gyrase. Gyrase binds to DNA by wrapping the DNA around itself. It then makes a cut in both strands of the DNA, pulls them apart and allows a separate portion of the DNA to pass through the cut. It then reseals the cut and lets go of the DNA. This action decreases the number of twists in DNA.

In modern organisms helicase, SSB and gyrase all are required at the replication fork. Mutants in which any of them are missing are not viable— they die. The questions for intelligent design theory are subtle. All of these parts interact but not directly. They do not necessarily even have to touch each other. All can be isolated and work by themselves, but in doing so they do not replicate DNA. Could a primitive cell have existed without these components? Could they each have been added individually, or must they all have been added together? One possible way for replication to proceed without any of these components is to do so very slowly. In that way the replication complex might be able to rotate as it proceeded down the DNA. How slowly would it have to go to do so? How small would the replication machinery have to be to avoid the frictional problems inherent in rotating once every turn of the double helix? If a cell already had a functioning replication system, could these other components be added without upsetting it? For example, if a cell were used to replicating its DNA without SSB, would the binding of a proto-SSB to the replicating DNA be a help or a roadblock? If the cell were used to going slowly to prevent the build up of torsional forces, would the presence of a new gyrase—decreasing that force—be useful or not?

The answers are not obvious. The questions may be able to be approached experimentally, but the exact approaches will require some clever thinking.

### The Replication Fork
When DNA polymerase I—the Kornberg enzyme—is thrown into a test tube

with DNA and activated nucleotides, it will replicate the DNA. However, PolI replicates just one strand at a time and displaces the other stand of the old helix as it moves along. Another enzyme then has to start at the opposite end of the displaced strand and replicate it. Some viruses replicate their DNA in much the same way. The viral polymerase replicates one strand, displacing the second strand; and then the second strand is replicated later.

Modern cells, however, do not replicate DNA one strand at a time. They do both strands at once. Electron micrographs of replicating DNA show that the double strand is opened up and that the replication machinery proceeds in one direction (this is called the replication fork). But new DNA is made using both strands as templates. This creates a problem. All known polymerases must make new DNA in the 5′_3′ direction. However, since the two strands of DNA run in opposite directions, then as the replication fork proceeds in one direction it would have to, it seems, make one new strand in the 5′_3′ direction, but the opposite new strand must be made in the 3′_5′ direction, contradicting what we know about polymerases.

It turns out, however, that the deduction is wrong. Both new strands are made in the 5′_3′ direction. This is done in a remarkably convoluted way. At the replication fork one strand is made continuously in the 5′_3′ direction; this is called the leading strand. The other strand, called the lagging strand, is made discontinuously, in relatively small pieces called Okazaki fragments. A piece is made beginning at the replication fork and proceeding for a while backward away from the fork. As the replication fork proceeds further away, the polymerase making the lagging strand hops back to the new location, again makes a new DNA chain proceeding away from the fork and continues until it bumps into the beginning of the last Okazaki fragment made.

When the end of the newly made fragment bumps into the beginning of the last-made fragment, several jobs have to be done to hook the two fragments together. The first job is that the primer that begins every Okazaki fragment and is made of RNA (not DNA) must be removed. This is the job of PolI 5′_3′ nuclease activity. The gap then has to be filled in, which PolI does with its polymerizing activity. Finally the two ends of the fragment have to be joined together; this is the job of an enzyme called DNA ligase.

After the completion of one Okazaki fragment, the equipment has to be recycled to the beginning of the replication fork again. PolIII has to be released, the clamp has to let go, and a new clamp has to be loaded at the beginning of the next fragment.

Clearly the formation and control of the replication fork is an enormously complex process. An intelligent design theorist would have many questions about the origin of this system. Supposing that a simple polymerase like PolI replicating each strand separately was the starting point, is it feasible that a replication fork could develop step by step? The PolIII activity is present as a dimer at the modern replication fork; suppose a primitive polymerase were duplicated and somehow started to replicate the second strand in the opposite direction while remaining attached to the first strand—would that have been an improvement? Or would the change slow down replication and clog things with short fragments that could not be used?

**Associated Problems and Viruses**

The problems I have brought up about DNA replication so far are only questions about the development of direct pieces of the replication machine itself—the parts that do the primary job. But many other factors have to be integrated into this picture. For example, replication of DNA has to be coordinated with cell division. If the two were unconnected, then many copies of genomic DNA might be present in a cell as it started to divide, which might make the mechanical process of division very difficult or downright impossible. If cell division were more rapid than DNA replication, the genetic information might be divided and lost. At the least the cell would be wasting resources making other cell structures that, when they were divided off from the parent cell, would carry no genetic instructions to continue. A second example of problems of control is seen in the effect in modern cells of an unbalanced nucleotide pool. If the four nucleotides that are the activated precursors to cellular DNA are not kept in a fairly even ratio with each other, many more mutations are introduced as the DNA is copied, launching the cell on the pathway to self-destruction.

If I may be permitted a homely analogy, throughout this chapter we have been wondering how a car could be put together step by step. We have concentrated mostly on getting the mechanical parts together and have not concerned ourselves with whether the oil was the right grade or whether the gasoline had been sufficiently refined. Nonetheless these other parts are also critical and require an intelligent design theorist's attention.

The final point I wish to mention about DNA replication brings up not only scientific problems that confront design theorists but also philosophical problems. Many viruses take over the cell's replication machinery when they invade and turn it to replicating viral DNA exclusively. However, viral replication frequently differs in a number of details from cellular replication. Let us look at just one of them.

Cellular DNA replication has to be primed by the prying apart of the DNA strands and the synthesis of a short piece of RNA, to which DNA is then attached. DNA synthesis cannot be started de novo. In adenoviruses (which cause cancer in certain animals), however, a piece of RNA does not have to be made, but DNA synthesis still must be primed. The priming is done by a protein that is covalently attached to each 5¢end of each viral strand (Kornberg and Baker 1992, 303-5). To the protein is covalently attached a cytidine. The cytidine attached to the protein acts as the primer for the synthesis of the complementary strand.

A question that looms large over design theory is this: Could this variation on the cellular replication mechanism have come about step by step, in a Darwinian fashion? And could other viral replication mechanisms, which differ from cellular mechanisms and from that of adenovirus, have come about in a Darwinian fashion? The conundrum is this: either the replication mechanisms could have come about at random, and thus there is a fair amount of plasticity in the replication process; or else the viral replication mechanisms were designed, and the philosophical problem of evil raises its head. Understanding the development of viral replication mechanisms may have large implications not only for science but for philosophy as well.

I should emphasize that design theorists have an absolutely clear field in all the areas of DNA replication that I have discussed. No one has ever published a paper in the professional science literature that explains in a detailed fashion how DNA replication in toto or any of its parts might have been produced in a Darwinian, step-by-step fashion. If you search the electronic databases for papers that have the words *evolution* and *replication* in their title, you come up completely empty. In 1992 Arthur Kornberg published the second edition of his well-known text, entitled *DNA Replication*. In the six thousand entries in the index to the text, there is only one to evolution. The referenced section talks mostly about origin-of-life issues, which are riddled with difficulties and in any event cannot explain the development of replication. Thus this area is wide open for analysis by intelligent design theory.

## The Job of Science

Since many readers do not enjoy lengthy articles about the details of biochemical systems, why have I gone on and on about DNA replication? I think my delving into details is necessary to remind us that the job of science is a difficult one and does not come to a standstill when we discover that some aspects of life were designed. The job of science is to describe, as closely as it can, the way the physical world works and, to the extent it can, the way it came to be. This cannot be shrugged off. As I have tried to show, DNA replication is an enormously complex process, but it can be broken down into conceptually and physically discrete subparts. Before we investigate, it may be the case that all of the subparts were explicitly designed, or that some parts were designed and others arose by natural mechanisms, or that all of the parts arose by natural mechanisms. It is the job of science to determine which of these possibilities is the correct one. The natural history of the development of life is an important question, and what we garner from that history may aid us in coping with present-day problems in science.

Design theorists have a more difficult job than do Darwinists. Most Darwinists realize that natural selection explains some things but not all things. Some biological features they ascribe simply to drift or accident. Is a certain enzyme present in some species and absent in others because of selection or because of accident? Darwinists have been known to have long and heated battles over such questions.

We face a more complex situation. William Dembski has written that in order to come to a conclusion of design, we must first rule out as explanations chance and law. Chance is of course chance, but law in this context we can see as Darwinian evolution. Although we conclude that some features of the cell have been designed, many may have arisen gradually through mutation or natural selection. Only if we rule out chance and law can we move on to conclude that a feature was designed.

So what difference does intelligent design theory make to the way we practice science? I believe it is this: a scientist no longer has to go to enormous lengths to shoehorn complex, interactive systems into a naturalistic scenario. When experiment and calculation reasonably exclude chance and law, then we should conclude, without going through metaphysical paroxysms, that a feature was designed. We should remain open to the possibility that further analysis will show our conclusion was wrong, but we should not be timid about reaching a conclusion of design and building on it.

## References

Alberts, B., D. Bray, J. Lewis, M. Raff, K. Roberts, and J. D. Warson. 1994. *Molecular biology of the cell.* 3rd ed. New York: Garland.

Behe, M. 1996. *Darwin's black box: The biochemical challenge to evolution.* New York: Free Press.

Kornberg, A., and T. A. Baker. 1992. *DNA replication.* 2nd ed. New York: Freeman.

Lohman, T. M., and M. E. Ferrari. 1994. *Eschericia coli* single-stranded DNA-binding protein: Multiple DNA-binding modes and cooperativities. *Annual Review of Biochemistry* 63:527-70.

Lohman, T. M., and K. P. Bjornson. 1996. Mechanisms of helicase-catalyzed DNA unwinding. *Annual Review of Biochemistry* 65:169-214.

Marians, K. J. 1992. Prokaryotic DNA replication. *Annual Review of Biochemistry* 61:673-719.

Shapiro, L. 1995. The bacterial flagellum: From genetic network to complex architecture. *Cell* 80:525-27.

Voet, D. and J. G. Voet. 1995. *Biochemistry.* 2nd ed. New York: Wiley.

Wang, J. C. 1996. DNA topoisomerases. *Annual Review of Biochemistry* 65:635-92.

# 8

# Basic Types of Life

## *Evidence for Design from Taxonomy?*

## SIEGFRIED SCHERER

*T*HE DIVERGING NUMBERS OF SPECIES ESTIMATED BY DIFFERENT authors are in part due to some uncertainty of species definitions. Depending on the way of counting, a dozen or more different species definitions exist. Häuser summarizes fifteen definitions that have been proposed between 1966 and 1985 (Häuser 1987). All definitions fall into one of four basic groups: ecospecies, chronospecies, morphospecies and genospecies. Genetic species concepts are most popular currently among biologists. The idea that gene flow is an important argument for defining species has been expressed by early biologists. In Mayr's definition, "Species are groups of actually or potentially interbreeding natural populations which are reproductively isolated from other such groups" (Mayr 1940). Other biologists contributed to the development of the biospecies concept as well (e.g., Dobzhansky, Huxley, Stresemann, Wright, and others; for references see Mayr 1963, 1982; Willmann 1985).

Thus no discussion of the problem of definition of species and higher taxonomic ranks in general will be given. The reader is referred to Scherer (1993a) in order to get a short introduction into this subject. Instead a definition of basic types, a higher taxonomic rank than that of species and genus, will be proposed. It is claimed that this category can be defined and verified rather objectively and is suitable to serve as a framework for the interpretation of a variety of biological data.

This chapter has not been written in order to present a solution to the species problem. For reasons that are to be discussed, a final solution probably does not exist. Although no valid species definition exists, there is no doubt that speciation processes occur in nature and in specifically designed experiments (e.g., Coyne 1992; Ereshefsky 1992; Mayr 1963).

**Interspecific Hybridization**
One aspect of similarity can be measured precisely these days by sequencing genes. But the information provided by gene sequences must be interpreted and may yield different classifications for different genes. More important, the most interesting differences between organisms are found in the genetic program package that leads to the formation of morphogenetic pattern during ontogeny. But this program cannot be localized in sequences of structural genes. It is also unlikely that mere sequences of various regulatory genes as such provide the basis needed in order to understand morphogenesis of an organism. It would seem that a complex interaction of a variety of regulatory genes with numerous structural genes, intimately bound to a specifically structured three-dimensional space of the zygote, must be known in order to describe pattern formation during ontogeny. However, we are very far from understanding such processes and therefore cannot use them for classification. But it is obvious that successful hybridization is a clear indication that the species from which the germ cells are derived are closely related. Can this important piece of information be used for classification?

Clausen, Keck and Hiesey proposed the taxonomic categories of ecospecies, coenospecies and comparium (Clausen 1951; Clausen, Keck and Hiesey 1939). An ecospecies has its own genetic system sufficiently differentiated and distinct from the genetic systems of other ecospecies to produce only hybrids with reduced fertility or viability. The ecospecies often corresponds to the species rank in common classifications. A coenospecies comprises ecospecies displaying the ability for restricted interchange of genes in spite of partial hybrid sterility. The comparium comprises coenospecies that are capable of producing sterile interspecific hybrids.

There have been a number of approaches using intergeneric hybridization as an argument to lump species from different genera into one genus (Ansell 1971; Buettner-Janusch 1966; Simpson 1961; Stains 1967; Stebbins 1956). Van Gelder suggested that "species in one genus should not be capable of breeding with species in other genera" (Van Gelder 1977). In other words, if interspecific hybrids are observed (irrespective of whether they are fertile or sterile), the parental species should be included in one genus. Consequently Van Gelder lumped 42 mammalian genera and created

17 genera instead; Stebbins (1956) suggested that it might be appropriate to merge 20 genera of Triticeae into a single genus. Probably genus numbers would be reduced further if systematic cross-fertilization experiments were undertaken. The genus definition of Van Gelder corresponds closely to the comparium of Clausen, Keck and Hiesey (1939). Van Gelder (1977) even wrote: "It seems to me that if the chromosomes of two taxa are compatible enough to develop a foetus to term, then the parents would seem to be more closely related than generic separation would suggest."

More recently Dubois (1988) also suggested using interspecific hybridization as a taxonomic criterion. He proposed that "whenever two species can give viable adult hybrids, they should be included in the same genus; if other valid criteria had led them previously to be placed into different genera, these must be merged." This approach corresponds closely to Van Gelder (1977). However, for the following reasons such a definition of a genus is probably not useful. First, the information storage capacity of biosystematic classifications is severely reduced since a variety of morphologically extremely different as well as highly similar species would be lumped together in one genus, comprising a large number of species. For instance, geese, swans and ducks would be members of the same genus (Scherer and Hilsberg 1982). Overall similarity, which is the basis for most classifications, even at the species level, would be excluded as a criterion. This is highly undesirable for the practical taxonomist. Second, it would dramatically change the nomenclature currently in use and therefore cause tremendous confusion. These two consequences must result in the rejection of such a genus definition by most taxonomists.

## The Basic Type Criterion
### *Definition of basic types*
A taxonomic rank termed "basic type" or "baramin," suggested by Frank L. Marsh (1941, 1976), comprises all individuals that are able to hybridize and therefore appears to be related to the genus definition of Clausen, Van Gelder and Dubois. Building on Clausen's, Marsh's, Van Gelder's and Dubois's work, it is submitted that hydridization data be used by the following primary membership criterion:

1. Two individuals belong to the same basic type if they are able to hybridize.

A secondary membership criterion greatly facilitates basic type recognition:

2. Two individuals belong to the same basic type if they have hybridized with the same third organism.

For practical reasons one may substitute the term *individual* for the term *species*, although in a strict sense only individuals are able to hybridize. Note that it is considered to be important neither whether hybridization occurs in nature or in captivity, nor if it is induced by artificial insemination or artificial pollination. Note further that fertility or sterility of the hybrid is not used as a criterion of relatedness, since sterility can be caused by rather minor genetic changes. In contrast, if hybridization is possible, morphogenetic programs of the parents obviously are highly similar, warranting the inclusion in one basic type.

In order to indicate basic types (bt) without confusing currently accepted taxonomic nomenclature, they will be labeled by adding the prefix *bt* to the acknowledged Latin name of the group.

### Advantages of the basic type definition

The basic type definition has several advantages. First, the criterion provides a category whose members share the same morphogenetic pattern. This has consequences for phylogenetic interpretations concerning such groups.

Second, a wealth of interspecific hybridization data already are available which have rarely been used in classification.

Third, if data are missing, one may introduce the experimental approach of artificial insemination or artificial pollination (Clausen, Keck, and Hiesey 1939). Therefore this criterion is a taxonomic category that is subject to empirical validation.

Fourth, this approach allows one to define the basic type taxon in much the same way as the biospecies. One of the advantages of the biological species taxon is that it can be defined without any reference to other species. Definitions of higher taxa, in contrast, "can only be relative to those of other categories, specifying relative ranks in the hierarchy and set relationships to taxa" (Simpson 1961). This limit can be overcome by the classification criterion suggested here (compare Dubois 1988).

Fifth, Schaefer (1976) stated correctly that until now it was impossible to answer the question of how a taxonomic category in one group (for instance, birds) can be made equivalent to the same category of another group (for instance, mammals or angiosperms). The criterion suggested here provides a taxonomic rank above the species level that is directly comparable within all kinds of sexually reproducing organisms.

Sixth, the criterion proposed leaves plenty of room for using morphological similarity in defining genera. Thus the information storage and retrieval capacity of such a classification scheme (i.e., species—genus—basic type) remains high.

Seventh, application of this criterion does not cause major changes in nomenclature since the binominal names remain unchanged.

### Problems of the basic type definition

The basic type criterion is not the ultimate solution of taxonomy. Some potential problems restrict the application of this taxonomic rank. Four of these problems are mentioned shortly. Further discussion can be found in Scherer 1993a.

First, classification can be performed only with sexually reproducing organisms.

Second, although there is a considerable data base on hybrids, for a variety of groups no hybrids are known. It is not always easy, for practical and conservational reasons, to obtain the data needed.

Third, in some cases hybridization fails when members of the same genus or even races of the same species are tested. Successful hybridization can be prevented by very small genetic changes. In this case one has to refer to similarity criteria by asking whether the individuals under discussion are sufficiently similar to members of a basic type that are known to be involved in hybridization. If such hybridization data are also missing, an annotation to a specific basic type is possible only by referring to taxonomic rankings currently in use. In such cases the development of additional membership criteria is necessary (Wise 1992).

Fourth, the preceding definition may eventually turn out to be not entirely objective: there exist grades in reproductive isolation at the species level, and these grades exist as well at the basic type level. Is the criterion of hybridization met if, for instance, a mammalian hybrid fetus dies before birth? I have therefore proposed a third membership criterion for basic types, which is a further development of Marsh's criterion (Marsh 1976):

3. Two individuals belong to the same basic type if embryogenesis of a hybrid continues beyond the maternal phase, including subsequent co-ordinated expression of both maternal and paternal morphogenetic genes.

Unfortunately almost no comparative data are known on gene expression during early embryogenesis of closely and only distantly related species, including the respective zygotes. Closer investigation of transcription during early embryogenesis in such cases eventually might reveal that some functional gene complexes are basic type specific while others are not. Clearly the development of a workable tertiary membership criterion is at best in its initial stages.

## Application of Basic Type Taxonomy

An overview on the taxonomic ranks of basic types is described in Scherer (1993a). The basic type rank depends on how one arranges the systematics of a particular group. For instance, according to Wolters (1983), *bt*Anatidae is at the family level but could also be assigned to the subfamily level (Johnsgard 1978; Scherer 1993b). Generally it appears that basic type rank is comparable with the subfamily or family level in Aves or Mammalia while it may range between tribe and family rank within plants. However, based only on a small number of 14 basic types described so far, no final statement is possible. Far more groups have to be studied, especially from other vertebrate classes and invertebrates and from other plant phyla.

Data on interspecific hybridization differ widely for the plant and animal groups investigated. For instance, within *bt*Equidae (1 genus, 6 species), from a total of 15 hybrids theoretically possible, 14 actually have been reported (Stein-Kadenbach 1993). In contrast, within the *bt*?Accipitrinae/Buteoninae (29 genera, approximately 150 species), only 7, including 2 intergeneric hybrids (between *Accipiter* and *Buteo* and between *Buteo* and *Parabuteo*) are known. Interestingly, one of the intergeneric hybrids connects the two subfamilies. It is therefore obvious that this basic type cannot yet be defined on the basis of hybridization (Zimbelmann 1993). Although the number of intergeneric hybrids actually found will depend on the number of genera within a basic type, other parameters also are responsible for such vastly different sets of data. For instance, within *bt*Anatidae (148 species, 40 genera), which is of a similar size to the *bt*?Accipitrinae/Buteoninae, a total of more than 300 intergeneric hybrids have been observed. This difference obviously is due to the fact that anatids can be bred easily in captivity while birds of prey can be bred only with difficulty. If birds of prey propagate in captivity, breeders usually try to avoid any hybridization for reasons of species conservation.

From this discussion an important bias of basic type classification emerges. It is restricted to groups of organisms that not only are very well known but also were kept in captivity or cultivation for some reason or the other. However, the perspective of planned hybridization, for instance by using artificial insemination or artificial pollination, should be considered carefully. First, induced by the rapid development of in vitro fertilization, the production of animal embryos gets easier. Second, comparatively few hybrids are necessary in order to discern a basic type. It is a general observation that species of the same genus with few exceptions will hybridize in captivity (by the way, this fact may shed some light on the feeling of taxonomists enabling them to assign species to a genus). Therefore intergeneric hybrids are far more important to study than interspecific hybrids, and experiments should be directed mainly to intergeneric crosses. Furthermore, it is not necessary that each intergeneric hybrid that is theoretically possible actually be produced. The basic type definition maintains that two species are assigned to the same basic type if they are connected indirectly by hybridization. For instance, consider *bt*Cercopithecidae (9 genera, which gives 36 different intergeneric combinations). Only 9 combinations actually have been reported (Hartwig-Scherer 1993), but these connect 8 of 9 genera, which delimits *bt*Cercopithecidae quite clearly. As a minimum, in order to delimit a basic type, one would need to produce only ($n$-1) hybrids, where $n$ is the number of genera. This task would appear to be quite feasible, at least when one is dealing with plants.

### Related Interpretations
*Polyphyletic versus monophyletic origin of basic types*
Where do basic types come from? Obviously the current explanation within the realm of biology is evolution: All basic types are thought to share a common ancestor that is more primitive than its descendants. Accordingly specific biological data available should fit mechanistic evolutionary models and should demonstrate transitions between fossil groups of forms that may be considered as basic types.

Alternatively basic types might have originated by design. If this assumption shall be taken seriously, biological data must make sense when interpreted within such an idea. Furthermore, predictions must be derivable from such a hypothesis, which can be tested by further experimental work.

Basic type biology and evolutionary biology can be described using the well-known terminology of polyphyletic versus monophyletic origin of life. Basic type biology implies a polyphyletic origin in the sense that each basic type originated, phylogenetically, independent from other basic types.

*Basic type biology provides a novel definition for microevolution and macroevolution*
Processes such as mutability in its broadest sense, variability, selection and isolation, as well as speciation (irrespective of the species definition used), are part of the biological database available. Generally these concepts are based on sound empirical evidence, leaving little room for controversial discussion. Evolutionary processes that are derived from empirical analysis are designated microevolution. The fact of microevolution must be accommodated for in all models dealing with the origin of life.

The term *macroevolution* does not have a clear-cut definition. For instance, Hansen and Martins (1996) try to describe mathematically how microevolutionary processes translate into macroevolutionary pattern. However, they do not even try to define macroevolution. Generally macroevolution is often associated either with the evolutionary acquisition of novel functional structures or with the evolution of more or less exactly defined higher taxonomic ranks such as classes and phyla. I submit that basic type biology helps to define microevolution and macroevolution more clearly, providing a test for the macroevolution concept.

*Microevolution: Variation within basic types.* Based on only about 14 basic types that have been investigated in some detail (Scherer 1993c), it appears that the hybridization criteria would place the basic type in taxonomic ranks that already have been recognized by traditional taxonomy. Generally it is acknowledged that taxonomical hypotheses below the family level are most controversial. Furthermore, speciation is a known phenomenon. Since the genomes of the species within a basic type must be very similar in terms of the regulation of morphogenetic processes, we tentatively suggest that processes of variation observed within basic types may be termed microevolution.

*Macroevolution: Descent of different basic types from a common ancestor.* Recognition of groups that I term basic types has always has been accompanied by pointing out that their members share clear synapomorphies and that they are clearly separated from other closely related groups. This holds for basic types at family rank as well as for those associated with tribe or genus rank. In other words, there seem to be substantial gaps between basic types when extant organisms are compared.

I submit that the term *macroevolution* be used to describe the formation of different basic types descending from a common ancestor. In contrast I suggest using the term *microevolution* for processes leading to the formation of species and genera within a basic type. It is postulated that species belonging to the same basic type form a monophyletic group.

*Macroevolution at the molecular level.* It is a major prediction of basic type biology that no molecular evolutionary mechanisms bridging the gaps between basic types will be found. Since we do not know enough on the morphogenetic differences between different basic types of animals and plants, this prediction cannot be tested using these organisms. However, at the level of bacteria, a little more is known. I have discussed possible delineations of microevolution versus macroevolution at the molecular level using bacteria as an example (Junker and Scherer 1992; Scherer 1983, 1984, 1995, 1996), but this discussion is outside the scope of this chapter. My conclusion is that no molecular mechanisms accountable for macroevolutionary processes are known.

### Polyvalent ancestral populations?

I have stated that basic type biology and evolutionary biology must accommodate all biological processes that can be demonstrated empirically (i.e., all microevolutionary processes). Both views hence will postulate that the species belonging to a single basic type have been derived from an ancestral population. However, there are major differences concerning the underlying mechanisms. Evolutionary biology usually assumes that this ancestral population was more primitive than the species that descended from it. In other words, the direction of evolution is from a more primitive state toward a more complex state. This chapter will not deal with mechanisms of speciation but rather with the distribution of characters throughout the members of a basic type, perhaps allowing some inference on the nature of the supposed ancestral population quite different from the evolutionary view.

When the results of the different basic types analyzed in Scherer (1993) are reviewed, some common features emerge that are found across the different groups of animals and plants. For this purpose we need to change levels and get back to the realm of the real biology.

Hybrids of two species often have morphological or behavioral features not found in their parents. Sometimes these characters were previously unknown, but quite regularly they turn out to be similar to a third species of the same basic type. For instance, this has been demonstrated within *bt*Anatidae (Scherer 1993b; Scherer and Hilsberg 1982), including both interspecific and intergeneric hybrids. As an extreme, it has been reported repeatedly that a hybrid between the two European species *Aythya fuligula* and *A. ferina* was indistinguishable from *A. affinis*, a third species from North America. Further examples were reported for *bt*Equidae (Stein-Kadenbach 1993), *bt*Estrildidae (Fehrer 1993) or *bt*Geeae (Junker 1993b). This means that the species involved in hybridization harbor an unrecognized potential of variability that is expressed upon hybridization. This potential of variation seems to be common to different species of the same basic type. A related observation concerns species within basic types that are impossible to classify. In case of *bt*Anatidae, these species are termed aberrant types, displaying a mosaic of characters usually found in quite different tribes of the anatids. Kutzelnigg (1993) mentions monotypic genera within *bt*Maloideae: for instance, the monotypic genus *Pseudocydonia* is similar to *Cydonia* but also to *Chaenomeles* and *Pyrus*. Hence it is impossible to assign this genus to either one of these genera. A large number of such problematic species or genera are known.

The same phenomenon has also been described for *Nyctereutes* (raccoon dog, *bt*Canidae). The basic type Canidae comprises three major groups: the wolflike canids, the South American canids and the *Vulpes*-like canids. The raccoon dog is similar to the wolflike canids when its limb morphology is considered. According to its masticatory characteristics, this animal groups toward the South American canids while the overall similarity of single-copy DNA indicates that it is most closely related to the foxlike canids (Crompton 1993).

There are two potential explanations for such observations. It may be speculated that this be explained by the common ancestor's already possessing a potential of variation (plesiomorphy). This does not mean that all characters of extant species were expressed in the ancestral population but that the genetic potential for such variation was hidden in the ancestral polyvalent gene pool. A hidden potential for variation suddenly becomes visible when different species or even races are hybridized; obviously the genetic balance of a species that results in a continuous expression of species-specific features becomes disturbed upon hybridization, revealing an astonishing potential of variability. Another interpretation would be convergence (homoplasy). In that case selective forces should exist that account for an independent origin of similar characters. Often such selective forces are unknown, which does not necessarily mean that they do not exist.

It is found throughout the basic types described so far (Scherer 1993c) that it seems impossible to construct a phylogenetic tree of all members of a particular basic type without numerous contradictions. Different characters yield different phylogenetic trees; for instance, when the six species of *bt*Equidae are considered (Stein-Kadenbach 1993). This is also true for a variety of characters from other basic types; for example, plumage pattern of anatids (Scherer 1993b) or carduelids (Fehrer 1993), the supposedly "highly reticulate evolution" within Triticeae (Junker 1993a) or a variety of characters within *bt*Maloideae (Kutzelnigg 1993). In the latter basic type, primitive characters are found regularly together with advanced characters (heterobathmy). However, there is no objective way to know which character is ancestral and which one is derived. Any such decisions are usually disputed. Characters therefore seem to form a network rather than a tree when species of a basic type are compared.

Again there are two potential explanations: plesiomorphy and homoplasy. Homoplasy requires mechanisms that evolve the same character independently. Such mechanisms (i.e., selective pressures) are yet to be demonstrated in each specific case. Application of the concept of plesiomorphy to such an extent that would explain the very common mosaic pattern of characters within basic types would lead to the idea of an ancestral population with an extremely high degree of polyallelism and hence with a large potential of variability. The evolution of different species from complex ancestors would scatter different characters and character combinations throughout the descendant species, the process being influenced by, for example, size of the descendant populations, migration pattern of populations, chance effects and the action of selective forces on random character combinations. Such a process might explain the network of characters without involving unknown selective pressures.

Furthermore, it is quite well known that speciation processes lead to specialization, which means that the descendant population has lost genetic potential when compared with the ancestral population. Speciation itself would therefore appear to support the concept of ancestral populations with a large hidden potential of variation. Adler (1993) pointed out that it is possible to interpret some characters of *bt*Funariaceae in terms of a morphologically complex ancestor. The five genera of this basic type are assumed to be reduced in morphological complexity to various degrees.

### Interpretation of the fossil record

In the few cases investigated, these gaps seem also to be present in the fossil record of those groups—for instance, for *bt*Anatidae, birds of prey, or *bt*Cercopithecidae. Is it possible that generally no fossil links can be demonstrated that would unequivocally connect two clearly delineated basic types? However, paleontological data have yet to be related to basic type taxonomy.

Basic type biology predicts that major discontinuities between basic types will continue to emerge at different levels of comparative biology.

## Evidence for Design?

What is evidence for design? I will not enter the complicated philosophical discussion concerning the design argument. I will stay at the level of biological data and continue to discuss them within different hypotheses. Walter ReMine (1993) suggested that biological data may be understood with respect to the message a hypothetical designer wanted to transmit via life. He submitted that the system of life was constructed to make it clear that life originated from a single source. The hypothesis that all life forms come from a single source is convincingly demonstrated by the overall similarity of life at all biological levels. Evolutionary biology uses these data to support a monophyletic history of life. Similarity, however, may likewise be used as an argument in favor of a single designer. It is not possible, using empirical arguments, to decide between these two worldviews. Overall similarity of life forms as such can therefore not be used as a final evidence for design or for evolution but can be interpreted within both frameworks. I will not deal with this question in this chapter.

Much more provocative is the idea of ReMine that the very peculiar pattern of diversity underlying life was designed to send the message that it did not result from a naturalistic process.

How could basic type biology contribute to the discussion that a message is transmitted by organisms?

### Polyvalent ancestors?

If the species and genera constituting a basic type descended from a polyvalent ancestral population, the existence of such ancestral populations is very unexpected and their origin difficult to explain within an evolutionary framework. A polyvalent (complex) ancestral population would, however, fit into a theory of design.

### Gaps between basic types

If it can be demonstrated that the existence of gaps between basic types is a general feature of extant life forms, such a feature of life would seem to be quite unexpected and difficult to explain within an evolutionary framework. It would, however, fit into a theory of design. The fossil record has to be analyzed accordingly.

### Evolution of features of ancestral population of basic types

For ancestral populations of basic types to originate, the evolution of biochemical pathways, cellular structures and morphogenetic programs (i.e., macroevolution) must have happened. It is my assertion that no evolutionary mechanisms have been found so far that could have led to the evolution of such traits. It is a prediction of a theory of design that such mechanisms will not be found in the future.

### Convergent characters between basic types

Between basic types there are not only differences but also a very peculiar pattern of similarity (conflicting characters) that is not easily predicted by evolutionary theory. This very common pattern of conflicting characters is usually interpreted to be due to convergent evolution. It is one of the most severe problems that renders the construction of unequivocal phylogenetic trees very difficult. Numerous examples could be given. Conflicting character distribution superimposes a networklike similarity over the nested-hierarchy similarity (treelike pattern) that is predicted by evolutionary theory.

I will mention one case of convergence at the molecular level; that is the existence of different holin/lysin proteins in bacteriophage. I pick this example because we work with this system in my laboratory. Bacteriophage are viruses that infect bacteria. Classification of bacteriophage as well as that of their hosts is extremely difficult and hence controversial. I will not discuss it in this chapter. The holin/lysin system comprises two functional proteins. One is an endolysin that is capable of cleaving the cell wall of bacteria after completion of the infection cycle. In order to get to its target, the endolysin must be secreted via the cytoplasmic membrane to the periplasmic space. However, with the exception of a *Bacillus cereus* phage (Loessner et al. 1997) no signal sequences have been found in endolysin genes. Endolysins are transferred by means of holins, proteins that form pores (holes) in the cytoplasmic membrane.

Holin/endolysin systems have been described for a wide array of grampositive and gramnegative bacteria such as *Escherichia coli* (Young et al. 1979), *Bacillus subtilis* (Steiner, Lubitz, and Bläsi 1993), *Lactobacillus gasseri* (Henrich, Binihofer, and Bläsi 1995), *Listeria monocytogenes* (Loessner, Wendlinger, and Scherer 1995), *Listeria innocua* (Zink, Loessner, and Scherer 1995) or *Staphylococcus aureus* (Loessner et al. 1998a). A total of 25 phage holins have been sequenced which are thought to form 11 or more unrelated gene families that share the functional and structural characteristics of holins (Young and Bläsi 1995). This holin/lysin system has been described recently to be "simple, but remarkably sophisticated" (Bläsi and Young 1996).

The important observation is that sequences of these holin families are unrelated; that is, no extensive sequence homology has been found. Evolutionary theory must propose that this is the result of multiple convergent evolution. Such a scenario would explain the observation just in case mechanistic processes can be demonstrated that lead to similar structures when evolution started from different ancestral sequences. Such processes have not been found experimentally and have not been modeled theoretically. Even the evolution of a single holin sequence from a nonholin sequence is a mystery.

### Odd molecular features of life
What is an odd feature of life? A provocative definition would be that this is a feature that cannot be predicted by and is not understandable within evolutionary theory. In other words, one may call it a signal that transmits the message that there was a designer at work.

The universal genetic code has been used as a major, very convincing argument for the monophyletic origin of life. The argument reads as follows: Once the genetic code has been established, each evolutionary diversion from that code would have changed the sequence of all proteins encoded by the genome, carrying the triplet that has been changed. However, an increasing number of slightly deviating genetic codes has been reported (Osawa et al. 1992) not only in mitochondria but also in the nucleus from different organisms. According to evolutionary theory, these different codes must have originated from the primary code independently. Again, it cannot be predicted through evolutionary theory why this should have happened or, more important, how this could have happened even once, not to speak from independent lines of origin.

Finally I would like to mention another odd feature that has been reported for different organisms. In a few cases, genes overlapping in different reading frames were reported. A recent example has been described for hemolysins coded for within the ribosomal RNA of *Entamoeba histolytica* (Aslög et al. 1994). We have discovered another example for a holin protein that is coded for out of frame by an endolysin sequence of this *Staphylococcus* phage (Loessner et al. 1998b). It was suggested by evolutionists that a selection pressure due to space limitation on plasmids and phage genomes have led to the evolution of these structures. However, most bacteriophage having genomes of a similar size do not show this features, surviving as well as the phage carrying the overlapping genes. Second, the modeling of an evolutionary origin of completely overlapping genes through a series of selectable intermediates seems to be exceedingly difficult and has not yet been reported.

**Conclusion**

Basic type classification applies to both animals and plants. This classification could comprise three main lower categories: the biospecies concept as a means to describe biodynamical processes, that is, speciation (comprising individuals genetically related through participation in the same gene pool); the genus category as a means to describe overall similarity (comprising morphologically related forms); and the basic type category as a means to describe monophyletic though potentially heterogeneous groups (comprising morphogenetically related forms).

The procedure recommended for delineating a basic type may be summarized as follows:

1. Collect all interspecific hybrids available within a particular group of organisms and produce a crossbreeding matrix (or polygon), placing special emphasis on intergeneric hybrids. Check if any reliable report indicates that different groups (e.g., subfamilies or tribes) are connected by hybridization.

2. Determine the overall range of variance that is indicated by those members of the group that are connected through hybridization. Then check whether other species that are not involved in hybridization would fall within the range of that variance. Some of the membership criteria given by Wise (1992) may be used accordingly. On the basis of these data, species can be assigned tentatively to a basic type.

3. Test such tentative assignments by artificial hybridization.

It is now necessary to test the basic type concept with as many animal and plant groups as possible. The results available so far (Scherer 1993c) seem to be encouraging. Critical test cases will be provided by groups that comprise a number of closely related families or subfamilies, such as Passeriformes. However, further work could also demonstrate that the basic type criterion submitted here will not hold up when it is put to test in daily classification work of practicing taxonomists.

Basic type biology or something equivalent to this approach will be a prerequisite to develop a theory of design that also accommodates the endless number of observations of microevolutionary processes. If basic type biology turns out to withstand the test of time, it will provide a framework for interpreting a variety of biological observations such as gaps between basic types, character distribution between the species within a basic type, character distribution between species of different basic types and the interpretation of seemingly odd features of life.

## References

Adler, M. 1993. Merkmalsausbildung und Hybridisierung bei Funariaceen (Bryophyta, Musci). In *Typen des Lebens,* ed. S. Scherer, 67-70. Neuhausen: Hänssler Verlag.

Ansell, W. F. H. 1971. Artiodactyla. In *The mammals of Africa: An identification manual,* ed. J. Meester and H. W. Setzer, 1-84. Washington, D.C.: Smithsonian Institution Press.

Aslög, J., F. Gillin, U. Kagardt, and P. Hagblom. 1994. Coding of hemolysins within the ribosomal RNA repeat on a plasmid in *Entamoeba histolytica. Science* 263:1440-43.

Bläsi, U., and R. Young. 1996. Two beginnings for a single purpose: The dual-start holins in the regulation of phage lysis. *Molecular Microbiology* 21:675-82.

Buettner-Janusch, J. 1966. A problem in evolutionary systematics: Nomenclature and classification of baboons, genus *Papio. Folia Primatologica* 4:288-308.

Clausen, J. 1951. *Stages in the evolution of plant species.* Ithaca, N.Y.: Cornell University Press.

Clausen, J., D. D. Keck, and W. M. Hiesey. 1939. The concept of species based on experiment. *American Journal of Botany* 28:103-6.

Coyne, J. A. 1992. Genetics and speciation. *Nature* 355:511-15.

Crompton, N. 1993. A review of selected features of the family Canidae with reference to its fundamental taxonomic status. In *Typen des Lebens,* ed. S. Scherer, 217-24. Neuhausen: Hänssler-Verlag.

Dubois, A. 1988. The genus in zoology: A contribution to the theory of evolutionary systematics. *Mem. Mus. Natn. Hist. Paris* (a) 140:1-124.

Ereshefsky, M., ed. 1992. *The units of selection: Essays on the nature of species.* Cambridge, Mass.: MIT Press.

Fehrer, J. 1993. Interspecies-Kreuzungen bei cardueliden Finken und Prachtfinken. In *Typen des Lebens,* ed. S. Scherer, 197-215. Neuhausen: Hänssler-Verlag.

Hansen, T. F., and E. P. Martins. 1996. Translating between microevolutionary process and macroevolutionary patterns: The correlation structure of interspecific data. *Evolution* 50:1404-17.

Hartwig-Scherer, S. 1993. Der Grundtyp der Meerkatzenartigen. In *Typen des Lebens,* ed. S. Scherer, 245-57. Neuhausen: Hänssler-Verlag.

Häuser, C. L. 1987. The debate about the biological species concept—a review. *Zeitschrift für Zoologische Systematik und Evolutionsforschung* 25:241-57.

Henrich, B., B. Binihofer, and U. Bläsi. 1995. Primary structure and functional analysis of the lysis genes of *Lactobacillus gasseri* bacteriophage Phiadh. *Journal of Bacteriology* 177:723-32.

Johnsgard, P. A. 1978. *Ducks, swans and geese of the world.* Lincoln: University of

Nebraska Press.

Junker, R. 1993a. Der Grundtyp der Weizenartigen (Poaceae; Tribus Triticeae). In *Typen des Lebens,* ed. S. Scherer, 75-93. Neuhausen: Hänssler-Verlag.

————. 1993b. Die Gattungen *Geum* (Nelkenwurz), *Coluria* und *Waldsteinia* (Geeae, Rosaceae)—ein Grundtyp? In *Typen des Lebens,* ed. S. Scherer, 95-111. Neuhausen: Hänssler-Verlag.

Junker, R., and S. Scherer. 1998. *Evolution-ein Kritisches Lehrbuck.* Giessen: Weyel.

Kutzelnigg, H. 1993. Verwandtschaftliche Beziehungen zwischen den Gattungen und Arten der Kernobstgewächse (Rosaceae, Unterfamilie Maloideae). In *Typen des Lebens,* ed. S. Scherer, 113-27. Neuhausen: Hänssler-Verlag.

Loessner, M., S. Gäng, and S. Scherer. 1998a. A dual start holin gene is fully embedded out-of-frame in the endolysin gene of *Staphylococcus aureus* phage 187 and can substitute for λS. Submitted for publication.

Loessner, M., S. Gäng, G. Wendlinger, S. Maier, and S. Scherer. 1998b. The two component lysis system of *Staphylococcus aureus* bacteriophage Twort: A large TTG start holin and an associated amidase endolysin. *FEMS Microbiology Letter,* in press.

Loessner, M. J., S. K. Maier, H. Daubek-Puza, G. Wendlinger, and S. Scherer. 1997. Three *Bacillus cereus* bacteriophage endolysins are unrelated but reveal high homology to cell-wall hydrolases from different bacilli. *Journal of Bacteriology* 179:2845-51.

Loessner, M. J., G. Wendlinger, and S. Scherer. 1995. Heterogeneous endolysins in *Listeria monocytogenes* bacteriophages: A new class of enzymes and evidence for conserved holin genes within the siphoviral lysis cassettes. *Molecular Microbiology* 16:1231-41.

Marsh, F. L. 1941. *Fundamental biology.* Lincoln, Neb.: n.p.

————. 1976. *Variation and fixity in nature.* Mountain View, Calif.: Pacific Press.

Mayr, E. 1940. Speciation phenomena in birds. *American Naturalist* 74:249-78.

————. 1963. *Animal species and evolution.* Cambridge, Mass.: Harvard University Press.

————. 1982. *The growth of biological thought: Diversity, evolution and inheritance.* Cambridge, Mass.: Belknap Press of Harvard University Press.

Osawa, S., T. H. Jukes, K. Watanabe, and A. Muto. 1992. Recent evidence for evolution of the genetic code. *Microbiology Review* 56:229-64.

ReMine, W. J. 1993. *The biotic message: Evolution versus message theory.* 1st ed. St. Paul, Minn.: St. Paul Science Publishers.

Schaefer, C. W. 1976. The reality of the higher taxonomic categories. *Zeitschrift für zoologische Systematik und Evolutionsforschung* 14:1-10.

Scherer, S. 1983. Basic functional states in the evolution of light-driven cyclic electron transport. *Journal of Theoretical Biology* 104:289-99.

————. 1984. Transmembrane electron transport and the neutral theory of evolution. *Origins of Life* 14:725-31.

————. 1993a. Basic types of life. In *Typen des Lebens,* ed. S. Scherer, 11-30. Neuhausen: Hänssler-Verlag.

————. 1993b. Der Grundtyp der Entenartigen (Anatidae: Anseriformes): Biologische und paläontologische Streiflichter. In *Typen des Lebens,* ed. S. Scherer, 131-58. Neuhausen: Hänssler-Verlag.

————, ed. 1993c. *Typen des Lebens.* Neuhausen: Hänssler-Verlag.

————. 1995. Höherentwicklung bei Bakterien: Ist ein molekularer Mechanismus bekannt? In *Streitfall Evolution,* ed. J. Mey, R. Schmidt, and S. Zibulla, 85-104. Stuttgart: S. Hirzel Verlag.

————. 1996. *Entstehung der Photosynthese—Grenzen molekularer Evolution bei Bakterien?* 2nd ed. Neuhausen: Hänssler-Verlag.

Scherer, S., and T. Hilsberg. 1982. Hybridisierung und Verwandtschaftsgrade innerhalb der Anatidae: Eine evolutionstheoretische und systematische Betrachtung. *Journal of Ornithology* 123:357-80.

Simpson, G. G. 1961. *Principles of animal taxonomy.* New York: Columbia University Press.

Stains, H. J. 1967. Carnivores and pinnipeds. In *Recent mammals of the world: A synopsis of families,* ed. S. Anderson and J. Knox-Jones, 325-54. New York: Ronald Press.

Stebbins, G. L. 1956. Taxonomy and the evolution of genera, with special reference to the family Gramineae. *Evolution* 10:235-45.

Stein-Kadenbach, H. 1993. Pferde (Equidae): Hybride, Chromosomen und Artbildung. In *Typen des Lebens,* ed. S. Scherer, 225-44. Neuhausen: Hänssler-Verlag.

Steiner, M., W. Lubitz, and U. Bläsi. 1993. The missing link in phage lysis of gram-positive bacteria: Gene 14 of *Bacillus subtilis* phage phi 29 encodes the functional homolog of lambda S protein. *Journal of Bacteriology* 175 (4):1038-42.

Van Gelder, R. G. 1977. Mammalian hybrids and generic limits. *American Museum Novitates* 2635:1-25.

Willmann, R. 1985. *Die Art in Raum und Zeit: Das Artkonzept in der Biologie und Paläontologie.* Berlin: Parey.

Wise, K. P. 1992. Practical baraminology. *CEN Technical Journal* 6:122-37.

Wolters, H. E. 1983. *Die Vögel Europas im System der Vögel.* Baden-Baden: Biotropic.

Young, R., and U. Bläsi. 1995. Holins: Form and function in bacteriophage lysis. *FEMS Microbiology Review* 17:191-205.

Young, R., S. Way, J. Yin, and M. Syvanen. 1979. Transposition mutagenesis of bacteriophage lambda: A new gene affecting cell lysis. *Journal of Molecular Biology* 132:307-22.

Zimbelmann, F. 1993. Grundtypen bei Greifvögeln. In *Typen des Lebens,* ed. S. Scherer, 185-95. Neuhausen: Hänssler-Verlag.

Zink, R., M. J. Loessner, and S. Scherer. 1995. Characterization of cryptic prophages (monocins) in *Listeria* and sequence analysis of a holin/endolysin gene. *Microbiology* 141:2577-84.

# 9

# Apes or Ancestors?

## Interpretations of the Hominid Fossil Record Within Evolutionary & Basic Type Biology

### SIGRID HARTWIG-SCHERER

**H**OMIN(O)ID FOSSILS OF THE THREE GEOLOGICAL PERIODS MIO-cene, Pliocene and Pleistocene are investigated within evolutionary and basic type biology. Both models are based on assumptions that determine the specific hypotheses. These hypotheses are aimed at explaining the observed facts such as geological occurrence, stratigraphical sequence and morphology. The quality of the specific set of explanatory hypothesis depends on the degree the data fit specific predictions.

The Miocene is a period of fossil hominoids with an exciting variety of families, genera and species. The following period, the Pliocene, is characterized by the australopithecine body plan. We know about 8 species depending on whether the researcher belongs to the lumpers or the splitters. The number of known species increased rapidly in the last fifteen years. In addition to the more traditional forms *(Australopithecus africanus, A. robustus, A. boisei, A. afarensis)*, new forms such as *A. aethiopicus, A. anamensis*, a yet-to-be-named species from Chad and the new genus *Ardipithecus ramidus*, which seems to be closely related to *Australopithecus*, have been described. They display humanlike traits (indicative of some kind of bipedal gait) in combination with more apelike (suspensory locomotion) as well as unique characters (facial shape).

The Pleistocene is characterized by the genus *Homo* with 3 to 8 species depending on the taxonomy: either all forms are lumped into *H. habilis, H. erectus, H. sapiens* or they are indicated separately as *H. habilis, H. rudolfensis, H.ergaster, H. erectus*, archaic Middle Pleistocene forms with *H. heidelbergensis, H. steinheimensis, H. sapiens* and finally *H. neanderthalensis*. With the exception of *H. habilis* and *H. rudolfensis*, members of the genus *Homo* display specific human traits, although the combination of species-specific characters is rarely found in extant humans. However, single traits may occur separately in extant population to some extent.

The morphology of these fossil forms as well as their distribution in space and time needs to be incorporated by any model aiming to explain their origin and history.

### Evolutionary Biology: Open Questions

Evolutionary theory assumes that all species originated exclusively by natural evolutionary processes, leading from more primitive to more derived bauplans. The evolutionary approach therefore is determined to identify fossils with potential ancestral-descendant polarities in respect to human ancestry. The following predictions can be derived from this basic assumption:

1. Generally a sequence should be observed of ancestral (i.e., more apelike) forms followed by more humanlike forms.

2. Specifically the identification of a fossil form close to the common ancestor of humans and apes should be possible.

3. The identification of fossils leading not only to humans but also to modern African apes and orangs is expected.

Roughly a number of the facts fit into these predictions: In the fossil record, a sequence is observed of apelike forms in the Miocene; australopithecine forms with a combination of apelike, humanlike and unique traits in the Pliocene; and humans in the Pleistocene. For humans and to some extent for orangs *(Sivapitecus, Lufengpithecus)*, fossil forms can be identified. No ancestors for African apes have been unearthed so far. With respect to human evolution, no general consensus has yet emerged considering the major evolutionary transitions toward modern humans (this is true for the other modern apes, too). Specifically five questions remain to be answered:

1. Which of the Miocene hominoids are potential ancestors for the hominid stock supposedly giving rise to early hominids? Although a number of forms were found in East Africa during Early and Middle Miocene, there are no adequate fossils in Africa at the time the origin of hominids presumably took place. During the late Miocene (10 and 5 million radiometric years before present), only a handful of fossils are available in Africa that could be interpreted to represent ancestors of the Plio-pleistocene australopithecines (Hill 1993). The available fossils, however, are discussed as being primitive

(i.e., nondiagnostic). In addition other features of them do not fit the morphological criteria expected for a hominid ancestry.

2. The evolutionary history of *Pan* and *Gorilla* is obscure. Forms known from Europe such as *Ankarapithecus* or *Ouranopithecus* (alias *Graecopithecus*) superficially display some traits similar to the gorilla, which, however, have been discussed as potentially primitive retentions.

3. Which of the early hominids—*Ardipithecus ramidus, Australopithecus anamensis, A. afarensis, A. africanus* or any other still unidentified early hominid—link Miocene hominoids to the genus *Homo?* The distribution of traits follows a mosaic pattern, rendering it difficult to assess which of the forms could be considered to represent the ancestor of humans. Some display bipedal adaptations in combination with a primitive head *(A. afarensis)*, others a derived cranium with somewhat more apelike limb proportions *(A. africanus)*. A form combining both has yet to be discovered.

4. Is *H. habilis* the first member of the genus *Homo,* linking earlier hominids to the true humans? As will be discussed, *H. habilis* is considered by most workers to be a composite of two or even three taxa *(rudolfensis, habilis, erectus)*. They reveal a similar mosaic pattern of trait distribution as the australopithecines: *rudolfensis* with an australopithecine face, large brain and bipedal adaptations, *habilis* with a more humanlike maxilla, small brain and apelike locomotion. *Homo ergaster* or *erectus* is the first form with human appearance lacking a suitable ancestor.

5. Which of the Pleistocene *Homo* forms (*H. ergaster, H. erectus,* Neanderthals, archaic sapiens, Middle Pleistocene mosaic forms) gave rise to modern humans, and where could this have happened? Again the mosaic combination of features prevents a generally accepted conclusion on the origin of modern humans. However, most workers agree that an archaic sapiens form originated in Africa and spread across the Old World, putting pressure on previous forms such as *H. erectus* in Asia or *erectus*-like forms in Europe as well as the Neanderthals. Whether previous populations were absorbed or became extinct remains to be discussed. New data required readaptation of the models. While it was previously assumed that *H. ergaster* left Africa at 1.9 million radiometric years, at the same time similar forms have been found in Southeast Asia. Not much time is left for migration or to date *ergaster* earlier in Africa, which would make them even more contemporaneous with their supposed precursors. In Israel the sequence of Neanderthals-sapiens as found in Western Europe is disturbed: Neanderthals, with traits somewhat less excessive than in Western Europe forms occurred before the sapiens forms and lived more or less contemporaneously, so to speak "cave to cave" in Skhul and Quafzeh.

In conclusion, some of the evolutionary predictions seem to fit the data.

With respect to other predictions, the fossil record does not (yet?) yield conclusive evidence, and a number of quite fundamental questions are left to be answered. Although new fossils have forced the alteration of some hypotheses, such changes never touch the underlying worldview.

## Basic Type Biology: An Outline

Basic type biology assumes that basic types originated by design. The Old and New World was (re)populated from a single place of origin. A single population of the ancestors of each basic type gave rise to all known extant and extinct species.

The basic type approach focuses on the delineation of basic types using biological and subsequently paleontological data. In a second step, the mode of biogeographic dispersion and speciation of primate and human basic types are investigated. Climatic, geophysical and ecological turnovers with subsequent immigration and emigration activities are generally acknowledged to trigger increased radiations (taxon pulses) and successions of ecological systems. Intrinsic traits such as genetic drift, reproduction rate, migration habits and survival strategies as well as external factors such as climatic conditions, resources, interaction with other members of the habitat and geographic isolation affected the gene pool of each basic type and lead to selection, adaptations, specializations, speciation, radiation, absorption by hybridization, survival or extinction. The following predictions may be derived from basic type biology:

1. Within extant hominoids, it should be possible to delineate distinct basic types by means of hybridization data. These specific basic types are characterized by sets of morphological, ontogenetic and behavioral characters providing supplementary membership criteria (for review see Scherer 1993).

2. By application of these supplementary sets of traits derived from extant basic types, an approximate identification of basic types in the hominoid fossil record should be possible.

3. Taxon pulses should follow the first appearance of members of a basic type in the fossil record, involving specific adaptations into open niches of the then-existing ecosystem.

4. Within a given body plan (which is a specific set of different basic types within the taxonomic category of the order), waves of taxon pulses should be observed in more than one part of the Old World at about the same geological period, followed by the next invading and more successful taxon.

5. Within a given body plan, r-selected pioneers should appear in the fossil record before the k-selected climax forms, which tend to be more specialized and highly adapted.

This chapter will deal with the first and second predictions. The third, fourth and fifth predictions appear to be interesting working hypotheses: Climatic, geological and ecological turnovers with subsequent immigration and emigration activities are generally acknowledged to trigger increased radiations (taxon pulses) and successions of ecological systems. In the woodlands of East African Miocene and Pliocene, the radiations of hominoid basic types are followed by the cercopithecid radiation (colobines and ceropithecines), while during the more arid Pliopleistocene habitats, the australopithecine radiation is followed by the radiation of the human basic type. Only the radiation of the latter will be discussed in some detail in the last section of this chapter.

## Basic Types in Extant Anthropoids

A given set of species belong to a basic type if they are connected directly or indirectly through hybridization. Hybridization data are available only for limited cases. In other cases supplementary membership criteria, such as morphological, behavioral or ontogenetic evidence, have to be used. For fossils, the morphological data base is the only evidence available.

### Identification of basic types based on hybridization

Basic type: Cercopithecinae (Primates: Cercopithecoidea). The superfamily Cercopithecoidea (colobine and cercopithecine monkeys) display a great diversity of species distributed all over the Old World. Although both colobines and cercopithecines are clearly distinguishable on various morphological, behavioral and chromosomal grounds, the taxonomic separation changed repeatedly between the family and the subfamily level. Within the Cercopithecinae the taxonomy is also characterized by various controversies concerning the number and distinction of species, genera and tribes. Taxonomies with more than 10 genera are opposing others that prefer to include all forms within one genus. Both approaches seem justified to some extent. The tendency to split reflects the enormous diversity of this group, while lumping takes into account the comparative unity of this group: eight of the nine genera described and acknowledged in Hill (1966) and Fleagle (1988) form intergeneric hybrids. Both approaches have been reconciled by creating the basic type (BT) Cercopithecinae supported by a great readiness to produce a number of interspecific and intergeneric hybrids both in captivity and in the wild. Species and tribe names of current taxonomies are retained for the description of this BT: it includes two tribes—the Cercopithecini and the Papionini—with 9 genera (Allenopithecus, Cercopithecus, Erythrocebus, Miopithecus, Cercocebus, Papio, Mandrillus, Theropithecus, Macaca) and 50 to 60 species altogether (for review see Hartwig-Scherer 1993b).

The high diversity of the tribe Cercopithecini with a great number of subspecies and possibly new forms may indicate a relatively recent radiation. Speciation within this basic type is still in progress. The existence of stable hybrid belts at the contact zones of the parent species are one indication for microevolution in action.

The species of this basic type are assumed to be derived from a common, yet unknown ancestor. Different cladistic analyses sought to establish a phylogenetic relationship within the Cercopithecinae. In order to explain the considerable proportional differences among the various members of this BT, ontogenetic scaling has been suggested as one mechanism to obtain these differences via relatively minor genetic modifications of growth parameters. Considerable morphological divergence may thus be obtained in relatively short time. The Cercopithinae provide an excellent opportunity to study a number of different mechanisms that may have led to rapid diversification and speciation within a basic type.

*Basic type: Hylobatidae (Primates: Hominoidea).* There exists good evidence for a basic type Hylobatidae: hybridization between both extant genera *Hylobates* and *Symphalangus* have been reported (Chiarelli 1973; Geissmann 1984; Myers and Shafer 1979; Shafer, Myers, and Saltzman 1984; Wolkin and Myers 1980). These hybrids labeled as siabons have been described in more detail by Myers and Shafer (1979) and Shafer, Myers, and Saltzman (1984).

Hylobatids radiated into Asia and became the sovereigns of the Southeast Asian tropical forest. Because of the highly adapted habits with strongly k-selected traits, it is a quite homogenous basic type easily perceived as a unit. Main differences are related to varying body size: *Hylobates* between 6 and 9 kg, *Symphalangus* more than 15kg. Besides this, similar overall growth patterns with specific differences have been reported (Jungers and Cole 1992).

*Basic type: Ponginae (Primates: Hominoidea).* The other Asian ape, *Pongo pygmaeus,* with two (sub)species on Borneo and Sumatra, seems to be the last and also vanishing relic form of the basic type ponginae with potential fossil members. Similar to the hylobatids, it is a highly k-selected and specialized form prone to extinction when the tropical forest is destroyed. This basic type comprises only a single living species.

*Basic type: Homininae (Primates: Hominoidea).* The name of the superfamily hominoidea was derived from some striking similarities of the (great) apes with humans. Despite unsupported claims in boulevard newspapers, however, no data are available for any hybridization between any of the great apes and humans. Ethical barriers prevent any experiments in this direction, thus leaving some unavoidable uncertainty. However, other data sets such as morphology, ontogeny and behavior clearly support a separate basic type Homininae. Despite the striking genetic similarities as far as nucleotide sequence is concerned, the greatly divergent allometric growth patterns of humans and chimps indicate an insurmountable incompatibility (see Hartwig-Scherer 1995). Needless to say, the basic type Homininae comprises but one living species.

### Identification of the basic type Gorillinae based on comparative ontogeny

On the African continent only one hominoid basic type has survived. The inferred basic type comprises the African ape genera *Gorilla* and *Pan* and is named Gorillinae. There is some evidence for possible hybridization among African apes, although discussion persists with respect to evidence of actual hybridization data between the two genera *Pan* and *Gorilla*. Shea and Coolidge (1984) summarize the evidence. Although they could not reach any firm conclusion, they noted that the congruence between gorilla and chimp "is so great that the production of viable hybrids remains a real possibility, although I emphasize that this has never been attempted in captivity nor demonstrated in the wild." Although not directly supported, hybridization is considered possible not only on morphological grounds but especially because of similar growth patterns.

The case of ambiguous hybridization data in African apes emphasizes the need of supplementary membership criteria (cf. Scherer 1993). Traditionally the comparison of morphological traits is used to determine the membership of a species to a given taxon. The problem of morphological traits (i.e., their generality and their polarity) have been discussed in numerous publications giving some model-depending indications how to distinguish primitive from derived traits or traits thought to be basic type specific. The application of basic type biology to fossil forms will have to use such static morphological comparisons.

In addition to this static approach, ontogenetic data may be exploited for additional support. Using hybridization data as final evidence for basic type membership means that the entire morphogenetic programs of two species have to match in order to produce a viable hybrid. Part of the morphogenetic programs are seen in ontogenetic development toward the adult morphology. Therefore comparative ontogeny is suggested to be the second-best membership criterion following hybridization.

Ontogenetic development can be studied by comparing allometric growth pattern of the species under investigation. This may contribute not only to identifying basic types but also to better understanding the origin of new shapes (and new species) within a given basic type. Here as in many other instances, the evolutionary and basic type approach converge because the study of allometric growth may be applied to support phyletic relationships as well as the determination of basic types. New forms are thought to arise by some form of ontogenetic modification (Bonner 1968; de Beer 1958). Closely related forms presumably have more aspects of ontogenetic patterns in common than less closely related forms (Alberch et al. 1979; Bonner 1982; Gould 1977). As size-related changes are supposedly fixed genetically, this is relevant for both phylogenetic considerations and basic type biology.

A review of the literature reveals how and to what respect ontogenetic trajectories may vary among forms of known close relationship (i.e., basic types delineated by hybridization). Hybridization has been assumed to indicate a relatively recent speciation event (Godfrey and Marks 1991) or at least the retention of similar growth programs. Only those cases are evaluated that fit the criterion of genealogical proximity: species that produce vital hybrids; forms that belong to a single breed; genetically transformed forms; the two sexes of a single species.

Within the cercopithecids known to hybridize extensively (Markarjan, Isakov, and Kondakov 1974; Southwick and Southwick 1983; Struhsaker Butynski, and Lwanga 1988), ontogenetic scaling is the predominant factor to acquire different proportions of species as differently sized as talapoin and patas monkey (Shea 1992). Skeletal ontogenies within cercopithecids revealed that the tiny *Miopithecus talapoin* is an ontogenetically scaled-down version of *Cercopithecus cephus* and an allometric consequence of a decrease in overall growth rates and terminal body size. However, not only ontogenetic scaling but also significant transpositions and slight slope differences may occur among closely related species. Cole (1992) found, in addition to ontogenetic scaling, parallel ontogenies in *Cebus apella* and *Cebus albifrons* (see also Jungers and Fleagle 1980). The ontogeny of hylobatid proportions indicates a clear parallel transposition between siamangs and gibbons (Jungers and Cole 1992). Therefore ontogenetic scaling, transposition and divergence of allometric slopes occur within basic types through microevolutionary processes (for review see Hartwig-Scherer 1993a).

In applying these results to the ontogenies of *Gorilla* and *Pan*, the observed allometric growth pattern—ontogenetic scaling, parallel disposition and divergence—are fully compatible with them belonging to the same basic type Gorillinae (Hartwig-Scherer 1995). Even within the closely related chimpanzee species—the common chimp and the Bonobo—there are significant size/shape dissociations relative to head-body length (Shea 1983) and relative to body weight (Hartwig-Scherer and Martin 1992). However, few would argue that the two chimpanzee species do not belong to the same basic type. Significantly, the comparison of ontogenies of Homo and Pongo to those of Pan and Gorilla clearly shows that neither Homo nor Pongo can be attributed to the basic type Gorillinae (Hartwig-Scherer 1993a).

## Basic Types in Fossil Anthropoids

*Fossil forms belonging to the basic type Homininae*

Indirect evidence such as morphological criteria and to a small extent the change in proportion during growth is the only means to infer basic types within the fossil record. Because of a comparatively unique combination of traits within the basic type Homininae, the Pleistocene hominid fossils, in contrast to other fossil hominoids, can easily be assigned to the basic type Homininae.

Roughly three main forms characterize the genus Homo on the basis of morphological criteria: *Homo ergaster/erectus, Homo sapiens* and Neanderthals. These forms share a number of features as being unique for the genus and are discerned by another set of traits making each of them more or less discrete entities. There are other forms displaying traits characteristic of two or even three of these forms giving a mosaic impression of *Homo*-specific traits. These forms that are disputed with respect to their specific attribution are often called Middle Pleistocene mosaic forms. They combine traits of two or more forms. This may be indicative of either hybridization or the continuous development of traits already contained genetically in the basic type hypodigm.

Many traits may be considered as effects of size variation, climatic stress, genetic drift and differential expression of the genes hidden in the (genetically polyvalent?) ancestral form. One of the diagnostic features is the varying degree of robusticity, which is high in *Homo erectus* but low in modern humans. For modern crania, robusticity was found to correlate with cranial size and shape (Lahr and Wright 1996): the greater the overall cranial size and the narrower the face (as in Australians with their long cranium and narrow face), the larger are the superstructures. Forty percent of the observed variation is explicable biomechanically (i.e., by the muscular and masticatory forces acting on the skull during ontogenetic bone remodeling). However, the regional pattern is a significant factor as well, indicative of genetic drift. Eskimos, although they load their teeth most extensively, do not belong to the most robust skulls. Also, there is little direct evidence for masticatory stress responsible for the development of the supraorbital torus (Hylander, Picq, and Johnson 1991; Turner 1985; but see Russel 1985). Thus size/shape and robusticity seem to form a functional unit that covary genetically during spreading and microevolution of the basic type Homininae.

*Fossil forms belonging to the basic type Ponginae*

Facial traits related to the airorhynchy of modern orangs are observed in *Sivapithecus* (including some of the Asian ramamorph forms) from the Indopakistan area and *Lufengpitecus* from China. If the facial traits are considered synapomorphic, these two Middle Miocene great ape genera could be included into the basic type Ponginae. However, the postcranials associated with *Sivapitecus* are not specialized toward the brachiating (arm-swinging) locomotion diagnostic for orangs. Whether these Miocene apes should be attributed to the basic type Ponginae cannot be settled so far.

### Basic type: Australopithecinae (Primates: Hominoidea)

The proposed fossil basic type Australopithecinae has no extant members. Fossils include *A. afarensis, A. anamensis, A. africanus, A. aethiopicus, A. robustus, A. boisei,* a yet-unnamed form and possibly *Ardipithecus ramidus.*

In addition to the South African forms *A. africanus, A robustus* or the East African forms *A. boisei, A. aethiopicus* and *A. afarensis,* there are a number of newly discovered fossils from East Africa as well as from the far west: *A. anamensis* and *Ardipithecus ramidus* from the East African Rift and *Australopithecus sp.* from Chad. Other finds supplement the assumed ancestral *A. afarensis.* In 1994 a robust male cranium of *A. afarensis* and other skeletal fragments were described (Kimbel, Johanson, and Rak 1994; compare Hartwig-Scherer 1994). They were found in Hadar, where the *A. afarensis* partial skeleton ("Lucy") and many other specimens have been found earlier.

Another, yet unspecified *Australopithecus* species has been found some two thousand miles west of the East African Rift Valley in Chad (Brunet et al. 1995), farther west than any other australopithecine. The morphology of the estimated 3-3.5 million radiometric years old australopithecine is similar to *A. afarensis* but also displays unique features suggesting a new species. Relatively thinner enamel is combined with australopithecine traits. Brunet et al. (1995) note that "it is not surprising that contemporaneous hominid populations as geographically distant as Chad and Tanzania would differ in morphology, regardless of whether they are classified as species or subspecies." Wood argues that this form "may turn out to be a new species; given its locality, this would not be surprising" (Wood 1995).

A definitively new australopithecine species *Australopithecus anamensis* was found in Kanapoi and Allia Bay, Kenya, and dated to the range of 3.5-4.2 millions radiometric years (Leakey et al. 1995). A number of cranial and postcranial fossils have been described. The postcranials suggest a body weight of 47-58 kg, which is more than that of earlier hominids. A somewhat older jaw of Allia Bayis is similar to *A. afarensis* from Laetoli. The tibia of Kanapoi has definite bipedal adaptations. Other traits are in common with *A. afarensis* indicating suspension or with quadrupedal arboreal climbers (Heinrich et al. 1993). The humerus also displays a very thick compacta indicative of an apelike power grip. Similarly, a handbone (Os hamatum) found in Tukwel is more similar to apes than to humans. A humeral fragment discovered in 1965 was included into the genus *Homo* because of its humanlike traits (Brandt 1995).

In 1992/1993 *Ardipithecus ramidus* was discovered in the Middle Awash Valley, Ethiopia, close to the village Aramis. This is fifty miles south of Hadar where the 3.2 million radiometric years old *A. afarensis* has been found. At three different localities the fossils were found on the surface, directly above a tuff dated approximately 4.4 million radiometric years (Wolde et al. 1994). Additional skeletal fragments were found in 1994, especially a partial skeleton of an adult including the crucial fragments of lower limb bones. However, they have not yet been described (as far as I know). This form was previously described as *Australopithecus* (White, Suwa, and Asfaw 1994) and later revised by introducing the new genus *Ardipithecus* (White, Suwa, and Asfaw 1995). It differs from the Miocene forms *Sivapithecus, Kenyapithecus, Ouranopithecus, Lufengpithecus* and *Dryopithecus* by the lack of a sectorial CP complex, smaller canines and a more anterior placed foramen magnum. It differs from the genus *Australopithecus* by displaying larger canines, less thick enamel on postcanine teeth (intermediate between apes and australopithecines), $C/P_3$ morphology considerably more apelike than *A. afarensis*, asymmetric $P^3$, postcranials displaying arboreal traits (great processus styloideus on the distal radius; strong trochlear ridge on the distal humerus). Whether *Ardipithecus ramidus* should indeed be included into the basic type *Australopithecus* or whether it belongs to a separate basic type has yet to be shown.

The diagnostic traits of the fossils tentatively assigned to the basic type Australopithecinae are summarized in table 9.1.

### The biotope and the diversification of australopithecines

*Australopithecus anamensis* lived at the border of a lake together with animals adapted to the life in savanna (Allia Bay) or open forest and bushland (Kanapoi) together with fossil baboons. *A. afarensis* dwelled in grassland with few trees (Laetoli) or in a mosaic of open grassland and closed forest (Hadar) (Johanson et al. 1982). *Ardipithecus ramidus* was a forest dweller in closed woodland (Wolde et al. 1994) indicated by floral and faunal elements such as colobus monkeys as typical forest dwellers. The more apelike features may be related to the woodland habitat (foli- and frugivorous diet, thinner enamel). Most of the following *Australopithecine* species had to face increasingly drier habitats, thus showing adaptations to graminivory (thicker enamel) and more bipedal locomotion. The (genetically polyvalent?) ancestral form possibly combined the potential to adapt to both types of habitats: the more arid the habitat, the more they adapted to heavy chewing and to bipedal locomotion, while in the woodland, less molarization with decreased enamel thickness as well as increased adaptation to suspensory locomotion is observed.

| | more Pan-like | intermediate | more human-like | unique |
|---|---|---|---|---|
| **Postcranium** | | | | |
| femoral head small | + | | | |
| femoral neck extremely long and flat | | | | + |
| humeral construction | | + | | |
| dorsally flexed phalanges | + | | | |
| intermembral index | | + | | |
| knee construction | | | + | |
| Os ilium extremely broad ("hyperhuman") | | | (+) | + |
| pelvis inlet proportions | | | | + |
| Spina iliaca anterior | | | + | |
| acetabulum ventral | | | + | |
| sacrum broad | | | + | |
| trait combination: suspension/bipedalism | | + | | + |
| trunk proportions | + | | | |
| **Cranium** | | | | |
| Fossa glenoidalis long and shallow | + | | | |
| position of F. glenoidalis very lateral | | | | + |
| Torus supraorbit, prominent, not massive | + | | | |
| cranial flexion | | + | | |
| hypermolarization | | | (+) | + |
| relatively thick enamel | | | (+) | + |
| bell-shaped cranium | | | | + |
| face construction | | | | + |

Table 9.1   The Most Important Traits Which Are Diagnostic for the Basic Type Australopithecinae

The ancestral form of the basic type Australopithecinae may have displayed arboreal as well as bipedal locomotor abilities, had mainly unique cranial and facial traits and possessed a brain larger than extant apes of its body size. It is expected that during the radiation of the basic type, different species increased different trends to different degrees. Some have expanded the arboreal trend to the expense of the bipedal activities, others the brain size, or exceeded the special australopithecine traits such as dished faces and megadontia (*A. robustus, A. boisei, A. arethiopicus*). New findings of South African australopithecines with extraordinary arboreal adaptations support the notion that there was an extension of the arboreal trend.

Suspension and bipedalism can be observed during more than 2 million radiometric years to varying degrees, not only within the australopithecines but also within the so-called *Homo habilis* (Clarke and Tobias 1995; Susman, Stern, and Jungers 1984), which will be treated next.

**The *Homo habilis* Complex: A Test Case**

*Homo habilis* is generally believed to link the small-brained *Australopithecus* with the larger-brained *Homo erectus* (for references see Tobias 1988), although there have been some dissenting interpretations (Leakey 1966). Advanced features such as enlarged brain size, indications of cerebral reorganization and possible indicators of a capacity for speech have been cited to justify inclusion in the genus *Homo* (Falk 1983; Holloway 1980; Leakey, Tobias, and Napier 1964; Tobias 1987, 1988). Although no long bones could be reliably assigned to *Homo habilis* prior to the discovery of OH 62, it was believed that this species was fully bipedal, in accordance with current ideas of human evolution (Day 1985; Howell 1978; Leakey, Tobias, and Napier 1964). The OH 8 foot attributed to *H. habilis* was originally described as human in major aspects (Day and Napier 1964), although a later study threw doubt on this interpretation (Lewis 1980). The notion of full bipedality in Lower Pleistocene hominids was also supported by isolated lower limb bones such as KMN-ER 1481 and 1472, which were found in strata dated at approximately 2 million radiometric years and have been clearly identified as attributable to *Homo* (Kennedy 1983; McHenry and Corruccini 1978).

Specimens attributed to *Homo habilis* have been reported from both East and South Africa and were all contemporary with at least one other hominid species. At Olduvai, temporal and spatial coexistence of the hyperrobust *Australopithecus boisei* and the gracile *Homo habilis* was recognized by Leakey and his coauthors (Leakey, Tobias, and Napier 1964). Stone tools found associated with *Homo* and *Australopithecus* at the same site have been assigned to the former in both East Africa (Leakey, Tobias, and Napier 1964) and South Africa (Hughes and Tobias 1977).

Discussion about the locomotor behavior of *Australopithecus* continues. The spectrum of possibilities extends from the extreme of fully bipedal (Latimer and Lovejoy 1989, 1990; Lovejoy, Heiple, and Burstein 1973; Wolpoff 1983b) to that of a nonhominid pattern (Oxnard 1975), although a growing number of authors now argue for a unique combination of terrestrial bipedal and arboreal features (Jungers 1982; Schmid 1983; Stern and Susman 1983; Susman, Stern, and Jungers 1984). For *Homo habilis*, however, the possession of bipedal gait remained largely unquestioned prior to the discovery of OH 62 (although see Lewis 1980). In contrast to the considerable discussion concerning the existence of *Homo habilis* as a species, there has been general agreement on the definition of all members of the genus *Homo* as fully bipedal with a "hind-limb skeleton . . . adapted to habitual erect posture" (Leakey, Tobias, and Napier 1964) and "lower limb more elongated and upper limb probably relatively shorter than in *Australopithecus*" (Howell 1978). Howell described the femur of *Homo habilis* as "relatively slender, elongate" (395-400) with a morphology of lower limb "much like other *Homo* species" (Howell 1978).

### Homo habilis *OH62: A partial skeleton with surprising features*

Johanson and colleagues (Johanson et al. 1987) modified this situation by introducing to the taxon *Homo habilis* the specimen OH 62 with features that were less humanlike than previously expected. They themselves noted that the humerofemoral index is "close to 95%" (AL 288-1 85%, *Homo* 72%, *Pan* approximately 100%). Korey's careful evaluation and cautious discussion also indicated that OH 62 may be less human than AL 288-1 as far as the humerofemoral index is concerned (Korey 1990). Whereas advanced features such as brain expansion, bipedal gait and tool production were emphasized in earlier discussions, Johanson and colleagues (Johanson et al. 1987) stressed traits formerly assessed as primitive (Lewis 1980; Susman and Stern 1982; Wood 1974).

In Hartwig-Scherer and Martin (1991), two partial skeletons of early hominids were compared with respect to their body proportions and inferred locomotor adaptations: the adult AL 288-1 (*Australopithecus afarensis,* "Lucy," dated to 3.1 My) (Johanson, Taieb, and Coppens 1982) and the adult OH 62 (*Homo habilis,* "Lucy's child," dated to 1.8 My; Johanson and Shreeve 1989; Johanson et al. 1987). They both include remains from upper and lower limbs. AL 288-1 has been inferred to show adaptation for terrestrial bipedality (Latimer and Lovejoy, 1990; Lovejoy 1988) or for a unique form of locomotion combining bipedality with climbing (Jungers 1982; Schmid 1983; Stern and Susman 1983; Susman, Stern, and Jungers 1984). Discussion as to whether AL 288-1 exhibited essentially human proportions or whether this skeleton had comparatively longer arms and/or relatively shorter legs than modern humans is not yet settled (Jungers 1982; Jungers and Stern 1983; Wolpoff 1983a, 1983b; Wolpoff and Lovejoy 1975).

Nevertheless, the humerofemoral index clearly indicates a position intermediate between African apes and humans. Specimen OH 62 is less complete than AL 288-1. In addition to a number of cranial fragments (parts of palate, face, calvaria, mandible and dentition), it incorporates an almost intact humeral shaft, two-thirds of the radial shaft (including the radial tuberosity), most of the ulna, the proximal shaft and neck of the femur, and a proximal fragment of the tibia (tibial tuberosity). The maxillary fragment of specimen OH 62 displays close similarity to Stw 53, an approximately contemporaneous specimen from Sterkfontein showing affinity to *Homo habilis* (Hughes and Tobias 1977). This led to the identification of OH 62 as *Homo habilis* (Johanson et al. 1987). Derived features characteristic of either *Australopithecus* or *Homo erectus* are lacking. The postcranium of OH 62 was described as being similar to that of AL 288-1 ("Lucy"), although the upper limb bones are reportedly longer and more robust than those of AL 288-1 while the legs seem to be smaller and more gracile (Johanson et al. 1987). Various limb bone dimensions of these skeletons are compared to those of modern African apes and humans. If *Homo habilis* is an intermediate between *A. afarensis* and *Homo* and if OH 62 belongs to this taxon, the partial skeleton of OH 62 assigned to *Homo habilis* in principle would present a special opportunity to test ideas concerning the transition from the unique locomotor pattern of *A. afarensis* to the fully bipedal pattern of *Homo* (*erectus*).

Pairwise comparison of available limb bone dimensions have been performed for AL 288-1 and OH 62 with respect to both African apes and humans. Twenty-eight out of 76 possible pairs of dimensions permitted a clear distinction between modern African apes and humans and have therefore been used to determine the position of AL 288-1 and OH 62 relative to these extant forms. Plots of these dimensions indicate whether a fossil of unknown association is more like African apes or *Homo*. In 24 out of 28 cases, OH 62 is closer to the African apes than is AL 288-1. In one case the opposite is true. For the remaining 3 cases, the position of the two fossil specimens relative to extant forms is similar (both are more apelike). In 16 out of 28 cases, OH 62 appears to be fully apelike, while AL 288-1 appears to be fully humanlike in 17 cases out of 28.

These results are quite unexpected in view of previous accounts of *Homo habilis* as a link between the australopithecines and humans. Earlier expectations concerning postcranial similarities between *Homo habilis* and later members of the genus *Homo* could not be corroborated. To the contrary, as reported here, a variety of measurements indicates that OH 62 displays much stronger similarities to African ape limb proportions than does AL 288-1.

Howell's definition (Howell 1978) of *Homo habilis* also included the expectation of "body weight unknown or as yet unestimated, but greater than *A. africanus* and probably within the range of *H. erectus*." It is obvious from inspecting the limb bones, as was pointed out by its describers (Johanson et al. 1987), that OH 62 could not have been heavier than AL 288-1. In fact, at 25 kg, the average body weight estimate for OH 62 (Hartwig-Scherer and Martin 1991) is almost 20 percent less than the average body weight estimate for AL 288-1. Yet AL 288-1 is a small representative of gracile *Australopithecus* with about half the estimated weight of *Homo erectus*. This also runs counter to previous expectations.

OH 62 fails to qualify as an intermediate link between *Australopithecus* and *Homo erectus* not only postcranially but also dentally. Johanson and his colleagues (Johanson et al. 1987) emphasize that "the degree of megadontia in *Homo habilis* may, in fact, be little changed from the *Australopithecus* condition."

Unfortunately, cranial capacity cannot be assessed for OH 62. However, it has been suggested "that small individuals of *Australopithecus* and *Homo habilis* were differentiated by cranial capacity and not by body size" (Johanson et al. 1987). The existence of a species with apelike limb proportions and therefore possibly apelike locomotion, as witnessed by OH 62, and an enlarged cranial capacity, as witnessed by certain other specimens attributed to *Homo habilis,* would revive a concept long thought to have expired: the brain-first theory of human evolution.

It is difficult to accept an evolutionary sequence in which *Homo habilis,* with apelike limb proportion and possibly apelike locomotor adaptations, is intermediate between *Australopithecus afarensis,* with more humanlike proportions and a certain kind of bipedality, and fully bipedal *Homo erectus.* The question arises as to how to fit fossil femora such as KMN-ER 1481 and 1472 into this picture: they display a clearly human morphology and are reported to date back as far as 2 million radiometric years (Kennedy 1983; McHenry and Corruccini 1978). OH 62 may furnish evidence for yet another hominid line coexisting in the Plio-Pleistocene of (East) Africa along with other gracile and robust forms (Tobias 1988; Wood 1978, 1985).

### Does Homo habilis *comprise specimens from different species?*

The acceptability of this species has, however, been controversial ever since its first description in the sixties (Leakey, Tobias, and Napier 1964). The holotype of *Homo habilis* is the Olduvai hominid OH 7, consisting of incomplete parietals, a damaged mandible and hand bones combined with four other cranial and postcranial specimens as paratypes (Leakey, Tobias, and Napier 1964), all recovered from Bed I in Olduvai. Additional material was attributed to this species later. Two opposite positions have been taken with respect to the validity of the taxon. For a summary of early opinions, see the comments associated with the article by Tobias (1965), and for a review including more recent discussions, see Stringer (1986). One group of authors holds that *Homo habilis* is a highly variable but valid species including all nonrobust and non*erectus* hominids occurring during the Plio-Pleistocene. Other authors cannot accept *Homo habilis* as a valid species and believe it to be either a mixture of two different genera (e.g., *Australopithecus* and *Homo;* Robinson 1965, 1966) or just a member of a (highly variable) *Australopithecus* species (Brace, Mahler, and Rosen 1972). Many commentators agree in suspecting that the identity of *Homo habilis* is obscured by the inclusion of ambiguous or dubious material in the taxon.

Due to the high variability of traits and the large size dimorphism observed in the *habilis*-complex, some propose *H. habilis* to be divided into two species: *H. habilis* (OH 4, 6-8, 10, 13-16, 21, 24, 27, 35, 37, 39, 48-45, 52, 62; KNM-ER 1478, 1501, 1502, 1805, 1813, 3735) with arboreal adaptation, small brain size, megadontia but humanlike maxilla, and the potentially bipedal

*H. rudolfensis* (KNM-ER 813, 819, 1470, 1472, 1481-83, 1590, 1801, 1802, 3732, 3891) with a relatively large brain size but an australopithecine facial and cranial morphology (Wood 1992).

Cranial resemblances are reported between OH 62 and the South African specimen Stw 53 attributed to *Homo habilis*. Dental characters are similar to the australopithecine pattern. At Sterkfontein, the humanlike maxilla Stw 53 is now supplemented by postcranials ("Little foot"; Stw 573) with a flexible big toe perfect for grabbing onto tree limbs (Clarke and Tobias 1995). Spoor, Wood, and Zonneveld (1994) showed by analyses of the labyrinth that Stw 53 was less specialized with respect to its locomotion, with little bipedal activity and retaining even a quadrupedal component.

### The Homo habilis *complex within evolutionary theory*

If OH 62 is a specimen of *Homo habilis*, this taxon should be excluded from the genus *Homo* sensu stricto. It does not form a suitable link between australopithecines and later *Homo* forms. It may belong to still another extinct hominid lineage or may be considered a late member of the australopithecine radiation with relatively larger brain, megadontia as in other australopithecines and increased suspensory activity to the expense of bipedal locomotor form. If *A. afarensis*, whose skeleton is dated more than 1 million radiometric years earlier, is commonly supposed to be the ancestor of *Homo habilis*, and if OH 62, classified as *Homo habilis* by its discoverers, does indeed represent a stage intermediate between *A. afarensis* and later *Homo*, a fundamentally revised interpretation of the course of human evolution is necessary. Both the large-brained, australopithecine-faced and assumed bipedal KNM-ER 1470 and the more humanlike faced, suspensory *habilis* OH 62 do not fulfill the expected morphology of an ancestral member of the genus *Homo* sensu stricto. Whether another *habilis* mandible of Malawi (putatively 2.4 My) (Schrenk et al. 1993) fills this gap remains to be shown, as no postcranial bones or other cranial elements have been described yet.

### The Homo habilis *complex within basic type biology*

The *habilis*-complex has been separated by some workers into three groups: a *habilis* group, a *rudolfensis* group and a *Homo erectus* group, the last being the bipedal tool maker. It is suggested that the *habilis*-complex may be an artificial combination of two inferred basic types: the Homininae (*H. erectus:* mainly the postcranial specimens of Kenya) and the Australopithecinae (*habilis* group). Whether the rudolfensis group belongs to the australopithecine basic type or to the human basic type or even to a third, hitherto undefined basic type is not yet settled. The evidence for more humanlike structures of the brain endocasts (for review see Brandt 1992) in combination with an australopithecine face makes the attribution of the *rudolfensis* group a difficult task. It cannot be excluded that it may belong to the basic type Australopithecinae.

## The Development of the Basic Type Homininae in Space and Time
### Multiregional versus single-origin hypothesis
Within the evolutionary framework *Homo ergaster* is considered an African species that descended from an unknown precursor from which *Homo erectus* is supposedly evolved in Southeast Asia as a descendant of early *H. ergaster* emigrants (Wood 1992).

With respect to the origin of modern *sapiens* two hypotheses are discussed in evolutionary biology. The first model is called multiregional evolution (Wolpoff 1989; Wolpoff and Thorne 1991), also known as regional continuity model, candelaber model, Noah's Sons or Neandertalphase model, and suggests that at two or more places of the Old World the evolution of modern forms took place independently. The second model is called single-origin model (Stringer and Andrews 1988), also known as Noah's ark model, the Garden of Eden model, Out of Africa 2, Mother Eve hypothesis (Cann, Stoneking, and Wilson 1987) or population replacement model and assumes that modern forms originated at a single part of the Old World (preferably Africa) from which the rest of the world was populated by replacing all previous *Homo*-forms. The latter model is generally preferred over the multiregional model, mainly because of probability reasons (Wilson and Cann 1992; but see Thorne and Wolpoff 1992).

The favored place of origin of the Noah's ark model is Africa (Bräuer 1984, 1992). Two main migration waves are considered to have occurred: the first by some form of primitive African *Homo ergaster* (Wood 1992) that emigrated out of Africa into Asia and perhaps into Europe. Before the second emigration wave occurred more than a million radiometric years later, some form of archaic sapiens evolved from some advanced *Homo ergaster/erectus*. These archaic sapiens forms are believed to have given rise to modern people. Most workers believe that during the Pleistocene an African population underwent a drastic reduction (bottleneck) in population size as genetic analyses of modern populations suggest. This archaic *sapiens* left Africa to spread all over the Old World and eventually to the New World. Previous populations of the genus *Homo*, such as *H. erectus* in Asia or later Neanderthals in West Europe, were either totally replaced by the newcomers or, as a modified version of the single-origin model allows, genetically absorbed.

A modified version of the single-origin model has been adapted to the basic type approach: three migration waves may have occurred originating from the Afro-Arabian shield. During the first migration, a population with unknown morphology spread into different directions and developed the typical *ergaster* morphology in Africa and the *erectus* traits in Southeast Asia. A second migration wave produced the Neanderthal morphology in the comparatively isolated Europe. Finally, a third migration wave filled the world with modern *Homo sapiens*. The mosaic features, a combination of *sapiens-*, *erectus-* and Neanderthal-like traits observed in European Middle Pleistocene forms, may be considered the consequence of either hybridization between members of the different migration waves or the expression of hidden traits in the (polyvalent?) ancestral gene pool or a mixture of both.

### Origin of the basic type Homininae in the Near East?

Besides the out of Africa hypothesis, the out of Near East model deserves specific emphasis as it is based on a series of arguments. Novel radiometric dates of the last few years urged some changes in the evolutionary hypotheses with respect to time and place of origin. Until the 1990s, the earliest occurrence of *Homo erectus* outside Africa was presumably not before the 1 million mark, leaving plenty of time (800000 radiometric years) to migrate from Africa (at about 1.8 million radiometric years) into Asia. Recently, redating (kalium-argon based radiometry) of fossiliferous sediments where *H. erectus* (Modjokerto child) has been found yielded the much higher age of 1.8-1.9 million radiometric years (Swisher et al. 1994). This urged either predating the emigration time or rethinking the place of origin. A more central place of origin—the Near East is about halfway between Africa and Asia—would reconcile both dates. In Ubeidiya, Israel, a more than 2-million-year-old horizon with *erectus* remains was reported (Repenning and Fejfar 1982), although it is disputed by others (Tchernov 1987, 1988).

Other redatings suggest that *H. sapiens* in the Near East (Israel) may have been as old as in Africa, and their morphological traits are also compatible with an ancestral condition for later *Homo sapiens* groups. Some recent publications may be interpreted in favor of the Near East as the center of origin on morphological and temporal grounds (Waddle 1994). Eighty-three Pleistocene crania were divided into 3 temporal and 4 geographic regions (time frame: 600000-125000, 125000-32000, 32000-8000 radiometric years; regions: Western Europe, eastern Europe, Southwest Asia, Africa). Based on matrix coefficient similarities, the single-origin model is supported with Israel as the more probable place of origin than Africa (correlation coefficient of 0.577 versus 0.407). Others have mentioned such an Afro-Levantic origin of modern humans before (Foley and Lahr 1992).

Thus the hypothesis based on the basic type approach supposing the Near East as place of origin for all human types is supported by the pattern of distribution of *erectus* as well as archaic *sapiens* both in time and place, the redatings and the morphological criteria.

In conclusion, based on the basic type model, a founder population presumably has undergone specific diversifications after a severe bottleneck. Assuming a genetically polyvalent ancestral population of the basic type Homininae and a single place of origin, the fossil sequences may be explained as the consequence of several migration waves: the first migration wave led to the microevolution of *ergaster* forms in Africa and *erectus* forms in Asia; the second led to the Neanderthal morphology; and the third and most extensive migration wave filled the world with modern people. The previous populations, developing various adaptations such as *Homo erectus, erectus* or Neanderthal traits, may have been replaced or genetically overridden with some, little or no genetic impact to following generations. The diversification of specific forms is expected to be the more pronounced the farther away they settled from the original population and the longer the genetic isolation lasted. Hybridization between the members of the migration waves may have produced mosaic forms such as those observed in the European Middle Pleistocene populations.

## References

Alberch, P., S. J. Gould, G. F. Oster, and D. B. Wake. 1979. Size and shape in ontogeny and phylogeny. *Paleobiology* 5:296-317.

Bonner, J. T. 1968. Size change in development and evolution. *Journal of Paleontology* 42 (5):1-15.

————. 1982. *Evolution and development.* New York: Springer-Verlag.

Brace, C. L., P. E. Mahler, and R. B. Rosen. 1972. Tooth measurement and the rejection of the taxon "Homo habilis." *Yearbook of Physical Anthropology* 16:50-68.

Brandt, M. 1992. *Gehirn und Sprache: Fossile Zeugnisse zum Ursprung des Menschen.* Berlin: Pascal-Verlag.

————. 1995. *Der Ursprung des aufrechten Ganges: Zur Fortbewegung der plio-pleistozänen Hominiden.* Neuhausen: Hänssler Edition "Pascal."

Bräuer, G. 1984. The Afro-european *sapiens*-hypothesis and the hominid evolution in East Asia during the Late Middle and Upper Pleistocene. *Courier Forschungsinstitut Senckenberg* 69:145-65.

————. 1992. Africa's place in the evolution of *Homo sapiens.* In *Continuity or replacement: Controversies in* Homo sapiens *evolution,* ed. G. Bräuer and F. H. Smith, 83-98. Rotterdam: Balkema.

Brunet, M., A. Beauvilain, Y. Coppens, E. Heintz, A. H. E. Moutaye, and D. Pilbeam. 1995. The first australopithecine 2500 kilometres west of the Rift Valley. *Nature* 378:273-75.

Cann, R., M. Stoneking, and A. Wilson. 1987. Mitochrondrial DNA and human evolution. *Nature* 325:31-36.

Chiarelli, B. 1973. Checklist of Catarrhina primate hybrids. *Journal of Human Evolution* 2:301-5.

Clarke, R. J., and P. V. Tobias. 1995. Sterkfontein Member 2 foot bones of the oldest South African hominid. *Science* 269:521-24.

Cole, I. T. M. 1992. Postnatal heterochrony of the masticatory apparatus in *Cebus apella* and *Cebus albifrons. Journal of Human Evolution* 23:253-82.

Day, M. H. 1985. Hominid locomotion—from Taung to the Laetoli footprints. In *Hominid evolution: Past, present and future,* ed. P. V. Tobias, 115-27. New York: Alan Liss.

Day, M. H., and J. R. Napier. 1964. Homind fossils from Bed I, Olduvai Gorge, Tanganyika: Fossil foot bones. *Nature* 201:967-70.

de Beer, G. R. 1958. *Embryos and ancestors.* Oxford: Clarendon Press.

Falk, D. 1983. Cerebral cortices of East African early hominids. *Science* 221:1072-74.

Fleagle, J. G. 1988. *Primate adaptation and evolution.* San Diego, Calif.: Academic Press.

Foley, R. A., and M. M. Lahr. 1992. Beyond "out of Africa": Reassessing the origins of *Homo sapiens. Journal Human Evolution* 22:523-29.

Geissmann, T. 1984. Inheritance of song parameters in the gibbon song, analysed in 2 hybrid gibbons (hylobates pileatus x h. lar). *Folia Primatologica* 42:216-35.

Godfrey, L., and J. Marks. 1991. The nature and origin of primate species. *American Journal of Physical Anthropology Supplement* 13:34-39.

Gould, S. J. 1977. *Ontogeny and phylogeny.* Cambridge, Mass.: Harvard University Press.

Hartwig-Scherer, S. 1993a. Allometry in hominoids: A comparative study of skeletal growth trends. Ph.D. thesis, University of Zürich.

————. 1993b. Hybridisierung und Artbildung bei den Meerkatzenartigen (Primates, Cercopithecoidea). In *Typen des Lebens,* ed. S. Scherer, 245-57. Neuhausen: Hänssler-Verlag.

————. 1994. Lebte "Lucy" mit Familie doch auf Bäumen? *Studium Integrale Journal* 1 (1):11-14.

————. 1995. Skeletal growth allometry and the human-chimpanzee clade. *Anthropologie et Préhistoire* 106:37-44.

Hartwig-Scherer, S., and R. D. Martin. 1991. Was "Lucy" more human than her "child"? Observations on early hominid postcranial skeletons. *Journal of Human Evolution* 21:439-49.

————. 1992. Allometry and prediction in hominoids: A solution to the problem of intervening variables. *American Journal of Physical Anthropology* 88:37-57.

Heinrich, R. E., M. D. Rose, R. E. Leakey, and A. C. Walker. 1993. Hominid radius from the Middle Pliocene of Lake Turkana, Kenya. *American Journal of Physical Anthropology* 92:139-48.

Hill, K. 1993. Life history theory and evolutionary anthropology. *Evolutionary Anthropology* 2:78-88.

Hill, W. C. O. 1966. *Primates: Comparative anatomy and taxonomy, 4, Catarrhini: Cercopithecoidea: Cercopithecinae.* Edinburgh: Edinburgh University Press.

Holloway, R. L. 1980. The OH 7 (Olduvai Gorge, Tanzania) hominid partial brain endocast revisited. *American Journal of Physical Anthropology* 53:267-71.

Howell, F. C. 1978. Hominidae. In *Evolution of African mammals,* ed. V. J. Maglio and H. B. S. Cooke, 154-248. Cambridge, Mass.: Harvard University Press.

Hughes, A. R., and P. V. Tobias. 1977. A fossil skull probably of the genus *Homo* from Sterkfontein, Transvaal. *Nature* 265:310-12.

Hylander, W. L., P. G. Picq, and K. R. Johnson. 1991. Masticatory stress hypotheses and the supraorbital torus of primates. *American Journal of Physical Anthropology* 86:1-36.

Johanson, D., and J. Shreeve. 1989. *Lucy's child: The discovery of a human ancestor.* New York: William Morrow.

Johanson, D. C., O. C. Lovejoy, W. H. Kimbel, T. D. White, S. C. Ward, M. E. Bush, B. M. Latimer, and Y. Coppens. 1982. Morphology of the Pliocene partial hominid skeleton (A.L. 288-1) from the Hadar formation, Ethiopia. *American Journal of Physical Anthropology* 57:403-51.

Johanson, D.C., F. T. Masao, G. G. Eck, T. D. White, R. C. Walter, W. H. Kimbel, B. Asfaw, P. Manega, P. Ndessokia, and G. Suwa. 1987. New partial skeleton of *Homo habilis* from Olduvai Gorge, Tanzania. *Nature* 327:403-51.

Johanson, D. C., M. Taieb, and Y. Coppens. 1982. Pliocene hominids from the Hadar formation, Ethiopia (1973-1977): Stratigraphic, chronologic and paleoenvironmental context, with notes on hominid morphology and systematics. *American Journal of Physical Anthropology* 57:373-402.

Jungers, W. L. 1982. Lucy's limbs: Skeletal allometry and locomotion in *Australopithecus afarensis*. *Nature* 297:676-78.

Jungers, W. L., and M. S. Cole. 1992. Relative growth and shape of the locomotor skeleton in lesser apes. *Journal of Human Evolution* 23:93-105.

Jungers, W. L., and J. G. Fleagle. 1980. Postnatal growth allometry of the extremities of *Cebus albifrons* and *Cebus apella:* A longitudinal and comparative study. *American Journal of Physical Anthropology* 53:471-78.

Jungers, W. L., and J. T. Stern. 1983. Body proportions, skeletal allometry and locomotion in the Hadar hominids: A reply to Wolpoff. *Journal of Human Evolution* 12:673-84.

Kennedy, G. E. 1983. A morphometric and taxonomic assessment of a hominine femur from the Lower Member, Koobi Fora, Lake Turkana. *American Journal of Physical Anthropology* 61:429-36.

Kimbel, W. H., D. C. Johanson, and Y. Rak. 1994. The first skull and other new discoveries of *Australopithecus afarensis* at Hadar, Ethiopia. *Nature* 368:449-52.

Korey, K. 1990. Deconstructing reconstruction: The OH 62 humerofemoral index. *American Journal of Physical Anthropology* 83:25-33.

Lahr, M. M., and R. V. S. Wright. 1996. The question of robusticity and the relationship between cranial size and shape in *Homo sapiens*. *Journal of Human Evolution* 31:157-91.

Latimer, B., and C. O. Lovejoy. 1989. The calcaneus of *Australopithecus afarensis* and its implications in the evolution of bipedality. *American Journal of Physical Anthropology* 78:369-86.

———. 1990. Metatarsophalangeal joints of *Australopithecus afarensis*. *American Journal of Physical Anthropology* 83:13-23.

Leakey, L. S. B. 1966. *Homo habilis, Homo erectus* and the australopithecines. *Nature* 209:1279-81.

Leakey, L. S. B., P. V. Tobias, and J. R. Napier. 1964. A new species of the genus *Homo* from Olduvai Gorge. *Nature* 202:7-9.

Leakey, M., C. S. Feibel, I. McDougall, and A. Walker. 1995. New four-million-year old hominid species from Kanapoi and Allia Bay, Kenya. *Nature* 376:565-71.

Lewis, O. J. 1980. The joints of the evolving foot. Part II: The fossil evidence. *Journal of Anatomy* 131:275-98.

Lovejoy, C. O. 1988. Evolution of human walking. *Scientific American* 259 (November):82-89.

Lovejoy, C. O., K. G. Heiple, and A. H. Burstein. 1973. The gait of *Australopithecus*. *American Journal of Physical Anthropology* 38:757-80.

McHenry, H. M., and R. S. Corruccini. 1978. The femur in early human evolution. *American Journal of Physical Anthropology* 49:473-88.

Markarjan, D. S., E. P. Isakov, and G. I. Kondakov. 1974. Intergeneric hybrids of the lower (42-chromosome) monkey species of the Sukhumi Monkey Colony. *Journal of Human Evolution* 3:247-55.

Myers, R. H., and D. A. Shafer. 1979. Hybrid ape offspring of a mating of gibbon and siamang. *Science* 205:308-10.

Oxnard, C. E. 1975. The place of the australopithecines in human evolution: Grounds for doubt? *Nature* 258:389-95.

Repenning, C. A., and O. Fejfar. 1982. Evidence for earlier date of Ubeidiya, Israel, hominid site. *Nature* 299:344-47.

Robinson, J. T. 1965. *Homo* "habilis" and the australopithecines. *Nature* 205:121-24.

———. 1966. Reply to Tobias. *Nature* 209:957-60.

Russel, M. D. 1985. The supraorbital torus: "A most remarkable peculiarity." *Current Anthropology* 26 (3):337-60.

Scherer, S. 1993. Basic types of life. In *Typen des Lebens*, ed. S. Scherer, 11-30. Berlin: Pascal-Verlag.

Schmid, P. 1983. Eine Rekonstruktion des Skelettes von A.L. 288-1 (Hadar) und deren Konsequenzen. *Folia Primatologica* 40:283-306.

Schrenk, F., T. G. Bromage, C. G. Betzler, U. Ringe, and Y. M. Juwayeyl. 1993. Oldest *Homo* and Pliocene biogeography of the Malawi Rift. *Nature* 365:833-36.

Shafer, D. A., R. H. Myers, and D. Saltzman. 1984. Biogenetics of the siabon (gibbon-siamang hybrids). In *The lesser apes: Evolutionary and behavioral biology*, ed. H. Preuschoft, D. J. Chivers, W. Y. Brockelman, and N. Creel, 486-97. Edinburgh: Edinburgh University Press.

Shea, B. T. 1983. Paedomorphosis and neoteny in the pygmy chimpanzee. *Science* 222:521-22.

———. 1992. Ontogenetic scaling of skeletal proportions in the talapoin monkey. *Journal of Human Evolution* 23:283-307.

Shea, B. T., and H. J. Coolidge. 1984. Between the gorilla and the chimpanzee: A history of debate concerning the existence of the kooloo-kamba or gorilla-like chimpanzee. *Journal of Ethnobiology* 4:1-13.

Southwick, C. H., and K. L. Southwick. 1983. Polyspecific groups of macaques on the Kowloon Peninsula, New Territories, Hong Kong. *American Journal of Primatology* 5:17-24.

Spoor, C. F., B. A. Wood, and F. Zonneveld. 1994. Implications of early hominid labyrinthine morphology for evolution of human bipedal locomotion. *Nature* 369:645-48.

Stern, J. T., and R. L. Susman. 1983. The locomotor anatomy of *Australopithecus afarensis*. *American Journal of Physical Anthropology* 60:279-317.

Stringer, C. B. 1986. The credibility of *Homo habilis*. In *Major topics in primate and human evolution*, ed. B. A. Wood, L. Martin, and P. Andrews, 266-94. Cambridge: Cambridge University Press.

Stringer, C. B., and P. Andrews. 1988. Genetic and fossil evidence for the origin of modern humans. *Science* 239:1263-68.

Struhsaker, T., T. M. Butynski, and J. S. Lwanga. 1988. Hybridization between redtail (*Cercopithecus ascanius schmidti*) and blue *(C. mitis stuhlmanni)* monkeys in the Kibale Forest, Uganda. In *A primate radiation: Evolutionary biology of the African guenons*, ed. A. Gautier-Hion, F. Bourlière, J. P. Gautier, and J. Kingdon, 477-97. New York: Cambridge University Press.

Susman, R. L., and J. T. Stern. 1982. Functional morphology of *Homo habilis*. *Science* 217:931-34.

Susman, R. L., J. T. Stern, and W. L. Jungers. 1984. Arboreality and bipedality in the Hadar hominids. *Folia Primatologica* 43:113-56.

Swisher, C. C., G. H. Curtis, T. Jacob, A. G. Getty, A. Suprijo, and C. Widiasmoro.

1994. Age of the earliest known hominids in Java, Indonesia. *Science* 263:1118-21.

Tchernov, E. 1987. The age of the Ubeidiya Formation, an Early Pleistocene hominid site in the Jordan Valley, Israel. *Israel Journal of Earth Sciences* 36:3-30.

———. 1988. The biochronology of the site of Ubeidiya (Jordan Valley) and the earliest hominids in the Levant. *Anthropologie* 92:839-62.

Thorne, A. G., and M. H. Wolpoff. 1992. Multiregionaler Ursprung der modernen Menschen. *Spektrum der Wissenschaft,* June:72-79.

Tobias, P. V. 1965. New discoveries in Tanganyika: Their bearing on hominid evolution. *Current Anthropology* 6:391-411.

———. 1987. The brain of *Homo habilis:* A new level of organization in cerebral evolution. *Journal of Human Evolution* 16:741-61.

———. 1988. Numerous apparently synapomorphic features in *Australopithecus robustus, Australopithecus boisei* and *Homo habilis:* Support for the Skelton-McHenry-Drawhorn Hypothesis. In *The evolutionary history of the "robust" Australopithecines,* ed. F. E. Grine, 293-308. New York: Aldine-de Gruyter.

Turner, C. G. II. 1985. Comments on "The supraorbital torus: 'A most remarkable peculiarity' " by M. D. Russel. *Current Anthropology* 26 (3):355.

Waddle, D. 1994. Matrix correlation tests support a single origin for modern humans. *Nature* 368:452-55.

White, T. D., G. Suwa, and B. Asfaw. 1994. *Australopithecus ramidus,* a new species of early hominid from Aramis, Ethiopia. *Nature* 371:306-12.

———. 1995. Corrigendum: *Australopithecus ramidus,* a new species of early hominid from Aramis, Ethiopia. *Nature* 375:88.

Wilson, A. C., and R. L. Cann. 1992. Afrikanischer Ursprung des modernen Menschen. *Spektrum der Wissenschaft,* June:72-79.

WoldeGabriel, G., T. D. White, G. Suwa, P. Renne, J. Heinzelin, W. K. Hart, and G. Heiken. 1994. Ecological and temporal placement of early Pliocene hominids at Aramis, Ethiopia. *Nature* 371:330-33.

Wolkin, J. R., and R. H. Myers. 1980. Characteristics of a gibbon-siamang hybrid ape. *International Journal of Primatology* 1:203-21.

Wolpoff, M. H. 1983a. Lucy's little legs. *Journal of Human Evolution* 12:443-53.

———. 1983b. Lucy's lower limbs: Long enough to be fully bipedal? *Nature* 304:59-61.

———. 1989. Multiregional evolution: The fossil alternative to Eden. In *The human revolution: Behavioral and biological perspectives on the origins of modern humans,* ed. P. Mellars and C. Stringer, 62-108. Edinburgh: Edinburgh University Press.

Wolpoff, M. H., and C. O. Lovejoy. 1975. A rediagnosis of the genus *Australopithecus. Human Biology* 4:275-76.

Wolpoff, M. H., and A. G. Thorne. 1991. A case against Eve. *New Scientist* 130 (June 22):37-41.

Wood, B. A. 1974. Olduvai Bed I postcranial fossils: A reassessment. *Journal of Human Evolution* 3:373-78.

———. 1978. Classification and phylogeny of East African hominids. In *Recent advances in primatology,* ed. D. J. Chivers and K. A. Joysey, 3, *Evolution,* 351-72. London: Academic Press.

———. 1985. Early *Homo* in Kenya, and its systematic relationships. In *Ancestors: The hard evidence,* ed. E. Delson, 206-14. New York: Alan Liss.

———. 1992. Origin and evolution of the genus *Homo. Nature* 355:783-90.

———. 1995. *Australopithecus* goes west. *Nature* 378:239.

# 10

# Evolutionary Accounts of Altruism & the Problem of Goodness by Design

## JEFFREY P. SCHLOSS

*The time has come to take seriously the fact that we humans are modified monkeys,
not the favored Creation of a Benevolent God on the Sixth Day. In particular,
we must recognize our biological past in trying to understand our interactions with others.
We must think again especially about our so-called "ethical principles."
The question is not whether biology—specifically, our evolution
—is connected with ethics, but how.*

*As evolutionists, we see that no [ethical] justification of the traditional kind is possible.
Morality, or more strictly our belief in morality, is merely an adaptation put in place
to further our reproductive ends. Hence the basis of ethics does not lie in God's will. . . .
In an important sense, ethics as we understand it is an illusion fobbed off on us
by our genes to get us to cooperate. It is without external grounding.
Like Macbeth's dagger, it serves a powerful purpose without existing in substance.*

*Ethics is illusory inasmuch as it persuades us that it has an objective reference.
This is the crux of the biological position.
Once it is grasped, everything falls into place. (Ruse and Wilson 1993)*

*I*T IS OFTEN CLAIMED THAT DARWIN, BY PROPOSING A NATURALISTIC
origin for biological diversity, removed a critical intellectual impedi-
ment to atheism and thereby helped to make belief in God
unnecessary (Dewey 1951; Himmelfarb 1968; Brooke 1991). Darwin's
challenge to theology was certainly not unprecedented. One can view Darwin
as presiding over the retirement of a deistic God who had been underem-
ployed since Enlightenment rationality and Newtonian mechanics no longer
required him (Fox 1989; Rachels 1990). Moreover, God's retirement con-

firmed the negative performance appraisals by outside reviewers like David Hume and Friedrich Nietzsche of a God whose carnage-filled creation looked like he had been doing dubious work even while gainfully employed as the watchmaker of natural theologians (Gliserman 1975; Dennett 1995). Against this some scholars have argued that Darwinian naturalism did not demonstrate but rather derives from prior commitments to metaphysical naturalism (Johnson 1991, 1995), explicit but unsubstantiated theological assumptions (Nelson 1996) and unexplicit though religiously significant ideological positions (Midgley 1980; Fox-Keller 1991).

The mere removal of impediments to atheism has become small beer for contemporary Darwinists. Accordingly Darwinism is said to do much more than suggest God's agency is unnecessary; it pronounces his existence untenable. Thus, according to Rachels (1990, 110), "Darwin's great contribution was the final demolition of the idea that nature is the product of intelligent design." How so? While any thoroughgoing naturalism might render God superfluous, the contingent, "dysteleological" character of Darwinian naturalism subverts and supplants the very possibility of God. Thus Dennett (1995, 15) writes, "Einstein famously said that the dear God is subtle but not malicious; [neo-Darwinism] turns that observation inside out: Mother Nature is heartless—even vicious—but boundlessly stupid." Hence natural selection, rightly understood, is not just operationally indifferent to but intrinsically incompatible with belief in an intelligent, purposeful Creator (Dawkins 1976; Williams 1988; Ruse and Wilson 1993; Bradie 1994).

Although other chapters in this volume will address what Dennett calls the "boundless stupidity" of nature by making a case for intelligent design, I want to focus on a different though related issue, namely, the "heartless, even vicious" character of the natural world (Dennett 1995, 15). It is not just that natural selection is claimed to leave no room for a designer but that the competition inherent in natural selection leaves no room for "goodness" in the emergence and development of life. Thus, even if we allowed that a designer might have used the naturalistic processes posited by Darwinism to create the world, a straightforward inspection of the world reveals that any such designer would have been monumentally wicked. As de Beer (1974, 7:23) put it:

> Darwin did two things: he showed that evolution was a fact contradicting scriptural legends of creation and that its cause, natural selection, was automatic, with no room for divine guidance or design. Furthermore, if there had been design it must have been very maleficent to cause all the suffering and pain that befall animals and men.

Even this assertion does not go far enough for many leading evolutionary thinkers (see Ghiselin 1974; Dawkins 1976; Barash 1977; Williams 1993;

Dennett 1995). They point out not only that natural processes entail much pain and carnage, but also that Darwinian natural selection specifically promotes suffering and ruthless self-interest and excludes the possibility of "natural goodness" in the form of biologically based sacrifice or beneficence. Darwin himself acknowledged that any character "formed for the exclusive good of another, would annihilate my theory, for such could not have been produced through natural selection" (Darwin 1967). As D. Oates (1988, 444) remarks, "For followers of Darwin, the familiar theological 'problem of evil' was turned inside out: evil could henceforth be assumed, and the existential paradox which demanded explanation became, in fact, *the problem of goodness*" (emphasis in the original).

A century after Darwin an important shift has occurred. The possibility of such sacrifice is no longer even entertained; rather its absence is a necessary consequence of an unquestioned commitment to Darwinian naturalism. As M. T. Ghiselin (1973, 967) puts it, to the extent we are persuaded that "natural selection is both sufficient and true, it is impossible for a genuinely disinterested or 'altruistic' behavior pattern to evolve." Alternatively "evolutionary biology is quite clear that 'What's in it for me?' is an ancient refrain for all life" (Barash 1977, 167). Whether life is indeed singing this glum refrain is the point of this investigation. In this chapter I will critique evolutionary accounts of altruism from the vantage of intelligent design.

**General Considerations**
Because natural selection by definition eliminates traits that reduce reproductive success relative to others, any trait that entails a reduction in fitness while increasing the fitness of others (i.e., "biological sacrifice") will be eliminated from populations. Biological altruism, defined as genetically "self-destructive behavior performed for the benefit of others," is incompatible with Darwinism (Wilson 1975, 578). If there are behaviors in animals (or for that matter in plants) that appear to entail such sacrifice, either it must be found upon closer scrutiny that there is no actual reduction in fitness or Darwin's theory fails as a sufficient, comprehensive biological explanation of the behavior of living systems.

Three points of clarification are worth making. First, some people who want to blunt the sting of Darwinism maintain that while altruism may be theoretically significant, it has no implications for design or divine character because it proceeds from an unwarranted "anthropomorphism" of nature and its organisms. Thus even if Darwinism is true, nature—an object, not a subject—is not really cruel or selfish. But this objection misses the point, which starts not with whether the world is cruel but with whether it suggests cruelty to human inquirers. When William Paley made a design argument, he took the adaptive complexity of insentient organisms to reflect intelligence in their maker. This argument from intelligence in objects to intelligence in the maker responsible for those objects applies as well to aesthetics and ethics. Thus beauty in an object reflects artistic awareness in its creator. The same holds true for goodness. Regardless whether the world has intrinsic moral qualities, our experience of its goodness has been used to underwrite faith in a God of providence (see Paul's sermon to the Athenians in Acts 17). This argument cuts both ways. Thus if the world is without features that suggest goodness, natural theology is in for a rough ride.

A second and related point is whether altruism should be understood in terms of intentions or consequences. The everyday notion of altruism is linked with the intention to sacrifice on behalf of another. But biological altruism is defined strictly as a behavior that reduces fitness on behalf of another and can be exhibited by organisms lacking intentionality. There has been regrettable confusion on these separate issues, and at times the emotionally laden imagery of motivational altruism has been inappropriately used to stimulate popular interest in the debate over biological altruism (see Schloss 1996). Nevertheless in the analysis of human behavior the two notions are closely linked.

Third and last, we must not sidestep the existential weight of natural evil but deal authentically with it, especially in the biological world and as it is uncovered through legitimate scientific discovery. To be sure, we have also unraveled great beauty and evidence of intelligent agency. But by itself that still leaves open Tennyson's problem of how beauty and creative intelligence are connected to goodness and moral purpose:

> This round of green, this orb of flame,
>
> Fantastic beauty; such as lurks
>
> In some wild Poet, when he works
>
> Without a conscience or an aim. (*In Memoriam*)

The first time I realized that after twenty years in field biology I could not think of a single, verifiable example of biological altruism, a single wind-pollinated flower that produces nectar, or anything else in all of living nature— "just to be nice"—it was a distressing revelation. I no longer believe such features are absent from nature, but the resolution of Tennyson's problem (at least for me) was not self-evident.

### Kin Selection

Let us start by considering a fact that had already puzzled Darwin years before he published the *Origin of Species*. Why are there characteristics, from ostensibly sacrificial social behavior to ungainly anatomical features, that appear to be an adaptive detriment to the individual possessor? It appears that organisms perform behaviors that help others while reducing the number of their own offspring. We shall call these counterreproductive or sacrificial behaviors. Some organisms, like the social insects, raised particular problems for natural selection theory because a large number of individuals do not mate at all and have biologically given up the ability to have offspring. Instead they tend the young of a reproductive queen. Nothing could appear to be more biologically altruistic than the nonreproductive lives of these sterile castes. Darwin did not resolve this problem, and it was more than a century before Darwinists made any progress in their resolution. Even the modern synthesis of Mendelian genetics and Darwinian selection theory failed to resolve this problem. Only in the last several decades have Darwinists made substantial progress.

The first significant advance came through the elucidation of kin selection and inclusive fitness in a seminal paper by William Hamilton (1964). Hamilton's argument began by observing that much behavior involving risk or sacrifice is directed toward offspring, which obviously ensures rather than compromises reproductive success or fitness. Moreover, if natural selection is understood as the "differential reproduction of genotypes," then fitness can be advanced by maximizing the genetic contribution to subsequent generations through the reproductive success of not only direct offspring (individual fitness) but also genetically related "kin" (inclusive fitness). Thus ostensibly sacrificial investments or risks on behalf of those who are not progeny but nevertheless have a shared genetic heritage may increase rather than decrease the proportionate representation of one's genome in the next generation. Hamilton predicted the degree of risk undertaken or investment expended should be proportional to the amount of genetic similarity between individuals. The notions of kin selection and inclusive fitness have successfully made sense of many previously observed but unexplained behaviors involving ostensible reproductive sacrifice in a wide variety of species and have been amply verified by subsequent experimental data. Moreover, they have effectively solved the enigma of sterile casts in social insects (see Trivers and Hare 1976).

Observational data indicate that cooperation between and reproductive sacrifice on behalf of genetically related kin are consistent with and predictable from selection theory. So potent appears the ability of inclusive fitness to make sense of counterreproductive helping behaviors, and so inadequate was our understanding of the possible genetic basis for social behavior prior to Hamilton's work that it is now described as facilitating a new synthesis that has "turned out to be the most important advance in evolutionary theory since the work of Charles Darwin and Gregor Mendel" (Trivers 1985, 47).

The modern synthesis integrated the hundred-year-old Darwinian and Mendelian theories but left the problem of cooperation and self-sacrifice unresolved. By solving a long-standing open problem with revolutionary new insights, the new synthesis hopes to integrate evolutionary biology more profoundly and comprehensively with the behavioral sciences than did the modern synthesis (see Hull 1978; Alexander 1993; Holcomb 1993).

Within the new synthesis, the new sociobiological synthesis engages the human behavioral sciences most directly and is therefore the most revolutionary and controversial as well as the most seriously incomplete (Holcomb 1993). When E. O. Wilson attempted to apply sociobiological ideas to human behavior in 1975, he broke what Mary Midgley (1982, xi) describes as a "precarious truce" in which "social scientists agreed not to deny the reality of human evolution, so long as nobody attempted to make any intellectual use of it." Reception outside the community of evolutionary biologists (and even within that community) was initially quite hostile. But as the triumphalist rhetoric of the popularizers gave way to more careful experimental work, interdisciplinary fields outside population genetics have emerged that attempt to relate natural selection to human behavior—for example, Darwinian anthropology, evolutionary psychology, biosociology and behavioral genetics.

What has become clear is that in human societies kin is a universal concept. And while there is considerable variance in kinship definitions, all of them correlate with genetic relatedness. Moreover, expectations for cooperativity tend to vary proportionally with kinship distance (Sahlins 1965). J. B. S. Haldane is purported facetiously to have remarked, "I'll gladly give my life for two brothers or eight cousins." Obviously we do not make such calculations consciously. But that is the point. Without having to calculate or even be cognizant of genetic similarity, virtually all cultures converge on behavioral values that are consistent with Hamilton's model. Of course consistency does not entail causality. Nevertheless here for the first time is a functional explanation of these patterns.

Even so, this particular functional explanation is also reconcilable with common grace and natural law (see 1 Timothy 5:8, where the apostle Paul asserts that anyone who deserts family is worse than an infidel and has forsaken the Christian faith). Moreover, for all the consistency between cultural universals and kin selection, there is still a wide variety of ethical concepts and actual behaviors that undeniably contradict it. While such anomalies are far more prevalent in human beings, counterreproductive behaviors that fail to enhance inclusive fitness are also common in other animal (and plant) species.

## Reciprocal Altruism

The next significant advance by evolutionists in explaining sacrificial behavior came from Robert Trivers's (1971) notion of reciprocal altruism. As with inclusive fitness, reciprocal altruism attempts to show that certain behaviors that appear to reduce reproductive success enhance fitness. The idea is simple, extending the notion of mutualistic interaction or shared benefit that we all know as "I'll scratch your back if you scratch mine." A large number of experimental studies and field observations has confirmed that reciprocal altruism, or prosocial behavior, can enhance fitness and has revealed the reciprocal benefits of many behaviors previously thought to be reproductively detrimental.

With respect to human social behavior, reciprocity is a cross-cultural universal, "no less universal and important an element of culture than the incest taboo" (Gouldner 1960, 171). Howard Becker (1956) went so far as to identify reciprocity as the defining, salient feature of human societies, even referring to the human species as *Homo reciprocus*. Becker expressed a significant but partial truth, for while subsequent studies confirmed the importance of reciprocity in human behavior and morality, reciprocal altruism has been found to play a significant role in many other social organisms as well. Should one do good to those who do good to you? Even the Gentiles, tax collectors and, for that matter, the passerine birds do the same. And while interspecific behavioral similarities do not demonstrate common causal mechanisms, it remains true that reciprocity in human behavioral systems is consistent with natural selection. At the same time reciprocity is also consistent with an intelligently designed human nature reflecting the capacity and need for mutually interdependent, personal relationships.

Reciprocal altruism is hardly a comprehensive theory of altruism. Consider, for instance, the origin of reciprocal behaviors. How could such a behavior, which requires the simultaneous existence of appropriate reciprocal behaviors to compensate for its cost, ever come about? Some applications of game theory have suggested scenarios that might account for cooperativity in extremely simple and stylized situations (e.g., a prisoner's dilemma with a limited number of stereotypic options). Reciprocal altruism is most common among organisms with the least simple behavioral repertoires (Holcomb 1993; Frank 1988). Or consider the maintenance of reciprocity once it has appeared inasmuch as "cheaters" not only incur benefits by cheating but at the same time destabilize cooperative paybacks. Much of the most recent work in evolutionary psychology and human moral evolution attempts to address this issue. But the most significant problem facing reciprocal altruism is that there exist numerous observable behaviors in plants and animals, and especially in humans, that are inexplicable on the basis of either kin selection or reciprocal altruism. Human behavior regularly exhibits noncompensatory sacrifice for nonkin. Explaining such phenomena constitutes one of the most controversial aspects of current evolutionary theory. Formulating an adequate explanation is widely regarded as the last roadblock to the theoretical completeness of evolutionary theory (Holcomb 1993).

## Recent Explanations of Sacrificial Behavior

While the theories of kin selection and reciprocal altruism have made great strides in explaining the biological basis for previously enigmatic animal behaviors, humans commonly exhibit behaviors that appear to violate these theories by incurring reproductive cost without conferring benefit to kin or compensatory reciprocation. Radical examples of such behaviors include voluntary celibacy, monastic orders of benevolence, vows of ascetic poverty, religious martyrdom and the life-threatening efforts of Holocaust rescuers. More common examples include adoption, heroic (one-time) efforts to save others across kinship and relational barriers, sacrificial philanthropy, blood and organ donation, acts of wartime or athletic (risk-entailing) valor, exclusive homosexuality, suicide, manic depression, and even drug use and gang violence. And while such acts are much more common in human beings, there are counterreproductive behaviors in other species as well. Three main theoretical approaches have emerged to explain these phenomena within a Darwinian context.

### Theoretical approaches

*Sexual selection and social status.* The first approach is to look for ways an ostensibly counterreproductive behavior might ultimately contribute to reproductive success. Darwin was the first person to explore this approach through his notion of sexual selection. Some biological characteristics, such as the bright and ungainly tail of male peacocks, would appear to confer adaptive detriment. Yet if the characteristic increases the ability of the individual to attract mates, the increased liability to predation associated with the tail could be compensated for by increased mating success. Fitness would be served. Another similar way sacrificial behaviors can serve reproductive ends is by enhancing social status. Increased social status can enhance fitness by enabling mate attraction (this would then be sexual selection), or by improving reputation (facilitating reciprocal exchange), or by contributing to dominance (and hence access to resources). In human beings sexual selection and the enhancement of social status have been proposed to explain blood donation, adoption, expenditure of resources for the acquisition of art and other counterreproductive investments, male acts of self-risking valor, and even gang behavior or flagrant drug use, here regarded as a display of potent risk taking (Diamond 1992, 202-3).

This attempt to explain ostensibly counterreproductive behavior faces several difficulties. First, there is no evidence that such behaviors have any genetic basis. Second, there are no studies to demonstrate that such behaviors are associated with social status. Third, there is not even consistent evidence that social status positively correlates with fitness in human populations. Lastly, there is substantial resistance to these explanations among evolutionary adherents (Gould 1977; Lewontin, Rose, and Kamin 1984; Singer 1981, 1984; Midgley 1994). None of these difficulties invalidate the approach, but they do testify to its limitations.

*Pleiotropic interactions and genetic lag.* The second approach openly acknowledges the existence of behaviors that do not confer reproductive benefit but then argues that they can nonetheless arise in systems formed through natural selection. One line of argument emphasizes pleiotropic or overdominant interactions, where a maladaptive characteristic is associated with adaptive benefits of a related genotype or phenotype. For example, while sickle-cell anemia is maladaptive, heterozygous carriers of the gene are resistant to malaria. Similarly, it has been proposed that while manic depression is a potentially fatal disease with a heritable component, related family members exhibit higher measures of intelligence and creativity. It has also been suggested that adoption is a maladaptive manifestation of the more common, more moderate and selectively advantageous inclination to parental care.

Another line of argument looks to genetic lag, in which the environment changes but the genotype (and concomitant phenotype) does not. Thus we can end up with a trait that was fully adaptive in the environment in which it arose but is not adaptive in the present one. Adoption is often presented as such a trait, where in earlier cultural environments it facilitated establishment of cooperative alliances (Alexander 1987). Wartime valor and gang-turf territoriality are presented as behaviors that made reproductive sense in the context of tribal units of kinship and reciprocal exchange. Now these tendencies result in counterreproductive, "vestigial" behaviors (Wright 1994). Although any species can exhibit genetic lag, because culture changes more rapidly than our genome, humans in particular are viewed as "a hodgepodge of special genetic adaptations to an environment largely vanished, the world of the Ice Age hunter-gatherer" (Wilson 1978, 196). None of these arguments has convincing empirical support.

*Manipulation and the extended phenotyype.* A third and more recent approach to counterreproductive behavior focuses on the recipient of the action rather than the actor. Within this approach reproductively sacrificial acts are viewed as manipulated by the beneficiary (Trivers 1985; Alexander 1987; Cronk 1994). The classic nonhuman example of this is interspecific parental care in birds, where one species (e.g., warblers) cares for the egg and feeds the hatchlings of another species (e.g., cowbirds), which lays its eggs in the first species' nest. This often results in failure of the warbler's own progeny to survive, and because it involves sacrificing reproductive success while enhancing that of another, it is a premier example of biological altruism— the very thing that natural selection should not allow. Even so, it becomes explainable from a Darwinian perspective if viewed as nest parasitism. The cowbird is manipulating, or parasitizing, the warblers' instincts for parental attentiveness, which were "designed to" ensure its own fitness.

From this perspective nearly any interaction that results in an asymmetric behavioral exchange, where one individual benefits at the expense of another, can be viewed as coercion or manipulation and takes the form of parasitism, competition or predation. Adoption of genetically unrelated infants has thus been explained as manipulation of parental care instincts by the neotinous attractiveness of newborns (Alexander 1987). Blood and organ donations have been explained as manipulation of compassionate or prosocial inclinations designed by selection to facilitate reciprocity (Williams 1988). In this way every act of apparent kindness becomes ultimately self-interested or involuntarily manipulated. In its favor, this view unmasks any saccharine ideal of human beneficence that denies the manipulation of prosocial instincts.

But the real scientific difficulty is how to demonstrate manipulation. Like the Aristotelian notion of violence, manipulation entails forcing something away from its intended end. The parental attentiveness of warblers is taken as having been "designed to" enhance the actor's reproductive success, but cowbirds manipulate it to another end. Thus a *telos* is introduced into evolutionary theory at this point, not unlike the teleonomic concepts used to describe physiological function and the attendant deviation from such function in pathology. Darwin himself was quite sensitive to this point and phrased himself with teleonomic precision when he observed his theory would be annihilated by the existence of any character "*formed for* [emphasis added] the exclusive good of another." Thus it is not mere sacrifice or even sacrifice resulting in another's benefit but only sacrifice "exclusively for" another that is evolutionarily inconceivable.

How we determine what behaviors are "for" and thus whether or not they have been "manipulated" are complicated phylogenetic and developmental questions that, as Alexander (1993) appropriately laments, we have not even begun to answer. Moreover, there remain substantial and unaddressed metalevel methodological questions about the role and testability of teleonomic hypotheses in science, as well as higher-order philosophical questions about the role of science vis-a-vis other disciplines in interpreting purpose in the natural world. As it now stands, evolutionary theory asserts that radical human sacrifice—which is undeniable in its prevalence—must be the result of manipulation because humanity and human morality are taken to be designed not for altruism but for keeping "the human genetic material intact. . . . Morality has no other demonstrable ultimate function" (Wilson 1978, 167).

Because natural selection is concerned with genetic outcomes and not with psychological motivation, even unwitting or manipulated reproductive sacrifice is still biologically altruistic: "With manipulation we have at last found true, albeit involuntary altruism" (Cronin 1991, 265). If it were common, such sacrifice would still be problematic for evolutionary theory. For this reason Richard Dawkins has taken the theoretically controversial but rhetorically astute move of dispensing with organisms in favor of genes. Dawkins contends that the unit of selection and repository of fitness is the gene—organismal phenotypes are the means by which genes interact with the environment to pass themselves on.

This is the familiar thesis of *The Selfish Gene* (Dawkins 1976). Accordingly the structure of an egg can be viewed as the phenotype of certain genes in a given environment. But the temperature of the egg and other characteristics related to its being cared for by its parents are also part of the phenotype of those genes. The behavior of parental care itself can be viewed as part of the phenotype of genes coding for egg characteristics, for if different genes resulted in sufficiently different colors or morphology, a different (or no) attentive response would be provoked. The fitness of the egg's genes is maintained by their phenotype of parental care. At this point, however, it is theoretically inconsequential which organism confers that care—the one who laid the egg (e.g., a cowbird) or another species altogether (e.g., a warbler). In either case the behavior is seen as the phenotype contributing to the fitness of the egg's genes.

Consequently there is no problem or even possibility of altruism, in which a characteristic, say, exists "for the exclusive good of another." The very notion of "another" refers to organisms. But characteristics (phenotypes) exist for genes, and benefits in turn accrue to genes. The whole idea of altruism, and the challenge to Darwinism it supposedly represented, becomes an artifact of an organism-centered rather than a gene-centered perspective on fitness. Dawkins argues, moreover, not only that we should focus on genes rather than organisms but also that our understanding of organisms themselves should expand beyond the skin—to entail all the phenotypic interactions between genes and their environments.

Just as a beaver's fur is part of the organismal phenotype of its genes, so is its dam part of its extended phenotype (Dawkins 1982). In a similar way spider webs, female crickets' muscular response to males' singing, women's erect nipples in the presence of a crying infant, and even the care received from warblers by cowbird eggs are also part of an extended phenotype of the genome receiving the behavior. Dawkins pushes the concept of a "skinless organism" to include all the interactions between a genome and its environment. Organismal sacrifice is no longer problematic, not only because it is genes rather than organisms that keep the tally but also because the very notion of an organism becomes a fluid conceptual construct. As Helena Cronin (1991, 265) ironically observes in her widely circulated exposition of sociobiological theory, "Only once it was solved was the problem clearly seen. . . . On a gene-centered understanding, the problem of altruism dissolves." Needless to say, the price of this solution is higher than many biologists are willing to pay.

### *Observational data*

The exciting thing about science is that the world pushes back against the concepts we use to describe it. How do the preceding theories fare in the face of observational studies? For lack of space I shall forgo animal and plant data and focus instead on human data. A large number of empirical studies on human behavioral altruism have been conducted over the last two decades (Breuer 1983; Badcock 1986; Batson 1987; Oliner and Oliner 1988; Rushton 1986, 1989; Wenegrat 1990; Vine 1992; Oliner et. al. 1993; Pope 1994; Sellick 1994; Monroe 1996). Several things become clear from these studies. First off, the existence, indeed the abundance, of human behaviors that are not explainable through direct benefits from kin selection or reciprocal altruism (i.e., behaviors that do not clearly contribute to reproductive success) is incontestable. A large number of ad hoc explanatory hypotheses have been proposed to explain these behaviors. These hypotheses remain controversial and have not gone unchallenged (see Sahlins 1976; Mattern 1978; Midgley 1980, 1982; Sayers 1982; Singer 1984; Kaye 1986; Schwartz 1986; Fox-Keller 1991; Ayala 1995; Gilkey 1995; Lash 1995; de Waal 1996).

Regardless of whether any of these hypotheses eventually prove successful, it is important to remember that their purpose is to make sense of why behavior fails to conform to the reproductive self-interest predicted for traits with an evolutionary origin. Human behavior displays unusually widespread nonconformity, so widespread that some leading theorists have been driven to conclude that characteristic aspects of the human behavioral repertoire actually "float free" from the influence of natural selection (Richards 1986,

1993; Bradie 1994; Ayala 1995; Sober 1995). This does not mean that natural selection cannot operate on the human genome, for if behavior is consistently counterreproductive, selection or even extinction will ensue. But it does mean that the genome on which selection acts has at best tentative ties with behavioral phenotypes.

In contrast sociobiology remains committed to seeing altruism as self-interest by another name. Thus over the last decade sociobiologists have developed a body of theory that attempts to explain not why ostensibly sacrificial behaviors do not contribute to fitness but how they end up doing so indirectly, by concealed means (Alexander 1987, 1993; Trivers 1991; Ruse and Wilson 1993; Cronk 1994). Their account begins with the observation that reciprocity is central to human social systems, and as with all mutualistic relationships, the optimal strategy is to manipulate the terms of exchange to one's benefit by "cheating," or taking more than one receives. A biologically common way of achieving this is by deceitful displays—for example, flowers that have no nectar may mimic the appearance of nectar-rich inflorescences. In the context of social reciprocity, individuals manipulate benefits by feigning cooperativity or resource possession. Detection of cheaters, however, pressures the development of ever more costly and therefore convincing altruistic displays. On this view guilt is the alarm that goes off when we are cheating in a way that is likely to be detected; that is, when we are risking reputationally mediated fitness penalties (Alexander 1987). Consequently, "What is in our genes' best interests is what seems 'right.' ... Moral guidance is a euphemism. Parents are designed to steer kids toward 'moral' behaviors only insofar as those behaviors are self-serving" (Wright 1994, 216).

But all this is highly counterintuitive. How do sociobiologists explain why no ordinary person believes this about morality? The reason people do not equate morality with self-interest is that in order to effectively deceive others for our own benefit, we first need to deceive ourselves. We deceive ourselves into believing that moral imperatives are legitimate and that we really ought to (and that we really do) care about others for two reasons. First, we accept the "illusion" of moral obligation because if we were good to others only in order to consciously manipulate them, then we would not be good enough to them to accomplish the manipulation! Morality—the impulse that we ought to do something—is natural selection's way of getting us to do the costly things that are ultimately necessary for self-benefit. But to work, morality has to seem real, functioning as "a collective illusion of the human race, fashioned and maintained by natural selection in order to promote individual reproduction" (Ruse 1988, 74). Alternatively, "we think that we have obligations to others because it is in our biological interests to have these thoughts" (Ruse 1993, 148).

The second reason for deceiving ourselves is this: Even if we could perform appropriate manipulative behaviors perfectly without deceiving ourselves, our manipulative intent would still be detected because the people we are manipulating would recognize themselves as manipulators too. Think of it this way: because I recognize that whenever I do $X$ for someone, I am manipulating him to do $Y$ for me, whenever someone does $X$ for me, I will suspect that he is manipulating me to do $Y$ for him. Human consciousness ushers in "a game of life in which the participants are trying to comprehend what is in one another's minds before, and more effectively than, it can be done in reverse" (Alexander 1987, 133). The best way of not having our self-serving or exploitive intentions detected by another is to make sure they do not enter our minds as conscious thoughts. Self-deception is therefore essential to achieving effective other-deception, and there is a growing literature on this topic (a sample of reviews and seminal treatments includes Trivers 1991; Barkow, Cosmides, and Tooby 1992; Alexander 1993; Cronk 1994).

It is certainly the case that sacrificial behaviors like adoption, heroism, philanthropy or tipping in an out-of-town restaurant potentially offer a reproductive payoff. Any one of these behaviors is likely to enhance reputation, and none of them entails reproductive defeat. Thus it is possible for their attendant risk to be more than offset by compensation from indirect or manipulated benefit. But certain more radical sacrificial behaviors—what Lopreato (1984) calls "ascetic altruism"—invariably incur grave risks and extreme renunciation, frequently produce reputational collapse and social ostracism, and often entail complete reproductive failure. Cronk (1994) tries to redeem these anomalies by observing that religious leaders may enhance personal fitness by using heightened social status to manipulate others to their own reproductive ends. In this vein Wright (1994, 366) will argue that even in the life of Christ preaching took the "form of exploitation . . . amplifying the power of Jesus." It is true that religious leadership or any socially esteemed role may yield access to resources. However, it is not the generic social institution of organized religion but the specific and distinctive behavior of ascetic altruism—often in the face of established religion—that requires explanation, in which social status is forfeited at the expense of marginalization and even martyrdom, and where even if life and resources were retained, there would be no progeny to profit from them. Appeals to reputationally mediated, indirect reciprocity is singularly unenlightening for understanding the lives of martyred celibates.

Wilson (1978) devotes the better part of a chapter to this problem and concludes that religious altruism, like that displayed by Mother Teresa, results from the "ossification" of self-serving in-group loyalty and out-group hostility, essentially no different from that of Marxists, Black Panthers or organized crime. Moreover, it may be selfishly motivated by the hope of heaven. Like Cronk, Wilson proposes a conceptual stereotype without offering empirical support. In particular he fails to address the numerous, observable cases where members of the out-group are served, very often at the cost of life and reproduction to the in-group. Furthermore, even if the behavior were selfishly motivated, the challenge to selection theory would still be to explain the consistently sacrificial reproductive outcomes. Trading fitness for eternal life is exactly the kind of swap that evolution cannot allow. Indeed any genes that calculate their return rate in heavenly currency will quickly lose their seat on the reproductive exchange (Schloss 1996, 126).

Ruse (1994, 1995) clearly recognizes this paradox and attempts to face it head on by arguing that the radical love commanded in Christianity is biologically and therefore ethically "perverse" since it requires us to do what an evolved nature cannot do. If there were any truth to completely self-disinterested moral obligation, "then at the substantival level, not only do we have a clash but we have a clear refutation of the evolutionist's case. No amount of careful talk or verbal juggling can save the day" (Ruse 1993, 154). All the same, claims Ruse, it is clear that although some people "pay lip service" to such notions, nobody believes them—and nobody lives by them. In the highly unlikely event we encountered somebody who did, it would be rare enough and bizarre enough to be considered pathological. And because such behavior constitutes a perverse departure from rather than an appropriate fulfillment of our evolved nature, perverse is exactly what it is. Natural selection, it is argued, cannot exclude maladaptive anomalies; it just prevents them from taking hold and becoming common or characteristic.

While Ruse appears to face the problem more squarely than others do, the problem with his proposal is that it begs the question. He treats radical altruism as a pathological deviation from rather than an essential manifestation of human nature precisely because his starting point is a humanity that has evolved via selection. Furthermore, observational data fail to confirm that ascetic altruism is uncharacteristic of our species. Unlike parthenocarpy in plants, ascetic altruism is not an anomalous but a universal and distinguishing feature of the human behavioral repertoire. Moreover, a large number of empirical studies have investigated whether such behavior is demonstrably associated with pathological deviance, marked self-deception or indirect reputational benefits (indirect reputational payoffs obviously could not contribute to the reproductive success of altruism in the case of celibacy or family martyrdom, but it could still contribute to their inclusive fitness if members of the extended family accrued benefits).

Batson (1987) has conducted a series of psychometric and experimental investigations of altruistic helping behavior. He has demonstrated that some individuals help others, at cost to themselves, where there is no possible material or reputational positive consequence for helping or negative consequence for not helping. The Oliners (1988, 1993) have conducted the most extensive comparative and longitudinal psychological investigations of Holocaust rescuers, as well as numerous related studies of altruism and altruistic personality. In their psychometric assessment of rescuers, they found no indication of pathology and no statistically significant deviance of any kind from control groups of nonrescuers.

Holocaust rescuers exhibited patterns of aid that uniformly violated selectionist expectations. Not only was the risk of death clear and ongoing, but also it was not confined to the rescuer. The rescuer's family, extended family and friends were all in jeopardy, and they were recognized to be in jeopardy by the rescuer. Moreover, even if the family escaped death, they often experienced deprivation of food, space and social commerce; extreme emotional distress; and forfeiture of the rescuer's attention. What is more, rescuing was unlikely to enhance the reputation of the rescuer: Jews, Gypsies and other aided individuals were typically despised, and assisting them so violated the laws and prevailing social values that the social consequences included ostracism, forfeiture of possessions and execution. While it is possible to speculate that reputation and group cohesion within subcultural enclaves could have been enhanced by rescuing, there is little evidence that such enclaves existed, and most rescuers do not testify to belonging to or knowing of a group that would have extended support or approval, much less reward or esteem for their actions. Moreover, the overwhelming majority were absolutely secretive about their behavior, not even disclosing it to closest friends or family members outside their immediate dwelling.

Finally, the "most unvarying" feature of the behavior and attitudes of all the rescuers was the complete absence of group or individual connections to those aided. Rescuers were not those who had strong ties to the Jewish community or culture or affectionate personal histories with Jewish individuals. Nor were they consciously motivated by the principle of equal rights for Jews or other groups (they were consistently unlikely to think in terms of either group identity or political causes). And significantly, the individuals they helped were not people they knew, or who lived in their neighborhood or region, or who were of the same nationality or socioeconomic class, or who shared similar ages, interests or personalities. Rescuers did not consider the individuals they assisted more likable or moral than others. None of the relational hallmarks of indirect benefit, group identity or reciprocal altruism were present. And even if they had been present, rescuers derived no compensatory reproductive benefit but only liability. The complete absence of group or individual connections between rescuers and those aided invalidates selectionist attempts to explain the rescuers' aid as manipulation or "reciprocity gone bad." Monroe (1996, 178) summarizes the matter thus:

> Altruism presents a particularly thorny theoretical problem for evolutionary biologists, who base their discipline on Darwin's notions of individual selection and survival of the fittest. Their general response to altruism has been to argue that individual selection works through either kin selection or group selection. There are few biological works on human altruism, and these do not specify the origin of altruism. Nor do biologists tend to focus on individual choices but rather on statistical trends in long-range genetic selection.

My overall conclusion concerning biological explanations of altruism is that they work reasonably well for behavioral patterns of rational actors in general and for some philanthropists but have nothing to contribute to our understanding of the more extreme forms of altruistic behavior. The individualistic paradigm and implicit assumption of self-interest on which Darwinian biology is based appears unable to account for situations of genuine self-sacrifice for people not of one's kin or social group. What evolutionary biologists are explaining is not altruism but rather the limited and isolated acts of charity or volunteer work in which even the most self-interested rational actor engages intermittently. To understand altruism and altruists themselves, we need another theoretical framework.

### An Alternative Framework
#### Theoretical instability of the current framework
What will such a framework look like? At the least it is clear we need a broader theoretical framework than Darwinian natural selection if we are to have an adequate understanding of human social behavior. Some second-generation sociobiologists already admit as much, maintaining that we need a biological explanation larger than Darwinian fitness, while others (including many biologists) concede that the moral and sacrificial aspects of human behavior most needing explanation cannot be understood in terms of biological causation at all (Sober 1993, 1995; Ayala 1995; Lash 1995; Gilkey 1995; Sagan and Margulis 1995). Such concessions arise not only because of incongruities between theory and observational data but also because of intrinsic explanatory inadequacies of the Darwinian framework. I shall briefly describe some of these inadequacies and then suggest how intelligent design offers a way around them.

Among the explanatory inadequacies facing sociobiology are its neglect of experiential data, the absence of connection with known genetic and developmental mechanisms, and its inability to predict patterns of age, gender or culture-related behavioral differences (Kitcher 1985; Alexander 1993; Holcomb 1993; Gilkey 1995). These widely treated issues represent an important research agenda for second generation research in sociobiology and related fields. Nonetheless I want to focus on two other explanatory inadequacies that have not been extensively acknowledged.

First, the theory as presently formulated does not distinguish between the evolutionary origin of human nature and the influence of evolution upon human nature. This tension is reflected in the virulent debate within the Darwinian community over whether natural selection explains every aspect or only some aspects of biological phenomena, especially human nature (Sober 1993, 1995; Dennett 1995; Gould 1997). Because many features of the natural world do not seem to agree with the predictions of selection theory, researchers are taking two conflicting approaches, either looking more imaginatively for the subtle hand of selection within the data or suggesting selection's hand is sufficiently slack that it may not account for all the data. It is important to note, however, that this debate over hyperselectionism betrays a more fundamental theoretical instability, namely, whether natural selection constitutes an ultimate, originating cause or merely a proximal, modifying influence. This question ties directly into the question of intelligent design, but one does not have to advocate intelligent design to posit the origin of major biological characters apart from natural selection.

This tension between natural selection as an originating cause and as a modifying influence is not new and has figured centrally in debates between creationists and evolutionists about biogenesis, macroevolution and the incompleteness of the fossil record. For the purpose of this study, how we resolve this tension is crucial to how we understand human altruism. To see this, imagine two scenarios. In one, humanity arose through natural selection, and its central behavioral impulses were linked to reproductive optimality, although changing environments, nonselective evolutionary forces, and our unusual phenotypic plasticity have yielded their share of counterreproductive behavior. Radical love represents an aberration (or as Dennett would say, natural selection does not guarantee adaptation, only extinction if one does not adapt).

Now consider a second scenario in which humanity was designed for loving interaction. The agency here is immaterial—without intending a supernatural referent Midgley (1994, 263) maintains that love is "part of animal nature, not a colonial imposition." As part of this scenario let us also assume that selection has profoundly influenced aspects of human nature since and perhaps even during its inception. In both scenarios the stamp of selection or reproductive interest is widely distributed across human behavior. How then to distinguish them? What we need is a more predictively specific formulation of the second scenario. A full-fledged theory of intelligent design would be extremely useful in fleshing out this second scenario.

Next, I wish to point out that not only are most sociobiological scenarios merely speculative possibilities, but also they are abiological possibilities. By "abiological" I do not mean that they are antibiological or contrary to biological theory but that they lack biological content. What characterizes the field is econometrics, wherein human behavior is assumed to be pitched toward maximizing the difference between resources acquired and resources expended in social interactions. This proceeds from the unexamined assumption that optimizing resource exchange will translate rather directly into optimized fitness. Thus "all organisms should have logically evolved to avoid every instance of beneficence or altruism unlikely to bring returns greater than the expenditure it entails" (Alexander 1975, 90).

Regardless whether this claim is true, it contains little biology, which no doubt is why so many economists and political scientists have contributed to evolutionary theory in this area (see Becker 1956; Frank 1988; Maxwell 1990; Simon 1990; Wilson 1993). We really do not learn anything from econometrics about the biological mechanisms (largely developmental) that mediate the connection between particular behaviors, resource states and the fitness-determining processes of growth and reproduction. This is not just a case of incomplete mechanistic explanations, as is the case with our understanding of gravitational attraction between two bodies. Most sociobiological accounts that purport to provide a biological explanation do not have a demonstrated link to organismal biology. Moreover, the assumed link through natural selection may be false. Here too is an open door for alternative paradigms, including design hypotheses.

### Implications for the design hypothesis
*Design as a scientific theory.* At the beginning of this chapter we considered Ghiselin's claim that if natural selection were both sufficient and true, there could be no genuinely disinterested behavior. Because Darwinists treat the truth and sufficiency of selection not as a hypothesis to be tested but as a given, they conclude that there are no disinterested behaviors. And this in turn requires them to deconstruct those behaviors that appear disinterested lest their theory be violated. But what if instead we treated the world as if human beings were created by a good God for loving relationship? Not only would this open the door to different interpretations of human behavior, but it would also encourage us to look for data that a hyperselectionist paradigm assumes cannot exist. Such a starting point is not committed to

supernatural causation. Moreover, it is free to generate testable hypotheses, which, unless dismissed on a priori grounds, can be confirmed or disconfirmed through the ordinary methods of science.

How might this happen? I have already commented on the abiological character of econometric sociobiological models, which bypass the organism by assuming that socially mediated resource budgets translate directly into reproductive output. Whatever else might be true about Darwinism, we know organisms are not passive tally sheets and that the bookkeeping analogy hardly captures the causal relationship between genes and phenotypes (Bradie 1994, 150). Rather organisms are integrated, dynamic systems that generate varying amounts of homeostatic and developmental return from their resources. They are alive. The key question for biology therefore is how human social behavior not only acquires resources but also mediates their conversion to fitness. This is a question about how life works and what kind of organisms human beings are.

If one believes human beings are designed to be loving organisms, then it is reasonable to hypothesize that behavior which is generous toward others might actually increase fitness—and not because it increases social status and therefore improves access to resources but because even if resources are relinquished, it may improve utilization efficiency or result in psychoneurological states that promote immunity, learning, vitality or other aspects of well-being. These are all testable hypotheses that do not require a commitment to supernatural agency before one investigates them, much less conceives of them. To be sure, this proposal flows naturally out of my commitment to intelligent design (Schloss 1996). But Fox-Keller and Ewing (1993, 93) make a similar proposal from a very different starting point: "Interactions that effectively generate new resources, or either increase the efficiency of resource utilization or reduce absolute requirement, are more directly damaging to the very principle of self-interest. These are exactly the kinds of interactions that are generally categorized as special cases."

Not only is the proposal testable, but also it conforms to a variety of emerging data in studies of well-being, psychoneuroimmunology and interpersonal relationships. Ayala (1995, 134) comments on how "the commandment of charity, 'Love thy neighbor as thyself,' often runs contrary to the inclusive fitness of the genes, even though it promotes social cooperation and peace of mind." Vine (1992, 100) proposes that we reconceptualize our entire understanding of how self-awareness develops, not in light of selection's emphasis on the individual but in light of the interpersonal bonding that we all experience:

> If initial awareness of self are "we-cognitions" of self-with-other, and "we-volitions" of self-for-other, the possibility of altruism becomes real.

And once the biological gulf between ego desires and other-concern has been crossed in prototypic form in this first social identity, there is no mystery in principle regarding our human power to escape from the enclosed worlds of evolutionary imperatives. These tied us rigidly to the pursuit of fitness only until humans jointly created and discovered their subjective, but still functionally real, social selves.

*Natural theology.* The preceding approach entails starting with design, reasoning to hypotheses about human social behavior and then confirming these hypotheses empirically. In natural theology one reasons back to design from observations of the world. There is a growing body of neuroscience literature that does just this. While the sociobiological perspective views consciousness as a tool for manipulating others, James Ashbrook (1994) maintains that consciousness and its neurological underpinnings reflect a "cry for the other." This cry for the other exists even prior to our conceptualizing the other. For instance, in maternal deprivation syndrome infants experience neurological deficits when they are deprived of maternal contact even if all their physical needs are met.

We know that relational intimacy, and not just the resources it might afford, is a condition for health throughout life. So is a sense of purpose and hope. We long for intimacy with people, beauty and meaning. These are necessary and real. Moreover, empirical data confirm that they are necessary and real. They are "there," as much as "warmth" or any other human processing of the external environment is there. As neuroscientist Rodney Holmes (1996, 451) puts it, "From our knowledge of how the brain constructs reality, we may conclude that there are realities that are not material: they include social reality, psychological reality, and metaphysical reality. It is a fundamental mistake to reduce them to material reality."

The question arises whether these social, psychological and metaphysical constructs grab hold of reality. Deception theory argues that our internal awareness of concern for others distorts the true state of our deepest motivations. Lopreato (1984) and Ruse (1994, 1995) claim that belief in a soul, nonmaterial forces and an objective basis for moral imperatives can effectively enable us to exhibit sacrificial behaviors at variance with selective constraints but that the objects of these beliefs are ultimately "fictitious" and "illusory." As usual this claim follows from presupposing Darwinism, not on independent grounds.

In contrast Holmes (1996, 453) argues—even though he assumes the brain is naturally selected—that what the brain does has "a fundamental root in reality and is fit for a real environment." Even Robin Fox (1989, 45) will admit that "instinct is the organism's demand for an appropriate environment." The implication for natural theology is that the fundamental longings and cognitive intuitions of the human psyche, including the cry for the other, entail real needs for environmental realities. Unlike the hypotheses that emerge from a scientific theory of design, such claims cannot be tested experimentally. Even so, and perhaps for this very reason, they deserve further philosophical and theological investigation, especially in the light of cognitive and behavioral neuroscience.

*Theology of nature.* I began this study by observing that many expositions of Darwinism claim that a world ruled by natural selection is incompatible with a good Creator. Even if we grant this claim, it is not clear that the scope of natural selection is all-encompassing. A more adequate understanding of the natural world views the world as fundamentally open to goodness. At the same time such an understanding need not be so naive as to view nature as one blissful frolic. The problem of evil remains a problem. Happily, good as well as evil receives full play in the biblical tradition. The biblical perspective, while affirming the goodness of God the Creator, also acknowledges the fallenness of creation. As Sloan (1995, 145) remarks,

> There would certainly be little warrant for assuming that the kinds of issues raised by Darwin present some kind of decisive critique, or even that the arguments raised by the existence of maladaptation, extinction, parasitism, or evolutionary "dead-ending" add something new to the awareness of a world in which death, evil, pain, suffering, and imperfection have deep theological significance. These arguments succeed as critiques only if it is assumed that Christian theology implies a natural order without evident defect or deficiency, able to reveal God's purposes and benevolence in some direct way without need at some point of a faith-response.

The world contains evil as well as beauty and goodness. The ability of goodness to emerge from a flawed process is itself good—a testimony to the grace of God, which can redeem good from evil (Gilkey 1995). As Lash (1995, 286) points out, "The context of the confession of God's good creation, the context of our celebration of God's good garden, remains (for the Christian) the garden of Gethsemane and the hill of Golgotha on which the tree of life was planted." To this Pascal would add that there is just enough light in creation to speak of God's purposes and just enough darkness to tell us we have lost sight of him and to convince us of our need for both faith and a Savior to restore it. But faith is not just a means for achieving understanding. It is also a way of preserving a healthy ignorance. This does not mean rejecting knowledge but rejecting the illusory confidence that we understand when we do not. Or as Lash (1995, 281) puts it, "Christian hope paradoxically enriches our knowledge by protecting our nescience from illusion."

## References

Alexander, R. D. 1975. The search for a general theory of behavior. *Behavioral Science* 20:77-100.

———. 1987. *The biology of moral systems.* Chicago: Aldine-de Gruyter.

———. 1993. Biological considerations in the analysis of morality. In *Evolutionary ethics,* ed. M. H. Nitecki and D. V. Nitecki, 163-96. Albany: State University of New York Press.

Ashbrook J. 1996. A rippling relatableness in reality. *Zygon* 31:469-82.

Ayala, F. J. 1995. The difference of being human: Ethical behavior as an evolutionary byproduct. In *Biology, ethics and the origins of life,* ed. H. Rolston, 3:113-36. Boston: Jones and Bartlett.

Badcock, C. R. 1986. *The problem of altruism: Freudian and Darwinian solutions.* Oxford: Basil Blackwell.

Barash, D. P. 1977. *Sociobiology and behavior.* New York: Elsevier.

Barkow, J. H., L. Cosmides, and J. Tooby, eds. 1992. *The adapted mind: Evolutionary psychology and the generation of culture.* New York: Oxford University Press.

Batson, C. D. 1987. Prosocial motivation: Is it ever truly altruistic? In *Advances in experimental social psychology,* ed. L. Berkowitz, 14:65-122. San Diego, Calif.: Academic Press.

Becker, H. 1956. *Man in reciprocity.* New York: Praeger.

Bradie, M. 1994. *The secret chain: Evolution and ethics.* Albany: State University of New York Press.

Breuer, G. 1983. *Sociobiology and the human dimension* (translation of *Der Sogenannte Mensch*). Cambridge: Cambridge University Press.

Brooke, J. H. 1991. *Sciences and religion: Some historical perspectives.* Cambridge: Cambridge University Press.

Cronin, H. 1991. *The ant and the peacock.* Cambridge: Cambridge University Press.

Cronk, L. 1994. Evolutionary theories of morality and the manipulative use of signals. *Zygon* 29:81-101.

Darwin, C. 1967. *On the origin of species by means of natural selection: Or, the preservation of favored races in the struggle for life.* 1859. Reprint, Cambridge, Mass.: Harvard University Press.

Dawkins, R. 1976. *The selfish gene.* Oxford: Oxford University Press.

———. 1982. *The extended phenotype.* Oxford: Oxford University Press.

de Beer, G. 1973-1974. Evolution. In *Encyclopedia Britannica,* 15th ed., 7:7-23. London: Encyclopedia Britannica.

de Waal, F. 1996. *Good natured: The origins of right and wrong in humans and other animals.* Cambridge, Mass.: Harvard University Press.

Dennett, D. C. 1995. *Darwin's dangerous idea: Evolution and the meaning of life.* New York: Simon and Schuster.

Dewey, J. 1951. *The influence of Darwin on philosophy, and other essays.* 1910. Reprint, New York: P. Smith.

Diamond, J. 1992. *The third chimpanzee: The evolution and future of the human animal.* New York: HarperCollins.

Fox, R. 1989. *The search for society: Quest for a biosocial science and morality.* New Brunswick, N.J.: Rutgers University Press.

Fox-Keller, E. 1991. Language and ideology in evolutionary theory: Reading cultural norms into natural law. In *The boundaries of humanity: Humans, animals, machines,* ed. J. J. Sheehan and M. Sosna, 85-102. Berkeley, Calif.: University of California Press.

Fox-Keller, E., and M. S. Ewing. 1993. The kinds of "individuals" one finds in evolutionary biology. In *Evolutionary ethics*, ed. M. H. Nitecki and D. V. Nitecki. Albany: State University of New York Press.

Frank, R. H. 1988. *Passions within reason: The strategic role of the emotions*. New York: Norton.

Ghiselin, M. T. 1973. Darwin and evolutionary psychology. *Science* 179:964-68.

———. 1974. *The economy of nature and the evolution of sex*. Berkeley: University of California Press.

Gilkey, L. 1995. Biology and theology on human nature: Ethics and genetics. In *Biology, ethics and the origins of life*, ed. H. Rolston, 3:163-90. Boston: Jones and Bartlett.

Gliserman, S. 1975. Early Victorian science writers and Tennyson's *In Memoriam:* A study in cultural exchange. *Victorian Studies* 18:277-308, 437-59.

Gould, S. J. 1977. *Ever since Darwin*. New York: Norton.

———. 1997. Darwinian fundamentalism. *New York Review of Books,* June 12.

Gould, S. J., and R. C. Lewontin. 1979. The spandrels of San Marco and the Panglossian paradigm: A critique of the adaptationist program. *Proceedings of the Royal Society of London* 205:581-98.

Gouldner, A. J. 1960. The norm of reciprocity: A preliminary statement. *American Sociological Review* 25:161-78.

Hamilton, W. D. 1964. The genetic evolution of social behavior. *Journal of Theoretical Biology* 7:1-16.

Himmelfarb, G. 1968. *Darwin and the Darwinian revolution*. New York: Norton.

Holcomb, H. R. 1993. *Sociobiology, sex and science*. Albany: State University of New York Press.

Holmes, R. 1996. *Homo religiosus* and its brain: Reality, imagination and the future of nature. *Zygon* 31:441-56.

Hull, D. 1978. Scientific bandwagon or traveling medicine show? In *Sociobiology and human nature*, ed. M. S. Gregory, A. Silvers and D. Sutch, 136-63. San Francisco: Jossey-Bass.

Johnson, P. E. 1991. *Darwin on trial.* Washington, D.C.: Regnery Gateway.

———. 1995. *Reason in the balance: The case against naturalism in science, law and education*. Downers Grove, Ill.: InterVarsity Press.

Kaye, H. L. 1986. *The social meaning of modern biology: From social Darwinism to sociobiology.* New Haven, Conn.: Yale University Press.

Kitcher, P. 1985. *Vaulting ambition: Sociobiology and the quest for human nature.* Cambridge, Mass.: MIT Press.

Lash, N. 1995. Production and prospect: Reflections on Christian hope and original sin. In *Evolution and creation*, ed. E. McMullin, 273-89. Notre Dame, Ind.: University of Notre Dame Press.

Lewontin, R. C., S. Rose, and L. J. Kamin. 1984. *Not in our genes: Biology, ideology and human nature*. New York: Pantheon.

Lopreato, J. 1984. *Human nature and biocultural evolution*. Boston: Allen and Unwin.

Mattern, R. 1978. Altruism, ethics and sociobiology. In *The sociobiology debate*, ed. A. L. Caplan. New York: Harper and Row.

Maxwell, M. 1990. *Morality among nations*. Albany: State University of New York Press.

Midgley, M. 1980. Rival fatalisms: The hollowness of the sociology debate. In *Sociobiology examined,* ed. A. Montagu, 15-38. New York: Oxford University Press.

———. 1982. Foreword to *Sociobiology and the human dimension,* by G. Breuer. New York: Cambridge University Press.

———. 1994. *The ethical primate: Humans, freedom and morality.* London: Routledge.

Monroe, K. R. 1996. *The heart of altruism: Perceptions of a common humanity.* Princeton, N.J.: Princeton University Press.

Nelson, P. 1996. The role of theology in current evolutionary reasoning. *Biology and Philosophy* 11:493-517.

Oates, D. 1988. Social Darwinism and natural theodicy. *Zygon* 23:439-54.

Oliner, P. M., S. P. Oliner, L. Baron, L. A. Blum, D. L. Krebs, and M. Z. Smolenska, eds. 1993. *Embracing the other: Philosophical, psychological and historical perspectives on altruism.* New York: New York University Press.

Oliner, S. P., and P. M. Oliner. 1988. *The altruistic personality: Rescuers of Jews in Nazi Europe.* New York: Free Press.

Pope, S. J. 1994. *The evolution of altruism and the ordering of love.* Washington, D.C.: Georgetown University Press.

Rachels, J. 1990. *Created from animals: The moral implications of Darwinism.* New York: Oxford University Press.

Richards, R. J. 1986. *Darwin and the emergence of evolutionary theories of mind and behavior.* Chicago: University of Chicago Press.

———. 1993. Birth, death and resurrection of evolutionary ethics. In *Evolutionary ethics,* ed. M. H. Nitecki and D. V. Nitecki. Albany: State University of New York Press.

Ruse, M. 1988. *Philosophy of biology today.* Albany: State University of New York Press.

———. 1993. The new evolutionary ethics. In *Evolutionary ethics,* ed. M. H. Nitecki and D. V. Nitecki. Albany: State University of New York Press.

———. 1994. Evolutionary theory and Christian ethics: Are they in harmony? *Zygon* 29 (1):5-24.

———. 1995. Evolutionary ethics: A defense. In *Biology, ethics and the origins of life,* ed. H. Rolston II, 89-112. Boston: Jones and Bartlett.

Ruse, M., and E. O. Wilson. 1993. The evolution of ethics. In *Religion and the natural sciences: The range of engagement,* ed. J. E. Huchingson. 1991. Orlando, Fla.: Harcourt Brace.

Rushton, J. P. 1986. Altruism and aggression: The heritability of individual differences. *Journal of Personality and Social Psychology* 50:1192-98.

———. 1989. Genetic similarity, human altruism and group selection. *Behavioral and Brain Sciences* 12:503-59.

Sagan, D., and L. Margulis. 1995. Facing nature. In *Biology, ethics and the origins of life,* ed. H. Rolston, 3:39-62. Boston: Jones and Bartlett.

Sahlins, M. D. 1965. On the sociology of primitive exchange. In *Relevance of models of social anthropology,* ed. M. Banton. New York: Praeger.

———. 1976. *The use and abuse of biology.* Ann Arbor: University of Michigan Press.

Sayers, J. 1982. *Biological politics.* New York: Tavistock.

Schloss, J. P. 1996. Sociobiological explanations of altruistic ethics: Necessary, sufficient or irrelevant? In *Investigating the biological foundations of human morality,* ed.

J. P. Hurd, 107-45. New York: Edwin Mellen Press.

Schwartz, B. 1986. *The battle for human nature: Science, morality and modern life.* New York: Norton.

Simon, H. 1990. A mechanism for social selection and successful altruism. *Science* 250:1665ff.

Singer, P. 1981. *The expanding circle.* New York: Farrar, Straus and Giroux.

————. 1984. Ethics and sociobiology. *Zygon* 19:141.

Sloan, P. R. 1995. The question of natural purpose. In *Evolution and creation,* ed. E. McMullin, 273-89. Notre Dame, Ind.: University of Notre Dame Press.

Sober, E. 1993. *Philosophy of biology.* Boulder, Colo.: Westview Press.

————. 1995. When natural selection and culture conflict. In *Biology, ethics and the origins of life,* ed. R. Holmes, 3:137-63. Boston: Jones and Bartlett.

Trivers, R. L. 1971. The evolution of reciprocal altruism. *Quarterly Review of Biology* 46:35-39.

————. 1985. *Social evolution.* Menlo Park, Calif.: Benjamin Cummings.

————. 1991. Deceit and self-deception: The relationship between communication and consciousness. In *Man and beast revisited,* ed. M. H. Robinson and L. Tiger, 175-91. Washington, D.C.: Smithsonian Institution Press.

Trivers, R. L., and H. Hare. 1976. Haplodiploidy and the evolution of the social insects. *Science* 191:249-63.

Vine, I. 1992. Altruism and human nature: Resolving the evolutionary paradox. In *Embracing the other: Psychological and historical perspectives on altruism,* ed. P. M. Oliner, S. P. Oliner, L. Baron, L. A. Blum, D. L. Krebs, and M. Z. Smolenska, 73-102. New York: New York University Press.

Wenegrat, B. 1990. *The divine archetype.* Lexington, Mass.: Lexington Books.

Williams, G. C. 1988. Huxley's evolution and ethics in sociobiological perspective. *Zygon* 23:383-407.

Williams, P. A. 1993. Can beings whose ethics evolved be ethical beings? In *Evolutionary ethics,* ed. M. H. Nitecki and D. V. Nitecki. Albany: State University of New York Press.

Wilson, E. O. 1975. *Sociobiology.* Cambridge, Mass.: Harvard University Press.

————. 1978. *On human nature.* Cambridge, Mass.: Harvard University Press.

Wilson, J. Q. 1993. *The moral sense.* New York: Free Press.

Wright, R. 1994. *The moral animal: The new science of evolutionary psychology.* New York: Pantheon.

# Part 4

## Philosophy & Design

# 11

# The Explanatory Relevance of Libertarian Agency as a Model of Theistic Design

## J. P. MORELAND

**M**ANY SCHOLARS HOLD THAT GIVEN THE NATURE OF SCIENCE, the concepts of divine action and theistic design are neither appropriate nor fruitful if they are employed to guide research and explain things in science. I and others have offered general criticisms of this ubiquitous opinion, and I shall not repeat them here (Meyer 1994; Moreland 1989, chaps. 1, 2, 6; 1994a, 2-13; 1994b, 22-25; Plantinga 1991a, 8-32; 1991b, 80-109). Rather I want to show that where primary causal divine miracles are depicted as libertarian acts, such acts of God can be appropriately and fruitfully employed to explain certain facts about the natural world that are otherwise inadequately explained or are not explained at all.[1]

In the first section of this chapter, I clarify the difference between event causation and libertarian agency and claim that when God acts by way of secondary causes, the mediating chains of events utilized may be treated as event causes for which a covering law model of explanation is appropriate. But when God acts as a first cause, at least the immediate effects should be explained by personal explanation. The last two sections of the chapter illustrate the value of personal explanation in two areas: the origin of the universe and the existence of mental entities. Main attention is given to the latter by comparing a theistic explanation of mental phenomena with a rival naturalist explanation offered by John Searle.

## Event Causation and Libertarian Agency

Event causation is a model of efficient causality widely employed in science. Suppose a brick breaks a glass. In general event causation can be defined in this way: an event of kind $K$ (the moving of the brick) in circumstances of kind $C$ (the glass being in a solid and not a liquid state) occurring to an entity of kind $E$ (the glass object itself) causes an event of kind $Q$ (the breaking of the glass) to occur. Here all causes and effects are events that constitute causal chains construed either deterministically (causal conditions are sufficient for an effect to obtain) or probabilistically (causal conditions are sufficient to fix the chances for an effect to obtain). Associated with event causation is a covering law model of explanation according to which some event (the explanandum) is explained by giving a correct deductive or inductive argument for that event. Such an argument contains two features in its explanans: a (universal or statistical) law of nature and initial causal conditions.

Some philosophers (e.g., compatibilists) describe human actions in terms of event causality and employ a covering law model to explain such actions. Advocates of libertarian freedom demur, and they have developed different versions of an alternative model of human action. In my view the core component of intentional action is intentional endeavoring (i.e., exercising a power in trying to bring about some effect for a reason).[2] We may incorporate this characterization of intentional action in the following depiction of libertarian agency:

(1) Person $P$ exercises libertarian agency and freely and intentionally brings about some event $e$ just in case $P$ is a substance that has the active power to bring about $e$;

(2) $P$ exerted his power as a first mover (an originator of change) to bring about $e$;

(3) $P$ had the categorical ability to refrain from exerting his power to bring about $e$;

(4) $P$ acted for the sake of a reason, which serves as the final cause or teleological goal for which $P$ acted.

Taken alone, the first three statements give necessary and sufficient conditions for a pure voluntary act. The four propositions state necessary and sufficient conditions for an intentional act.

By "substance" I mean a member of a natural kind, an essentially characterized particular that sustains absolute sameness through (accidental) change and that possesses a primitive unity of parts, properties and capacities or powers at a time. "Active power" is an epistemically primitive notion that has a sense that is ultimately understood ostensively in acts of first-person introspective awareness of one's own initiation of change.[3] A characteristic mark of active power is the ability to initiate motion, to bring something about. Active power is a dual ability. So understood, it is impossible for an exercise of active power to be causally necessitated by prior events. A "first mover" is a substance that has active power. The notion of "categorical ability" in the third statement has two important aspects to it. First, it expresses the type of ability possessed by a first mover that can exercise active power, and as such it contrasts with the conditional ability employed by compatibilists. Second, categorical ability is a dual ability: If one has the ability to exert his power to do or will to do *A*, then one also has the ability to refrain from exerting his power to do or to will to do *A*. Finally, the fourth statement expresses a view of reasons as irreducible, teleological goals for the sake of which a person acts. In general we may characterize this by saying that person *S W'd* (e.g., went to the kitchen) in order to *Y* (e.g., get coffee or satisfy *S's* desire for coffee). This characterization of action, according to the fourth proposition, cannot be reduced to a causal theory of action that utilizes belief/desire event causation.

Three things should be mentioned about this definition of libertarian agency. First, there are two basic schools of thought regarding libertarian agency. Advocates of the first school hold to agent causation and thus believe that the first mover in (2) causes his actions. Advocates of the second school accept a noncausal view of agency in which the actions of unmoved movers are uncaused events done for reasons as final causes. Either way an unmoved mover is an agent that can act without sufficient causal conditions necessitating that the agent act—the agent is the absolute source of his own actions. Second, libertarian agency theorists are divided about the role or reasons in an overall theory of agency. Noncausal theories of agency are clear in seeing reasons as final causes—teleological goals for the sake of which someone acts. Advocates of agent causation either accept this view of reasons or else hold reasons to be necessary (efficient) causal conditions that, together with the agent's own active exercise of power (and perhaps other conditions), cause the action. Therefore some agent causationists would adjust (4) accordingly. Third, it is broadly logically impossible for a person to be caused to agent-cause something. Libertarian acts are spontaneous in the sense that there are no causal antecedents sufficient to determine that an agent acts with libertarian freedom.

Advocates of libertarian agency employ a form of personal explanation that stands in contrast to a covering law model. To understand this form of explanation, we need to look first at a distinction that is part of action theory: the difference between a basic and nonbasic action. To grasp the difference between a basic and nonbasic action, note first that often more than one thing is accomplished in a single exercise of agency. Some actions are done by doing others (e.g., I perform the act of going to the store to get bread by getting into my car and by driving to the store). Basic actions are fundamental to the performance of all others but are not done by doing something else. In general *S's W-ing* is basic if there is no other nonequivalent action description *'S's Y-ing'* such that it is true that *S W-ed* by *Y-ing*. My endeavoring to move my arm to get my keys is a basic action. A nonbasic action contains basic actions that are parts of and means to the ultimate intention for the sake of which the nonbasic action was done. To fulfill a nonbasic intention, I must form an action plan: a certain ordered set of basic actions that I take to be an effective means of accomplishing my nonbasic intention. The action plan that constitutes going to the store to get bread includes the acts of getting my keys and walking to my car.[4]

In my view an action is something contained wholly within the boundaries of the agent. Thus, strictly speaking, the results of an action are not proper parts of that action. A basic result of an action is an intended effect brought about immediately by the action. If I successfully endeavor to move my finger, the basic result is the moving of the finger. Nonbasic results are more remote intended effects caused by basic results or chains of basic results plus more remote intended effects. The firing of the gun or the killing of Lincoln are respective illustrations of these types of nonbasic results.

With this in mind, a personal explanation (divine or otherwise) of some basic result $R$ brought about intentionally by person $P$ where this bringing about of $R$ is a basic action $A$ will cite the intention $I$ of $P$ that $R$ occur and the basic power $B$ that $P$ exercised to bring about $R$. $P$, $I$ and $B$ provide a full explanation of $R$: agent $P$ brought about $R$ by exercising power $B$ in order to realize intention $I$ as an irreducibly teleological goal. To illustrate, suppose we are trying to explain why Wesson moved her finger $(R)$. We could explain this by saying that Wesson $(P)$ performed an act of endeavoring to move her finger $(A)$ in that she exercised her ability to move or will to move her finger $(B)$ intending to move the finger $(I)$. If Wesson's moving her finger was an expression of an intent to move a finger to fire a gun to kill Smith, then we can explain the nonbasic results (the firing of the gun and the killing of Smith) by saying that Wesson $(P)$ performed an act of killing Smith $(I_3)$ by endeavoring to move her finger $(A)$ intentionally $(I_1)$ by exercising her power to do so $(B)$, intending thereby to fire the gun $(I_2)$ in order to kill Smith. An explanation of the results of a nonbasic action (e.g., going to the store to get bread) will include a description of the action plan.[5]

We are now in a position to discuss personal explanation and divine action.[6] First we should distinguish between God acting as a productive or conserving cause and as a transforming cause. The former refers to God's actions in creating and sustaining the universe. God is directly responsible for the fact that there is something rather than nothing, the universe is radically contingent, and God is the creator and sustainer of the world. There are two different ways of depicting God's relationship to the world as a productive or conserving cause. First, some hold that God created the world but that once it exists, it does so moment by moment under its own steam. Second, others hold that God created and sustains the world each moment of its existence. Most who hold this view take it that there is no difference between the type of action God exercises in creating versus conserving the world. It is important to note that this second view need not be interpreted in an Edwardsian way, namely, that things do not endure through time but rather come into existence anew at each moment of their being. It is consistent with this second position to hold that substances endure and God sustains them and their causal powers in existence while they exist. In what follows I shall not discuss God's activity as a productive or conserving sustainer of the world's existence because it is not as relevant to my thesis as is God's activity either as a productive cause of the world's (or something in the world's) coming to be ex nihilo or as a transforming cause.

There are debates about the precise nature of the world's own causal activity, but I want to set these aside and concentrate on explaining the difference between primary causal, miraculous acts by God in the natural world versus the use of secondary causes by God.[7] In the ordinary course of natural events (e.g., weather patterns or chemical reactions) God sustains natural entities in existence along with their own causal powers, but those entities have causal dispositions to bring about changes themselves if they are affected in certain ways. In ordinary causal chains God does not move natural entities; he simply sustains them. In such cases God is not directly responsible for the changes of states of affairs in things, and event causation along with a covering law model of explanation are appropriate, even if God employs natural causal sequences to secure a divine intent.

However, when it comes to primary causal, direct miraculous acts by God in creating ex nihilo or in producing changes in the world (e.g., parting the Red Sea, creating the universe from nothing, bringing into existence new kinds of life, creating souls, raising Jesus from the dead), God exercises libertarian agency, and personal explanation is required. Some have conceived of such activity as God either bringing something into existence ex nihilo or momentarily supplying natural entities with new causal powers different from their normal powers that in turn sets off a chain reaction of divergence in the universe. But irrespective of the precise nature of divine primary causal activity, at least the basic results of such acts are caused by an exercise of divine libertarian agency and are to be explained by personal explanation. We will consider two illustrations of the value of personal explanation, namely, the origin of the universe and the existence of mental entities.

### The origin of universe

Let us grant that the past is temporally finite and that the universe had a beginning. There are at least two classical big bang models of the initial singularity of time $t = 0$. The first model depicts a time interval that is closed at $t = 0$. On this model $t = 0$ is a singular, temporally first event of physical space-time. The second model features a time interval that is finite, open in the past and excludes $t = 0$ as a point of space-time. Rather $t = 0$ is construed as a boundary of space-time. In both models there is no instant of time prior to the initial singularity.

If the origin of the universe is not to be taken as a brute fact, what sort of explanation should we give for it? For at least two reasons it is obvious that an event-causal explanation will not suffice.[8] First, whether $t = 0$ is the first event in time or the boundary of time and therefore not an event, it is the case that if causal priority entails temporal priority, then there can be no event-cause for $t = 0$; and if causal priority does not entail temporal priority (i.e., a cause can be simultaneous with its effect), then the event cause for $t = 0$ would itself be the explanatorily first event rather than the initial singularity, and an event-causal explanation would in turn be needed for it ad infinitum.[9] Second, as William Lane Craig has argued, the cause of the universe's beginning must be uncaused, eternal and changeless (sans the creation). Moreover, the cause must be personal "[f]or the only way in which a temporal effect could originate from an eternal, changeless cause would seem to be if the cause is a personal agent who eternally chooses to create an effect in time. A changeless, mechanically operating cause would produce either an immemorial effect or none at all; but an agent endowed with [libertarian] free will can have an eternal determination to operate causally at a (first) moment of time and thereby to produce a temporally first effect" (Craig 1994a, 219).

It would seem then that not only is an event-causal explanation inadequate for the beginning of the universe but also that a personal explanation is adequate. However, this has been hotly contested, and a series of articles by Craig and Grünbaum has brought this debate to center stage in recent years (Craig 1992, 1994a, b, c; Grünbaum 1989, 1991, 1994). Grünbaum has inveighed against an agent-causal, personal explanation of the beginning of the universe. His main criticisms are

(1) The notion of a divine agent cause of the initial singularity is incoherent because causation is essentially a temporal activity or relation in which the cause must be temporally prior to its effect.

(2) The notion of a divine agent cause of the initial singularity is too inscrutable, mysterious and obscure to do any explanatory work.

(3) Divine personal explanation is inferior to scientific explanation because the former fails to provide what the latter proffers: a specification of intermediate causal processes, mediating causal links that connect causes (divine or otherwise) with their effects.

(4) It does not follow from the causal premise "whatever begins to exist has a cause" that the first cause is a conscious agent.

(5) Only events can qualify as the momentary effects of other events or of the actions of agents, and if the singularity $t = 0$ is taken as a nonevent, then the singularity cannot be taken as an effect of any cause.

Part of Craig's response to Grünbaum, especially to (1), is the specification of three cogent models of theological creationism, of which two are relevant to my concerns. Model 1 is that the Creator may be conceived to be causally but not temporally prior to the origin of the universe, such that the act of causing the universe to begin to exist is simultaneous with its beginning to exist. The Creator sans the universe exists changelessly and (most likely) timelessly and at the singularity creates both the universe and time. Model 2 is that the Creator may be conceived to exist timelessly and to cause tenselessly the origin of the universe at the big bang singularity.

Further reflection on the nature of libertarian agency will, I hope, support the intelligibility of Craig's models and provide further refutations of Grünbaum's objections. For the purpose of brevity, let us assume without argument a volitional theory of action according to which normal actions like raising one's arm are to be parsed thusly: the bodily movement is caused by a specific sort of event—a volition (endeavoring)—that in turn is brought about in some way or another by the agent.

There is a certain difficulty for the libertarian theory of agency if we grant that whatever has a beginning has a cause. The raising of one's arm is an event with a beginning, and it is caused by another event—a volition. But the volition is an event with a beginning; and it has a cause as well, namely, the agent. What does the agent do to cause his volition? If the agent does something, is what he does itself an event, and if so, does it need a cause? Let us side with the majority of philosophers and grant that this solution to the difficulty is inadequate: the agent causes an infinite hierarchy of events in causing his volition. What other solutions are available? Three have been widely recognized (Rowe 1991, 30-40, 145-61).

AC I: The agent does not do anything to cause his volition. The volition is a basic act produced directly by the agent without exercising any power to produce it. The agent is simply the first relatum that stands in a primitive causal relation to the second relatum, the volitional event. The following objection has been raised against AC I: If the volition occurs at a particular time $t_1$ and the cause is an enduring substance that existed for some time prior to $t_1$, then why did the volition occur when it did? One reason this problem arises is that in cases of libertarian agency, no set of conditions within an agent is sufficient to produce a volition. There may be necessary conditions (e.g., motives, beliefs and desires), but these may exist in an agent over a protracted time period with no volition brought about. If the agent does not do something to cause the volition, why does it happen at $t_1$? So far as I can see, short of abandoning AC I, the best solution to the problem is to work with the second relatum. An agent does not just cause a volition simplicatur, a volition-to-$f$. The agent causes a volition-to-$f$-at-$t_1$ (or now).

AC II: The agent does do something to cause her volition, namely, she exercises a power. According to this view, the causal relation between an agent and her volition is not primitive; it is grounded in an exercise of power. In AC II we should revise the causal principle and recognize that an exercise of power is not an event in the sense relevant to this revised principle. The causal principle should read "every substance that begins to exist or every change that a substance undergoes has a cause." An exercise of power is the exertion of a self-moving power or principle of self-determination that is not itself a change undergone by the agent. In libertarian acts agents are unmoved or first movers. They do not first undergo a change (an exercise of power) before they can cause a change (a volition). Rather agents qua substances directly cause their volitions by virtue of possessing and exercising their power to do so. Since an exercise of power is not a change undergone by an agent (nor a coming-to-be of a substance), it is not an event with a beginning in the sense relevant to the causal principle, even though there was a time before and after which the agent caused her volitions. Besides coming into existence, only the changes (internal or relational) need a cause.

AC III: A third response to the problem is that the correct causal principle is "every event that can broadly logically have a cause does have a cause." As we saw earlier, it is broadly logically impossible for someone to be caused to agent-cause something else (e.g., a volition). So if we grant that an exercise of power is an event (i.e., a change within the agent), when we recognize that such an exercise just is the event of an agent directly agent-causing his volition (the exercise of power is not an event caused by the agent that in turn event causes the volition), it becomes clear that it does not have an efficient cause because it cannot (though it may have a reason that serves as the final cause of the exercise of power).

Let us apply these insights to Grünbaum's criticisms of divine agent causality. It turns out that his objections take exception to agent causation and not divine action per se. Regarding objection (1), the notion of divine agent causality is not incoherent. There is a well-developed literature about agent causality as well as its application to divine action, and most philosophers who reject agent causation do not do so on the grounds that it is incoherent. Moreover, Craig's first response to the charge of incoherence (God's act of causing the origin of the universe was simultaneous with its beginning) is quite plausible. God's volition (AC I-III) or his exercise of power and his volition (AC III) could be taken as simultaneous or coincident with the basic result of God's volition—the creation of the initial singularity. AC I-III render intelligible the notion that a timeless God sans creation could spontaneously bring about the initial singularity. On AC I God timelessly causes the volition to create the universe at $t = 0$, and this volition is simultaneous or coincident with the initial singularity. AC II depicts God's exercise of power as something brought about by God but that is not itself a change within God. So it becomes intelligible to suppose that God could changelessly exist and exercise his power to bring about a volition to cause the creation of the universe at $t = 0$. Again the volition would be simultaneous or coincident with the initial singularity. If God could do this changelessly, I see no reason to deny that he could also do it timelessly because temporality is relevant to efficient causality largely because it is sometimes mistakenly thought that an exercise of efficient causality involves change and change is temporal. On AC III God's exercise of power would be the uncaused event of directly agent-causing his volition to bring about the initial singularity. Such an exercise would not, indeed could not, be preceeded by a prior event that brought it about.

Craig's second model (God exists timelessly and tenselessly causes the initial singularity) is plausible as well (setting aside problems of reconciling this model with an *A* series view of time) if we abandon the volitional theory of action: an agent brings about an effect without doing so by way of an internal, volitional change within the agent. On AC I God could timelessly cause from eternity the beginning of the universe at $t = 0$. On AC II an exercise of power would bring about the initial singularity, but the exercise of power would not itself be an event. AC III would not be applicable to Craig's second model because it depicts an exercise of power as an event within the agent.

Objection (2) is wide of the mark as well. For one thing, the divine creation of the initial singularity is precisely analogous to human libertarian acts (e.g., both involve first movers who initiate change). There is nothing particularly mysterious or inscrutable about the latter, so in the absence of some good reason to think that there is some specific problem with the initial divine creation, the charge of inscrutability is question begging. Moreover, we understand exercises of power primarily from introspective awareness of our own libertarian acts, and we use the concept of action so derived to offer third-person explanations of the behavior of other human persons. There is nothing obscure about such explanations for the effects produced by other finite persons, and I see no reason to think that this approach is illicit in the case of divine initial creation. In fact naturalists like John Searle, John Bishop and Thomas Nagel all admit that our basic concept of action itself is a libertarian one (Searle 1984, 98; Bishop 1989, 58, 72, 69, 95-96, 103-4, 126-27, 140-41, 144; Nagel 1986, 110-37). Searle goes so far as to say that our understanding of event causality is conceptually derived from our first-person experience of our own causation (Searle 1983, chaps. 3, 4). There is a major tradition in philosophy that agent causation is clearer and more basic than event causation, and it may be that if any sort of causation is inscrutable, it is event causation. By claiming that God created the initial singularity, we mean that there was no sufficient causal antecedent for the initial singularity, temporal or otherwise, apart from either God directly causing the initial singularity without first doing something (AC I) or an exercise of divine power to bring about the initial singularity (AC II or AC III); in a basic libertarian act, God freely and spontaneously brought about a volition that caused $t = 0$ as a basic result.

Objection (3) is also wide of the mark. A basic libertarian act that produces a basic result does not have intermediate causal links between the act and the result. Theists depict the creation of the initial singularity as a basic divine act in which a First Mover brought about an initiation of change. Whatever caused $t=0$ could not have done so by way of an intermediate temporal causal process of the type Grünbaum heralds as a virtue of scientific explanation, since $t = 0$ is either the first event or the initial boundary from which events ensue. Thus it is a virtue of the theistic model that it requires no such intermediate causal linkage.

Regarding (4), so far as we know only conscious agents endeavor or will anything. So even if it is logically possible that the First Cause was not conscious, it is not epistemically possible in light of what we know about the types of agents who are capable of libertarian action. Further, Bishop has argued that given the nature of contemporary scientific naturalism, "the idea of a responsible agent, with the 'originative' ability to initiate events in the natural world, does not sit easily with the idea of [an agent as] a natural organism" (Bishop 1989, 1).[10] Elsewhere Bishop notes that "the problem of natural agency is an ontological problem—a problem about whether the existence of actions can be admitted within a natural scientific perspective. . . . [A]gent causal-relations do not belong to the ontology of the natural perspective. Naturalism does not essentially employ the concept of a causal relation whose first member is in the category of person or agent (or even, for that matter, in the broader category of continuant or 'substance'). All natural causal relations have first members in the category of event or state of affairs" (Bishop 1989, 40).[11] If we grant that abstract objects do not have efficient causal powers, then Bishop's remarks, if correct, would seem to imply that the efficient cause of the initial singularity is not only conscious but also supernatural.

Objection (5) is false. Agents bring about their own exercises of power, and these may reasonably be taken as nonevents (AC II). Moreover, in nonbasic actions, agents are first movers who generate a chain of events. If we take an exercise of power or a volition to be the first event in such a chain, the agent brought about this event. However, if we take a nonbasic action to be the initiation of a temporal, causal sequence to follow, such that the exercise of power or volition forms an initial boundary for that sequence, the agent still brought about the exercise of power or volition. So even if we grant that $t = 0$ is a nonevent, libertarian action theory has the resources to allow that it could be an effect of a free, divine, creative act.

### Mental phenomena

Frequently theists have advanced what is called the argument from consciousness [AC] for God's existence, which starts with the existence of mental phenomena and uses personal explanation (Adams 1992; Swinburne 1979, chap. 9; 1986, 183-96):

(1) Mental events are genuine nonphysical mental entities that exist.

(2) Specific mental event types are regularly correlated with specific physical event types.

(3) There is an explanation for these correlations.

(4) Personal explanation is different from natural scientific explanation.

(5) The explanation for these correlations is either a personal or natural scientific explanation.

(6) The explanation is not a natural scientific one.

(7) Therefore the explanation is a personal one.

(8) If the explanation is personal, then it is theistic.

(9) Therefore, the explanation is theistic.

Space forbids me to comment on all the premises of AC, but I should point out that there have been a number of variants on (1) that have been cited as problems that science cannot explain but that can be given a theistic personal explanation: the existence of mental properties themselves (Armstrong 1978, 262); the fact that mental properties have come to be exemplified in the spatiotemporal world; the nature of the relation (e.g., causal or supervenient) between mental and physical entities (Horgan 1993, 313-14);

the fact that certain particular mental events are correlated with certain particular physical events; the fact that the correlations mentioned in the preceding point are regular; the existence of libertarian freedom and the type of agency necessary for it (Bishop 1989, 36-44, 74-76);[12] the aptness of our noetic equipment to serve as truth gatherers in our noetic environment (Plantinga 1993, 194-237); the evolutionary advantage of having mental states as opposed to the evolution of organisms with direct stimulus-response mechanisms that have no mental intermediaries (Swinburne 1986, 191-95).

The crucial premises of AC in dispute are (3) and (6). Rather than consider these directly, it will be more profitable to look at them in light of Searle's biological naturalism, which arguably is the chief current rival to AC. According to Searle, philosophy of mind has been dominated by scientific naturalism for fifty years, and scientific naturalists have advanced different versions of strict physicalism, however implausible they may be in light of what is obviously known by us about consciousness, because strict physicalism was seen as a crucial implication of taking the naturalistic turn. For these naturalists, if one abandons strict physicalism one has rejected a scientific naturalist approach to the mind/body problem and opened oneself to the intrusion of religious concepts and arguments about the mental.

Searle offers his analysis of the mind as a naturalistic account because, he says, no one in the modern world can deny "the obvious facts of physics—for example, that the world is made up entirely of physical particles in fields of force" (Searle 1992, 28). An acceptance of naturalism is constituted by an acknowledgment of the atomic theory of matter and evolutionary biology, both of which allow for micro to micro or micro to macro causal explanations but not macro to micro ones (Searle 1992, 85-91). According to Searle, dualism in any form is widely rejected because it is correctly considered to be inconsistent with the scientific worldview (Searle 1992, 3, 13-16). But a commitment to naturalism and a concomitant rejection of dualism have blinded people to the point that they feel compelled to reject what is obvious to experience, namely, the nature of consciousness and intentionality.

Searle's own solution to the mind/body problem is biological naturalism: consciousness, intentionality and mental states in general are emergent biological states and processes that supervene upon a suitably structured, functioning brain. Brain processes cause mental processes, which are not reducible to the former. Consciousness is just an ordinary (i.e., physical) feature of the brain and as such is merely an ordinary feature of the natural world (Searle 1992, xii, 13-19, 25-28, 85-93). Despite the frequent assertions by a number of philosophers that Searle is a property dualist, he denies the charge and seems puzzled by it (Searle 1992, 13, 16). However, in my view Searle is indeed a property dualist and an epiphenomenalist one at that, though he denies the latter charge as well.

Why does Searle claim that there are no deep metaphysical implications that follow from biological naturalism? More specifically, why is it that biological naturalism does not represent a rejection of scientific naturalism, which in turn opens the door for religious concepts about and explanations for the mental? Searle's answer to this question is developed in three steps. First, he cites several examples of emergence—liquidity, solidity, properties of digestion—that he takes to be unproblematic for a naturalist and argues by analogy that the emergent properties of consciousness are likewise unproblematic.

Searle's second step is a formulation of two reasons why, appearances to the contrary notwithstanding, consciousness is not a problem for naturalists. First, Searle identifies why so many people have taken the existence of irreducible mental entities to be a problem for naturalism. We are misled into thinking that the following is a coherent question that needs an answer: "How do unconscious bits of matter produce consciousness?"(Searle 1992, 55).[13] Many people "find it difficult, if not impossible to accept the idea that the real world, the world described by physics and chemistry and biology, contains an ineliminably subjective element. How could such a thing be? How can we possibly get a coherent world picture if the world contains these mysterious conscious entities?" (Searle 1992, 95).

For Searle the question of how matter (e.g., the brain) produces consciousness is a request about how the brain works to produce mental states even though individual neurons in the brain are not conscious. This question is easily answered in terms of specific though largely unknown neurobiological features of the brain. However, Searle thinks that many philosophers are misled into thinking this question is about something deeper and more puzzling. Setting consciousness aside, in all other cases of entities arranged in a part/whole hierarchy of systems we can image how emergent features arise because these systems and all their features are objective phenomena. Our problem is that we try to image how consciousness could arise from a system of unconscious bits of matter in the same way, but this is not possible because consciousness itself is not imageable, and we cannot get at it through a visual metaphor. Once we give up on trying to imagine consciousness, any deep puzzlement about the emergence of consciousness, given a naturalist worldview, evaporates, and the only question left is one about how the brain produces mental states.

There is another reason Searle offers as to why the emergence of consciousness has no deep metaphysical significance (Searle 1992, 118-24). In standard cases of reduction (e.g, heat and color), an ontological reduction (color is nothing but a wavelength) is based on a causal reduction (color is caused by a wavelength). In these cases we can distinguish the appearance of heat and color from the reality, place the former in consciousness, leave the latter in the objective world, and go on to define the phenomenon itself in terms of its causes. We can do this because our interests are in the reality and not the appearance. The ontological reduction of heat to its causes leaves the appearance of heat the same.

However, when it comes to mental states like pain, even though an ontological reduction cannot be found, there is a similar causal pattern (e.g, pain is caused by such and such brain states). So why do we regard heat as ontologically reducible but not pain? In the case of heat, we are interested in the physical causes and not the subjective appearances, but with pain the subjective appearance itself interests us. If we wanted to, we could reduce pain to such and such physical processes and go on to talk about pain appearances analogous to the heat case. However, in the case of consciousness, the reality is the appearance. Since the point of reductions is to distinguish and separate reality from appearance in order to focus on underlying causes by definitionally identifying the reality with those causes, the point of a reduction for consciousness is missing, since the appearance itself is the reality of interest. Therefore the irreducibility of consciousness has no deep metaphysical consequences and is simply a result of the pattern of reduction that is itself a result of the way we have decided on pragmatic grounds to carry out our definitions and investigations.

In the third step Searle claims that an adequate scientific explanation of the emergence of consciousness is a set of very detailed, even lawlike correlations between specific mental and physical states (Searle 1992, 89, 100-4). Searle considers and rejects an argument by Nagel that, if it were successful, would deny that mere correlations amount to a scientific explanation. In terms of AC, Searle accepts while Nagel denies that a mere correlation would count as a scientific explanation. Nagel would accept premise (6) of AC and deny that Searle's correlations count as scientific explanations. Searle rejects (6) and believes such correlations count as adequate scientific explanations. Nagel claims that in other cases of emergence like liquidity, a scientific explanation not only tells us what happens but also explains why liquidity must emerge when a collection of water molecules gather under certain circumstances. In this case scientific explanation offers physical causal necessity: given certain states of affairs, it is causally necessary that liquidity emerge, and it is inconceivable that it not supervene. But, argues Nagel, no such necessity and no answer to a why question is given by a mere correlation between mental and physical states in the brain.

Searle's response to Nagel is threefold (Searle 1992, 101-4). First, he says that some explanations in science do not exhibit the type of causal necessity Nagel requires (e.g., the inverse square law is an account of gravity that does not show why bodies have to have gravitational attraction). I think this response is clearly question begging against Nagel, because the inverse square law is merely a description of what happens and not an explanation of why it happens. Newton himself took the inverse square law to be a mere description of how gravity works but explained the nature of gravity itself (due to his views about action at a distance, the nature of spirit, and the mechanical nature of corpuscularian causation by contact) in terms of the activity of the Spirit of God. The point is not that Newton was right. The point is that he distinguished a description of gravity from an explanation of what it is, and his explanation cannot be rebutted by citing the inverse square law. Rather one needs a better explanatory model of gravity. So Searle's own example works against him.

Moreover, even if we grant that covering law explanations are in fact explanations in some sense, they are clearly different from explanations that offer a model of why things must take place given the model and its mechanisms. Since the argument from consciousness assumes the correlations and offers an answer to the why question, Searle's solution here is not really a rival explanation but merely a claim that such correlations are brute facts that just need to be listed and not explained. For at least two reasons Searle's claim should be rejected.

First, it is question begging and ad hoc for Searle to assert that these correlations are basic. Why? Because such correlations are natural and bear a relevant similarity to other entities, properties and relations in theism (e.g., God as spirit who can create and causally interact with matter), but they are unnatural given the nature of contemporary scientific naturalism. In this regard Terence Horgan says that "in any metaphysical framework that deserves labels like 'materialism,' 'naturalism,' or 'physicalism,' supervenience facts must be explainable rather than being *sui generis*" (Horgan 1993, 313-14). And D. M. Armstrong goes so far as to admit, "I suppose that if the principles involved [in analyzing the single all-embracing spatiotemporal system that is reality] were completely different from the current principles of physics, in particular if they involved appeal to mental entities, such as purposes, we might then count the analysis as a falsification of Naturalism" (Armstrong 1978, 262).

Horgan and Armstrong say this precisely because mental entities, the supervenience relation or a causal correlation between mental and physical entities are not natural given a consistent naturalist paradigm. Their reality constitutes a falsification of naturalism for Horgan and Armstrong, and, given AC, they provide evidence for theism. It is question begging and ad hoc to adjust naturalism as does Searle, given the presence of AC as a rival explanation.

Second, as Richard Swinburne points out, a correlation can be either an accidental generalization or a genuine law (which exhibits at least physical necessity), and we distinguish the two in that laws are (but accidental correlations are not) noncircular correlations that fit naturally into theories that are simple, have broad explanatory power and fit with background knowledge from other, closely related scientific theories about the world (Swinburne 1979, chap. 9; 1986, 183-96). By "fit" Swinburne means the degree of naturalness of the correlation and entities correlated in light of both the broader theory of which the correlation is a part and background knowledge. Searle admits that mental phenomena are absolutely unique compared to all other entities in that they "have a special feature not possessed by other natural phenomena, namely, subjectivity" (Searle 1992, 93). Precisely this radical uniqueness makes mental phenomena unnatural for a naturalist worldview and prevents Searle from distinguishing an accidental correlation from a genuine law of nature regarding mental and physical correlations.

So much for Searle's first response to Nagel. His second response is to say that the apparent necessity for some scientific causal explanations may be a function of the fact that we find some explanation so convincing that we cannot conceive of certain phenomena behaving in a different way. Medieval people may have thought modern explanations of the emergence of liquidity mysterious and lacking in causal necessity. Similarly our current belief that there is no causal necessity to specific mind/brain correlations may be due to our ignorance of how the brain works.

It is hard to see what is supposed to follow from Searle's point. Just because it is logically possible or that it has been the case that someone made a mistake about using conceivability as a test for causal necessity, it does not follow that conceivability is never a good test for it. Only a case-by-case study can in principle decide the appropriateness of its employment. When it comes to things like liquidity or solidity, Nagel is right. Precisely because of what we know about matter, we cannot conceive of certain states of affairs obtaining and these properties being absent. That medievals would not be so convinced is beside the point since they were ignorant of the relevant atomic theory. If they possessed the correct theory, their intuitions would be as are ours. But when it comes to the mental and physical, they are such different entities, and the mental is so unnatural given the rest of the naturalist ontology that there is no clearly conceivable necessity about their connection. This judgment is based not on what we do not know about the two types of states but on what we do know. Moreover, a more detailed correlation in the future will not change the situation. There is no noncir-cular, non-ad-hoc way to formulate such a correlation, and we will merely be left with a more detailed dictionary of correlations that will leave intact the same type of problem of causal necessity true of less detailed correlations. Our current lack of belief in such a causal necessity is not due to ignorance of more and more details of the very thing that lacks the necessity in the first place. Rather it is based on a clear understanding of the nature of the mental and physical, an understanding that Searle himself accepts.

But Searle had another line of defense against Nagel. Even if we grant Nagel's point about the lack of causal necessity in the mental/physical case, nothing follows from this. Why? Because in the water and liquidity case, we can picture the relation between the two in such a way that causal necessity is easily a part of that picture. But since consciousness is not pictureable, we are not able to imagine the same sort of causal necessity, but that does not mean it is not there.

Here Searle simply applies his earlier point that, given naturalism, our puzzlement about the emergence of consciousness from unconscious bits of matter is due to our attempt to picture consciousness. It seems to me that this point is false, and egregiously so. I have no temptation to try to picture consciousness. And other naturalists like Paul Churchland have put their finger on the real difficulty about the emergence of consciousness:

> The important point about the standard evolutionary story is that the human species and all of its features are the wholly physical outcome of a purely physical process. . . . If this is the correct account of our origins, then there seems neither need, nor room, to fit any nonphysical substances or properties into our theoretical account of ourselves. We are creatures of matter. And we should learn to live with that fact. (Churchland 1984, 21; cf. Peacocke and Gillett 1987, 211; Armstrong 1968, 30)

Churchland notes two reasons the naturalist should opt for strict physicalism: there is neither need nor room for anything else. Regarding need, I take it he means that everything we need in order to explain the origin and workings of human beings can be supplied by physicalist causal explanations. Regarding room, entities do not come into existence ex nihilo, nor do radically different kinds of entities emerge from purely physical components placed in some sort of complex arrangement. What comes from the physical by means of physical processes will also be physical. Charles Darwin himself realized that it was difficult if not impossible to find a place for mental entities given evolutionary naturalism (Gruber 1974, 211). It seems then that Searle is wrong about the problem being the imageability of consciousness. The problem for naturalism is ontological, not epistemological, as most natural-ists have seen.

I conclude therefore that Nagel is right and Searle is wrong: premise (6) of AC is correct, and Searle's correlations are not examples of scientific explanation that count against (6). But what about premise (3)? Why isn't it reasonable to take mental entities and their regular correlations with physical entities to be brute natural facts for which there is no explanation? The answer is the same as the arguments just mentioned about why Searle's correlations are not really scientific explanations. Mental entities are not natural or at home in the naturalist epistemology, etiology and ontology. Given theism and AC as a rival explanatory paradigm and given the fact that mental entities and correlations are natural for theism, it is question begging and ad hoc to announce that these entities and correlations are natural entities. Searle could respond that biological naturalism is not question begging because we already have reason to believe that naturalism is superior to theism prior to our study of the nature of the mental. Apart from a few sociological musings about what it means to be a modern person, the only support Searle gives for this claim is that it is an obvious fact of physics that the world consists entirely of physical particles moving in fields of force. It should be clear, however, that this claim is itself question begging and clearly false. When there is a statement in a physics text about the world in its entirety, it is important to note that this is not a statement of physics. It is a philosophical assertion that does not express any obvious fact of physics. Moreover, it is a question-begging assertion by naturalists prior to a consideration of the evidence and arguments for theism, including AC. If Searle denies this, then he should inform advocates of AC of exactly what obvious fact of physics they deny in their employment of the argument.

One final issue in Searle's defense of biological naturalism needs to be addressed, and that is his claim that the emergence of consciousness fits a broad pattern of emergence (e.g., cases of liquidity, solidity, digestion) and therefore, since the latter present no problem for naturalism, neither does the former. I have three things to say in response to this claim. First, if we take liquidity or solidity to be the degree of rigidity, flexibility or viscosity of a collection of particles, then these properties are not good analogies to consciousness because they turn out to be nothing more than group behavior of particles placed in a relatively compressed, stable, ordered structure for solids or a more viscous, less compact arrangement for liquids. So there is no problem about emergence, since we can easily understand how liquidity and solidity are related to groups of material particles as they are depicted in physical theory.

Second, when we are dealing with genuinely emergent properties that are categorially different from what physical theory takes to characterize subvenient entities, I think that it could be argued that the naturalist has the same difficulty here as with the emergence of consciousness. Recall Searle's point about the pragmatics of reduction: we reduce heat to its causes because we happen to be interested in the objective causes and not the subjective appearances; but in cases of pain we are interested in the painful appearance itself, so we do not reduce pain to its causes. In my view the decision to reduce heat to its causes is not primarily a scientific matter, nor it is a matter of our pragmatic interest. I think it has been a function of two things. First, if we take heat, color, liquidity or solidity to be identical to the qualia we experience in certain circumstances (e.g., heat is identical to warmth; red is a color, not a wavelength; liquidity is wetness), then an ontological puzzle arises analogous to the one about the emergence of mental states: How could warmth emerge in a physical structure as a result of increased atomic agitation? Second, there was a way of avoiding this question in light of a widely held Lockean view of secondary qualities and sense perception. We can locate these secondary qualities in consciousness and identify them as appearances of the real objective phenomena, namely, the objective causes for our experiences of secondary qualities.

John Yolton has shown that during late seventeenth and early eighteenth century debates about materialism, immaterialist philosophers (e.g., Ralph Cudworth) regularly argued against the idea that mental entities could emerge from properly structured matter (Yolton 1983, 4-13, esp. 6-7). A standard rebuttal to this claim was that light and heat were very different from matter but could be generated in material bodies given the right conditions; so mind could likewise emerge. Cudworth and others responded by asserting that light, heat and other secondary qualities were not in material bodies but rather were sensations in minds; thus the problem does not arise as to how they could arise in a material structure devoid of such qualities prior to the right conditions obtaining. It is clear from this debate at the beginning of the emergence of modern materialism that one philosophical motive for locating secondary qualities in consciousness was to avoid a straightforward metaphysical problem: *ex nihilo nihil fit.*

If I am right about this, then the ontological puzzle is really the driving force behind what Searle calls normal naturalist cases of emergence. The problem is that these cases are not natural any more than the emergence of consciousness, and that is why they were located in consciousness. For example, both secondary qualities like redness or warmth and painfulness are dissimilar to the properties that constitute an ideal physics. Jaegwon Kim has argued that in Nagel-type reductions, the relevant bridge laws should be taken as biconditionals and not as conditionals, because we need materially equivalent correlations between entities (or terms) in the reduced and base theories in order to assert identities between the entities in question (Kim

1996, 214-15).[14] Moreover, says Kim, the identity of reduced and base entities is preferable to mere correlations because the latter raise potentially embarrassing questions as to why such precise correlations arise in the first place.

Kim's point is not confined to mental and physical correlations. All a naturalist can do with them (if we keep these so-called secondary qualities or other categorially distinct emergent qualities in the external world) is to offer a detailed correlation to describe regular relations between physical structures and emergent entities. No amount of knowledge whatever of subvenient entities would take us one inch toward predicting or picturing why these particular entities regularly emerge in such and such circumstances and not others. In discussions of emergence over a century ago, it was precisely their unpredictability from knowledge of subvenient entities that was identified as the hallmark of an emergent property. In more modern terms, it is the inability to either image or understand why warmth emerges regularly here and not somewhere else or why it emerges at all given our knowledge of molecular agitation. Note carefully that Searle himself seems to accept pictureability as a necessary condition for the acceptance of a claim that one entity emerges from another in the "normal" cases, but pictureability is no more available for heat (warmth) emerging from matter than it is for mental states (Searle 1992, 102-3). Nagel's conceivability test applies here just as it does to mental states.

However, even if I am wrong about the problematic nature of "normal" cases of emergence for naturalists, I still think a third response can be given to Searle. There are two features of mental states that make their emergence disanalogous to, say, the properties of digestion. First, mental states are so unique and different from all other entities in the world that it is far more difficult to see how they could emerge from physical states than it is for the so-called normal cases. Second, mental states are quite natural in a theistic worldview and have a higher prior probability given theism over against naturalism even if we agree that, say, the emergence of the properties of digestion are equally natural and probable on both worldviews.

In my view these two features of mental states make them more analogous to value properties than to characteristics of digestion. Concerning moral properties, it is interesting to note that J. L. Mackie argued, correctly in my view, that the supervenience of moral properties would constitute a refutation of naturalism and evidence for theism: "Moral properties constitute so odd a cluster of properties and relations that they are most unlikely to have arisen in the ordinary course of events without an all-powerful god to create them" (Mackie 1982, 115; cf. Moreland and Nielsen 1993, chaps. 8—10).[15] Presumably Mackie's reasons for this claim involve some of the points I have just made: moral properties have the two features that make them natural for theism but unnatural for naturalism. No matter how far future physics advances our understanding of matter, it will not make the emergence of moral properties the least bit more likely, more pictureable or more natural. And the same claim could easily be made for mental properties even if features of digestion are granted equally natural for theism and naturalism. Searle himself admits that of all the entities in the world, mental states are absolutely unique and radically different from all the others. To the degree that this is so, the analogy between the emergence of mental states and other cases of emergence is weakened.

In this chapter I have argued that if primary causal divine miracles are depicted as libertarian acts, such acts of God can be appropriately employed by way of personal explanation to explain certain facts about the natural world that are otherwise inadequately explained or are not explained at all. I have also claimed that the origin of the universe and the existence of mental phenomena are two places where this strategy is highly justified, though I would not limit its employment to these areas.[16]

## Notes
[1] I assume at least partial univocity between human and divine action. For more on this see Alston 1988.

[2] This is not quite correct, because sometimes an agent performs an intentional action by allowing a certain sequence of events to take place. An agent gives a sort of passive permission and does nothing to stop a sequence of events that accomplish the agent's intent. The agent refrains from endeavoring.

[3] Timothy O'Connor holds that the primitive, core element in our concept of causality is that of the "production" or "bringing about" of an effect (see O'Connor 1995, 175-78). For O'Connor this core element is a genus of which agent and event causation are distinct species. My claim that active power is epistemically primitive is consistent with O'Connor's claim in this way. Through introspective awareness of my own free acts, I am aware of my own active power. By reflection I may then form a concept of active power. By reflection on the concept of active power, I may then form a concept of causal production per se by removing from my concept of active power the component of being able to refrain.

[4] There is some debate about whether each of these basic actions requires its own intending. Swinburne argues that in performing actions that take a long time (writing a chapter), we do not exercise a separate volition for each intentional action (e.g., willing to write the first sentence) that is part of the long-term act. Rather we intend to bring about the long-term effect by bringing about a generally conceived series of events, and the body unconsciously selects a particular routine to accomplish that effect (see Swinburne 1986, 94-95). I leave the matter open except to note that to the degree that a nonbasic action contains subacts of a discontinuous nature (picking up keys and getting into a car versus a series of steps in taking an hour-long walk), then it is more likely that subintentions are required to characterize adequately those subacts.

[5] Thus we see that there are at least three kinds of intentional actions: basic actions

with a basic intent (intentionally moving a finger), basic actions with nonbasic intents (ultimate intents that have other intents as means—e.g., intentionally squeezing one's finger to fire a gun to kill Smith) and nonbasic actions (those that contain subacts—subendeavorings and intendings—as parts, such as going to the store to buy bread).

[6]For excellent treatments of divine action relevant to this article, see the chapters by Jonathan L. Kvanvig and Hugh J. McCann, Philip L. Quinn, Peter van Inwagen and William P. Alston in Morris 1988.

[7]The main views of the world's causal activity in relationship to God's are the full secondary causality view (God sustains the world in existence, but in the normal course of things the entities of the world exert their own causal powers, and such exertions are sufficient to produce changes in the world), occasionalism (there are no autonomous, distinct causal powers possessed by created objects; God is the only true cause, and no effect in nature is brought about by natural entities) and concurrentism (every event cause has God collaborating with the natural causal entity, cooperating with its causal activity by ratifying that activity). My own view is the first position.

[8]I am assuming here that there is no metaphysical time prior to physical time.

[9]If the initial singularity is taken to be an event, then the event cause would be simultaneous with the initial singularity in the sense of being at the same time as the singularity. If the initial singularity is taken as a boundary of time, then the cause, strictly speaking, would not be an event (in which case, event causality would not be applicable) but could still occur coincidentally in that both the cause and the effect occur at $t = 0$ (for more on this, see Craig 1994a, 222).

[10]Bishop's own solution eschews libertarian agency in favor of a version of the causal theory of action.

[11]An interesting implication of Bishop's view is that naturalism cannot allow for there to be a first event in the absolute sense of not being preceded by other events because all events are caused by prior events or else they are simply uncaused. In the latter case the coming to be of the event cannot be natural since it is a brute fact. In the former case this means that if the kalam cosmological argument is correct and there was a beginning to the universe, then the beginning itself was not a natural event, nor was its cause if it had one. For more on this, see Craig and Smith 1993.

[12]Selmer Bingsjord rejects Swinburne's version of AC because it focuses on the regular correlations of specific types of mental and physical events. But Bingsjord thinks that a version of AC that starts with agent causation is likely to be successful (see Bingsjord 1986, 140-41).

[13]Compare a passage in which Searle considers and rejects as incoherent a closely related question formulated in terms of intelligence and intelligent behavior and not consciousness (Searle 1992, 32, 56-57). If intelligence and intelligent behavior are interpreted from a third-person perspective in behavioristic terms (e.g., as regular and predictable behavior), then it is false that bits of matter are not intelligent. If first-person subjective criteria are formulated for intelligence, then the question reduces to the one asked in terms of consciousness. So this is the correct question to ask on Searle's view.

[14]See G. K. Chesterton's claim that the regular correlation between diverse entities in the world is magic that requires a Magician to explain it (Chesterton 1950, chap. 5).

[15]Mackie found it easy to deny the objectivity of moral properties and opted for a form of moral subjectivism. But he could not bring himself to deny the mental nature of qualia. So he adopted a solution for qualia similar to Searle's. I shall not look at Mackie's case, because Searle's is more forceful and better developed. Moreover, part of Mackie's case rests on his critique of AC, and I have already interacted with some of his major points of critique.

[16]I have argued elsewhere that when an agent exercises libertarian agency, he or she leaves a gap in the natural causal fabric that at least in principle can be discovered and explained by a divine primary cause, especially if one had antecedent reason to suspect that such a gap would be present (e.g., if one takes revelation to specify that the basic kinds of life were created by a divine primary causal miracle). When an agent exercises libertarian agency, the act is supernatural in the sense that it cannot be subsumed under a law of nature plus initial conditions, and in this sense agent acts transcend nature. See Moreland 1997a, b.

## References

Adams, R. 1992. Flavors, colors and God. In *Contemporary perspectives on religious epistemology*, ed. R. D. Geivett and B. Sweetman, 225-40. 1987. Reprint, New York: Oxford University Press.

Alston, W. P. 1988. Divine and human action. In *Divine and human action*, ed. T. V. Morris, 257-80. Ithaca, N.Y.: Cornell University Press.

Armstrong, D. M. 1968. *A materialist theory of mind*. London: Routledge and Kegan Paul.

———. 1978. Naturalism, materialism and first philosophy. *Philosophia* 8:261-76.

Bingsjord, S. 1986. Swinburne's argument from consciousness. *Philosophy of Religion* 19:127-43.

Bishop, J. 1989. *Natural agency*. Cambridge: Cambridge University Press.

Chesterton, G. K. 1950. *Orthodoxy*. 1908. Reprint, San Francisco: Ignatius.

Churchland, P. 1984. *Matter and consciousness*. Cambridge, Mass.: MIT Press.

Craig, W. L. 1992. The origin and creation of the universe: A reply to Adolf Grünbaum. *British Journal for the Philosophy of Science* 43:233-40.

———. 1994a. Creation and big bang cosmology. *Philosophia Naturalis* 31:217-24.

———. 1994b. Prof. Grünbaum on creation. *Erkenntnis* 40:325-41.

———. 1994c. A response to Grünbaum on creation and big bang cosmology. *Philosophia naturalis* 31:237-49.

Craig, W. L., and Q. Smith. 1993. *Theism, atheism and big bang cosmology*. Oxford: Clarendon Press.

Gruber, H. E. 1974. *Darwin on man: A psychological study of scientific creativity*. Chicago: University of Chicago Press.

Grünbaum, A. 1989. The pseudo-problem of creation in physical cosmology. *Philosophy of Science* 56:373-94.

———. 1991. Creation as a pseudo-explanation in current physical cosmology. *Erkenntnis* 35:233-54.

———. 1994. Some comments on William Craig's "Creation and big bang cosmology." *Philosophia Naturalis* 31:225-36.

Horgan, T. 1993. Nonreductive materialism and the explanatory autonomy of psychology. In *Naturalism*, ed. S. J. Wagner and R. Warner, 295-320. Notre Dame, Ind.: University of Notre Dame Press.

Kim, J. 1996. *Philosophy of mind.* Boulder, Colo.: Westview Press.

Mackie, J. L. 1982. *The miracle of theism.* Oxford: Clarendon Press.

Meyer, S. C. 1994. The methodological equivalence of design and descent. In *The creation hypothesis,* ed. J. P. Moreland, 67-112. Downers Grove, Ill.: InterVarsity Press.

Moreland, J. P. 1989. *Christianity and the nature of science.* Grand Rapids, Mich.: Baker.

—————. 1994a. Conceptual problems and the scientific status of creation science. *Perspectives on Science and Christian Faith* 46:2-13.

—————. 1994b. Response to Bube and Meyer. *Perspectives on Science and Christian Faith* 46:22-25.

—————. 1997a. Complementarity, agency theory and the God of the gaps. *Perspectives on Science and Christian Faith* 49 (March):2-14.

—————. 1997b. Miracles, agency theory and the God of the gaps. In *Miracles: Has God acted in history?* ed. R. D. Geivett and G. Habermas, 132-48. Downers Grove, Ill.: InterVarsity Press.

Moreland, J. P., and K. Nielsen. 1993. *Does God exist?* 1990. Reprint, Buffalo, N.Y.: Prometheus.

Morris, T. V., ed. 1988. *Divine and human action: Essays in the metaphysics of theism.* Ithaca, N.Y.: Cornell University Press.

Nagel, T. 1986. *The view from nowhere.* New York: Oxford University Press.

O'Connor, T. 1995. Agent causation. In *Agents, causes and events,* ed. T. O'Connor, 173-200. New York: Oxford University Press.

Peacocke, A., and G. Gillett, eds. 1987. *Persons and personality.* Oxford: Basil Blackwell.

Plantinga, A. 1991a. When faith and reason clash: Evolution and the Bible. *Christian Scholar's Review* 21 (1):8-32.

—————. 1991b. Evolution, neutrality and antecedent probability: A reply to McMullin and Van Till. *Christian Scholar's Review* 21 (1): 80-109.

—————. 1993. *Warrant and proper function.* New York: Oxford University Press.

Rowe, W. 1991. *Thomas Reid on freedom and morality.* Ithaca, N.Y.: Cornell University Press.

Searle, J. 1983. *Intentionality.* Cambridge: Cambridge University Press.

—————. 1984. *Minds, brains and science.* Cambridge, Mass.: Harvard University Press.

—————. 1992. *The rediscovery of the mind.* Cambridge, Mass.: MIT Press.

Swinburne, R. 1979. *The existence of God.* Oxford: Clarendon Press.

—————. 1986. *The evolution of the soul.* Oxford: Clarendon Press.

Yolton, J. W. 1983. *Thinking matter: Materialism in eighteenth-century Britain.* Minneapolis: University of Minnesota Press.

# 12

# Design, Chance & Theistic Evolution[1]

## DEL RATZSCH

T THE CORE OF INTELLIGENT DESIGN THEORY ARE SEVERAL KEY contentions. One is that appeal to nonnatural intelligent design in explanation of natural phenomena is in principle scientifically legitimate. Another is that in specified cases, such design explanations can be supported in a scientifically legitimate manner by specifiable empirical considerations. A claim frequently subsidiary to those two in specific cases is that intelligent design is the only viable explanation and is hence scientifically not only permissible in principle and supportable in fact but also essential in practice.

Evolution, however, especially Darwinian evolution, is typically interpreted as excluding in principle any hint of design in its processes. The basis of its operation is blind chance. The means of its operation is genetic mistake and death. The result of its operation is a random walk through some morphological and genomic phase space. There is no ultimate goal of its operation. The ultimate actual destination of its operation is unforeseen and lacking any special significance, whatever it is.

That would suggest that any rapprochement between evolution and design, to which theistic evolution is committed at some level—let alone between evolution and intelligent design theory—would be out of the question. Nevertheless determining whether this is so requires a detailed look both at what design involves and at what resources theistic evolution can legitimately claim. In what follows I try to go at least some distance toward those goals.

## Design: Initial Foray

Design, whatever its source, can be located, introduced, initiated, implemented or exhibited in only a limited number of logical arenas. The relevant ones fall into two broad categories. First, design can be introduced into the historical course of and against the background of an already existing nature by humans, aliens, other finite beings or God. Watches, for instance, embody design that humans introduce into the history of the cosmos and that are not natural manifestations in history of some built-in cosmic design. Second, design could be built protohistorically into the very fabric of nature and nature's operations. For instance, a fine-tuning of natural constants for some specific purpose would involve a design not introduced into nature but a designing of nature itself. This second broad category, involving as it does the giving of definition even to what nature is, is obviously an option only for supernatural agents.[2] Each of those broad categories can be separated into further subcategories as follows.

### Initiation in cosmic history

There are three areas where design as initiated within cosmic history may be exhibited.

*Products/properties.* Designedness is frequently evident in human products—spoons, watches, bulldozers—that do not appear in nature and that have properties at scales that also do not appear in nature. The same can also be true of some products of divine activity, for example, a Roman coin, directly created, in a fish's mouth. In this latter case both the introduction and the evidence of design would be at the product/property level.

*Processes.* Design can be embodied in processes, even when the products of those processes exhibit no direct evidences of design. For instance, a molecule of some protein might be produced by purely natural processes, or it might be the result of some high-tech artificial synthesis. Examination of the product itself or its empirical properties would not reveal which, any more than examination of the wine at Cana revealed that it was the result of a miraculous process.

*Initiating conditions.* Some products that do not exhibit direct (spoon-like or watch-like) evidence of design and whose productive processes do not reveal direct evidences of design may spring ultimately from special conditions, initiated within history, that were themselves products of design. For instance, living cells are natural and operate by purely natural processes.

They do not reveal their designedness to simple inspection: they do not wear their design characteristics in the same way as do, say, bulldozers. Nor does their production exhibit direct evidences of design, as would examination of the means of artificially synthesizing some protein, let alone of synthesizing a bulldozer. We can watch cell production from parent cells in minute detail for generations without seeing anything that is not wholly explainable by normal, natural laws, conditions and processes.

But suppose that cells could not have originally arisen by purely natural means. In that case the initiating of the cell line—the line whose products, properties and reproductive processes are purely natural and exhibit no direct evidences of design—would embody direct design. That could occur in a number of ways. For instance, it might involve the direct, complete, de novo originating of an ancestor cell from which all other cells descended by purely ordinary means. Or it might involve constructing specially designed "artificial" conditions from which the ancestor cell itself could arise. For instance, suppose that we finally discover that life can arise spontaneously but only under exactly one set of conditions. One must begin with 4003.6 gallons of eight specific, absolutely pure chemicals, exactly proportioned down to the molecule. The mixture must then be sealed into a large, light green Tupperware container with one sterile copy of "Sergeant Pepper's Lonely Hearts Club Band." Do that, and life develops spontaneously by natural means (catalyzed by the precise surface characteristics of "Sgt. Pepper"). Its development, subsequent reproductions and characteristics are completely according to normal natural laws. And life in this case was not directly specially created. But those initial conditions involve interjection of deliberate intent and design with a vengeance.

There are more prosaic examples involving human initiation of special conditions. For instance, researchers recently introduced genes for bioluminescence into the tobacco mosaic virus. That was a deliberate, designed, initiating intervention. That combination did not and, we may suppose, might never have arisen by natural means. But once the initiating was complete, the subsequent generations, complete with bioluminescence, arose by perfectly ordinary reproductive means, and their possession of genes for bioluminescence did not violate any laws, scream "design," or anything of the sort. The initiating event did exhibit design directly visible to anyone observing it (test tubes, labs smocks, grant applications, coffee pots), but nothing past that point did.

### Implications: Concepts
Pursuing some of the relevant issues will require a number of terms, concepts and preliminary implications. Some of the more crucial ones follow.

*Intervention.* Introduction of design into history in any of the above locations (product, process or initiating conditions in history) involves a de novo initiation or creation in at least one of the three loci. More exactly, any design initiative in either of the latter two areas will inevitably involve an initiation in the first area, either in triggering or directing the process in question or in producing the relevant initiating conditions. It is part of the force of saying that some specific design was introduced into the world, at some point in its historical course, that any such introduction involves agent intervention in history, whether human, alien or supernatural, and in whichever locus.

*Counterflow.* There is another, even more fundamental implication. Linked to the intervention just mentioned, there will now be something about the cosmos, its history or its path that did not flow out of its prior states. The intervention will in effect involve the pushing of nature out of a path that nature, if left to itself, otherwise would have taken and into one it would not have; otherwise it would not be intervention. (Some technical qualifications are required later.) Nature moving in paths it would not of itself have taken I shall term *counterflow.* Counterflow is both defined and identified against a background of what nature might otherwise have done in contrast to the normal flow of nature.[3]

*Artifactuality.* The result of counterflow intervention into the course of nature is what we generally term an artifact. I shall use that term to refer to such results, whether by human, alien or supernatural agents, and whether physical (bulldozers, physical processes), immaterial (mathematical algorithms) or whatever.

*Nomic discontinuity.* The natural causal history of most instances of artifactuality will involve a gap precisely at the point of intervention, in that the reigning natural laws will not define a path from the state immediately preceding the intervention to that immediately following the intervention. That will mean that in most instances (not all), nature could not produce the artifact in question (e.g., diesel bulldozers; for related remarks see Thaxton, Bradley and Olsen 1984, 201-2).

### Implications: Relations

Although the preceding points are all closely linked, they are distinct and for the most part are not coextensive. Most important for the moment is that neither counterflow, artifactuality nor intervention entails nomic discontinuity. Consider this sort of case: Suppose that emergence of a specific innovation in some organism requires a subtle alteration at a particular gene site. Spontaneous decay of a specific atom at that site would, via purely natural processes, trigger the desired alteration. Spontaneous decay of that atom is completely within the bounds of governing natural law, and there is a specifiable probability of its doing so. However, suppose that if left to itself it will not decay. God, being omniscient, knows that, so he intervenes, decreeing the decay. All then proceeds as indicated. (This approach to biological history may be called quantum progressive creation, although some persons who call themselves theistic evolutionists fit here. Some discussion of this general idea is in Ratzsch 1996a, 186-88.)

In this case there is intervention, but since the decreed decay is within the bounds of the governing quantum laws and even has a certain probability of spontaneous occurrence under such laws, there is no nomic discontinuity. The relevant laws do not bar the state transition from stability to decay, a transition that would naturally trigger the innovation. The decay could have happened naturally; it just did not and was not going to.

There is also counterflow in this case. Something was brought about that would not have happened had nature been left to itself. But again, the event could have happened. It was not prohibited by the relevant laws, and given the specifiable probability of its spontaneous occurrence, natural law did define a path between the two states in question. There was thus again no nomic discontinuity. Note that in this sort of case even a complete and perfect science could not empirically detect specific instances of counterflow. (Note that this implies that quantum progressive creationism would be empirically indistinguishable from some forms of theistic evolution but significantly different theologically and metaphysically.)

Essentially identical considerations apply to artifactuality and nomic discontinuity. Furthermore, it might be noted that for similar reasons, deliberately destructive intervention might not necessarily involve nomic discontinuity.[4]

Connections to design are a bit trickier. For instance, artifactuality and designedness cannot be equated. Someone idly, unmindfully whittling on a stick with neither purpose nor intention will still produce an artifact, indeed a recognizable artifact. But that artifact will not be designed or a product of design. It will not be the result of deliberate intent, plan or anything of the sort. And as will be seen later, supernatural design does not necessarily imply counterflow or intervention in history (as human and alien designing nearly without exception do), much less nomic discontinuity.

One distinction already suggested should perhaps be made more explicit. That an object is a product of intent, plan and intervention via counterflow processes does not necessarily imply that that object itself displays any detectable properties definitive of or indicative of design. Pick any object that is notoriously lacking in signs of design. That object obviously could be the result of deliberate, intentional activity; it might have been deliberately produced to serve as a paradigm example of designlessness at the National Bureau of Lack of Standards. Thus that something was a result of deliberate intent, planning and even counterflow processes does not entail that the object itself exhibits design. But typically the two do go together, and since any case for deliberate intent in nature's producings would fulfill substantially the same functions as cases for the designedness of nature's products, I shall unless otherwise noted treat them as roughly equivalent. Thus

(1) counterflow entails artifactuality but not nomic discontinuity,

(2) intervention entails counterflow but not nomic discontinuity, and

(3) artifactuality entails neither nomic discontinuity nor designedness.

And as we will see a bit later,

(4) designedness (especially supernatural) entails neither counterflow nor intervention, at least not in their most straightforward senses.

### Recognizing historically initiated design

Employing design as a scientific explanatory resource obviously requires a capability of recognizing design. When it comes to instances of human design and other historically initiated design, recognition of design is typically subordinate to recognition of artifactuality. It is perhaps possible in principle to recognize something as being designed and then conclude that it must therefore be an artifact. But with human products it usually works the other way. What we recognize immediately seem to be indications of counterflow, and we then (nearly instantaneously) identify their carriers as made. But even having recognized counterflow and artifactuality, we sometimes do not recognize designedness, let alone identify what the intent or purpose of the design might be. For instance, one might recognize an apparently amorphous jumble on the floor of an avant-garde art gallery as an artifact but might not realize that it was designed. (Reportedly a mess left by workers in a gallery once won a prize, and in another instance an artwork was swept up by the museum janitor.) Or we might easily recognize scraps produced by a metal lathe as artifacts. But those scraps are not designed, and they are produced by intention only in a derivative sense. Such scraps would clearly evidence counterflow.

Moreover, the specifics of design—purpose, plan, intent, function—may be unrecognized even when designedness is evident. The Smithsonian Institution has a collection of obviously designed human artifacts, concerning the purposes of which no one has a clue. In any case designedness and artifactuality, although they are closely linked, are not coextensive, and recognition of designedness is typically subordinate to, even dependent upon, recognition of artifactuality. That recognition in turn typically involves recognition of indications of counterflow (in a related context see Thaxton,

Bradley and Olsen 1984, 203-4).

The claim that we typically get to designedness indirectly through counterflow and artifactuality might sound counterintuitive. But imagine what a manual for identifying traces of alien cultures on alien planets might contain. It is at least possible that aliens (presuming such) might have intentions, concepts, desires, needs and thought processes so incommensurable with ours that we could not even grasp either the content of the purposes behind their designs or even what an intention was in the context of their consciousness. Yet even in such a case planetary explorers would not necessarily be reduced to bringing home bags of random debris, having no idea whether anything in the bags was of alien origin or not. They could still confidently and accurately identify some things as alien artifacts, and that would provide a legitimate basis for believing that the objects were indeed designed.

If we do typically get at designedness indirectly via artifactuality and counterflow, then wild improbability or various sorts of complexity are only secondary indications of designedness and are relevant only to the extent that they themselves serve as signals of counterflow and artifactuality. And they do not always do so. For instance, complexity on the one hand and counterflow and artifactuality on the other do not always track together. A four-ton, absolutely pure, absolutely cubical chunk of titanium screams "artifact" and "counterflow" but does not itself exhibit much complexity. The Oklo natural reactor, however, involves some astonishing complexities but does not seem to suggest artifactuality or counterflow (Cowan 1976).

How then do we recognize counterflow? As a practical matter I think that we recognize counterflow most frequently in human artifacts through geometric properties in objects on a scale (a human scale) that nature typically does not produce. Think of nearly anything identifiable as an obvious human artifact, especially one of unknown purpose. The observable tip-offs are mathematizable (often geometrizable) uniformities—edges, areas, spacings, patterns, regularities, purities, symmetries. Those are our usual clues and provide the basis on which we propose to identify alien artifacts as well. Search for Extraterrestrial Intelligence (SETI), for instance, looks for certain patterns of a sort and in regions where nature presumably would not generate them. (It is interesting in this context that artificial-flower makers have learned to make their products look more natural by introducing nonuniformities such as irregular variations in color.) I am not claiming that there are any clear conceptual links or necessary links or logical links or invariant links but only that as a practical matter such uniformities and counterflow are linked in our recognition of artifactuality and ultimately of designedness.

Positive cases for intelligent design theories depend upon recognizing identifying marks linked to designedness. Such cases frequently if not routinely involve instances of nature allegedly being unable to produce whatever phenomenon is in question.[5] Such dependence is not surprising. We typically, albeit often intuitively and tacitly, associate design with counterflow; and counterflow in ordinary circumstances (not invariably) involves (i) an inability of nature to do the job alone, (ii) intervention in the historical course of nature and (iii) discontinuity in the usual course of nature.

But we should not forget that we typically do not recognize counterflow directly; that counterflow itself is direct evidence not for designedness but for artifactuality; and that although artifactuality is closely linked to designedness, it does not entail it. Thus our usual clues—e.g., these geometrizable properties—are several conceptual levels removed from design. For present purposes, however, even cases for artifactuality in nature would be a telling achievement. Moreover, this holds true regardless of any characteristics the artifact might or might not have.

It should be noted that there is nothing worrisome about design theory's frequent evidential dependence upon claims of nature's inability to generate specified phenomena. Positive theoretical cases for nature's inability to produce such are importantly different from mere inability to see how nature could have. That is a key possible difference between design theory and widely disparaged reliance upon gaps. Theoretical impossibility cases, such as for the impossibility of perpetual motion machines, are scientifically respectable. Such cases are, however, theoretical, indirect, often tricky and seldom rationally obligatory.

### (Protohistorical) design of nature

Design can be introduced into the course of history by humans, aliens or supernatural beings. But there is, recall, a second broad category: design built (protohistorically) directly into the fabric of nature and nature's operations. This option, again, would seem to be open only to supernatural beings. Only two design loci fall under this second category. Inbuilt design can be located either in the structure of the laws governing (or defining) the pathways of nature or in the primordial, ultimate starting conditions upon which those laws will operate.

*Primordial conditions.* A supernatural being could adjust primordial, protohistorical conditions to bring about desired results in the context of and by the normal operation of reigning natural laws. Leibniz and Augustine seemingly held versions of this view. Given a fixed background of operative laws, a supernatural being could have, at the very beginning or before it, set up primordial conditions in the precise ways required to give rise to desired results (e.g., life, diversity of species, human beings).

Those results would ex hypothesi be the outcome of deliberate activity, intent and design. There would not, however, be any direct empirical evidences, either present or historical, of deliberate interventions or of design-related discontinuities in any causal path in the natural realm. There might not even be indirect toolmarks connected with the phenomena in question. Everything in the natural realm throughout all of history would be a result of purely natural processes operating upon prior cosmic conditions.

Some sorts of inferred primordial conditions we would probably be inclined to classify as unnatural (e.g., a primordial version of the earlier Tupperware case would strike us as a bit odd). But specifying the meaning of *natural* would be a bit tricky in this sort of case. We could not define *natural* as we often intuitively do—"resulting by ordinary processes from prior conditions"—since there would be no prior conditions. But regardless of how that turned out, any intended results of primordial conditions deliberately chosen and structured with the intent of achieving just those results would have to be classified as products of design regardless of their empirical identifiability, their characteristics (whether simple or exhibiting varying types of complexity), and so forth.

*Law structures.* A second option available to a supernatural being goes even deeper, and that is the possibility of deliberately structuring the laws and principles of nature themselves in ways aimed at generating desired results. In this case the results would be natural, expectable, predictable, in accord with all reigning natural principles, and so on, precisely because the occurrence of the processes and products in question would result, intentionally so, from the reigning laws that defined the very concept of nature. But while they would be natural, they would be products of design as well. They typically would not, however, demonstrate the observable characteristics by which we directly identify human products or processes of design—much to the detriment of analogical teleological arguments, as we shall see.

There is in principle a wide range of potential possible tradeoffs and balancing off of relevant constraints between these last two areas. It might be that most of the work could be done in the structuring of laws and principles, so that nearly any primordial conditions would ultimately give rise to intended results. Or the laws and principles could be left much looser, with the necessary constraints being concentrated in precisely arranged primordial conditions. Or the balance could fall somewhere in between.

It might be possible that constraints for, say, life were so tight, so demanding, that there was no way of constructing any combination of laws and primordial conditions such that those laws operating upon those conditions could result in the natural emergence of life from nonlife. It might be, in other words, that under any set of laws the constraints upon conditions would be so demanding as to themselves constitute life; in short, it might be that the only possible ultimate source of biological life was direct creation of biological life itself. That seems to me to be a respectable possibility, but I leave it to others to establish or refute it.

### Recognizing protohistorical design

Design resulting from those preceding two alternatives need not involve any of the foregoing three implications: inability of nature (if nature is deliberately set up to do it, then nature obviously can do it), intervention in the historical course of nature (if everything is set up beforehand, primordially, to lead naturally to the phenomenon in question, no further input is needed), or discontinuity in nature (if nature is structured exactly to produce of itself the results in question by means deliberately made available to nature, then no gaps will appear). In particular counterflow—recognition of which typically underlies our capacity for artifact and design recognition—will be systematically missing from cases of supernatural design anchored in laws or primordial conditions and generally will be indirect and inferential in cases involving structuring of initial conditions.

In short, the primary and fundamental means by which we recognize artifact designedness, human or alien, will be of no direct use in the case of natural objects since we distinguish the natural from the artificial in terms of presence or absence of counterflow. So the cues by which we normally recognize designedness will be systematically missing in nature, and the clues that we can identify in nature will generally be at best derivative with respect to design. Their significance as design indicators will be supported at best by indirect, theoretical cases. But if the familiar indications of designedness are absent, and if the usual means by which we recognize designedness are of no direct relevance, how then would we recognize design that had been built into either primordial conditions, the structure of cosmic law itself, or both?

The previous basic intuition is still operative. It must still be true that something on some level is different than it otherwise would have been. But the focus is now in a different arena. With human and alien and some supernatural designedness, that "something being otherwise" translates as counterflow, as intervention in the normal flow of nature. But when design is interjected at the level either of primordial conditions or the structure of governing law, in what might jointly be termed initializing circumstances, the results cannot be counterflow since the circumstances both define what constitutes nature and establish the starting points of subsequent historical paths of nature. Further, whereas design-indicating counterflow is identified against the background of nature, it is not clear that there even is some ultimate background of how things otherwise would have been, against which design-indicating differences in the actual initializing circumstances of the actual cosmos could be identified. That may be one consequence of the doctrine of creation ex nihilo.

So how could we identify design in initializing circumstances? The answer, I think, must be in terms of something like the presence or absence of significant, qualitatively discontinuous, distinguishing properties, the presence of which is extremely sensitive to initializing circumstances. What might that mean? Consider the following situations: primordial conditions and law structures that, due to their precise shape, ultimately result in a pattern of cratering on the back side of the moon spelling out "John 3:16"; and primordial conditions and law structures that, due to their precise shape, ultimately result in the exact present jumbled pattern of cratering on the back side of the moon.

Both cases involve extreme sensitivity to initializing circumstances. The exact pattern of cratering on the back side of the moon may even be beyond sensitive in the sense that even identical initializing conditions would never reproduce it exactly. But the only relevant sensitive, discontinuous property—identity of pattern or nonidentity of pattern—seems to have no obvious significance whatever. The pattern is a jumble, and even vast alterations leave it in that respect utterly unchanged, still a jumble.

In the other case, change a few key parameters even slightly and the meaningful "John 3:16" would be lost, replaced by a jumble that conveyed no immediate content at all (if a moon, much less a cratered moon, even did result). Few would have doubts concerning the pattern's designedness. The disputes would likely concern whether the pattern was an outgrowth of initializing cosmic conditions or was, say, the work of aliens. The most crucial feature that would distinguish it from the present impact jumble would not be the improbability of the specific impact locations, the sensitivity to initializing conditions, or anything of that sort (which are similar in both cases) but the inarguable significance of the pattern.

Now consider primordial conditions and law structures that, due to their precise shape, ultimately give rise to life. Here the case is a bit more difficult, in part because we do not yet know enough. Toss a rock into space, and eventually it will fall into a gravity well somewhere. Is something similar true with life: toss out nearly any initializing circumstances and something will eventually fall into some viability island? Or is the origin of life extremely sensitive to initializing conditions, viability islands in the total initializing circumstances phase space being enormously rare?

I am assuming that the latter is the case. It seems close to inarguable that only a vanishingly small portion of the total possible initializing circumstances would generate life. Change a few initializing parameters (laws or primordial conditions) even slightly, and life would never develop. And in the switch from life to nonlife (a discontinuous difference), a significant property—life—would be lost.

I do not know how to specify *significant* very clearly, although I mean the term at least to suggest value or importance or meaning or the like. The sense in which "John 3:16" is significant and the sense in which life is significant are quite different. But neither are trivial matters of indifference, and neither are inconsequential in the way that a crater jumble pattern typically would be. It must be conceded that the inclusion of *significant* in the preceding characterization means that the proposed cases are not *purely* empirical. (Whether anything ever is remains a reasonably vexed question, which here I do not propose to get anywhere near.) But I do not think that there is any workable way to avoid that inclusion. That is connected to my earlier suggestion that improbability or complexity by themselves will not do the evidential job.[6]

### Theistic Evolution, Design Theories and Design Loci
Theistic evolution and design theory need not be in disagreement over some kinds of design in some loci. On the face of it, nothing whatever in theistic evolution requires that its advocates refuse to admit that phenomena in nature be results of deliberate, foresighted, active intent or that such phenomena exhibit evidences of such design. Theistic evolution can readily incorporate design that tracks back (continuously) to primordial conditions or to the ultimate structuring of natural laws and principles.[7] Cosmological anthropic cases might fit here. Indeed one theme frequently heard from theistic evolutionists is that God designed and set up the cosmos in such a way that life, species and humans, not to mention *E. coli* motors, would naturally, indeed inevitably, result. On that view what we see around us was deliberately intended and designed, although intervention into the flow of nature is not needed to account for it, and there thus need be no counterflow in any straightforward sense. Design and intent, on this view, are absolutely appropriate in explanations of life, humans and the broader structure of the cosmos but do not need to be appealed to in ways demanding discontinuous historical interjections. (In this sort of case, the probability of life, given those laws and primordial conditions, would be quite high, as a direct result of that designedness.)

Thus where design theory potentially differs from theistic evolution will be precisely in the potential for explanatory appeals to design of a sort that requires intervention into cosmic history. Theistic evolutionists have available all the explanatory resources of any design theory in cases where supernatural design is located either in ultimate primordial conditions or in the initial decreeing of the laws of nature. Nothing prevents theistic evolutionists from admitting, even insisting, that specific phenomena in nature are ultimately products of deliberate design and that there are sound, empirically based reasons for thinking that. But they do not have the option of tracking that designedness to some discontinuity within history, at which point the specific design in question entered history (at least not to discontinuities beyond those possible within quantum bounds). Theistic evolutionists can thus employ the concept of design as descriptive of natural phenomena and can employ design as explanatory of natural phenomena so long as that explanation tracks completely and naturally to the protohistorical (whether to primordial conditions, law structures, or both).[8]

But a thoroughgoing theistic evolution cannot employ design as explanatory de novo (involving nomic discontinuity) within cosmic history. That, however, has one often-misunderstood consequence. Any properties whatever taken as evidence of design, but for which the design initiation does not involve direct intervention and discontinuity in nature at the locus of the particular phenomenon, will be explainable in terms of laws and prior conditions within cosmic history, just as if the phenomenon in question were not designed. The difference attaching to the two cases—noninterventive initializing design and nondesign—would not enter at that level of explanation but would enter at deeper levels. So the sort of design claims thus consistent with theistic evolution (noninterventive, nondiscontinuous design) do not add anything at the immediate empirical causal explanatory level concerning phenomena in nature, just as critics of theistic evolution usually charge.

Theistic evolutionists thus apparently cannot make use of—indeed must reject—the design arguments and evidences most popular among creationists and many other design theorists, those being arguments resting upon degrees of improbability and specific types of complexity purporting to show the inability of nature and natural processes to produce the phenomena in question from prior natural conditions—that is, proposed indications of counterflow. According to a consistent theistic evolution, nothing wholly within, say, the biological realm exhibits counterflow, although such things may exhibit design. And here again is evidence that our typical clues to designedness—counterflow—are irrelevant to some key types of supernatural design.

### Design, Chance and Theistic Evolution

Two major issues separate most design theorists from most theistic evolutionists. First, theistic evolutionists tend to believe that appeal to supernatural design involving intervention or discontinuity in the actual history of nature is scientifically or even theologically impermissible. Design theorists nearly by definition believe it to be permissible in principle (for specific cases see Meyer 1994 and Dembski 1994 in Moreland 1994; Moreland 1989, chap. 6). I think that design theorists are right about that. I have frequently argued for related positions elsewhere and will not pursue the arguments here (see Ratzsch 1996a, 166-71, 192-95; Ratzsch 1986, 108-11, 141-49; Ratzsch 1995; Ratzsch 1996b).

Second, theistic evolutionists nearly by definition believe that appeal to supernatural design involving intervention or discontinuity in the actual postcreation history of nature is scientifically unnecessary. Design theorists nearly universally believe such appeal to be supported, if not demanded, by the data. I do not propose to take a position here—that is all in other people's territory.

But a deeper issue has a long history and underlies some important stretches of theistic evolution/creationism/design theory tensions. Creationists of most types, including some design theorists, believe that theistic evolution is logically incompatible with divine design in any robust sense of that term—maybe even internally incoherent. That is a reasonable position given the notion of design that many work with—a concept demanding exactly the intervention and historical, causal discontinuity that theistic evolution forbids.

But as we have seen, design does not entail intervention or causal discontinuity within cosmic history in the course of nature. Still, design does intuitively involve activity somewhere affecting the way things are as distinct from ways they otherwise would or might have been had such activity been otherwise or absent. It involves either historically or protohistorically a hands-on directing. Evolution is, notoriously, supposed to be undirected and fundamentally dependent upon random, chance-driven processes. There is an apparent tension here: evolution is stochastophilic; design is stochastophobic. Thus trying to reconcile evolution and design, as any theistic evolution that is genuinely theistic and genuinely evolutionary seems committed to doing, is going to be problematic.

### Types of randomness

But is there really no way of reconciling design and fundamentally random, chance processes? The answer depends in part upon what *chance* and *random* are taken to mean.[9] In this context there are three different notions that need to be separated.

*Epistemological randomness.* An event can happen at random from our perspective in the sense that we cannot predict it or handle the relevant variables. It was in this epistemic sense that gas molecule behavior was classically considered to be random, despite its being on Newtonian principles totally determined. There is obviously no difficulty reconciling that sense of randomness, or an evolution embodying that sense, to designedness. This sense need not be considered further.

*Teleological randomness.* A more problematic sense we might call "teleological" randomness or chance. An event or other phenomenon is teleologically random if no future state, aim or goal is in the empirical causal or explanatory postcreation historical chain leading up to that event or phenomenon. On Darwin's view, variation was random in this sense in that whether an absolutely essential variation occurred or not was completely independent of the needs, desires or prospects of the organism in question. This notion of randomness is consistent with a complete determinism (which Darwin also accepted).[10] Back to this in a bit.

*Nomic randomness.* Suppose that every relevant process was governed by laws that were ultimately, purely stochastic—that every relevant process was driven fundamentally by utterly random, chance events. In that situation key events would be random not merely in the sense that they came as surprises to epistemically limited and imperfect humans but in the sense that the relevant principles themselves were ultimately nomically random, involving, perhaps, mutations triggered by completely uncaused, indetermined, spontaneous quantum events. Would not an evolution fueled by that sort of randomness, in the context of a complete lack of supernatural intervention along the way, be completely irreconcilable with design?

*Nomic randomness: Some implications*

I do not think so. Let us begin with a simple example. Suppose that it was important to me that a strawberry ice cream cone be sold at the neighborhood ice cream parlor at exactly 2 p.m. One way I could prompt that to happen is as follows. Knowing quite well the preference for strawberry ice cream of one of my children, I take him to the ice cream parlor at 2 p.m. and allow him to freely choose any sort of ice cream cone he wishes—knowing that after examining every flavor, he will completely freely choose strawberry. I know that the following counterfactual of freedom is true:

(1) Were my son allowed to freely, uncausedly choose a flavor, he would choose strawberry.

Knowing the truth of that counterfactual of freedom, I can take advantage of it by establishing the appropriate conditions: taking him there and giving him a free choice. My aim—a strawberry cone sold at 2 p.m.—has been realized, and I have played a key, indirect role in that realization. But I have not caused it, I have not abridged my son's freedom, his choice was genuinely free, and the sale was not causally determined by me or anyone or anything else.

*Subjunctive governance.* Now it may well be that there are counterfactuals of nature that are not only true but known by God. Here is a simple example. Given the fundamentally indeterministic character of the basic natural laws, there would be no way (remaining within the context of those laws) to create some radioactive atom that would be causally guaranteed to decay exactly at 2 p.m. Yet it is possible that that atom, so created, would in fact spontaneously decay at precisely that moment. Of course it might very well not. But suppose that the truth of the matter was that it would do so. Were it going to do that in fact, God would know that fact. Thus, although its creation plus complete specification of relevant conditions plus the relevant laws would not entail that it would decay at that moment, it is nonetheless true that

(2) Were God to create that atom in the specified state and in the specified conditions, it would in fact decay at that precise moment.

By knowing that subjunctive and by taking advantage of it by creating the requisite atom in the requisite way, God could thus indirectly bring it about that the desired result—radioactive decay at the precise specified moment— did occur. Bringing that about would involve no intervention in what would in fact be spontaneous, uncaused, and purely random and purely natural quantum decay processes.

Let us extend that case. Suppose that God creates a world by setting up some set of primordial initial conditions and mandating a set of laws to govern developments out of those conditions. If some of those laws involve irreducible randomness, then there will be no one inevitable and law-driven outcome. But it may still be true that given the way that all the purely random, uncaused quantum events would just happen to go, an evolutionary process resulting in human beings would in fact (and completely depending on those random events) occur. It is thus possible that the following sort of subjunctive is true:

(3) Were God to set up the requisite primordial initial conditions and laws, the evolution of human beings by a path essentially incorporating nomically uncaused, random events would ensue.

If such a subjunctive were true and foreknown by God, then by beginning the creation in the requisite way, God could achieve the desired end of there being human beings, incorporating the foreknown results of utterly random processes. That achieving would be deliberate and intentional and would involve no supernatural intervention at any point during the process.

So if there are subjunctives of nature of the requisite sort, then the following are all mutually logically consistent:

(a) specific evolutionary outcomes depending essentially upon genuinely nomically random, uncaused processes,

(b) there being no supernatural intervention in normal, natural processes within history,

(c) those specific evolutionary outcomes being the result of deliberate supernatural intention and choice.

There are a number of alternative formal possibilities depending upon the exact nature of the subjunctives employed.[11] I will not develop all those alternatives here, although there is one substantively different alternative worth brief discussion.

*Subjunctive supervision.* Doubtless some people will be vehemently skeptical of the very existence of these sorts of subjunctives in cases involving fundamentally random, uncaused, undetermined processes. Although I think such subjunctives are largely unproblematic, let us for the moment suppose that there are none, or perhaps none that are in fact true, or perhaps none that are even truth-valued.[12] Given any of those situations, there would be no possibility of knowing in advance of initiating the relevant conditions what the relevant outcome was. The only way to find out would be to try it and find out what begins to ensue and then perhaps take appropriate steps if necessary.

Consider this simple analogy. Suppose that someone is teaching a child to ride a bicycle. At some point the trainer usually finds himself or herself running alongside the moving bicycle, not holding it but ready instantly to grab should the learner show reliable signs of beginning to topple over. If the learner shows no such signs, the trainer does not intervene. Thus the stance of the trainer is described by the following subjunctive:

(4) Were the learner otherwise going to topple over, the trainer would intervene and keep things upright.

That general stance I shall call *subjunctive supervision.*

Should it turn out that the learner did not begin to fall, then the successful continuation of the learner would be a result solely of the unaided activity of the learner. That would be true despite the facts that the preceding supervision subjunctive would be true and that had a fall been imminent, there would have been intervention. Notice further that the trainer typically does not know at the beginning of the run whether or not intervention will be required or will occur. It may, or it may not, depending upon how the learner does on his or her own.

Now consider the corresponding case involving divine intervention. If no appropriate subjunctive is true (or even has a truth-value), then a creator (if creating at all) would be in a position of having to give things the most promising-looking start and then having to take a subjunctive-supervision stance of being prepared, if necessary, to intervene in order to keep things on a proper track. Should it turn out that things stay on an acceptable track—and that may well be in part a result of the way various undetermined, uncaused, random quantum events happen to go—then no intervention would be necessary.

So at the outset it may be true that were specified primordial conditions and laws initiated, certain desired results might occur. Of course it may be that were those specified conditions and laws initiated, those same desired results might not happen. Similarly intervention might be required to attain those results. And it might not be required. If intervention turns out not to be required, then—assuming that the resultant world is an evolutionary world—evolutionary results may well depend crucially upon nomically random occurrences, yet the results will still be in a sense intended. In fact the sense of *intended* is fairly robust, since there will be a continual supernatural, active subjunctive supervision involving a continual stance of readiness to steer things right should they show signs of going in directions contrary to that intent if left to themselves.

It might sound slightly counterintuitive to attribute design in such a case. But consider two worlds, in both of which a specific phenomenon might or might not develop depending upon the occurrence or failure of some nomically random event. Suppose that in one it occurs on its own but that in the other the supernatural subjunctive supervision must be and is *activated* to bring it about. The outcomes in these cases are identical, so any empirical property exhibited in the one will be exhibited in the other. Thus if either displays properties constituting empirical criteria of or evidence of designedness, both will. Presumably then one should give the same assessment concerning presence or absence of design in both cases. Thus one must apparently say either that in the one case there is no design despite criteria of design being the direct result of deliberate intervention or else that in the other there is design despite there being no counterflow, no nomic discontinuity and no intervention (and the result not being built into created initializing circumstances). The latter seems to me more intuitively plausible. In any case genuine randomness and chance are consistent with genuine intent and plan in a way that does not require divine intervention initiating design in the causal history of phenomena in question.

### Teleological randomness

Teleological randomness would appear initially to be irreconcilable with design.[13] Of course one might ask how it could be established that events were random in this sense. Suppose for instance that it were demonstrable that the vast majority of variations (or mutations, or whatever) were unnecessary or even disastrous. It is not evident that that would show that those which were crucially useful were not deliberate, planned or designed. Surely nothing in the basic concept of design requires that all relevant factors affecting all organisms must be deliberately intended. If that is right, then even demonstration that the overwhelming majority of such events are indeed teleologically random (however one might do that) would be interesting but not decisive. (And obviously everything that exists at present did get whatever it needed to get here.)

But what if every relevant event were indeed teleologically random in the sense that need, aim, goal, plan, intent or purpose attaching to organisms played no immediate role ever in the postcreation causal paths leading to those events. Would not design be out of the question in that sort of case and any evolution, theistic or otherwise, that incorporated that sort of teleological randomness be flatly inconsistent with design? Counterintuitively enough, the answer to this question is, "Not necessarily."

Were nature completely deterministic, then, as we have seen, intended results could be built into primordial conditions and laws, the causal system itself guaranteeing not only those results but also whatever empirical factors internal to the history and character of nature might underlie the conclusion, perhaps empirically quite legitimate, that all relevant events were teleologically random. Design, plan, intent—none of those would play any immediate causal or explanatory role within the postcreation historical causal path to any phenomenon. There could well be nothing with any links to design, intervention or deliberate discontinuity that was part of the immediate causal history of any relevant event, genetic variation, transition in chemical evolution, or anything of the sort. All events would in that sense be teleologically random. But specific outcomes could still be the desired, planned, intended, designed results, having specific characteristics for specific reasons—the foundation of those results tracking back to ultimate, primordial creation.

But that turns out not to be crucial, for the simple reason that the causal fabric of the world appears not to be deterministic; it contains small quantum gaps, and the reigning fundamental principles of nature are indeterministic. And we already know what the consequences of that are for present purposes. We are confronted with the sorts of counterfactual situations discussed in the previous section. And just as it is perfectly possible that

(3) Were God to set up the requisite primordial initial conditions and laws, the evolution of human beings by a path essentially incorporating nomically uncaused, random events would ensue,

it is also perfectly possible that

(5) Were God to set up the requisite primordial initial conditions and laws, the evolution of human beings by a path crucially dependent upon events all of which were teleological random would ensue.

After all, any such events that are uncaused are obviously not caused by needs, aims or goals. (Or if no such subjunctive is even truth-valued, an alternative exactly paralleling subjunctive supervision is possible here also.)

What that possibility shows is that specific features of the world following upon deliberate, intentional activity and design are logically consistent with the immediate causal ancestry of those features—indeed, their entire post-creation causal ancestry—consisting entirely of events that are teleologically random. Although not a causal factor in the teleologically random events, the intent, aim and goal are still relevant. Were it not for goal-sensitive protohistorical activity, those crucial, specific, teleologically random events would have been replaced (or better, preempted) by others.

## Larger Implications

So if any of the preceding sorts of subjunctives were true (or if all were nontruth-valued), then were God to create the requisite system of laws and primordial conditions, then the result would or might be the evolutionary development of human beings by means that did not involve any deterministic inevitability and involved no intervention. The resultant evolutionary path would at various points directly and crucially depend upon purely random, uncaused, undirected, spontaneous, chance events. Were we able to construct a quantum detector or a teleology detector that infallibly told us whether or not some event was completely nomically random or teleologically random, that detector would tell us that every one of the events of the relevant sort that had affected evolutionary history was indeed random.

But that would not imply that the results were not intentionally and deliberately—and successfully—aimed for. The choice of which primordial conditions, which laws, to initiate would have been deliberately made in order to appropriate precisely the results that would or might arise, utterly by natural and random means, from random events stemming from those primordial beginning points but caused neither by those beginning points nor by the target end points. That means that one cannot accuse theistic evolution of being inherently logically incoherent on grounds that genuine Darwinian evolution is profoundly chance-driven whereas theism is profoundly committed to supernatural design, control, superintendence and guidance. The various interrelationships are not as simple as has been widely thought.

Suppose that is all right. That would still not close the gap to design theory unless theistic evolutionists could also, consistent with other of their commitments, take various empirical data as evidence for this sort of designedness. Can they? I do not have a totally worked-out answer to that question. But the answer may be yes. Earlier, extreme sensitivity to initializing circumstances was cited as possibly constituting design-relevant empirical evidence (under some additional conditions). In the present case it may be possible to construct an empirical case for design that involves precreation appropriation of foreknown teleologically random factors, that case being based upon extreme path sensitivity, rather than initialization sensitivity. Intuitively, a long ordered sequence of wild but utterly essential "coincidences" all involving events that taken individually are teleologically random and that function in service to some significant, discontinuous (etc.) property, should raise suspicion (for a brief discussion of coincidence see Pletcher 1982). Again, I do not know how the details of that would all go, but it seems to me that there is some substantial promise there.

**Conclusion**

That brings us back to what seems to me to be the core of the disagreement. Theistic evolutionists can agree to, indeed insist upon, the designedness of the cosmos and can take empirical data as indicating design in primordial conditions and the structure of natural law. Theistic evolutionists can even take specific features of the cosmos, of organisms, as empirical evidence of design—design built into the founding of the cosmos. And if the foregoing argument is correct, theistic evolutionists can maintain those positions without being logically forced to abandon admission of randomness, whether nomic or teleological, into their theories. God might appropriate such processes without altering their fundamentally random character. No commitment that a theistic evolutionist might have to evolutionary processes being fundamentally random, chance processes automatically, by any straight formal logical principles, destroys any of that.

There are more serious differences in the matter of intervention, of introduction of design into natural processes, of design that enters nature at some point other than initializing circumstances. But even here, if the foregoing arguments are correct, subjunctive governance and subjunctive supervision each in its own specific way offers the possibility of the ensured but not causally driven occurrence within history of intended design, that occurrence being achieved without either intervention or nomic discontinuity, and without being causally built in from the beginning. And one possible variant of subjunctive supervision would, like quantum progressive creation, allow incorporation of counterflow and intervention-based design, while still remaining within quantum bounds and involving no nomic discontinuity.

But although the gap between design theory and theistic evolution is thus not as broad as generally believed, in the area of empirically supported arguments involving introduction of design into postcreation history, and involving counterflow, intervention, and nomic discontinuity, design theory has available to it resources beyond the reach of theistic evolution.

**Notes**

[1] I am indebted to my colleagues in the Calvin College philosophy department for their insightful comments and criticisms, which have deprived readers of this chapter of a number of entertaining errors.

[2] One can distinguish between having design and being designed, where the former involves no agent whereas the latter does. Plato and Immanuel Kant might be seen as endorsing the former but not the latter. However, I prefer to restrict design to cases involving agent activity somewhere and thus instead distinguish between actual design and apparent design. Also of interest in this context is Gardner (1983, 57-67, especially 62 and 66).

[3] This general idea can be found in various creationist writings, among them Parker (1994, 13-17) and Morris and Parker (1987, 32-35).

[4] Many theistic evolutionists claim that God upholds all things at every instance and that laws describe his usual ways of dealing with the cosmos. On that view, talk of intervention is inappropriate, as is talk of laws and ontological distinctions between the miraculous and the natural. Even talk of natural causation might be inappropriate. Everything on this view is designed, and as designed as any other thing. Thus, according to advocates of this position, theistic evolution, as opposed to deistic evolution, embodies as much affirmation of design as it is logically possible to have, since everything at every instant is a direct and immediate product of design. For a technical exploration of this concept of law see Ratzsch 1987.

If that is the case, then we cannot properly distinguish things designed from things not designed (there are none), and we cannot cite any interesting distinguishing properties on the basis of which we might recognize design as opposed to nondesign. We might be able to recognize the designedness of some things via particular properties, although we are unable to recognize the designedness of other, equally designed things. But if that is so, then there apparently would be no property shared by human artifacts and all products of design in nature (at least, that we had access to). That would restrict the scope of analogical design arguments.

And even if one agreed that the distinction between "designed" and "undesigned" is an empty one, the distinction that most people intuitively make, the categorization that most people intuitively accept could still be effected in different terms—things that occur in the course of the ways that God usually governs and directs "nature" (e.g., water flowing downhill, bacteria reproducing) versus things that appear to involve God governing and directing "nature" in some unusual way (life suddenly appearing with no precursors, for instance). The same categories extensionally would be generated. And one could, even on this view, see design theory as an apologetic tool—taking distinctions mistakenly admitted by even some unbelievers and attempting to show that for at least some phenomena design conclusions are unavoidable even on that basis.

[5] Most of Behe's (1996) cases fall into this category (e.g., 1996, 203-5). See also Thaxton, Bradley, and Olsen (1984); Davis and Kenyon (1993, 6-7); and various of the essays in Moreland (1994). That approach has a long history (e.g., Brooke 1991). Also fairly common are implications that intelligent design suggests at least minimal de novo creations within postcreation history (e.g., Davis and Kenyon 1993, 85, and Behe 1996, 231).

[6]To object that a much larger portion of the actually nomically possible sets of initial conditions might generate life is, even if true, irrelevant here since the present issue concerns possible explanations for the present actual nomic conditions prevailing. Should it turn out that given the actual laws of nature, the emergence of life would have been quite probable no matter what the primordial conditions, or should it turn out that given the actual primordial conditions, the emergence of life would have been quite probable no matter what laws of nature reigned, the case could still support design construals provided that few other initializing circumstances incorporating other possible sets of laws (in the first case) or incorporating other primordial conditions (in the second case) could result in the production of life. In either case the sensitivity to initializing circumstances would be preserved, and the actualization of one of the few sets of laws (or the few primordial conditions) that would not only produce life but would nearly guarantee it would again meet the basic requirements for interpretability as evidence of designedness.

[7]Many design theorists readily admit this (e.g., Moreland 1994, 31). Behe (1996, 193) defines intelligent design in a way that does not preclude products of evolution being designed or, for that matter, the process of evolution itself being a result of intelligent design. The underlying intuition predates evolution (see, e.g., Brooke 1991, 125, 143).

[8]There are complications. For instance, suppose that, unknown to earth astronomers, twenty or so multimegaton meteors are on a collision course with the earth annually. Some sympathetic aliens, however, have for eons been systematically diverting them before they come into detectable range. (They missed one about 65 million years ago, but that turned out all right.) Recently, however, interstellar space has become unbearably polluted by sleaze broadcast by daytime television talk shows, and the aliens have finally had enough. After several years of waiting, they find a meteor of just the right mass, composition and trajectory to destroy human life on earth without triggering the extinction of all life. That one they deliberately let through without interference, and things take their predicted course; that is, what would happen were nature left to itself does happen. Was the destruction deliberate and designed? If so, then things are a bit trickier than previously indicated, since it is the aliens' deliberate inactivity (nonintervention) that is important here.

[9]There are differences in the concepts (see Dembski 1991), but those differences do not, I think, have significant consequences for the present project.

[10]Brooke (1991, 304) characterizes chance of this sort as "an intersection of otherwise independent causal chains."

[11]For instance, counterfactuals of this general sort but which have disjunctive consequents (where no similar counterfactuals having only any one of the disjuncts as consequent are true, but where any one of the disjuncts would be an acceptable outcome), will allow the same sort of conclusions as the subjunctive governance counterfactuals.

[12]Van Fraassen-type truth-value-gap semantics can be plausibly appealed to in this sort of case.

[13]This has been and is still a common intuition. For one representative present example see Morris and Parker (1987, 190). For discussion of one historical example see Ratzsch 1992. But see also, for example, Horigan (1979, 19-20, 23,

chaps. 10—11) and Brooke (1991, 315).

## References

Behe, M. 1996. *Darwin's black box: The biological challenge to evolution.* New York: Free Press.

Brooke, J. H. 1991. *Science and religion: Some historical perspectives.* Cambridge: Cambridge University Press.

Cowan, G. A. 1976. A natural fission reactor. *Scientific American* July, 36-37.

Davis, P., and D. Kenyon. 1993. *Of pandas and people.* 2nd ed. Dallas: Haughton.

Dembski, W. A. 1991. Randomness by design. *Nous* 25:75-108.

———. 1994. On the very possibility of intelligent design. In *The creation hypothesis,* ed. J. P. Moreland, 113-18. Downers Grove, Ill.: InterVarsity Press.

Gardner, M. 1983. Order and surprise. In *Order and surprise,* ed. M. Gardner, 57-67. Buffalo, N.Y.: Prometheus.

Horigan, J. 1979. *Chance or design?* New York: Philosophical Library.

Meyer, S. 1994. The methodological equivalence of design and descent. In *The creation hypothesis,* ed. J. P. Moreland, 67-112. Downers Grove, Ill.: InterVarsity Press.

Moreland, J. P. 1989. *Christianity and the nature of science.* Grand Rapids, Mich.: Baker.

———, ed. 1994. *The creation hypothesis.* Downers Grove, Ill.: InterVarsity Press.

Morris, H., and G. Parker. 1987. *What is creation science?* Rev. ed. El Cajon, Calif.: Master Books.

Parker, G. 1994. *Creation: Facts of life.* Colorado Springs, Colo.: Master Books.

Pletcher, G. K. 1982. Coincidence and explanation. In *Philosophy of science and the occult,* ed. P. Grim, 169-77. Albany: State University of New York Press.

Ratzsch, D. 1986. *Philosophy of science.* Downers Grove, Ill.: InterVarsity Press.

———. 1987. Nomo(theo)logical necessity. *Faith and Philosophy* 4:383-402.

———. 1992. Abraham Kuyper's philosophy of science. *Calvin Theological Journal* 27:277-303.

———. 1995. Science. In *New dictionary of Christian ethics and pastoral theology,* ed. D. Atkinson and D. Field, 761-64. Downers Grove, Ill.: InterVarsity Press.

———. 1996a. *The battle of beginnings.* Downers Grove, Ill.: InterVarsity Press.

———. 1996b. Tightening some (loose) screws: Prospects for a Christian natural science. In *Facets of faith and science, 2, The role of beliefs in mathematics and natural sciences: An Augustinian perspective,* ed. J. M. van der Meer, 173-90. Lanham, Md.: Pascal Center for Advanced Studies in Faith and Science/University Press of America.

Thaxton, C. B., W. L. Bradley, and R. L. Olsen. 1984. *The mystery of life's origin: Reassessing current theories.* Dallas: Lewis and Stanley.

# 13

# God of the Gaps

## Intelligent Design &
## Bad Apologetic Advice

### JOHN MARK REYNOLDS

T HE FAMOUS BAYEUX TAPESTRY DEPICTS THE DESTRUCTION OF THE
Saxon Harold, king of England, by the Normans. Prominent in the
background of this master work of the Middle Ages is a flaming
comet. It is a warning of the doom and judgment that is about
to fall on Harold by command of heaven. As Andrew D. White is at great
pains to show in *A History of the Warfare of Science with Theology in Christendom*,
belief in the supernatural nature of comets was almost universal in Christendom (White 1995, 171-208).

This idea did not last. Halley and his fellow naturalists destroyed the
notion that comets were sublunar,[1] products of human sinfulness or special
creations of the Almighty. Published sermons and tracts advocating moral
behavior based on the appearance of comets were rendered useless. Natural
explanations triumphed over secular ones. Such a triumph was seen as
consistent with more modern and intellectually tenable religious belief.
White says, "Happily none of the fears expressed by Conrad Dieterich and
Increase Mather were realized. No catastrophe has ensued either to religion
or to morals. In the realm of religion the Psalms of David remain no less
beautiful, the great utterances of the Hebrew prophets no less powerful. . . .
In the realm of morals, too, serviceable as the idea of firebrands thrown by
the right hand of an avenging God to scare a naughty world might seem, any

competent historian must find that the destruction of the old theological cometary theory was followed by moral improvement rather than by deterioration." This confidence regarding religious and moral improvement must have seemed much more justified to a late Victorian than it does to a person standing at the end of the twentieth century. It has been felt, however, that this picture of God being squeezed out of the picture by natural science contained powerful warnings for the modern theist engaged in either science or apologetics.

Does God act directly in the cosmos in detectable ways? As natural science gave more and more convincing explanations for all natural phenomena once viewed as the sole preserve of the deity, thinking people came to have their doubts. Finally many became convinced that science had either explained the great underlying laws of nature or was very close to doing so. Divine action was confined only to the gaps in scientific knowledge. Even such non-Christians as Voltaire feared that in the end God would be removed from the picture altogether (Roe 1990, 417-39). Every time science advanced, one more potential area of divine action was removed. Given past success in disposing of these gaps in the natural sciences, why not remove the God hypothesis altogether? This sort of reasoning was convincing to many late Victorians such as Thomas H. Huxley (1894) and is still found in popular antitheistic writings such as the work of the late Isaac Asimov.

Religious thinkers have responded in at least four major ways. First, many followed White into a religion lacking historical claims. White repeatedly said that the Christian religion was found only in the ethical and moral claims of some of the Old Testament and all of the New Testament. Science has aided the theologian in finding those parts of Scripture central to the message of the Christian church. "For the one great, legitimate, scientific conclusion of anthropology is, that, more and more, a better civilization of the world, despite all it survivals of savagery and barbarism, is developing men and women on whom the declarations of the nobler Psalms, of Isaiah, of Micah, the Sermon on the Mount, the first great commandment, and the second, which is like unto it, St. Paul's praise of charity, and St. James' definition of 'pure religion and undefiled,' can take stronger hold for the most effective and more rapid uplifting of our race" (White 1995, 327). Confined to the realm of morality, God was safely out of the way for the scientist.

Many Christian theists found this move repugnant on theological, philosophic and scientific grounds. They continued to try to make science fit with the text of Genesis. Such a thinker might accept some scientific discoveries, such as mechanisms for microevolution, while continuing to point out deficiencies in other areas of scientific reasoning.[2] These weak areas are often taken as evidence for the inadequacy of the modern scientific paradigm and as good reason to return to a more religious understanding of the causes of certain natural phenomenon. Opponents have often accused these concordist theories of simply repeating the God-of-the-gaps problem in biology (Giberson 1993, 138-54).

To Christian theists for whom both the White and concordist movements were wrong-headed, a different sort of solution commended itself. They rejected all concordist views, those that tried to bring the Genesis text and the latest scientific advances into line, for something that has been called the historical-cultural approach (Hummel 1986, 213). This exegetical method preserves the theological message of Genesis. It also allows for truthful statements to appear in the text dealing with science or the metaphysics undergirding a good philosophy of science. This differentiates it from White's approach, or at least that of his more radical disciples. Genesis may be allowed to teach broadly about God's creation of the cosmos, without letting worrisome and archaic details about creation intrude on the methodological naturalism of the good scientist. Writers like Howard J. Van Till[3] (Van Till 1993, 32-38) and Karl Giberson may disagree on the details of God's interaction with the world, but they do agree in rejecting any scientifically discernible action of God outside the theologically important salvation history.

Recently a fourth response has become popular. Phillip E. Johnson labeled it "theistic realism" in *Reason in the Balance* (Johnson 1995). A group of thinkers who may have little or nothing to say about the putative harmony of Genesis and biology have suggested that modern science, when it is not viewed through the lens of naturalistic metaphysics, supports the idea of God's direct intervention in the natural world. Nonetheless they deny that they are guilty of the God-of-the-gaps argument.

One of the seminal works in this new response to the religion and science question, *The Creation Hypothesis,* explicitly denies that it falls into the God-of-the-gaps problem. Philosopher J. P. Moreland describes the gaps argument and argues that theistic realism does not fall prey to this objection (Moreland 1994, 41-66).[4] Moreland claims this new theistic science[5] is safe for three reasons. First, it allows for divine action outside the gaps. It is not a form of soft deism, since it postulates God's continued sustaining activity in the cosmos. Second, the theistic scientist has reasons independent of naturalistic ignorance for invoking divine intelligence and a Designer. These reasons are philosophic and theological. Finally Moreland suggests theistic science functions best in historical as opposed to empirical science. Most commonly cited examples of the failure of theistic science, such as Newton, are from the latter, not the former (Moreland 1994, 59-60).

Other thinkers distinct from the writers of *The Creation Hypothesis,* such as philosopher Alvin Plantinga of the University of Notre Dame, agree with Moreland and dismiss concerns about a God of the gaps (Plantinga 1994). They argue that the gaps criticism misses the theological, philosophic and scientific point of the advocates of intelligent design. Why is this so? What is the God-of-the-gaps argument?

Plantinga says of the God-of-the-gaps argument: "The following, therefore, are the essential points of God-of-the-gaps theology. First, the world is a vast machine that is almost entirely self-sufficient; divine activity in nature is limited to those phenomena for which there is no scientific, i.e., mechanical and naturalistic explanation. Second, the existence of God is a kind of large-scale hypothesis postulated to explain what cannot be explained otherwise, i.e., naturalistically. Third, there is the apologetic emphasis: the best or one of the best reasons for believing that there is such a person as God is the fact that there are phenomena that natural science cannot (so far) explain naturalistically" (Plantinga 1994, 33). According to Plantinga, critics of the God-of-the-gaps position are correct in their dismissal of such a position. What is the difficulty? Proponents of theistic science like Plantinga do not advocate the God-of-the-gaps theology. God of the gaps does not, therefore, provide a sufficient reason for accepting total methodological naturalism and for rejecting the possibility of a theistic science. The theistic realist who advocates a theistic science does not agree with the three basic premises of the gaps theology. According to Plantinga, the God-of-the-gaps problem is therefore "a red herring in the present context" (Plantinga 1994, 35).

Moreland concurs (Moreland 1997). He describes the gaps argument as based on two basic assumptions. "First, natural science is making these gaps increasingly rare, and thus, there is less need to believe in God if such a belief is justified solely or largely by the God-of-the-gaps strategy. Second, this strategy is based on a faulty understanding of the integration of science and theology and the proper model of human and divine action as depicted in the complementarity model. In particular, the strategy fails because there are simply no such gaps in the natural world" (Moreland 1996, 8). The theist worried by the gaps argument also is concerned that God's actions have been limited to the gaps. The belief that God has acted is based only on the failure of natural science. Moreland describes such representations of theistic science as a "gross caricature" (Moreland 1996, 9).

Moreland points out that logically gaps are still possible. Following an overview of agency theory, Moreland even argues that certain theists may have a philosophical and theological reason for postulating the existence of such gaps. This reason could be reached prior to any putative failure of natural science to explain a phenomenon. It is not necessary to review Moreland's impressive case to see that he is not placing divine agency in the gaps of scientific reason because those gaps exist. He also explicitly denies that God's intervention in cosmic affairs is limited to any gaps. If Moreland and Plantinga have correctly described the gaps objection, then Moreland is not guilty of transgressing it.[6]

What is the gaps argument in this historical sense? Can the argument briefly described and emphatically rejected by Moreland and Plantinga be spelled out more carefully? The following is a summary of the argument as it is traditionally presented:

**Traditional God-of-the-Gaps Argument (Apologetic Version)**[7]

(1) The universe is governed by natural laws.

(2) If God exists, God would not by his free actions violate natural laws.

(3) Therefore if God is to have full freedom to act, then it must be in an area not governed by natural law.[8]

(4) If God exists, then God has freedom to act.

(5) Deism is for a priori theological reasons known to be false; therefore if he exists, God does act.[9]

(6) Therefore if God exists, there must be an area in the cosmos not governed by natural law.

(7) Science discovers natural laws that explain phenomena according to the working of natural laws.

(8) If there exists no natural cause for the existence of a phenomenon, then the phenomenon was caused by God.

(9) In the current state of scientific knowledge, there exists some phenomenon $x$ such that science has discovered no natural law to explain $x$.

First Major Conclusion:

(10) Therefore it is possible that science will never explain phenomenon $x$.

Or (in some cases such as alleged to have been suggested by Newton)

(10′) In the current state of scientific knowledge, there exists some phenomenon $x$ such that a reasonable person can be sure that no natural law exists to explain $x$.

Second Major Conclusion:

(11) Therefore it is possible that God is responsible for $x$, so God possibly exists.

Or

(11′) Therefore necessarily God is responsible for $x$, so God exists.

Even this very crude summary of the traditional God-of-the-gaps argument shows the many problems with it. As we have seen, Plantinga and Moreland summarize some of them. Both correctly observe that the God-of-the-gaps argument is dependent on a post-Enlightenment theology of God's action and an Enlightenment understanding of natural law. Why must the contemporary theist accept such outdated ideas of the late nineteenth century?

Many more problems exist than those cited by Plantinga and Moreland. A fuller explication of the arguments makes this clear. For example, it is hard to see how one can make this argument work without assuming things about God that a non-Christian theist might not be willing to grant. Premise 5 is the prime example of this problem. How could someone not already inclined to certain forms of theism know that deism is false? It is also evident that one could do theistic science without being committed to a number of these premises. For example, premise 2 is vague at best. There is no reason to think philosophers like Moreland would be committed to the simplistic views about natural laws that are implied by it. If this version of the gaps argument was used by anyone, and I know of no clear examples, it could only have been used by a thinker of the Enlightenment.

Moreland and Plantinga are not the only ones to object to modern uses of the gaps argument as it is used to oppose theistic science. Philosopher of science Del Ratzsch also dismisses the God-of-the-gaps problem. He points out that in principle, in areas like biochemistry, a scientist could appeal to design without falling into the God-of-the-gaps difficulty (Ratzsch 1996, 192-95). Ratzsch concludes that "such objections do not seem compelling." Phillip Johnson avoids a God-of-the-gaps problem by rejecting premises 2 and 3 of the traditional argument (Johnson 1995, 206). Instead he simply postulates the possibility of divine action in the natural world. All the same, Johnson insists on examining the scientific evidence for such divine activity.[10]

Why do critics of theistic science or intelligent design continue to press this gaps argument? Van Till says, "In discussions of this sort Johnson adamantly denies that he is espousing a God-of-the-gaps strategy, but I must admit that I cannot distinguish his argumentation on this point from that of the young-earth creationist, which is built on the assumption that there must exist gaps in the developmental economy of the created world—gaps that can be bridged only by acts of supernatural intervention into the course of otherwise natural phenomena" (Van Till 1993, 34). Having followed an Internet electronic mail exchange between the two camps, I know that each group is aware of the main criticisms of the other. If Van Till believes that Johnson advocates the approach described by Plantinga and Moreland, he is mistaken. Given the volume and amount of discussion regarding this topic, it is difficult to believe that the contemporary critic of theistic science has made such an elementary error. Is there a more charitable way of reading contemporary uses of the God-of-the-gaps argument?

## A New Gaps Argument?

It is common for critics of detectable divine intervention to invoke the God-of-the-gaps argument. We have already seen that this criticism is viewed as problematic by philosophers in the theistic science camp, like Plantinga and Moreland, and by at least one philosopher who is undecided about the merits of theistic science, namely, Ratzsch. As Plantinga points out, there is no precise formulation of the God-of-the-gaps argument (Plantinga 1994, 32). Even a crude description of the argument makes it plain that putting it in logical form or in a compelling manner would be very difficult, if it were possible at all. Nor is this an unfair characterization of the argument as it is commonly presented. Plantinga's description of the argument is very much like that of Giberson, even to the use of Newton as the paradigm case for a gaps argument.[11] Plantinga's and Moreland's brief against such simplistic gaps arguments seem persuasive.

Van Till, however, makes a gaps claim against Johnson that I think different in important ways from the descriptions of Plantinga and Moreland. If it is supplemented with a passing comment by Stanley Jaki (1990, 68-69), then Van Till and other gaps critics may be capable of making an argument not subject to the criticism advanced by Plantinga, Moreland and Ratzsch. This new reading of the gaps objection may go some way toward capturing the problem dimly perceived by the critic of the God of the gaps. Van Till's full response to what he understands as Johnson's gaps problem is most illuminating. Van Till (1993, 34-38), after the earlier quotation charging Johnson with gaps reasoning, writes:

> Gaps in our scientific understanding are not important in themselves, but they gain profound significance by being recognized as indicators of gaps in the economy of the created world. Hence Johnson is tolerant of a great deal of "microevolution" within the limits of some category of classification, provided that such phenomena (or any other natural processes) not be presumed capable of warranting a macroevolutionary theory concerning how these distinct categories of creatures "came to exist in the first place."
>
> Caught in the jaws of this fruitless apologetic debate, in which the existence or nonexistence of an *active* Creator is to be decided on the basis of whether there are or are not gaps in the genealogical history of life forms, Johnson speaks as if the only conceivable reason for favoring an unbroken genealogical continuity is that it appears to give the proponents of antitheistic naturalism an apologetic advantage. Against the background of the dynamics of this apologetic struggle, we can see why Johnson wishes to place under a dark cloud of doubt and suspicion those Christians who are caught in the act of favoring the concept of a created world endowed with a gapless economy that could conceivably provide the basis for the full genealogical

continuity envisioned in the macroevolutionary paradigm. They must be identified publicly as persons of questionable intelligence and dubious faith who seek a "compromise" of irreconcilable perspectives, who have "embraced naturalism with enthusiasm" and strive to "baptize" it for incorporation into the body of contemporary Christian belief. Beware, dear friends, of those theistic naturalists, whose twisted reasoning "establishes a remarkable convergence of Christian theism and scientific naturalism." So goes the accusatory rhetoric.

But we must get back to the issue of what kind of activity divine creation is and how we would recognize it. Johnson and other skeptics of macroevolutionary continuity appear to be looking expectantly for "evidence" (I presume this to mean the kind of evidence to which natural science has privileged access) that confirms that God's creative activity has "made a difference." To the question, "What difference would it make if there were no Creator?" traditional Judeo-Christian theism has replied, "If no Creator, then no created world." In other words, the very existence of the world of which we are a part is sufficient evidence for the action of the Creator. No further proof, no even modern scientific argument, is necessary. Contrary to all of the rhetorical bluster of materialism in its many forms, neither the existence of the world nor the character of its functional economy is self-explanatory.

It appears, however, that this traditional answer is not sufficiently convincing to the law professor. Hence we must seek evidence for divine creative action of the sort that would convince any honest and intelligent twentieth-century person that we had proved our case beyond the shadow of doubt in the court of scientific rationality. In Johnson's words, "If God stayed in that realm beyond the reach of scientific investigation, and allowed an apparently blind materialistic evolutionary process to do all the work of creation, then it would have to be said that God furnished us with a world of excuses for unbelief and idolatry."

This remarkable statement follows Johnson's appeal to Romans 1, from which he presumably derives his claim that we should expect to find, by unbiased scientific analysis of the empirical data relevant to the formative history of distinctly differing life forms, evidence of the kind of "supernatural assistance" that had "made a difference." One cannot help but wonder concerning the sorry plight of all those poor folks who, "ever since the creation of the world" and before the advent of modern biological science, were deprived of this essential evidence.

In personal correspondence, I once asked Johnson to help me understand how this evidential test would work by telling me just how one would establish a "no divine action baseline" to which actual processes and events could be compared. Armed with a knowledge of this baseline we could perform the crucial test and settle the apologetic question of the ages once and for all. Johnson chose not to answer my question. Perhaps he would be willing now to do so for the reader of *First Things* and tell us just what biological history would have been like if left to natural phenomena without "supernatural assistance."

Van Till is passionately opposed to something that he believes he sees in Johnson's writings. He connects this problem with the God-of-the-gaps argument. Leaving aside the question whether he has correctly interpreted Johnson, Van Till suggests a new and subtle variation of the traditional gaps argument and attributes it to Johnson. Johnson is not guilty of the traditional gaps fallacy, or at least he need not be guilty of it. Van Till has, however, made modifications to the old claims. Having found a revised gaps argument in Johnson, Van Till discovers in it many of the defects of the bad old Enlightenment God of the gaps. What has Van Till discovered? How does it relate to the God-of-the-gaps argument? If we examine the criticism of Johnson by Van Till, then we can derive the following argument.

### Johnson's Putative God-of-the-Gaps Argument
### (Modern Apologetic Version)[12]

(1) God exists if and only if God acts in nature.[13]

(2) God acts in nature if and only if God uses a succession of extraordinary acts in the course of time whereby God forces matter and material systems to do things beyond their resident capacities and therefore different from what they ordinarily would do.

(3) Such action on the part of God would be in principle verifiable by means of empirical science.

(4) If matter and material systems do nothing beyond their resident capacities (i.e., nothing different from what they ordinarily would do), then God did not act in nature.

(5) If matter or material systems do things beyond their resident capacities (i.e., things different from what they ordinarily would do), then God did those things.

(6) Scientific knowledge of the world is incomplete, and there exists one physical state of affairs $y$ such that there is no current scientific knowledge of resident capacities of matter or material systems $z$ such that $z$ produces $y$.

(7) Given 5, the theist is justified in concluding that matter and material systems are incapable of producing $y$.

(8) Given 6, the theist is justified in concluding that natural science has verified God's action in nature.

(9) Therefore God exists.

## Van Till's Response: The Modern God-of-the-Gaps Problem
### (A Bit of Apologetic Advice)

(A1) There is a time $t$ such that at $t$ scientific knowledge of nature was incomplete and there existed one physical state of affairs $y$ such that there was no current scientific knowledge at $t$ of resident capacities of matter or material systems $z$ such that $z$ produces $y$.

(A2) At $t+1$, there was scientific knowledge of $z$ such that $z$ produces $y$.

(A3) Therefore given the God-of-the-gaps argument at $t$, one was justified in believing God existed on the basis of A1 and at $t+1$ one was not justified in believing in God on the basis of A1.

Apologetic Advice: Given A3—

(A4) Theism is hurt by the God-of-the-gaps argument.

(A5) Though there will never be a time such that all gaps will be filled, a person is rationally justified in believing that no such gaps exist.[14]

Therefore:

(A6) The theistic realist is committed to an argument that suffers from the same apologetic problems as the God of the gaps and should be avoided for the same reasons.

Van Till has placed a new gaps argument in the mouth of Johnson. This God of the gaps is not dependent on an Enlightenment picture of what God would not do. Instead the argument makes predictions about what Johnson's God would do. The old God-of-the-gaps argument worried about God breaking natural laws. The new God-of-the-gaps argument is concerned that God must do something detectable. Under the old argument, a fully naturalistic account of the cosmos would have left God with nothing to do after creation. Under the new case, a similarly naturalistic cosmology would leave God free to act but in a manner undetectable to the human investigator. Using Ockham's razor, the investigator would be given good reason for dismissing God's existence altogether.

The first difficulty with the new gaps argument is that it is directed toward a putative apologetic purpose on the part of Johnson. Books like Michael Behe's *Darwin's Black Box* and articles like those by Plantinga and Moreland may have apologetic value, but they do not seem solely or even mostly apologetically motivated. If they are so motivated, then this is an accidental feature of the psychology of persons drawn to theistic science, not a necessary condition. In other words, is it possible that even a naturalistic scientist would come to the conclusion that an object was the product of intelligent design? Not only is this conceivable, but theistic realist William Dembski has provided a hypothetical case (Dembski 1994, 120-22). In fact such situations are so easy to imagine that they form the basis for numerous science fiction accounts.[15]

It is also crucial to make one further point. Johnson need not believe that this gaps argument is the only reason or even a compelling reason for believing in God's existence. He might think the ontological argument for God's existence is sound, true and rationally compelling. Or he might think the gaps argument sound and true but not rationally compelling to a nontheist. In other words, there is no reason to think that the Johnson God-of-the-gaps argument is necessary for theism to be true and or worthy of rational belief.

What is the purpose of such arguments, if this is the case? God's existence, like the existence of any being, has intrinsic interest to the researcher. She might propose such an argument as one test for God's (as of yet) hypothetical existence. She need not make any commitment to the argument on a theological level.

Van Till attacks the argument he attributes to Johnson on two fronts. As we have seen, he believes it apologetically fruitless. He also thinks it theologically suspect. It denies the gapless economy that Van Till believes he has found (albeit inconsistently) in such Christian thinkers as Augustine and Basil. As Plantinga has pointed out, Van Till has turned the table on the old gaps argument. It is now Van Till who suggests what God would not do. Premise 2 is false from Van Till's point of view, and apologetic disaster lurks around the corner if theists adopt it.

Let us assume for the sake of argument that Van Till is right about the apologetic situation. The God-of-the-gaps argument is not beneficial to the case for Christian theism. What would follow from that? The question of God's existence and how a theist might know God's existence is interesting in its own philosophical right without any apologetic motive whatsoever. An atheist could advance arguments for God's existence. She or he would be under no obligation to follow Van Till's apologetic advice. Furthermore, suppose Johnson believes the argument is both valid and true. He might agree with Van Till that it would hurt theism to make the case and still feel compelled to argue for it on altruistic grounds. It is a dubious proposition indeed to make a case for or against an argument based on some hazy notion of the sociological outcome of such reasoning. There is no reason to follow advice that shuts off philosophic discourse in the name of apologetic safety.

Even so, the argument Van Till attributes to Johnson remains deeply flawed. To see how flawed one need only turn to each premise of the argument. The first premise is quite acceptable. For a traditional Christian theist like Van Till, premise 1 must be believed. If God exists, then it is quite sensible to think he acts. Even an Aristotelian Prime Mover acts, even if it is only in thinking thought itself.

It is premise 2 that gives the first difficulty. It is very strong. There is no reason to believe that Johnson holds such a position. In fact it seems false on its face. As Van Till frequently points out, God can act to sustain the universe. The Aristotelian god does not even act in this manner, yet he still exists. We have already seen that both Plantinga and Moreland reject such ideas about divine action. Moreland, for example, postulates continuous divine actions (sustaining) of the very sort advocated by Van Till. Perhaps 2 should be modified to read:

(2′) If God uses a succession of extraordinary acts in the course of time whereby God forces matter and material systems to do things beyond their resident capacities and therefore different from what they ordinarily would do, then God exists.

This revised premise allows for the possibility of divine action that is not detectable to modern science. The conclusion (9) still follows from revised premise 2′. It does force the abandonment of premise 4, which was never necessary to the argument in the first place.

Premise 5 is at best unclear and is most likely false if Christian theism is true. Since Johnson is a Christian theist, this is important. Matter and material systems do things beyond their capacity whenever manipulated by intelligence. Is there intelligence other than God? Humans, angels, demons and other beings are all candidates for such action from a traditional Christian perspective. Are humans more than matter and energy? This is part of the very question under debate. In any case the premise is too hasty. The theist cannot assume that all gaps of this sort are products of divine action. This premise must be modified as well:

(5′) If matter or material systems do things beyond their resident capacities (i.e., things different from what they ordinarily would do), then it is possible God did those things.

The conclusion now no longer follows. The argument now can only show that it is possible that God exists—not a very interesting claim. If the more powerful original conclusion is to hold, then an additional premise will have to be added at some point in the argument. I would suggest:

(7.1) There exists some theological prediction $G$ such that a theist is justified in assuming God did $y$.

Or

(7.2) There exists some fact or set of facts $F$ regarding $z$ such that only God could have caused $z$ to produce $y$.

The addition of these premises might in fact undercut any apologetic natural theology use of Johnson's putative gaps argument. It is difficult to think of circumstances such that a committed nontheist could be convinced to accept the truth of 7.1 or 7.2. The theistic investigator into God's action and existence need not be concerned with this apologetic problem. She would be able to seek empirical support for her theological predictions regarding the natural world. Why not allow her theology to shape her considerations of what intelligent beings could be responsible for *y*? Secondly, the theistic realist may believe that certain facts of the world are such that only a being with the attributes of God could be responsible for such a system. For example, in the case of cell biology she could conclude that only a being with the power of God and the wisdom of God could be the cause of such a system on the basis of her scientific knowledge of the system as a whole and of the natural capacities of the cell.

The belief that Johnson's putative gaps argument is similar to the traditional God-of-the-gaps argument results from premise 6. This premise asserts a gap in natural science's knowledge of the world. However, there is an important difference between the traditional gaps argument and the one attributed to Johnson (as revised). The traditional argument is based on mere scientific ignorance. Even on Van Till's reading of Johnson, the gaps argument contains positive knowledge of the cosmos in addition to this gap. Premise $5'$ states the antecedent condition that matter and material systems do things beyond their natural capacities. If the scientist knows this condition obtains, then he knows what the matter or material system cannot produce. This knowledge is positive knowledge about the natural world. The scientist knows the natural capacities of a thing and knows (positively) that this particular action is not one of them. Such a scientist is not merely guessing out of ignorance but deducing what a thing did not do based on what she knows it can do. The gap in scientific knowledge is in fact implied by any valid use of modus ponens on premise $5'$. If matter or a material system[16] does what scientists know to be beyond the natural capacity of the matter or system, then there is a necessary gap in the natural explanation for that thing or system.

It might be objected that no one could know, in the strong sense of *know*, that matter or a material system was incapable of doing *y*. Why should this be the case, however? It is certainly logically possible that humans should know everything there is to know about one small field of science. One need not know everything about the natural world, merely everything there is to know about some small piece of it. If the piece of the world is small enough, then exhaustive human knowledge might be possible.

Perhaps, however, the objection centers on humans' knowing that they "know everything there is to know" about some piece of matter or material system. This an interesting question but beyond the scope of this discussion. Epistemological questions of this sort are notoriously difficult. It is sufficient for this examination simply to modify premise 6.

($6'$) Scientific knowledge of the world is incomplete, and there exists one physical state of affairs *y* such that there is no current scientific knowledge of resident capacities of matter or material systems $z$ such that $z$ produces $y$, and it is probable on the basis of the best contemporary scientific knowledge of $z$ that no such properties exist that could produce $y$.

This leads to a second modification of premise 5:

(5″) If matter or material systems do things that, based on the best contemporary scientific knowledge, are beyond their resident capacities (i.e., things different from what our best contemporary scientific knowledge tells us they ordinarily would do), then it is possible God did those things.

If this is so, the gaps argument as presented by Van Till and other critics of intelligent design is simply a form of the argument from design for the existence of God. In this case design or intelligence is manifested in a particular design detail. The Designer has left himself a direct role in the production of certain cosmic states of affairs. How does the researcher know this is so? She examines the natural world and discovers that God has left a back door of direct divine intervention. She makes this discovery on the basis of her hard-gained knowledge of material systems and her theological insight. There are many reasons to be concerned about design arguments, but the "mere gaps" worry (i.e., the worry that we fill a gap with design simply to cloak ignorance) is not one of them.

I am not the only one to make the connection between gaps and design arguments. Some have viewed gaps arguments as degenerate design arguments. Jaki (1990, 69) has expressed this concern about William Paley's design argument. Jaki worries that Paley's argument is based only on ignorance of the natural methods of producing apparent design. The revised version of Johnson's putative gaps argument does not fall into this trap of mere gaps. It depends on knowledge of a natural system's actual abilities, not on ignorance. Suitably revised, Johnson's putative gaps argument is not a gaps argument at all.

That leaves the traditional gaps argument of the Enlightenment period. Giberson (1993, 81) and others claim God-of-the-gaps arguments were the stock in trade of theologians over multiple centuries (Giberson looks to White for examples of this history of bad reasoning). Was the Christian church guilty of gaps reasoning throughout the late Middle Ages? First, no unmodified gaps argument would have been possible during that time. The theology of the period, for example that of Thomas Aquinas in the West or Maximos in the East, was simply too sophisticated. Neither the scholastic nor the Byzantine scholar postulated divine action only in those places where the science of the day failed. In fact, like Augustine, both were willing to allow for direct and indirect divine action. The philosopher-theologians of the period gave natural and theological reasons for any postulated instance of direct, divine action.

Second, it is not necessary to examine or modify the Enlightenment gaps argument to see that it could not possibly be applied to the period of the Middle Ages. Take for example the stunning appearance of Halley's comet at the time of the battle of Hastings. The thinkers of the Middle Ages did not assume God created the comet directly for theological reasons. White (1995, 171-248) describes the theological arguments in favor of the "divine" comet as rather weak and equivocal. Rather than being seen as a mere prop of theology, the comet was understood in the context of a well-developed Aristotelian or neo-Platonic cosmology.

Some of the parameters of this theory were constant throughout the Middle Ages. Change could not take place in the heavens as heavens. The comet must therefore be sublunar. Theories about its material composition were mixed. All described one of several different substances condensing in the atmosphere and catching fire. This physical mechanism of formation was carefully combined with the theological input. God used the flaming comets, each one of which was a singular event, to warn humankind of his wrath. Far from being the result of ignorance about the natural world, the view of the Middle Ages was the product of sophisticated cosmological and theological concerns. The thinker of the Middle Ages was not looking to plug a hole but to save the appearances. If he failed in the task, it is not a greater failure than that suffered by any modern philosophical or scientific reasoner who tries to capture the nature of a phenomenon only to discover either his facts or his metaphysical assumptions are in error.

Giberson and Van Till would be hard pressed to find any examples of the traditional gaps argument outside the narrow period of Enlightenment thought. The cosmology of the Middle Ages is, in the words of C. S. Lewis, a discarded image. It is not, however, an image that can be criticized for gaps reasoning. Nor can the ancient philosophers be found guilty of gaps reasoning. Plato, for example, developed a new philosophy of science centered around a teleologically motivated examination of the cosmos (Reynolds 1996, 179-86). Plato postulated solutions to problems of natural science based on two principles: induction from astronomical observation and deduction from recollected Forms. When God or demigod is invoked as explanation, it is for carefully described teleological or observational reasons. For example, the craftsman or demiurge of *Timaeus* 30 is invoked to act as a mediator between the World of the Forms and the World of Becoming in which humans live. He is postulated not because of a gap in human knowledge but as the only entity fit to fill such a metaphysical space. Neither God nor a demigod is ever invoked merely to cover a gap in knowledge.

Even the ancient critics of design did not claim that advocates of design used design merely to cover up their ignorance. Lucretius, in his famous work *On Nature,* feels the need to attack teleology again and again. He cannot simply invoke a naturalistic explanation and hope that the gods will retreat. Naturalism in the ancient world recognized the power of both design and purpose in the cosmos in forming scientific theories.

The bad God-of-the-gaps argument of the Enlightenment is of historical interest. In the modern era, however, invoking the language of gaps to criticize theistic science too often obscures what is actually being attacked. The gaps complaint amounts to a criticism of design arguments. It is rarely used with any precision. It is impossible to formalize a gaps argument for modern theistic science without rendering it useless to the critic of theistic science. If it fits the actual position held by theistic scientists, it is no longer a gaps argument. If it fits the form of the bad old gaps argument, then it describes no actual person's beliefs. Opponents of theistic science should abandon the claim that such reasoning is or ever was widespread. They should also make clear that their complaint is primarily theological. The gaps critic is entitled to her or his theology. But no one has the right to confuse an issue by inflammatory labeling.

### Appendix: Revised Version of Johnson's Putative Gaps Argument

(1) God exists if and only if God acts in nature.

(2) If God uses a succession of extraordinary acts in the course of time whereby God forces matter and material systems to do things beyond their resident capacities and therefore different from what they ordinarily would do, then God exists.

(3) Such action on the part of God would be in principle verifiable by means of empirical science.

(Premise 4 is deleted.)

(5″) If matter or material systems do things that, based on the best contemporary scientific knowledge, are beyond their resident capacities (i.e., things different from what our best contemporary scientific knowledge tells us they ordinarily would do), then it is possible God did those things.

(6′) Scientific knowledge of the world is incomplete, and there exists one physical state of affairs $y$ such that there is no current scientific knowledge of resident capacities of matter or material systems $z$ such that $z$ produces $y$, and it is probable on the basis of the best contemporary scientific knowledge of $z$ that no such properties exist that could produce $y$.

(7) Given 5″, the theist is justified in concluding that matter and material systems are incapable of producing $y$.

(7.1) There exists some theological prediction $G$ such that a theist is justified in assuming God did *y*.

Or

(7.2) There exists some fact or set of facts *F* regarding *z* such that only God could have caused *z* to produce *y*.

(8) Given 6, the theist is justified in concluding that natural science has verified God's action in nature.

(9) Therefore God exists.

## Notes

[1] A sublunar comet allowed the naturalists of the Middle Ages to save important features of Aristotle's cosmology. See *De Caelo* and *Metaphysics*.

[2] The best popular treatment of this position is found in Ratzsch 1996. See especially, chapters five through seven.

[3] This article repeats arguments found in fuller form in Van Till 1989.

[4] Moreland does not use Johnson's terminology of "theistic realism" but argues for much the same position.

[5] Moreland (1996) defines "theistic science" by means of the following three propositions:

(1) God, conceived as a personal, transcendent agent of great power and intelligence, has through direct, immediate, primary agency and indirect, mediate, secondary causation created and designed the world for a purpose and has directly acted through immediate, primary agency in the course of its development at various times (including prehistory, history prior to the arrival of human beings).

(2) The commitment expressed in proposition 1 can appropriately enter into the very fabric of the practice of science and the utilization of scientific methodology.

(3) One way this commitment can appropriately enter into the practice of science is through various uses in scientific methodology of gaps in the natural world that are essential features of direct, immediate, primary divine agency *properly understood.* [emphasis added]

[6] This does not mean that no one is guilty of this gaps reasoning. There are numerous historical examples cited by gaps critics. I am convinced most of them fail to be examples of the bad sort of reasoning feared, but that is beside the point. Contemporary theistic realists are innocent.

[7] Again, I do not require that anyone has ever made this full argument. I am trying to summarize what critics of gaps arguments believe has taken place in cases like Newton. I am skeptical that Newton is guilty as charged. The apologetic argument can be modified to assume that God exists. This nonapologetic God-of-the-gaps argument would provide the reasons for assuming divine action in the case of scientific ignorance. Since Van Till and other critics focus on the apologetic problems of the gaps argument, I shall use this form of it.

[8] My goal is not to defend this crude libertarian notion of freedom. I am merely stating the normal assumptions implicit in a gaps appeal.

[9] By deism I mean the belief that God may have caused the world in the beginning but that he does nothing in the cosmos after that beginning.

[10]See Johnson 1993a and his favorable citation of Michael Behe's work in biochemistry (Johnson 1995).

[11]The gaps critic suggests that Newton "fixed" some difficult details of his cosmology by having God "prod" the system (Giberson 1993, 78).

[12]Again, I am not saying that this argument exists anywhere in Johnson's thought but that Van Till and antigaps theorists ascribe such arguments to intelligent design proponents like Johnson.

[13]Johnson is defending the notion of a Christian-style god. A deistic god is excluded on theological grounds.

[14]Van Till asserts this in his writings on theological grounds (cf. his "gapless economy"). To carry any weight, however, it needs at least in principle to be capable of scientific verification.

[15]Arthur C. Clarke's 2001 provides a good example.

[16]By placing material systems in this description, we prevent the naturalist from begging the question by pushing the problem off onto human intelligence. Humans are part of the material system. Do we have nonnaturalistic intelligence? Such a gap would be just as problematic to Van Till as a divine gap.

## References

Aquinas, T. 1948. *Summa theologica.* In *Introduction to Thomas Aquinas,* ed. A. C. Pegis. New York: Modern Library.

Augustine. 1984. *City of God.* Translated by H. Bettenson. New York: Penguin.

———. 1995. *On Genesis.* Translated by R. J. Teske, S.J. Washington, D.C.: Catholic University Press.

Calvin, J. 1960. *Institutes of the Christian religion.* Edited by J. T. McNeill. Philadelphia: Westminster Press.

Dawkins, R. 1987. *The blind watchmaker.* New York: Norton.

Dembski, W. A. 1994. On the very possibility of intelligent design. In *The creation hypothesis,* ed. J. P. Moreland, 113-38. Downers Grove, Ill.: InterVarsity Press.

Freddoso, A. J. 1983. *The existence and nature of God.* Notre Dame, Ind.: University of Notre Dame Press.

Giberson, K. 1993. *Worlds apart: The unholy war between religion and science.* Kansas City, Mo.: Beacon Hill Press.

Harre, R. 1984. *The philosophies of science.* Oxford: Oxford University Press.

Hummel, C. E. 1986. *The Galileo connection.* Downers Grove, Ill.: InterVarsity Press.

Huxley, T. H. 1894. *Science and the Hebrew tradition: Essays.* New York: D. Appleton and Co.

Jaki, S. 1990. *The purpose of it all.* Washington, D.C.: Regnery.

Johnson, P. E. 1993a. *Darwin on trial.* Downers Grove, Ill.: InterVarsity Press.

———. 1993b. Creator or blind watchmaker. *First Things* 34:38-41.

———. 1995. *Reason in the balance.* Downers Grove, Ill.: InterVarsity Press.

Lewis, C. S. 1964. *The discarded image.* Cambridge: Cambridge University Press.

Losee, J. 1993. *A historical introduction to the philosophy of science.* Oxford: Oxford University Press.

Lucretius. 1946. *On the nature of things.* Translated by C. Bennett. Roslyn, N.Y.: Walter J. Black.

McMullin, E. 1985. *Evolution and creation.* Notre Dame, Ind.: University of Notre Dame Press.

Maximos the Confessor. 1981. Various texts on theology, the divine economy, and virtue and vice. In *The philokalia*. Edited by G. E. H. Palmer, P. Sherrard, and K. Ware.

Moreland, J. P. 1989. *Christianity and the nature of science*. Grand Rapids, Mich.: Baker.

———. 1994. Theistic science and methodological naturalism. In *The creation hypothesis*, ed. J. P. Moreland, 41-66. Downers Grove, Ill.: InterVarsity Press, 1994.

———. 1996. Complementarity, agency theory and the God of the gaps. In *Detecting design in creation*, ed. S. Meyer, P. Nelson, and J. M. N. Reynolds. Manuscript under review with Rutgers University Press.

Morris, T. V., ed. 1988. *Divine and human action: Essays in the metaphysics of theism*. Ithaca, N.Y.: Cornell University Press.

Peacocke, A. 1984. *Intimations of reality*. Notre Dame, Ind.: Notre Dame University Press.

Plantinga, A. 1994. Methodological naturalism? In *Detecting design in creation*, ed. S. Meyer, P. Nelson, and J. M. N. Reynolds. Manuscript under review with Rutgers University Press, 1996.

Plato. 1989. *Timaeus*. Translated by R. G. Bury. Cambridge, Mass.: Harvard University Press.

Ramm, B. 1954. *The Christian view of science and Scripture*. Grand Rapids, Mich.: Eerdmans.

Ratzsch, D. 1996. *The battle of beginnings*. Downers Grove, Ill.: InterVarsity Press.

Reynolds, J. M. N. 1996. Human psyche in the *Timaeus*. Ph.D. dissertation, University of Rochester. UMI Dissertation Services.

Roe, S. 1990. Voltaire versus Needham: Atheism, materialism and the generation of life. In *Philosophy, religion and science in the seventeenth and eighteenth centuries*, ed. J. W. Yolton, 417-39. Rochester, N.Y.: University of Rochester Press.

Ross, H. 1993. *The Creator and the cosmos*. Colorado Springs, Colo.: Navpress.

Ruse, M. 1994. Philosophical preference, scientific inference and good research strategy. In *Darwinism: Science or philosophy?* ed. J. Buell and V. Hearn, 29-40. Richardson, Tex.: Foundation for Thoughts and Ethics.

Van Till, H. 1989. *The fourth day*. Grand Rapids, Mich.: Eerdmans.

———. 1993. God and evolution: An exchange. *First Things* 35:32-41.

White, A. D. 1995. *A history of the warfare of science with theology in Christendom*. 1896. Reprint, Buffalo, N.Y.: Prometheus.

Wierenga, E. R. 1989. *The nature of God*. Ithaca, N.Y.: Cornell University Press.

# 14

# Design & the Cosmological Argument

## WILLIAM LANE CRAIG

ROM EARLIEST TIMES THE COSMOLOGICAL ARGUMENT AND THE TELE-
ological argument have served the natural theologian as "weapons
of righteousness for the right hand and for the left" (2 Cor 6:7
RSV) in his defense of philosophical theism. Both arguments were
employed by Plato (*Laws* 10.884-899d; *Timaeus* 29, 47; *Philebus* 28) and
Aristotle (*Physics* 8.1-6.250b5-260a15; 8.10.266a10-267b25) in support of
their theism. Both are to be found in Aquinas's famous Five Ways of
demonstrating God's existence (*Summa theologiae* 1a. 2. 3). And both were
vigorously attacked by Hume (1947)[1] and Kant (1933, A603/B631-
A630/B658, 507-24). In our own day both have been dramatically resusci-
tated by discoveries in astronomy and astrophysics, which have prompted
lively debates over the metaphysical implications of big bang cosmology and
the fine-tuning of the universe for intelligent life.

The cosmological argument aims to prove that there exists a First Cause
or Sufficient Reason for the existence of the cosmos; the teleological argument aspires to show that there is an Intelligent Designer of the order in the
cosmos. The teleological argument shows that the First Cause demonstrated
by the cosmological argument is not some mindless ground of being but a
personal, intelligent Mind; the cosmological argument shows that the Cosmic Designer is not a mere artificer or demiurge working on preexistent

materials but the Creator of all space-time reality. The arguments are thus clearly complementary and together comprise a considerable part of a cumulative case for theism.

## The *Kalam* Cosmological Argument and the Teleological Argument

In this chapter I wish to examine more closely the relationship of the cosmological argument to the teleological argument. More precisely, I want to examine the relationship of one particular version of the cosmological argument, the so-called *kalam* cosmological argument,[2] to the teleological argument. This version of the cosmological argument originated in the attempt of early Christian philosophers like John Philoponus to rebut the Aristotelian doctrine of the eternity of the universe and was developed by medieval Islamic and Jewish theologians who bequeathed it to the Christian West, where it became the subject of heated debate, pitting Bonaventure against Aquinas. It was championed by Bentley and defended by Locke and eventually found its way into the thesis of Kant's First Antinomy concerning time.

As formulated by one of its greatest proponents, the medieval Islamic theologian al-Ghazali, the argument is extremely simple:

(1) Whatever begins to exist has a cause.

(2) The universe began to exist.

(3) Therefore, the universe has a cause.

In defense of the second premise, Ghazali presented various philosophical arguments to show the impossibility of an infinite regress of temporal phenomena and, hence, of an infinite past. The limit at which the finite past terminates Ghazali calls "the Eternal" (al-Ghazali 1963, 32), which he evidently takes to be a state of timelessness. Given the truth of the first premise, the finite past must therefore "stop at an eternal being from which the first temporal being should have originated" (al-Ghazali 1963, 33).

If the *kalam* version of the cosmological argument is sound, it has obvious relevance to the teleological argument. One of its most important implications is that infinite past time is not available for the realization of the vanishingly small probability of the origin and evolution of intelligent life apart from a Cosmic Designer. Hume's suggestion that "many worlds might have been botched and bungled, throughout an eternity, ere this system was struck out" (Hume 1947, 167) is excluded, as is Wheeler's speculation concerning an eternally oscillating universe with different sets of physical constants and laws for each cycle (Wheeler 1973). Of course, the detractor of the hypothesis of design might insist that while the number of prior oscillations or universes was finite, nonetheless it was just enough for the realization by chance of the probabilities calculated by the proponent of teleology. But such a response has an ad hoc air about it. As Swinburne has pointed out, the postulation of any finite number of universes seems to cry out for explanation (Swinburne 1979, 94). We should want to know why the universe has completed just that number of oscillations which it has, a number that is put in by hand to fill the bill presented by teleology. By demonstrating that the universe had a beginning, the cosmological argument thus diminishes the plausibility of the hypothesis of a chance origin of anthropic fine-tuning and biological complexity.

However, I want to focus on another, more directly relevant implication of the *kalam* cosmological argument for the hypothesis of a Cosmic Designer. The unique genius of the medieval Islamic formulation of the cosmological argument was that it aimed to show not merely that a cause of the universe exists but that this cause is a Personal Creator. It thus entails virtually the same conclusion as the teleological argument: that behind the cosmos stands a Personal Mind.

How does this conclusion follow from the *kalam* argument? The answer is that that argument is a remarkably fecund source for deduction of traditional divine attributes through conceptual analysis of what it is to be a cause of the origin of the universe. For example, the cause must be uncaused, since an infinite regress of causes is impossible. One could, of course, arbitrarily posit a plurality of causes in some sense prior to the origin of the universe, but ultimately, if the *kalam* argument is sound, this causal chain must terminate in a cause that is absolutely first and uncaused. There being no reason to perpetuate the series of causes beyond the origin of the universe, Ockham's razor, which states that we should not posit causes beyond necessity, strikes such causes in favor of an immediate First Cause of the origin of the universe. The same principle dictates that we are warranted in ignoring the possibility of a plurality of uncaused causes in favor of assuming the unicity of the First Cause. This First Cause must also be beginningless, since by contraposition of premise (1) whatever is uncaused does not begin to exist. Moreover, this cause must be changeless, since an infinite temporal regress of changes cannot exist. We should not be warranted, however, in inferring the immutability of the First Cause, since immutability is a modal property, and from the Cause's changelessness we cannot infer that it is incapable of change. But we can know that the First Cause is changeless, at least insofar as it exists sans the universe. From the changelessness of the First Cause, its immateriality follows. For whatever is material involves incessant change on at least the molecular and atomic levels, but the uncaused First Cause exists in a state of absolute changelessness.

Given some relational theory of time, the Uncaused Cause must therefore also be timeless, at least sans the universe, since in the utter absence of events time would not exist. It is true that some philosophers have argued persuasively that time could continue to exist even if all events were to cease (Shoemaker 1969; Forbes 1993), but such arguments are inapplicable in the case at hand, where we are envisioning not the cessation of events but the entire absence of any events. In any case the timelessness of the First Cause sans the universe can be more directly inferred from the finitude of the past. Given that time had a beginning, the cause of the beginning of time must be timeless.[3]

Finally, this Cause must also be spaceless, since it is both immaterial and timeless, and no spatial entity can be both immaterial and timeless. If an entity is immaterial, it could exist in space only in virtue of being related to material things in space; but then it could not be timeless, since it undergoes extrinsic change in its relations to material things. Hence the uncaused First Cause must transcend both time and space and be the cause of their origination.

### Abstract Objects and Personhood

The personhood of the First Cause is already powerfully suggested by the preceding considerations. For there appear to be only two candidates that can be described as immaterial, beginningless, uncaused, timeless and spaceless beings: either abstract objects or unembodied mind. If the former can be ruled out, then that fact implies that the First Cause is unembodied mind, or the Personal Creator of the universe. That is, we can argue as follows:

(4) If the universe has a cause, then the cause of the universe is either an abstract object or unembodied mind.

(5) An abstract object cannot be the cause of the universe.

(6) Therefore, if the universe has a cause, then the cause of the universe is unembodied mind.

Together (3) and (6) imply

(7) Therefore, the cause of the universe is unembodied mind.

With respect to the two candidates mentioned in premise (4), abstract objects like numbers, sets, propositions and properties are typically construed by philosophers who include such things in their ontology as being precisely the sort of entities that exist necessarily, timelessly and spacelessly. Similarly philosophers who hold to the possibility of disembodied minds would describe such substances as immaterial and spaceless, and there seems no reason to think that a Cosmic Mind might not also be beginningless and uncaused. For my part, I cannot think of any other candidates that could be suitably described as immaterial, beginningless, uncaused, timeless and spaceless beings. Nor has anyone else, to my knowledge, suggested any other such candidates. The disjunction would therefore seem to be complete, and, hence, premise (4) is not question-begging.

With respect to premise (5), some thinkers have suggested that the cause of the origin of the universe is indeed some sort of abstract object. For example, John Leslie, the foremost authority on the Anthropic Principle, champions a Neo-Platonic concept of God as the creativity of ethical requiredness (Leslie 1989, 165-74). That is to say, the universe exists because it should; it is morally necessary that a universe of free agents exist. This ethical requiredness of the universe has a sort of creative power that makes the world exist.

Less seriously, Oxford University scientist P. W. Atkins, drawing on John Wheeler's notion of a pregeometry which somehow underlies existing space-time structure, suggests that "at the time before time" there existed a chaotic "dust" of mathematical points, which, constantly reassembling, finally combined by chance into the geometrical structure of space-time; and thus did our universe "come into existence without intervention, and . . . there is no *need* to invoke the idea of a Supreme Being" (Atkins 1992, vii, 129). If it be asked where the points came from, Atkins will reply, "time brought the points into being, and the points brought time into being" (Atkins 1992, 141). This piece of metaphysical bravado is obviously self-contradictory and incoherent. The postulation of a time before time is a clear self-contradiction, nor can this notion be written off as a mere rhetorical flourish, for Atkins's idea of a collection of points constantly combining into various structures and then dissolving until they organize into our space-time geometry presupposes the reality of time. The sort of causation that he posits between time and the pregeometrical points is viciously circular and hence incoherent. More fundamentally, Atkins's confusion of abstract and concrete objects makes it impossible to state the difference between actually existing space-time and an uninstantiated space-time (say, with a Bolyai-Lobachevskian geometry), since both are composed of mathematical points. In a sense the implication of Atkins's view is not that the universe was caused by an abstract object but that it is an abstract object, which is absurd.

Nor does it seem to me any more plausible, despite Leslie, to claim that any sort of abstract object can be the cause of the origin of the universe. For, quite simply, abstract objects are not involved in causal relations. Since they are not agents, they cannot volitionally exercise a causal power to do anything. If they are causes, they would be so not as agents but as mindless events or states. But they cannot be event-causes, since they do not exist in time and space. Even if we allow that some abstract objects exist in time (for example, propositions that change their truth-value in virtue of the tense in the sentences that express them), still, in view of their abstract nature, it remains utterly mysterious how they could be causally related to concrete objects so as to bring about events, including the origin of the universe. Nor can they be state-causes of states involving concrete objects, for the same reason, not to mention the fact that in the case at hand we are not talking about state-state causation (that is, the causal dependence of one state on another), but what would amount to state-event causation (namely, the universe's coming into being because of the state of some abstract object[s]), which seems impossible. Thus premise (5) is most certainly true.

Perhaps the most promising route for the nontheist to take at this point is to assert that neither is it possible for unembodied mind to be the cause of the universe. Thus, despite first appearances, (4) is false (there is some third, unknown alternative) or else (3) is false. But if we are to reject those premises despite their prima facie warrant, then the nontheist must give us warrant for the negation of (7) that is sufficient to overwhelm the warrant for (3) or (4). What does he have to offer? Perhaps he might agree that an unembodied mind could be beginningless, immaterial and spaceless but deny that such a mind could be timeless. Temporality, he might claim, is essential to personhood. But I must say that, having written on this question at some length elsewhere (Craig 1997), I have been unable to find any good reason to think that a personal being cannot be atemporal.[4]

Perhaps the nontheist will claim, even more radically, that mind cannot be unembodied, because mental states are either identical with brain states or dependent upon brain states. But this sort of critique constitutes an argument against theism as such, since God's immateriality and personhood are essential divine properties, not merely a defeater aimed at a premise in the *kalam* cosmological argument. It would be as if I had rejected (5) on the basis of the nominalist claim that abstract objects do not exist. It opens up an entirely different topic with its own proper set of issues and wealth of literature, which cannot divert us here. If nonphysicalists working in neurology and the philosophy of mind succeed in turning back the force of this objection to theism,[5] then it cannot be used to defeat (7); au contraire, the *kalam* cosmological argument, with its prima facie warrant for (3)-(5), constitutes a small part of the case against physicalism.

So in the catalog of attributes deducible from the *kalam* cosmological argument, we have good grounds for inferring that the First Cause of the universe is a Personal Creator.

### A Temporal Effect from an Eternal Cause

But the *kalam* argument affords a more direct demonstration of this same conclusion. The philosophers whom al-Ghazali opposed held that the world must be sempiternal because they rejected "the procession of the first temporal being from the Eternal" as impossible (al-Ghazali 1963, 32). They took it "as a self-evident fact that nothing can be distinguished from its like, unless there be something which gives it a special character" (al-Ghazali 1963, 24); that is to say, something must account for why one of the two similar alternatives is actualized. They held in effect that the hapless animal that later came to be known as Buridan's ass would have starved to death caught between two equally appetizing bundles of hay. Now, they reasoned, "in the case of the world, which was possible of existence as well as of non-existence, . . . there was nothing to give existence a special character" (al-Ghazali 1963, 24), since there was nothing prior to the beginning of the universe.

If it be said that the First Cause lent to existence its special character and thus brought the universe into being, then the First Cause is causally (if not temporally) prior to the beginning of the universe. But then the question arises, How could a first temporal effect arise from an eternal cause? Either the causal conditions sufficient for the existence of the universe were eternally actual or not. If not, then they must have arisen at some moment of past time, indeed at the first moment of time, the same moment at which the universe, its causally sufficient conditions now present, sprang into being. The problem with this alternative is that now we must ask why the causal conditions arose when they did, and off we go on an infinite regress—which has been shown to be impossible.

Suppose, then, we say that the causal conditions for the world's existence are never absent from the First Cause. In that case the world should exist coeternally with its Cause. If the causally sufficient conditions for an effect exist, then the effect must also exist. It would be impossible for the First Cause to exist alone sans the universe, for it constitutes the causally sufficient conditions for the world's existence. Therefore, the philosophers conclude, if the Eternal is causally prior to the world, "it will be necessary that both should be either eternal or temporal. It will be impossible for one to be eternal, while the other is temporal" (al-Ghazali 1963, 36). In effect the philosophers were arguing that it is impossible to have state-event causation, especially where the state is atemporal and the event is temporal.

This is a powerful objection, and al-Ghazali subverts it only by appealing to a different analysis of causation. He agrees that there must be something that gives special character to the existence of the world over its nonexistence, and he finds it in the notion of an agent cause. The Islamic theologians who developed the *kalam* argument adhered to the so-called principle of determination, which I shall formulate as follows:

PD: If two physical states of affairs, S and its complement ~S, are physically possible at a time $t$ and $S$ obtains at $t$, then there must be a personal agent who, by the free choice of his will, instantiates $S$ rather than $\sim S$ at $t$.

For example, if it is physically possible at $t$ for me to raise or not raise my left arm, then it is not determined by the causal antecedents prior to $t$ that I raise my arm. If it were so determined, then it is not in fact physically possible for me to not raise my arm. Suppose, then, that at $t$ I raise my arm. It follows from (PD) that my arm's rising is the result of the free choice of my will, that I am in effect the agent cause of my arm's rising. On the basis of the principle of determination, al-Ghazali reasoned that the First Cause of the origin of the universe must be a personal agent who freely chooses to create the temporal world. So Ghazali responds to the philosophers,

> The (eternal) will produced the world as it is, wherever it is, and whatever it is like. As regards the will, it is an attribute of which the function it is to distinguish something from its like. If it had no such function, then power would have had to be regarded as an adequate principle. But since power bears an equal relation to two opposite things, and since it becomes necessary to posit a cause which gives one of these two things a special character, therefore, it must be said that, over and above power, the Eternal has an attribute whose function is to distinguish something from its like . . . so the answer to the . . . question should be: "Will is an attribute of which the function—rather nature—is to distinguish something from its like." (al-Ghazali 1963, 24-25)

The origin of the universe requires not merely power to produce the world but power that is exercised through free agency. The Eternal must, in order to produce a temporal world, be an agent with the freedom to bring about the beginning of the universe wholly in the absence of any antecedent determining conditions. Ghazali's argument that the cause of the universe is a Personal Creator is thus

(8) If the universe has a cause, then the cause is either a set of impersonal causal conditions or a free, personal agent.

(9) The cause of the universe is not a set of impersonal causal conditions.

(10) Therefore, if the universe has a cause, then the cause of the universe is a free, personal agent.

Together (3) and (10) imply

(11) Therefore, the cause of the universe is a free, personal agent.

On behalf of (8), it can be said that this appears to be a necessary truth, since a cause that is not a free, personal agent just is a set of impersonal causal conditions. The argument for (9) is the argument given by the philosophical opponents of Ghazali. Even if one accepts (8) and (9), however, one might be led to reject (3) if (11) could be shown to be a metaphysical impossibility. One would need in that case overwhelming warrant for denying (11) in face of the warrant for (3). It might be claimed, for example, that the relation of the Personal Creator of the universe to time cannot be coherently sorted out on this view or that the very notion of agent causation is unintelligible. I have discussed the first issue elsewhere, however (Craig 1996), and believe that a coherent doctrine of divine eternity and creation can be formulated. As for the latter issue, there is some latitude for maneuvering here, and I shall leave the formulation and defense of personal agency and freedom in the able hands of others (Moreland 1998; O'Connor 1995; Taliaferro 1994; Morris 1988).

Rather I wish to discuss a serious challenge presented by contemporary physics to (9). It is a commonplace of quantum physics that due to indeterminacy on the fundamental level, events occur for which fully determinate causes do not exist. It cannot be precisely predicted, for example, when an atom of radium will decay into radon. Nor is this unpredictability an epistemic affair only; rather it is due to an ontic indeterminacy on the quantum level. At best probabilities can be calculated for the occurrence of quantum physical events; but precision is impossible because reality itself is indeterminate in this respect. If quantum indeterminacy is a fact of nature, then it follows that (PD) is false. If $S$ is the decay of a radium atom and $\sim S$ is the continued existence of that atom, then both states are physically possible at some time $t$, being indeterminate with respect to the state of the atom prior to $t$, and yet no personal agent is required to choose which state is instantiated at $t$. Nothing determines whether the atom decays at $t$ or not; it just happens. Accordingly (PD) would have to be replaced by

> (PD*): If two physical states of affairs, $S$ and its complement $\sim S$, are physically possible at a time $t$ and $S$ obtains at $t$, then either (i) there must be a personal agent who, by the free choice of his will, instantiates $S$ rather than $\sim S$ at $t$ or (ii) $S$'s instantiation at $t$ is the result of an indeterminate, quantum physical transition.

Since the assumption of (PD) underlies the *kalam* cosmological argument for a Personal Creator, the substitution of (PD*) suggests an alternative explanation in quantum indeterminacy.

## Ontic Quantum Indeterminacy

But must we accept (PD*) rather than (PD)? The answer to that question will depend on whether we take quantum indeterminacy to be ontic or not.[6] Although the majority of physicists and philosophers of science hold quantum indeterminacy to be ontic and although such an interpretation of quantum theory is almost universal on the popular level, such an understanding is by no means inevitable. For there are a number of interpretations of quantum theory that are fully deterministic and yet are both mathematically consistent and wholly compatible with the experimental data. For example, there is the ensemble interpretation of quantum theory, according to which that theory is not applicable to individual particles but is a theory of ensembles of particles.[7] This interpretation holds that the behavior of individual particles is deterministic but that quantum mechanics is concerned only with calculations about averages over a large number of similar systems. Hence indeterminacy does not lodge at the most fundamental level.

Or there is de Broglie-Bohm pilot-wave model, according to which hidden variables exist along with a force field that permits superluminal influences.[8] "Like it or lump it," says J. S. Bell, "it is perfectly conclusive as a counter example to the idea that vagueness, subjectivity, or indeterminism are forced on us by the experimental facts covered by nonrelativistic quantum mechanics" (Bell 1984, 70). There is even the many worlds interpretation of quantum physics, which holds that every result of a quantum measurement is actualized in some universe. Not only are these interpretations deterministic, but some of them are every bit as plausible as indeterministic views such as the realist construal of the Copenhagen interpretation, according to which quantum entities acquire determinate values of dynamic properties only when measured by a classical apparatus or observed by a conscious being. Contrary to popular impression, ontic indeterminacy is not an implication of quantum theory itself but rather of certain interpretations of quantum theory that are speculative and controversial and that enjoy no privileged status over deterministic interpretations. One recent commentator remarks, "Seventy years after the discovery of modern quantum mechanics, there is still no consensus as to how the theory should be understood" (Lockwood 1996, 159). In fact, my sense is that there is a growing discontent with the received Copenhagen interpretation and a renewed interest in deterministic interpretations of quantum theory.

More than that, however, even if we accept the received Copenhagen interpretation, ontic indeterminacy follows only on a realist construal of that interpretation. But the orthodox Copenhagen interpretation is notoriously antirealist in orientation. According to Bohr, there really is no quantum world such as the theory describes. There is only an abstract quantum physical description.[9] The theory is purely instrumentalist in nature; it enables us to make accurate predictions but should not be taken as a literal description of the way the world is. Schrödinger also resisted any interpretation of quantum theory that implied ontic indeterminacy. After a week of indecisive discussion with Bohr in September 1926, Schrödinger grumped, "If all this d— quantum jumping *(Quantenspringerei)* were really to stay, I should be sorry I ever got involved with quantum theory!" (reported by Heisenberg 1971, 75). The whole point of his famous cat was to show how intolerable a realist construal of quantum indeterminacy is by providing an illustrative means of magnifying its effects to the macroscopic world, where indeterminacy is completely counterintuitive. He never anticipated that otherwise sensible people would believe that a cat exists in a superposition of states until somebody opens the chamber and looks inside.

Instrumentalism with respect to quantum theory does not commit one to scientific antirealism in general and may be justified with respect to quantum theory in light of its counterintuitive consequences. The measurement problem illustrated by Schrödinger's cat is probably insoluble within the context of a realist construal of the Copenhagen interpretation.[10] Therefore an instrumentalist construal of the Copenhagen interpretation of quantum theory is not implausible and is in line with the orthodox understanding of that interpretation.

Given the availability of deterministic interpretations of quantum theory that are no more implausible than the received Copenhagen interpretation and the plausibility of a nonrealist construal of the Copenhagen interpretation itself, I see no reason to believe that ontic indeterminacy exists and therefore no reason to prefer (PD*) over (PD). But I recognize that this is a minority viewpoint and that it would be imprudent to stake my claim on such hotly contested ground. Therefore let us concede ontic indeterminacy as described in quantum theory and accept (PD*). How would this affect the *kalam* argument for a Personal Creator of the universe?

### Vacuum Fluctuation Cosmogonic Models
What (PD*) seems to allow is that the origin of the universe may be the result of an indeterminate quantum physical transition. At first blush this seems absurd. If the universe began to exist, then there was nothing prior to the beginning. Thus it is incoherent to speak of any sort of process or transition as a result of which the universe came into being. An absolute beginning of existence cannot be a change of any sort, because there is no enduring subject whose properties change while the subject lasts from one state to the next; rather the subject with its properties just begins to exist at a certain time $t$. Incredibly, however, many physicists have spoken of the origin of the universe precisely in terms of a quantum transition out of nothing. One finds frequent statements to the effect that "the universe quantum tunneled into being out of nothing," or that "nothingness is unstable" to fluctuations that grow into universes, or that "the universe is a free lunch" because in this case "we got something for nothing."

If such statements were taken literally, they would be absurd because they treat nothing as though it were something, a sort of substance possessing properties and governed by the laws of quantum physics. In fact such statements turn out to be just rhetorical flourishes, which, while unfortunately misleading the public, no informed scientist takes literally. Most of these statements have reference to the quantum vacuum, which underlies all of space-time reality and is a fluctuating sea of energy. Some quantum physical models postulate the origin of our universe not in an initial space-time singularity but as a fluctuation in the energy of the primordial vacuum. Because the primordial vacuum is a physical state existing in space and time, such models do not envision a genuine origin of the universe out of nothing, as Kanitscheider (1990) emphasizes:

> The violent microstructure of the vacuum has been used in attempts to explain the origin of the universe as a long-lived vacuum fluctuation. But some authors have connected with this legitimate speculations *[sic]* far-reaching metaphysical claims, or at most they couched their mathematics in a highly misleading language, when they maintained "the creation of the universe out of nothing."
>
> From the philosophical point of view it is essential to note that the foregoing is far from being a spontaneous generation of everything from naught, but the origin of that embryonic bubble is really a causal process leading from a primordial substratum with a rich physical structure to a materialized substratum of the vacuum. Admittedly this process is not deterministic; it includes that weak kind of causal dependence peculiar to every quantum mechanical process (Kanitscheider 1990, 346-47).

If we consider the primordial vacuum to be a state of the universe, what the proponents of such models really deny is our premise (2), not (9). But suppose we take "universe" to refer only to that expanding matter/energy field in which we find ourselves. In that case the universe did begin to exist according to such models, and the cause of the universe was the primordial vacuum. Since the universe originates out of the vacuum via a spontaneous fluctuation of its energy, the proponent of such models will deny (9), while affirming (PD*). He will not deny (1), contrary to oft-repeated assertions that quantum physics falsifies that premise (Post 1991, 85; Oppy 1995, 240-41; Worthing 1996, 50),[11] for, as Kanitscheider's comments indicate, there are causal conditions of such quantum mechanical transitions, though they are not fully deterministic. The unique contribution of these models lies rather in their denial of a material cause of the universe. Since the positive energy associated with mass is precisely offset by the negative energy associated with gravitation, the sum total of the universe's energy/matter is zero.

This has unfortunately led to some silly statements to the effect that even now nothing exists. John Gribbin, for example, declares that in this case we got "not something for nothing, after all, but *nothing* for nothing" (Gribbin

1986, 374). Karl Philberth differentiates between the "interior" and "exterior" aspects of the cosmos, claiming that from the interior aspect there is existence, but from the exterior aspect there is nothingness—apparently oblivious to the self-contradiction that from the exterior aspect, in his words, "Cosmic spacetime is closed on itself" and "Objects subject one another to the collective gravitational potential" (Philberth 1977, 127).

What such models imply is not that nothing exists now (after all, positive and negative energy are very real[12]) but that the universe lacked a material cause. No energy was borrowed from the vacuum to produce the universe. But, as Christopher Isham emphasizes, there is still a "need for ontic seeding" to produce the energy, even if on balance it is naught (Isham 1994, 8). The primordial vacuum was the efficient cause of the origin of the universe, but not its material cause. In this sense the quantum vacuum plays a role very analogous to God in the biblical doctrine of *creatio ex nihilo:* it spontaneously brings the universe into being without a material cause. Accordingly the proponent of such vacuum models will affirm that the cause of the universe is indeed a set of indeterministic, impersonal causal conditions, just what is needed to subvert the *kalam* argument for a Personal Creator.

The defender of *kalam* might reject such an alternative account of the causal origin of the universe on philosophical grounds. Since there cannot be an infinite regress of fluctuations, the primordial vacuum would have to be absolutely quiescent; but the quantum vacuum is the very antithesis of quiescence. Therefore it would itself have required a cause.[13]

But to consider the theory on its scientific merits, such models turn out to be fatally flawed. For given the infinite, homogeneous past of the primordial vacuum, there is no way to determine when and where fluctuations that produce universes will occur. Thus for any point in space there is within any finite time interval a nonzero probability of a universe-generating fluctuation occurring. Given an infinite past, universes will form at every point in space and, as they expand, begin to collide and coalesce with one another. Thus we should observe either an infinitely old universe or else "worlds in collision" with our own, which we do not. About the only way to avoid this problem is to postulate an expansion of the primordial vacuum itself, but then we must ask about its origination, and we have solved nothing. Isham has called this objection "fairly lethal" to such models and says that therefore they "have not found wide acceptance" (Isham 1990, 10; 1988, 387). They were "jettisoned twenty years ago" and "nothing much" has been done with them since (Isham 1994, 8). These theories are now obsolete, having been abandoned even by their original proponents (Brout and Spindel 1989).

It is sobering to note, however, how eagerly and uncritically these theories have been adopted by popular science writers, even long after their demise.

For example, referring to the quantum vacuum as "the originating power [which] gave birth to the universe," Brian Swimme and Thomas Berry of the so-called Center for the Story of the Universe substitute for the Genesis story what amounts to a scientific mythology for our time: "In the beginning was a flashing forth of evanescent beings," particles that dissolve back "into the same night that had given them forth, into non-existence, absorbed back into that abyss, that originating and annihilating power that is the marrow of the universe" (Swimme and Berry 1992, 17, 20). In the same way Daniel Matt, a pantheist and cabalistic mystic, begins *God and the Big Bang* with the words, "In the beginning was the big bang, fifteen billion years ago. The primordial vacuum was devoid of matter, but . . . pregnant with potential. . . . Through a quantum fluctuation, . . . there emerged a sort of hot dense seed . . . containing all the mass and energy of our universe" (Matt 1996, 19). The primordial vacuum does not exactly replace God. Rather "'God' is the name we give to the oneness of it all. . . . The entire world is God in myriad forms and disguises" (Matt 1996, 36, 39). How God can begin to exist is not explained. Again, in an issue of the Phi Kappa Phi magazine *National Forum,* J.-M. Wersinger, while acknowledging that theories of "the appearance of the universe out of the nothingness of vacuum" are "highly speculative" and "not corroborated experimentally," nevertheless touts such theories as the first milestone of "a plausible scenario for the appearance and evolution of our universe" (Wersinger 1996, 15). In contrast to the standard big bang model, which seemed "to give in to the Judeo-Christian idea of a beginning of the world" and "also seemed to have to call for an act of supernatural creation," now "science has come up with a theory of Genesis that does not have to rely on a supernatural intervention" but "is entirely described by mechanisms rooted in the currently known laws of physics" (Wersinger 1996, 9, 15).

Reading these accounts, one can only agree with Isham's judgment that aversion to the theism seen to be implicit in big bang cosmology has at times led to scientific ideas—in this case, vacuum fluctuation models—being advanced with a tenacity that so exceeds their intrinsic worth that one can only suspect that psychological factors rather than scientific evidence is the driving force behind them (Isham 1988, 378).

Such models may not, however, be entirely without worth, even to the natural theologian. Some detractors of the doctrine of *creatio ex nihilo,* such as Hume, have charged that that doctrine is incompatible with the maxim *ex nihilo nihil fit* (Hume 1975, 12.3.132, 164). That is not the case, since the doctrine of *creatio ex nihilo* denies only a material cause of world but insists on the presence of an efficient cause. Still, insofar as vacuum fluctuation models render it plausible that the universe lacks a material cause, they are of service to theism, since any dispute that might exist between theists and the proponents of such theories will concern only the identity of the efficient cause of the universe. There is no reason that the theist could not explain *creatio ex nihilo* by saying that the sum total of the matter/energy in the universe is zero and thus God in creating the universe required no material substratum.

The only person I know of who has adumbrated such a position is Philberth, who holds that "the Universe is creation in the proper sense of the word: produced by the free will of a personal creator, of God, who Himself is not subject to space, time, or matter" and then proceeds to affirm, after explaining the balance of positive mass energy and negative gravitational energy, that "matter was generated because the Creator wanted its generation; and the non-applicability of local energy conservation is nothing but the method, the mode of this generation's realization without violation of physical laws in the cosmos" (Philberth 1977, 115, 126). Philberth does retain the empirically untenable hypothesis of a primordial, undifferentiated gas in which the universe forms, a sort of analogue of the quantum vacuum. But it must be said that any such an entity is wholly unnecessary as a material cause; the universe on such models has zero energy/matter and so borrows nothing of the *Urstoff*. It needs the quantum vacuum only as an (indeterministic) efficient cause. But the theist who affirms God as the Creator has no need of the vacuum and so can ascribe creation directly to God as its efficient cause.

### Quantum Gravitational Models

At any rate, theoretical cosmology has moved beyond the old vacuum fluctuation models in search of the Holy Grail of physics: a unified theory, including a quantum theory of gravitation. Such a theory will be required to describe the state of the universe prior to $10^{-43}$ sec after the big bang, where space-time curvature becomes so extreme that the classical general theory of relativity (GTR) will not apply. Since quantum effects normally dominate on such scales, gravitation will likely have to be quantized. Unfortunately, since quantum theory and gravitational theory are in their present formulations incompatible, something has got to give; and nobody knows what. As a result, the brief moment prior to the Planck time has become fertile ground for cosmological speculation.

Many theorists hope that a unified theory will serve to remove the initial cosmological singularity that characterizes classical big bang models. Undoubtedly the most well-known quantum gravitational model is the Hartle-Hawking model popularized by Stephen Hawking in his bestselling *A Brief History of Time*. Less famous but also important is the cosmological model of Alexander Vilenkin. Both models eliminate the initial singularity by converting the conical hypersurface of classical space-time terminating in an initial point into a smooth, curved hypersurface having no edge. This is accomplished by the introduction of imaginary numbers for the time variable in Einstein's gravitational equations, which has the effect of converting time into a dimension of space. Thus our classical space-time emerges from a four-dimensional space that Vilenkin characterizes as a "state in which all our basic notions of space, time, energy, entropy, etc., lose their meaning" (Vilenkin 1983, 2851) and that Hawking describes as "completely self-contained and not affected by anything outside itself. It would be neither created nor destroyed. It would just BE" (Hawking 1988, 136).

Here is a God-substitute worthy of the name: this Euclidean four-space is uncaused, immaterial, beginningless and transcendent with respect to both time and space (classically conceived). It is the indeterministic cause of the origin of the universe. Yet it is not a personal agent; it is comprised of a set of impersonal causal conditions. To put it in Kanitscheider's words, "In quite an amazing way the quantum principle came to the aid again to rescue the rationality of science of the universe from miraculousness" (Kanitscheider 1990, 346).

Hawking is not at all reticent about what he sees as the theological implications of his model:

> The idea that space and time may form a closed surface without boundary . . . has profound implications for the role of God in the affairs of the universe. . . . So long as the universe had a beginning, we could suppose it had a creator. But if the universe is really completely self-contained, having no boundary or edge, it would have neither beginning nor end. What place, then, for a creator? (Hawking 1988, 140-41)

Not only are such models said to obviate the need of a Personal Creator in the sense envisioned by the *kalam* cosmological argument, but both Hartle-Hawking and Vilenkin also claim that their theories serve to explain the origin of the universe out of nothing. Hartle-Hawking interpret their equations as giving the amplitude for some three-geometry "to arise from a zero three-geometry, i.e. a single point. In other words, the ground state is the amplitude for the Universe to appear from nothing" (Hartle and Hawking 1983, 2961). More recently Hawking has claimed that on their model the universe "would quite literally be created out of nothing: not just out of the vacuum, but out of absolutely nothing at all, because there is nothing outside the universe" (Hawking and Penrose 1996, 85). Similarly Vilenkin claims that his model postulates the creation of the universe "from literally *nothing*" (Vilenkin 1982, 26).

These lofty claims, however, are easily dismissed. By "nothing" Vilenkin meant merely "a state with no classical spacetime" (Vilenkin 1983, 2851). As metaphysician John Post points out, "In fact the 'nothing' out of which the universe tunnels in this scenario is a space, even though it is not a space-time with all the structure that that implies" (Post 1991, 89; cf. Isham 1993, 72-74[14]). As for Hartle-Hawking's claim, a three-space having zero volume and subject to the laws of physics is not the same as nothing (Drees 1987, 940). Moreover, since time is imaginary in the Planck region, that zero volume point exists timelessly and does not come into being. When Hawking says that there is nothing outside the universe on their model, he is forgetting the Euclidean four-sphere itself. Thus these scenarios do not envision an origination of the universe out of nothing but (taking "universe" to refer to classical space-time) the origination of the universe via a transition from a timelessly subsisting, Euclidean four-space into classical space-time. Given such an entity, there is no need for a Personal Creator such as is implied by the *kalam* cosmological argument.

In assessing these quantum gravitational models, we need to have a clear realization that their force in obviating the need for a Creator depends entirely on (i) the plausibility of a realist construal of such theories and (ii) a physically reductionistic understanding of time. With regard to the first question, one of the chief obstacles to a realistic understanding of such theories is their use of so-called imaginary time. Imaginary quantities in science are without physical significance.[15] Use of such numbers is a mathematical trick or auxiliary device to arrive at physically significant quantities represented by real numbers. It makes no more sense to speak of an imaginary duration than of an imaginary length or an imaginary volume. The Euclidean four-space from which classical space-time emerges is thus a mathematical fiction, a way of modeling the early universe that should not be taken as a literal description.

One might consider profitably the analogy of the use of imaginary numbers for the time coordinate in the metric of Minkowski space-time, a mathematical trick that suppresses the curvature in space-time and so allows one to treat a pseudo-Euclidean four-space as a Euclidean four-space. Space-time itself, as an *(ex hypothesi)* objectively existing reality, is not changed by this redescription. It is still a pseudo-Euclidean four-space, but we can treat it as if it were Euclidean by using imaginary numbers for the time coordinate. The only change that occurs is on paper. As early as 1920, Sir Arthur Eddington remarked, "It is not very profitable to speculate on the implication of the mysterious factor $\sqrt{-1}$, which seems to have the property of turning time into space. It can scarcely be regarded as any more than an analytical device" (Eddington 1987, 48). Illustrations like imaginary time, he said, "certainly do not correspond to any physical reality" (Eddington 1987, 281). In a similar way Hawking's use of imaginary numbers for the time variable allows one to redescribe a universe with an initial cosmological singularity in such a way that that point appears as a nonsingular point on a curved hypersurface. Such a redescription suppresses and also literally spatializes time, which makes evident the purely instrumental character of the model. Such a model could be of great utility to science, but it would not, as Hawking boldly asserts, eliminate the need for a Creator.

Remarkably, Hawking has recently stated explicitly that he interprets the Hartle-Hawking model nonrealistically. He confesses, "I'm a positivist. . . . I don't demand that a theory correspond to reality because I don't know what it is" (Hawking and Penrose 1996, 121). Still more extreme, "I take the positivist viewpoint that a physical theory is just a mathematical model and that it is meaningless to ask whether it corresponds to reality" (Hawking and Penrose 1996, 3-4). In assessing the worth of a theory, "All I'm concerned with is that the theory should predict the results of measurements" (Hawking and Penrose 1996, 121; 4).

The clearest example of Hawking's instrumentalism is his analysis of electron/positron pair creation in an electric field as a combination of an electron quantum tunneling in Euclidean space (with time being imaginary) and an electron/positron pair accelerating away from each other in Minkowski space-time (Hawking and Penrose 1996, 53-55). This analysis is directly analogous to the Hartle-Hawking cosmological model; and yet no one would construe particle pair creation as literally the result of an electron transitioning out of a timelessly existing four-space into our classical space-time. It is just an alternative description employing imaginary numbers rather than real numbers. Ironically, Hartle-Hawking stands indicted by the same charge leveled by Hawking against certain GTR theorists: "People were so pleased when they found a solution that they didn't care that it probably had no physical significance" (Hawking and Penrose 1996, 3). But then what becomes of Hawking's vaunted claim to have eliminated the need for a Creator? It turns out to have been sensationalist, theological bunkum, which left theists wringing their hands in consternation and Hawking laughing all the way to the bank.

It might be said that so-called imaginary time just *is* a spatial dimension and to that extent is physically intelligible and so is to be realistically construed. Our world of three spatial dimensions plus one temporal dimension originated in a realm comprised of four spatial dimensions, one dimension of which gradually evolved into time (Hartle-Hawking model) or out of which our space and time world arose via a sort of quantum tunneling (Vilenkin model). But now the metaphysician must surely protest the reductionistic view of time that such an account presupposes. Time as it plays a role in physics is not the full-blooded notion of time known to us by experience but is an operationally defined quantity varying from theory to theory: in the special theory of relativity as a quantity defined via clock synchronization by light signals, in classical cosmology as a parameter assigned to spatial hypersurfaces of homogeneity, in quantum cosmology as a quantity internally constructed out of the curvature variables of three-geometries. In physics time is so *defined*, not merely measured.

But clearly these are but pale abstractions of time itself.[16] For a series of mental events alone, a succession of contents of consciousness, is sufficient to ground time itself. An unembodied consciousness that experienced a succession of mental states, say, by counting, would be temporal; that is to say, time would in such a case exist, and that wholly in the absence of any physical processes. I take this simple consideration to be a knockdown argument that time as it plays a role in physics is at best a measure of time rather than constitutive or definitive of time. In short, Isaac Newton was correct when he distinguished between time itself and what are merely our "sensible measures thereof" (Newton 1966, 1.8). Confirmation of this distinction comes from the further fact that physics knows nothing of the tense determinations of past, present, and future in its concept(s) of time, though such determinations are, I should argue, essential to time itself (Smith 1993; Craig 1994, 241-43; forthcoming c). Hence even if one were to accept at face value the claim of quantum cosmological models that physical time really is imaginary prior to the Planck time, that is to say, is a spatial dimension, that fact says absolutely nothing at all about time itself.

When it is said that such a regime exists timelessly, all that means is that our physical measures of time (which in physics are taken to define time) break down under such conditions. That should hardly surprise. But time itself must characterize such a regime for the simple reason that it is not static. I am astonished that quantum theorists can assert that the quantum regime is on the one hand a state of incessant activity or change and yet is on the other not characterized by time. If this is not to be incoherent, such a statement can only mean that our concepts of physical time are inapplicable on such a scale, not that time itself disappears. But if time itself characterizes the quantum regime, as it must if change is occurring, then one can regress mentally in time back along the imaginary time dimension through concentric circles on the spherical hypersurface as they converge toward a nonsingular point that represents the beginning of the universe and before which time did not exist. Hartle and Hawking themselves recognize that point as the origin of the universe in their model, as we have seen, but mistakenly identify it as nothing. How that point came into being (in metaphysical, that is, ontological time) is not even addressed by their theory.

Hence, even on a naive realist construal of such models, they at best show that that quantity which is defined as time in physics ceases at the Planck time and takes on the characteristics of what physics defines as a spatial dimension. But time itself does not begin at the Planck time but extends all the way back to the very beginning of the universe. Such theories, if successful, thus enable us to model the origin of the universe without an initial cosmological singularity. Despite Hawking's assertions, such models, by positing a finite imaginary time on a closed surface prior to the Planck time rather than an infinite time on an open surface, support rather than undercut the *kalam* cosmological argument. It is the doctrine of reductionism, which is a metaphysical, not a scientific issue, that the defender of the *kalam* argument rejects.

Thus it seems to me that the introduction of quantum gravitational models—what Vilenkin calls exercises in "metaphysical cosmology" (Vilenkin 1983, 2854)—do not at all undermine premise (9) of the *kalam* cosmological argument. For their dependence on so-called imaginary time requires us either to adopt an antirealist approach to such theories or to make explicit the untenability of any physically reductionistic construal of time. Significantly this conclusion is not based on some scientific shortcoming of such theories—and these are, it must be confessed, legion—that might be remedied at some future date but rather on an inherent feature of these models that is of metaphysical significance (Isham 1993, 56).

Again, one can only shake one's head in bewilderment at how uncritically popularizers of science have swallowed Hawking's claim to have eliminated the need for a Creator. For example, an exuberant John Gribbin proclaims, "The kind of unified theories that physicists are now groping toward, and may discover (or invent) before the end of this century, ought to be able, combined with Hawking's universe, to explain every phenomenon that ever has happened or ever could happen in the universe. . . . Hawking's universe holds out the prospect of combining General Relativity and cosmology in one grand theory of creation. . . . There is no need to invoke miracles, or new physics, to explain where the universe came from" (Gribbin 1986, 391).

Thus Gribbin solemnly declares that Hawking's quantum cosmology spells "the end of the road for metaphysics" (Gribbin 1986, 392). In Gribbin's words,

Hawking has already indicated an end, not to physics but to *metaphysics*. It is now possible to give a good scientific answer to the question "Where do we come from?" without invoking either God or special boundary conditions for the universe at the moment of creation. As of the Vatican Conference of 1981, it is the metaphysicians who are out of a job. (Gribbin 1986, 392)

What makes this pompous proclamation so amusing is that Hawking's claim to have eliminated the need for a Creator rests, as we have seen, precisely on crucial metaphysical assumptions about the nature of time—assumptions that too often go unexamined.

Finally a word should be said on behalf of the beleaguered cosmological singularity of classical big bang cosmology. John Barrow has rightly cautioned that "one should be wary of the fact that many of the studies of quantum cosmology are motivated by the desire to avoid an initial singularity of infinite density, so they tend to focus on quantum cosmologies that avoid a singularity at the expense of those that might contain one" (Barrow 1994, 113).[17] Noting the same tendency, Roger Penrose states, "I have gradually come around to the view that it is actually misguided to ask that the space-time singularities of classical relativity should disappear when standard techniques of quantum (field) theory are applied to them" (Penrose 1982, 4). For if the initial cosmological singularity is removed, then "we should have lost what seems to me to be the best chance we have of explaining the mystery of the second law of thermodynamics" (Penrose 1982, 5).

What Penrose has in mind is the remarkable fact that as one goes back in time the entropy of the universe steadily decreases. Just how unusual this is can be demonstrated by means of the Bekenstein-Hawking formula for the entropy of a stationary black hole. The total observed entropy of the universe is $10^{88}$. Since there are around $10^{80}$ baryons in the universe, the observed entropy per baryon must be regarded as extremely small. By contrast in a collapsing universe the entropy would be $10^{123}$ near the end. Comparison of these two numbers reveals how absurdly small $10^{88}$ is compared to what it might have been. Thus the structure of the big bang must have been severely constrained in order that thermodynamics as we know it should have arisen. So how is this special initial condition to be explained?

According to Penrose, we need the initial cosmological singularity, conjoined with the Weyl curvature hypothesis, according to which initial singularities (as opposed to final singularities) must have vanishing Weyl curvature.[18] In standard models the big bang does possess vanishing Weyl curvature. The geometrical constraints on the initial geometry have the effect of producing a state of very low entropy. So the entropy in the gravitational field starts at zero at the big bang and gradually increases through gravitational clumping. The Weyl curvature hypothesis thus has the time asymmetric character necessary to explain the second law. By contrast the Hartle-Hawking model "is very far from being an explanation of the fact that past singularities have small Weyl curvature whereas future singularities have large Weyl curvature" (Hawking and Penrose 1996, 129). On Hawking's time symmetrical theory, we should have white holes spewing out material, in contradiction to the Weyl curvature hypothesis, the second law of thermodynamics and probably also observation (Hawking and Penrose 1996, 130). Penrose illustrates the difference (see figure 14.1).

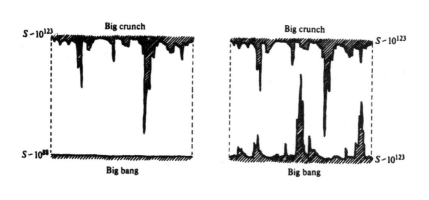

**Figure 14.1  Contrast Between Two Universes**
Contrast between the universe as we know it (assumed for convenience to be closed) with a more probable universe. In both cases the big crunch is a high-entropy (~$10^{123}$), complicated, unconstrained singularity. For the left-hand picture the big bang is a low-entropy ($\leq 10^{88}$), highly constrained initial singularity, while for the right-hand picture it is an unconstrained, much more probable big bang. The "stalactites" represent singularities of black holes, while the "stalagmites" represent singularities of white holes.

If we remove the initial cosmological singularity, we render the Weyl curvature hypothesis irrelevant, and "we should be back where we were in our attempts to understand the origin of the second law" (Penrose 1982, 5). Could the special initial geometry have arisen sheerly by chance in the absence of a cosmic singularity? Penrose's answer is decisive: "Had there not been any constraining principles (such as the Weyl curvature hypothesis), the Bekenstein-Hawking formula would tell as that the probability of such a 'special' geometry arising by chance is at least as small as about one part in $10^{1000B(3/2)}$ where B is the present baryon number of the universe [~$10^{80}$]" (Penrose 1981). Thus Penrose calculates that, aiming at a manifold whose points represent the various possible initial configurations of the universe, "the accuracy of the Creator's aim" would have to have been one part in $10^{10^{(123)}}$ in order for our universe to exist (Penrose 1981, 249; cf. Hawking and Penrose 1996, 34-35). He comments, "I cannot even recall seeing anything else in physics whose accuracy is known to approach, even remotely, a figure like one part in $10^{10^{(123)}}$" (Penrose 1981, 249).

This puts the detractor of a Cosmic Intelligence in an awkward dilemma. If the universe began with an initial cosmological singularity, then the *kalam* cosmological argument implies that since a temporal effect cannot arise from an impersonal, eternal cause, a Personal Creator of the universe therefore exists. On the other hand, if one removes the initial singularity, then we are left with the inexplicable and incomprehensibly finely-tuned initial conditions of the universe, which supply grist for the mill of the teleological argument for a Personal Designer of the universe. Take your pick.

### Conclusion

I hope to have shown the close links between the *kalam* cosmological argument and the teleological argument. The former provides good reason to believe that behind the existence of our universe stands a Personal Creator, whom the teleological argument shows to be also a Cosmic Designer. That the cause of the universe is a Mind is already implied by the causal impotence of the only alternative, abstract objects. The attempt of some quantum cosmologists to explain how a temporal effect could arise from an eternal cause by supplying *Ersatzgötter* in the form of a quantum vacuum or a Euclidean four-space ultimately misfires. Even if we concede ontic indeterminacy on the quantum level, such models fail to obviate the need for a Personal Creator due to the finitude of past (ontological) time as implied by those very models. Thus the cause of the origin of the universe must be a transcendent Personal Agent.

## Notes

[1] The *Dialogues* in general are a critique of the teleological argument; the cosmological argument comes under attack in part 9.

[2] For background and a defense of the argument, see Craig 1979; for a debate on its cogency, see Craig and Smith 1993.

[3] This needs some qualification, since the *kalam* argument strictly demonstrates only that metric time had a beginning. For discussion, see Craig 1996; 1997.

[4] See also Mann 1983, 270; Helm 1988, 64-65; Yates 1990, 173-75; Leftow 1991, 285-90. For an intriguing nontheistic analysis, see Walker 1978, 34-41.

[5] Important defenses of a nonphysicalist account of mind may be found in Popper and Eccles 1993; Swinburne 1986; Smythies and Beloff 1989; Foster 1991; and Robinson 1993.

[6] For some discussion of the two routes I mention in the text, see Shimony 1986.

[7] For a defense of this interpretation, see Brody 1993.

[8] For a recent review of this model, see Holland 1993.

[9] For a discussion see Petersen 1963.

[10] Unless one invokes God as the ultimate observer to break the measurement chain (Craig forthcoming b).

[11] Post's objections to a transcendent First Cause are strangely question-begging. For he begins with the assumption, "by definition the universe contains everything there is or ever was or will be" (Post 1991, 85), which rules out a transcendent cause by definition. The only way to escape a vicious circle is to hold that the definition leaves open the possibility of a timeless being not in the universe. But Post never even considers such a possibility. Thus his argument is either question-begging or unsound. He is also guilty of the non sequitur that because "the singularity cannot be caused by some earlier *natural* event or process," therefore "the universe has an uncaused beginning. . . . It seems contemporary physical cosmology cannot be cited in support of the idea of a *divine* cause or creator of the universe" (Post 1991, 87 [emphasis added]). Not content with making this mistake once, he again states that the initial four-space in the Vilenkin model "cannot be caused by some earlier *natural* event or process" and therefore "talk of *divine* creation . . . appears to contradict physical accounts according to which the universe has an uncaused beginning via tunneling from literally nothing. It is not easy to make friends of science and religion" (Post 1991, 89, 91 [emphasis added]). Perhaps it would help if they were introduced to each other by logic.

Kanitscheider's own remarks on this head are curiously inconsistent. He doggedly insists that if the universe began to exist in a singularity, "the only inescapable conclusion would be the existence of *an absolute zero of time.* Nothing could be read into this formula beyond physics. An absolute zero of time would transcend just as little the realm of naturalistic ontology as the existence of an absolute zero of temperature does" (Kanitscheider 1990, 344); this despite the fact that "if taken seriously, the initial singularity is in head-on collision with the most successful ontological commitment that was a guiding line of research since Epicurus and Lucretius," viz., *out of nothing nothing comes,* which Kanitscheider calls "a metaphysical hypothesis which has proved so fruitful in every corner of science that we are surely well-advised to try as hard as we can to eschew processes of absolute origin" (Kanitscheider 1990). Contra Kanitscheider, the crucial disanalogy between an absolute zero of temperature and of time is that only in the case of the latter is it a matter of something's coming into being out of nothing. This is in such violation of the metaphysical principle extolled by Kanitscheider that it propels us beyond physics and the realm of naturalistic ontology.

Funnily enough, Kanitscheider's exposition of the standard model refutes the uninformed assertion of Mario Bunge that "the model assumes explicitly that the universe existed prior to that time" at which the expansion started (Bunge 1985, 238); Bunge thinks that otherwise "it would be unscientific, for science abides by the principles that nothing comes out of nothing or turns into nothingness . . . and that everything happens according to law rather than miracles" (Bunge 1985, 239). Kanitscheider says, "This principle seems to be self-evident from common sense knowledge and it has been defended in a long philosophical tradition" (Kanitscheider 1990, 345). But that is true only of the first principle enunciated by Bunge; Kanitscheider ignores the long philosophical tradition that has shown the vacuousness of arguments against the impossibility of miracles and freedom of the will. When Bunge belatedly remonstrates, "Natural theology cannot be revived at this late date" (Bunge 1985, 239), and Kanitscheider mistakenly asserts that the singularity "cannot have a cause *of any kind*," not even a supernatural cause, so that there is "no help in natural theology," (Kanitscheider 1990, 345), it is evident that the force driving their conclusions is fear of the bogeyman of natural theology.

[12]See the quite sensible remarks by Drees 1991, 70. Unfortunately Drees does not distinguish clearly efficient causation from material causation in his critique of the *kalam* argument. What he says supports the *kalam* argument by showing that what is required for *creatio ex nihilo* is an efficient, not a material, cause.

[13]See the related discussion in Craig 1991.

[14]Contra Smith, who in Craig and Smith 1993, 301-2, imagines two Vilenkin models despite Vilenkin's explicit statements to the contrary in Vilenkin 1983, 2849; 1988, 888.

[15]In the case of quantum mechanics, for example, "the state vector in the Schrödinger equation is not a physical magnitude, for it is an imaginary function and such functions do not represent real physical magnitudes" (Liu 1993, 622). Liu contends that in the mature theory of quantum gravity a fundamental arrow of time will obtain.

[16]See the interesting lecture by Rovelli 1993, 17, where he lists eight properties of time as characterized in natural language and compares the concepts of time found in thermodynamics, STR, GTR, and so forth; time as it is defined in quantum gravity has none of the properties usually associated with time. Compare Isham 1992, 17-19, who describes ten different definitions of time in quantum gravity alone.

[17]Elsewhere Barrow observes that the singularities that GTR renders inevitable do not require infinite density and temperature and that if in fact they do not possess these properties, then quantum gravity will not save us from their reality (Barrow 1988, 310).

[18]Weyl curvature is the curvature of space-time that is not due to the presence of matter and is described by the Weyl tensor. Space-time curvature due to matter is described by the Einstein tensor. Together they make up the Riemann tensor giving the metric for space-time.

## References

Al-Ghazali. 1963. *Tahafut al-falasifah*. Translated by S. A. Kamali. 1095. Reprint, Lahore: Pakistan Philosophical Congress.

Atkins, P. W. 1992. *Creation revisited.* Oxford: Freeman.

Barrow, J. 1988. *The world within the world.* Oxford: Clarendon Press.

———. 1994. *The origin of the universe.* New York: BasicBooks, HarperCollins.

Bell, J. S. 1984. On the impossible pilot wave. In *Quantum, space and time—The quest continues,* ed. A. O. Barut, A. van der Merwe, and J.-P. Vigier, 66-76. New York: Cambridge University Press.

Brody, T. 1993. *The philosophy behind physics,* ed. L. de la Pena and P. E. Hodgson. Berlin: Springer-Verlag.

Brout, R., and P. Spindel. 1989. Black holes dispute. *Nature* 337:216.

Bunge, M. 1985. *Treatise on basic philosophy, 7, Epistemology and Methodology 3: Philosophy of Science and Technology,* part 1, *Formal and physical sciences.* Dordrecht: D. Reidel.

Craig, W. L. 1979. *The* kalam *cosmological argument.* London: Macmillan.

———. 1991. The *kalam* cosmological argument and the hypothesis of a quiescent universe. *Faith and Philosophy* 8:104-8.

———. 1994. Response to Grünbaum on creation and big bang cosmology. *Philosophia Naturalis* 31:237-49.

———. 1996. Timelessness and creation. *Australasian Journal of Philosophy* 74:646-56.

———. 1997. Divine timelessness and necessary existence. *International Philosophical Quarterly* 37:217-24.

———. 1997. Divine timelessness and personhood. *International Journal for Philosophy of Religion,* 1-16.

———. Forthcoming a. The tensed versus tenseless theory of time: A watershed for the conception of divine eternity. In *Questions of time and tense,* ed. R. LePoidevin. Oxford: Oxford University Press.

———. Forthcoming b. Cosmos and creation. In *Detecting design in creation,* ed. S. C. Meyer and J. M. Reynolds.

———. Forthcoming c. *God, time and eternity.* Under consideration.

Craig, W. L., and Q. Smith. 1993. *Theism, atheism and big bang cosmology.* Oxford: Clarendon Press.

Drees, W. B. 1987. Interpretation of "the wave function of the universe." *Journal for Theoretical Physics* 26:939-42.

———. 1991. Potential tensions between cosmology and theology. In *Interpreting the universe as creation,* ed. V. Brümmer, 65-89. Kampen, Netherlands: Pharos.

Eddington, A. 1987. *Space, time and gravitation.* 1920. Reprint, Cambridge: Cambridge University Press.

Forbes, G. 1993. Time, events and modality. In *The philosophy of time,* ed. R. Le Poidevin and M. MacBeath, 80-95. Oxford: Oxford University Press.

Foster, J. 1991. *The immaterial self.* London: Routledge.

Gribbin, J. 1986. *In search of the big bang.* New York: Bantam.

Hartle, J., and S. Hawking. 1983. Wave function of the universe. *Physical Review D* 28:2960-75.

Hawking, S. 1988. *A brief history of time.* New York: Bantam.

Hawking, S., and R. Penrose. 1996. *The nature of space and time.* Princeton, N.J.: Princeton University Press.

Heisenberg, W. 1971. *Physics and beyond.* Translated by A. J. Pomerans. New York: Harper and Row.

Helm, P. 1988. *Eternal God.* Oxford: Clarendon Press.

Holland, P. 1993. *The quantum theory of motion.* Cambridge: Cambridge University

Press.

Hume, D. 1975. *An enquiry concerning human understanding.* In *Enquiries concerning human understanding and the principles of morals.* Edited by P. H. Nidditch. 3rd ed. 1777. Reprint, Oxford: Clarendon Press.

———. 1947. *Dialogues concerning natural religion.* Edited by N. K. Smith. 1779. Reprint, Indianapolis, Ind.: Bobbs-Merrill.

Isham, C. 1988. Creation of the universe as a quantum process. In *Physics, philosophy and theology: A common quest for understanding,* ed. R. J. Russell, W. R. Stoeger, and G. V. Coyne, 375-408. Vatican City: Vatican Observatory.

———. 1990. Space, time and quantum cosmology. Lecture to the Science and Religion Forum conference "God, Time, and Modern Physics." England.

———. 1992. Canonical quantum gravity and the problem of time. Lectures presented at the NATO Advanced Study Institute "Recent Problems in Mathematical Physics," Salamanca, June 15-27.

———. 1993. Quantum theories of the creation of the universe. In *Quantum cosmology and the laws of nature,* ed. R. J. Russell, N. Murphy, and C. J. Isham, 49-89. Vatican City: Vatican Observatory.

———. 1994. Quantum cosmology and the origin of the universe. Lecture presented at the conference "Cosmos and Creation," Cambridge University, July 14.

Kanitscheider, B. 1990. Does physical cosmology transcend the limits of naturalistic reasoning? In *Studies on Mario Bunge's "Treatise,"* ed. P. Weingartner and G. J. W. Dorn, 337-50. Amsterdam: Rodopi.

Kant, I. 1933. *Critique of pure reason.* Edited by N. K. Smith. 1781. Reprint, London: Macmillan.

Leftow, B. 1991. *Time and eternity.* Ithaca, N.Y.: Cornell University Press.

Leslie, J. 1989. *Universes.* London: Routledge.

Liu, C. 1993. The arrow of time in quantum gravity. *Philosophy of Science* 60:619-37.

Lockwood, M. 1996. "Many minds" interpretations of quantum mechanics. *British Journal for the Philosophy of Science* 47:159-88.

Mann, W. 1983. Simplicity and immutability in God. *International Philosophical Quarterly* 23:267-76.

Matt, D. 1996. *God and the big bang.* Woodstock, Vt.: Jewish Lights Publishing.

Moreland, J. P. 1998. The explanatory relevance of libertarian agency as a model of theistic design. In *Mere creation: Science, faith and intelligent design,* ed. W. A. Dembski, chap. 11. Downers Grove, Ill.: InterVarsity Press.

Morris, T. V., ed. 1988. *Divine and human action: Essays in the metaphysics of theism.* Ithaca, N.Y.: Cornell University Press.

Newton, I. 1966. *Sir Isaac Newton's "Mathematical Principles of Natural Philosophy" and his "System of the World."* Translated by A. Motte and Rev. F. Cajori. 2 vols. 1685. Reprint, Los Angeles: University of California Press.

O'Connor, T. W., ed. 1995. *Agents, causes and events.* Oxford: Oxford University Press.

Oppy, G. 1991. Craig, Mackie, and the *kalam* cosmological argument. *Religious Studies* 27:189-97.

———. 1995. Professor William Lane Craig's criticisms of critiques of *kalam* cosmological arguments by Paul Davis, Stephen Hawking and Adolf Grunbaum. *Faith and Philosophy* 12:237-50.

Penrose, R. 1981. Time-asymmetry and quantum gravity. In *Quantum gravity 2,* ed. C. J. Isham, R. Penrose, and D. W. Sciama, 245-72. Oxford: Clarendon Press.

——. 1982. Some remarks on gravity and quantum mechanics. In *Quantum structure of space and time*, ed. M. J. Duff and C. J. Isham, 3-10. Cambridge: Cambridge University Press.

Petersen, A. 1963. The philosophy of Niels Bohr. *Bulletin of the Atomic Scientists* 19 (September):8-14.

Philberth, K. 1977. The generation of matter and the conservation of energy. In *Cosmology, history and theology,* ed. W. Yourgrau and A. D. Breck, 113-29. New York: Plenum.

Popper, K., and J. Eccles. 1993. *The self and its brain: An argument for interactionism.* London: Routledge and Kegan Paul.

Post, J. 1991. *Metaphysics: A contemporary introduction.* New York: Paragon House.

Robinson, H., ed. 1993. *Objections to physicalism.* Oxford: Clarendon Press.

Rovelli, C. 1993. What does present days *[sic]* physics tell us about time and space? Lecture presented at the 1993-1994 Annual Series of Lectures of the Center for Philosophy of Science of the University of Pittsburgh, September 17.

Shoemaker, S. 1969. Time without change. *Journal of Philosophy* 66:363-81.

Shimony, A. 1986. Events and processes in the quantum world. In *Quantum concepts in space and time,* ed. R. Penrose and C. J. Isham, 182-202. Oxford: Clarendon Press.

Smith, Q. 1993. *Language and time.* New York: Oxford University Press.

Smythies, J. R., and J. Beloff, eds. 1989. *The case for dualism.* Charlottesville: University Press of Virginia.

Swimme, B., and T. Berry. 1992. *The universe story.* San Francisco: HarperSanFrancisco.

Swinburne, R. 1979. *The existence of God.* Oxford: Clarendon Press.

——. 1986. *The evolution of the soul.* Oxford: Clarendon Press.

Taliaferro, C. 1994. *Consciousness and the mind of God.* Cambridge: Cambridge University Press.

Vilenkin, A. 1982. Creation of the universe from nothing. *Physics Letters* 117B (25):25-28.

——. 1983. Birth of inflationary universes. *Physical Review D* 27 (12):2848-55.

——. 1988. Quantum cosmology and the initial state of the universe. *Physical Review D* 37 (4):888-97.

Walker, R. 1978. *Kant.* London: Routledge and Kegan Paul.

Wersinger, J.-M. 1996. The origin of the universe. *National Forum* 76 (winter):9-15.

Wheeler, J. 1973. From relativity to mutability. In *The physicist's conception of nature,* ed. J. Mehra, 202-50. Dordrecht: D. Reidel.

Worthing, M. W. 1996. *God, creation and contemporary physics.* Minneapolis: Fortress Press.

Yates, J. 1990. *The timelessness of God.* Lanham, Md.: University Press of America.

# Part 5

## Design in the Universe

# 15

# Big Bang Model Refined by Fire

## HUGH ROSS

N OT SINCE THE COPERNICAN REVOLUTION HAVE SCIENTISTS AND theologians battled so ferociously over an astronomical theory as they have in the twentieth century over the big bang. The only casualties in this protracted conflict have been falsehoods and fears, though some remain slow to die. The protracted fighting has not been futile. Rather it has solidified and amplified the scientist's understanding of the cosmos and the Christian's case for faith in the biblical Creator.

In *The Fingerprint of God* I gave some background on this big bang battle, especially how and why it began. Two key players were Immanuel Kant and Albert Einstein. Kant turned the philosophical and scientific tide toward belief in an infinite universe, thereby attempting to make God irrelevant. Einstein surprised himself and the world with brilliant theoretical work that was observationally supported, that contradicted an infinite universe and that demanded a beginning (and a relatively recent one at that). The scientific community, even Einstein himself, went through contortions to escape the creation event, which came to be known as the big bang. They understood its implication—the necessity of an Initiator, someone who initiated and carefully controlled the progress of that event.

Philosophy drifted along in denial while science madly scrambled to discredit the religious and therefore repugnant idea of a beginning. Cosmologists proposed one bizarre hypothesis after another—some ancient, some science fiction—in attempting to counter the growing conviction that the universe had a beginning. Ironically all their efforts only highlighted the beauty and accuracy of the big bang model.

Only with difficulty did Christian theology make sense of these developments. Perhaps still staggered by the weight of Darwinism and the Scopes debacle, some Christians mistook Einstein's theory of relativity for relativism and reacted against it. Others, remembering that Kant gave lip service to God's existence, saw themselves as defending God by opposing Einstein. Still others, thinking a creation date of several billion years back would certainly support atheistic evolution, resisted the big bang to defend biblical truth.

In *The Creator and the Cosmos* and *Creation and Time* I treated the challenges to the big bang model stemming respectively from science and theology. *The Creator and the Cosmos* marshaled the scientific evidence supporting the big bang, evidence augmented by the search for alternate models. It also described how this evidence revealed divine design more graphically and irrefutably than anyone might have imagined. In *Creation and Time* I showed how a reexamination of the biblical text, especially the Hebrew manuscripts and the writings of early church scholars, more clearly and consistently support the big bang model—namely, an old-universe, old-earth interpretation of the text—than they do any recent-creation scenario (i.e., one in which the universe is only a few thousand years old).

My latest book, *Beyond the Cosmos,* addresses the fear that advancing scientific knowledge may contradict biblical truths and undercut the Christian understanding of God as Creator-Redeemer. Thus in *Beyond the Cosmos* I show how recent developments in string theory support Christianity's foundational, and too often divisive, doctrines. Understanding string theory also gives us a renewed and enlarged sense of awe for the indescribably magnificent capacities of the Creator.

As the empirical support for big bang cosmology mounts and as the model becomes increasingly well understood, signs of a personal, transcendent, loving Creator become increasingly evident. Despite the skepticism of our age, we find the Creator revealed in clear and exciting ways. Many new discoveries are continually enlarging and enhancing the list of features that signal design behind the universe, our solar system, the earth and living things. The aim of this chapter is to present some of these key features that signal design. I begin with a brief review of how astronomy and astronomers work.

## Astronomy's Unique Perspective

Unlike other scientific disciplines, astronomy directly observes and measures the past. Because light travels at a fixed, finite velocity, we see and measure the conditions of astronomical objects as they were when the objects began radiating light toward us. When we look at the sun, for example, we see its conditions eight minutes ago, when the visible light and other radiation we now detect left the sun. When we map the Orion Nebula, we see it as it was 1,200 years ago. When we examine the center of our galaxy, we discover what was happening there 30,000 years ago. When we study the core of the Andromeda Galaxy, we observe what took place 2 million years ago.

Astronomers witness the past. To see how the creation was taking shape a certain number of years ago, we need only focus our instruments on objects the appropriate distance away. With recent technological advances, we can actually see all the way back to a split second after the cosmic explosion with which all the universe's time, space, matter and energy began.

In 1992 the Cosmic Background Explorer (COBE) satellite brought us the first image of the moment when light separated from darkness, an event that occurred when the cosmos was just one ten-thousandth of a percent of its current age. Heralded by Stephen Hawking as "the discovery of the century, if not of all time" (quoted in Hawkes 1992, 1), this finding made front-page headlines around the world for days. It was widely acknowledged by scientists as the strongest proof yet for a hot big bang and thus for the existence of a transcendent Initiator (Ross 1995a, 19-20).

The COBE image made such a splash because it solved one of the puzzling anomalies of the big bang model—the mystery of the clumpy, rather than smooth, distribution of matter throughout the universe. COBE research as well as subsequent research (Ross 1995a, 31-47; 1995b, 5; 1996c, 3-4) indicates that exotic matter (i.e., matter that does not strongly interact with radiation) is about four to eight times more abundant in the universe than ordinary matter. This constitution of matter explains why it would clump and gives credence to the big bang model. Most recently astronomers have identified at least three distinct kinds of exotic matter.

A later, less widely publicized set of COBE measurements provided even more direct and dramatic proof of the hot big bang (creation) model. These measurements showed that the cosmic background radiation (the radiation remaining from the creation event) fits the spectral profile of a perfect radiator to better than 0.03 percent precision over the entire range of wavelengths. In other words, the universe is a half billion times more entropic (i.e., more efficient in radiating heat and light) than a burning candle. Only one scientific explanation accounts for this extreme entropy measure: The universe must have started from a nearly infinitely hot and infinitely compact volume.

## The Latest Observations

With the dual 400-inch Keck telescopes, astronomers have been able to verify the cooling down of the big bang by measuring the effects of the cosmic background radiation in extremely distant gas clouds. According to the big bang, at such great distances we are seeing the universe in a much younger and more compact state than today. Hence the radiation from the creation event should be hotter than it is now. The cooling curve astronomers observe precisely matches what the big bang model predicts.

In addition to measuring the cosmic cool-off, astronomers can now observe the maturation of galaxies from infancy to middle age (their current developmental stage). By sending us images of different types of galaxies at distances ranging from 50 million to 14 billion light years (Flam 1994, 1806; Goldsmith 1996, 450), the Hubble space telescope has given us a stop-action view of galaxy development, like a photo album of our life from babyhood until today. One of the latest sets of photo images shows us an epoch before galaxies existed, like a photo of your parents just before you were born. Only the building blocks—small clumps of hot young stars—of galaxies are visible in these shots (Glanz 1996a, 756). Such images of the prehistories and life histories of various galaxies give the most visually convincing testimony yet that the cosmos arose from a powerful creation event.

Additional convincing evidence for the hot big bang creation event has come from research into the relative abundances of various elements throughout the cosmos. Since stars can synthesize only some of these elements, an independent nuclear furnace must have generated the remainder. The only plausible candidate for this quantity and quality of nuclear fusion is the big bang itself, and only when the cosmos was between three and four minutes old. The combined effects of the big bang and 15 billion years of stellar burning result in exactly the abundance of elements we find in the universe. No other model comes close.

In 1995 a space shuttle telescope measured an abundance of helium in some distant intergalactic clouds. These clouds predate stars, galaxies and all other compact astronomical bodies. Whatever helium exists there could only have come from the first four minutes of the big bang. This measurement then gives us a reality check on the big bang model. We know that helium comprises 26 percent of all ordinary matter in the universe and that only 2 percent of the helium comes from stellar burning. If the universe did indeed arise from a hot big bang, the quantity of helium in these ancient clouds should amount to 24 percent. That is exactly the proportion measured by the shuttle. This finding ranks as one of the most direct and unambiguous confirmations of the hot big bang creation event (Ross 1995b, 5).

## Resolution of Expansion Rate "Crisis"

For more than a decade two groups of astronomers, using different measuring techniques, have been producing discordant values for the universe's expansion rate. One group claimed a value of 80 km/sec/megaparsec (one parsec = 3.26 light years) while the other group stood by a value of 55 km/sec/megaparsec. The higher value yields a creation date of 8.4 to 12.5 billion years ago (the difference depends on the universe's mass density). The lower yields a creation date between 12.2 and 18.2 billion years ago. These dates were at odds with those indicated by the oldest stars and by the abundances of radiometric elements (17 and 16 billion years, respectively).

To help clear up this discrepancy (along with the resulting feud among astronomers), measuring the cosmic expansion rate became the Hubble space telescope's (HST's) top priority. One of the first such measurements to come from the HST suggested a value of 877 km/sec/mpc. Assuming a mass density for the universe large enough (though clearly improbable) to eventually halt its expansion, the research team made a bold announcement to the press: "The universe is only about half as old as scientists formerly thought—about 8 billion years old." Because of the huge discrepancy with the dating of the oldest stars and other age indicators, the big bang model was declared "in crisis."

The public heard nothing about two earlier sets of HST measurements indicating expansion rate values of 7311 and 529 km/sec/mpc. Few if any newspapers reported that the universe's mass density measures to be only about one-fifth the value that would be needed to eventually halt the universe's expansion.

Since that controversial announcement appeared, seven more sets of expansion rate measurements have been published, all with smaller error bars (Cowen 1996a, 292; Saha et al. 1995, 8-26; Sandage et al. 1996, L15-L18; Sandage and Tammann 1995, pp. 1-11; Schaefer, 1996, pp. L19-L23; Tammann and Sandage 1995, 16-24; Tanvir et al. 1995, 27-31). The methods used as well as the expansion values are given in table 15.1. The creation-date calculations are based on the mean of five recent, independent mass density measures (Coles and Ellis 1994, 609-13; Cowen 1996b, 246; Glanz 1996c, 1590; Hogan 1994, 374-75; Peebles 1993, 475-83).

Meanwhile, research dating the oldest stars, which are contained in globular clusters, has advanced significantly. Four American and Canadian astronomers have just completed exhaustive calculations of stellar burning rates in the seventeen oldest globular clusters associated with our galaxy (Chaboyer et al. 1996, 957-61). The mean age the team derived for such stars was 14.6 ± 1.3 billion years. The best determinations for the time interval between the creation event and the formation of these early stars range from 0.1 to 1.0 billion years. Therefore the so-called discrepancy between the age of the universe and the ages of the oldest stars has been completely removed. As table 15.2 indicates, all the methods for measuring the date of the universe's creation are tending toward the same answer, giving us yet more support for the big bang creation event.

| method | expansion rate | creation date |
| --- | --- | --- |
| cepheid stars in NGC 4639 | $57 \pm 4$ km/s/mpc | 16 Gyr |
| cepheid stars in NGC 4496 | $62 \pm 5$ km/s/mpc | 15 Gyr |
| cepheid stars in NGC 5253 | $52 \pm 8$ km/s/mpc | 18 Gyr |
| globulars in Virgo Cluster | $55 \pm 7$ km/s/mpc | 17 Gyr |
| supernovae recalibration | $57 \pm 4$ km/s/mpc | 16 Gyr |
| cepheids in M96 | $69 \pm 8$ km/s/mpc | 14 Gyr |
| cepheids in NGC 1365 | $73 \pm 8$ km/s/mpc | 13 Gyr |

mean date for creation: $15.31 \pm 1.6$ Gyr

**Table 15.1   Best Measurements of the Expansion of the Universe up to 1996.8**

| method | creation date |
| --- | --- |
| expansion rate of the universe | $15.3 \pm 1.6$ Gyr |
| burning and formation times of the oldest stars | $15.1 \pm 1.6$ Gyr |
| decay of the radiometric elements | $16.0 \pm 4.0$ Gyr |
| time interval when intelligent physical life is possible | $17.0 \pm 7.0$ Gyr |

mean date for creation: $15.4 \pm 1.6$ Gyr

**Table 15.2   Four Independent Measures of the Date for the Cosmos's Creation Method**

## Loopholes Tighten

The preponderance of evidence has all but eliminated secular opposition to the hot big bang model. Five astronomers who still resist the evidence admit that they do so for nonscientific reasons, disliking the theistic implications. When the five recently collaborated on an article for *Nature,* the famed British journal printed a black frame around each page, boldly imprinted with the warning "hypothesis"—an unprecedented editorial decision.

For these holdouts one of the despised implications of the hot big bang model issues from the work of Stephen Hawking, George Ellis and Roger Penrose. In 1970 these three proved that if the equations of general relativity are valid and if the universe contains any measurable mass, then space and time must have originated concurrently with matter and energy. In other words, time itself is finite and had a beginning outside of the universe's boundaries.

Obviously the universe contains mass. But in 1970 a small shadow of doubt still hovered over general relativity, leaving room for speculation. Ten years later, however, a NASA rocket experiment all but erased that shadow, shrinking it to less than a hundredth of a percent. In 1994 a team led by radio astronomer Joseph Taylor used 21 years of measurements on the orbital periods of binary pulsar PSR 1913+16 (two neutron stars orbiting one another) to confirm general relativity to a precision of 99,999,999,999,999 parts in a hundred trillion. In Penrose's words, this finding made Einstein's theory of general relativity "the most accurately tested theory known to science" (Penrose 1994, 230).

The origin of matter, energy, space and time in a singular hot big bang establishes that the source of the universe is independent of its space-time dimensions. Indeed its source is a Creator who exhibits both personality and complete transcendence.

## Extradimensional Creation

The Creator's transcendence has been dramatically confirmed and extended. The breakthroughs came as physicists and astronomers tackled two previously intractable problems facing the big bang models. The first dilemma was this: treating fundamental particles as point entities (the traditional view) made unifying any of the four forces of physics impossible. Since we have both theoretical and experimental proof that this unification can and did occur for the weak nuclear force and the electromagnetic force, a new approach to fundamental particles was required. That new approach introduced lines or loops of energy, called strings. When theoreticians treated fundamental particles as highly stretched, vibrating, rotating elastic bands undergoing the extreme heat of the first split second of creation, the dilemma disappeared. Strings behave as points under subsequent cooler conditions but not in the crucial beginning moment. Counterintuitively strings require more than three spatial dimensions. To operate they need more room than three dimensions have to offer; they need several dimensions beyond the ones of ordinary experience.

The second dilemma was that in the current space-time dimensions of the universe, all gravitational theories imply that quantum mechanics is impossible, and all quantum mechanical theories imply that gravity is impossible. Andrew Strominger hypothesized a brilliant resolution in the form of "extremal" (i.e., very small) black holes, which become massless at critical moments (Breckenridge et al. 1996, 423-26; Callan and Maldacena 1996, 591-608; Maldacena and Strominger 1996, 428-29; Strominger and Vafa 1996, 99-104; Taubes 1995, 1699). At first, however, he seemed merely to have traded one dilemma for another. Black holes are massive objects so highly collapsed that their gravity attracts anything within proximity. How can a black hole be massless without violating the definition of a black hole or without violating the principles of gravity? Simply put, how can there be gravity without mass?

The answer lay once again in extradimensionality. Strominger discovered that in six spatial dimensions the mass of an extremal black hole is proportional to its surface area. As the surface shrinks, the mass eventually becomes zero. The resolution works given the existence of at least six extra spatial dimensions.

String theory therefore solves the two troubling dilemmas (Ross 1996a, 21-33). Accordingly the theory tells us that the universe was created with ten rapidly expanding space-time dimensions. When the universe was just $10^{-43}$ seconds old, the moment when gravity separated from the strong-electroweak force, six of these ten dimensions ceased to expand. Today these six dimensions still remain as a component of the universe, but they are as tightly curled up as when the universe was only $10^{-43}$ seconds old, having a diameter of $10^{-33}$ centimeters, so small as to be virtually undetectable.

Four lines of evidence indicate that this theory is correct (Ross 1996a, 28-30). Perhaps the most convincing is that string theory produces as a bonus all of the equations of special and general relativity. In other words, if we knew nothing at all about relativity, this ten-dimensional string theory would have revealed relativity theory in complete form. Such profound, precise corroboration is both rare and wonderful in scientific research. Moreover, it has important implications for Christian theology, helping to explain certain mysteries and paradoxes that have puzzled biblical scholars for centuries.

1. God existed before the universe. God exists totally apart from the universe and yet can be everywhere within it (Gen 1:1; Col 1:16-17).

2. Time has a beginning. God's existence and cause-and-effect activities precede time (2 Tim 1:9; Tit 1:2).

3. Jesus Christ created the universe. He has no beginning and was not created (Jn 1:3; Col 1:16-17).

4. God created the universe from what cannot be detected with the five senses (Heb 11:3).

5. After his resurrection Jesus could pass through walls in his physical body, an evidence of his extradimensionality (Lk 24:36-43; Jn 20:26-28).

6. God is very near, yet we cannot see him—a further suggestion of his extradimensionality (Ex 33:20; Deut 30:11-14; Jn 6:46).

7. God designed the universe in such a way that it would support human beings (Gen 1—2; Neh 9:6; Job 38; Ps 8:3; Is 45:18).

**Table 15.3  Biblical Cosmology Confirmed via Extradimensionality**

**Design Parameters**

As helpful as big bang cosmology has been in attesting to the Creator's existence and transcendence, it has provided even greater service in attesting to the Creator's personality. The more we learn about the physics of the universe, the more clearly we see reflected not only the awesome power but also the mind and heart of the One who planned and initiated and sustains all things, inanimate and animate. Big bang cosmology is elucidating the universe and in so doing rendering the design of the universe irrefutable. Astronomers and physicists widely acknowledge that the only reasonable explanation for the intricately harmonious features of the universe, our solar system, our planet—all ingeniously focused on the requirements for life—is the action and ongoing involvement of a personal, intelligent Creator.

In 1961 Robert Dicke was the first to suggest that gravity required fine-tuning if life—any conceivable kind of life—were to be possible anywhere and at any time in the universe. In 1963 Carl Sagan calculated two more characteristics requiring fine-tuning, namely, the mass of a star and the distance of a planet from its star. In the first printing of *The Fingerprint of God* (1989), I listed sixteen characteristics of the universe and another nineteen of the solar system that must be fine-tuned to make life possible and sustainable. In the most recent edition of *The Creator and the Cosmos* (1995), those lists had grown to twenty-six characteristics for the universe and forty-one for the solar system. The pace of new discoveries demonstrating design in the universe and solar system has escalated dramatically, so much so that I now publish a quarterly update. The most recent of these updates describes thirty-two characteristics for the universe and seventy-five for the solar system.

A summary of the twenty-nine characteristics of the universe that must be fine-tuned for any kind of physical life to be possible appears in table 15.4. Table 15.5 describes the fine-tuning necessary in forty-five characteristics of the solar system. Table 15.6 gives a conservative calculation of the probability that all these (and more) characteristics of the solar system, acknowledged as fine-tuned for life, could be met without invoking design. References to the discoveries on which these tables and calculations are based but not published in my previous works are Burrows and Lumine 1995, 333; Editors 1996, 18, 21; Glanz 1996b, 449-50; Gonzalez 1997; Jayawardhana 1994, 1527; Kerr 1996, 814-15; Lieb, Loss, and Solowej 1995, 985-989; Mayor and Queloz 1995, 355-59; Muller and MacDonald 1995, 107-8; Ross 1995c, 1-3; 1996a, 32-33; 1996b, 1-3; 1997, in press; Rye, Kuo, and Holland 1995, 603-5; Snow and Witt 1995, 1455-57; Wetherell 1995, 470; White and Keel 1992, 129-30; White, Keel, and Corselice 1996; Zuckerman, Forveille, and Kastner 1995, 494-96.

---

1. strong nuclear force constant

    if larger: no hydrogen; nuclei essential for life would be unstable

    if smaller: no elements other than hydrogen

2. weak nuclear force constant

    if larger: too much hydrogen converted to helium in big bang, hence too much heavy element material made by star burning; no expulsion of heavy elements from stars

    if smaller: too little helium produced from big bang, hence too little heavy element material made by star burning; no expulsion of heavy elements from stars

3. gravitational force constant

    if larger: stars would be too hot and would burn up quickly and unevenly

    if smaller: stars would be so cool that nuclear fusion would not ignite, thus no heavy element production

4. electromagnetic force constant

    if larger: insufficient chemical bonding; elements more massive than boron would be unstable to fission

    if smaller: insufficient chemical bonding

5. ratio of electromagnetic force constant to gravitational force constant

    if larger: no stars less than 1.4 solar masses, hence short and uneven stellar burning

    if smaller: no stars more than 0.8 solar masses, hence no heavy element production

6. ratio of electron to proton mass

    if larger: insufficient chemical bonding

    if smaller: insufficient chemical bonding

7. ratio of number of protons to number of electrons

    if larger: electromagnetism dominates gravity preventing galaxy, star and planet formation

    if smaller: electromagnetism dominates gravity preventing galaxy, star and planet formation

8. expansion rate of the universe

    if larger: no galaxy formation

    if smaller: universe collapses prior to star formation

9. entropy level of the universe

    if larger: no star condensation within the protogalaxies

    if smaller: no protogalaxy formation

10. mass density of the universe

    if larger: too much deuterium from big bang, hence stars burn too rapidly

    if smaller: insufficient helium from big bang, hence too few heavy elements forming

11. velocity of light

    if larger: stars would be too luminous

    if smaller: stars would not be luminous enough

12. age of the universe

    if older: no solar-type stars in a stable burning phase in the right part of the galaxy

    if younger: solar-type stars in a stable burning phase would not yet have formed

13. initial uniformity of radiation

    if smoother: stars, star clusters and galaxies would not have formed

    if coarser: universe by now would be mostly black holes and empty space

14. average distance between galaxies

    if larger: insufficient gas would be infused into our galaxy to sustain star formation for a long enough time

    if smaller: the sun's orbit would be too radically disturbed

15. galaxy cluster type

    if too rich: galaxy collisions and mergers would disrupt solar orbit

    if too sparse: insufficient infusion of gas to sustain star formation for a long enough time

16. average distance between stars

    if larger: heavy element density too thin for rocky planets to form if smaller: planetary orbits would become destabilized

17. fine structure constant (a number used to describe the fine structure splitting of spectral lines)

if larger: no stars more than 0.7 solar masses

if smaller: no stars less than 1.8 solar masses

if larger than 0.06: matter is unstable in large magnetic fields

18. decay rate of the proton

if greater: life would be exterminated by the release of radiation

if smaller: insufficient matter in the universe for life

19. $^{12}$C to $^{16}$O nuclear energy level ratio

if larger: insufficient oxygen

if smaller: insufficient carbon

20. ground state energy level for $^4$He

if larger: insufficient carbon and oxygen

if smaller: insufficient carbon and oxygen

21. decay rate of $^8$Be

if slower: heavy element fusion would generate catastrophic explosions in all the stars

if faster: no element production beyond beryllium and hence no life chemistry possible

22. mass excess of the neutron over the proton

if greater: neutron decay would leave too few neutrons to form the heavy elements essential for life

if smaller: proton decay would cause all stars to rapidly collapse into neutron stars or black holes

23. initial excess of nucleons over antinucleons

if greater: too much radiation for planets to form

if smaller: not enough matter for galaxies or stars to form

24. polarity of the water molecule

if greater: heat of fusion and vaporization would be too great for life to exist

if smaller: heat of fusion and vaporization would be too small for life; liquid water would be too inferior of solvent for life chemistry to proceed; ice would not float, leading to a runaway freeze-up

25. supernovae eruptions

if too close: radiation would exterminate life on the planet

if too far: not enough heavy element ashes for the formation of rocky planets

if too infrequent: not enough heavy element ashes for the formation of rocky planets

if too frequent: life on the planet would be exterminated

if too soon: not enough heavy element ashes for the formation of rocky
planets

if too late: life on the planet would be exterminated by radiation

26. white dwarf binaries

if too few: insufficient fluorine produced for life chemistry to proceed

if too many: disruption of planetary orbits from stellar density; life on the
planet would be exterminated

if too soon: not enough heavy elements made for efficient fluorine
production

if too late: fluorine made too late for incorporation in protoplanet

27. ratio of the mass of exotic matter to ordinary matter

if smaller: galaxies would not form

if larger: universe would collapse before solar type stars can form

28. number of effective dimensions in the early universe

if smaller: quantum mechanics, gravity and relativity could not coexist,
and life would be impossible

if larger: quantum mechanics, gravity and relativity could not coexist, and
life would be impossible

29. number of effective dimensions in the present universe

if smaller: electron, planet, and star orbits would become unstable

if larger: electron, planet, and star orbits would become unstable

---

**Table 15.4  Evidence for the Fine-Tuning of the Universe**

The following parameters of a planet, its moon, its star and its galaxy must
have values falling within narrowly defined ranges for life of any kind to exist.
Characteristics 4 and 5 are repeated from table 15.4 since they apply to both
the universe and the galaxy.

---

1. galaxy size

if too large: infusion of gas and stars would disturb sun's orbit and ignite
too many galactic eruptions

if too small: insufficient infusion of gas to sustain star formation for long
enough time

2. galaxy type

if too elliptical: star formation would cease before sufficient heavy element buildup for life chemistry

if too irregular: radiation exposure on occasion would be too severe and
heavy elements for life chemistry would not be available

3. galaxy location

if too close to a rich galaxy cluster: galaxy would be gravitationally disrupted

if too close to very large galaxy(ies): galaxy would be gravitationally disrupted

4. supernovae eruptions

if too close: life on the planet would be exterminated by radiation

if too far: not enough heavy element ashes would exist for the formation of rocky planets

if too infrequent: not enough heavy element ashes present for the formation of rocky planets

if too frequent: life on the planet would be exterminated

if too soon: not enough heavy element ashes would exist for the formation of rocky planets

if too late: life on the planet would be exterminated by radiation

5. white dwarf binaries

if too few: insufficient fluorine would be produced for life chemistry to proceed

if too many: planetary orbits disrupted by stellar density; life on planet would be exterminated

if too soon: not enough heavy elements would be made for efficient fluorine production

if too late: fluorine would be made too late for incorporation in proto-planet

6. proximity of solar nebula to a supernova eruption

if farther: insufficient heavy elements for life would be absorbed

if closer: nebula would be blown apart

7. timing of solar nebula formation relative to supernova eruption

if earlier: nebula would be blown apart

if later: nebula would not absorb enough heavy elements

8. parent star distance from center of galaxy

if farther: quantity of heavy elements would be insufficient to make rocky planets

if closer: galactic radiation would be too great; stellar density would disturb planetary orbits

9. parent star distance from closest spiral arm

if farther: quantity of heavy elements would be insufficient to make rocky planets

if closer: radiation from other stars would be too great; stellar density would disturb planetary orbits

10. number of stars in the planetary system

if more than one: tidal interactions would disrupt planetary orbit of life support planet

if less than one: heat produced would be insufficient for life

11. parent star birth date

if more recent: star would not yet have reached stable burning phase; stellar system would contain too many heavy elements

if less recent: stellar system would not contain enough heavy elements

12. parent star age

if older: luminosity of star would change too quickly

if younger: luminosity of star would change too quickly

13. parent star mass

if greater: luminosity of star would change too quickly; star would burn too rapidly

if less: range of planet distances for life would be too narrow; tidal forces would disrupt the life planet's rotational period; ultraviolet radiation would be inadequate for plants to make sugars and oxygen

14. parent star color

if redder: photosynthetic response would be insufficient

if bluer: photosynthetic response would be insufficient

15. parent star luminosity relative to speciation

if increases too soon: runaway greenhouse effect would develop

if increases too late: runaway glaciation would develop

16. surface gravity (escape velocity)

if stronger: planet's atmosphere would retain too much ammonia and methane

if weaker: planet's atmosphere would lose too much water

17. distance from parent star

if farther: planet would be too cool for a stable water cycle

if closer: planet would be too warm for a stable water cycle

18. inclination of orbit

if too great: temperature differences on the planet would be too extreme

19. orbital eccentricity

if too great: seasonal temperature differences would be too extreme

20. axial tilt

if greater: surface temperature differences would be too great

if less: surface temperature differences would be too great

21. rotation period

if longer: diurnal temperature differences would be too great

if shorter: atmospheric wind velocities would be too great

22. rate of change in rotation period

if longer: surface temperature range necessary for life would not be sustained if shorter: surface temperature range necessary for life would not be sustained

23. age

   if too young: planet would rotate too rapidly

   if too old: planet would rotate too slowly

24. magnetic field

   if stronger: electromagnetic storms would be too severe

   if weaker: ozone shield would be inadequately protected from hard stellar and solar radiation

25. thickness of crust

   if thicker: too much oxygen would be transferred from the atmosphere to the crust

   if thinner: volcanic and tectonic activity would be too great

26. albedo (ratio of reflected light to total amount falling on surface)

   if greater: runaway glaciation would develop

   if less: runaway greenhouse effect would develop

27. asteroidal and cometary collision rate

   if greater: too many species would become extinct

   if less: crust would be too depleted of materials essential for life

28. mass of body colliding with primordial earth

   if smaller: earth's atmosphere would be too thick; moon would be too small

   if greater: earth's orbit and form would be too greatly disturbed

29. timing of body colliding with primordial earth

   if earlier: earth's atmosphere would be too thick; moon would be too small

   if later: sun would be too luminous at epoch for advanced life

30. oxygen-to-nitrogen ratio in atmosphere

   if larger: advanced life functions would proceed too quickly

   if smaller: advanced life functions would proceed too slowly

31. carbon dioxide level in atmosphere

   if greater: runaway greenhouse effect would develop

   if less: plants would be unable to maintain efficient photosynthesis

32. water vapor level in atmosphere

   if greater: runaway greenhouse effect would develop

   if less: rainfall would be too meager for advanced life on the land

33. atmospheric electric discharge rate

   if greater: too much fire destruction would occur

   if less: too little nitrogen would be fixed in the atmosphere

34. ozone level in atmosphere

   if greater: surface temperatures would be too low

if less: surface temperatures would be too high; there would be too much ultraviolet radiation at the surface

35. oxygen quantity in atmosphere

if greater: plants and hydrocarbons would burn up too easily

if less: advanced animals would have too little to breathe

36. seismic activity

if greater: too many life forms would be destroyed

if less: nutrients on ocean floors from river runoff would not be recycled to continents through tectonics; not enough carbon dioxide would be released from carbonates

37. volcanic activity

if greater: too many life forms would be destroyed

if less: not enough carbon dioxide and water would be released into the atmosphere

38. oceans-to-continents ratio

if greater: diversity and complexity of life forms would be limited

if smaller: diversity and complexity of life forms would be limited

39. global distribution of continents (for earth)

if too much in the southern hemisphere: seasonal differences would be too severe for advanced life

40. soil mineralization

if too nutrient-poor: diversity and complexity of life forms would be limited

if too nutrient-rich: diversity and complexity of life forms would be limited

41. quantity of forest and grass fires

if too many: too much destruction of plant and animal life

if too few: not enough charcoal returned to soil, limiting biomass and diversity of life

42. gravitational interaction with a moon

if greater: tidal effects on the oceans, atmosphere and rotational period would be too severe

if less: orbital obliquity changes would cause climatic instabilities; movement of nutrients and life from the oceans to the continents and vice versa would be insufficient; magnetic field would be too weak

43. Jupiter distance

if greater: too many asteroid and comet collisions would occur on earth

if less: earth's orbit would become unstable

44. Jupiter mass

if greater: earth's orbit would become unstable

if less: too many asteroid and comet collisions would occur on earth

45. drift in major planet distances

    if greater: earth's orbit would become unstable

    if less: too many asteroid and comet collisions would occur on earth

---

**Table 15.5   Evidence for the Fine-Tuning of the Galaxy-Sun-Earth-Moon System for Life Support**

| Parameter | Probability of Galaxy, Star, Planet or Moon Falling in Required Range |
|---|---|
| galaxy size | .1 |
| galaxy type | .1 |
| galaxy location | .1 |
| star location relative to galactic center | .2 |
| star distance from closest spiral arm | .1 |
| proximity of solar nebula to a supernova eruption | .01 |
| timing of solar nebula formation relative to supernova eruption | .01 |
| number of stars in system | .2 |
| star birth date | .2 |
| star age | .4 |
| star mass | .001 |
| star luminosity relative to speciation | .0001 |
| star color | .4 |
| star's long term distance from galactic plane | .1 |
| supernovae rates and locations | .01 |
| white dwarf binary types, rates and locations | .01 |
| $H_3+$ production in galaxy | .3 |
| planetary distance from star | .001 |
| inclination of planetary orbit | .8 |
| axis tilt | .3 |
| rotation period | .1 |
| rate of change in rotation period | .05 |
| orbit eccentricity | .3 |
| surface gravity (escape velocity) | .001 |
| tidal force | .1 |
| magnetic field | .01 |
| albedo | .1 |
| density | .1 |
| thickness of crust | .01 |
| oceans to continents ratio | .2 |
| rate of change in oceans to continents ratio | .1 |
| global distribution of continents | .3 |
| asteroidal and cometary collision rate | .1 |
| mass of body colliding with primordial earth | .002 |
| timing of body colliding with primordial earth | .05 |
| rate of change in asteriodal and comet collision rate | .1 |
| position and mass of Jupiter relative to earth | .01 |
| eccentricity and regularity of Jupiter's and Saturn's orbits | .05 |

| | |
|---|---|
| drift and rate of drift in major planet distances | .1 |
| atmospheric transparency | .01 |
| atmospheric pressure | .1 |
| atmospheric electric discharge rate | .1 |
| atmospheric temperature gradient | .01 |
| carbon dioxide level in atmosphere | .01 |
| oxygen quantity in atmosphere | .01 |
| ozone quantity and location in atmosphere | .01 |
| water vapor level in atmosphere | .01 |
| oxygen to nitrogen ratio in atmosphere | .1 |
| quantity of greenhouse gases in atmosphere | .01 |
| soil mineralization | .1 |
| quantity of forest and grass fires | .1 |
| tectonic activity | .1 |
| rate of decline in tectonics | .1 |
| volcanic activity | .1 |
| rate of decline in volcanic activity | .1 |
| dependency factors | 10,000,000,000 |
| longevity requirements | .0001 |

Probability for occurrence of all 55 parameters = $10^{-69}$
Maximum possible number of planets in universe = $10^{22}$

Much less than 1 chance in one hundred billion trillion trillion trillion exists that even one such planet would occur anywhere in the universe.

**Table 15.6   An Estimate of the Probability for Attaining the Necessary Parameters for Life Support**

Thirty-five years of research on the anthropic principle (i.e., the principle that the universe tends to provide every necessity for human life) has steadily confirmed that the universe is designed. What we see is the exact opposite of the old God-of-the-gaps fallacy. As knowledge and understanding of the natural realm have advanced, it is those scientific explanations of the cosmos that avoid design that have run into trouble. Thirty-five years of research have moved so conclusively in the direction of design that astronomers who reject design no longer have a scientific basis for their position. As Ed Harrison remarks, any honest appraisal of the cosmos's finely tuned features leads to a moment of truth:

Here is the cosmological proof of the existence of God—the design argument of Paley—updated and refurbished. The fine tuning of the universe provides *prima facie* evidence of deistic design. Take your choice: blind chance that requires multitudes of universes, or design that requires only one. . . . Many scientists, when they admit their views, incline toward the teleological or design argument. (Harrison 1985, 252, 263)

To place one's confidence in blind chance and the unknowable existence of a virtually infinite number of universes is to commit a type of gambler's fallacy. For consider someone who argues that a single coin flipped ten thousand times and coming up heads all ten thousand times provides no evidence that the coin is biased in favor of heads over tails—after all, there might be $2^{10,000}$ coins and $2^{10,000}$ different coin flippers producing $2^{10,000}$ outcomes different from the observed result of 10,000 consecutive heads. What is the problem here? With no evidence whatsoever for the existence of $2^{10,000}$ coins, $2^{10,000}$ coin flippers or $2^{10,000}$ distinct outcomes, one posits an extremely large sample size simply to ensure that the improbability of the event in question will not be too small. This is both tendentious and fallacious. All we have evidence for in the case of the coin flipper is a sample of size one. Given one coin and one coin flipper and a finite number of flips, the most reasonable interpretation is that someone rigged either the coin or the flips to land heads 10,000 times in a row.

There is only one universe for which we have any evidence, and ours is it. General relativity tells us that since the first split second of the universe's existence, the space-time manifold of the universe has been thermodynamically closed. This means the space-time envelope of our universe cannot overlap the space-time envelope of any other hypothetical universe(s). Therefore either we can place our bets on the only universe we can ever possibly know, or we can speculate about hypothetical universes that will forever remain beyond human knowing. To bet that our universe fell in place exactly as it did, precisely suited for life, because innumerable chance events were taking place in universes causally inaccessible to ours makes even less sense than to bet that on the 10,001st toss the same coin that has come up heads on the previous 10,000 observed tosses will come up tails.

**Conclusion**
Christian theology has no reason to fear and every reason to embrace scientific research into the origin and characteristics of the universe. The more cosmologists learn, the stronger the evidence for the existence of God and for his identity as revealed in the Bible. Those who fight hardest against the design of the universe often produce the most powerful new evidences for it. As technology improves our tools for measuring the universe and as the scope and power of our scientific theories increases, the more compelling becomes the case for God as Creator and Redeemer. Though not many scholars who write about the new developments in cosmology acknowledge Jesus as Lord and Savior, they do admit that the best and perhaps the only explanation for the universe we observe is a Designer beyond the space-time continuum of the universe. In this admission they testify eloquently to the God who made us and wants to be known by us.

## References

Breckenridge, J. C., P. A. Lowe, R. C. Myers, A. W. Peet, A. Strominger, and C. Vafa. 1996. Macroscopic and microscopic entropy of near-extremal spinning black holes. *Physics Letters B* 381:423-26.

Burrows, A., and J. Lumine. 1995. Astronomical questions of origin and survival. *Nature* 378:333.

Callan, C. G., Jr., and J. M. Maldacena. 1996. D-brane approach to black hole quantum mechanics. *Nuclear Physics B* 472:591-608.

Chaboyer, B., P. Demarque, P. J. Kernan, and L. M. Krauss. 1996. A lower limit on the age of the universe. *Science* 271:957-61.

Coles, P., and G. Ellis. 1994. The case for an open universe. *Nature* 370:609-13.

Cowen, R. 1996a. Age of the cosmos: A first consensus. *Science News* 149:292.

———. 1996b. Deep images favor expanding universe. *Science News* 149:246.

Editors. 1996. The vacant interstellar space. *Discover* April:18, 21.

Flam, F. 1994. The space telescope spies on ancient galaxy menageries. *Science* 266:1806.

Glanz, J. 1996a. Galactic building blocks found. *Science* 271:756.

———. 1996b. Planets remind astronomers of home. *Science* 271:449-50.

———. 1996c. Precocious structures found. *Science* 272:1590.

Goldsmith, D. 1996. Digging deeply into galaxies' pasts. *Science* 271:450.

Gonzalez, G. 1997. Solar system bounces in the right range for life. *Facts & Faith* 11 (1):4-5.

Harrison, E. 1985. *Masks of the universe*. New York: Collier Books, Macmillan.

Hawkes, N. 1992. Hunt on for dark secret of the universe. *London Times*, 25 April.

Hogan, C. J. 1994. Cosmological conflict. *Nature* 371:374-75.

Jayawardhana, R. 1994. No alien Jupiters. *Science* 265:1527.

Kerr, R. A. 1996. Revised Galileo data leave Jupiter mysteriously dry. *Science* 272:814-15. Eleven technical papers on the Galileo Data appear in the same issue of *Science* (May 10, 1996).

Lieb, E. H., M. Loss, and J. P. Solovej. 1995. Stability of matter in magnetic fields. *Physical Review Letters* 75:985-89.

Maldacena, J. M., and A. Strominger. 1996. Statistical entropy of four-dimensional extremal black holes. *Physical Review Letters* 77:428-29.

Mayor, M., and D. Queloz. 1995. A Jupiter-mass companion to a solar-type star. *Nature* 378:355-59.

Muller, R. A., and G. J. MacDonald. 1995. Glacial cycles and orbital inclination. *Nature* 377:107-8.

Peebles, P. J. E. 1993. *Principles of physical cosmology*. Princeton, N.J.: Princeton University Press.

Penrose, R. 1994. *Shadows of the mind*. New York: Oxford University Press.

Ross, H. 1995a. *The Creator and the cosmos*. 2nd ed. Colorado Springs, Colo.: NavPress.

———. 1995b. Hot new evidence for the big bang creation event. *Facts & Faith* 9 (3):5.

———. 1995c. Lunar origin update. *Facts & Faith* 9 (1):1-3.

———. 1996a. *Beyond the cosmos*. Colorado Springs, Colo.: NavPress.

———. 1996b. New developments in Martian meteorite. *Facts & Faith* 10 (4):1-3.

———. 1996c. Refined maps help refine creation model. *Facts & Faith* 10 (2):3-4.

———. 1997. Wild fires under control. *Facts & Faith* 11 (1):1-2.

Rye, R., P. H. Kuo, and H. D. Holland. 1995. Atmospheric carbon dioxide concentrations before 2.2 billion years ago. *Nature* 378:603-5.

Saha, A., A. Sandage, L. Labhardt, H. Schwengeler, G. A. Tammann, N. Panagia, and F. D. Macchetto. 1995. Discovery of cepheids in NGC 5253: Absolute peak brightness of SN Ia 1895B and SN Ia 1972E and the value of Ho. *Astrophysical Journal* 438:8-26.

Sandage, A., et al. 1996. Cepheid calibration of the peak brightness of type Ia supernovae: Calibration of SN 1990N in NGC 4639 averaged with six earlier type Ia supernova calibrations to give Ho directly. *Astrophysical Journal* 460:L15-L18.

Sandage, A., and G. A. Tammann. 1995. Steps toward the Hubble constant: X the distance of the Virgo cluster core using globular clusters. *Astrophysical Journal* 466:1-11.

Schaefer, B. E. 1996. The peak brightness of SN 1960F in NGC 4496 and the Hubble constant. *Astrophysical Journal* 460:L19-L23.

Snow, T. P., and A. N. Witt. 1995. The interstellar carbon budget and the role of carbon in dust and large molecules. *Science* 270:1455-57.

Strominger, A., and C. Vafa. 1996. Microscopic origin of the Bekenstein-Hawking entropy. *Physics Letters B* 379:99-104.

Tammann, G. A., and A. Sandage. 1995. The Hubble diagram for supernovae of type Ia: II, The effect on the Hubble constant of a correlation between absolute magnitude and light decay rate. *Astrophysical Journal* 452:16-24.

Tanvir, N. R., T. Shanks, H. C. Ferguson, and D. R. T. Robinson. 1995. Determination of the Hubble constant from observations of cepheid variables in the galaxy M96. *Nature* 377:27-31.

Taubes, G. 1995. How black holes may get string theory out of a bind. *Science* 268:1699.

Wetherill, G. 1995. How special is Jupiter? *Nature* 373:470.

White, R., III, and W. C. Keel. 1992. Direct measurements of the optical depth in a spiral galaxy. *Nature* 359:129-30.

White, R., III, W. C. Keel, and C. Corselice. 1996. Seeing galaxies through thick and thin: I, Opticalical opacity measures and overlaping galaxies. *Astrophysical Journal* (in press).

Zuckerman, B., T. Forveille, and J. H. Kastner. 1995. Inhibition of giant-planet formation by rapid gas depletion around young stars. *Nature* 373:494-96.

# 16

# Design in Physics & Biology

## Cosmological Principle &
## Cosmic Imperative?

### ROBERT KAITA

**F**OR MUCH OF THE HISTORY OF WESTERN THOUGHT, IT WAS NOT considered improper for natural philosophers—or what we now call scientists—to think about design in nature. With the rise of modern science in the seventeenth century, however, this began to change. As Hansen observes,

> One example from the physics of harmony and resonance may clarify the transformation [of science]. In a world of essences and sympathies—the world of natural magic and medieval science—the qualitative differences between strings made of sheep gut and wolf gut sufficed to explain why the strings would be discordant, for there was natural antipathy between sheep and wolves. . . . [However,] by the 1630's the work of Galileo, Mersenne, and others established a mathematical relationship for the vibrating string, which came to be known as Mersenne's law. This scientific triumph epitomizes a transformation both of the terms of physical explanation and of the character of the fundamental units of nature. (Hansen 1986, 135-36)

Hansen concludes that the "new quantitative and mechanistic approach eventually established a new metaphysics that left no room" for design in nature and relegated anything that implied design to the realm of "something unreal, something supernatural in the modern sense" (Hansen 1986, 136).

This view of the history of modern science ignores that the very revolutionaries responsible for modern science embraced design in nature. For example, Johannes Kepler is widely admired as a great modern scientist, but as Gingerich points out, he never wavered in his "views of God as a geometer and of a universe filled with God's geometrical designs" (Gingerich 1994, 45). He quotes from Kepler's *Astronomia nova:*

> I implore my reader not to forget the divine goodness conferred on mankind, and which the psalmist urges him especially to consider. When he has returned from church and entered on the study of astronomy, may he praise and glorify the wisdom and greatness of the creator¼ Let him not only extol the bounty of God in the preservation of living creatures of all kinds by the strength and stability of the earth, but also let him acknowledge the wisdom of the Creator in its motion, so abstruse, so admirable. (Gingerich 1994, 45)

Kepler is here concerned with observation (i.e., what the data reveal), not proof. While the universe reflects the Creator, it does not demonstrate his existence. Nonetheless the worldview of the earliest modern scientists held that the book of Scripture reveals how the book of nature reflects the Creator. As expressed at the beginning of Psalm 19 (KJV), "The heavens declare the glory of God; and the firmament showeth his handiwork." Moreover Psalm 136 asserts that by wisdom God made the heavens. The universe is thus not a jumble of random, unconnected phenomena but instead follows certain laws of nature. This made science, or the search for these laws, a rational activity for Kepler and his contemporaries, and this is still implicitly assumed by all scientists. Far from abandoning it, therefore, modern science presupposed design to make the "new quantitative and mechanistic approach" possible.

Because the stated task of the physical sciences is to study the laws of nature, its practitioners have been among the most outspoken in alternately opposing or embracing design in the universe. It is not the purpose of this chapter to review the cosmological evidence for design in detail, as this has been done elsewhere (cf. Ross 1989, 121-32). Rather the purpose is to critique two principles that attempt to rid science of design, namely, Christian de Duve's cosmic imperative (CI) and the anthropic cosmological principle (ACP).

Hawking provides a brief statement of the ACP in *A Brief History of Time* by writing, "We see the universe the way it is because we exist. . . . [It is as old as it is because] it takes about that long for intelligent beings to evolve" (Hawking 1988, 124). In *Vital Dust: Life as a Cosmic Imperative* de Duve begins by asserting that "life is increasingly explained strictly in terms of the *laws of physics and chemistry*" and then attributes anthropic significance to these laws:

"the universe was—and presumably still is—pregnant with life. To me, this conclusion is inescapable. It is based on logic, not on an a priori philosophical tenet" (de Duve 1995a, 9). On the contrary, CI is precisely that, an a priori philosophical tenet. De Duve admits as much elsewhere when he asserts that natural processes alone are permitted "if we wish to remain within the realm of science" (de Duve 1995b, 428). This is the common basis CI shares with the ACP. It is also the source of their mutual difficulties, which are ultimately philosophical.

### The Physical Universe and Biological Systems

In his lectures on physics Richard Feynman compared scientific research with learning a game simply from watching it being played. Feynman focused specifically on chess. At first the reason for the variety of pieces is not obvious, and their motions seem arbitrary. After a while, however, it becomes clear that pieces of a certain type move in the same way. There may still be occasional surprises, such as the way pawns capture pieces and become queens, or castling, but the rules of the game are eventually learned from the patterns that are observed (Feynman 1967, 59-60). How does this analogy apply to physics? First, the rules in physics are simple enough so the game can be learned. Just as the rules of chess are finite, the equations governing the so-called physical laws, while often difficult to solve in specific cases, are relatively few in number.

For example, the basis for the entire discipline of plasma physics is Maxwell's equations. As reproduced in the *Plasma Formulary* (Huba 1994, 19), they are as follows (in Gaussian units):

$$\text{curl } \mathbf{E} = -(1/c)\partial\mathbf{B}/\partial t \text{ (Faraday's law)} \tag{1}$$

$$\text{curl } \mathbf{H} = (1/c)\ \partial\mathbf{D}/\partial t + 4\pi\mathbf{J}/c \text{ (Ampere's law)} \tag{2}$$

$$\text{div } \mathbf{D} = 4\pi\rho \text{ (Poisson equation)} \tag{3}$$

$$\text{div } \mathbf{B} = 0 \text{ (Absence of magnetic monopoles)} \tag{4}$$

$$q(\mathbf{E} + (1/c)\ \mathbf{v} \times \mathbf{B}) \text{ (Lorentz force on a charge q)} \tag{5}$$

$$\mathbf{D} = \varepsilon\mathbf{E} \text{ and } \mathbf{B} = \mu\mathbf{H} \text{ (Constitutive equations)} \tag{6}$$

Here, the variables have the usual definitions: $\mathbf{E}$ is the electric field strength, $\mathbf{D}$ is the electric displacement, $\mathbf{B}$ is the magnetic induction, $\mathbf{H}$ is the magnetic field strength, and $\mathbf{J}$ and $\rho$ are the current and charge densities, respectively. The names of the individual equations illustrate the process of how scientists initially formulated the individual laws named after them, as Ampere did when he first related the magnetic field and the electric current. This is analogous to assuming initially that the rules for the black and white chess pieces are different. The realization that they are in fact the same would then correspond to the relationship in Maxwell's equations between electricity and magnetism. It is particularly evident in the "free space" case where

$\rho = \mathbf{J} = 0$ and the permittivity ($\varepsilon$) and permeability ($\mu$) are both unity, so that the constitutive relationships as well as the first four equations clearly indicate a symmetric relation between the electric and magnetic fields.

Maxwell's work is often cited as the first example of a theoretical unification in modern physics. This has led to the belief that the rules of the game are indeed simple and the quest for a "theory of everything" that unifies the electromagnetic, weak, strong and gravitational forces is not futile. Maxwell's equations indicate that a few rules can make a vast number of physical phenomena comprehensible.

Contrast this with biology. For biology, de Duve has formulated what he calls the "constraints of chance." According to him, "evolution does not operate in a world of infinite possibilities in which a throw of the dice decides which possibility will become reality" (de Duve 1995a, 294). Rather he begins with the following rule:

> Mutations are not truly random events, in the sense of being ruled entirely by chance. Some areas in the genome are more sensitive to mutagenic influences than others, and this sensitivity itself varies according to genetic and environmental influences. Gene mutability has been woven by natural selection within a network of responses that all, one way or another, facilitate or hamper the mutability of certain genes in a manner favorable to the organism. This complex control has even some researchers to speculate about the possibility of "selective" or "adaptive" mutations. (de Duve 1995a, 294-95)

What sort of rule is this? Consider again the analogy with chess. Chess requires not only rules governing the movement of the pieces but also that the pieces have the right size. If they are too small to be seen by the participants or too large to be moved by them, the game cannot be played. Gingerich has pointed out a physical analog: differences of only a half a percent in the nuclear resonance levels of oxygen and carbon would have made the production of the latter impossible through stellar nucleosynthesis (Gingerich 1991, 392). Since nucleosynthesis is presently believed to be the source of carbon, on which life on earth depends, this important piece of the universe depends critically on a coincidence between what the universe needs to be to support life and what it actually is. Such coincidences suggest design. Ross lists sixteen further coincidences that suggest the universe was designed to be a fit habitat for human existence (Ross 1989, 121-28).

A biological analog, according to de Duve, is the scale of DNA modification required by macroevolution:

> Not all genetic changes are equally significant. It is now generally agreed that simple point mutations, those that result merely in the replacement of one nucleotide by another in a nucleic acid or of one amino acid by

another in a protein, rarely play a role in what is known as macroevolution, the kind of evolution we are talking about. Most often, the truly creative mutations involve whole chunks of DNA that are duplicated, inverted, transposed, or otherwise reshuffled. (de Duve 1995a, 295)

Moreover,

> Not all genes are equally significant targets of mutation. The genes concerned in nontrivial evolutionary steps most often belong to the small class of regulatory genes, such as homeotic genes. Run-of-the-mill "housekeeping" genes are rarely involved. It is striking that loss of enzymes, rather than gain of enzymes, has often accompanied evolutionary "progress." We humans are particularly indigent in this aspect, which is why we must find in our food so many vitamins and essential nutrients manufactured by so-called "lower" forms of life, which are, in fact, biochemically richer than we are. (de Duve 1995a, 295)

Finally we need to be sure our starting positions allow us to play an interesting (i.e., nontrivial) game. A form of chess can be imagined where only two kings are placed next to each other in the middle of the board, and whoever goes first wins by taking the opponent's king. Neither chess nor the universe appears to be designed that way. The standard big bang cosmology requires fine-tuning in the starting position of the universe. This model predicts too many regions that are causally disconnected (i.e., these regions have not yet had time to communicate with each other as the universe expanded; Guth 1981, 560). Furthermore, "a universe can survive approximately $10^{10}$ years only by extreme fine tuning of the initial values of [the energy density] and [the Hubble expansion constant (H)]" according to the standard model" (Guth 1981, 560).

The accuracy this requirement imposes on the energy density is around one part in $10^{55}$, depending on one's assumptions about the initial temperature (Guth 1981, 561). This conclusion follows because the entropy per comoving volume (S) of the universe is expressible in terms of H and an energy density factor ($\Omega$). In the standard model there is no reason why S should not start out on the order of unity and stay that way as the universe evolves. Because S is proportional to $[H^2(\Omega-1)]^{-2/3}$, and $H \approx (10^{10}\text{yr})^{-1}$, the constraint on the energy density results from the need for $\Omega-1$ to be extremely small (Blau and Guth 1987, 533).

The inflation model appears to resolve such difficulties. It has been described in terms of a phase transition, roughly similar to what occurs when a liquid solidifies. In classical thermodynamics, the change in molar entropy is exhibited in the latent heat of fusion. The analog in the inflation model is the energy provided by the symmetry breaking that is responsible for the different forces we now observe (Blau and Guth 1987, 579). Inflation permits the universe to expand by a factor of Z within the first $10^{-30}$ seconds or so of the universe. Since S(after inflation) $\gg$ $Z^3$S(before inflation), and the inflation model predicts Z to be as high as $10^{10,000,000,000}$, S can be very large. Therefore, $\Omega = 1$ to great accuracy, and the need for extreme fine-tuning of the energy density disappears (Blau and Guth 1987, 548). The problem of causally disconnected regions in the standard model is also solved, because communication between them occurred when the universe was much smaller than a simple extrapolation backward in time without inflation would imply.

There are still difficulties in the details of the inflation model, as even its originator admits (Blau and Guth 1987, 595). The symmetry breaking is part of what is referred to as the grand unified theory (GUT) for elementary particles. There are several candidates for such a theory, but none so far seem to satisfy both the drive mechanism for inflation and the properties of the universe as we presently observe them (Blau and Guth 1987, 589). Guth and Blau reply that "inflation is not a specific theory, but rather a mechanism that can be implemented in a number of different ways" (Blau and Guth 1987, 525), and this has led some to claim that "If you can find an inflationary theory which gives you anything you want, it's useless as a predictive theory" (Glanz 1996, 1168).

The best response to such criticisms is not to deny the inflation model's validity. Rather it is to examine the consequences of a successful GUT. There is no a priori reason why a GUT that accurately describes the workings of the universe cannot be found. If the quest is successful, it will be a triumph for the idea that rules govern every aspect of the universe. In addition it would lead to a conclusion even more remarkable than the fine-tuning of initial conditions. Clever indeed would then be the designer whose rules for the motion of the pieces actually dictate where they must be placed at the beginning of the game.

According to de Duve (1995a, 295), initial conditions are also important in biology, where they constrain the mutations that organisms can undergo:

Only in a given organismic context can a given genetic change be evolutionarily influential. Pre-existing body plans limit the possibilities of viable change. Once a direction has been taken, the possible scope of future change narrows, and it narrows even further with each subsequent evolutionary step. This explains the occurrence of evolutionary lines, as well as the increasing pace at which evolution often proceeds along such lines. The evolution of the horse is a textbook example. The ape-to-human transformation is a particularly striking one. (de Duve 1995a, 295)

Furthermore,

Related to the preceding condition, there is the historical, hierarchical factor. At each level of complexity, a different kind of genetic change becomes relevant. To take just a few examples, very early in the development of life, the most decisive changes were those that increased the accuracy of RNA replication. In the course of the prokaryote-eukaryote transition, the emergence of structured proteins, such as actin and tubulin, was an essential condition of cellular enlargement. In the formation of multicellular animals, cell adhesion molecules (CAM's) and the substrate adhesion molecules (SAM's) became pace-setting innovations. And so on. To each evolutionary phase its own type of mutations. (de Duve 1995a, 295)

De Duve stresses the importance of the rule that the environment drives natural selection and that "not every genetic change retained by natural selection is equally decisive" (de Duve 1995a, 295-96) He explains that "most changes have but a marginal impact on the unfolding of evolution," but "[k]ey mutations are those that determine a major fork in the tree of life" (de Duve 1995a, 296). However, de Duve is vague about the relationship between specific environmental factors and evolution through key mutations. For instance, in commenting on the role of natural catastrophes in evolution, he writes,

> Evolution is punctuated by massive extinctions, sometimes of cataclysmic proportions. Almost invariably, life's response has been remarkably innovative. Apparently, when evolution becomes sluggish, it is not so much for want of an appropriate chance mutation as for the lack of a worthy environmental challenge. (de Duve 1995a, 213)

The preceding observations about physics are uncontroversial. Davies summarizes our current thinking thus: "Even the most atheistic scientist accepts as an act of faith that the universe is not absurd, that there is a rational basis to physical existence manifested as a lawlike order [i.e., the rules of the game] in nature that is at least in part comprehensible to us. So science can proceed only if the scientist adopts an essentially theological worldview" (Davies 1995, 32).

However, de Duve's astonishment at "life's innovations" and the importance he attaches to the "worthiness" of an environmental challenge suggests that evolutionary biology does not yet possess the predictive power of physical theories. This, however, is not the key problem. Even if the ambiguities concerning the mechanism of evolution were resolved, the universe would still constitute an intelligently designed game, with rules, pieces and initial conditions that render it nontrivial. This nontriviality must hold for all sensible theories, whether they be in physics or biology.

## The Response to Design

The observations of physics and biology make sense only against a theoretical backdrop of rules. Aharoni has described the relationship between what he calls experimental (or observational) fact and theory:

It is wrong to say, "The apple falls from the tree because it is pulled by Earth's gravitational field." It is wrong because the Earth's gravitational field is a *theory*, while the falling of an apple is an experimental *fact*, which can be measured and verified. The *correct* way for a physicist to phrase the above statement is, "We *hypothesize* the existence of a gravitational field because we *observe* the apple falling from the tree." The difference between these two statements is the basis for the whole philosophy of physics. (Aharoni 1995, 33, emphasis added)

If the analogy between formulating scientific hypotheses and learning the rules of a game is sound, then so is design. Apart from an underlying design of the universe, the entire scientific enterprise of formulating scientific hypotheses becomes an exercise in futility.

This claim is controversial. Barrow and Tipler (1988) challenge it by formulating the ACP mentioned earlier. Barrow and Tipler formulated this principle in *The Anthropic Cosmological Principle*, which in de Duve's words is a "massive, vastly documented opus—700 pages, 600 mathematical equations, 1,500 notes and references" (de Duve 1995a, 289). Much of the mathematics in this book attempts to confirm that the pieces are indeed the right size for the game to be played. This is the upshot of the first of their anthropic principles:

Weak Anthropic Principle (WAP): The observed values of all physical and cosmological quantities are not equally probable but they take on values restricted by the requirement that there exist sites where carbon-based life can evolve and by the requirement that the universe be old enough for it to have already done so. . . . [T]hose properties we are able to discern are self-selected by the fact that they must be consistent with our evolution and present existence. (Barrow and Tipler 1988, 16)

Carter has introduced the still more speculative strong anthropic principle (SAP): "The Universe must have those properties which allow life to develop within it at some stage in its history" (Barrow and Tipler 1988, 21). This exceeds the WAP, which merely constrains whether a particular experimental observation is sensible, by requiring that the constants and laws of nature (the "rules, pieces, and initial conditions of the game") must enable life to exist. Barrow and Tipler claim that one interpretation of this principle is "religious" and "continue[s] in the tradition of the classical Design Arguments" of natural theology (Barrow and Tipler 1988, 22). "There exists one possible Universe 'designed' with the goal of generating and sustaining 'observers'" (Barrow and Tipler 1988,22).

Wheeler's interpretation of quantum mechanics puts another spin on the anthropic principle: "Observers are necessary to bring the Universe into existence" (Barrow and Tipler 1988, 22). Barrow and Tipler call this the participatory anthropic principle (PAP), and they add that it is closely related to an additional conclusion: "An ensemble of other different universes is necessary for the existence of our Universe" (Barrow and Tipler 1988, 22). They elaborate:

> This statement receives support from the 'Many Worlds' interpretation of quantum mechanics and a sum-over-histories approach to quantum gravitation because they must unavoidably recognize the existence of a whole class of *real* 'other worlds' from which ours is selected by an optimizing principle. (Barrow and Tipler 1988, 22)

The many worlds viewpoint is best illustrated by the famous two-slit diffraction experiment. In Feynman's version, a beam of electrons impinges on a tungsten plate with two holes in it. On the one hand electrons behave as bullet-like "lumps" because they can be detected individually by any electrical system that can pick up their discrete charge. On the other hand the electrons that are detected past the plate follow the distribution expected if they were waves (i.e., the maxima and minima characteristic of an interference pattern; Feynman 1967, 130-37). Furthermore, any experiment that attempts to determine which hole the electron actually passes through perturbs it in such a way that it indeed behaves like a bullet passing through armor plate and does not exhibit wave-like interference (Feynman 1967, 138-42). The reason, according to quantum theory, is that the probability of the outcome of a particular measurement is the square of its probability amplitude, or the wave function solution ($\psi$) of the time-dependent Schroedinger equation (Dirac 1958, 111):

$$i(h/2\pi)\partial\psi/\partial t = H\psi. \tag{7}$$

This is yet another example of our ability to predict the state of motion of a system by a simple equation, or rule, with just one real linear operator H, which corresponds to its total energy. The difficulty here is interpreting the solutions. According to Feynman,

> When an event can occur in several alternate ways, the probability amplitude [$\psi$] is the sum of the [$\psi$]'s for each of the various alternatives. If an experiment is performed which is capable of determining which alternative is taken, the probability of the event is changed; it is then the sum of the probabilities for each alternative. That is, you lose the interference. (Feynman 1967, 144-45)

One way to interpret this is that once the experiment is performed, the universe divides into a world that contains the outcome we observe, as well as another world that is forever separate and unobservable to us, where both alternatives are consistent with the probability amplitudes. This is the essence of the many worlds viewpoint (Barrow and Tipler 1988, 472-89).

The PAP's attraction to physicists, according to Barrow and Tipler, is that by making the other worlds real, the PAP promises to resolve certain fundamental questions in quantum mechanics and cosmology. Barrow and Tipler (1988, 503-4) also claim that "it has consequences that are potentially testable," because the PAP imposes specific boundary conditions on the wave function solution to the Schroedinger equation for the universe. They admit, however, that they do not yet know how to translate those boundary conditions into predictions that can be tested experimentally (Barrow and Tipler 1988, 505). It is thus not clear that the ability to resolve certain logical or conceptual difficulties alone, independent of experimental verification, offers particularly persuasive support of a hypothesis like the PAP.

Midgley offers a more fundamental criticism of the PAP. Her key point is that observation requires some kind of physical detection device, like a photographic plate or particle counter. An electron or photon may behave like a particle or a wave depending on how the measurement is performed. However, such observations are perfectly objective since for a given experimental configuration anybody will see the same interference pattern or record the same counts at a particular physical location. As a result, Midgley argues,

> the vast cosmic claims collapse into absurdity. Measuring devices, if they are really detached from human intentions, are just physical objects. On their own, in a world where no mind uses or understands them, grains of silver bromide can no doubt exist and respond to photons. But they do not measure or register or record anything at all. These words only have a sense when they describe acts carried out by enquirers. The grains could indeed still be affected causally by quantum events. But then so would other physical things, for instance the particles surrounding those events. None of these effects would have any meaning, any significance, any importance. None could possibly be credited with exciting roles in creating the cosmos. (Midgley 1992, 208)

Given these difficulties with the PAP, Barrow and Tipler consider yet one more anthropic principle:

> Suppose that for some unknown reason the SAP is true and that intelligent life must come into existence at some stage in the Universe's history. But if it dies out at our stage of development, long before it has had any measurable non-quantum influence on the Universe in the large, it is hard to see why it *must* have come into existence in the first place. This motivates the following generalization of the SAP: Final Anthropic Principle (FAP): Intelligent information-processing must come into existence in the Universe, and, once it comes into existence, it will never die out. (Barrow and Tipler 1988, 23)

They claim that the "FAP is a statement of physics and hence *ipso facto* has no ethical or moral content" (Barrow and Tipler 1988, 23). In fact it is very much a philosophical statement that not only asserts that the universe appears to be designed (the SAP) but that it would somehow reflect a "wasted effort" if intelligent life, as embodied in humanity as we know it, was all there was going to be. It is very much like the longing of many an agnostic that given all we are able to experience, feel and do, there must be a point to our existence beyond an ignominious return to dust after we die.

Barrow and Tipler share this longing. In the FAP they equate the meaning of intelligent life with immortality. Moreover, they claim to establish the immortality of intelligent life as follows (Barrow and Tipler 1988, 659):

(1) Any living creature is fundamentally a type of computer.

(2) What is really important in a computer is the program, not the hardware on which it runs.

(3) Humans may very well become extinct, but intelligent programs do not have to run on the "special hardware" of their bodies.

(4) Intelligent life can thus continue to exist forever as long as there is some type of construction material for the computer hardware and the energy to run them.

In the tradition of Aristotle and Aquinas they thus argue for something like an immortal soul (Barrow and Tipler 1988, 659). Their reduction of the human person to a computer program, however, remains highly controversial.

Though a biologist, de Duve draws conclusions largely similar to those of Barrow and Tipler. De Duve admits that a living cell exhibits such a high level of complexity that "there must, by necessity, be a very large number of steps, often modular in nature" (de Duve 1995a, 9) to construct it, as his list of rules for life attests. De Duve responds with his own version of the SAP. He explains that in the card game of bridge, each of four players are dealt thirteen cards from a deck with hearts, diamonds, spades and clubs (de Duve 1995a, 8). The odds of any player receiving all thirteen spades is one in 635 billion. He then goes on to describe how even more remarkable is the origin of life:

We are dealt thirteen spades not once but thousands of times in succession! This is utterly impossible, unless the deck is doctored. What this doctoring implies with respect to the assembly of the first cell is that most of the steps involved must have had a *very high likelihood of taking place under the prevailing conditions* [emphasis in the original]. Make them even moderately improbable and the process must abort, however many times it is initiated, because of the very number of steps involved. (de Duve 1995a, 9)

The universe, by de Duve's logic, must then be "pregnant with life" precisely because its emergence would be so improbable if it were not. The processes by which life originated, he goes on to state, must be natural, and since "[l]ife is increasingly explained strictly in terms of the laws of physics and chemistry" (de Duve 1995a, 10), he is convinced a physical basis for life's origins can be found. As noted earlier, however, de Duve supports this view by appealing to the philosophically dubious claim that "life arose spontaneously by natural processes—a necessary assumption if we wish to remain in the realm of science" (de Duve 1995b, 428) rather than by looking to empirical evidence. For de Duve empirical evidence seems to shed more darkness than light. Consider his discussion of the development of winged insects:

> Nobody knows how dragonflies, butterflies, bees, mosquitoes, and other flying insects won their wings. It is not even known whether they inherited their wings from a common ancestor or achieved flying separately by convergent evolution. Unlike the wings of other flying animals, those of insects are not modified limbs. They are formed by flattened outfoldings of the chitinous covering of the animal's back, which are moved by muscles of extraordinary performance efficiency. How such an amazing arrangement ever came into being is anybody's guess. (de Duve 1995a, 210)

The specter in the background here is reductionism. Polkinghorne, though agreeing that molecular biology has been successful in showing that no vital force is needed "to turn inanimate matter into a living being" (Polkinghorne 1986, 86), criticizes those who err on the other extreme of what he calls "thorough-going reductionism":

> I believe that those who defend the autonomy of their subject against the imperialist claims of physics are right to do so. Animals are made of atoms but that does not imply that biology is just a complicated corollary of atomic physics. Characteristically, biological concepts need for their understanding the total living setting in which they find their expression. Consider a sentence like: Molecular biology has given us considerable biochemical insight into how the genetic blueprint is encoded onto DNA and how messenger RNA transfers the appropriate parts of that plan to control the production of proteins. It speaks in a hopelessly mixed language. Biochemistry can talk about the molecular dynamics of aggregating amino acids to form proteins. The information-carrying 'blueprint' and 'plan' refers to a different and disjoint type of discourse which only begins to make sense in a cellular context. (Polkinghorne 1986, 87)

The consequences of reductionism and the problems it raises for science can be illustrated by comparing two rock formations. One is located in the Black Hills of southwestern South Dakota, namely, Mount Rushmore. Mount

Rushmore is a huge relief of the heads of George Washington, Thomas Jefferson, Abraham Lincoln and Theodore Roosevelt. There is no question that it was designed, as we know its sculptor, Gutzon Borglum (Caswell 1968, 962).

Now contrast Mount Rushmore with the most famous geological feature in the White Mountains of New Hampshire, namely, the "Profile" or the "Old Man of the Mountains." Nathaniel Hawthorne referred to it as the "Great Stone Face," and the formation became widely known through his short story by the same name. His description of it is as follows:

> The Great Stone Face, then, was a work of Nature in her mood of majestic playfulness, formed on the perpendicular side of a mountain by some immense rocks, which had been thrown together in such a position as, when viewed at a proper distance, precisely to resemble the features of a human countenance. It seemed as if an enormous giant, or a Titan, had sculpted his own likeness on the precipice. There was the broad arch of the forehead, a hundred feet in height; the nose, with its long bridge; the vast lips, which if they could have spoken, would have rolled their thunder accents from one end of the valley to the other. True it is, that if the spectator approached too near, he lost the outline of the gigantic visage, and could discern only a heap of ponderous and gigantic rocks, piled in a chaotic ruin one upon another. Retracing his steps, however, the wondrous features would again be seen; and the farther he withdrew from them, the more like a human face, with all of its original divinity intact, did they appear; until, as it grew dim in the distance, with the clouds and glorified vapor of the mountains clustering about it, the Great Stone Face seemed positively to be alive. (Pearson 1937, 1171)

I chose these two formations because of their similarity in scale and granite composition. Each head on Mount Rushmore is about sixty feet high, and although Hawthorne exaggerates, the "Great Stone Face" still stands at an impressive forty feet. Thoroughgoing reductionism would focus only on the comparable "heap of ponderous and gigantic rocks, piled in a chaotic ruin one upon another" at the base of both of these formations and demand that only the physical mechanism of how they got there fall within the purview of science. Although the laws of physics and chemistry operate identically at each location to describe how rocks fall and fracture, the laws of physics and chemistry alone cannot distinguish the designed sculpture from the natural geological feature.

All the same, science is not coextensive with these rules of the game. Science can distinguish the two rock formations precisely because it permits us to consider their total settings. This includes the ability to cite criteria that make Mount Rushmore recognizable as an intentional representation of four American presidents, and this is the basis for its meaning. De Duve, like Barrow and Tipler, implicitly acknowledges this when he too is not content in leaving all to reductionism. While not going as far as articulating the equivalent of the FAP, he expresses his discomfort by comparing the world-views of Pierre Teilhard de Chardin and Jacques Monod.

De Duve explains Teilhard de Chardin's vision as follows.

[M]ind and matter coexist in elementary form from the beginning of time and are jointly driven toward increasing complexity by the combined and complementary powers of these two forms of energy. Life emerged naturally from this "complexification" and went on to weave an increasingly elaborate fabric of living organisms on our planet. The evolution of this "biosphere" culminated in the appearance of humankind and consciousness. (de Duve 1995a, 287)

The meaning of our existence is then in the next step, which sounds very much like the FAP. It involves the creation of a "noosphere (from the Greek word for spirit or soul)" (de Duve 1995a, 287).

[The noosphere] is a planetary spiritual entity destined finally to converge, perhaps in association with other noospheres produced elsewhere in space, into point Omega, which is Teilhard's 'scientific' name for the God of his religion. (de Duve 1995a, 287)

This contrasts with de Duve's summary of Monod's views.

[B]iological evolution, far from being in any way directed by some sort of *élan vital*, radial energy, or other mystical force, depends entirely on random mutations (chance) screened by natural selection (necessity). There is no meaning, purpose, or design to be read in the appearance and evolution of life, even intelligent life. (de Duve 1995a, 288)

De Duve's writings betray a tension between advocating CI, which clearly conflicts with Monod's conclusion, and preferring Monod's conclusion over Chardin's separation of mind and matter in order to be consistent with the reductionist view that "all is physics and chemistry." De Duve's more fundamental problem, however, is his failure to recognize that reductionism is not required to do science. A strict adherence to reductionism creates difficulties for the scientist, as Polkinghorne and the discussion of the rock formations show. Instead of admitting this, de Duve holds that the structure of the universe is such that intelligent life had to emerge (as in the SAP) and finds its meaning in intelligent life. De Duve ends his book as follows:

I shall leave the last words to two other Frenchmen. Here, out of Pascal's *Pensées*, is God's message to the researcher: "Be consoled; you would not look for me if you had not already found me." Not all may find solace, or even meaning, in the message. Those who prefer to steer clear of metaphysics may, with Medawar, be content to follow the concluding advice

Voltaire put in the mouth of Candide: "We must cultivate our own garden." (de Duve 1995a, 302)

This is reminiscent of Weinberg's contention that in an otherwise pointless universe, the cultivating process of seeking answers to such questions through scientific research "is one of the very few things that lifts human life a little above the level of farce, and gives it some of the grace of tragedy" (Weinberg 1977, 144). This hardly inspires confidence in the scientific enterprise. The only way to have confidence in the scientific enterprise is by recognizing design in the universe and appropriately responding to its implications.

**Conclusion**

At the beginning of modern science, evidence for design in the universe was unproblematic. Scientists were motivated by "a desire to trace God's handiwork" (Gingerich 1994, 45). Even today, it should not disturb us to assert, in a paraphrase of Aharoni: "We hypothesize the existence of a designer because we observe the 'rules' governing the universe, and the 'fine tuning' of the conditions that allow us to exist." Such a claim does present a difficulty, however, for those who object to its philosophical implications. The ACP in its various incarnations and the CI are alternatives to design.

A determinism underlies the ACP and the CI. Hawking captures this determinism with his "no boundary proposal":

Einstein once asked the question: "How much choice did God have in constructing the universe?" If the no boundary proposal is correct, he had no freedom at all to choose initial conditions. He would, of course, still have had the freedom to choose the laws that the universe obeyed. This, however, may not really have been all that much of a choice; there may well be only one, or a small number, of complete unified theories, such as heterotic string theory, that are self-consistent and allow the existence of structures as complicated as human beings who can investigate the laws of the universe and ask about the nature of God. (Hawking 1988, 174)

Given Hawking's "no boundary proposal," there is no place for a creator save a creator who had no choice but to create our particular universe. Such a creator is hardly a creator in any traditional sense.

What place, then, for a creator? De Duve implicitly asks this question when he recognizes that the probability for the random occurrence of the sequence of events required for life to emerge is too small to conceive. The origin of life is therefore a necessity, he argues, and reflects the determinism in the laws of physics and chemistry. A creator now becomes superfluous because the creator has no options from which to choose.

This blanket rejection of design results not from any lack of evidence but from prejudice. Prejudice against design can be quite pedestrian. Consider the recent case of crop circles in Great Britain (Nickell 1995, 41-43). During the past few years, mysterious patterns were found in wheat fields taking the form of large, distinct geometric patterns. Nobody observed these patterns being formed, and speculation ran from intelligent causes, such as ingenious pranksters, or the perennial favorite, extraterrestrial beings, to natural phenomena. Finally a couple of men admitted responsibility and revealed that their equipment consisted of very large versions of the stylus and string that people have been using to make geometric figures since antiquity. These men worked at night and quickly—hence the difficulty in detecting them at work. In spite of this unequivocal evidence for design, some insisted that this did not explain all of the crop patterns and persisted in suggesting highly improbable natural causes.

We need always keep in mind two separate questions: How well does the evidence support design? and, Are we predisposed to reject design apart from the evidence? The first is a scientific question. The second is a philosophical question. Only if we reject the second question can we agree with Hamlet that "there are more things in heaven and earth, Horatio, than are dreamt of in your philosophy" (Wells and Taylor 1987, 1131-132).

### References
Aharoni, A. 1995. Agreement between theory and experiment. *Physics Today* 48 (6):33-37.
Barrow, J. D., and F. J. Tipler. 1988. *The anthropic cosmological principle*. Oxford: Oxford University Press.
Blau, S. K., and A. H. Guth. 1987. Inflationary cosmology. In *Three hundred years of gravitation*, ed. S. W. Hawking and W. Israel, 524-603. Cambridge: Cambridge University Press.
Caswell, J. E. 1968. Mount Rushmore National Memorial. *Encyclopedia Britannica* 15:962.
Davies, P. 1995. Physics and the mind of God. *First Things* 55:31-35.
de Duve, C. 1995a. *Vital dust: The origin and evolution of life on earth*. New York: Basic-Books.
———. 1995b. The beginnings of life on earth. *American Scientist* 83 (5):428-37.
Dirac, P. A. M. 1958. *The principles of quantum mechanics*. Oxford: Oxford University Press.
Feynman, R. 1967. *The character of physical law*. Cambridge, Mass.: MIT Press.
Gingerich, O. 1991. Let there be light: Modern cosmogony and biblical creation. In *The world treasury of physics, astronomy and mathematics*, ed. T. Ferris, 378-94. Boston: Little, Brown.
———. 1994. Is there a role for natural theology today? In *Science and theology: Questions at the interface*, ed. M. Rae, H. Regan, and J. Stenhouse, 29-45. Edinburgh: T & T Clark.

Glanz, J. 1996. Debating the big questions. *Science* 273:1168-70.

Guth, A. 1981. Inflationary universe: A possible solution to the horizon and flatness problems. *Physical Review D* 23 (2):560-69.

Hansen, B. 1986. The complementarity of science and magic before the scientific revolution. *American Scientist* 74 (2):128-36.

Hawking, S. J. 1988. *A brief history of time.* New York: Bantam.

Huba, J. D. 1994. *Plasma formulary.* Washington, D.C.: Naval Research Laboratory Publication NRL/PU/6790—94-265.

Midgley, M. 1992. *Science as salvation: A modern myth and its meaning.* London: Routledge.

Nickell, J. 1995. Crop circle mania wanes: An investigative update. *Skeptical Inquirer* 19:41-43.

Pearson, N. H., ed. 1937. *The complete novels and selected tales of Nathaniel Hawthorne.* New York: Random House.

Polkinghorne, J. 1986. *One world: The interaction of science and theology.* Princeton, N.J.: Princeton University Press.

Ross, H. 1989. *The fingerprint of God.* Orange, Calif.: Promise Publishing.

Weinberg, S. 1977. *The first three minutes: A modern view of the origin of the universe.* New York: Bantam.

Wells, S., and G. Taylor, eds. 1987. *The complete Oxford Shakespeare.* Oxford: Oxford University Press.

# 17

# Gödel's Question[1]

## DAVID BERLINSKI

*The affirmation of being is the purpose and the cause of the world.—Kurt Gödel*

**D**ESPITE A RICH AND MARVELOUSLY UNINTERESTING BODY OF WORK devoted to mathematical population genetics, the claims of Darwin's theory and of Darwinian theories generally have often seemed fantastic, especially to mathematicians. "[T]he formation within geological time of a human body," Kurt Gödel remarked to the logician Hao Wang, "by the laws of physics (or any other laws of similar nature), starting from a random distribution of elementary particles and the field, is as unlikely as the separation by chance of the atmosphere into its components" (Wang 1995, 173).

"The complexity of living bodies," Gödel went on to say, Hao Wang listening without comment, "has to be present either in the material [from which they are derived] or in the laws [governing their formation]." In this Gödel seemed to be claiming without argument that complexity is subject to a principle of conservation, much like energy or angular momentum. Every human body is derived from yet another human body; complexity is in reproduction transferred from one similar structure to another. The immediate complexity of the human body is thus present in the matter from which it is derived; but on Darwin's theory, human beings as a species are, by a process of random variation and natural selection, themselves derived from other structures, the process tapering downward until the rich panorama of organic life is driven into an inorganic and thus a relatively simple point. The origin of complexity thus lies—it *must* lie—with laws of matter and thus with laws of physics.

In these casual inferences Gödel was in some measure retracing a version of the argument from design. The manifest complexity of living creatures suggested to William Paley an inexorably providential designer. Cancel the theology from the argument and a connection emerges between complexity and some form of intelligence.[2] And with another cancellation, a connection between complexity and the laws of physics.

These algebraic operations shift the argument's shape without entirely altering its conclusions. They suggest that on Gödel's view, complexity has no ultimate metaphysical source. It may be transferred, as when an artist fabricates a painting or a statue, endowing durable pigment or stone with the complexity already latent in his mind; it may be shuffled by various combinatorial processes, but it cannot be created. The inferential trail that begins in wonder ends not with an infinitely accomplished designer but with a principle instead, one that assimilates complexity to conserved quantities in mechanics.[3] This is not, needless to say, a position to which the Reverend Paley would have given his ungrudging assent.

### Irreducible Complexity

In expatiating grandly on biology, Gödel chose to express his doubts on a cosmic scale, his skepticism valuable as much for its sharp suggestiveness as anything else; but the large question that Gödel asked about the existence of life in a world of matter has an inner voice within biology itself, interesting evidence that questions of design and complexity are independent of scale. Living systems have achieved a remarkable degree of complexity within a very short time, such structures as the blood clotting cascade or the immunodefense system or human language suggesting nothing so much as a process of careful coordination and intelligent design.

Darwin's theory of evolution is widely thought to have exploded this suggestion, complexity in nature arising by means of random variation and natural selection. It is instructive to regard these claims from an oblique, a mathematical perspective, if only for the sake of the harsh revealing light that mathematics may sometimes provide.

Evolution is a stochastic process, one that moves forward by means of inconclusive humps. Those humps having for a time humped themselves, the mathematician observes the outline of a Markov process or a Markov chain, the standard mathematical structure for the depiction of conditional change.[4] At any given time, a Markov process occupies one of a finite or a countably infinite number of states $\Omega = \varepsilon_1, \varepsilon_2, ..., \varepsilon_n$. These function as bursts of information, a form of memory. In the context of theoretical biology, each state is the buoyant expression of some organism sliced sideways in the stream of time. Starting at $t = 0$, the system changes randomly at $t = 1, 2, \ldots$ and times thereafter. The evolution of the system is described by the crabwise movement of a random variable $\xi(t)$:

$$\xi(0) \to \xi(1) \to \xi(2) \to \ldots$$

Further details: an initial probability distribution defined over $\Omega$ recounts the likelihood $\mathbf{P}\{\xi(0) = \varepsilon_j\}$ that at $t = 0$, the system is in state $\varepsilon_j$. A scheme of transition probabilities $\mathbf{P}\{\xi(n+1) = \varepsilon_j \mid \xi(n) = \varepsilon_k\}$, $(j, k = 1, 2, \ldots)$, describes the chances that a system in state $\varepsilon_k$ will in a single enlightened step change to the state $\varepsilon_j$. A state $\varepsilon_j$ is accessible from some other state $\varepsilon_k$ if there is some probability $\mathbf{P}(n) > 0$ of going from $\varepsilon_k$ to $\varepsilon_j$ in $n$ steps.

There is no very deep theoretical content to the concept of a Markov process. Its purpose is to stiffen an intellectual structure with a tendency otherwise to sag. The metaphor of a skeleton is valuable nonetheless; skeletons are load-bearing structures, and skeptical doubts about Darwinian theories almost always resolve themselves to the question whether such structures can bear their intended weight. In *Darwin's Black Box* the biochemist Michael Behe has argued that with respect to the irreducibly complex systems the answer is unequivocally no. Such structures are comprised of parts designed to work with one another or not to work at all.[5] A common padlock is an example, the key matched to a specific locking cylinder and vice versa. Lacking functional intermediates, the padlock remains inaccessible to any process of random variation and natural selection. So too, Behe argues, many biochemical systems.

**Example**[6] Eukaryotic replication takes place at the rate of perhaps 50 nucleotides per second. The process thus must take place at many thousands of points simultaneously—to lay down 3 billion nucleotides at 50 nucleotides per second would take 16,667 hours or about 9 months. That means that specific enzymes must make thousands of cuts at predetermined forks; other enzymes must straighten twists in the resulting strands, still other enzymes acting to disentangle them; it is then that an RNA primer roughly five nucleotides in length has to be attached to the replicating strand. This too requires the action of additional enzymes. Energy for the process must be supplied by the convenient release of a pyrophosphate group from each incoming nucleotide. That group is either added to the old nucleotides (by one process) or made with new ones (by another process). Because the two separated strands are now moving in opposite directions, two different enzymes are pressed into service to lay down new nucleotides on each strand but in opposite directions, one starting from the crotch of the forking strand, the other from an initial tip. Thousands of these nucleotides must be joined.

RNA primer must be removed; this requires the action of yet another enzyme. The ends have to be collected and put together in the right order; still another enzyme is required. Mistakes occur despite the pairing rule. In prokaryotes, the polymerase that catalyzes synthesis of a new DNA strand also checks errors and fixes them.[7] In Eukaryotes it is not known how checking and repairing are done.[8]

Irreducibly complex processes seem quite beyond the reach of any mechanism of change requiring functioning intermediates and for this reason beyond the reach of any mechanism governed by Darwinian principles. These are strong and daring claims, but they are not self-evident. The mathematician having provided the big picture, the biologist must provide the details.

Which follow: the set of states $\Omega$ — this remains, but each $\varepsilon$ in $\Omega$ now admits of a dissection $\varepsilon = \{\rho_1, \rho_2, \ldots, \rho_n\}$ into parts, the parts themselves arranged in various complicated ways.

Darwin's theory envisages complexity emerging by means of the double action of chance and selection. Things happen. Good accidents survive; the bad are washed away. Fitness plays a prominent role in this scheme; it is the curiously featureless Factor X that accounts for biological success and explains biological failure. For purposes at hand, the content to the concept may be expressed by a function $f: \Omega \to \mathfrak{R}$, one taking elements in $\Omega$ to their numerical reward.

For every $\varepsilon = \{\rho_1, \rho_2, \ldots, \rho_n\}$ in $\Omega$, that $f$ is

*Additive*     $f(\varepsilon) = f(\rho_1) + f(\rho_2) + \ldots + f(\rho_n).$[9]

This is the first of three assumptions required to bring about the transmogrification of the skeleton of a Markov process into the torso of a Darwinian mechanism.[10]

Within the ambit of that torso, biological structures and their parts are selected, and so retained, because they make a contribution to the whole. A Darwinian system is in this respect unlike a social organism: there are no free riders. For every $\varepsilon = \{\rho_1, \rho_2, \ldots, \rho_n\}$ in $\Omega$, fitness is thus

*Partwise Positive*     $f(\varepsilon) > f(\{\rho_1, \ldots, \rho_{t\text{-}1}\}) > \ldots > f(\{\rho_1\}).$

This too is an assumption, but one inexpungible from Darwinian theories.[11]

A third and mercifully final assumption deals not with fitness but with chance and distance. Whatever the fossil record may say, within a Darwinian universe organisms change one step at a time if they are likely to change at all. Alterations in any given state arise in a neighborhood of that state. Given $\varepsilon_j$ and $\varepsilon_k$, let $\mu$ represent their degree of difference. At $\mu = 0$, $\varepsilon_j$ and $\varepsilon_k$, are entirely the same; at $\mu = 1$, entirely different. The details, which can prove vexing, are left as an exercise, but however those details are settled, the scope of change must be conservative, various probabilities

*Serially Ordered*   $\mathbf{P}\{\xi(n+1) = \varepsilon_j \mid \xi(n) = \varepsilon_k\}$ ($j, k = 1, 2, \ldots$) $\to 0$

as $\mu \to 1$.

A Darwinian mechanism $\mathcal{DM}$ thus emerges on the scene, all torso but no head, just as its creators have always claimed.[12]

What of irreducible complexity now that a Markov process has been provided with independent counsel? Intuition reports itself unclouded. If $\varepsilon_j$ is irreducibly complex it is unlikely to be accessible from any other state. A Darwinian mechanism, mathematicians say, is closed to irreducible complexity.

A formal argument requires a number of details, but the argument's force, its large-limbed suggestiveness, may be conveyed by a cooked-up case, one in which a state $\varepsilon = \{\rho_1, \rho_2\}$ consists of two and only two parts.

A definition first: $\varepsilon$ is irreducibly complex if and only if $f(\rho_1) = 0$ for every $\gamma$ in $\Omega$ such that $\rho_2 \notin \gamma$. Ditto for $f(\rho_2)$.

A minitheorem next.[13] If $\varepsilon$ is irreducibly complex

**THEOREM** *There is no state $\gamma$ in $\Omega$ such that $\varepsilon$ is accessible from $\gamma$.*

The argument proceeds by contradiction. Suppose that $\varepsilon$ were accessible from $\gamma$. It follows that $\varepsilon = \{\rho_1, \rho_2\}$ and $\gamma = \{\zeta_1, \zeta_2\}$ differ by only a single part—$\rho_1$, say—so that $\rho_2 = \zeta_2$. Otherwise $\mu = 1$ and the probability that $\varepsilon$ is accessible from $\gamma$ drops to 0. Now $f(\gamma) = f(\zeta_1) + f(\zeta_2)$. By the definition of irreducible complexity, $f(\zeta_2) = 0$. But $f(\gamma) > f(\zeta_1)$ and thus $f(\zeta_1) + f(\zeta_2) > f(\zeta_1)$, whence $f(\zeta_1) > f(\zeta_1)$.

Disorderly impulses are plainly at work, the tension evident even in Richard Dawkins's *Climbing Mount Improbable,* a book otherwise free of intellectual tension altogether. In speculating on the evolutionary development of the mammalian eye, Dawkins imagines improvements occurring one at a time, the eye's photoreceptive array acquiring new cells incrementally. This satisfies a principle of serial order. Changes are concentrated in the neighborhood of a given structure. But the mammalian eye is irreducibly complex, or so it would appear, the eye's parts working together in a tightly coordinated hierarchical system, the structure as a whole ranging from the biochemical to the neurological.[14] The blue shadow of a contradiction may now be observed falling over the discussion.

The definition of irreducible complexity makes strong empirical claims. It is foolish to deny this and foolish as well to suggest that these claims have been met. The argument having been forged in analogy, it remains possible that the analogy may collapse at just the crucial joint. The mammalian eye seems irreducibly complex; so too, Eukaryotic replication and countlessly many biochemical systems, but who knows? Still, the concept of irreducible complexity is surely not empty. A modern airplane, a wristwatch, a nuclear reactor or even a mousetrap all contain a core of critical parts designed specifically to work with other parts designed specifically to work with them. This we know because we have done the designing. Gödel's words may now be heard again both as an overtone and as a warning: "The complexity of living bodies has to be present either in the material [from which they are derived] or in the laws [governing their formation]." What holds for human bodies holds for human artifacts, irreducible complexity transferring itself backward from the inorganic world of things and artifacts to the biological world in which plans are made and things and artifacts designed.

An odd, an exhilarating and unexpected consequence now follows. Darwinian theories if they are falsifiable in principle are false in fact.[15] In this regard they are unique. Intuition and argument now seem to be describing a closed circle.

### General Irreducible Complexity

A Markov process is in the context of Darwinian thought useful because it expresses the stochastic character of Darwinian theory. Whatever else it may be, evolution is, on Darwin's theory, an essentially serial process—one damn thing after the other. A finite state automaton is the simplest of devices that expresses the serial order of behavior and useful thus in precisely this regard; but a finite state automaton is also a device whose memory is fixed and so is independent of its inputs, indifferent to its fate. And this too is a characteristic of Darwinian theories.[16] Another mathematical model is now in prospect.[17]

An automaton is defined first in terms of a finite alphabet $\Sigma$.[18] This reflects the three-way interpretation of the subject in logic, linguistics and computer science, but an alphabet in this context is no more intrinsically linguistic than symbols are intrinsically symbolic in the context of symbolic dynamics; the origins of finite state devices in neural modeling should suggest the relevance of a biological interpretation of those very mutable symbols.[19]

Given a finite alphabet $\Sigma$, it is the business of an automaton either to recognize or to generate a finite sequence of symbols drawn on the alphabet.[20] Such are the words,

$$x = a_1 a_2 \ldots a_n;$$

these are structures entirely determined by their shape or internal configuration. The set of all words on $\Sigma$ is recorded as $\Sigma^*$. It has the structure of a free monoid.[21]

An automaton $\mathcal{A}$ over $\Sigma$ comprises four parts

| | |
|---|---|
| *States* | A finite set $Q$ of elements |
| *Initial States* | A subset I of $Q$ |
| *Terminal States* | A subset T of $Q$ |
| *Edges* | A subset $E$ of $Q \times \Sigma \times Q$ |

A particular edge $(p, \sigma, q)$ begins at $p$ and ends at $q$. The symbol $\sigma$ serves as the label of the edge. An edge may also serve as the expression of a function $\sigma : p \to q$, or as the expression of a function from symbols and states to states themselves: $\sigma : Q \times \Sigma \to Q$, or as the expression of a rule, one in which the automaton is instructed to move from a state and a symbol to a new state.

Edges first, paths next. A path $c$ in $\mathcal{A}$ is a finite sequence of consecutive edges

$$c = (q_0, \sigma_1, q_1)(q_1, \sigma_1, q_2) \ldots (q_{k-1}, \sigma_k, q_k).$$

If a path $c\colon i \to t$, $i \in \mathbf{I}$, $t \in \mathbf{T}$, conducts itself from an initial to a terminal state, it is said to be successful; the successful paths form a subset $|A|$ of $\Sigma^*$. They embody, they represent, the behavior of $\mathcal{A}$.

The behavior of a finite state automaton may be illustrated by a simple schema. Small circles indicate states of the system. Initial states are marked by an inward (or facing) arrow; terminal states by an outward arrow.

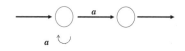

This automaton may do one of two things: it may move directly from an initial to a terminal state, or it may loop through its initial state. Its extraordinary simplicity notwithstanding, this machine is capable of recognizing all structures of the form: **a, aa, aaa, aaaa,** this up to $\boldsymbol{a^m}$.

There is finally the crucial concept of recognizability. Herewith the obvious definition. A subset $A$ of $\Sigma^*$ is recognizable if there exists an automaton $A$ over $\Sigma$ such that $A = |\mathcal{A}|$. With the larger project of interpreting finite state automata in the context of evolutionary theories, recognizability is one step from accessibility. Thus for some biological organism or structure $\varepsilon = \{\rho_1, \rho_2, \ldots, \rho_n\}$ in $\Omega$, $\varepsilon$ is accessible from some Darwinian mechanism $\mathcal{DM}$, if and only if (i) $\mathcal{DM}$ and $\mathcal{A}$ are isomorphic (or otherwise the same) for some automaton $\mathcal{A}$, (ii) $\{\rho_1, \rho_2, \ldots, \rho_n\}$ is a subset of $\Sigma^*$, and (iii) $\{\rho_1, \rho_2, \ldots, \rho_n\}$ is recognizable to $\mathcal{A}$. Nothing more.

Finite state automata are interesting for the promise they hold of permitting the mathematician to draw a limpid connection between what a finite state automaton is and what it does.[22] In this, the theory of finite state automata is decisively characterized by a single absolutely fundamental theorem, one known for more than half a century.

Let $\Sigma$ be an alphabet. The rational expressions[23] on $\Sigma$ are defined with respect to its subsets. There are just three pertinent constructions:

*Union* $X \cup Y$
*Product* $XY = \{xy \mid x \in X, y \in Y\}$
      *Star* $X^* = \{x_1 \, x_2 \, \ldots \, x_n \mid n \geq 0, \, x_1 \in X\}$.

The rational subsets of $\Sigma$ are just those that can be derived from the finite subsets of $\Sigma$ using the rational operations of union, product and star formation.

Now let $\Sigma_S$ designate the subsets of $\Sigma$. That absolutely fundamental theorem:

**THEOREM** (Kleene) *A set $X \subset \Sigma_S$ is recognizable if and only if $X$ is rational.*

Rationality is the mark of those structures accessible to a finite state automaton; and a finite state automaton is that device capable of recognizing them. It is sobering to think that nowhere else in evolutionary theory is there anything like the precise matching of a device to what it can do that is available in this context and by means of this result.

Having come this far through the badlands of symbolism, the reader may well wonder what the connection—the precise connection—between Darwinian mechanisms and finite state automata. The question, although fascinating, is ill posed. The finite state automata have received a precise definition. Not so the Darwinian mechanisms. They are half Markov chain and half some shambling Other. There is still room for conjecture, guesses playing over the undiscovered country in which everything is ultimately made clear. My conjecture, recorded in the definition of accessibility, is that any finite state automaton may be approximated by some Darwinian mechanism.

The case is circumstantial but nonetheless compelling, or if it is not compelling then at least suggestive. Finite state automata are inherently serial. They achieve their effects by looping and by iteration, but lacking any memory beyond their states, they are incapable of intricate acts of deferral and subordination. Hoping to electrify the community of linguists, Patrick Suppes demonstrated in the late 1960s that any finite state automaton could be asymptotically approximated by some stimulus sampling theory. His theorem rested on a connection between Markov processes and finite state automata that was antecedently obvious; but it had the merit of fixing stimulus sampling theories in psychology precisely in a region of space.

**THEOREM** (Suppes) *Given any connected finite automaton $\mathcal{A}$, there is a stimulus response model $\mathcal{SR}$ such that in the limit $\mathcal{SR}$ and $\mathcal{A}$ are isomorphic* (see Suppes 1969, 411-53).

Now stimulus sampling theories in psychology stand to Darwinian theories in biology as sister to long-lost sister. They are both theories embedded in Markov chains; they share the same vocabulary; and they appeal to the same mechanism, one in which the trigger of chance is followed by the filter of selection or reinforcement.[24] This suggests a revision of Suppes's theorem, one in which psychology gives way to evolutionary biology. The perspective afforded is oblique, but an oblique perspective is all that the mathematician can ever offer, so while little may be gained, absolutely nothing has been lost.

CONJECTURE *Given any connected finite automaton A, there is a Darwinian model DM such that in the limit DM and A are isomorphic.*

Although shallow mathematically, theorem and conjecture do send a shaft of sunshine into a discussion that might otherwise remain dark. Two facts stand illuminated. Kleene's theorem specifies, and specifies precisely, what a finite state automaton can do. Suppes's theorem and the conjecture that follows establish that whatever a finite state automaton may do, this may also be done by a device randomly shooting changes into the wilderness and trusting in the wilderness to select those changes that do some good.

Theorems and conjecture settle only half the vexing issue of theory. They describe what a particular mechanism or device can do. The other half remains. What is it that such devices need do? Suppes evidently believed that by demonstrating his theorem for stimulus-response models in psychology he was coming to their defense. Another, more medical interpretation is possible. The identification achieved between structures serves only to permit a certain contagion to spread, the limitations of finite state automata infecting the stimulus response theories and so the Darwinian mechanisms as well.

### Apropos Those Limitations

If rationality offers an absolute standard of accessibility, it suggests—and it must provide—a correlative concept of inaccessibility. And so it does. The inaccessible structures are those that cannot be recognized by a finite state automaton. This makes for a voluptuously general scheme of classification, simplicity identified with the rational events and complexity with everything else. Behe's irreducible complexity now emerges as a special case of the more wide-ranging concept of general irreducible complexity.

Surprisingly enough, examples often turn on properties of symmetry.[25] A partial list follows, given in terms of strings drawn on a finite alphabet or directly in terms of languages:

$L = \{a^n b^n\}$, *where $n > 0$*

*The set of strings over a finite alphabet in which parentheses are mated*

*Parenthesis-free propositional calculus in prefix notation*

*The set of palindromes over a finite alphabet*

$L = \{aXa\}$, *where $X$ is a point of symmetry.*

Though short, this list reveals sharp and unsuspected limitations on what finite state devices can do. A finite state machine cannot produce arbitrary structures of the form $\{a^n b^n\}$. This may suggest that it is the promiscuity of an arbitrary $n$ that is at fault. Not so. The same finite state machine can generate structures of the form $\{a^n b^p\}$, where $p$ is a fixed integer. Difficulties lie elsewhere.

A finite state machine is inherently serial—a point in its favor. Now imagine $n$ for the moment fixed, time frozen at $t$. There is no way that by $t$, a serial device could have realized $\{a^n b^n\}$; at any particular point in its deliberations, it can have reached only $\{a^n b^p\}$, where $p < n$. Before winding things up with a grunt of satisfaction, the automaton must loop through $b$: $b \rightarrow b^{2k} \rightarrow b^{ik}$, the effect of the routing indicated by placing a symbol in context: $b \rightarrow Rb^{2k} \rightarrow Rb^{ik}$. The index $i$ counts the number of loops. But the automaton must bring some $Rb^k$ to an end at, say, $b^l$, if $b$ is ever to count as a terminal symbol.

It is thus that at some point the automaton contemplates a structure of the form $a^m b^p R$. It has reached $m$ of the $a$'s, and $p$ of the $b$'s, and completed who knows how many $R$'s, and is set to loop for the last time. But this means that the automaton is poised to recognize infinitely many strings of the form $\{a^m,\ b^{p+ik+l}\}$—a gloomy monstrosity, not at all the intended result.

This tight little argument has a large, a percussive charge, one that explodes a convenient superstition. General irreducible complexity has nothing whatsoever to do with size or indeed with any of the standard measures of complexity, such as that "degree of irregularity" to which Stephen Jay Gould appeals in *Full House*. There are very simple symmetrical structures whose organization lies beyond the reach of any serial process.

It is the push down storage automata that are capable of recognizing or generating structures such as $\{a^n b^n\}$—capable, in fact, of recognizing the entire class of context-free events or languages or structures. This little fact yields the pleasurable sense that something is under construction, a hierarchy of sorts, the finite state machines neatly matched to the regular languages, machines that are slightly more powerful matched to languages that are slightly more complicated. From the perspective of automata theory or algebra, it is no doubt the hierarchy that is of interest; but from the perspective of theoretical biology, there is something else at work here, some faint but ineffably important conceptual line that is crossed when finite state machines give way to push down storage automata.[26]

A push down storage automaton is a finite state device, one augmented by a stack or memory. Three objects are required:[27]

$X = \Gamma^* \times \Sigma^*$

$\alpha: \Sigma^* \rightarrow \Gamma^* \times \Sigma^*$

$X_\omega = \Gamma^* \times 1$.

$\Gamma^*$ denotes the stack or memory. It is derived algebraically from $\Gamma$, which is an output alphabet. Whereas a finite state automaton had only one alphabet in $\Sigma$, now it has two, $\Sigma$ of old functioning as an initial or input alphabet. Both $\Gamma^*$ and $\Sigma^*$ denote sets of words and both have the structure of a free monoid. The set $X$ denotes the Cartesian product of the two sets of words. The function $\alpha \colon \Sigma^* \to \Gamma^* \times \Sigma^*$ maps words from the input alphabet onto $X$. It serves to instruct the automaton whether symbols or structures should go to memory or pass onto the output. The stack is unbounded: hence $X_\omega$.

The (superficial) complexity of notation notwithstanding, the action of a push down storage automaton is simple. It is given a finite string of symbols, these having a particular shape—*aaabbb,* say. It is often convenient to imagine those symbols being conveyed to the automaton by a tape. The machine acts via the function *a* to place symbols in memory or to assign them to its output. This too can be thought of as a tape, so that the action of the machine is in the end a curious concourse between two tapes, the machine acting to evacuate one and fill the other. Detours occur when some symbols are sent to the stack; but when the stack is empty, the automaton has done its work.

A context-free language or structure is any language or structure accessible to a push down storage automaton.[28] This easy association serves the intellectually valuable purpose of illuminating the powers of a device by reference to the objects that it can recognize. But unlike the regular events, the class of context-free structures has remained undefined, their appearance so far a matter only of unobtrusive examples. Whatever the definition to come, general irreducible complexity is nonetheless an absolute property of certain systems.[29] The burden of these remarks is suggested by two classical results, both of them given in the old-fashioned language of formal linguistics

**THEOREM** (Chomsky, Schützenberger) *If $\phi$ is any set of finite state productions, and $\gamma$, any set of context free productions, then $\phi$ is a proper subset of $\gamma$.*

This theorem establishes the first step on the full, the famous ascending Chomsky hierarchy, which stretches from the finite state automata to the Turing machines on the left, and the regular languages to the unrestricted rewriting systems on the right; but what gives the theorem its intellectual force is the unequivocal nature of the distinction that it draws.

The second theorem goes further by establishing that context-free structures cannot in general even be approximated by finite state structures

**THEOREM** (Parikh) *There exists a push down storage automaton PDS, whose productions are $PDS(Pr)$, with the following property: given a finite state automaton $FSA_1$, whose productions are $FSA_1(Pr) \subset PDS(Pr)$, it is possible to construct a finite state automaton $FSA_2$, with productions $FSA_2(Pr)$, such that (i) $FSA_1(Pr) \subset FSA_2(Pr)$; and moreover (ii) $FSA_2(Pr)$ contains infinitely many structures not in $FSA_1(Pr)$.[30]*

It follows from the asymptotic identification of Darwinian mechanisms with finite state automata that

**CONJECTURE** *There exists a push down storage automaton* PDS *that cannot be approximated by any Darwinian mechanism* DM.

Despite the number of assumptions that have been built into this conjecture, it is nonetheless a disturbing and controversial claim, suggesting as it does that an empirical theory might be fatally compromised by a chain of logical circumstances. The association between stimulus sampling and evolutionary theories is a source of irony as well as insight, behavioral theories in psychology having themselves been brought low by arguments very similar to those that I am now advancing.

## The Serial Order of Behavior

Behe's irreducibly complex structures lie beyond the reach of any Darwinian mechanism, and for this a waterproof argument suffices. Doubts crept in on the argument's far side, when biological structures were sifted for signs of irreducible complexity. The pattern repeats itself in the case of general irreducible complexity but with little sense of real scruples being scrupled. Biology is essentially the study of nonserial behavior, the point overwhelmingly clear in the case of natural languages, where the facts by now are unassailable. Elsewhere, more of the same.[31]

In addition to the creation of proteins, DNA creates proteins in a significant order. In some cases it is the order in which the proteins are coded that is essential for the proper development of some feature of the organism. But this sort of development is very limited in the overall construction of the organism. So far as we know, it is limited only to items such as the formation of insect exoskeletons. In these instances the actual development is, like the DNA plan itself, serial; it goes from front to back or top to bottom. Most of the organism for one or another very different sorts of reasons cannot be serially organized, and certainly not the whole of an organism, as though it were laid down in a series of planes like the slices seen in an MRI scan. This is no doubt obvious, but if we look at some of the reasons against such a suggestion, we see the nature of the problem:

1. Embryological development is not serial. Where it is visible, it seems to be systematic; that is, the physical systems, whether skeletal, circulatory or nervous, have their own schedules and procedures. What little truth there is to the notion of ontogeny recapitulating phylogeny shows not serial planar construction but rather some process of system building and integration.

2. There are not only many systems within every living creature that have to be integrated into an organic whole—they must be put together in some sort of balance. The legs have to be the right size and strength to support

the body and to carry out the appropriate activities of the animal; the same can be said of a stem or a leaf or the cilia of a paramecium. And this is to say that the whole has a superordinate influence on its parts. One is likely to imagine that the parts just naturally fall into the right scale and proportion, but in the purely chance driven mechanism of the DNA molecule, there is nothing to justify such a conclusion.

3. An animal crawls, walks, swims or flies by a characteristic coordination of appendages. Hence there are central nervous specifications to this end. The central nervous system is a physical organ, to be sure, and as such might be serially accessible to some Darwinian device. However, it is the function of the nervous system that characterizes it as an organ, and unlike the leg, its function is not apparent in its movement. It makes no sense to speak of the executive properties of the nervous system in serial terms, as though the various programs were set up in and because of an order corresponding to the physical relationship of the neurons (starting from the top of the head or some other point of origin). It makes no sense because while there is only one physically realizable serial order to parts of the nervous system, there are—there must be—an extraordinary number of distinct executive programs; for example, if there is a walking program, it must be modified each time the organism walks so as to adjust to the ground and the destination.

4. All animals have sense organs of some sort even if primitive ones. A sense organ is of no use by itself. Its purpose comes from its informational contribution. Typically doing $x$ is preceded by perceiving $x$ or signs of $x$ as warnings or indications. Hence those organs of sense have to be tied to other circuits in the central nervous system that are first evaluative and then executive. Putting it this way makes it sound as though only higher animals are included, but a worm that turns abruptly from contact with a dry rock has evaluated the problem and withdrawn from it as part of its program, much as the human somatic nervous response to touching a hot stove does not involve consciousness, not even figuratively. If the central nervous system, the peripheral nervous system and the muscles all operated together because they were constructed in the same serial order, then the events in the world would have to cooperate by placing demands on them in the same serial order.

5. Within the higher organisms, the geometry and mechanical arrangement of the muscles and appendages of movement do not prescribe their use. The antelope does not have to run faster, the eagle does not have to fly. Their tendency to run or to fly is located in a program quite separate from the one that expresses their powers of running or flight. The eagle must develop the will to fly, along with its muscles and its wings. In concentrating on the higher organisms, let us not forget the remarkable coordination DNA

codons impose on the design of protein groups in the manufacture of insects, where will is not involved. The wasp equipped with an ovipositor and some special faculties detects the presence of larva under the ground and then pierces the ground and the body of the larva to the appropriate depth, whereupon she inserts her eggs. There is no way to understand this talent as developed piecemeal and no way to justify thinking that the various coordinated components are close to one another in the DNA metric.

Such are the various facts. What of their significance? The mammalian eye is an organ that has exerted a magnetic influence on Darwinists and doubters alike. It is plain that the eye is organized as a hierarchical structure, one extending over at least three levels[32]: that of the visual system **VS;** that of the anatomical system **Anat;** and that of the biochemical system **Bio** = $\{b_1,$ ... , $b_n\}$. One way in which to depict the hierarchy is by means of labeled brackets [**VS**[**Anat**[**Bio**[$\{b_1, \ldots, b_n\}$]]]], this indicating that every group of right elements belong to the next leftmost category.[33]

The effect of the labeling may be conveyed as well by a series of rules

$$\textbf{VS} \rightarrow \textbf{Anat,}$$
$$\textbf{Anat} \rightarrow \textbf{Bio}$$
$$\textbf{Bio} \rightarrow b_1, \ldots, b_n.$$

And the effect conveyed by the rules conveyed in turn by an equation

$$\textbf{VS} = \textbf{Anat} + \textbf{Bio} + b_1, \ldots, b_n,$$

or more generally by a polynomial

$$\textbf{A} = f_1 + f_2 + \ldots + f_k,$$

where **A** is any biological category including $f_i$ as subcategories and the + sign indicates not straightforward addition but logical alternation. The polynomial in turn goes over to a system of equations in $n$ variables

$$A_1 = f_1(A_1, \ldots, A_n)$$

$$\cdot$$
$$\cdot$$
$$\cdot$$

$$A_n = f_n(A_1, \ldots, A_n).$$

Each step in this scheme is not only plausible but natural as well. Since time immemorial, mathematicians have found it useful to represent systems by means of simultaneous equations; it is their canonical instrument for the representation of complexity, its employment a sign that some process cannot be represented in the straightforward terms in which a single function undertakes to map one thing onto another. The equations at hand, it is true, are defined in terms of words and not numbers, but words are mathematical objects in their own right, the algebraic machinery that proceeds smoothly over systems of numerical equations proceeding smoothly here as well.

Like many biological structures, the context-free languages, and so the push down storage automata, admit of definition in terms of a system of equations, a natural circle now forming, one moving from general irreducible complexity to systems of equations to context-free languages and back again to systems of equations. There is a mediating operation that has so far gone unremarked, one that is needed to close the circle and that is the specification of the context-free languages in terms of a grammar. The definitions are straightforward and by now a part of a general academic culture. A context-free grammar $G = (V, A, P, S)$ consists of a finite alphabet $V$; a subset $A$ of $V$ designating terminal symbols; a finite set of productions $P \subset (V—A)$, and a distinguished element $S \in (V—A)$, one functioning as an axiom. The grammar works by means of derivations or rewriting rules.

Consider, as an example, a grammar consisting of one symbol $F$ and two terminal symbols $a$ and $b$. The axiom is

$$F \rightarrow aFb.$$

Productions are all of the form

$$F \rightarrow aabb.$$

The language $L$ associated with these rules consists of all and only the terminal strings, expressions of the form $\{a^n b^n\}$, evidence of the deep and surprising power of the notation.

Now let $X$ be a variable ranging over symbols in $(V—A)$, and let $P_X$ be the right hand sides of productions having $X$ on their left side. The set of productions can obviously be rewritten as

$$X \rightarrow P_X.$$

This gives rise to a system of equations, one associated with a particular grammar—$G$, say. A solution to the system is given by a family $L_X$ of subsets of $A$, such that

$$L_X = P_X(L),$$

where

$$P_X(L) = \bigcup_{p \in P_x} p(L),$$

and where $p(L)$ is the product of the language obtained by replacing in $p$ each occurrence of a variable $Y$ by the language $L_Y$.

A far-reaching theorem now follows, one that draws close a conceptual circle.

**THEOREM** (Schützenberger) *Let $G$ be a context-free grammar. The family $L = (L_X)$, where $L_X = L_G(X)$, is the least solution of its associated set of equations.*

This theorem rests on certain algebraic machinery; theorem and machinery have the effect of ratifying certain natural forms of representation and so indirectly of ratifying certain intuitions. A context-free grammar is a way of expressing a system of equations and vice versa, the vice versa collapsing the distinction between grammar and equations entirely so that both devices lend themselves to the description of structures in which there is nesting, domination, hierarchy, pattern and symmetry.

It is perhaps time for a retrospective. Two hierarchies have made an appearance, those comprised of automata and those comprised of their accessible structures—the regular events in the case of finite state devices, the context-free languages in the case of push down storage automata. Structures and automata alike give every indication of vanishing into a purely algebraic void; but while the algebra has the effect of vacating the familiar from a class of concepts, it also has the effect of throwing a sharp, clean, hard light on the essentials. Defined over words, equations are the algebraic middle men in what has passed. This takes some getting used to, but familiarity breeds assent, the more so since the universe of words seems strangely to mimic the universe of numbers, rather like those parallel universes in which one may observe a character identical to oneself in all respects save one. In elementary analysis, the solution to a system of equations is specifiable in terms of power series. Here, too, but with the difference that the underlying variables do not commute.

The introduction of formal power series marks a third abstractive level—things, devices and structures to equations, equations to power series. It preserves, this third step, distinctions in place down the line. Regular and accessible events coincide in the case of finite state automata. So too their associated power series. This is the burden of a remarkably lovely and far-reaching theorem by M. P. Schützenberger. Power series recognizable by a finite state automata are rational and vice versa

$$\mathcal{A}^{\,\mathrm{rat}}\langle\Sigma*\rangle = \mathcal{A}^{\,\mathrm{rec}}\langle\Sigma*\rangle.$$

Does the same hold for push down storage automata as well? Not in terms of rational structures, of course; that would defeat the distinction it has taken so many definitions to enforce. Beyond the rational power series, there are those that algebraic, the extraordinarily illuminating pattern almost repeating itself once again. With reservations signified by that guarded "almost" in mind, there is the altogether remarkable

$$\mathcal{A}^{\,\mathrm{alg}}\langle\Sigma*\rangle = \mathcal{A}^{\,\mathrm{rec}}\langle\Sigma*\rangle,$$

where $\Sigma*$ is the free monoid of a context-free language.

These purely algebraic identities have a wickedly alluring gleam: they glitter and they glare. A compression of identity is at work, the husks of finite state and push down storage automata dropping away to reveal an algebraic incarnation. This is always an exciting process to watch, but however compelling mathematical pupation, my attention is inexorably drawn elsewhere. Things that stay the same as other things are changing are invariant;

reification yields invariants. A subgroup S of a group G in which right and left cosets coincide is an invariant; the dimension of a finite dimensional vector space is another.

Now the line dividing finite state and push down storage automata corresponds in a very intuitive way to the division between natural and artificial processes and between systems of descriptions that apply to material events and systems of descriptions that apply to biological events. If this seems too rich a claim for many tastes, I have a lite version in mind as well. The line between finite state and push down storage automata corresponds to a division between two concepts of complexity, or between degrees of complexity as one polyvalent concept displays itself. Whatever the content to the distinction, it is less important than the fact that the distinction is refulgent; and if Factor X is good enough for evolutionary theorists casting about for content to the concept of fitness, Factor X can again be pressed into service here, as whatever it is that the distinction defines.

Whatever it is, the distinction is provided with an invariant, one set of cases expressed by the rational power series, the other by the algebraic power series.

I would say that these are invariants first of matter and second of life; but I am content to claim only that the invariants serve to characterize Factor X, leaving matters for the moment at that.

### Explanation by Algorithm

And yet a troubling point remains. My argument has washed on alien shores. Automata and algorithms are by their nature scientifically anomalous instruments.[34] They do not express laws of nature in the sense made familiar by mathematical physics. They play an interesting but poorly understood role in the local economy of explanation. The idea that psychological processes are inherently computational is hardly a model of sturdy common sense. But the identification of Darwinian devices with finite state automata was my idea, evidence, if any were needed, that however unwholesome the algorithmic category, I for one have not scrupled at its employment. The proverbial camel is now within the tent, peering indignantly out. Finite state automata cannot express a certain order of complexity. Very well. Let us go to the next best thing, and that is the devices that can do the job. Is there a reason that Darwinian theories should not be cast directly in push down terms, the baleful conclusions of my own argument short lived because short circuited?

It is a reasonable question, one that touches on a number of dark places in the philosophy of science. Push down storage automata mark the place where what a computational device does is determined in part by what it remembers, memory functioning as an ancilla to design and so playing the role in such devices that it plays elsewhere. It is evidence of design that must itself be explained, if Gödel's question is ever to be answered; and plainly if the device doing the explanation itself requires an explanation of precisely the same sort, we are in the position of a man bailing water from the front end of his boat and depositing it in the rear.

The unhealthy effect of something so simple as a stack on the larger Darwinian project emerges when specific cases come under scrutiny. Consider structures of the form $\{a^m\}$; plainly they are accessible to an $\mathcal{A}$ of old

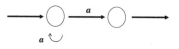

the result of its action a set of paths, one increasing in length $a, aa, aaa, aaaa,$ ..., $a^m$.

With the details left in decent obscurity, it is easy to imagine a Darwinian mechanism $\mathcal{DM}$ coming in its behavior to coincide with the paths specified by the automaton, fitness a function of ever lengthening paths

$$f(a) < f(aa) < f(aaa) < f(aaaa) < ... < f(a^m).$$

Consider, on the other hand, structures of the form $\{a^n b^n\}$. These lie in the Great Beyond that a finite state automaton cannot reach and does not know. Suppose that $n = 3$ so that $\{a^n b^n\}$ has the form $\{aaabbb\}$. Symbols are presented to a machine on a tape, one that functions purely as a device of presentation

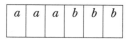

The machine turns now to a second tape, this one blank

It is this second tape that functions as the useful embodiment of an imaginary stack. Reading the first tape from left to right, the machine divides its action, printing the symbol $c$ in its stack every time it spots the symbol $a$. By the time the machine has finished with the $a$'s, the stack is half full

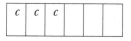

Ah, but on encountering $b$, the automaton reverses its operations, erasing instead of writing $c$. When the stack is again empty, the machine has done its work. There is in this design something devilishly clever, the stack

managing to achieve the effect of counting without counting at all, action over the stack having first swept in $n$ counters and then swept out $m$ counters and so leaving the stack empty if and only if $n = m$.

But if a simple push down storage automaton is a marvel of ingenuity, it seems hardly a model for those natural processes in which complexity is constructed by accretion. The problem is the difficult one of distributing fitness to intermediate steps. In the case of structures of the form $\{a^m\}$, increasing path length is a convenient proxy for fitness. One can imagine natural selection for whatever reason relentlessly favoring length. Structures of the form $\{a^n b^n\}$ are different, the attempt to distribute fitness over intermediate cases leading to contradiction.

Thus $f(c^n) < f(c^m)$, if $n < m$, and thus again

$$f(c) < f(cc) < f(ccc) \ldots,$$

whence

$$f(a^n) > f(a^n b^{m-2}) > f(a^n b^{m-1}) > f(a^n b^m).$$

But equally,

$$f(a^n b^{m-1}) < f(a^n b^m),$$

if $f$ is partwise positive, assessment over the stack and assessment over the output failing to cohere.

Two impulses are plainly at work and plainly in conflict. The difficulty is that increasing path length has nothing whatsoever to do with any measure of fitness, however loose. The example of $\{a^m\}$ is a lurid distraction. Structures of the form *aaabb* are not slightly more symmetrical than structures of the form *aaab*. The latter are not symmetrical at all. Symmetry arises only when the structure has been completed, a vivid example of irreducible complexity, and one incidentally that has nothing to do with function.

Cases such as this are by no means artificial; they are a staple in the literature of evolutionary theory; they occur whenever target sentences or words are supposedly discovered by means of an evolutionary search.[35] If the cases are a staple, so too the defective strategies for their analysis. Almost always those defective strategies involve a discovery procedure in which a description of the desired object is illicitly smuggled into the search procedure itself. If symmetry is at issue, it plainly does little good to resolve contradictory impulses by arguing that $f(aaabb) > f(aaab)$ in virtue of the fact that *aaabb* is *closer* to *aaabbb* than *aaab*. A Darwinian mechanism having access to a definition of distance could no longer be a Darwinian mechanism. Such a device is designed to achieve certain ends, that element of carefully contrived intelligence that was to disappear from Darwinian theories reappearing now in models of those theories, rather like a spirit indignantly refusing to stay exorcised. An old, a painful dilemma.[36]

The point is informal, but it is also quite general. Finite state automata occupy a position in the uncharted region between natural laws and complex algorithms. Darwinian theories have always commended themselves to biologists as a bridge between the physical and the living; and insofar as the finite state automata and the Darwinian mechanisms coincide, so too the finite state automata. But in a curious reprise of the third man argument, intellectual difficulties have divided themselves without diminishing themselves, the line between the physical and living now reappearing as the distinction between finite state and push down storage automata, evidence, if any were needed, that the distinction is itself irrefragable.[37]

### Whence Complexity?

Scientists and philosophers often imagine that they are in the business of liberating men and women from their illusions: it is their common boast, although whether men and women find those illusions burdensome or are grateful for the liberation is another matter entirely. The idea that there is an absolute character to the distinction between life and matter and so between biology and physics is among the more stubbornly held illusions, perhaps because it is not an illusion at all but simply the plain, the ineradicable truth. For reasons that are anything but clear, scientists willing to champion materialism as nothing less than the plain evidence of their senses often treat its denial as a logical impossibility, a contradiction in prospect to which they are singularly indifferent.

In careless conversation, Gödel asked for an account of biological complexity, but however careless the conversation, his question has an intellectual force that transcends its circumstances, if only because nothing suggests or even plausibly hints that it has in any way been satisfactorily answered. We have no reason to assume that complexity is conserved but no reason to doubt it either; and whenever issues are pressed beyond the anecdotal, it quickly emerges that the conservation of complexity functions as a limit, one vacating schemes for the generation of complexity, at least when they are made precise.

In one very large respect, however, the discussion has had something of a toy-like quality. It has been largely static, a matter of adjusting certain structures to certain devices without concern for much beyond their fit. Biology is preeminently the discipline in which living creatures pursue living ends, their lives marked by continually evolving trajectories that carry them from what they wish and desire and need to what they achieve, attempt and gain. We know little about the analysis of such activities; beyond the superficial, we know nothing at all. And yet any serious study of complexity must deal with functional complexity, an assessment of biological organisms by reference to the tasks that they undertake.[38] Is sight a more complicated task for an organism than digestion or thermoregulation? On what basis the determination, and what parameters are involved? How should the maintenance of long-range biological rhythms be compared with activities taking place on fractional time scales? What is the correct or even the pertinent mathematical space for the representation of the characteristic triplet of desire, undertaking and satisfaction?

Questions such as these are easy to come by and free for the asking. They tend to mask in a flurry the extent to which the relationship between structure and function is analytically obscure on even the simplest level. Does a biological structure, for example, obey a principle of compositionality, so that what the whole of what the structure does is a function of what its parts do? I have in general no idea. Nor does anyone else.

Theoretical computer science is a discipline confronting problems that are cognate if not common. "In programming linguistics," Peter Mosses writes, "as in the study of natural languages, 'syntax' is distinguished from 'semantics.'" He continues:

> The syntax of a programming language is concerned only with the *structure* of programs: whether programs are legal; the connections and relations between the symbols and phrases that occur in them. Semantics deals with what legal programs *mean:* the behavior they produce when executed by computers. (Mosses 1992, 577)

This sense of semantics already goes far beyond the sense common in philosophy or even formal logic and seems reminiscent in an odd way of Wittgenstein's unhappy dictum that the meaning of a word lies with its use. To a limited extent, it makes sense to speak of a theory of computer behavior, one in which structure and function receive some measure of coordination. The larger project of amplifying that distinction so that it comes to cover biological structure and function remains incomplete, and for all anyone knows, incompleteable.

But until that distinction is clarified, the distinction between structural and functional complexity will remain obscure. And so long as that distinction remains obscure, what evidence can be forthcoming that any mechanism is in any sense an adequate answer to Gödel's question?

### Notes

[1]In writing this chapter I have benefited greatly from my correspondence with Arthur Cody. We have discussed every issue at length, agreeing in almost all respects, disagreeing in but a few. Our hope is to write at greater length on this topic.

[2]I have pursued this theme in Berlinski 1996a. It has seldom been noted, but criticism of Darwin's theory forms a chapter in the history of idealist thought.

[3]Physicists often say that information is neither created nor destroyed; it is a thesis that would appear to have a counterexample in the case of a physical signal passing beyond the event horizon of a black hole. If complexity is defined in terms of

information—a generous assumption, to be sure—then the conservation of complexity is no less plausible than the conservation of information. No less, note, but unfortunately no more either.

[4]Genetic algorithms, currently a subject of interest among theoretical biologists, are themselves finite state Markov chains. See Goldberg 1989 for details.

[5]This is not Behe's definition. A system is irreducibly complex, Behe argues, if it is critically contingent upon its parts: withdraw any of them from the system and the system fails (see Behe 1996 for details). On Behe's definition, an ordinary three-legged foot stool would appear to be irreducibly complex. The definition at hand entails Behe's definition.

[6]The discussion that follows is almost entirely Arthur Cody's work; I have adjusted his remarks just slightly so that they agree in style with my own.

[7]Where, one might ask, does its information come from?

[8]In correspondence, a distinguished mathematician once remarked to me that "organic chemicals have an affinity for one another that chemistry cannot explain." Indeed.

[9]It is obviously possible to specify a more complex relationship. Exploring the so-called NK model of epistatic interaction, Stuart Kauffman defines the fitness of a genotype as the average of the fitness of its parts. This has the somewhat bizarre consequence that a structure of N parts interacting K ways could be less fit than some N-$k$ of its parts (see Kauffman 1993, 42).

[10]Change within Darwinian systems is always in the direction of increasing fitness: $\mathbf{P}\{\xi(n+1) = \varepsilon_j \mid \xi(n) = \varepsilon_k\}$ $(j, k = 1, 2, \dots)$ $= 0$ if $f(\varepsilon_j) < f(\varepsilon_k)$; this is an assumption collapsing fitness and selection. It is, by the way, almost certainly false as stated and probably false when stated any other way. It is the central assumption of any mountain-climbing metaphor. It is not needed in what follows.

[11]It may seem at first cut that I am confusing two quite separate processes: the discovery by evolution of certain biological structures and the creation by morphogenesis of an organism from an initial cell. Morphogenesis is a concession to the twin requirements of miniaturization and replication. It is hardly needed conceptually. The problem of evolutionary discovery is logically prior. If this seems paradoxical, the reader might imagine evolution as a process $k_1 \to k_2 \to \dots \to k_n$, extending over $n$ fully formed generations such that for every $i, j$, either $k_i = k_j$, or $k_j$ is derived from $k_i$ by means of augmentation of parts or by means of a change in the nature or structure of one of its parts. These are in fact the only logical possibilities for any evolutionary process driven by point mutations. In this sense, the questions how a complex structure is assembled and how a complex structure evolves turn out to be one and the same.

[12]The three assumptions just given do not logically specify a theory or anything like a theory. They must be taken for what they are—three assumptions merely.

[13]A theorem, note. The argument is entirely conceptual. I am not for a moment arguing that there are no intermediates in fact for irreducibly complex systems. I am arguing that such intermediates could not logically exist. Suggesting nothing so much as a man proposing gamely to trisect an angle, Orr (1996) has argued the contrary.

[14]See page 418 et seq.

[15]This is such a paradoxical conclusion that it might be worthwhile to spell out the argument. Herewith a sketch. Three premises:

(1) There exist irreducibly complex objects inaccessible to any Darwinian mechanism $\mathcal{DM}$.

(2) Some irreducibly complex objects are made by human beings.

(3) Complexity is neither created nor destroyed.

The first premise is itself the conclusion of a theorem; the second is a plain fact; and the third is a frank assumption. It follows that human beings have at least the same degree of complexity as the irreducibly complex objects. And from this it follows that some biological structures—namely, human beings—are also inaccessible to any *DM*. To make this argument valid would require some precise quantitative definition of complexity and some more perspicuous account of the conservation of complexity. These are very large projects.

[16]Dennett (1995) has argued that evolution is an algorithmic process; but beyond saying that it exists, he has not specified the algorithm. If by an algorithmic process he means one that is effectively computable, the claim is uninteresting. As a philosopher, Dennett seems unaware of the very significant issues raised when a physical process is explained by an appeal to an algorithm. If we were to notice that the rivers of the world express a correlation between the position of their names in the alphabet and their size, so that rivers whose names begin with A are invariably larger or longer than rivers whose names begin B, would we conclude that we had explained the phenomenon in question by appealing to a sorting algorithm?

[17]Markov process and finite state automata are closely related objects.

[18]The discussion is taken from Eilenberg (1974). The subject has in recent years been infused with algebraic techniques and concepts. Readers familiar with early discussions from formal linguistics will require a short period of orientation before the new notations become compelling.

[19]An alphabet consists of a finite list of discrete items, and syntax is pursued in terms of shapes. There is no reason whatsoever that those symbols may not receive an interpretation in terms of any other finite and discrete set of structures—tissues or organs, for example, or more generally, "elements of an abstract set of events in the case of an analysis of the behavior of a system," as Perrin puts it (Perrin 1994, 4). It is for this reason that I use languages, events and structures with a certain lack of specificity.

[20]In what follows I draw no distinction between recognition and generation, swallowing both concepts in the all-purpose notion of a word being accessible to an automaton.

[21]A free monoid is a grouplike object, but one without an inverse. DNA is a word, of course; so too any of the proteins. In dealing with such structures, their associated free monoid is of an astonishing cardinality, an interesting and important fact, one pertinent to any assessment of the plausibility of Darwinian claims.

[22]Before any evolutionary theory may rationally be addressed, two logically prior questions need to be asked. The first: What are the properties of living systems that must be explained? The second: What are the capabilities of the devices invoked to explain them? Neither question is ever pursued in a serious way; but it is only when both questions have received an answer that anyone is in a position to determine whether in principle a particular theory could account for a particular fact or evolutionary development. The point is widely understood in other disciplines but stoutly resisted in biology.

[23]These are also known as regular expressions or events.

[24]The connection between behavioral theories in psychology and evolutionary theories in biology is one that typically goes unremarked by biologists, no doubt because of the stain of the association.

[25]This should provoke an intellectual twitch. From the point of view of Kolmogorov complexity, symmetry is the mark of structures that are simple; symmetry in physics marks the appearance of a local group. Just how these concepts are to be integrated is yet unknown.

[26]I have been calling attention to this point for years on end (see Berlinski 1972).

[27]See p. 407.

[28]Context-free language may also be defined directly in terms of grammatical rules or systems of equations. See p. 416 for details.

[29]The use of the term *absolute* is meant to suggest Gödel's own well-known remarks about recursiveness.

[30]For an example, see p. 411.

[31]The examples that follow are again due to Arthur Cody.

[32]There is a fourth level, that of experience itself. Without an account of such a level, no description of vision can possibly be complete; it is the purpose of the eye, after all, to enable an organism to see. Needless to say, we are in no position whatsoever to undertake a scientific analysis of experience.

[33]A labeled bracket is a static description of a biological structure. Like every other biological organ, the eye is designed to achieve a certain function, namely, sight; at the level of biological realism, one would expect to find very complicated transformations obtaining among various labeled brackets, so that even the simplest visual act must be described by a sequence $\Phi_1 \rightarrow \Phi_2 \rightarrow \ldots \rightarrow \Phi_n$, where each $\Phi$ is a labeled bracket. The description of such a sequence is utterly beyond our analytical abilities. Behe (1996) gives a fine sense of the complexity of a small part of the biochemistry of vision, but while we know something of the biochemistry and something too of the algorithmic properties of the visual system at a very abstract level, this through the work of David Marr and his collaborators, what we lack is any understanding of their dynamic interaction. See pp. 418 et seq.

[34]In the late 1950s analytic philosophers often wondered whether contextual definitions (in the sense of Carnap) filled an unused space between definitions and laws of nature. Their discussion was inadvertently prophetic. The question needs to be asked about algorithms instead.

[35]The obvious example is Richard Dawkins's *The Blind Watchmaker;* for comments, see Berlinski 1996b; but even sophisticated authors often fail to see the problem. See Keen and Spain 1992 for details.

[36]See Berlinski 1986, section 5, for further details.

[37]One is reminded of those superb lines by Gottfried Benn: *Leben ist Brückenschlagen über Ströme die vergehn.*

[38]In his final interview in *La Récherche,* this was a point to which M. P. Schützenberger recurred again and again. The interview, together with comments from critics, is available on the Web: http://www.mrccos.com/arn/odesign/od172/schutz.htm.

## References

Behe, M. J. 1996. *Darwin's black box: The biochemical challenge to evolution.* New York: Free Press.

Berlinski, D. 1972. Philosophical aspects of molecular biological systems. *Journal of Philosophy* 69 (June):319-35.

———. 1986. *Black mischief: Language, life, logic and luck.* New York: Harcourt Brace.

———. 1996a. The end of materialist science. *Forbes ASAP,* December:146-58.

———. 1996b. The deniable Darwin. *Commentary,* June:19-29.

Dennett, D. 1995. *Darwin's dangerous idea.* New York: Simon and Schuster.

Eilenberg, S. 1974. *Automata, languges and machines.* Vol. B. New York: Academic Press.

Goldberg, D. E. 1989. *Genetic algorithms.* Reading, Mass.: Addison-Wesley.

Kauffman, S. 1993. *The origins of order.* New York: Oxford University Press.

Keen, R. and J. Spain. 1992. *Computer simulation in biology.* New York: Wiley.

Mosses, P. 1994. Denotational semantics. In *Handbook of theoretical computer science,* ed. J. van Leeuwen, B:527-629. Cambridge, Mass.: MIT Press.

Orr, H. A. 1996. H. A. Orr responds. *Boston Review,* February:35.

Perrin, D. 1994. Finite automata. In *Handbook of theoretical computer science,* ed. J. van Leeuwen, B:3-53. Cambridge, Mass.: MIT Press.

Suppes, P. 1969. *Studies in methodology and foundations of science.* New York: Humanities Press.

Wang, H. 1995. On "computabilism" and physicalism: Some problems. In *Nature's imagination,* ed. J. Cornwell, 161-89. Oxford: Oxford University Press.

# 18

# Artificial Life &
# Cellular Automata

## ROBERT C. NEWMAN

RTIFICIAL LIFE (AL) IS A FLEDGLING SCIENCE THAT DIDN'T BEGIN IN earnest until the 1980s.[1] Unlike biology, AL studies life not in nature or in the laboratory but in the computer.[2] AL attempts to simulate life mathematically, generating known features of life from certain simple computational building blocks (Langton 1989, 2-5). Some of the more gung-ho researchers in AL see themselves as actually creating life in the electronic medium (Ray 1994, 180). Others are more modest and think they are only imitating it (Harnad 1994, 544-49). At any rate, AL presupposes that life does not have to be manifested in biochemistry.

AL research is dominated by metaphysical naturalism, the view that the cosmos is all that is, or ever was, or ever will be. Metaphysical naturalism demands a purely nonsupernatural origin and development of life, unguided by any mind. For metaphysical naturalism, no other causality exists. Theists, by contrast, believe that a mind—God—is behind it all, irrespective of how he worked. Perhaps God created matter with built-in capabilities for producing life; perhaps he intervened to structure matter with the informational patterns characteristic of living things; perhaps he used some combination of the two.

Current naturalistic explanations of life may be characterized by three basic claims. First, life arose here on earth or elsewhere without any intelligent oversight—a self-reproducing system somehow assembled itself. Second, the (essentially blind) Darwinian mechanism of mutation and natural selection, which then came into play, was so effective that it produced all the variety and complexity we see in modern life forms. Third, the time taken for the assembly of the first self-reproducer was short enough and the rate at which mutation and natural selection operates is fast enough to account for the general features of the fossil record and such particulars as the Cambrian explosion. Much of the AL research attempts to establish one or more of these claims.

What sort of world do we actually live in: the "blind watchmaker" universe of metaphysical naturalism or one structured by a designing mind? AL hopes ultimately to resolve this question in favor of naturalism. Meanwhile AL remains a large and rapidly growing field of inquiry. Although I cannot give a comprehensive picture of this field, I shall try to whet your appetite and provide some suggestions for further research. To do this I shall look briefly at several proposals from AL and see how these proposals are faring in the light of AL's naturalistic presuppositions. First we shall look at the cellular automata devised by von Neumann, Codd, Langton, Byl and Ludwig, both with respect to the origin of significant self-reproduction and the question of how life might have developed. Second, we shall sketch Mark Ludwig's work on computer viruses, which he suggests are the nearest thing to artificial life that humans have yet devised. Third, we shall examine one of Richard Dawkins's programs designed to simulate natural selection. Fourth, we shall look at Thomas Ray's "Tierra" environment, which explores the effects of mutation and natural selection on a population of electronic creatures.

### Cellular Automata

Beginning nearly half a century ago, long before there was any discipline called AL, computer pioneer John von Neumann sought to investigate the question of life's origin by designing a self-reproducing automaton. This machine was to operate in a very simplified environment to see just what was involved in reproduction. For the building blocks of this automaton, von Neumann chose computer chips fixed in a rigid two-dimensional array rather than biochemicals swimming in a three-dimensional soup. (In practice his machine was to be emulated by a single large computer to do the work of the many small computer chips.)

Each computer chip is identical but can be made to behave differently depending on which of several operational states it is currently in. Typically we imagine the chips as wired to their four nearest neighbors, each chip identifying its current state via a number on a liquid crystal display like that on a wristwatch. The chips change states synchronously in discrete time-steps rather than continuously. The state of each chip for the next time-step is determined from its own current state and those of its four neighbors using a set of transition rules specified by the automaton's designer (see figure 18.1).

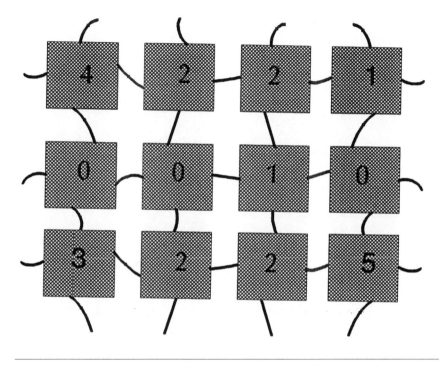

Figure 18.1  2-D Array of Chips for Cellular Automaton

The idea in the design of a self-reproducing automaton is to set up an initial array of states for some group of these chips in such a way that they will turn a neighboring set of chips into an information channel and then use this channel to build a copy of the original array nearby.

Von Neumann in the late 1940s and early 1950s attempted to design such a system (called a cellular automaton) that could construct any automaton from the proper set of encoded instructions. As a special case it could make a copy of itself. Unfortunately von Neumann died in 1957 before he could complete his design, and it was finished by his associate Arthur Burks (von Neumann 1966). Because of its complexity—some 300×500 chips for the memory control unit, about the same for the constructing unit, and an instruction "tape" of some 150,000 chips—the machine von Neumann designed was not built.[3]

Since von Neumann's time, self-reproducing automata have been greatly simplified. E. F. Codd (1968) reduced the number of states needed for each chip from 29 to 8. But Codd's automaton was also a "universal constructor"— able to reproduce any cellular automaton including itself. As a result it was still about as complicated as a computer (see figure 18.2).

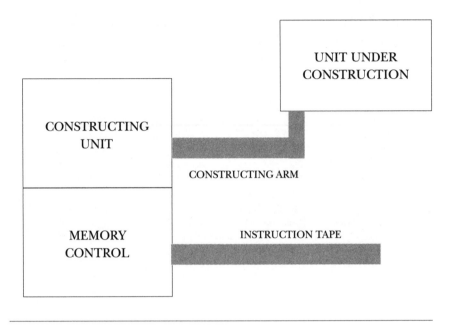

**Figure 18.2   Codd's Automaton**

Christopher Langton (1984) made the real breakthrough to simplicity by modifying one of the component parts of Codd's automaton and from it producing a simple automaton (see figure 18.3) that will reproduce itself in 151 time-steps. It reproduces by extending its arm (at the bottom right of figure 18.3) by six units, turning left, extending it six more units, turning left, extending six more, turning left a third time, extending six more, colliding with the arm near its beginning, breaking the connection between mother and daughter and then making a new arm for each of the two automata. Langton's automaton by design will not construct other kinds of cellular automata as von Neumann's and Codd's would. His device consisted of some 10×15 chips, including an instruction tape of 33 chips, plus some 190 transition rules.

```
                  2 2 2 2 2 2 2 2
                2 1 7 0 1 4 0 1 4 2
                2 0 2 2 2 2 2 2 0 2
                2 7 2         2 1 2
                2 1 2         2 1 2
                2 0 2         2 1 2
                2 7 2         2 1 2
                2 2 2 2 2 2 2 2 1 2 2 2 2 2
                2 0 7 1 0 7 1 0 7 1 1 1 1 1 2
                  2 2 2 2 2 2 2 2 2 2 2 2 2
```

**Figure 18.3   Langton's Automaton**

Just a few years later John Byl (1989a, b) simplified Langton's automaton further (see figure 18.4) with an even smaller automaton that reproduced in just 25 time-steps. Byl's automaton consisted of an array of 12 chips—of which 4 or 5 could be counted as the instruction tape—and 43 transition rules.

```
    2 2             2 2             2 2     3
  2 6 3 2         2 3 4 2         2 4 6 2
  2 6 4 2         2 6 6 4 3 3     2 3 6 6 4 3 6 3
    2 5             2 2 1 2         2 2 1 2 2 2

    T = 0           T = 5           T = 10


    2 2     3             2 2           2             2 2             2 2
  2 6 6 2         3     2 6 3 2       3 6 2       2 3 4 5       2 6 3 2
  2 4 3 6 6 4 3 6 2     2 6 4 3 6 6 4 3 2     2 6 6 2       2 6 4 2
  2 2 1 2 2 2 2         2 2 1 2 2 2 2         2 2     2     2 5

    T = 15                 T = 20               T = 25
```

**Figure 18.4   Byl's Automaton**

Most recently Mark Ludwig (1993, 107-8) has carried this simplification to its apparent limit with a minuscule automaton that reproduces in just 5 time-steps. This automaton consists of 4 chips, only one of which is the instruction "tape," and some 22 transition rules (see figure 18.5).

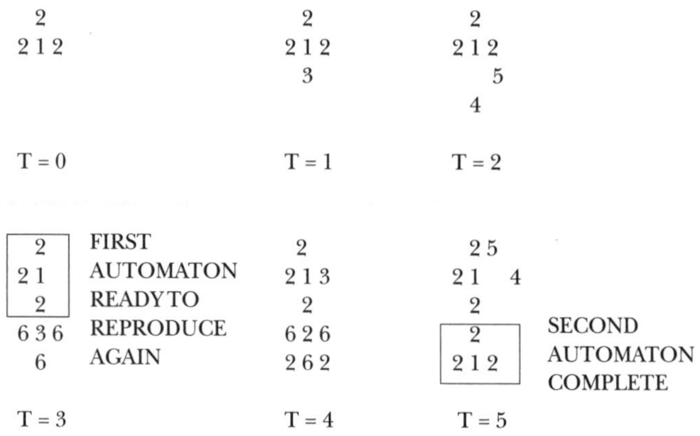

```
        2                          2              2
      2 1 2                      2 1 2          2 1 2
                                   3              5
                                                 4


      T = 0                      T = 1          T = 2
```

```
      ┌───┐  FIRST                2              2 5
      │ 2 │  AUTOMATON          2 1 3          2 1    4
      │ 2 1│  READY TO            2              2
      │ 2 │  REPRODUCE                        ┌─────┐
      └───┘                                   │  2  │   SECOND
      6 3 6  AGAIN              6 2 6          │ 2 1 2│   AUTOMATON
        6                      2 6 2          └─────┘   COMPLETE


      T = 3                      T = 4          T = 5
```

---

**Figure 18.5  Ludwig's Automaton**

It is interesting to note that the information contained in each of these self-reproducing automata may be divided into three parts: the transition rules, the geometry of the chips and the instruction tape. The transition rules, which tell us how state succeeds state in each chip, are supposed to resemble the physics or chemistry of a biological environment. The geometry of the automaton would correspond to the structure of a biological cell. The instructions resemble the DNA. Thus in both AL and biology, self-reproduction depends not only on an instruction set but also upon the structure of the reproducer and the nature of the physical realm in which it operates.

For the von Neumann and Codd automata, since they are universal constructors, the size of the machine and its instructions are enormous. One could not seriously entertain a naturalistic origin of life if the original self-reproducing system had to have anything like this complexity. The smaller automata look much more promising, however. Perhaps a self-reproducing biochemical system at this level of complexity could have arisen by a chance assembly of parts. In a previous work (Newman 1988) I suggested that the random formation of something as complex as the Langton automaton (even with very generous assumptions) was out of the question in our whole universe in the 20 billion years since the big bang, as the probability of formation with all this space and time available is only 1 chance in $10^{129}$.

In response to Byl's proposed automaton, I found it necessary (Newman 1990a) to revise this probability, but even so I found that Byl's automaton had only 1 chance in $10^{69}$ of forming anywhere in our universe since the big bang. Ludwig's automaton, however, looks so simple as to be a sure thing in a universe as vast and old as ours. By the assumptions used in doing my probability calculation for Byl's automaton, we would have a Ludwig automaton formed every $7 \times 10^{-15}$ seconds in our universe.

Nonetheless an enormously favorable assumption is contained in this calculation—that all the carbon in the universe is tied up in 92-atom molecules that exchange material to try out new combinations as quickly as an atom can move the length of a molecule at room temperature. If, however, we calculate the expected fraction of carbon that would actually be found in 92-atom polymers throughout our universe, the expected time between formation of Ludwig automatons in our universe jumps to about $10^{86}$ years. Thus it would still not be wise to put one's money on the random formation of self-reproduction even at this simple level.[4]

Besides the problem of formation time, the physics (transition rules) of these smaller automata was specially contrived to make the particular automaton work, and it is probably not good for anything else. Since the automata of Langton, Byl and Ludwig were not designed to be universal constructors, self-reproduction typically collapses for any mutation in the instructions. To avoid this, the constructing mechanism in any practical candidate for the first self-reproducer will have to be much more flexible so that it can continue to construct copies of itself while it changes.

The physics of such automata could be made more general by going back toward the larger number of states used in von Neumann's automaton. Langton, for instance, has a signal for extending a data path in his information tape but none for retracting one; a signal for a left-turn but none for a right-turn. These could be included rather easily by adding additional chip states to his eight, thus making the physics more flexible. Of course this would significantly increase the number of transition rules and the consequent complexity of his automaton.

This obviously makes self-reproduction even less likely to have happened by chance. But it would also help alleviate the problem that these simpler automata do not have a big enough vocabulary in their genetic information systems to be able to do anything but a very specialized form of self-reproduction, and they have no way to expand this vocabulary, which was designed in at the beginning. This problem seems to me a serious one for the evolution of growing levels of complexity in general.

As for building an automaton that is more general in its constructing abilities and not tied to a particular physics especially contrived for it, Karl Sigmund (1993, 27-39) has described an attempt by John Conway to use the environment of his game of "Life" as a substrate on which to design a universal constructor. He succeeds in doing so, but the result is outrageously complex, back in the league with von Neumann's and Codd's automata.

We should be able to design a reasonably general self-reproducing automaton on a substrate not especially designed for it. This would be a good project for future research. We would then have a better handle on what complexity appears to be minimal for significant self-reproduction and what would be the likelihood it could occur by chance in a universe such as ours.

The environment in which each of these self-reproducing automata operates is empty in the sense that nothing else is around and happening. By design, the sea of unused cells is quiescent. This is certainly unlike the scenario imagined for the origin of biochemical life. What will happen to our automata if they are bumped by or run into other objects in their space? Are they too fragile to be real candidates for the hypothetical original self-reproducer? The Langton automaton certainly is. By running the program with a "pimple" placed on the surface of the automaton (i.e., the structure is touched by a single cell in any of the states 1-7), we find that the automaton typically "crashes" in about 30 time-steps (the time taken for the data to cycle once around the loop). It appears that the automaton is very fragile or brittle rather than robust. This would certainly not be satisfactory in a real-life situation.

### Computer Viruses

Ludwig is an expert on computer viruses (see Ludwig 1991). Recently he has written *Computer Viruses, Artificial Life and Evolution* (1993). In it Ludwig argues that computer viruses are closer to artificial life than anything else humans have produced so far, especially since such viruses have gotten loose from their creators (or been set loose) and, like the biochemical viruses for which they are named, are fending for themselves quite successfully in a hostile environment.[5]

Like the cellular automata, computer viruses have the ability to reproduce themselves. What is more, they can hide themselves from predators (antivirus programs) by lurking inside the instructions of some regular computer program that they have infected. They may also function as parasites, predators or clever annoyances as they ride programs from disk to disk, computer to computer and user to user. Some viruses (by design or not) damage files or programs in a computer's memory; others clutter up memory or diskettes or send humorous and irksome messages to the computer screen.

Although no one claims that computer viruses arose spontaneously in the memories of computers, one can still ask how likely it would be for something as complex as a simple computer virus to form by chance in a computational environment. Early in 1993 Ludwig sponsored "The First International Virus

Writing Contest," awarding a prize for the shortest virus that could be designed having a certain rather minimal function (Ludwig 1993, 319-21). Ludwig provides the code (computer program) for the virus that was grand prize winner as well as for several runners-up, plus a sample virus that he sent out with the original announcement of the contest (Ludwig 1993, 322-31). These programs all turned out to be over 100 bytes in length.

Ludwig calculates that for the shortest of these (101 bytes) there are $10^{243}$ possible files of length 101 bytes. If we could get all the 100 million PC users in the world to run their machines full-time with a program that generates nothing but 101-byte random sequences at 1000 files per second, then in 10 years the probability of generating this particular virus is $2 \times 10^{-224}$ (Ludwig 1993, 254-25). If they ran for the whole history of the universe, the probability would be $4 \times 10^{-214}$. If all the elementary particles in our universe were converted into PCs generating 1000 random 101-byte files per second, the probability of forming this particular virus would be $6 \times 10^{-110}$ (Ludwig 1993, 255). Obviously our universe does not have the probabilistic resources to generate this level of order by random assembly.

Ludwig then discusses two much smaller programs. One is a crude virus of 42 bytes, which copies itself on top of all the programs in a computer's directory. He notes that one might just expect to form this virus in the history of the universe if all those elementary particles were PCs cranking out 1000 42-byte random files per second but that if one only had the 100 million PCs and ten years for the job, the probability would be only $4 \times 10^{-81}$ (ibid., pp. 254-55). This would improve to $8 \times 10^{-72}$ if one had all the time since the big bang to work with.

The smallest program Ludwig works with is not a virus, since it cannot make copies of itself that are saved to disk but only copies that remain in memory so long as the computer is running. This program is only 7 bytes long. It could easily be formed in ten years with 100 million PCs turning out 1000 7-byte sequences per second, but it would take a single computer about 2.5 million years to do so. It is doubtful that this is the long-sought self-reproducer that will show how life arose by chance. The actual complexity of this program is considerably greater than 7 bytes because it uses the copying commands provided by the computer, which actually makes the duplicates.[6] The environment provided for computer viruses is thus much more helpful for self-reproduction than is the biochemical environment.

Ludwig also considers forming a virus by accidental mutation of an existing computer program (Ludwig 1993, 259-63). This is an interesting discussion, but it tells us more about how a biochemical virus might get started in a world that already has a lot of life than it does about how life might get started in abiotic circumstances. Thus, as in the case of cellular automata, we see that a random search for self-reproduction (before mutation and natural selection can kick in) is an extremely inefficient way to reach even very modest levels of organized complexity. Yet for naturalism, that is the only path available.

### Dawkins's "Weasel" Program

Richard Dawkins claims there is no need for a mind behind the universe. Random processes, operating long enough, will eventually produce any level of order desired. "Give enough monkeys enough time, and they will eventually type out the works of Shakespeare." If indeed we grant that we live in a universe totally devoid of mind, then something like this must be true. And granting this, if we broaden our definition of "monkey" sufficiently to include anthropoid apes, then it has already happened. An ape evolved into William Shakespeare, who eventually wrote—and his descendants typed— his immortal works.

But this is merely to beg the question. As Dawkins points out (Dawkins 1987, 46-47), the time required to reasonably expect a monkey to type even one line from Shakespeare—say, "Methinks it is like a weasel" from *Hamlet*— would be astronomical. To get any significant level of order by random assembly of gibberish is out of the question in a universe merely billions of years old and a similar number of light-years across.

But Dawkins (who, after all, believes our universe was devoid of mind until mind evolved) claims that selection can vastly shorten the time necessary to produce such order. He programs his computer to start with a line of gibberish the same length as the target sentence and shows how the target may be reached by selection in a very short time.

Dawkins accomplishes this (Dawkins 1987, 46-50) by having the computer make a random change in the original gibberish and test it against the target sentence, selecting the closer approximation at each step and then starting the next step with the selected line. For instance, starting with the line

WDLTMNLT DTJBSWIRZREZLMQCO P

Dawkins's computer reaches its target in just 43 steps or generations. In two other runs starting with different gibberish, the same target is reached in 64 and 41 generations.

This seems impressive. Yet it does not tell us much about natural selection (i.e., selection as it occurs in nature as opposed to in a computational environment). A minor problem with Dawkins's program is that he designed it to converge far more rapidly than real mutation and natural selection. I devised a program SHAKES (Newman 1990b) that allows the operator to enter any target sentence plus a line of gibberish of the same length. The computer then randomly chooses any one of the characters in the line of gibberish, randomly chooses what change to make in that character, and then tests the result against the target. If the changed line is closer to the target than it was before the change, it replaces the previous gibberish. If not, then the previous version remains.

Dawkins did something like this, but his version closes on its target far more rapidly. For instance, his version moves from

METHINKS IT IS LIKE I WEASEL

to

METHINKS IT IS LIKE A WEASEL

in just three generations (Dawkins 1987, 48). For Dawkins, once the computer gets a particular character right, it never allows mutation to work on that character again. That is certainly not how real mutation works. My version took several hundred steps to move across a gap like the preceding one because the mutation had to both randomly occur at the right spot in the line and randomly find a closer letter to put in that place. My runs typically took over a thousand steps to converge on the target from the original gibberish.

But a far more serious problem with Dawkins's simulation is that real mutation and natural selection do not have a template to aim at unless we live in a designed universe (see Ludwig 1993, 256-59). A better simulation would be an open-ended search for an unspecified but meaningful sentence, something like my program MUNSEL (Newman 1990b). This program makes random changes in the length and the characters of a string of letters without a template guiding it to some predetermined result. Here a randomizing function either adds a letter or space to one end of the string or changes one of the existing letters or spaces to another. This mimics the action of mutation in changing the nucleotide bases in a DNA molecule or the amino acids in a protein.

In this program, natural selection is simulated by having an operator decide whether the resulting string consists of nothing but English words. If it does, then the mutant survives (is retained); if it does not, the mutant dies (is discarded). This could be done more efficiently (and allow for much longer computer runs) if one programmed the computer to use a spell-checker from a word-processing program to make these decisions instead of a human operator.

The mutants must satisfy even more stringent requirements to simulate the development of higher levels of order. For instance, the operator might specify that each successful mutant conform to English syntax or even that it have coherent semantic content. This would give us a better idea of what mutation and natural selection can do to produce the higher levels of organization needed for macroevolution really to work.

### Ray's "Tierra" Environment

One of the most interesting and impressive attempts to simulate evolution computationally is the ongoing experiment called "Tierra" by Thomas Ray at the University of Delaware (Ray 1991). Ray designed an electronic organism that is a small computer program that copies itself. In this it resembles cellular automata and in particular computer viruses. It differs from these in that it lives in an environment—"the soup," also designed by Ray—that explicitly includes both mutation and a natural competition between organisms.

To avoid problems that can arise when computer viruses escape captivity, the soup is a virtual computer, a text file that simulates a computer, so the programs are not actually roaming around loose in the computer's memory. For most of Ray's runs, the soup contains 60,000 bytes, equivalent to 60,000 instructions. This will typically accommodate a population of a few hundred organisms, so the dynamics will be those of a small, isolated population.

To counter the problem of fragility or brittleness that arises with cellular automata, Ray invented his own computer language. This "Tierran" language is more robust than the standard languages and therefore not as easily disrupted by mutations. It is a modification of the very low-level assembly language used by programmers, but with two major differences: it has very few commands—only 32 (compare the assembly language for 486 computers, with nearly 250 commands; see Brumm, Brumm, and Scanlon 1991, 136-41)—and it addresses other locations in memory by means of templates rather than address numbers, a feature modeled on the biochemical technique by which molecules find each other. The program is set up so the operator can vary the maximum distance that an organism will search to locate a needed template.

Ray starts things off by introducing a single organism into the soup. There it begins to multiply, with the mother and resulting daughter organisms taking turns at copying themselves until they have nearly filled the available memory. Once the level of fullness passes 80 perecent, a procedure kicks in which Ray calls "the Reaper." This keeps the soup from overcrowding by killing off organisms one by one, working down from the top of a hit list. An organism at birth starts at the bottom of this list and moves upward as it ages, but will move up even faster if it makes certain errors in copying. Alternatively it can delay moving upward somewhat if it can successfully negotiate a couple of difficult procedures.

The master computer that runs the simulation allows each organism to execute its own instructions in turn. The turn for each organism can be varied in different runs of the experiment so as to make this allowance some fixed number of instructions per turn, or dependent on the size of the organism so as to favor larger creatures, smaller ones, or be size-neutral.

Ray introduces mutation into the system by fiat and can change the rate of mutation from zero (to simulate ecological situations on a timescale much shorter than the mutation rate) up to very high levels (in which the whole population perishes).

One form of mutation is designed to simulate that from cosmic rays. Binary digits are flipped at random locations in the soup, most of which will be in the organisms' genomes. The usual rate that Ray sets for this is one mutation for every 10,000 instructions executed. Another form of mutation is introduced into the copying procedure. Here a bit is randomly flipped during reproduction (typically for every 1000 to 2500 instructions transferred from mother to daughter). This rate is similar in magnitude to the cosmic ray mutation. A third source of mutation Ray introduces is a small level of error in the execution of instructions, making their action slightly probabilistic rather than strictly deterministic. This is intended to simulate occasional undesired reactions in the biochemistry (Ray 1994, 187). Ray does not specify the rate at which error is introduced by this channel.

Ray's starting organism consists of 80 instructions in the Tierran language, each instruction being one byte (of 5 bits) long. The organism begins its reproduction cycle by reading and recording its length, using templates that mark the beginning and end of its instruction set. It then allocates a space in the soup for its daughter and copies its own instructions into the allocated space, using other templates among its instructions for the needed jumps from place to place in its program (subroutines, loops, etc.). It ends its cycle by individuating the daughter as a separate organism. Because the copying procedure is a loop, the original unmutated organism actually needs to execute over 800 instructions before it completes one full reproduction. Once there are a number of organisms in the soup, this may require an organism to use several of its turns to complete one reproduction.

Ray has now run this experiment on his own personal computer and on much faster mainframe computers many times, with some runs going for billions of instructions. (With 300 organisms in the soup, 1 billion instructions would typically correspond to some four thousand generations.) Ray has seen organisms both much larger and much smaller than the original develop by mutation, and some of these have survived to do very well in the competition.

Ray has observed the production of parasites, which have lost the instructions for copying themselves, usually due to a mutation in a template that renders it useless. These are sterile in isolation, but in the soup they can often use the copy procedure of a neighbor by finding its template. This sort of mutant typically arises in the first few million instructions executed in a run (less than 100 generations after the soup fills). Longer runs have produced organisms with some resistance to parasites; hyperparasites, which cause certain parasites to reproduce the hyperparasite rather than themselves; social hyperparasites, which can reproduce only in communities; and cheaters, which take advantage of the social hyperparasites. All these Ray would classify as microevolution. Under the category of macroevolution, Ray mentions one run with selection designed to favor large-sized organisms, which produced apparently open-ended size increase and some organisms longer than 23 thousand instructions.

Ray notes two striking examples of novelty produced in his Tierra simulations: an unusual procedure one organism uses to measure its size and a more efficient copying technique developed in another organism by the end of a 15-billion-instruction run. In the former of these, the organism, having lost its template that locates one end of its instructions, makes do by using a template located in the middle and multiplying this length by two to get the correct length. In the latter, the copying loop has become more efficient by copying three instructions per loop instead of just one, saving the execution of several steps.

With size-neutral selection, Ray has found periods of stasis punctuated by periods of rapid change. Typically the soup is first dominated by organisms with length on the order of 80 bytes for the first 1.5 billion instructions executed. Then it comes to be dominated by organisms 5 to 10 times larger in just a few million more instructions. In general it is common for the soup to be dominated by one or two size-classes for long periods of time. Inevitably, however, that will break down into a period (often chaotic) in which no size dominates and sometimes no genotypes are breeding true. This is followed by another period of stasis with one or two other size classes now dominating.

Ray's results are impressive. But what do they mean? For the origin of life, not much. Ray has not attempted to simulate the origin of life, and his creatures at 80 bytes in length are complex enough to be very unlikely to form by chance. Each byte in Tierran has 5 bits or 32 combinations, so there are $32^{80}$ combinations for an 80-byte program, which is $2 \times 10^{120}$. Following Ludwig's scheme of using all the earth's 100 million PCs to generate 1000 80-byte combinations per second, we would need $7 \times 10^{100}$ years for the job. If all $10^{90}$ elementary particles were turned into computers to generate combinations, it would still take $7 \times 10^{18}$ years, 300 million times the age of the universe. Not a likely scenario, although one can hope a shorter program that initiates reproduction might kick in much earlier.

In fact Ray's experiments have apparently generated a 22-instruction creature that reproduces by itself (i.e., is not a parasite).[7] This is much more likely to form accidentally from scratch than an 80-instruction program, but it is still quite unlikely. The number of possible 22-byte programs is $32^{22}$, which is $1.3 \times 10^{33}$. Using Ludwig's scheme for calculation, we would expect 100 million PCs generating 1000 22-byte combinations per second to take $4 \times 10^{14}$ years to find this combination.

What about the type of evolution experienced in the Tierra environment? Can it reach the levels of complexity seen in biology? This is not an easy question to answer. The Tierra simulation is typically run with a very high rate of mutation, typically on the order of 1 in 5000 or higher. Copying errors in DNA are more like 1 in a billion (Dawkins 1987, 124), some 200,000 times smaller. Thus we get a lot more variation in a short time and many more mutations per generation per instruction. Ray justifies this by claiming that he is simulating the hypothetical RNA world before the development of the more sophisticated DNA style of reproduction and that a much higher level of mutation is to be expected. Besides, for the sake of simulation, one wants to have something to study within the span of reasonable computer times. All this is true, but there is also the danger of simulating a world that is far more hospitable to evolution than ours is (see the remark of Pattee and Ludwig's discussion, both in Ludwig 1993, 162-64).

The consequences of mutation seem considerably less drastic in Tierra also, making that world especially favorable for evolution. No organism in Tierra dies before it gets a shot at reproducing, whereas dysfunction, disease, predators and accidents destroy many organisms (fit or not) before they reproduce in our world. This effectively raises the mutation rate in Tierra still higher while protecting against its dangers, and it increases the chance that an organism may be able to hop over a gap of dysfunction to land on an island of function.

In Tierra the debris from killed organisms remains in the environment. But instead of being a danger to living organisms, as it so often is in our world, the debris is available as instructions for parasites whose programs are searching the soup for templates. This enormously raises the mutation rate for parasites, producing something rather like sexual reproduction in a high mutation environment.

Tierran organisms have easy access to the innards of other organisms. The program design allows them to examine and read the instructions of their neighbors but not write over them. The organisms are designed to be able to search in either direction from their location some distance to find a needed template. This is typically set at 200-400 instructions but on some runs has been as high as 10,000, giving access to one-third the entire environment. This feature is not used by any organism whose original templates are intact, but it provides the various types of parasites with the opportunity to borrow genetic material from up to one-third of the creatures in Tierra and probably permits many of them to escape their parasitic lifestyle with a whole new set of genes.

The innards themselves, whether part of a living or a dead organism, are all nicely usable instructions. Every byte in each organism is an instruction, and once an organism has inhabited a particular portion of the soup, its instructions are left behind after its death until they are written over by the instructions of another organism inhabiting that space at a later time.

The Tierran language is robust in that every mutation of every byte produces a mutant byte that makes sense within the system. Gibberish arises only in the random arrangement of these bytes rather than in any of the bytes themselves. Thus the Tierran language cannot help but have meaning at the level of words. The real test for macroevolution in Tierra will be how successful it is in producing meaning at the level of sentences, and this does not appear impressive so far.

In a more recent paper Ray attempts to mimic multicellular life (Thearling and Ray 1994). So far they have been unable to produce organisms in which the cells are differentiated. Moreover, they have skipped the whole problem of how to get from unicellular to multicellular life.

One might respond that the Tierran language is too limited to mirror all that has happened in the history of life on earth. Even so, Maley (1994) has argued that the Tierran language is computationally complete—that it is equivalent to a Turing machine[8]—so that in principle it can accommodate any function that the most sophisticated computer can perform. It might take an astronomically longer time to accomplish this than it would with an ordinary computer, but this brings us back to the question whether simulations are more or less efficient than biochemistry at producing the degree of complexity we actually find in nature. Until we can answer this question, it will be hard to use AL to prove that life in all its complexity could or could not have arisen by undirected natural processes in our universe and in the time available. In any case these simulations should be able to tell us whether mutation and natural selection can actually generate structures with a significant amount of irreducible complexity (Behe 1996).

What do the evolved programs of Tierran mutants look like, and how do they compare with the programs found in the DNA of biochemical life? Are they comparable in efficiency, elegance and function? Does the DNA in our world look as though biochemical life has experienced a history similar to these Tierran creatures? Thomas Ray's experiment needs to be continued for it provides a tractable computational model of what an evolutionary process can actually accomplish. But the details of its design need to be continually revised to bring it in line with biochemical reality.[9] Ray has shown that the Tierra environment can produce a certain degree of complexity.

Can it produce enough to explain the complexity we observe in biochemical life on earth? I, for one, remain skeptical.

## Conclusion

In this chapter I have briefly reviewed some of the high points of artificial life research. Many open problems remain. Even the definition of self-reproduction requires clarification. Within AL the temptation is to make self-reproduction much easier than it is in biology. It is, for instance, all too easy to ride on the copying capabilities of the host computer and its language. Our computational models need to approximate biochemical reality. In biochemical life, multicellular organisms function and reproduce differently from unicellular organisms. The transition from one to the other appears to have occurred roughly at the Cambrian explosion. How did it occur? So far, nothing we have seen in computer simulations of evolution has even come close to mirroring this event.

Because AL is a rapidly growing field of research, in the coming years we should obtain a better handle on how complex self-reproduction is and what mutation and natural selection can accomplish in building complex machines. For now it appears a self-reproducing automaton needs to be considerably closer to a universal constructor than the simplest self-reproducers that have been proposed. In order that it not immediately collapse when subjected to mutation, a self-reproducing automaton must be robust. Also, it must be able to continue constructing itself as it changes from simple to complex. In fact it must somehow change both itself and its instructions in synchrony in order to continue to reproduce and develop the levels of complexity seen in biochemical life.[10] This is a tall order for any self-reproducer that could be expected to form in a universe as young and small as ours. However, even though this is a short order for a universe infinite in extent or duration, there is no evidence that ours is such a universe. Currently artificial life looks more like an argument for a designer than for a blind watchmaker.

## Notes

[1] See Langton (1989, 6-21) for the "prehistory" of artificial life studies.

[2] Taylor and Jefferson (1994, 1-4) would define artificial life more broadly to include synthetic biochemistry and robotics; so too Ray (1994, 179-80).

[3] Pesavento (1995) announces the recent implementation of von Neumann's machine.

[4] These calculations do not take into account the possible multiplicity of self-reproducers of a particular size scale. It is not known in complex cases how numerous these might be, so that the calculations may be some orders of magnitude too pessimistic. Ludwig (1993) has done some estimates along these lines for simple

cellular automata.

[5]See also Spafford 1994, who does not want to call viruses artificial life but admits they are closer to it than anything else humans have made.

[6]The various "move" commands do not just move the information from one location to another, but also they leave the same information behind in the original location, thus effectively copying it.

[7]Assuming that none of Ray's graduate students slipped a designed creature into his soup.

[8]See Dewdney 1989 for a discussion of Turing machines.

[9]Some helpful attempts in this direction have been made by Adami and Brown 1994 and Shanahan 1994.

[10]Ray finesses this problem by collapsing the genotype and phenotype into one.

## Bibliography

Adami, C. 1995. On modeling life. *Artificial Life* 1:429-38.

Adami, C., and C. T. Brown. 1994. Evolutionary learning in the 2D artificial life system "Avida." In *Artificial life*, ed. R. A. Brooks and P. Maes, 377-81. Cambridge, Mass.: MIT Press.

Agarwal, P. 1995. The cell programming language. *Artificial Life* 2:37-77.

Behe, M. J. 1996. *Darwin's black box: The biochemical challenge to evolution.* New York: Free Press.

Bonabeau, E. W., and G. Theraulaz. 1994. Why do we need artificial life? *Artificial Life* 1:303-25.

Brooks, R. A., and P. Maes, eds. 1994. *Artificial life 4.* Cambridge, Mass.: MIT Press.

Brumm, P., D. Brumm, and L. J. Scanlon. 1991. *80486 Programming.* Blue Ridge Summit, Penn.: Windcrest.

Byl, J. 1989a. Self-reproduction in small cellular automata. *Physica D* 34:295-99.

―――. 1989b. On cellular automata and the origin of life. *Perspectives on Science and Christian Faith* 41 (1):26-29.

Codd, E. F. 1968. *Cellular automata.* New York: Academic.

Dawkins, R. 1987. *The blind watchmaker.* New York: Norton.

Dennett, D. 1994. Artificial life as philosophy. *Artificial Life* 1:291-92.

Dewdney, A. K. 1989. *The Turing omnibus.* Rockville, Md.: Computer Science Press.

Fontana, W., G. Wagner, and L. W. Buss. 1994. Beyond digital naturalism. *Artificial Life* 1:211-27.

Harnad, S. 1994. Artificial life: Synthetic versus virtual. In *Artificial life 3*, ed. C. G. Langton, 539-52. Reading, Mass.: Addison-Wesley.

Koza, J. H. 1994. Artificial life: Spontaneous emergence of self-replicating and evolutionary self-improving computer programs. In *Artificial life 3*, ed. C. G. Langton, 225-62. Reading, Mass.: Addison-Wesley.

Langton, C. G. 1984. Self-reproduction in cellular automata. *Physica D* 10:135-44.

―――. 1989. Artificial life. In *Artificial life*, ed. C. G. Langton, 1-47. Reading, Mass.: Addison-Wesley.

―――, ed. 1989. *Artificial life.* Reading, Mass.: Addison-Wesley.

―――, ed. 1994. *Artificial life 3.* Reading, Mass.: Addison-Wesley.

Langton, C., C. Taylor, D. Farmer, and S. Rasmussen, eds. 1991. *Artificial life 2.* Redwood City, Calif.: Addison-Wesley.

Ludwig, M. 1991. *The little black book of computer viruses.* Tucson, Ariz.: American Eagle

Publications.

———. 1993. *Computer viruses, artificial life and evolution.* Tucson, Ariz.: American Eagle Publications. Current address: American Eagle Publications, P.O. Box 1507, Show Low, AZ 85901.

Maley, C. C. 1994. The computational completeness of Ray's Tierran assembly language. In *Artificial life 3,* ed. C. G. Langton, 503-14. Reading, Mass.: Addison-Wesley.

Neumann, J. von. 1966. *The theory of self-reproducing automata.* Edited by A. W. Burks. Urbana: University of Illinois Press.

Newman, R. C. 1988. Self-reproducing automata and the origin of life. *Perspectives on Science and Christian Faith* 40 (1):24-31.

———. 1990a. Automata and the origin of life: Once again. *Perspectives on Science and Christian Faith* 42 (2):113-14.

———. 1990b. *Computer simulations of evolution.* MS-DOS diskette of computer programs. Hatfield, Penn.: Interdisciplinary Biblical Research Institute.

Pesavento, U. 1995. An implementation of von Neumann's self-reproducing machine. *Artificial Life* 2(4):337-254.

Ray, T. S. 1991. An approach to the synthesis of life. In *Artificial life 2,* ed. C. G. Langton, C. Taylor, D. Farmer, and S. Rasmussen, 371-408. Redwood City, Calif.: Addison-Wesley. An updated and expanded version of the paper (as of August 1995), under the title "Evolution, ecology and optimization of digital organisms," is available on the Internet at www.htp.atr.co.jp/~ray/pubs/tierra/tierrahtml.html.

———. 1994. An evolutionary approach to synthetic biology: Zen and the art of creating life. *Artificial Life* 1:179-209.

Shanahan, M. 1994. Evolutionary automata. In *Artificial life 4,* ed. R. A. Brooks and P. Maes, 388-93. Cambridge, Mass.: MIT Press.

Sigmund, K. 1993. *Games of life: Explorations in ecology, evolution and behavior.* New York: Oxford University Press.

Sipper, M. 1995. Studying artificial life using a simple, general cellular model. *Artificial Life* 2:1-35.

Spafford, E. H. 1994. Computer viruses as artificial life. *Artificial Life* 1:249-65.

Taylor, C., and D. Jefferson. 1994. Artificial life as a tool for biological inquiry. *Artificial Life* 1:1-13.

Thearling, K., and T. S. Ray. 1994. Evolving multicellular artificial life. In *Artificial life 4,* ed. R. A. Brooks and P. Maes, 283-88. Cambridge, Mass.: MIT Press.

# Afterword

# How to Sink
a Battleship

*A Call to Separate
Materialist Philosophy
from Empirical Science*

PHILLIP E. JOHNSON

*I*WANT TO BEGIN BY REMEMBERING THREE IMPORTANT EVENTS THAT
occurred when I was a young adult, events that symbolize the ideological shift that occurred in the second half of the twentieth century.
The first event was the Darwinian centennial of 1959, commemorat-
ing the hundredth anniversary of the publication of Darwin's *Origin of Species*.
The celebration was held at the University of Chicago, where I entered law
school shortly thereafter. Chicago was a particularly appropriate place to
have the Darwinian centennial, because it was associated with other seminal
events in modern science: the first atomic reactor was built there under Stagg
Field, and in 1952 the famous Miller-Urey experiment had given scientists
confidence that the Darwinian principle of materialistic evolution could be
extended back to the ultimate beginning of life.

So in 1959 the mood at the Darwinian centennial was one of triumphalism. Darwinism had gone through a rocky period when there was much
dispute about the mechanism, but then the neo-Darwinian synthesis had
come to the rescue with its mathematical population genetics. Neo-Darwinism seemed like the ultimate truth, a biological theory of everything.

Julian Huxley, grandson of Thomas Henry Huxley and brother of Aldous,
was the most prominent speaker. He declared that supernatural religion was

finished and that a new religion of evolutionary humanism based upon science would become the worldwide creed. We might say he proclaimed the death of an aged tyrant called God and then credited Charles Darwin with supplying the murder weapon.

The second event to recall was the 1960 Stanley Kramer movie of *Inherit the Wind*, starring Spencer Tracy as the agnostic lawyer patterned after Clarence Darrow. It was one of the great propaganda masterpieces of all time. In the context of presenting a distorted account of the notorious Scopes trial, the film portrayed the moral side of the Darwinian triumph over Christianity.

*Inherit the Wind* is a simple morality play in which the Christian ministers are evil manipulators and their followers are bumpkins who sing mindlessly in praise of "that old-time religion." In the movie it appears that the theological content of Christianity amounts to threatening people with damnation if they dare to think for themselves. The overthrow of this caricature provides a liberation myth, which goes with the triumphalism of the Chicago celebration. The movie teaches that the truth shall make us free, and the truth, according to science and Hollywood, is that biblical religion is an oppressor to be overthrown.

The film embodied a stereotype that has dominated public debate over evolution ever since the Scopes trial. As far as the media are concerned, all critics of Darwinism fit into what I call the *Inherit the Wind* stereotype. No matter how well qualified the critics are and no matter how well grounded their criticisms, the reporters assume that they are Bible-thumping fanatics challenging scientific fact in order to impose political oppression. The review in *Nature* of Michael Behe's *Darwin's Black Box* (Free Press, 1996) fits squarely in that tradition. Behe made solid scientific arguments demonstrating the existence of irreducible complexity in biochemical systems, arguments that the reviewer did not dispute on scientific grounds. Instead the review began and ended with irrelevant attacks on fundamentalists who want to substitute the book of Genesis for science. Like Marxism, Darwinism is a liberation myth that has become a new justification for ordering people not to think for themselves.

The third event in my trio is the 1962 school prayer decision of the United States Supreme Court, *Engel v. Vitale*. The school prayer involved in that case came not from the Bible Belt but from the state of New York. The school authorities wanted to approve a prayer that would unite Christians and Jews, and so the prayer was not distinctively Christian. It read: "Almighty God, we acknowledge our dependence upon Thee, and we beg Thy blessings upon us, our parents, our teachers, and our Country." The phrase "under God" had recently been added to the pledge of allegiance, and so the educators had good reason to suppose that Americans of all races and creeds believed in honoring our common Creator.

I am not concerned here with the merits or demerits of school prayer but with the question of what unites us as a people and what we regard as divisive. Before 1962 the United States were unified by the concept that people of different races and religious traditions all worship their common Creator, the God of the Bible. By 1962 that had been reversed. The 1959 Centennial proclaimed that a blind material process of evolution is our true creator. In 1962 the Supreme Court decided that even a very general evocation of God was a divisive sectarian practice, warning that government endorsement of religion is inherently associated with religious strife and oppression.

These three events symbolized a tremendous change in the ruling philosophy in the United States. Science now teaches us that a purposeless material process of evolution created us; the artists, poets and actors teach us that biblical morality is oppressive and hateful; and the courts teach us that the very notion of God is divisive and so must be kept out of public life. The pledge of allegiance may say that we are "one nation, under God," but we have become instead a nation that has declared its independence from God.

### What Went Wrong?

I believe that at some time well before 2059, the bicentennial year of Darwin's *Origin of the Species,* perhaps as early as 2009 or 2019, there will be another celebration that will mark the demise of the Darwinist ideology that was so triumphant in 1959. The theme of this anticentennial will be "What Went Wrong?" or perhaps, "How Could We Ever Have Let It Happen?"

What went wrong is that scientists committed the original sin, which in science means believing what you want to believe instead of what your experiments and observations show you. In small matters you cannot afford as a scientist to indulge in the original sin because your colleagues will show you up and make a fool out of you. If, however, you are leading the whole research community in a direction it wants to go, your colleagues might lack the motivation or might even be afraid to challenge you.

What happened in that great triumphal celebration of 1959 is that science embraced a religious dogma called naturalism or materialism. Science declared that nature is all there is and that matter created everything that exists. The scientific community had a common interest in believing this creed because it affirmed that in principle there is nothing beyond the understanding and control of science. What went wrong in the wake of the Darwinian triumph was that the authority of science was captured by an ideology, and the evolutionary scientists thereafter believed what they wanted to believe rather than what the fossil data, the genetic data, the embryological data and the molecular data were showing them.

What are we going to do to correct this deplorable situation? Most of us who attended this conference are in academic life, and we will be doing the academic job of research, writing and teaching. We have launched a new journal, *Origins & Design,* and we have had a very successful first conference at Biola. Many more people have attended than we originally expected, and a lot of very able people are now making a contribution in the area of intelligent design. We hope to schedule future conferences at major secular universities. We are developing a research agenda. We have confidence in our intellectual position. We are observing that the materialists have to rely on distortion and appeals to prejudice to defend their position. This is a sign that we have taken the high intellectual ground.

We also have our healthy disagreements about all sorts of specifics. But we are united on a common approach, a shared determination to define the issues correctly. It is an approach that everyone can contribute to—not just people with academic positions but also schoolteachers, parents, youth workers and everyone who has some influence over the education of the next generation of thinkers.

## The Basis for Rationality

I was asked to supply a theme for this conference, and the theme I chose was this: "The first step for a twenty-first-century science of origins is to separate materialist philosophy from empirical science." That is the basis not just for a science of origins; it is the basis for a proper understanding of rationality. To materialists, rationality starts with the realization that in the beginning were the particles and that mind itself is a product of matter. That makes it difficult to understand how there can even be knowledge of objective reality in science.

In chapter six of *Reason in the Balance* I compared two prominent philosophers, John Searle and Richard Rorty. Searle argues that there are objective standards of value in academic life and that mind is not reducible to matter. Yet he also insists that all thinking must be based on materialistic and Darwinian assumptions, thus undercutting his own conclusions.

Rorty has a poorer philosophy, but he is far more discerning about the implications of materialism and Darwinism. Rorty notes that Darwinian selection promotes only what is useful for survival and reproduction and concludes that "the idea that one species of organism is, unlike all the others, oriented not just toward its own increased prosperity but toward Truth, is as un-Darwinian as the idea that every human being has a built-in moral compass—a conscience that swings free of both social history and individual luck." When materialism is fully understood, objective truth goes into the trash can along with objective morality.

The postmodernist irrationalism that is sweeping our universities is thus the logical outcome of the scientific rationalism that prepared the ground by undermining the metaphysical basis for confidence in objective truth. A wrong view of mind has come out of science because science has become confused with materialist philosophy. And that wrong view has become a compulsory dogma for every discipline and for the intellectual culture in general.

Richard Dickerson, a professor of molecular biology at UCLA, provides a good example of how the basis of modern science has been articulated. He states as rule number one of scientific investigation, "Let us see how far and to what extent we can explain the behavior of the physical and material universe in terms of purely physical and material causes without invoking the supernatural."

That is a rational project, but another sentence has to be added for the rule to make any sense, and that is "At some point we'll stop to audit the books and see how far we've gone." For example, if your investment adviser suggests plunging wildly in the corn futures market, then at some point you will want to know if you have anything left or whether you have made any money. If he tells you, "Let's just always assume that corn futures go up in value," you know you are giving your money to somebody who has lost touch with reality.

Dickerson's first rule requires that at the end of the day you have to come in without a materialist bias and analyze what has been happening. You have been trying to explain the complexity of biology by mutation and selection; now what does the evidence really show? How successful have you been? Does the fossil record fit when you look at it objectively and without a Darwinian bias? We know the answer to that is no. We ask, "Does finch beak variation really show how you can get finches in the first place?" No, of course not. Neo-Darwinism is a failed project—give it up! "Not yet!" you say. "We're still trying to succeed." Good luck to you, friend, but the evaluation for now is you are not making it. It is what in tenure cases we call the midcareer review; you have not published and you are going to perish!

The naturalists say, "Let's protect naturalism for a while longer to give us a fair chance to succeed." It was reasonable to say that a few decades ago. But now it is time to audit the books.

Most philosophers, literary critics and Supreme Court justices assume the materialist picture of reality, even if they are not consciously aware of it. As Paul Feyerabend put it, "Scientists are not content with running their own playpens in accordance with what they regard as the rules of the scientific method; they want to universalize those rules, they want them to become part of society at large, and they use every means at their disposal—argument, propaganda, pressure tactics, intimidation, lobbying—to achieve their aims." With these tactics they have been successful in imposing a naturalistic religious philosophy on the entire culture.

## Rule 1: Do Not Fool Yourself

In his famous 1974 commencement address at Caltech, Richard Feynman provided an inspiring counterexample of how science ought to be practiced. He began by warning against self-deception, the original sin of science, saying that "the first principle is that you must not fool yourself, and you are the easiest person to fool." To avoid self-deception scientists must bend over backward to report data that cast doubt on their theories. Feynman applied this principle specifically to scientists who talk to the public:

> I would like to add something that's not essential to the science, but something I kind of believe, which is that you should not fool the laymen when you're talking as a scientist. . . . I'm talking about a specific, extra type of integrity that is not lying, but bending over backwards to show how you're maybe wrong, [an integrity] that you ought to have when acting as a scientist. And this is our responsibility as scientists, certainly to other scientists, and I think to laymen.

That is such a magnificent statement I wish it could be set to music. Richard Feynman's kind of science has the virtue of humility at its core. Honesty and humility. This is what has to be brought into evolutionary science: an understanding of the obligation of science to separate materialist philosophy from scientific investigation, to maintain that separation and be honest about it, and not to mislead the public about what has been demonstrated and what has not.

When science aspires to establish a ruling philosophy for all aspects of life and to replace God as the basis of rationality and human unity, it has to resort to the methods Paul Feyerabend condemned rather than the humility that Richard Feynman commended. It has to employ the bluster of such as Carl Sagan and Richard Dawkins, both of whom have been highly honored by the scientific establishments of their respective countries for promoting naturalism and materialism in the name of science. We need to replace Dawkins-style and Sagan-style science with a science that is humble about what it can do. A science that sticks to its data, that is careful to consider alternative explanations, and that does not allow itself to be ruled by a philosophical or religious agenda of any kind. A science that does not commit the original sin of believing what you want to believe. A science in which the scientists do not fool themselves and therefore do not try to fool the public either.

Separating empirical science from materialistic philosophy is a big job, and everyone with the right spirit can contribute to it. If you are a scientist, you can follow the path set by Michael Behe and others and bring out the crucial information that is not widely reported because it does not fit materialist preconceptions. If you are a philosopher, you can encourage your colleagues to speak out against other philosophers and scientists who abuse their authority by using it to promote dubious philosophies as if they had been empirically confirmed. Lawyers also have an important role to play, especially in persuading judges that constitutional principles of freedom of expression apply to criticism of evolutionary naturalism. Too many judges have the idea that criticism of naturalism and materialism constitutes religion and hence is forbidden on public property.

In some respects parents, schoolteachers and youth workers have the most important role in preparing the next generation of thinkers to understand the difference between real science and materialist philosophy. It is never too early to learn good critical thinking—but sometimes, after years of indoctrination in a biased educational system, it is too late. Some of us are preparing teaching materials to help home-schoolers, private schools and even adventurous public schoolteachers to teach the kids what the textbook writers and curriculum planners do not want them to know. Of course the Darwinists and their lawyers will resist this ferociously. Recently some of them have even taken to saying that "critical thinking" is a code word for creationism and hence for religious oppression. They have cause to worry, because when the young people learn to spot hidden assumptions and know about the evidence the textbooks slide over, they will be very hard to indoctrinate.

We need people who have enough courage to say this to the scientific materialists: "We're going to challenge the claims you're making that go beyond what you know. You can tell us what you know as biologists, and we want to know and honor that specialized knowledge. But when, as biologists, you tell us that you are believers in materialism as philosophy, we will reply, 'Who cares? You don't know that as biologists, and we're going to call you on your false claims of expertise over philosophical issues.'" We need to have lots of people doing just that.

**Freeing Up Inquiry**

What we need for now is people who want to promote genuine inquiry, not people who have all the answers in advance. In good time new theories will emerge, and science will change. We should not try to shortcut the process by establishing some new theory of origins until we know more about exactly what needs to be explained. Maybe there will be a new theory of evolution, but it is also possible that the basic concept will collapse and science will acknowledge that those elusive common ancestors of the major biological groups never existed. If we get an unbiased scientific process started, we can have confidence that it will bring us closer to the truth.

For the present I recommend that we also put the biblical issues to one side. The last thing we should want to do or seem to want to do is to threaten the freedom of scientific inquiry. Bringing the Bible anywhere near this issue just raises the *Inherit the Wind* stereotype and closes minds instead of opening them.

We can wait until we have a better scientific theory, one genuinely based on unbiased empirical evidence and not on materialist philosophy, before we need to worry about whether and to what extent that theory is consistent with the Bible. Until we reach that better science, it is best to live with some uncertainties and incongruities, which is our lot as human beings—in this life, anyway. For now we need to stick to the main point: In the beginning was the Word. Moreover, the "fear of God"—recognition of our dependence upon God—is still the beginning of wisdom. If materialist science can prove otherwise, then so be it. But everything we are learning about the evidence suggests that we do not need to worry.

One by one the great prophets of materialism have been shown to be false prophets and have fallen aside. Marx and Freud have lost their scientific standing. Now Darwin is on the block.

Some of us saw a clip of Richard Dawkins being interviewed on public television about his reaction to Michael Behe's book. You can see how insecure that man is behind his bluster and how much he has to rely on not having Mike Behe on the program with him, or even a lesser figure like Phil Johnson. Darwinists have to rely on confining their critics in a stereotype. They have learned to keep their own philosophy on the stage with no rivals allowed, and now they have to rely almost exclusively on that cultural power.

These are exciting times. When I finished the epilogue to *Darwin on Trial* in 1993, I compared evolutionary naturalism to a great battleship afloat on the ocean of reality. The ship's sides are heavily armored with philosophical and legal barriers to criticism, and its decks are stacked with 16-inch rhetorical guns to intimidate would-be attackers. In appearance it is as impregnable as the Soviet Union seemed a few years ago. But the ship has sprung a metaphysical leak, and that leak widens as more and more people understand it and draw attention to the conflict between empirical science and materialist philosophy. The more perceptive of the ship's officers know that the ship is doomed if the leak cannot be plugged. The struggle to save the ship will go on for a while, and meanwhile there will even be academic wine-and-cheese parties on the deck. In the end the ship's great firepower and ponderous armor will only help drag it to the bottom. Reality will win.

# Postscript

# The Twenty-first Century Has Arrived

## BRUCE CHAPMAN

*T*HE PRECEDING CHAPTERS HAVE CHALLENGED MATERIALISM (OR what throughout this volume also has been called naturalism) on scientific grounds and announced the formation of a new scientific movement known as intelligent design. The Mere Creation Conference on which this volume is based was pivotal in creating a new "community of thought" (to use Henry Schaefer's phrase from the foreword) dedicated to the empirical investigation of design in nature. Science, philosophy and theology are all destined to feel the influence of this growing community of thought. The road is now clear for a parade of new articles, books, conferences and media productions that detail the flaws in materialist thinking across academic disciplines and that advance the theory of intelligent design. We are well down that road, with a new generation of scholars picking up the materialist challenge.

This became especially evident when Christian Leadership Ministries and the Discovery Institute jointly sponsored a Consultation on Intelligent Design in Dallas in the fall of 1997 (about a year after the Mere Creation Conference). The consultation provided an opportunity to review the research underway as well as the impact that the intelligent design movement is having. The consultation demonstrated remarkable progress in the actual scientific research on intelligent design and also in awakening the public's interest in intelligent design.

Fifteen out of the twenty-two scholars who contributed to this volume are now affiliated with the Discovery Institute's Center for the Renewal of Science and Culture. These and other Discovery fellows have begun producing a steady stream of articles and books that in the coming years promises to become a torrent. The Discovery Institute also is promoting their work by giving it visibility in university and media settings. Not only are Discovery fellows working to overthrow the materialist interpretation of natural science, but they are also exploring how such disciplines as history, sociology, psychology and education will need to be reconfigured once materialism is cast aside and a transcendent designer regains acknowledgment.

In conjunction with Access Research Network, five Discovery fellows—Paul A. Nelson, William A. Dembski (editor of this volume for Christian Leadership Ministries), Stephen C. Meyer, Jonathan Wells and Bruce Gordon—are editing a top-quality interdisciplinary quarterly, *Origins & Design*, which examines theories of origins and all aspects of the idea of design. What is more, these and other Discovery fellows are with increasing frequency seeing their writing appear in mainline academic journals. The criticism that intelligent design is not legitimate because it publishes in all the wrong places is thus no longer supportable.

Nelson recently received his doctorate from the University of Chicago for his pathbreaking work challenging common descent. His dissertation, though entirely heterodox to the Darwinian establishment, will nonetheless be published this year through the University of Chicago Press in its monograph series on evolutionary biology. Dembski is the author of the forthcoming Cambridge University Press monograph *The Design Inference: Eliminating Chance Through Small Probabilities*. The publication date is set for the fall of 1998. (In 1996 the University of Illinois at Chicago awarded it the best dissertation in the humanities for that year.) Stephen C. Meyer, who received his Ph.D. several years ago from Cambridge University for his dissertation on methodological issues in origins-of-life biology, recently has published several scholarly articles legitimating design inferences within science. In particular, he has done extensive work on the evidence for design in the sequencing of DNA. Together Dembski, Meyer and Nelson are working on a book entitled *Uncommon Descent*, which will present a comprehensive theory of biological design. That book is expected to appear in 1999.

Amidst all these preparations, Michael J. Behe's *Darwin's Black Box* (Free Press), after twelve hardcover printings and six foreign-language printings, is now out in paperback. *Darwin's Black Box* promises to become a classic, presenting an unanswerable challenge to Darwinian orthodoxy. It was *Christianity Today*'s 1997 Book of the Year, largely because of its unprecedented role in stimulating the debate over evolution. Behe's concept of "irreducible complexity" has gained such currency that it is no longer necessary to cite his name with it.

Likewise Phillip E. Johnson's arguments against Darwinism and materialism have worked their way into the public imagination, especially those put forth most recently in *Defeating Darwinism by Opening Minds* (published by InterVarsity Press). Since the Mere Creation Conference, Johnson, when he is not teaching law at the University of California at Berkeley, spends much of his time on speaking and debating tours that carry him all over the United States, as well as overseas. Increasingly, Johnson is the keynote speaker at the growing number of academic conferences pitting Darwinism against intelligent design. Most of these conferences would never have been held but for the work of Johnson. His efforts have opened the debate and are forcing scientists to consider the evidentiary case for design.

The critique by Johnson and others of the materialist philosophy that is so prevalent in our educational system was surely at least in part responsible for the National Association of Biology Teachers' backpedaling when in 1997 they revised their definition of evolution. The NABT dropped the words *impersonal* and *unsupervised* from their official definition of evolution, no longer characterizing evolution through that language. This represents a fundamental concession even if it was motivated by public-relations concerns.

The Foundation for Thought and Ethics in Dallas is in the forefront of getting public schools to acknowledge the growing questions about evolution and the scientific evidence for design. Long before the Mere Creation Conference and also since, the FTE has been an important publisher of textbooks that provide an alternative to the overreaching materialism of secondary school instruction.

The media also have been invaluable in getting the debate between Darwinism and design back on the academic table. In November 1997 the PBS program *TechnoPolitics* visited Seattle and the Discovery Institute, home of the Center for the Renewal of Science and Culture. The resulting television program, its producers said, garnered more response by far than any in the series' history—ten times as much viewer response as usual. As a result *TechnoPolitics* decided to produce a second program on this same debate a few weeks later. In these programs, Johnson and Discovery fellows Meyer and Behe made a compelling case against the materialistic interpretation of modern biology, using three-dimensional computer animations produced by Discovery Media Productions. They also showed some of the compelling evidence for design within the microcosm of the cell.

To be sure, proponents of Darwinism and materialism defended the reigning paradigm in these programs. Even so, the *TechnoPolitics* programs plainly represented a breakthrough for the intelligent design movement. Shortly thereafter, in December 1997, another debate on another PBS program, William F. Buckley's *Firing Line,* drew still further attention to the growing debate over materialism. This time Johnson and Behe were joined by David Berlinski, as well as Buckley himself, in challenging the dogmatic presentation of Darwinism.

At the time of the Mere Creation Conference, intelligent design proponents could easily keep track of the number of scholarly and popular articles that treated their position. What is more, representation in the popular media was almost nil. A year later, print media coverage of the debate over materialism, Darwinism and intelligent design occurs daily. As for radio and television coverage, there continue to be notable developments. Thus, in addition to the publicity Johnson and Behe have been receiving, Meyer has appeared on PBS's *Freedom Speaks* and CNBC's *Hardball with Chris Matthews* in the past year. When in early 1997 the subject came up on Bill Maher's *Politically Incorrect* on cable television—though hardly a forum for sober deliberation—one knew this debate was entering the mainstream.

Sometimes the debate is clouded by confusion over terms like *creationism,* wherein opponents of design insist on reenacting old battles, since these are the ones they won. There is also the entertaining but distracting attention in the news media given to the growing dissension among the orthodox defenders of neo-Darwinism (e.g., the vitriolic exchanges between Stephen Jay Gould and Richard Dawkins). Moreover, the complexity of the scientific issues are at times difficult to communicate to the general media.

Even so, not only has there been progress in refuting the materialist implications of Darwinism, but also observers outside science are beginning to see the significance of this battle for the future of the culture as a whole. Within the religious community, Christian Leadership Ministries has played a key role in grappling with the implications of materialism both in the academic sphere and for the Christian faith.

But changes in our understanding of science affect the population as a whole, regardless of faith. And changes in science, philosophy and theology, however vast, are only the beginning. Materialism is not limited in its implications to natural science. Materialism is a way of understanding day-to-day existence and responding to it. Materialism has influenced public standards and policies on morals, law and criminology, education, medicine, psychology, race relations, the environment, and many other areas.

It can be argued that materialism is a major source of the demoralization of the twentieth century. Materialism's explicit denial not just of design but also of the possibility of scientific evidence for design has done untold damage to the normative legacy of Judeo-Christian ethics. A world without design is a world without inherent meaning. In such a world, to quote Yeats, "things fall apart; the center cannot hold."

Materialism not only prevails in the natural sciences but has also been adopted by such soft sciences as sociology and psychology. In his widely acclaimed recent book on the Scopes trial, *Summer for the Gods*, University of Georgia law professor and historian Edward J. Larson briefly describes the fascinating case that attorney Clarence Darrow handled just before he went to Dayton, Tennessee, in 1925 to combat William Jennings Bryan at the Scopes trial. Darrow's case prior to the Scopes trial was the infamous Leopold-Loeb murder case in Chicago. It was in that earlier trial that Darrow first introduced Darwinian arguments into criminology.

Two rich and well-educated youths, ages eighteen and nineteen, admitted to killing a fourteen-year-old boy for the thrill of it. They thought they were too smart to get caught. Brilliantly and successfully, Darrow, their attorney, argued against the death penalty, asserting that the "distressing and unfortunate homicide" happened mainly because a normal emotional life failed to "evolve" properly in the defendants. Speaking of Richard Loeb, he demanded, "Is Dickie Loeb to blame because . . . of the infinite forces that were at work producing him ages before he was born . . . ? Is he to blame because his machine is imperfect?"

Leopold and Loeb—Darrow repeatedly called them children—were really helpless agents of their genes. "Nature is strong and she is pitiless. She works in her own mysterious way, and we are her victims. We have not much to do with it ourselves. Nature takes this job in hand, and we play our parts."

In its own way the Leopold-Loeb defense was as important to the future of the law as Darrow's next case on the teaching of evolution—the Scopes trial—was to education. It foreshadowed decades of legal theory that rationalized outrageous and irresponsible behavior. Think, for example, of the Menendez brothers' murder case. Darrow brought noted scientists as witnesses to bolster his case for biological determinism. This is not to say that science per se was responsible for the demoralization of our culture. Rather it was the materialist interpretation of science that was responsible.

Right or wrong, materialism fundamentally shaped twentieth-century culture. The results can be seen in medicine (think of the battles over euthanasia), technology (where it is claimed that computers will soon take over the evolutionary process) and the entire field of morality and ethics. Exploring the role of materialism in these and other fields must become the task of a new generation of scholars, many of whom will take the work of this volume as their starting point. For if the materialist view of science is wrong, so surely is its application and misapplication in public policy and culture.

These Mere Creation Conference proceedings are a gold mine. Nonetheless, if you are looking for the final wisdom on the subject of origins and design, you will not find it here. If you are looking for the final wisdom on the implications of design for culture, you will not find it here. People of many backgrounds and convictions—and certainly scholars and critics who adhere to diverse faiths or no faith at all—will need to enter this debate and contribute to it. The important thing for now is that materialism can no longer be assumed unquestioningly and that intelligent design is on the table for discussion.

For those overly enthusiastic about the end of the millennium, historians will point out that the millennium is already here. As it turns out, Jesus was really born around 6 B.C., not in A.D. 1 as one might think (there is no year zero). Due to a computational error by an early Christian monk named Dionysius Exiguus, Christ's birth was placed about six years late, and all subsequent calendars have perpetuated that mistake.

A new century and millennium have already begun, not just temporally but also intellectually. Just as the nineteenth century closed in a burst of fashionable despair mixed with exciting new ideas about nature, humanity and society, so too we are already witnessing the rejection of many of the prevalent ideas of the twentieth century and their replacement by new ones. The Mere Creation Conference and the intellectual activity that is issuing from it stand as a historic marker in the progress of ideas and will prove critical in reclaiming the natural world from materialism.

# Contributors

**Michael Behe,** Ph.D. (biochemistry, University of Pennsylvania), associate professor in the department of biological sciences at Lehigh University, author of *Darwin's Black Box: The Biochemical Challenge to Evolution* (Free Press). Behe's biochemical research focuses on the structure and function of chromatin and has been funded by the National Institutes of Health and the National Science Foundation. He is a member of the Biophysical Society and the American Society for Molecular Biology and Biochemistry. In *Darwin's Black Box* he argues that the irreducible complexity of cellular biochemical systems shows that they were designed by an intelligent agent. *Darwin's Black Box* has been reviewed in *Science, Nature,* the *New Scientist, National Review,* the *Wall Street Journal* and the *New York Times.* It was selected as *Christianity Today's* 1996 Book of the Year. Behe is a fellow of the Discovery Institute's Center for the Renewal of Science and Culture.

**David Berlinski,** Ph.D. (mathematics, Princeton University), lecturer, essayist, author of *Black Mischief* (Harcourt Brace) and *A Tour of the Calculus* (Pantheon). Berlinski is an outspoken critic of Darwinism. His June 1996 article in *Commentary* entitled "The Deniable Darwin" provoked a maelstrom of response both from participants at the Mere Creation Conference and from doctrinaire evolutionists like Richard Dawkins and Daniel Dennett. Berlinski was a longtime friend of the late Marcel Schützenberger, with whom he collaborated on the mathematical critique of Darwinism. Berlinski is a fellow of the Discovery Institute's Center for the Renewal of Science and Culture.

**Walter Bradley,** Ph.D. (mechanical engineering, University of Texas at Austin), professor of mechanical engineering at Texas A & M University, author of more than one hundred publications in materials science, coauthor of *The Mystery of Life's Origin* (Philosophical Library). Bradley taught for eight years at the Colorado School of Mines before assuming his current position at Texas A & M University in 1976. He served from 1989 to 1993 as department head. He has also served as the director of the Polymer Technology Center at Texas A & M University (1987-1989; 1994-present). He oversees an active research program and publishes widely. He has received several research awards, including Senior TEES Research Fellow. He was elected a fellow of the American Society for Materials in 1991 and a fellow of the American Scientific Affiliation in 1992. With Charles Thaxton he coauthored a seminal work on the chemical basis of life entitled *The Mystery of Life's Origin: Reassessing Current Theories.* Bradley lectures widely on design and origins. He is a fellow of the Discovery Institute's Center for the Renewal of Science and Culture and a faculty affiliate of Christian Leadership Ministries.

**Bruce Chapman,** B.A. (Harvard), president of the Discovery Institute in Seattle, formerly fellow of the Hudson Institute in Indianapolis. Chapman is a specialist in public policy development with a long career in government service at all levels as well as a private career as an editorial writer, publisher and public policy fellow. In addition to his duties as president of the Discovery Institute, Chapman writes an editorial column every Friday in the *Seattle Post-Intelligencer.* He is the author of *The Party That Lost Its Head* (with George Gilder) and *The Wrong Man in Uniform* and is currently completing a book on changes in the nature of public life and the political vocation. From 1981 to 1983 Chapman was director of the United States Census Bureau. Later he served as deputy assistant to the president, from which position he directed the White House Office of Planning and Evaluation. In 1985 he was appointed U.S. Ambassador to the United Nations Organizations in Vienna, Austria, serving until 1988. He received the State Department's Superior Honor Award at the end of his service.

**William Lane Craig,** Ph.D. (philosophy, University of Birmingham under John Hick), Ph.D. (theology, University of Munich under Wolfhart Pannenberg), lecturer, debater, author of numerous articles and books, including (with Quentin Smith) *Theism, Atheism and Big Bang Cosmology* (Oxford University Press). Craig's research and publications are far ranging. He has published in the *Journal of Philosophy,* the *British Journal for the Philosophy of Science, Faith and Philosophy, Religious Studies,* and the *International Journal for Philosophy of Religion.* He has written extensively on the cosmological argument, Christian apologetics, divine omniscience and divine eternity. Craig is a fellow of the Discovery Institute's Center for the Renewal of Science and Culture.

**William Dembski,** Ph.D. (mathematics, University of Chicago), Ph.D. (philosophy, University of Illinois at Chicago), M.Div. (Princeton Theological Seminary), writer, lecturer, author of *The Design Inference* (forthcoming with Cambridge University Press, 1998). Dembski has done postdoctoral work at MIT, University of Chicago, Northwestern, Princeton, Cambridge and Notre Dame. He has been a National Science Foundation doctoral and postdoctoral fellow. His publications range from mathematics *(Journal of Theoretical Probability)* to philosophy *(Nous)* to theology *(Scottish Journal of Theology).* In *The Design Inference* he describes the logic whereby rational agents infer intelligent causes. Dembski is a fellow of the Discovery Institute's Center for the Renewal of Science and Culture.

**Sigrid Hartwig-Scherer,** Ph.D. (physical anthropology, University of Zurich with R. D. Martin), research fellow at the Institute for Anthropology and Human Genetics, Ludwig-Maximilian University, Munich, author of *Ramapithecus—Vorfahr des Menschen? [Ramapithecus—Progenitor of Humans?]* (Pascal Verlag). Hartwig-Scherer's doctoral work was in the field of skeletal ontogeny and hominoid phylogeny. She has published articles in such journals as the *American Journal of Physical Anthropology* and the *Journal of Human Evolution.* As a member of American and German anthropological and primatological societies she lectures widely. Her research deals with comparative pre- and postnatal skeletal development in primates.

**Phillip Johnson,** J.D. (University of Chicago), Jefferson Peyser Professor of Law at the University of California at Berkeley, well-known speaker on the philosophical significance of Darwinism, author of *Darwin on Trial, Reason in the Balance* and *Defeating Darwinism by Opening Minds* (all InterVarsity Press). After completing his law degree at the University of Chicago, Johnson was a law clerk for Chief Justice Earl Warren of the United States Supreme Court. Johnson has taught law for thirty years at the University of California at Berkeley. He is the author of two massive textbooks on criminal law: *Criminal Law: Cases, Materials and Text* (4th ed., West, 1990) and *Cases and Materials on Criminal Procedure* (2nd ed., West, 1994). Johnson entered the creation-evolution controversy because he found the books defending Darwinism dogmatic and unconvincing. He is an adviser to the Discovery Institute's Center for the Renewal of Science and Culture.

**Robert Kaita,** Ph.D. (physics, Rutgers University), principal research physicist at Princeton University's Plasma Physics Laboratory, teaches in Princeton's department of astrophysical sciences, author of more than 180 publications in nuclear and plasma physics. Kaita is a member of the American Association for the Advancement of Science, the American Physical Society and the American Scientific Affiliation. His interest in the creation-evolution debate dates from his anthropology studies and field work as an undergraduate at New York University and the State University of New York at Stony Brook. He is on the editorial board of the journal *Origins & Design.* Kaita is a fellow of the Discovery Institute's Center for the Renewal of Science and Culture.

**Stephen Meyer,** Ph.D. (history and philosophy of science, Cambridge University), associate professor of philosophy at Whitworth College, senior research fellow at the Discovery Institute (Seattle), director of the Discovery Institute's Center for the Renewal of Science and Culture. Meyer's research focuses on the nature of scientific rationality as it relates to design. He has several books in preparation, including *Uncommon Descent* (with conference participants Dembski and Nelson) and *Detecting Design in Creation* (with conference participants Nelson and Reynolds). These books seek to reestablish the legitimacy and fruitfulness of design within biology. In addition to his scholarly work on design, Meyer is a frequent contributor to public policy debates, with articles appearing in such places as the *Wall Street Journal* and the *Los Angeles Times.*

**J. P. Moreland,** Ph.D. (philosophy, University of Southern California), Th.M. (Dallas Theological Seminary), professor of philosophy, Talbot School of Theology, author and editor of numerous books, including *Christianity and the Nature of Science* (Baker) and *The Creation Hypothesis* (InterVarsity Press). Moreland publishes widely in the philosophical literature and has had his work appear in such publications as *Philosophy and Phenomenological Research, American Philosophical Quarterly, Australasian Journal of Philosophy* and *Faith and Philosophy.* Moreland served for eight years as a bioethicist for PersonaCare Nursing Homes, Inc., headquartered in Baltimore, Maryland. His research interests lie in metaphysics, philosophy of science and philosophy of mind. Moreland is a fellow of the Discovery Institute's Center for the Renewal of Science and Culture.

**Paul Nelson,** Ph.D. (philosophy, University of Chicago), editor of the journal *Origins & Design.* Nelson's work in design dates back to his undergraduate days in philosophy and biology at the University of Pittsburgh, where he wrote a senior thesis with Nicholas Rescher entitled "The Possibility of Design." Having recently completed his doctorate in philosophy at the University of Chicago, Nelson will shortly begin postdoctoral research there in evolutionary and developmental biology. His article "The Role of Theology in Current Evolutionary Reasoning" appeared in *Biology and Philosophy* and has provoked international response. Nelson is a member of the International Society for the History, Philosophy and Social Studies of Biology as well as a fellow of the Discovery Institute's Center for the Renewal of Science and Culture.

**Robert Newman,** Ph.D. (astrophysics, Cornell University), M.Div. (Faith Theological Seminary), professor of New Testament at Biblical Theological Seminary, director of the Interdisciplinary Biblical Research Institute. Newman has been national president of the Evangelical Theological Society (1996). He is also a fellow of the American Scientific Affiliation, for which he chairs the commission on creation. He is coauthor with Herman Eckelmann of *Genesis One and the Origin of the Earth* (InterVarsity Press). Newman is an expert in Christian apologetics, especially at rebutting arguments that claim to show the incompatibility of Christian faith with science.

**Nancy Pearcey,** M.A. (Covenant Theological Seminary), fellow and policy director of the Wilberforce Forum, Washington, D.C. For the past five years Pearcey has worked with Charles Colson as executive editor of his award-winning daily radio program *BreakPoint*, a program analyzing current affairs and culture, reaching a weekly audience of five million listeners. She is the author of numerous articles on science and religion, with her work appearing in such periodicals as *First Things, Books & Culture* and *Christianity Today*. She is a contributor to *Of Pandas and People* (Haughton), the supplemental biology text advocating intelligent design. She is also a coauthor with Charles Thaxton of *The Soul of Science* (Crossway), a nonnaturalistic account of the rise of modern science. Pearcey is a fellow of the Discovery Institute's Center for the Renewal of Science and Culture.

**Del Ratzsch,** Ph.D. (philosophy, University of Massachusetts, Amherst), professor of philosophy at Calvin College, author of *Philosophy of Science* and *The Battle of Beginnings* (both InterVarsity Press). Much of Ratzsch's work over the last seventeen years at Calvin College has sought to relate science and religion (and more recently creation and evolution) in a way that is philosophically informed, scientifically defensible and theologically meaningful. Although Ratzsch is optimistic that design theory can avoid past mistakes in the creation-evolution controversy, he stresses that fundamental clarifying work remains to be done in this area.

**John Mark Reynolds,** Ph.D. (philosophy, University of Rochester), founder and director of the Torrey Honors Institute at Biola University (a Great Books program for undergraduates), specializes in ancient philosophy, especially as it relates to design. Reynold's dissertation at the University of Rochester focused on Plato's psychology. Reynolds specializes in ancient cosmology and the philosophy of religion. He has recently completed a two-year postdoctoral fellowship in the philosophy of science at Biola University under the supervision of Phillip Johnson of the University of California, Berkeley, and J. P. Moreland of Biola University. Reynolds has taught philosophy at several colleges and universities. He is currently completing a book about the history of ancient philosophy for InterVarsity Press. Reynolds is a fellow of the Discovery Institute's Center for the Renewal of Science and Culture.

**Hugh Ross,** Ph.D. (physics [astronomy], University of Toronto), director of Reasons to Believe, well-known lecturer on the relation between cosmology and creation, author of *The Fingerprint of God* (Promise), *The Creator and the Cosmos, Creation and Time* and *Beyond the Cosmos* (all NavPress). As a postdoctoral fellow at the California Institute of Technology, Ross conducted research for several years on some of the most distant objects in the universe. As president of Reasons to Believe, he has written extensively on issues pertaining to science and faith. His most recent book is *Beyond the Cosmos*. His articles have appeared in scientific journals as well as in popular magazines, including *Christianity Today, Moody Monthly, World* and *Canadian Challenge*.

**Henry F. Schaefer III,** Ph.D. (chemical physics, Stanford), professor of chemistry at the University of California, Berkeley, for eighteen years, since 1987 the Graham Perdue Professor of Chemistry and Director of the Center for Computational Quantum Chemistry at the University of Georgia. Schaefer is the author of more than 750 scientific publications, the majority appearing in the *Journal of Chemical*

*Physics* or the *Journal of the American Chemical Society.* He has been the research director of fifty successful doctoral students and has presented plenary lectures at more than 125 national or international scientific conferences. He is the editor-in-chief of *Molecular Physics* and president of the World Association of Theoretically Oriented Chemists. His major awards include the American Chemical Society Award in Pure Chemistry (1979), the American Chemical Society Leo Hendrik Baekeland Award (1983) and the Centenary Medal of the Royal Society of Chemistry (London, 1992). The science citation index shows that Schaefer is the third most highly cited chemist in the world. His research involves the use of state-of-the-art computational hardware and theoretical methods to solve important problems in molecular quantum mechanics. The *U. S. News & World Report* cover story of December 23, 1991, describes Schaefer as a "five-time nominee for the Nobel Prize." Schaefer is a fellow of the Discovery Institute's Center for the Renewal of Science and Culture.

**Siegfried Scherer,** Ph.D. (biology, University of Konstanz), professor of microbial ecology and director of the Institute of Microbiology at the Technical University of Munich, edited *Typen des Lebens [Basic Types of Life]* (Pascal Verlag), coauthored the biology textbook *Entstehung und Geschichte der Lebewesen [Origin and History of Living Forms]* (Weyel Biologie). With his coworkers, Scherer has published numerous papers in international peer-reviewed journals. He is a member of several scientific societies, including Sigma Xi, American Association for the Advancement of Science, American Society for Microbiology, Society for the Study of Evolution, and Society for Molecular Biology and Evolution. His current research deals with food microbiology, microbial ecology, molecular evolution and taxonomy.

**Jeffrey Schloss,** Ph.D. (ecology and evolutionary biology, Washington University), professor of biology at Westmont College in Santa Barbara, California. Schloss attended Wheaton College, where he earned his B.S. in biology, and was subsequently a Danforth fellow during his doctoral studies in ecology and evolutionary biology at Washington University. Schloss conducts research in population genetics, ecophysiology and the sociobiology of human morality and altruism. He is concerned with the social implications of evolutionary and environmental biology. He is a member of the Society for the Study of Evolution, the International Society for the History, Philosophy and Social Studies of Biology and the American Scientific Affiliation. Schloss is a fellow of the Discovery Institute's Center for the Renewal of Science and Culture.

**Jonathan Wells,** Ph.D. (religious studies, Yale), Ph.D. (developmental biology, University of California at Berkeley), postdoctoral research biologist in the department of molecular and cell biology at the University of California at Berkeley, author of *Charles Hodge's Critique of Darwinism* (Edwin Mellen). Wells's primary interest is the conflict between Darwinism and Christianity. Thus in 1978 he entered a Ph.D. program in theology at Yale, where his dissertation (later published as a book) defended Charles Hodge, a nineteenth-century Presbyterian theologian who criticized Darwinism for excluding design. In 1989 Wells entered Berkeley for a second Ph.D., this time in molecular biology. His Berkeley dissertation research (recently published in the journal *Development)* dealt with processes in early frog embryos that help to determine the future shape of the animal. Now, as a postdoctoral research biologist at Berkeley, Wells focuses on recent developments in embryology that signify the end of the Darwinian paradigm. Wells is a fellow of the Discovery Institute's Center for the Renewal of Science and Culture.

# Index